FOOD BRITANNIA

*Andrew Webb* | Food Britannia

BOOKS

Published by Random House Books 2011

2 4 6 8 10 9 7 5 3 1

Copyright © Andrew Webb 2011

First published in Great Britain in 2011 by
Random House Books

Random House
20 Vauxhall Bridge Road
London SW1V 2SA

www.randomhouse.co.uk

Addresses for companies within The Random House Group Limited
can be found at: www.randomhouse.co.uk/offices.htm

The Random House Group Limited Reg. No. 954009

A CIP catalogue record for this book is available from the British Library

ISBN 9781847946232

The Random House Group Limited supports The Forest Stewardship
Council (FSC), the leading international forest certification organisation.
All our titles that are printed on Greenpeace approved FSC certified paper
carry the FSC logo. Our paper procurement policy can be found at
www.randomhouse.co.uk/environment

Maps by Darren Bennett
Design by Richard Marston
Typeset by Palimpsest Book Production Limited
Falkirk, Stirlingshire
Printed and bound in China by
C&C Offset Printing Co., Limited

*For Kate and Matilda*

# Contents

# Introduction

The journey that ultimately led to this book began very early one bright April morning in 2008, when I set off from London bound for Land's End. I had been commissioned by Channel 4 to present *The Big British Food Map*, I had a creative carte blanche, and as it was just me, a car, a laptop and a couple of cameras, I could do anything and go anywhere. And so, with the roads out of London almost to myself and the satnav set for Cornwall, I began a seven-month, 11,500-mile food tour that took me all the way round the UK. As you can imagine, I met some truly amazing people and saw many tucked-away areas of this wonderful country, which only served to confirm my view that it is far more beautiful and interesting than we often give it credit for. During my tour I learned new recipes and cooking ideas, and gained a much better knowledge of plant and animal breeds. I was constantly impressed by the skill and expertise I witnessed, and even my UK history and geography improved.

Seven months might sound a long time, but they positively flew by, and after my role on the Channel 4 project came to an end in November 2008, I still felt there were areas, products and producers I had missed. So, after taking some time out to get married and become a father, I began researching and visiting more people and places. The result is this book: over 300 entries spanning everything from one-man-band operations that do what they do more for love than for profit to the fascinating histories of much-loved household staples, many of which are nowadays produced by large corporations. Alongside organically reared beef and lamb, and food gathered from the wild, you'll also find such things as After Eight mints (p. 238), stottie cakes (p. 222) and Edinburgh chippie sauce (p. 167). Why? Well, because they're eaten and enjoyed and have stories worth telling, and it's these stories that interest me.

Another reason to include a broad range of products is that food needn't always be fancy. All too often, supposedly 'good food' is presented as part of some sort of bucolic lifestyle that harks back to a bygone age. Complex recipes invariably produce 'simple mid-week suppers', while ingredients are described in cloyingly effusive terms like 'toothsome', with flavours forever 'cutting through' other ones. All these clichés wind me up no end, and you'll find none of them in this book. But beyond being my personal bête noire, this sort of talk alienates people and doesn't reflect the way in which we eat. Food shouldn't be something a few 'foodies' are into, but a daily chance for us all to experiment with the abundance that surrounds us, to strengthen our local communities, and to improve our health and ultimately our happiness. It's important stuff, is eating.

Since setting off on that April morning much has changed in the world, and food production and retail, like the rest of society, have felt those changes. The summer of that year was awful, and I witnessed first-hand the sodden wheat harvests. Then there was the fuel crisis, followed, in 2009, by the financial meltdown. While this did affect some areas of the food sector, particularly those producing organic food, I also spoke to people who had feared an apocalypse and yet were amazed to find themselves not only still in business, but in some cases even growing. Indeed, some restaurateurs I spoke to have positively enjoyed the challenge; yes, it's been hard, they say, but it's forced them to offer value and redouble their efforts on service, as well as shaking a lot of dead wood out of the industry. People still go on dates, have birthdays or want to buy, cook and eat good food, and smart businesses still provide that. The food sector today is one of incredible dynamism for those who want to seek, if not their fortune, then at least their own destiny. It's hard, yes, but plenty of new people are coming into the industry. As Guy Tullberg of Tracklements (p. 11) told me, 'When we started you were very limited in your routes to market; now, if I think I've made the finest chilli sauce since time began, I can get a pitch at a farmers' market for £20 and get going.'

Online retail is another key area in which the public has become more experienced. When I was dreaming up *The Big British Food Map* in the winter of 2007, I thought it odd that, although people were at ease using Amazon and eBay, not much food came via online mail-order services, and few food producers offered their goods that way. Not any more: you can get nearly everything in this book, including lobster (p. 149), saffron (p. 91) and sea salt (p. 58), delivered to your home or work in just a few clicks. As Paul and James from Cocoa Mountain (p. 164) told me, delivery services in the UK are now so good that they can get a box of their chocolates anywhere in the country within twenty-four hours. Today, any producers worth their salt have a website detailing, at the very least, what the company does and providing contact information. Particularly entrepreneurial producers like Michael Dallaway (p. 492) are using the internet to help sell a crop before it has even grown. By allowing people to rent one of his cherry trees for twelve months, Michael is guaranteed an income right from the start of the year.

And so today, despite its small size and sometimes clone-town high streets, Britain still remains sufficiently different from district to district and from region to region to make exploring it worthwhile. Most areas now boast excellent artisan cheeses, a local brewer or two, some well-produced meat and unique regional specialities. You don't have to spend a year travelling and researching like I did; just pick a region, book a long weekend off work, get in the car and you're away. Take in a farm, some local shops and a good restaurant or pub, and you've got your own little food adventure right there. What I hope you'll find in this book is solid evidence that Britain's food soul, so nearly lost, is now firmly returning. There are people doing brilliant, creative and exciting things with food all over the British Isles. Go and find them. Just make sure you take this book.

It's worth taking a moment here to explain a distinction that crops up for a number of the products in this book, namely that of PFN (Protected Food Name) status. European recognition of a product or production method comes in three flavours: PDO (Protected Designation of Origin) covers agricultural products and foodstuffs produced, processed and prepared in a given geographical area; PGI (Protected Geographical Indication) is a touch broader, covering agricultural products and foodstuffs closely linked to the geographical area; finally, TSG (Traditional Speciality Guaranteed) highlights traditional character, either in the composition or means of production.

The UK lags behind even Germany in PFN-recognised products, and a long way behind France and Italy. There are a number of reasons for this, ranging from Britain having thrown overboard much of its artisanal food-production techniques in the twentieth century, to contemporary Euroscepticism. Even when UK products *do* have PFN status, it's mainly beers and cheeses, predominantly from the central region of the country, and meat from breeds of animals at the periphery of farming. Like a teenager's diet, there's a distinct lack of fruit and vegetables, although Yorkshire forced rhubarb (p. 255) has recently joined Jersey Royals and a few others in the scheme.

PFN status really is worth fighting for, as it not only ensures and protects a certain standard of production to an agreed recipe using an agreed set of ingredients, but it also exposes products to European markets where the scheme is better known.

# 1 | The South-West

W  A

Swansea
o

Barnstaple
o

★
King's Nympto

DEVO

Dartmoor

★
Rock

Newquay o

Lostwithiel

CORNWALL          ★

Looe
★

Plymouth
★

Totnes

o
St Austell

Newlyn

Marazion

St Just ★        ★        ★ Helston

Treen ★    ★

Mousehole

St Keverne
★

Newlyn
Bay

## BATH, SOMERSET
# *Bath chaps*

Time was, traditional British dishes were under threat. In the 1980s and 1990s we – especially 'the young', according to the press – were filling our stomachs with the wondrous produce of the world while neglecting our own food heritage. After seemingly sating ourselves with rustic peasant dishes from around the globe, we began to look anew at our own. A rise in national pride as well as the sharp shock of the economic downturn and you couldn't move for articles about cheap cuts and wartime austerity and 'making the most of . . .' features.

And so just as Bath chaps were about to be relegated for ever to the food history books, along with such culinary oddities as the cockatrice (a medieval dish in which the front of a chicken was sewn on to the back of a pig), they were saved and brought back in from the cold. Perhaps their most well-known evangelist is Fergus Henderson, proprietor of St John restaurant in London, whose nose-to-tail eating ethos sits at the heart of the pride in British cooking.

Bath chaps are made from the pig's cheeks. If that makes you feel a bit squeamish, it's worth considering that most cheap mass-produced sausages will contain bits of pigs' heads as there is a fair old amount of good meat there – the temple (a small nugget that sits behind the eye socket), the snout, the cheeks and the jowl. Bath chaps are made from these last two cuts: first, the meat is removed and brined for a couple of days in salted water. Then it's boiled slowly for three hours in slightly salted water, flattened, rolled, and chilled. To serve, you can either cut a thick wedge and flash-fry to crisp a little, or slice it very thin on a bacon slicer and treat it the same way as you would ham.

But can you get Bath chaps in the city itself? Well, yes. The world may have shrunk, but Bath is still home to some quality chaps, particularly the Garrick's Head pub in St John's Place. Or you could head to the Albion pub in nearby Bristol, where a slice of pig's face comes with onion purée, poached duck egg and watercress. Chaps are by their nature fatty, and so need something sharp to contrast. If you see them on a menu, try them: they take a lot of effort to prepare and the chef – as well as your stomach – will thank you for it.

*See also* BURY MARKET, GREATER MANCHESTER (p. 99); DINGWALL, HIGHLAND (p. 160); HAROME, NORTH YORKSHIRE (p. 249); HEREFORD, HEREFORDSHIRE (p.296); SMITHFIELD, ISLINGTON (p. 401); STONEHALL COMMON, WORCESTERSHIRE (p. 312).

## Bath's many buns

The city of Bath is well known for its waters and, to a lesser extent, its buns and biscuits. These take the form of the Sally Lunn bun, the Bath bun, Bath Olivers and the London Bath bun, and their histories – some might say 'mysteries' – are as follows.

Sally Lunn buns are, according to the Sally Lunn tea shop, which sells them, the creation of one Solange Luyon, a young Huguenot refugee who fled to England in the 1680s and found work earning an honest crust at a baker's in Lilliput Alley, Bath. She is said to have baked rich, round and generous brioche-style bread, which became known as the 'Sally Lunn' bun. However, there are other theories; one being that the name is a corruption of *sol et lune* (sun and moon), due to the round, golden shape of the crust and the soft white-as-the-moon interior. Then there is the French brioche-style bread known as *solilemmes* to consider; this is spongy, enriched with egg and served hot. In all these tales there is a French connection.

In time, popularity of the bun grew and it soon became the thing to nibble on while ambling around admiring the city's architecture and taking the waters. Moreover, many people in the town seemed to have made products prefixed with 'Sally Lunn'. Gye's 1819 Directory of Bath contains an advert for W. Needes, bread and biscuit maker to the Prince Regent. Needes operated from 2 Westgate Street, and his advert proudly declares that he makes not only Sally Lunn *cakes*, but also Brown Georges, a kind of apple turnover popular in the south of England. Other books and periodicals carried similar adverts, and as the recipe appears in many nineteenth-century cookery books, it seems many producers jumped on Sally's bun wagon.

Next in the breadline are Bath buns, made with a sweetish dough and often containing caraway seed. These were said to have been invented by Dr William Oliver, who extolled the virtues of drinking Bath's waters, saying in his 1716 book on the subject, 'What the ancient Poets feigned of their Nectar, or Drink of their Gods, may be truly said of our Bath-Waters.' His patients, however, enjoyed his buns rather too much, so he invented the Bath Oliver, made from flour, milk, fresh butter, malt and hops. It is a light, easy-to-digest biscuit, and helped some of his more rotund patients to slim down. They're still available, though now made by Huntley & Palmers of Sudbury, Suffolk.

Then there is something called the London Bath bun, which is an even sweeter bread made with lumps of sugar and a further dusting of sugar on top. These sugar-rush-inducing buns were sold at the Great Exhibition of 1851, where, according to *Fireside Facts from the Great Exhibition*, 311,731lb of London Bath buns and 460,657lb of plain old buns kept visitors well fed.

Today the humble bun as a foundation for jam and cream has rather been eclipsed by the scone and the teacake, and the merry buns of Bath are no longer first and foremost in the minds of the public.

*See also* HOW RECIPES BEGIN (p. 496); LARDY CAKE (p. 26); ALBERT EMBANKMENT, LAMBETH (p. 368); ALDERLEY EDGE, CHESHIRE (p. 96); BISHOP AUCKLAND, COUNTY DURHAM (p. 201); ECCLES, GREATER MANCHESTER (p. 103); HOOK NORTON, OXFORDSHIRE (p. 328); LLANDEILO, CARMARTHENSHIRE (p. 74); MANCHESTER, GREATER MANCHESTER (p. 119); MELTON MOWBRAY, LEICESTERSHIRE (p. 341); NAVENBY, LINCOLNSHIRE (p. 344); OTLEY, WEST YORKSHIRE (p. 252); STANBRIDGE, BEDFORDSHIRE (p. 360); WHITBY, NORTH YORKSHIRE (p. 269).

## BATH, SOMERSET
### Tony Eades, gentleman greengrocer

The Royal Crescent: Grade I listed and the jewel in Bath's architectural crown. To view it from the front is to behold some of England's finest Georgian buildings. View it from the rear, however, and you'll find a tiny greengrocer's shop made from two garages knocked together. When I visited I met the owner, fourth-generation greengrocer Tony Eades, who told me the story. 'We used to be a bit further down, but the shop was blown out during the war. My dad just picked up what was left, set the table up in one of the old mews and carried on.' In the 1950s, the council knocked down the mews and replaced it with garages. They wanted to evict the Eades, but the residents of the Crescent – which at that time included minor gentry – objected and the council allowed two of the garages to be turned into Tony's shop. It's been the same ever since. 'I did want to update it,' he says, but every time he talks about modernising the shop there's a howl of protest from his regulars. 'When people ask, "How long have you been a grocer?" I tell 'em I've got Jaffa printed on my arse! My mother would save the blue tissue paper the oranges came wrapped in to use in the lav.'

Tony Eades picks the flowers from his purple sprouting broccoli

One of the reasons why his produce is so good is that, unusually for a greengrocer, Tony grows some of his own stock in nearby Swainswick. He tends a beautiful spot with a stunning view over the city, which nestles in the valley below. 'I've had offers for it from developers – "Name your price," they say, but I won't sell it, ever. It's important for Bath to keep this hillside green.' Here Tony grows broccoli, cauliflower, potatoes and, surprisingly, Christmas trees. He has a fairly laid-back attitude to growing: 'I let crops go to seed: it's good for the bees, and we need to do everything to encourage them. If I was more intensive I would have ploughed all this back under now it's been harvested, but it can't all be take, you've got to give something back.'

CHEDDAR, SOMERSET
## *West Country Farmhouse Cheddar*

Cheddar may have hailed from a small village in Somerset, but it went on to conquer the world. Over 50 per cent of the cheese eaten in the UK is Cheddar, and huge volumes are made and eaten in North America, Australasia and elsewhere; Cheddar, it seems, is clearly the world's cheese. That's fine if you're not that bothered what your Cheddar actually tastes like. Sadly, most of the world's Cheddar is to cheese what poor old plain vanilla is to ice cream: the standard default option and often little more than industrial rubber-tasting gunk.

A proper traditional Cheddar is no middle-of-the-road choice, but a glorious journey through the taste and flavour of the west of England. And though Cheddar is made worldwide, West Country Farmhouse Cheddar has Protected Designation of Origin (PDO) status, and so can only be made in Cornwall, Dorset, Devon or Somerset by a group of producers using primarily milk from their own herd and traditional production techniques.

For one pound of Cheddar, you need approximately a gallon of milk – to which you add a starter culture before heating gently. Rennet, which causes the milk to set, is added, and the semi-solid mixture is cut and stirred. The next step is to drain off the whey (the watery bit), leaving the curds to settle into a layer twenty-five centimetres thick. Then the curds are cheddared, i.e. cut into blocks and turned repeatedly to ensure no moisture remains. After this, they are 'milled' (or ground), salt is added, and everything is put into a mould and pressed. If the Cheddar is being made in a round truckle shape, it will be wrapped in cheesecloth that has been greased with lard. It is then stored and aged for a minimum of ten to twelve months.

There are many producers making West Country Farmhouse Cheddar. The 'big three' are Keen's, based at Moorhayes Farm, Wincanton; Montgomery's in Shepton Mallet; and Westcombe, also of Shepton Mallet. These three producers have formed a Slow Food presidium, 'Artisan Somerset Cheddar'.

The other ten producers in the region include Parkham's on the North Devon coast, Denhay in West Dorset and Barber's in Somerset. There are a host of little subtleties – even down to the mood of the cow – that mean that each company's cheese tastes slightly different, whether it has a pronounced acidic tang, or is more mellow in the mouth. George Keen believes his Cheddar has a long, intricate, creamy flavour – 'long' as in the amount of time the taste lingers in your mouth; 'Cheese should have miles in it, so the flavour will last several miles down the road,' says George. Perhaps the best option is to explore a few at the same time.

A final word of advice: whichever Cheddar you choose, it'll prefer being stored in a cool, damp environment (like the caves that give it its name) rather than the cold dryness of the refrigerator. So think pantry, cellar or garage: a bit of a pain to run and fetch it, but it will taste and keep better, I assure you.

See also BRITISH CHEESE (p. 290).

## Wild boar from the Real Boar Company

It's thought that British indigenous wild boar were hunted to extinction by the thirteenth century. Subsequently, there have been various attempts at reintroduction, particularly by royalty. James I and later Charles I

Julian the boar, owner Simon's nemesis and progenitor of the 'sounder'

brought in boar from the Continent for hunting during the seventeenth century, and killing a wild boar was a mark of ascendance to manhood for many a dashing young blade – in part, perhaps, because boar do not die easy. In fact, boars don't do anything easy, to which wild-boar farmer Simon Gaskell can attest.

Simon started farming on twenty acres of woodland that was a perfect home for boars (luckily, as it suited little else). That was in 2005, and the 'sounder', as a group of boar is known, now numbers over 200 animals. Simon tends to leave them to get on with things until they're needed, at which point he has his work cut out as you can't really 'round up' boar. 'When I first went to gather them in to take to slaughter, it took me nine days,' says Simon. After years of building up trust, Simon has eventually succeeded in gathering most of them in more quickly by bribing them with food, but they're an unruly bunch. And the most stubborn, obstinate and downright mean of his charges is stud boar Julian, who will regularly have a gore at Simon, as the scars on his legs prove.

All this pain and effort is worth it, however, when the meat comes back from the abattoir. Boar flesh has an unmistakable smell to it: a sweet gamey tang reminiscent of porcini mushrooms; earthy and natural rather than high or musky. Simon hangs the sides for ten days before even beginning to work with them. The meat is butchered on site, the loin and prime cuts being sold into the restaurant trade and the rest of the animal going into Simon's salamis and chorizo. There are precious few producers of higher-welfare cured meats in Britain; as Simon explains, historically the British climate lent itself more to hams and fresh meat rather than air-dried products. However, public tastes have changed, and Simon and others are charging forward to meet that demand. He now supplies three of the top five restaurants in the UK, as well as the London Eye – accolades that go some way to soothing the pain Julian inflicts, you'd imagine.

*See also* ACOMB, NORTHUMBERLAND (p. 195); AUCHTERMUCHTY, FIFE (p. 144); BLAXHALL, SUFFOLK (p. 419); BROMPTON-ON-SWALE, NORTH YORKSHIRE (p. 236); FRILSHAM, BERKSHIRE (p. 479); KENDAL, CUMBRIA (p. 114).

# Onion marmalade from Tracklements

Disney's *Peter Pan* begins with the line 'All of this has happened before, and it will all happen again.' It's what Guy Tullberg, the current owner of Tracklements, could have said to the officer from trading standards when he told Guy he couldn't name his product 'onion marmalade' as everyone knew marmalade was made from citrus fruits. Instead, Guy and his father William patiently presented twenty-seven pages of notes on historical recipes. Chief among them were instructions for making 'Marmulate of Red Currants' from a fantastic book entitled *The Closet of the Eminently Learned Sir Kenelme Digbie Kt. Opened*. Sir Ken might have served as the inspiration for Lord Flashheart in *Blackadder*, being very much the Elizabethan swashbuckler, and he also happened to be a bit of a foodie. His closet contains many recipes for mustards, sauces and condiments, as well as advice on roasting meat, stuffing chickens and a large selection of recipes for ales, ciders and other alcoholic beverages; a guy after my own heart then. So thanks to evidence from 1669 provided by Sir Ken, along with French chef Michel Guerard's twentieth-century recipe for *Marmelade d'Oignons*, trading standards saw sense.

Tracklements started in 1970 when William Tullberg read a recipe for wholegrain mustard in John Evelyn's diary. All mustard was wholegrain until the eighteenth century and Mrs Clement's invention of Durham mustard, which milled the grain like flour (*see* p. 227). William experimented by part blitzing a batch in a coffee grinder to release some of the pungency, yet keep the grain texture, and the results were good. He made some more for friends, and the local pub said they'd take a few jars. The rest, as they say, is history.

The name of the company comes from a word that William's grandmother, who hailed from Lincolnshire, used to describe a collection of such things as salt, pepper, sauce and condiments. Dorothy Hartley, author of *Food in England* (1953), said she invented the word 'tracklement', and the *OED* notes her book as the first citation, defining the term as 'an article of food, specifically a jelly, prepared to accompany meat'. However, it probably has roots in earlier dialect and meant a collection of things.

Tracklements' wholegrain mustard is now joined by over fifty other lines, of which the onion marmalade remains the most popular, selling something like 250,000 jars a year. The year 2010 saw their fortieth anniversary, and a trawl through the old order books reveals that the Continental Delicatessen in Devizes has been stocking it ever since the very early days of the company.

One of Tracklements' other sauces is horseradish, the traditional accompaniment to roast beef. Tracklements believes it is the only manufacturer in the UK using fresh horseradish, without any fillers like turnip. Indeed, the company would welcome new suppliers, as Guy tells me horseradish is not a popular crop with farmers. 'Once you've planted it you never get rid of it. If you do want to grow it in your garden, plant it in a bucket.' More or less every culture has invented some sort of strong-tasting stiffish substance to flavour food; everything from sweet chilli sauce and wasabi to the classic French sauces. All foods need a blob of something, and when sauces and condiments are done right they enhance the flavour of what they accompany by throwing it into relief. For me it's almost as if you appreciate the taste of the beef *because* of the horseradish; it provides an alternative view.

Today Tracklements is still going strong, but for anyone else starting out Guy offers this piece of advice: 'When we started you were very limited in your routes to market; now, if I think I've made the finest chilli sauce since time began, I can get a pitch at a farmers' market for £20 and get going.' We're a nation of tinkerers, testers and fiddlers, and men and women with an 'I wonder if . . .' and 'Mmm, now that's interesting' mentality have given us some of our greatest inventions. And so it should be in food. As Guy says, 'We sometimes see ourselves as a little bit of a trailblazer, but we're not really doing anything new, we're just doing it as it's meant to be done.'

*See also* BISHOP'S STORTFORD, HERTFORDSHIRE (p. 321); EDINBURGH, EDINBURGH (p. 167); FAVERSHAM, KENT (p. 477); MOFFAT, DUMFRIES & GALLOWAY (p. 183); NORWICH, NORFOLK (p. 451); OXFORD, OXFORDSHIRE (p. 351); ROSSENDALE, LANCASHIRE (p. 131); ST HELENS, MERSEYSIDE (p. 132); SHEFFIELD, SOUTH YORKSHIRE (p. 258); SPENNYMOOR, COUNTY DURHAM (p. 227); WORCESTER, WORCESTERSHIRE (p. 317).

# Smoked eel from Brown and Forrest smokery

Jesse Pattisson has been the sole owner of the Brown and Forrest smokery since 2007, when he bought the business from founder and old friend Michael Brown. It started up in 1981 with smoked eels and crayfish, and now supplies some of the UK's finest restaurants, including the Ivy and J. Sheekey, with artisanal smoked salmon. The fish comes from a unique farming operation in Loch Duart in Scotland (see p. 187), and is first brined in water, sugar and a little bit of whisky, then laid flat on racks and cold smoked. Despite the big-name London contracts, you can get a whole side of his salmon delivered for £29 – handy if you can't get a table at the Ivy.

As well as smoking various kinds of fish, Brown and Forrest produce a very good smoked duck breast

His eels come from closer to home, namely the rivers Avon, Test, Stour and Piddle. They're brought in to the smokery live and then killed, skinned and placed in the hot smoker, over beech and apple wood. They are available to order too, either portioned or whole. The latter, depending on size, will serve four to ten people. Jesse recommends you serve smoked eel at room temperature to really appreciate the flavours.

'Smoking is all about the quality of ingredient you put in, then adding a flavour that enhances that ingredient,' says Jesse. Hot smoking involves roasting the food over a large fire for twenty minutes to cook it, and then adding sawdust to the fire to kill the flames and produce smoke that imparts flavour. Cold smoking is a much longer process, in which the product goes in raw or brined over a slow-burning dynamite-style trail of sawdust. This produces lots of smoke but no heat, and the process can typically last for twenty hours or more. And that's it: no gas or electricity or firelighters, just wood and flame.

Jesse uses native woods in his smokery: 'There are some really interesting African woods, but what's the point in using African wood in an English smokery?' Attached to the smokery is a small shop and restaurant that allows Brown and Forrest to show off its wares, a combination of wholesale, shop and restaurant that means Jesse's eggs aren't all in one basket. I wonder if he's ever tried smoking an egg?

See also ARBROATH, ANGUS (p. 143); CLEY NEXT THE SEA, NORFOLK (p. 424); FINDON, ABERDEENSHIRE (p. 169); GREAT YARMOUTH, NORFOLK (p. 433); NIDDERDALE, NORTH YORKSHIRE (p. 251); SEAHOUSES, NORTHUMBERLAND (p. 224); WHITBY, NORTH YORKSHIRE (p. 268).


## HAMPRESTON, DORSET
### Dorset blueberries

Blueberries rather came out of the blue in recent years, suddenly appearing in the late 1980s or early 1990s along with other American imports such as American Football and *The Cosby Show*. I think I first saw them dyeing the inside of a blueberry muffin an alarming colour. Their commercial history, though, would fit on the back of an envelope. Despite being enjoyed by Native Americans, and known since colonial times, blueberries didn't really come under the scrutiny of horticulturists until the turn of the last century. As for their first ever entry into the UK, well, if you've got an OAP bus pass, you were around when it happened.

In 1951 an advert appeared in the *Grower* magazine offering 100 free blueberry bushes to anyone who would pay the shipping costs. The late David Trehane, a market gardener from Wimborne, Dorset, responded, along with three other growers from the south-west. 'The plants were offered by a Methodist minister from Lulu Island, British Columbia, who wanted to add a little cheer to post-war Britain,' says Jennifer Trehane, David's daughter. The initial batch took well, and ten years later when the decision was made to start producing them commercially, 1,000 plants arrived on the *Queen Mary*, with Jennifer arriving dockside at Southampton to collect them with her father. Jennifer, along with her son, also called David, now runs the Dorset Blueberry Company, and with over fifty years and a brace of books on the subject, she may arguably be considered the UK's leading blueberry expert. The varieties they originally received included Rubel, Concord, Jersey and Pemberton, which are all highbush varieties heralding from the north-east of the USA. Lowbush 'wild' variants are grown in Maine, as well as on the Canadian West Coast.

'Blueberries can take six or seven years to establish and deliver a return,' says Jennifer. 'Once they're in, though, they're good for sixty or seventy years.' A fact supported by her father's original 1957 commercial plantings, which are still producing fruit. The Trehanes now produce about eighteen tonnes a year in a season that runs from mid July to late September. As for buyers, they range from Marks & Spencer and Tesco to farm shops and the public, who can visit and 'pick their own'.

Today the demand for blueberries is huge, but, according to Jennifer, 'Twenty years ago people thought these were sloes or something – they'd never seen them before.' Nowadays, blueberries are fêted as an antioxidant-packed superfood. However, the long establishment time is a problem for would-be UK growers, and consequently some have tried to shorten this by growing in pots under plastic. Bear in mind the fact that any UK grower also has to compete with Dutch and Polish counterparts, as well as those in America, which is still the world's largest producer, and you'll see that it's not the easiest business to get into. The Dorset Blueberry Company doesn't have to worry about establishing the crop however, thanks to a forward-thinking patriarch and the generosity of a Canadian minister.

*See also* CORBRIDGE, NORTHUMBERLAND (p. 207); EGTON BRIDGE, NORTH YORKSHIRE (p. 243); HONITON, DEVON (p. 17); INVERGOWRIE, PERTH &

## HELSTON, CORNWALL
### *Picnics*

Ahhh, the classic British summer! The thwack of leather on willow, the zip of a frisbee, the pleasure of dozing under a tree or feeling the grass between your toes . . . all of which are no doubt enhanced by a picnic. I like proper picnics: they're sophisticated and civilised, while often being more fun and less fraught than barbecues. Whether it's a gang of mates on a patch of grass in a park with everything bought from the nearby mini-mart and a footy to kick around, or a well-planned affair laid out in a picturesque spot or overlooking a majestic vista, when it's sunny – which is by no means certain – there's nothing finer.

Of course, if you want to have a sophisticated picnic but don't have the time to prepare the hamper, you can always let someone else do the hard work. Gourmet Picnics, based in Cornwall, does just that. Rather than just a hamper with a few biscuits and a bottle of wine, each cool bag contains fresh food all made properly by a chef and delivered to your door in twenty-four hours. The company was set up by London-born Sam Sheffield-Dunstan, who met and married a Cornish man while attending art school in the county. Initially she just supplied people in Cornwall: 'There's a huge alfresco-eating mindset down here. If the sun's out, people'll get on the beach.' Soon the operation went nationwide, and she now offers dressed Cornish crabs, dressed lobsters, West Country cheeses, Parma ham and melon, and a range of salads, all chilled and packed in biodegradable containers. 'We get a lot of requests from guys getting ready to propose,' says Sam. 'You look pretty cool with your dressed lobster and chilled champagne.'

Dining outside is nothing new: many rural workers ate outside come (frequent) rain or shine. But a picnic isn't just about eating alfresco. It's about taking the inside, outside. Though picnics first appeared at the fag end of the Regency period, picnics found mass appeal during the Victorian era, perhaps in response to the ever-stiffening rules of etiquette at Victorian mealtimes. That's not to say, however, that picnics didn't have a sense of propriety. Mrs Beeton gives a list of things to take for a picnic for forty: 'A joint of cold roast beef, a joint of cold boiled beef, two ribs of lamb, two shoulders of lamb, four roast fowls, two roast ducks, one ham, one tongue, two veal-and-ham pies, two pigeon pies, six medium-sized lobsters, one piece of collared calf's head' . . . and that's just the meat. Outside eating was taken very seriously: if Manet had been British he'd have no doubt painted *Le déjeuner sur l'herbe* without the lady in the nip and with the addition of Scotch eggs, bottles of beer, cheese, cold chicken, salads, apples, and all the produce and paraphernalia of a proper picnic hamper. He would have also probably painted an ominous-looking cloud on the horizon.

HONITON, DEVON

## *Home-grown peaches from Otter Farm*

A harvesting high-point for climate-change farmer Mark Diacono was picking the first peach at his farm on the banks of the River Otter in Devon. Alongside peaches, Mark grows apricots, olives, pecans and persimmon. It's not all exotics, though he also turns his hand to seldom-seen natives such as mulberries, medlars and quinces.

'The idea is driven entirely by flavour. I made a list of food I liked, looked into how much of it was realistic to grow here, saw some that was at the edge of viability but with climate change would be more likely,' says Mark. The aim is to create a virtuous circle: growing commonly imported foods and by doing so reducing the carbon that is associated with those foods in the UK.

When Mark began Otter Farm in 2005, the seventeen acres had formerly belonged to the council. The soil had been farmed intensively for years and was in pretty poor condition. Mark set about restoring the hedges and ditches, and encouraging the wildlife, and the farm now has Soil Association organic status. Everything is produced on the farm in small quantities at the moment, partly because farms and orchards take time to develop; Mark's oldest tree is only five years old, after all. Gradually, as things become more viable and established, a more formal retail option may emerge. Mark readily admits his farm is a work-in-progress; right now he's attempting to prove the concept works, whether on a farm his size, on an allotment or even a garden-sized plot. 'Food is the way into dealing with climate change. It accounts for 30 per cent

# Cornish Pasties

Board a train bound for the Home Counties leaving any of the London stations at eight or so in the evening and you'll see them: office workers who've obviously been in the pub since five (or earlier), trying to soak up a skinful with a sausage roll, a pie or, more often than not, a pasty. Their clothing soon becomes flecked with golden dandruff, and they make the whole carriage smell like a bakery; I call these the pasty trains.

Historically, though, the pasty is associated with another kind of worker: the Cornish tin miner. He too needed something quick, hot and filling to eat, and the pasty fitted the bill. There's been a great deal of 'hoo' and indeed 'ha' over the pasty of late: where it should be made, what shape it should be and what it should contain have all been hotly debated. The Cornish Pasty Association, consisting of fifty or so of the county's bakers, defines a genuine Cornish pasty thus: a distinctive 'D' shape, with the crimped edge around the curved side. The filling should be chunky, and contain mince or roughly chopped beef (skirt being traditional), diced swede or turnip, diced potato, onion, salt and plenty of pepper.

The association's aim is to get Protected Designation of Origin (PDO) status for their product, meaning that if it's called a Cornish pasty, it's made only in Cornwall, and in the traditional way. Admittedly, this is unlikely to stop people all over the UK making pasties; it will just halt the perceived misuse of the 'Cornish' prefix. Their campaign aims to source the ingredients from within the county itself, supporting farmers, creating jobs and putting a stop to the environmental madness of trucking in a load of raw ingredients, part assembling them, then trucking them out again to be baked and sold.

Of course, the pasty isn't alone. There is its poorer relative, the hoggan, which also comes from Cornwall and is a blob of pastry with bits of potato or meat pushed into it. On occasion, dried fruits are used instead, and the result is called a figgy hobbin. The spelling 'hobban' also appears, and one – or indeed all – of these variants are related to the oggie, which is the name of a Welsh pasty. This too was said to be tough enough to drop down a mineshaft – just like its Cornish cousin.

Why the pasty has become so popular in recent years is, at least in my eyes, due to the fact that the pastry-to-filling ratio is just right, making it easy to eat on the move. When eating a pie – and oh how I love them also – you always run the risk of getting your chin scalded by dripping hot filling, but the pasty's wide girth spreads the filling load. So it's perfect if you're hungry and about to board the 19.55 to Basingstoke from Waterloo.

See also BOGHALL, WEST LOTHIAN (p. 146); BRIGHOUSE, WEST YORKSHIRE (p. 235); CARDIFF, CARDIFF (p. 59); CLACHNACUDDIN, HIGHLAND (p. 154); FORFAR, ANGUS (p. 172); MELTON MOWBRAY, LEICESTERSHIRE (p. 342); SANDY, BEDFORDSHIRE (p. 358).

of our carbon footprint and it may be the single major contributor.' But what surprises him most is the interest the idea has generated. 'It's got people thinking creatively – it almost doesn't matter whether it works or not. It's about being creative, adapting as well as mitigating.'

*See also* CORBRIDGE, NORTHUMBERLAND (p. 207); EGTON BRIDGE, NORTH YORKSHIRE (p. 243); HAMPRESTON, DORSET (p. 14); INVERGOWRIE, PERTH & KINROSS (p. 180); LYTH AND WINSTER VALLEYS, CUMBRIA (p. 117); NORTHIAM, EAST SUSSEX (p. 492); WALMERSLEY, GREATER MANCHESTER (p. 137); WIMBLEDON, MERTON (p. 415).

## KING'S NYMPTON, DEVON
### *A multi-bird roast from Heal Farm*

The 'Turduken' is the recent portmanteau creation of New Orleans chef Paul Prudhomme; it's a chicken stuffed inside a duck stuffed inside a turkey, all liberally rubbed with his range of ready-made sauces and spice mixes. It is, however, a mere spring chicken to Anne Petch's twelve-bird roast. Anne and her husband Richard started Heal Farm in North Devon with a few pigs in 1974. It's now a fully fledged mail-order food business selling everything from fresh meat and soups to pies, puddings and cakes, and it specialises in multi-bird roasts, which have become increasingly popular in recent years. Hugh Fearnley-Whittingstall successfully made one on *River Cottage* a few years ago for a medieval-themed feast. Anne's monster twelve-birder feeds around 125 diners, takes eight hours to cook and comes in its own roasting tray and hamper. You will, however, need a catering-sized oven to cook it in.

'We only sold six in the end, all made to order, but it gave us some great publicity,' she says. Her more pedestrian five-bird roast is her most popular; it's a boned farm turkey stuffed with chicken breasts, guinea-fowl breasts, pheasant breasts and boned quail. The reasons multi-bird roasts have become popular are manifold: they make an interesting centrepiece for the Christmas table, there's something for everyone and it gives people the opportunity to try something different – say pheasant – without upsetting the traditionalists at the table who still want turkey. Moreover, because it's all boned out, there is very little left over, it's easy to cook and they're a cinch to carve. 'I remember the tension in my father-in-law's house when anything difficult to carve was brought out,' Anne says. Unlike the Russian-doll method, where one bird is inside another, Anne's bird roast contains layers of breast meat with different flavoured stuffing in between, which helps to keep the bird moist.

If, however, a bird stuffed with twelve common game birds is just too pedestrian for you, there is always the *roti sans pareil*, or 'roast without equal'. A few recipes abound, though one of the best has to be from *Venus in the Kitchen* (1952), edited by sexual miscreant and bon viveur Norman Douglas. It calls for an olive at the heart of a succession of boned-out birds, all placed one inside the other. First the olive goes inside a garden warbler, which goes inside an ortolan (a type of finch and already the victim of one of gastronomy's more sadistic preparations), which goes in a lark, which goes in a thrush, which goes in a fat quail. The quail is then put inside a lapwing, the lapwing in a golden plover, and the plover in a fat red-legged partridge. This, we're told, then fits inside a well-hung woodcock, the woodcock inside a teal, the teal inside a guinea fowl; the fowl then goes in a pheasant, the pheasant in a wild goose, the goose in a turkey and finally the turkey somehow fits inside the largest bird native to these islands and now protected, namely the bustard bird. After cooking and eating this you can quite rightly expect a visit from the RSPB.

*See also* GOOSNARGH, LANCASHIRE (p. 106); HARLOW, ESSEX (p. 436); HINDOLVESTON, NORFOLK (p. 437); MAIDENHEAD, BERKSHIRE (p. 487); THUXTON, NORFOLK (p. 458).

LOOE, CORNWALL
## *Bocaddon Farm Veal*

It is a fact often overlooked that if you take milk in your morning cuppa or splash it on your cornflakes, you are complicit in the production of veal. To keep the UK's 1.9 million dairy cows producing the 13.5 million litres of milk that we drink yearly in the UK, they all need to have a calf. Female calves can join the herd, replacing older animals, but the laws of chance dictate that about half those calves will be bulls. Their fate used to be live export to Continental Europe, or, more often than not, being shot soon after birth; not much of a life, then.

It was partly an awareness of this that led Jonathan and Vicky Brown to start Bocaddon Farm Veal. Milk runs in the blood for Vicky: her parents were dairy farmers. Husband Jonathan's background is rather different: he

At Bocaddon Farm, male calves are reared to produce rose veal

worked for a jewellery wholesaler before leaving with a dream of becoming a chef. On the way, though, he got diverted: 'I'd just finished reading Hugh Fearnley-Whittingstall's *Meat* book, and discovered it was possible to rear veal nicely. I saw that no one was doing it.'

And so John and Vicky took six calves from a pedigree Holstein and Guernsey herd and got started. 'We had no idea what we were doing. We didn't know how big they were going to get, how old to take them, and the really ridiculous thing was we didn't know how our product was going to taste.' They finally slaughtered one when they thought it was big enough – about five months old – and were delighted with the results.

But who would buy it? Jonathan began knocking on the kitchen doors of fine-dining restaurants in Cornwall and telling them what he was up to. Being restaurants, they all want the same high-value 'cheffy' cuts: the loin, the fillet and the much-prized liver. Even on a small animal like a calf that leaves plenty of other bits, so they got a stall at Lostwithiel farmers' market selling the roasting joints, escallops, mince and home-made sausages.

As for the public's perception of veal, Jonathan and Vicky have heard it all. 'One woman at a farmers' market came up to me and said, "I think it's disgusting you're selling the foetuses of unborn calves,"' proving that this particular meat is surrounded by a great deal of misinformation and misconception. Bocaddon's veal – sometimes called rosé or pink veal – has nothing to do with any of the cruel production techniques from the past. It's more akin to lamb, in that it's just the meat of a young tender animal. 'We're saving an animal from being shot at birth and being wasted,' says Jonathan. His calves get to move around inside and out, and they live on a varied diet including milk, cereals and straw from their own bedding.

The diet certainly seems to work, as the veal is extraordinary. I tasted a flash-fried escallop served with picked-right-then wild garlic between two slices of freshly baked bread. It was quite possibly one of the nicest sand-wiches I've ever eaten. The raw garlic leaves had a punch, the veal was as soft and delicate as a first-date kiss, and the bread was warm and nutty: as delicious and as rustic a lunch as you could hope for.

LOSTWITHIEL, CORNWALL
## Clotted cream

As well as bartering saffron for Cornish tin (*see* p. 37), the Phoenicians are also said to have introduced the process of making clotted cream to the peninsula, which was very generous of them; nice lot, those Phoenicians. This observation is espoused by everyone from Charles Dickens and the Revd Sabine Baring-Gould, who in the early twentieth century was something of an expert on Cornish Celtic history, right up to eminent food historian Alan Davidson, so who am I to argue? Other myths and legends about its creation do abound, often featuring hungry giants and unwatched pots on the fire, but in the present day it is worth noting that only in the West Country and the Middle East (where it is known as *kaymak*) is clotted cream made.

Cornish clotted cream has PDO (Protected Designation of Origin) status, thanks in part to the leadership of the Rodda family, who for five generations have been making cream in Redruth. There are many other producers in the county though, and indeed all across the south-west. One is the Trewithen Dairy, based in Lostwithiel, where sales manager Paul Worden talked me through the process. The milk comes from one of the seventeen farms that Trewithen work with, all of whom are within a twenty-mile radius. First, it's pasteurised, then put through a separator which draws off most of the cream. This is warmed in a vat before being transferred to individual pots and baked in an oven at around 80 °C for about an hour, which allows the beautiful nutty crust to form. The cream is then placed in a fridge to cool before the lids are put on and it's ready to be slathered on anything you fancy. 'In the old days, housewives would milk the cow, and set the pan on the Rayburn overnight. Come morning the cream would be ready to have with your toast,' says Paul. Which is not a bad idea, and along with the rarely seen Cornish splits (small cake-like buns) is far more traditional than perhaps that modern interloper, the scone.

See also STOURHEAD, WILTSHIRE (p. 39).

## LYME REGIS, DORSET
# Baker's eggs from the Town Mill Bakery

The Town Mill Bakery in Lyme Regis, Dorset, isn't hard to find, despite being tucked down an alleyway; all you have to do is follow the waft of freshly baking bread. As the name suggests, the bakery began life in the old town mill up the road, but moved to its current location in an old boatyard in 2007. The larger venue allows for the whole thing – mixers, ovens, shop and eatery – to take place in one open-plan space, so you really get to see the flour flying.

When I talked to Clive Cobb, the aptly named owner, he told me that 'Baking has become a devalued word. A lot of places that say they're bakeries are just reheating – it's like making instant coffee. Very few are making the product from scratch.' At the Town Mill Bakery they use the classic sponge and dough method, which takes longer but uses less yeast and gives a much better flavour. The white flour comes from Shipton Mill in Gloucestershire, with N. R. Stoates in Shaftesbury providing the wholemeal and malt flour. Everything else that can be sourced nearby is done so; exceptions are things like olive oil, as unfortunately there is not much of that in Dorset.

One of the best complements to wonderful fresh bread is the humble egg. Like Doctor Who and his assistants these two ingredients have appeared in

A range of breads — as well as cakes, buns and muffins — are made daily at the Town Mill Bakery

many guises over time, yet their relationship remains fundamentally the same, namely one of contrasting textures. So there are scrambled eggs on toast, a boiled egg and a regiment of soldiers, and one you might not have heard of: baker's eggs. This is the name given to a particular egg and bread partnership at the Town Mill Bakery, but it goes by others around the world: egg in a nest, egg in a basket, bull's eye, or perhaps my favourite, a one-eyed jack.

At the Town Mill bakery they take a decent doorstep-sized slice of bread and cut a circle out with a pastry cutter, then place the bread on an ovenproof tray. Into the resulting hole goes a fresh free-range egg, and the tray is popped into the oven to toast the bread and cook the egg. The difference at the Town Mill bakery is that they bake the dish rather than fry it, giving a less oily and more toasty taste while keeping the barely set dunkability of a fried egg. Finally the cut-out piece of circular bread is toasted alongside and comes served on top at a jaunty angle like a little hat.

# Lardy Cake

You have to feel sorry for lard. It has none of the sweet, rosy connotations of butter, none of the Continental sun of oil, and none of the honest beefy goodness of dripping. This is no doubt because it comes from pigs, and so maintains the pig's unfortunate baggage of sloth and gluttony. This is a shame, because nearly all our greatest pastry-based dishes feature lard in some way, and none celebrates the joy of lard more than lardy cake. Lardy cake is the heady combination of lard and bread, with a few dried fruits that, at a push, count towards your five a day. It is the sort of pudding that separates those who live to eat from those who eat to live; dieters, the gluten-intolerant and fatophobes recoil in horror at the very mention of it. With lardy cake, though, you at least know what you're in for: there is no hidden fat here.

To make it, the bread dough is rolled out, spread with lard, sugar, dried fruit and warm spices (nutmeg, cinnamon and such) before being folded over. The process is then repeated several times. Some recipes call for the folded pastry to be rolled into a coil and baked into a round shape, while others maintain that it ought to be kept flat and baked square. During cooking, the sugars caramelise, the fat becomes flavoursome, the bread rises and the raisins become chewy.

The cake's richness is due to the fact that it was traditionally made as a celebration of harvest, and though it was made all over the UK (wherever there was pig fat going begging) lardy cake's homeland is the pig-producing counties of Suffolk, Oxfordshire, Gloucestershire and Wiltshire. The name occasionally changes, too. In Suffolk it's fourses cake; in Wiltshire it's sharley cake. Despite having the word 'cake' in its name, the finished article looks more like a loaf or bun than a cake. A well-made one is surprisingly tasty, and shouldn't be greasy as the dough absorbs much of the lard. It should, however, leave your fingers shiny.

Like some reintroduced rare species, lardy cake is establishing a foothold in pubs and restaurants that have come to realise how lovely it can be, and it makes a change from profiteroles and ice cream. You can also find it in good bakeries where they know the joy of mixing the scent of all those spices with the scents of freshly baking bread and melting fat. Two Wiltshire bakeries produce particularly good lardy cake: the Bakery in Great Bedwyn and Marshall's in Wootton Bassett, which sells both a standard and a deluxe version – the latter basically being the former but with more of everything.

We are constantly told we all eat too much fat, but then, as I've said elsewhere in this book, fat is flavour. Lard is surely set for a return, in moderation, as it is essentially a tasty and natural product. Welcome back old friend.

*See also* BATH, SOMERSET (p. 5); CHELSEA, KENSINGTON & CHELSEA (p. 373); SWANSEA, SWANSEA (p. 87)

## *Cornish earlies*

The Cornish early potato is one of England's little-known treasures; like golden nuggets these tiny tubers grow in the rich mineral earth of the Cornish peninsula, aptly named the Golden Mile. They have a sweet buttery taste that is complemented by an almost zincy mineral flavour; all of this packed into something no bigger than the end of your thumb. John Wallis, potato farmer and champion of Cornish produce, goes so far as to describe earlies as the Cornish truffle, and tells of a time, not so long ago, when 'new' potatoes really meant something, usually that you'd survived the winter. The very tip of Cornwall enjoys a much milder climate than the rest of the country, meaning that Cornish earlies were traditionally the first potatoes harvested in the UK. With the arrival of the railways, the very first earlies would be sent up to London as soon as they were ready, where they would fetch an excellent price; hard to imagine in these

John Wallis harvesting his crop on Cornwall's Golden Mile, overlooking Mount's Bay

days of air-freighting when it is easy enough to get 'new' potatoes all year round.

*See also* CORNHILL-ON-TWEED, NORTHUMBERLAND (p. 208); NEWCASTLE, TYNE & WEAR (p. 218); SHEFFIELD, SOUTH YORKSHIRE (p. 260).

# The Somerset Cider Brandy Company

The world of cider is a book in itself (and I recommend James Cowden's excellent *Ciderland*). The tradition of making beverages from apples exists not only in the West Country, but also in the West Midlands, Kent, Suffolk and Wales. This was no doubt due to the favourable climatic conditions in the south of the country, though in recent times production has stretched as far as Cumbria and Yorkshire, and there is even one producer in Scotland. Uniquely, cider producers are allowed to make 1,500 gallons before paying any duty.

But as venerable as the cider tradition is in these parts of the country, the point at which cider could be said to have become sexy happened sometime in the mid 2000s, thanks to some very successful marketing by the Magner's cider company. The adverts featured shots of apples, orchards and beautiful people enjoying the drink. The summers of 2004 and 2005 were good ones, and crucially Magner's suggested serving cider over ice (something we'd only seen previously in the film *Withnail and I*).

'What Magner's did was come to the West Country, steal our ideas of cider, take them to Ireland and say they were theirs. And they did a wonderful job,' says Julian Temperley from the Somerset Cider Brandy Company. Love it or loathe it, the Magner's effect introduced a new generation, especially women, to the ancient and revered beverage of cider. Off the back of that, artisan cider producers got much more of a look-in as drinkers began to try different styles and look for new tastes, paying particular attention to organic and premium ciders. In the past ten years it is amazing to think just how gentrified the drink has become. Some producers are even looking to the wine industry and making single-apple varieties of cider – rather than blends – in order to exploit the apple's different characteristics.

Of course, there is more you can do with cider than simply drink it (as delicious as it often is), and since 1989 Julian Temperley has been making

Julian Temperley and his cider-distilling equipment

cider brandy. He was the first to restart the process of distilling light frothy apple juice into a crystal-clear auburn spirit. The apple juice is first fermented for six months to make cider, then distilled to remove the colour, creating a clear spirit. Being an apple man, Julian knows all about windfall – when fruit is blown off a tree. A windfall of a slightly different kind happened in January 2007 when the container ship MSC *Napoli* got into difficulty in the Channel. Washed ashore were several oak wine casks en route to South Africa. Julian obtained a few with the permission of the Receiver of Wrecks. He then matured some of his ten-year-old cider brandy in them for twelve months. The barrels are Allier oak from the central region of France. 'The low rainfall there gives a tighter grained wood that imbibes a stronger taste,' says Julian. The result is a strong oaky nose and flavour, sitting on mellow appley back notes. 'It has all the tale of the wild West Country – apples, cider, shipwrecks and larceny,' he laughs.

*See also* AMPLEFORTH, NORTH YORKSHIRE (p. 234).

MOUSEHOLE, CORNWALL
## *Stargazey pie at the Ship Inn*

One could say that stargazey pie achieved international notoriety when it was served as the main course at the British Embassy in Paris on the BBC's *Great British Menu* programme in 2007. The chef on that occasion was Mark Hix, and his version of the dish featured rabbit and crayfish under the pastry cover, with four of the crustaceans poking through and gazing longingly up at the sky. Hix's dish was a clever use of two species normally considered vermin. 'Rabbits and crayfish are doing their fair share to ruin crops and destroy other water life,' he says in his book *Seasonal Food*. Traditionally, however, the dish eschews these environmental ne'er-do-wells and contains that Cornish staple of old, the pilchard. Dorothy Hartley mentions stargazey pies in her 1953 *Food in England*. Here there is a small drawing of each individual fish lovingly wrapped in pastry, like a fishy sausage roll, with the heads protruding. The reason she gives for this is that covering the inedible head with edible pastry was a waste of good pastry, yet removing the head let all the oils and juices out. Hartley also describes a large family-sized pie version, and attributes the 'head-poking-out' effect to the Victorians, although her fish are all arranged in a circular pattern with the heads lying at the edge of the pie like numbers on a clock face.

The pie is said to have been created in Mousehole (pronounced *mow-zul*) by one Tom Bawcock, a brave sailor – some say a widower with nothing to lose – who sailed out in violent stormy seas when the village was facing starvation. The fish he returned with were made into a pie and shared among the townsfolk, thus saving them from famine. His heroic deeds are celebrated every 23 December in the town to this day.

The only place worth eating a stargazey is the Ship Inn on Mousehole harbour, although owner and chef Colin Perkin only makes the pies for the Tom Bawcock eve celebrations. His recipe consists of seven types of white fish in a white sauce, on to which is added a layer of chopped boiled egg, followed by a layer of mashed potato. A pastry lid is rolled out, placed on top, then sardines or baby mackerel heads and tails are pushed through cuts made in the pastry. Colin gives out portions of the pie throughout the evening's festivities free of charge, and the fish is kindly donated by local fishermen.

As for Tom Bawcock, well, it's pinches of salt all round as to whether the events ever took place. It seems that the townsfolk couldn't have been that lacking in food if they somehow found pastry, potatoes and eggs to make the pie. But facts be damned. Perhaps he is best left as the inspiration for a great pie and an excuse for the people of Mousehole to have a good old knees-up in the December cold.

*See also* HOW RECIPES BEGIN (p. 496); CARDIFF, CARDIFF (p. 59); CHINLEY, DERBYSHIRE (p. 285); DENBY DALE, WEST YORKSHIRE (p. 240); GLASGOW, GLASGOW (p. 178); GREENWICH, GREENWICH (p. 380).

NEWLYN BAY, CORNWALL
## Albacore, or 'white meat', tuna

According to the Marine Stewardship Council, albacore tuna (sometimes called 'white meat' tuna) is plentiful, unlike the nearly extinct blue- or yellow-fin tuna, and Quentin Knights – a big bloke with a big smile and big hands like half pounds of sausages – is nigh on obsessed with it. During the summer months Quentin crews on the *Nova Spero*, a 19.2-metre wooden beamer, and, along with another beamer called the *Charisma*, goes after albacore tuna. 'For fifteen years no one had brought the tuna in, not since the end of drift

Quentin Knights keeps his catch fresh in these ice-filled boxes

netting. But I'd always wanted to do it. I'd dreamed of it,' he told me. A study in 2003 showed it to be viable, and in 2007 they went out for a test run. At that point they struggled to sell it back on the quay as there just wasn't a market for it, but in 2008, thanks to a partnership with M&J Seafood, things worked out much better: the price was agreed before putting to sea, and in 2009 Morrison's became the first UK supermarket to take it for their fish counters.

I asked him how he can be sure he'll catch the right species of tuna, and he answers, 'For one, hook and line is very selective. Your breaking pound of line dictates what fish you can catch, with the average being around six kilos in weight. The breeding stock are larger, but they're down deeper. We're just after the juveniles – the teenagers if you like – who are higher up feeding.' It seems incredible, but he assures me it works. 'Everything's so finely tuned. It's like angling, but on a commercial scale.'

## NEWLYN, CORNWALL
# *Cornish sardines*

The transformation of the Cornish pilchard into the Cornish sardine is all down to one reason: public perception. Sardines remind shoppers of sunny Mediterranean holidays and delicious barbecues, whereas plain old pilchards remind them of tea at some old auntie's house that smelled of mothballs. So, seeing which way public opinion was swimming, the Cornish Sardine Management Association (CSMA) was set up in 2004 to do something about it. The renaming was just one part of a drive to protect an age-old tradition and a key part of Cornish maritime life; the association also manages catches to protect stock levels. To earn the new nomenclature, and the all-important accompanying EU protected food status, the fish must be caught within six miles of the Cornish coast.

In the past this was done with a cliff-top spotter guiding the boats via semaphore; now sonar does that job. The fish used to be preserved with salt and packed in wooden barrels before being exported to the Continent, a trade that has been going on since Elizabethan times. The first recorded exports were from Looe in East Cornwall in 1555, and the main buyers were in Italy. Nick Howell is chairman of the CSMA and also runs the pilchard works in Newlyn. He's been leading the rebrand, having seen the market for the traditional barrel-preserved fish dry up. He made his last barrel in 2005 – 'One family, the Borzone, had been taking the fish since 1905' – but Italian tastes were changing. As well as fresh sardines, Nick still offers the classic tinned version, which is landed and prepped in Cornwall before being sent to Brittany for canning. Here, in a small canning firm, the fish are cooked before being placed in the tin. Most canning firms in the UK would place the fish in raw, seal the tin, then cook them, leaving you with a mushy, poor-tasting product.

Now there is protection for the name and the process, and Marine Stewardship Council certification on the way, it's up to us as consumers to make the most of this wonderful fish. Nick would like to see the season, which runs from midsummer until autumn, become a cause for celebration, much like the grouse season. During this time, the sardine's flesh is plump and full of good flavourful oils; it really deserves a spot on your barbecue.

*See also* DERWENTWATER, CUMBRIA (p. 102); DOVER, KENT (p. 473);
GLOUCESTER, GLOUCESTERSHIRE (p. 288); HASTINGS, EAST SUSSEX (p. 483);

PLYMOUTH, DEVON
# Plymouth Gin

Gin, like other spirits, is produced by the seemingly magical process of distillation, where a liquid is vaporised, then condensed by cooling the resulting vapour back to a liquid. And so while wine or other liquids go in at one end, by a simple heating process, a totally different – and stronger – liquid comes out the other. And perhaps it was this strange new alchemy that led to the thought that gin, along with other spirits, was a magical nostrum for many ills. Pepys tried 'strong water made of juniper' to cure his constipation in 1633, and gin was once known as 'plague water', guaranteed to protect the drinker from the deadly disease.

Today, according to Sean Harrison, head distiller at Plymouth Gin, quality gin is still distilled, but now cheaper gins are made using the compound method. This sees the spirit mixed with essences of the main flavouring ingredients to produce a cheaper, less interesting and more chemically tasting gin worthy of one of Hogarth's *Gin Lane* ladies. 'Distilling technology is a thousand years old, and it hasn't needed to change very much because fundamentally nature knows best,' says Sean. He then tells me about all the ingredients that go into the distinctive flavour, and how every year the firm must scour the world to find the right suppliers. Lemons and oranges are sourced from Spain, coriander from Russia, juniper and orris root from Italy, angelica root from Saxony and cardamom pods from Guatemala.

All of these ingredients add different flavours to the gin. So although juniper is the lead flavour, it is flanked by some sweetness from the orange, and some citrus tang from the lemon, while the roots add drier, earthy tones, and the coriander and cardamom a touch of spicy, pepperlike heat.

Gin has always had a relationship with the military. British troops watched their Dutch allies take a swig before battle, which gave us the phrase 'Dutch courage'. And when the Admiralty decided that officers must drink something different from the common rum given to ratings, it was gin, not brandy or whisky, that they chose.

The Plymouth Gin brand is now owned by Pernod Ricard, but production began in 1792 in the city when one Mr Coates, a local businessman, began distilling gin on Southside Street. The building he chose had once been the site of a Dominican Order monastery built in 1431, and it was also where the Pilgrim Fathers are said to have lodged before sailing for America in September 1620. It then went through other ecclesiastical hands before Mr Coates got the keys to the place. And though the firm he founded has changed ownership over the years, the gin is still made in the same location to this day, under Sean's careful eye. At its peak in the 1800s the firm was supplying the Royal Navy with 1,000 barrels of 100 per cent (57 per cent abv) proof gin a year. Its popularity at sea no doubt improved in 1848, when pink gin, featuring a shot of angostura bitters, was touted as a cure for seasickness. The angostura was the element doing all the work, the gin just making the former palatable.

*See also* HAMMERSMITH, HAMMERSMITH & FULHAM (p. 382).


ROCK, CORNWALL
## Nathan Outlaw's hog's pudding

When I first met Kent-born Nathan Outlaw he was cooking at the Marina Hotel in Fowey. There I found his cooking both bold and confident. Each dish was incredibly well presented, without fusions or foams or other cheffy tricks. Of course, it takes a huge amount of skill to make it look that easy.

Since then he has moved to the St Enodoc Hotel in Rock, and a new restaurant split between a twenty-six-cover fine-dining room, and a much larger and informal seafood and grill room that can take up to eighty covers. There is the same ethos and dedication, only this time an even better selection of fish and seafood. 'The big advantage is our fish and shellfish; I can get better than anyone in the country,' he says. But what particularly caught my eye was his dish of scallops with hog's pudding.

Hog's pudding has been made all over the UK since medieval times, wherever a hog was killed. Eventually it became associated with both Cornwall and Devon, with the two versions differing slightly in seasoning. It was designed to use up the lungs, heart, liver and any other bits of the freshly killed pig, and was highly seasoned with spices such as cumin, coriander and nutmeg. In the past dried fruit was also added, while other recipes include almonds or cayenne. This was all bulked out and bound with bread, maybe an egg or two, and placed into hog skins. A recipe featuring most of the ingredients above can be found in Mary Kettilby's *Collection of Above Three Hundred Receipts in Cookery, Physick, and Surgery* from 1734, but plenty of other examples exist, some of which suggest adding groats (unpolished barley) rather than bread.

'I make it all myself, whereas most people buy it ready-made from the butchers,' says Nathan. He doesn't make his to a traditional recipe, but uses pork fillet, chicken, bread, thyme, cumin, shallots, cream, salt and pepper, which he cooks in a terrine and serves in slices with the scallops. 'I've made it lighter and a bit less breakfasty for the restaurant – more like a boudin blanc. The dish is completely south-west,' says Nathan. 'You've got south-west scallops, home-made hog's pudding, and the garnish is locally foraged sea beet, with Jerusalem artichokes pickled and puréed.' A local dish from a chef who's gone native.

## *Saffron cake from W. T. Warren & Son*

The story goes that saffron, the dried stigmas of the *Crocus sativus* flower, was introduced to Cornwall by Phoenician merchants who traded it for tin around 1000 BC. This was long before the Romans – who generously introduced, among other things, carrots, turnips and wine to Britain – landed at Dover in AD 43. The story, of course, may be apocryphal. Phoenicia, after all, was located in present-day Lebanon, and that's a hell of a way to come for some tin. Sir Christopher Hawkins's 1811 work *Tin Trade of the Ancients in Cornwall* doesn't mention saffron, though the ancient Greek historian Strabo states that there was a great deal of trade with Britain for tin. Personally, I think it odd that the tough Iron Age mining men of Cornwall, having hacked tin ore out of the ground and smelted it down, would be inclined to swap it for a few dried flower stigmas but there you go, that's legends for you.

Many cultures outside saffron's original homeland of south-west Asia have recipes featuring the precious warming spice; the Swedes, for example, make a saffron-infused Lucia bread in honour of an Italian saint, and saffron-infused cakes and buns have long been baked throughout Britain. Saffron Walden in Cambridgeshire, of course, was named for the spice's trade, and on the other side of the island the Cornish peninsula has made the bread – or the cake – its own.

There are many bakers, both large and small, who make it, but W. T. Warren & Son are notable for the fact that they won a Great Taste award for their saffron cake in 2009. Their headquarters are still in the Cornish town of St Just, where the business started in the 1860s. The original Queen Street bakery delivered bread and cakes using horse and cart for over 100 years. Their version is made with La Mancha saffron from Spain to a secret 100-year-old recipe, and consists of wheat flour, mixed fruits, lard, vegetable fat, sugar, yeast, peel, egg, butter, salt and the all-important saffron. Jason Jobing, product development manager for Warren's, recommends eating it either as it is, or toasted and liberally spread with butter. If you really want to gild the lily (and who doesn't like gold-plated lilies from time to time), you can add a blob of Cornish clotted cream.

*See also* WREXHAM, WREXHAM (p. 91).

## ST KEVERNE, CORNWALL
### A traditional ox roast

In 1953 the Ministry of Food granted applications for communities to roast a whole ox to celebrate the Coronation, but only if they could prove that by tradition an ox had been roasted at previous coronations (154 applications were received; of those 40 were withdrawn, 33 refused and 81 approved).

One such permission was granted to St Keverne in West Cornwall. The community still holds an ox roast every August, although these days it's used to raise funds for the St Keverne Brass Band, which does great work encouraging children to take up an instrument. The first slice of the done-to-a-turn beef is auctioned off, and the winning bid in 2009 was £350.

The village hasn't always been so fond of royalty, however. It was home to local blacksmith Michael An Gof, who in 1497 led an army of 20,000 Cornishmen to London in a rebellion against King Henry VII. The Cornishmen were protesting about taxes on tin to fund the war in Scotland. Henry met the force with one greater, and An Gof found his head on a pike soon after.

But back to 1953. The matter of the applications was raised many times in the House of Commons. Rationing was still in place, and getting one's hands on anything, as well as permission, must have been tricky. On 1 April, two months before the Coronation itself, Norman Dodds, MP for Dartford, asked the Minister of Food 'why sheep-roasting is forbidden during the Coronation celebrations when ox-roasting is permitted'. Sir Gerald Nabarro, MP for Kidderminster, added that Hallow in rural Worcestershire had roasted oxen in the past, but now, due to a smaller population, wanted to roast a sheep instead. To this the Minister of Food Major Gwilym Lloyd George replied, 'I am not prepared to extend these arrangements to animals other than oxen.' After more toing and froing Robert Boothby, MP for Aberdeenshire East, added, 'In the absence of sheep, will my Right Honourable and gallant friend consider inaugurating a national campaign for the Coronation for the roasting of herrings?' The wag!

The view of the Ministry on ox-roasting in general remained thus: 'While meat is still rationed, this is difficult. [We] are reluctant, however, to stand in the way of traditional festivities of this kind. [The minister] has, therefore, decided that any local authority ... which has made a custom of ox-roasting at Coronations, will be permitted to obtain an ox for this purpose ... provided the cooked meat is given away free.'

For those unable to get roast ox, there was a 'bonus' of one pound of sugar and a quarter pound of margarine, although most thought this a little derisory, especially the Housewives' League, a right-wing Christian organisation that aimed to act as the voice of the housewife. The nation, it seemed, had had enough, and all they wanted to do was celebrate in front of their new television sets.

STOURHEAD, WILTSHIRE
## A National Trust cream tea

The eighteenth-century landscaped gardens and parkland of Stourhead sit a stone's throw over the Somerset border in Wiltshire. On the day I visited the weather was bright and sunny, which naturally meant the car park was overflowing into adjacent fields. Hordes of visitors were thronging to the gardens for the annual Festival of the Voice. Upon entering, I was greeted by the sight of a slowly ambling mass of pastel-clad pensioners freshly disgorged from coaches and all cocking an ear to the assembled choir.

As the melodies and harmonies drifted through the air, I paused to think, 'What could be more English on a summer's day than a nose round a National Trust property, followed by a nice cream tea? And yet what better represents

Jam or cream first?

British food pedantry than the star of that cream tea, the scone?' This is no humble baked product but in fact a powerful prism for splitting the white light of Britishness into the minute spectra of class, education and social standing.

First there's the pronunciation. Is it 'scone' to rhyme with John, or 'scone' to rhyme with Joan? Those who favour the latter – let's call them Joans – number around 35 per cent according to a 1998 survey by University College London. They are seen as posh and aloof by the other 65 per cent – let's call them the Johns – who are in turn seen as common and unable to speak correctly by the Joans. As of December 2008 there were fifty-three groups on Facebook all hurling abuse at each other over this very issue. As George Bernard Shaw said, 'It is impossible for an Englishman to open his mouth without making some other Englishman hate or despise him.'

But let's say you find yourself breaking this particular bread product with someone who pronounces it the same way you do. You're by no means out of the woods yet. There's the dilemma of whether to put the cream or the jam on first. Cream on first is apparently the Devonshire way of doing it; jam on first is the Cornish way. However, in my travels I've seen the complete opposite of this in both counties. What's more, Ellen Easton in a 2004 article entitled 'Etiquette Faux Pas and Other Misconceptions About Afternoon Tea' declares it 'improper to slice a scone in its entirety' and recommends breaking off small chunks and applying jam and cream to these, as one might a croissant. It seems the whole issue exists to beset and befuddle the middle classes. (You notice no one gives a monkey's about whether it's the salt or the vinegar that goes on chips first.)

But since you're asking, I personally favour clotted cream on first – yes, on top of butter – then just a small blob of either strawberry or raspberry jam. The reason why I think this works is that if the cream is on top, it hits your mouth first, completely filling your taste buds like grouting on a bathroom wall. When the jam (which should be at room temperature) is on top, it hits your mouth with that citrus sugar sharpness before the mouth-wide cooling effect of the cream. Finally, I pronounce 'scone' to rhyme with John, but that's just me. No doubt some readers are raising a pitchfork-armed militia against me for my heretical views, but here I call that iconoclastic Englishman Stephen Fry as witness for the defence: 'If you're the kind of person who insists on this or that "correct" use . . . abandon your pedantry as I did mine. Dive into the open flowing waters and leave the stagnant canals be . . . Above all, let there be pleasure!' Because whichever way you eat it, a cakey, bready bun with some dairy product and preserved fruit slathered on it in a manner of your choosing remains one of the joys of England.

*See also* LOSTWITHIEL, CORNWALL (p. 23).

TOTNES, DEVON
## Sloe Tavy

'Poets have been mysteriously silent on the subject of cheese,' said G. K. Chesterton in 1910. The girls staffing Totnes Country Cheeses, on the other hand, can wax lyrical on the subject. The shop was started by Gary and Elise Jungheim in the 1980s when they realised that nearly all the local cheeses were being sent up to London.

All artisanal cheese-making pretty much stopped after the war as milk was pooled, which meant it was bought, managed and distributed for the common good. The only cheese that could be made went by the name of 'Government Cheddar', and wasn't worthy of the name. Still, there was a nation to feed and rebuild, and a bright modern future to strive towards. The world moved on, and in this corner at least, the art of the local artisanal cheese nearly died out, and took decades to return. Gary and Elise started out with a stall on Tavistock Market selling what they could source from the region, and things grew from there. They now have three shops in the south-west and a thriving mail-order service.

Not only are all the 100 or so cheeses in the shop British, but 95 per cent of them are from the West Country. The only out-of-towners are big favourites like Stilton, as you can't have a British cheese shop without the classics. It's the West Country ones that hold the most interest, however, particularly 'Sloe Tavy' made by Pete Humphries at White Lake Cheeses. This cheese is unique and is only sold in Totnes Country Cheeses and a few other selected outlets. It's an aged goat's milk cheese whose rind is washed in Plymouth Sloe Gin. It tastes amazing, with a nutty tang and a slight back-

Sloe Tavy is a thing of rare beauty

of-the-nose 'woo' that no doubt comes from the gin. It's also a delicate pink colour due to the sloes and is shaped like a heart. Who says goat's cheese can't be romantic?

*See also* BRITISH CHEESE (p. 290).

*See also* BRITISH CHEESE (p. 290).

TREEN, CORNWALL

## *Chris Hall's fresh unpasteurised milk*

Milk, as the 1980s advert featuring two football-loving Scouse kids informed us, is what Ian Rush drinks. And thirty years on, milk is still thought of as something primarily for children, Liverpool strikers aside. For the rest of us it's simply the ever-present, ever-the-same semi-skimmed white stuff in the fridge, only there for wetting cereal or diluting tea or coffee, right? Well, not quite. There's that milk, and then there's real milk in its purest form, unpasteurised and straight from the cow.

Chris Hall has a small organic herd of thirty Guernsey cows on land his grandfather used to farm in the village of Treen at the tip of Cornwall. Those caramel-coloured beauties produce 80,000 litres a year, but Chris can only sell a fraction of that, some 10,000 litres, unpasteurised, and then only from a small hatch in the wall of his milking shed or from a milk round he runs locally. In short, he's not allowed to sell it in any shops.

'A Guernsey produces less milk than a Holstein, but it's of a better quality,' says Chris. 'It's almost golden in colour.' It did look thicker and perhaps more cream-coloured, but I assumed that was because it had just come out of the cow. That is, until we compared it to some ordinary, shop-bought milk I had brought along for a blind taste test. I took a pint of semi-skimmed made by Robert Wiseman's dairies, and a pint of Tesco's own brand full-fat blue top. With something to compare it to, Chris's milk stands out by a country mile, taking on the golden hue of a Turner sunset, while the contents of the other two glasses had a bluish tinge, as if someone had washed a paintbrush in them after touching up their gloss work.

I began the taste test, despite knowing instantly which one was Chris's. The two shop-bought ones tasted a little thin and plasticky and had very little depth. Chris's, on the other hand, goes mental in your mouth. 'It's a food, not a drink,' says Chris. It doesn't just taste like thicker milk – as that would be cream – it tastes like the sum of all milk, seeming to explode

Spot the milk that's come straight from the cow

after you swallow it, coating the inside of your mouth with a thin film of butter. It's complex and intense, and not so much creamy as grassy and fatty.

I asked Chris about the future of a product like this: 'All I want is to be allowed to sell my milk in shops so more people can try it. It's freedom of choice.'

The Food Standards Agency's line remains very much that raw milk should not be given to the sick, infants and the elderly. My experience is that if it's coming from small, healthy, naturally farmed herds, you shouldn't have a problem. Until the law is relaxed, visiting people like Chris directly is the only way to get it, and perhaps that's the best way too. But get it you should, and don't be scared by it – it's not Japanese blowfish, just really great-tasting, natural milk.

*See also* WHITLAND, CARMARTHENSHIRE (p. 90).

# *Dorset Naga, the British chilli*

Of all the edible plants to come from South America to the UK as part of the Columbian exchange (when foodstuffs were traded all around the globe), some did better than others. Potatoes, tomatoes and chocolate became, after some initial reluctance, part of our food landscape hundreds of years ago. Yet avocados and chillies were practically ignored until very recently. You could say that we're making up for it now. Though native to hotter climes, in the past ten years a band of commercial producers and growers have sprung up in the UK, mainly in the southern counties and the south-west. And it's here we find the Dorset Naga, Britain's only home-grown chilli.

Michael and Joy Michaud established Peppers by Post at Sea Spring Farm in Dorset in 1995. They both have PhDs in agriculture, but started market gardening on the side. 'The hotter chillies tend to be *Capsicum chinense*, and are slow growing; on top of that they're always eaten ripe.' The Dorset Naga was developed in 2001 from the Naga Morich, which is native to Bangladesh and traditionally sold green, giving Michael and Joy an extra month to sell it.

Though developed from a Bangladesh original, the Dorset Naga is now its own unique variety, recognised as being 'extensive, uniform and stable'. Joy says they couldn't have done it without support from the Bangladeshis in the region. 'They come back again and again to pick our chillies, and we feel confident we're producing something authentic.' The attraction is not only the Dorset Naga's short growing period, but also the combination of heat and flavour. 'It has a great smell, just one broken in a room will perfume the air. It's a really powerful, beautiful flavour.'

A chilli's heat is measured in Scoville units, which tell us how many times a solution of the chilli pepper extract needs to be diluted before the heat can no longer be detected. A red sweet pepper, for example, has a Scoville rating of zero. The Dorset Naga ranges from 661,451 SHU for a green fruit up to 1,032,310 SHU for ripe fruit. Pepper spray, it's worth noting, is about 5 million, and pure capsaicin has a rating of 15 to 16 million.

David Floyd from Dorset runs the Chile Foundry, a website for UK chilli fans, and says the UK chilli scene is particularly vibrant right now, with many

The Dorset Naga, Britain's only home-grown chilli

producers developing a range of sauces, pickles and marinades. No doubt there are those who choose ultra-hot chilli and sauces out of bravado, as some test of manhood. The result? People get burned, or rather their innards do. However, there are those who actively enjoy the sensation and who use it correctly and sparingly in cooking influenced by South-East Asian recipes through to native Mexican cuisine.

Macho nonsense aside, the chilli deserves a place in the British spice rack as much as anything else. When used correctly it can deliver heat, piquancy and flavour: enjoy a dab of chilli sauce with the traditional Sunday lunch of roast beef, the chilli taking the place of horseradish or mustard; and at the milder end of the spectrum, chilli jams and chutneys go with anything from oysters to toast.

## Willoughby Hedge Café

The old Willoughby Hedge Café on the A303 has a special place in my heart because it was the very first place I stopped on the journey that ultimately led to the book you're now holding. Its positioning is key: 100 miles or so from London, 80 from Exeter, it's a natural stopping point for those who want to stretch their legs and have a bite to eat – a tea 'n' pee stop. Five minutes after pulling up I was washing down the last of egg in a bap with a cup of tea strong enough to creosote a fence.

Unlike most lay-by cafés, Willoughby Hedge isn't run by an ex-con, a thug or a nutter, but by the charming Dave Thomas, who, as I pulled up, was giving the café a clean with a bucket and sponge. The entire thing – kitchen, counter and seating area – is just a small Portakabin. The current one, which Dave had custom built, is four years old, and there have been a handful of predecessors going back to 1980, when he first acquired the pitch.

Also (perhaps) unlike most roadside cafés, Dave likes to take a bit of care when sourcing his ingredients, aiming for local food where possible. His tea comes from D. J. Miles, a Somerset-based family firm that has been blending tea since the 1930s, and his bread and baps arrive every day at 9 a.m. from the Cottage Bakery in Gillingham. Dave makes no apologies for his café's menu, nor should he. It's a caff, and rightly sells your café favourites – egg, bacon, sausage, burgers, chips and the like – all cooked fresh to order.

The place is popular with everyone from truckers and bikers (the field next door used to be a grass racing track) to classic car enthusiasts and famished families. It's never going to be heralded as gourmet, but it does what a good roadside café should do, namely serve you a big cup of tea and something hot between two pieces of bread that you can wolf down as you stretch your legs, look at the sky and listen to the traffic roll by.

*See also* GRINDLEFORD, DERBYSHIRE (p. 294); LLANBERIS, GWYNEDD (p. 71).

Willoughby Hedge excels at good strong tea and something hot between two slices of bread

## WINCANTON, SOMERSET
### *Charles Dowding's leaves*

The West Country, in salad-and-leaves grower Charles Dowding's opinion, is becoming one of the best food-producing regions in the world. Things grow well in Somerset soil. Salad is also one of those crops where the quality starts to decline from the moment it's picked. Various methods are used to slow this, from sealed bags to 'living salads' that you sometimes see in the larger supermarkets. However, you can't beat the taste of freshly picked, quickly rinsed leaves: the crunch is much more pronounced and the flavours come through swiftly. A blood-veined sorrel leaf's astringent citric taste shoots across the mouth like forked lightning, then other sweet notes start to play.

Charles grows around twenty-five different types of leaves, including tango lettuce, cress flower, Freckles lettuce, orache (a tallish plant that's also known as mountain spinach; you eat the leaves), chervil, pea shoots and a bit of dill, and is able to grow salad and greens all year round by carefully choosing varieties that work with the seasons. In summer he grows more basil and endives, and so salads from that time of year are milder and more juicy. Towards autumn he grows chicory, rockets, pak choi and mustards. Then at wintertime it's lambs lettuce and others, grown under the polytunnel.

Charles is also well known for extolling the 'no dig' method, though this isn't about being work-shy with a shovel. He set up an experiment in 2007 sowing various crops in four beds, two with the manure dug through, and two with it placed on top of the soil. The yield was 49.5kg for the dug, and 54.2kg for the non-dug – almost a 10 per cent improvement. Indeed, soil is where people should concentrate their efforts in the garden: 'Feed the soil, not the plant,' is his advice.

*See also* CHICHESTER, WEST SUSSEX (p. 471); CRYMYCH, PEMBROKESHIRE (p. 63); GOMERSAL, WEST YORKSHIRE (p. 247).

WINTERSLOW, WILTSHIRE
# Truffles

Like snails, gooey cheese and fizzy white wine, truffles may be considered out-and-out French, but they can also be found right here in Blighty. Britain's last working truffle hunter was Alfred Collins, who tracked down summer truffles with two Spanish poodles in Winterslow, Wiltshire. He retired in 1930, but the truffles are still there, if you know where to look – and, indeed, what you're actually looking for.

Truffles are subterranean members of the fungus family, growing five centimetres or so below ground. They work in symbiosis with the roots of the tree (often beech, ash, cherry or hazel), extending the roots' surface area and, in return, taking sugar and glucose in order to grow (as truffles cannot photosynthesise). To germinate, the mycelium coils into the distinctive ball shape and hopes to get eaten by an animal so that it can be spread.

That role was traditionally performed by pigs, who sought them out because a truffle's odour is similar to boar saliva, and so a real turn-on for your amorous sow. In Wiltshire, what you're most likely to find is the summer truffle, *Tuber aestivum*, between the months of July and September. It's a delicate truffle, not as strong or as pungent as the continental black truffle, which is found later in the year. Pigs are useful for finding truffles, but pooches are better, as they are less likely to eat their finds and, at £200 a kilogram, you don't want to take the risk. Another option, employed by Michelin-starred chef Roger Jones, patron of the Harrow Inn in Little Bedwyn, Wiltshire, is a twelve-year-old boy, and father and son can often be found, eyes scanning the ground of a Wiltshire wood looking for summer truffles for Roger to use back at the restaurant. Guided, perhaps, by the ghost of Alfred.

*See also* HEBRON, CARMARTHENSHIRE (p. 67); LYMINGTON, HAMPSHIRE (p. 486); LLANGADOG, CARMARTHENSHIRE (p. 78).

# 2 | Wales

## KEY

| | |
|---|---|
| BG. | BLAENAU GWENT |
| BR. | BRIDGEND |
| CA. | CAERPHILLY |
| CAR. | CARMARTHENSHIRE |
| CD. | CARDIFF |
| CER. | CEREDIGION |
| DEN. | DENBIGHSHIRE |
| FL. | FLINTSHIRE |
| MON. | MONMOUTHSHIRE |
| MT. | MERTHYR TYDFIL |
| NP. | NEWPORT |
| NT. | NEATH PORT TALBOT |
| PEM. | PEMBROKESHIRE |
| RH. | RHONDDA CYNON TAF |
| SW. | SWANSEA |
| TO. | TORFAEN |
| VG. | VALE OF GLAMORGAN |
| WR. | WREXHAM |

*Irish Sea*

*St. George's Channel*

Little Haven  *PEM*
★

★
Pembroke
Dock

0   5   10   15   20   25   30 mi

0   10   20   30   40   50 km

# *Laver bread*

Laver bread is as Welsh as leeks, rugby and Tom Jones. Found clinging to rocks all round the British Isles, the seaweed (*Porphyra umbilicalis*) has been eaten by many different peoples over the centuries, but it's the Welsh who have taken it most to heart. After washing then boiling it for several hours, what you're left with is a dark, spinach-like purée with an iodine tang and a saline taste like the smack of a wave. Most people baulk at their first mouthful, and it's not much to look at (it resembles make-up searching for a face) but it certainly rewards perseverance.

Though it can be served as a sauce with lamb, its traditional form in the eighteenth and nineteenth centuries was as small cakes, coated in oatmeal and fried in the fat of the breakfast bacon. It was just the sort of thing to set you up for a day standing underground waist-deep in water, hitting a wall of rock with a pickaxe. Nowadays it tends to be included in a standard 'full Welsh' fry-up, and a tinned variety is available from Parson's Pickles in Carmarthenshire if you'd like to give this a go.

Laver bread is also being used more imaginatively by a new breed of Welsh chefs. Bryan Webb, head chef at Tyddyn Llan, a restaurant with rooms in Snowdonia, serves wild bass with laver bread *beurre blanc*. The famous Victorian chef Alexis Soyer suggests laver *ramifolle*:

> Roll out some mashed potatoes to a quarter of an inch thickness then cover with some nicely seasoned cold, stewed laver. Put another layer of mashed potatoes on top, and allow it to get quite cold. When it's set, cut into square pieces, cover with egg and breadcrumbs and sauté.

Greta's Wholefoodies makes laver-bread burgers, adding Caerphilly cheese, mustard and fresh parsley as well as oats to the patties – they're particularly good with a poached egg for breakfast. However, my favourite has to be the special Welsh maki rolls made by Kai and Josephine Chan from Sushi Day in Abercynon, who use laver along with lamb and leeks. If California can lend its name to a Western-style maki roll, why not Abercynon?

*See also* THE UNITED KINGDOM OF FRY-UPS (p. 354).

# Glamorgan sausages from Greta's Wholefoodies

Despite having some of the best lamb and beef in the country, Wales still gave the world the Glamorgan sausage. Skinless and meatless, it's a combination of leek, onions and cheese coated in breadcrumbs and fried to produce crunchy croquettes filled with a tasty, cheesy, leeky goo. Traditionally, Glamorgan cheese was used, so called because it is made with milk from the Glamorgan cow. Between the 1920s and the late 1970s, this breed was thought to be extinct, but in 1979 farmer and ex-military man Major 'Teddy' Savage from East Sussex put his herd up for sale, stating there were some Glamorgans among the stock. Glamorgan County Council bought them, and they're now housed at Margam Country Park, although sadly there still aren't enough to meet the demand for Glamorgan cheese. As a result, most modern recipes substitute Caerphilly cheese, as it's very similar in texture and taste.

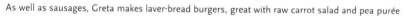

As well as sausages, Greta makes laver-bread burgers, great with raw carrot salad and pea purée

The sausage was first mentioned in print in George Borrow's 1862 book, *Wild Wales*. He states:

> The morning was moist and dripping, and nothing could look more cheerless and uncomfortable than the entire scene. I put on my things, which were still not half dry, and went down into the little parlour, where I found an excellent fire awaiting me, and a table spread for breakfast. The breakfast was delicious, consisting of excellent tea, buttered toast, and Glamorgan sausages.

Borrow had the sausages in the tavern of 'Y Gwter Fawr' ('The Big Gutter') in the historic county of Glamorgan. The town is now known as Brynamman, and the Tregib Arms in the village is thought to date back to around 1860, so could be a contender for the place where his breakfast was served. Wales may not be quite so wild these days as it was in Borrow's time, and modern-day explorers in search of a Glamorgan sausage should seek out Greta's Wholefoodies' version, available from independent delis and shops in the region. Greta Watts-Jones makes Glamorgan sausages by hand, using local ingredients including Gorwydd (pronounced *Gor-with*) Caerphilly, made by Trethowan's Dairy to a traditional recipe with unpasteurised milk (see p. 73).

The original Glamorgan may have been meatless due to poverty as meat was expensive. During the Second World War they appeared once more as meat was scarce. Today, when people are choosing vegetarian products for ethical or dietary reasons, they could do worse than the Glamorgan, the original veggie sausage.

*See also* SAUSAGES (p. 122).

*See also* SAUSAGES (p. 122).

BLAENAFON, TORFAEN
## Big Pit cheese

Coal was the fuel of the Industrial Revolution, and a great deal of that fuel came from Wales. It's easy to forget, nowadays, just how dangerous mining could be. Between 1851 and 1920 there were 3,000 deaths in South Wales mines alone. The history of this profession is now on display at Big Pit: National Coal Museum. Pwll Mawr, or 'Big Pit', was the biggest producer of coal and steel in the nineteenth century, finally closing in 1980 and leaving a massive man-made cave. So what to do with it apart from turning it into a world heritage site dedicated to our industrial past? Well, Susan Flander-Woodhouse thought it would make a great space to mature her Cheddar cheese.

Susan started Blaenafon Cheeses in 2006, and has won nationwide recognition for her business, which has food, tourism and heritage at its heart. At present she sells eight flavours of Cheddar and four varieties of goat's cheese. Her Cheddar cheeses are made with milk collected from Welsh farms, and produced by First Milk dairy in Haverford West. The medium-strength one she brings straight to her shop in Blaenafon town centre and begins adding subtle and interesting Welsh flavours. But the mature one is taken 300 feet down the pit, where the temperature remains a constant 9.5°C – this is the perfect atmosphere for maturing the cheese. Once a fortnight, 120 kilograms is brought up for sale.

All this came about because the management at Big Pit decided to forge links with local businesses to bring more visitors to the area. Susan had a meeting with manager Neil Walker, who supported the idea, and she then went on to prove to the Environmental Health Officer that the product was safe. Now the twenty-kilogram cheeses are stored in six specially made metal caskets with small gaps at the top and bottom that allow the air to pass through, but keep errant fingers out. 'It's the atmosphere down there that really makes the cheese,' says Susan.

Cave-ageing cheese is as old as the hills above. Cheddar was originally aged in the caves of the Cheddar Gorge; Rocquefort, too, gets its distinctive mould from spending time in a cave. The key to ageing is to provide a constant temperature and humidity. Even at home, cool, moist rooms such as outhouses or garages are much better places to store cheese than refrigerators, which are not only too cold, but also too dry.

It's nice to see that although the making of the Welsh cheese Caerphilly by Cheddar makers in the West Country has been happening for years now, cheese-making-ideas have not all been travelling one way over the Severn Bridge and there are plenty of dairies and creameries all over Wales now having a go at making Cheddar.

See also BRITISH CHEESE (p. 290).

## *Sea salt from Halen Môn*

David and Alison Lea-Wilson have been involved in Anglesey aquatic activities for many years. First they had an oyster farm, then they became fishmongers, then they ran a public aquarium, and now they produce sea salt as well. 'We knew the waters around here were pure because we were keeping things like sea horses in them, and they're very particular,' says Alison.

As the aquarium's visitors dwindle a bit during the winter months, the Lea-Wilsons looked into salt production. The first batch was made in a frying pan on the family Aga, and subsequent ones were made in a large bath. Now, of course, it's a much more professional operation, but the process is the same: seawater is heated in a pan until the water has evaporated and a residue is left.

Halen, meaning 'salt', and Môn, the Welsh word for Anglesey, gave the company its name. The water is drawn from the Menai Straits and before it enters the facility it has already passed through a mussel bed and a sandbank, both of which work as natural filters. It's then heated until it becomes a salty brine, which is released into crystallisation tanks where the snow-white flakes form. These are scooped out and left to dry before being boxed. The whole process takes ten days from start to finish.

The government drive against excessive salt consumption has actually helped Halen Môn: 'People are more conscious about what goes into or onto their food, and are prepared to pay more money for a purer product that delivers more taste for less sodium,' says Alison.

Part of the charm of sea salt is its crunch, shape and feel in the mouth. Halen Môn salt doesn't have that mouth-puckering chemical effect that industrial salt can sometimes have. You can get it via mail order, or if you happen to be in North Wales you can even visit the factory and see how it's made. After that, you can pop next door and admire the sea horses cantering round their tanks and enjoying the salt in its original form.

*See also* MALDON, ESSEX (p. 446)

## Clark's Pies

The story of the Clark's pie would be worthy of an episode of top genealogical show *Who Do You Think You Are?* It's a tale of a family business spanning five generations and 100 years. Things started in 1912, when Mary and Arthur Clark opened a pie shop at 93 Donald Street, Cardiff. During the First World War it had to close, due to meat shortages, and things didn't get going again until the 1920s. Mary made the pies in her own kitchen, and delivered them around the neighbourhood. In 1928 they opened a proper shop in Paget Street, Grangetown, and her daughter Winifred opened her own shop across town in Canton in 1932. It was in 1934 that the trademark 'CLARPIE' was registered and stamped on to the bottom of every pie they made, just as it is today. Mary's other children spread out like mushrooms propagating themselves around Wales and the south-west, from Bristol, Newport and Gloucester to Swindon and Reading. Soon a second world war came, with harsher rationing measures, and some of these shops had to close. Mary's shop survived the war, however, by switching to vegetarian pies.

Nowadays there are two shops left in Cardiff – one in Canton, one in Grangetown – as well as a shop in Bristol. Ceri Dutch-John is the fourth generation of her family to work in the Canton shop, and the Grangetown shop is owned by a different member of the family. They work closely together, though, and are forging links with their second cousins in Bristol: 'Although we've always had contact, we don't really have any involvement with Bristol, other than a hello at a funeral or a wedding.'

This history is all very well, but what about the pies? Ceri says they're simply 'beef and vegetable pies in a thick gravy, made to a secret family recipe, encased in shortcrust pastry'. A pretty standard pie, then, but with pastry that's thicker than your average pie casing, meaning the pie comes without the need for a supporting foil tray. 'It's sold as an open, unwrapped product that stands by itself,' says Ceri.

Both Cardiff shops produce about 1,500 to 2,000 pies, six days a week. At the Canton branch they do everything by hand except roll out the pastry, whereas in Grangetown they have a fully automated system. To the trained eye, and indeed palate, there are subtle differences between the Canton and

Grangetown versions. 'People tend to favour the one they were brought up on,' Ceri adds. Any rivalry, it seems, comes from their loyal customers rather than inside the family.

What's lovely about the Clark's pie story is not only the history, but the consistency. They have not been swayed by fashion, nor had designs to take over the world. They have just made pies, decade in, decade out. On the streets on which the Clark's pie shops stand, particularly the Grangetown branch, you can see there were once lots of little shops. Most have had their fronts bricked up and been turned somewhat awkwardly into homes. But when you hear people say that we're no longer a nation of shopkeepers and that we're all now squashed under a carpet of mass retail homogeny, send them to Clark's pies. As Ceri says, 'You get generations and generations who come through our door and purchase our product. I've worked here since 1997, but it's taken until now to realise how special and loved our product is by this community.'

*See also* CORNISH PASTIES (p. 18).

## CONWY, CONWY

*Sausages from Edwards of Conwy*

Ieuan Edwards has seen his business grow over the last twenty-five years from a tiny shop staffed by just himself to a regional institution that employs more than fifty people and supplies most of North Wales with quality sausage and meats. Ieuan is one of the younger sons of a farming family, but growing up he felt 'the farm wasn't big enough . . . and I was too thick to go to university.' So he got an apprenticeship at a butcher's in Llanrwst where he learned his trade. It was there that he found out that he wanted to be in retail. In the early 1980s a lease came up on a butcher's shop in Conwy and things grew from there.

From the start Ieuan wanted to do things differently. 'I saw the sawdust-on-the-floor and blood-on-the-apron approach and I thought, "Why does it have to be like this?"' So he spent some time researching the Continental approach to butchery. 'I was amazed how skilled they were in places like Holland, how – because the meat was poorer quality than ours – the butchery skill had to be higher.' They were also ahead of the game on selling and cooking produce: 'Over there, butchers seemed to be half chef, half butcher.' The feeling in the UK at the time was 'We cut meat,

Edwards of Conwy still make all of their sausages by hand

and that's it.' You can see the legacy of this research in Edwards today. Ieuan sums it up in this way: 'I've got this product called meat; how many ways can I sell it?' That's why he offers everything from traditional cuts to cooked and cured to sliced and in a bun. He's also been doing mail order for over ten years.

His pork comes from Anglesey, and the lamb is Welsh and seasonal, starting with new-season lamb from March onwards, salt-marsh from May, and Welsh mountain lamb from September. His beef is all female and hung whole on the bone for three weeks before being boned out and sold on the fourth week. This drying and maturing process costs Ieuan several hundred pounds a carcass, but what they lose in weight they gain in flavour.

Moving on to sausages: 'I believe the perfect British sausage should have a meat content of around 75 per cent,' he says. 'Some types of sausage, the borwust or merguez, for example, have higher meat contents, but not the British breakfast sausage, otherwise you end up with mince in a bag. The key is the quality of the meat put in.' Despite a large demand from his shop, the local area and the likes of ASDA, Edwards still makes all its sausages in small batches and they remain the artisan products they always were. Consistency, it seems, is the key. 'If for some reason you don't like my sausage, you won't like it next week either,' he says.

See also SAUSAGES (p. 122); BROMYARD, HEREFORDSHIRE (p. 283); CAMBRIDGE, CAMBRIDGESHIRE (p. 422); FORRES, MORAY (p. 173); LOUTH, LINCOLNSHIRE (p. 336); MARYLEBONE, WESTMINSTER (p. 387); MELTON CONSTABLE, NORFOLK (p. 447); NANTWICH, CHESHIRE (p. 125); WOODHALL SPA, LINCOLNSHIRE (p. 364); YORK, NORTH YORKSHIRE (p. 271)

## CORWEN, DENBIGHSHIRE
# Organic beef from the Rhug estate

The Rhug (pronounced *Reeg*) Estate in Denbighshire, North Wales, has passed down the male line of the Wynn family since the 1700s, carrying with it the title of Lord Newborough. The family was originally granted the title for defending the Menai Straits against French invasion. In the second half of the twentieth century, war hero and Colditz veteran Robert C. M. V. Wynn made many improvements to the estate's farm, and his son, Robert V. Wynn, current Lord Newborough and the 8th Baron, has built on this, converting the farm to organic production in 1998 and gaining accreditation two years later.

The estate lands comprises some 12,500 acres, most of which is let to tenants and put to a variety of uses including rally-car driving, outdoor pursuits and public events. The family once owned Bardsey Island, where whisky was first said to have been invented (see p. 83). In 1971 this was sold to the Bardsey Trust to help meet death duties. The 2,500-acre organic farm – one of the largest in Wales – forms the core of the estate, and produces around 1,000 head of cattle, 7,400 lambs, 2,400 chickens and 400 pigs annually.

The estate supplies Waitrose and Sainsbury's as well as hotels and Michelin-starred restaurants. Although the supermarkets' meat is graded and assessed while hanging on the hook to ensure it meets their requirements, 'All the chefs are into is taste,' says Lord Newborough. 'They couldn't give a damn what the meat looks like on the hook.'

Rhug now employs forty-three people and has its own cutting plant to allow it to tailor the product for a variety of markets. Chefs, for example, might want larger cuts that they can break down themselves, whereas supermarkets go for consistency, and farm shops like something in the middle. A stall in London's Borough Market has helped to increase the profile of the company and give direct access to the public.

Lord Newborough is in many ways an organic farming pioneer, and he has great hopes for its future: 'I do believe it is a sustainable form of agriculture. We've gone through the fertility build and now, in our eleventh year, the farm is twice as productive as it's ever been in my history. I believe that the principles of organic farming are right; the better welfare and standards are important to people and certainly to me.'

One of Lord Newborough's predecessors once said, 'Vigorous let us be in attaining our ends, and mild in our method of attainment' – as sage a piece of advice today as it ever was.

*See also* UPTON UPON SEVERN, WORCESTERSHIRE (p. 315).

*See also* UPTON UPON SEVERN, WORCESTERSHIRE (p. 315).

CRYMYCH, PEMBROKESHIRE
## *Micro leaves and edible flowers from First Leaf*

Derek Lewis's farm in rural Pembrokeshire is tiny: about the size of one and a half tennis courts. This pocket-sized plot, however, provides plenty of room for his crop of shoots, edible flowers and micro leaves. 'You'd be surprised what you can actually eat,' says Derek. His crop includes rose geraniums, blue cornflowers, rocket flowers, chrysanthemum, even the humble daisy – and all will enliven your salad bowl no end. For the most part, Derek works with wholesale clients: chefs, of course, and also cocktail makers, theatre companies and even London Zoo. 'They had a new gorilla arrival and wanted a photo of her eating flowers.' One of the benefits of being a small company with a small product is being able to adapt day by day, and if a customer wants something in particular, Derek can grow it in just over two weeks.

Derek started in 2004 growing micro leaves such as baby basil, chives and sage, which were then the 'Next Big Thing' with chefs. These are sold live in the punnet. In 2006 he began to grow edible flowers and pea shoots, which are available mail order all over the UK. Chef Vivek Singh at the Cinnamon Club in London used Derek's flowers to create a stunning vegetarian garden-themed lunch menu to celebrate the Chelsea Flower Show.

Flowers carry a hint of the taste of the plant they're from; the tiny lemon yellow broccoli flowers have an unmistakable trace of the mother plant, for example, and are quite delicious. Wild garlic flowers are also stunning, both raw and dipped in a cold tempura batter and deep-fried for seconds. Most of the flowers of things we already eat are edible: horseradish, fennel, the brassicas like kale, broccoli and mustard, onions, even apples and other blossoms are fair game.

Gardeners may have always nibbled on the odd shoot, and the Chinese, of course, have been eating them for centuries, but they've really only arrived on our plates in the past five years or so. Of course, what chefs get up to in fine-dining establishments eventually trickles down to the rest of us, and micro leaves have got to be the easiest thing to grow; all you need is a windowsill.

*See also* CHICHESTER, WEST SUSSEX (p. 471); GOMERSAL, WEST YORKSHIRE (p. 247); WINCANTON, SOMERSET (p. 48).

## ELAN VALLEY, POWYS
# *Elan Valley mutton*

In the middle of Wales, in one of the remotest parts of the country, lies Elan Valley. Here Tony and Angela Davies farm Welsh mountain sheep, a breed as hard as the nails on a Welsh miner's boot and perfectly at home 1,700 feet up a mountain. All of Tony's sheep have over four years to get acquainted with the gradient, however, as they're all destined for mutton – some, even, for Angela's traditional Welsh mutton cawl (see p. 68).

It's one of our national food hypocrisies that we eschew veal but love lamb, and conversely love beef and ignore mutton; in fact the latter has come in for some real stick over the years. In *The Two Gentlemen of Verona*, Shakespeare uses the phrase 'a laced mutton' to describe a lady disparagingly. The sentiment lives on in the saying 'mutton dressed as lamb'. Founded in 2004 by the National Sheep Association and the Academy of Culinary Arts and launched by the Prince of Wales, the mutton renaissance campaign works to counter this anomaly. It maintains that age is part of the beauty of the meat. From the farmer's side of the gate it means that they get to sell their older animals as well as the young ones. But proper mutton as endorsed by the campaign isn't just 'old sheep', it's an animal that has spent time growing slowly and putting on flavour from a diet of grasses and wild herbs. Furthermore, the meat must be matured by hanging for at least two weeks. The best time to enjoy it is in the cooler months, when the animal has had a chance to spend a summer eating and so is at its prime when slaughtered.

As well as the regular cuts like chops, breast and leg, Tony is keen to develop new products. A few years ago he noticed that in Iceland smoked mutton was still very popular, and so he developed 'macon' (like bacon, but made with mutton; it was popular in the past in places like Scotland where pigs were in short supply). However, it wasn't a big hit and has been discontinued. Looking again to Scandinavia, he took a leaf out of the Norwegians' book and developed his mutton salamis. One hundred and fifty grams of his mutton goes into each hundred grams of salami, meaning a third of the weight is lost to shrinkage as the meat cures. They come in a range of flavours: a traditional one, a spicy one flavoured with paprika, one flavoured with juniper and another with rosemary.

For all this innovation mutton, like veal, remains a niche product, but one definitely worth seeking out. Tony recommends long, slow cooking: 'Imagine lamb but with a fuller, meatier, more succulent taste,' he says.

*See also* ELWY VALLEY, DENBIGHSHIRE (BELOW); HIMBLETON, WORCESTERSHIRE (p. 297); THE ISLE OF MAN (p. 110).

ELWY VALLEY, DENBIGHSHIRE
## *Elwy Valley lamb*

It was once said that there were more sheep in Wales than people, and while this is still true – 8.2 million sheep to about 3 million people – the ratio is reducing. Welsh sheep are some of the finest in the world, often bred and managed by farming families with generations of experience and skill in animal husbandry. This, coupled with the terrain and weather, both of which are perfect for sheep farming, has given Welsh lamb not only a distinct taste and flavour, but also a well-earned PDO (Protected Designation of Origin) status. Welsh lamb is so good, in fact, it's even exported to France, which took some 22,203 tonnes in 2008, by far the most of any EU country. Its PDO status has much greater resonance with French consumers, and when they see *Agneau Gallois* in the shops they know it means quality.

It was to Welsh lamb that Jamie Oliver turned when he cooked for the G20 leaders in Downing Street in 2009, specifically slow-roast shoulder. That lamb came from Daphne and William Tilley's farm in the Elwy Valley, Denbighshire. Their lamb and mutton also graces the tables of many a top London restaurant, and is admired by the likes of chef Richard Corrigan among others.

The animals start out as a blend of Beulah Hill ewes and Blue Faced

Leicesters, which gives what is called the Welsh mule (just a name, as the animal isn't infertile like an equine mule). The results of this cross-breeding are then bred with Texels and Beltex, which give the animals a larger frame and bone structure.

The Tilleys are constantly adjusting the breeding of the animals, refining characteristics and attributes. The most valuable part of any animal is the back and the loin; the shoulder provides the cheapest cuts, but can contain a huge amount of flavour. William Tilley tells me that often it is the better chef who will order the cheaper cuts. This is partly because of the flavour, but also because these cuts need work and skill to raise the meat to a fine-dining level, and that is where chefs make their money.

*See also* ELAN VALLEY, POWYS (p. 64); HIMBLETON, WORCESTERSHIRE (p. 297); THE ISLE OF MAN (p. 110).

## HALKYN, FLINTSHIRE
# *British buffalo*

The Romans introduced a huge number of new species to these islands, many of which we now consider native (the term for this is 'archaeophyte', trivia fans). One they didn't introduce, however, was the water buffalo. That was accomplished, in Wales at least, by John Sigworth, who in 1998 introduced forty Asian water buffalo from Romania to his farm in Halkyn, Flintshire.

Having made the switch from traditional dairy farming, where all his milk went to the Milk Marketing Board (as then was), John now enjoys being able to talk and sell direct to his customers. What's more, water buffalo are easy to keep; they will eat pretty much anything, and unlike American bison, they don't fall under the Dangerous Animals legislation, but instead are considered equivalent to standard domestic bovine breeds.

The herd, which now numbers around 200 animals, was originally intended for producing the milk so beloved by Italian mozzarella makers. Though it may look similar, it has twice the fat of cow's milk, as well as more protein, both of which are essential in cheese-making. This means that 100 litres of buffalo milk will produce twenty-four kilos of mozzarella, while using the same amount of cow's milk will give you only thirteen kilos.

The milk was popular, but soon the deliveries to London, Leicestershire and elsewhere became a bit much to cope with, and so John switched to meat production. Around six animals a month are slaughtered and the cuts sold via farmers' markets or simply at the farm gate. John uses an abattoir eleven miles down the road, and all the butchery is done on the farm. Buffalo meat, despite being butchered into familiar beef cuts such as topside, silverside, steaks and so on, is noticeably different as it is much leaner. Consequently, cooking a buffalo steak the same way as you would a beef steak is a sure way to make something as inedible as shoe leather. Buffalo steaks are for people who like their meat *rare*.

Interestingly, the Newa people of Nepal's Kathmandu Valley have a dish called *kachila*, a raw, tartare-style dish made with buffalo meat. (The rest of the population of Nepal are Hindu and consequently don't eat water buffalo.) The meat is chopped, then mixed with grated ginger, salt and hot peppers. At the same time, mustard oil is heated in a pan, fenugreek seeds are added, and when the oil is smoking it is poured over the raw meat. If you don't quite fancy scaling the peaks of Nepalese gastronomy, you could always opt for one of John's water-buffalo burgers. 'We've kept the recipe the same since day one and people love them,' he says.

*See also* WEM, SHROPSHIRE (p. 316).

HEBRON, CARMARTHENSHIRE
## *Foraging with Mountain Foods*

Collecting wild food has been romanticised as a panacea for these anodyne times. Who, during a particularly gruelling commute, hasn't imagined a more sanguine way of life spent harvesting nature's bounty, living off the land and generally getting 'in touch' with the rhythms of the seasons?

Yun Hider does just that, and is best placed to dispel some of the myths and dispense a supersized portion of reality, namely that making a living from foraging is hard, hard work. It's an all-weather, all-week job, but one he loves. Yun runs Mountain Foods, and supplies chefs all over the UK with wild herbs, leaves and vegetables that he's foraged, mainly from neighbouring Pembrokeshire. 'There are lots of wild plants out there, but only so many you can talk people into using,' he says. Bordered on three sides by the sea, Pembrokeshire is perfect foraging country, as it contains not only stunning beaches, as you'd expect, but streams, meadows, woods, lanes, mountains, fields and estuaries.

# Cawl

Cawl (pronounced *cowl*) lays easy claim to being the national dish of Wales. The word hasn't really got a definitive translation, and can mean a soup, broth or stew featuring anything. Today it has come to mean a stewy soup made with lamb and leeks, although in the past whatever was available (usually pork) was used. Cawl, then, is as old as meat, root veg and a pot to cook them in; a basic and fundamental food born of the need for sustenance rather than gastronomy. It was certainly enjoyed in the eleventh century, when Gruffydd ap Llywelyn, a feckless prince who, upon hearing that one piece of meat kept rising to the top of the cawl during cooking, took it to be a prophecy and went on to unite all of Wales, albeit briefly.

Cawl is a rhapsody on the theme of thrift and simple flavours, one of many similar dishes found circling the Irish Sea, including Liverpudlian scouse, Lancashire hotpot and Irish stew. Where cawl differs from the others is in its two-stage process. First, the lamb is cooked slowly in water and left to cool. The solidified fat is skimmed off and the meat picked from the bones. The next day the vegetables – any combination of potatoes, carrots, swedes, cabbage and turnip – are softened and then cooked in the remaining lamb stock. The meat is returned to the dish, and towards the end of the cooking process, chopped leeks are added. Another way to serve it is in two parts: first the broth, then the bits of meat and veg. Like all slow-cooked stews, cawl improves in flavour when heated up the next day. The dish was traditionally eaten with a large carved wooden spoon with a deep 'bowl' (the receptacle end of the spoon), and ornate versions of these would have been given by suitors as 'love spoons'.

Mimosa in Cardiff Bay is a contemporary bar and restaurant replete with large windows, dark wood and minimalist chic, and yet has a menu that features Welsh classics including Glamorgan sausages, cockles and laver bread as well as cawl. 'We get lots of comments, especially from older diners, that it reminds them of their mum's cawl,' says head chef Alun Roberts. In his recipe he features good-quality Welsh lamb from Howells butchers in Swansea. 'In season (May to October) we get their salt-marsh lamb, which grazes practically across the road from their shop,' says Alun. This is cooked until tender, and then the potatoes, parsnips, swede and carrots are added. Once these are cooked through, the leeks go in. He serves his cawl with a slice of granary bread made by the Sugarcraft Bakery in Pontypridd, topped with a slice of Todd Trethowan's Gorwydd Caerphilly (p. 73) for you to dunk in the juices. The accompaniment of a slice of cheese is how most cawl comes served these days. 'There's nothing special to it really, just good quality ingredients,' says Alun.

See also BLACKBURN, LANCASHIRE (p. 99); LIVERPOOL, MERSEYSIDE (p. 116); SAUNDERSFOOT, PEMBROKESHIRE (p. 90).

'There's no money in foraging,' a friend once told Yun. 'And I've proved him right!' Yun jokes, as he also spends time doing a spot of tree surgery. But what you do find in foraging is soul. If you spend some time talking to Yun, you can see that picking and collecting from nature nearly every day for fifteen years has left him with a deep respect for the land. 'It's brought a whole flavour to my life. The most important thing is interacting with the environment. It's so special.'

So where to begin? 'My message is to learn one plant at a time, plants you can recognise and that are safe. Even pros can make mistakes,' says Yun. Blackberrying is the thin end of the wild-food wedge, so widespread it has become a verb. Most people know a blackberry when they see one, and what's more (if my childhood is anything to go by) these little beauties grow on urban wasteland just as well as country hedgerows. Gorse is another good thing to start with as it's safe and easy to recognise. It also offers a bit more of a culinary challenge when back indoors, but brewing it into a drink is a popular treatment. Of course, massive blackberries from Chile are available in the shops all year round, and your corner shop sells Oz plonk, so why bother? Well, there is the satisfaction of spending time doing it, of enjoying the journey and the walk in the woods. As Yun says, 'When you've collected a few kilos of bluey-black sloes, scarlet hawthorns and deep red rosehip berries, they're like a handful of rubies.' Foraging can lead to a different kind of wealth, it seems.

*See also* LYMINGTON, HAMPSHIRE (p. 486); LLANGADOG, CARMARTHENSHIRE (p. 78).

## LITTLE HAVEN, PEMBROKESHIRE
### *Spider crab from Dash Shellfish*

You're never very far from the sea in Pembrokeshire, so as you'd expect, fish and seafood grace many a local plate. The fishing villages of Little Haven and Broad Haven are home to a number of crab boats that fish along the stunning coastline. In more recent years the native lobster and brown crab have been joined by a Continental cousin, the spider crab, which is normally found in Mediterranean waters. No one is entirely sure why, it could be due to warming waters, or a change in currents or migration patterns, but the fact is they're here, they're plentiful and they're tasty. The spider is much fêted by the Spanish, who will pay good money for its sweet flesh. Getting it out of its shell, however, can prove a bit tricky.

It's something crab processor Danny Curtis of Dash Shellfish knows well. 'People think that the spider crab is cheap. I often hear 'em joking, "We'll mix a bit of spider in to bulk it out," but a cock spider crab is the same price, if not more, as a cock brown, but there's less meat in it.' Consequently, six kilos of brown crab, say, will give you roughly one kilo of meat, while for one kilo of spider-crab meat you would need to process fourteen kilos. This obviously ups the final price, but it's definitely worth trying.

The season for crab runs from March to September. Danny gets his from two of his mates: the aptly named Gareth Rudder, who skippers a boat out of Milford Haven, and another pal with a smaller boat that docks at Broad Haven who also handles lobster.

The business began in 2007, and from the start Danny put in a weapons-grade processing facility custom-made for handling shellfish. 'When we started we'd struggle to clean 80 kilos a day. Now we can easily handle 200 kilos a day.' It's all down to practice and process, it seems, and during a busy summer week he can manage half a ton. What is different about Dash, though, is that they don't boil their shellfish, they steam them. Danny took a gamble installing a £5,000 oven steamer rather than buying a burner and large pot, but he believes the results are well worth it. Steaming, rather than boiling, helps to keep the flavour in and produces a sweeter, firmer meat, although Danny, ironically, is not a true expert in this. 'I personally hate the taste of shellfish, the smell ... the lot!' he laughs.

See also BUCKIE, MORAY (p. 149); CHINATOWN, WESTMINSTER (p. 374); CROMER, NORFOLK (p. 426); MORECAMBE BAY, LANCASHIRE (p. 121); SALTHOUSE, NORFOLK (p. 454).

LLANBERIS, GWYNEDD
## Pete's Eats Café

Pete Norton has been running the eponymous Pete's Eats Café for over thirty years. He is therefore something of an institution among the day-trippers and landscape thrill-seekers of Snowdonia national park; Pete's Eats is not so much a café as a community hub. Downstairs there is a library of donated books, board games, free newspapers and a community noticeboard. Upstairs there is a shower (£2 a go), Internet access, a schools area and the map room, to which other walkers have donated maps and walking routes from all over the world.

Pete's monster chip butty, a sandwich in the loosest, chippiest sense of the word

The food fuels up fresh-faced, carb-craving customers with a broad range of café favourites: the full English breakfast, omelettes, toasted sandwiches, and meat and two veg. Pete's a vegetarian, and veggies are well catered for. The changing specials take in such family favourites as chilli con carne, ham-and-leek pasta bake, three-bean casserole and lasagne, all of which are made on site. Pete takes a man-sized attitude to his menu. 'Our idea of portion control is stopping when it's falling off the plate,' he says with a grin. This mantra is most manifest in their legendary chip butty, which isn't so much a sandwich as a slice of white bread crushed under a rugby scrum of freshly cooked chips, with another slice teetering on top. You don't need a fork so much as an ice pick and crampons to make an ascent on this. It's probably fair to say that the 4th Earl of Sandwich didn't have this in mind when he allegedly invented the thing, but for me, a chip butty remains one of life's simple pleasures.

If you've room for pudding there are home-made pies, cakes, crumbles and biscuits galore. You can wash all this down with a whole pint of hot steaming tea. If you're after tea in china pots, dainty sandwiches and paper doilies, this ain't the place for you. Cheap filling meals in a friendly warm café, however – take a seat.

*See also* GRINDLEFORD, DERBYSHIRE (p. 294); WEST KNOYLE, WILTSHIRE (p. 47).

# Caerphilly cheese from Trethowan's Dairy

Cheese-makers are a pretty friendly bunch, keen to share knowledge more than most other professions. 'Maybe because all products aren't exactly the same,' says Todd Trethowan, cheese-maker and -monger, and the man behind Gorwydd (pronounced *Gor-with*) Caerphilly. Todd has been making cheese for fourteen years, originally starting out doing apprenticeships with various cheese-makers, including Chris Duckett, who was then making Caerphilly in Somerset. Caerphilly is the quintessential Welsh cheese, said to have been invented in the 1880s, although its production probably went unrecorded before then. It was originally sold in the market town of Caerphilly, which gave it its name.

However, it wasn't long before the cheese-makers on the other side of the Bristol Channel took note and started to make their own versions. Cheddar may be the West Country's most famous cheese, but part of its charm is that it takes months to mature. Caerphilly, being a semi-hard cheese, takes weeks. Canny Cheddar-makers therefore saw a way to get a young cheese to market early, while their Cheddar was still ageing.

Then the Second World War happened, and all milk that wasn't drunk fresh went into the production of 'Government Cheddar'. This resulted in a product as bland, manufactured and uniform as an *X-Factor* winner, and until 1954 was still the only cheese allowed to be made. Much artisan cheese-making knowledge, and indeed many cheese-makers and dairymen, were lost during that time. What also disappeared was the making of Caerphilly in small batches on farms and dairies in Wales.

Thankfully, the tradition has been resurrected by people like Todd. 'There are three special things about my cheese. First, it's unpasteurized, second, we use animal rennet, which is crucial, and third, it's totally handmade.' The raw milk Todd uses comes from a dairy herd over the road. Raw milk not only gives a greater depth of flavour and complexity, but it does so for longer as the flavour lingers in the mouth. The length of the ageing process also has a part to play. Todd takes his cheeses to two months, rather than a few weeks as most producers do, which adds to the complexity and character. As for the most important part of the process, the eating, Todd recommends eating the rind, which has a wonderfully earthy taste. Immediately under this, the cheese is beginning to break down, giving a slightly brie-like quality, and beyond that there is the familiar Caerphilly crumbly interior. Enjoy.

See also BRITISH CHEESE (p. 290).

# Bara brith

The Welsh, like pretty much everyone else in the United Kingdom, aren't averse to sitting down with a slice of cake and a cup of tea; and there is a broad range of traditional Welsh breads, cakes and pastries to choose from. The most well known (after Welsh cakes themselves) is probably bara brith, which translates as speckled bread. Originally it was made with yeast, before the arrival of modern raising agents such as bicarbonate of soda in the nineteenth century, and indeed good bara brith should still be made this way according to Bobby Freeman in her classic guide to Welsh food.

Besides the dough, the other ingredients are currants, raisins or sultanas, as well as candied peel and spices. It's these that give the interior a speckled look. The key to getting these fruits nice and plump is the soaking of them overnight in cold tea.

Laura Mason and Catherine Brown could find no early written history in their audit of national dishes, *Traditional Foods of Britain* (1999), and point to the fact that the bread was known as 'teisen dorth' in the south, and only as 'bara brith' in the north.

Like tea bread is in England, bara brith is made in many small bakeries all over Wales. Welsh Cottage Cakes in Llandeilo, Carmarthenshire, picked up a Great Taste award for theirs in 2007. Other companies have riffed on the bara brith flavour too. Pemberton's chocolates in Llanboidy, Carmarthenshire, flavoured a ganache (double cream and chocolate) with tea and bara brith spices and dried fruits, before adding a final cloak of chocolate.

Bara brith falls in alongside Lincolnshire plum bread, barm bracks in Ireland, fruit loaf, malt loaf and a dozen other regional heavy cakes that can also take a spread of butter. Wherever they're found on these islands, these cakes, loaves and breads are the heavy artillery of the cake world, able to deliver a solid rich taste and soak up tea like a sandbag.

See also ALBERT EMBANKMENT, LAMBETH (p. 368); ALDERLEY EDGE, CHESHIRE (p. 96); BISHOP AUCKLAND, COUNTY DURHAM (p. 201); ECCLES, GREATER MANCHESTER (p. 103); HOOK NORTON, OXFORDSHIRE (p. 328); MANCHESTER,

GREATER MANCHESTER (p. 119); MELTON MOWBRAY, LEICESTERSHIRE (p. 341); NAVENBY, LINCOLNSHIRE (p. 344); OTLEY, WEST YORKSHIRE (p. 252); STANBRIDGE, BEDFORDSHIRE (p. 360); WHITBY, NORTH YORKSHIRE (p. 269).

## LLANDINAM, POWYS
# *Neuadd Fach Baconry*

Ithyl Brown has been farming his thirty-five-acre smallholding, Neuadd Fach, since 1963. He was joined in 1979 by his wife, Linda, and together they have been farming pigs for over twenty years. In 1999 the market value of pigs collapsed, but the Browns kept at it, borrowed more money from the bank, and built a 'baconry'. One for future lexicographers, the word 'baconry' was invented by Ithyl and Linda's son, and perfectly sums up the room where their pork is prepared. The flesh in question comes from their herd of 400 large whites, fed on a diet mixed by Ithyl himself. The animals go off to slaughter on a Wednesday, come back and are hung until the Monday so they're firmer to work with.

The Browns have to take their animals into Shropshire to get them killed, a trip of forty miles. 'There's an abattoir two minutes down the road from us, but they don't handle pigs.' The pigs come back from the abattoir split down the middle and with their heads removed. The butchery is done, the belly is taken off for bacon and the legs are cured, some with a dry cure, others with brine. Shoulders that aren't cured and any bits left over go into their sausages and hamburgers, of which they make over 100 kilos a week.

What is appealing about the Browns is their small-scale simplicity. Their farm is small and lies deep in mid Wales, which, as Linda says, has yet to be subjected to the media and cultural spotlight currently being shined so brightly on the Brecon Beacons. Their customers are small local village shops and post offices – exactly the sort of places that serve a community well and yet are threatened with closure. Linda and Ithyl care deeply for their animals: they're not units or items to them, but charges. The Browns are a shining example of animal husbandry, producing products that have won True Taste of Wales awards to sell locally. Their passion for their work is clear. As Linda puts it, 'I love it. Both my husband and I should have retired, but we don't really want to!'

*See also* LOWICK, NORTHUMBERLAND (p. 216); MARYLEBONE, WESTMINSTER (p. 387); MEOPHAM, KENT (p. 489); NEATH, NEATH PORT TALBOT (p. 80); PEASENHALL, SUFFOLK (p. 452).

## Welsh Rabbit

The 'Welsh rabbit' versus 'Welsh rarebit' debate mirrors the one that surrounds the pronunciation of 'scone'. However, the rabbits do seem to be winning, slowly. They have not only the *OED* and Delia Smith on their side, but also the English language commentator Henry Watson Fowler, who said in 1926, 'Welsh rabbit is amusing and right, and Welsh rarebit is stupid and wrong.'

And yet 'rarebit' persists. It is Francis Grose with his *Classical Dictionary of the Vulgar Tongue* (1785) who may have begun the confusion, as he defined Welsh rabbit as a corruption of 'rare bit'. Indeed, Mrs Beeton used this phrase in her book seventy-six years later, but then the poor lass also described Stilton as the British Parmesan, so we shouldn't put too much faith in her knowledge of cheese matters. The late food blogger Ken Thorne looked into the issue in 2005 and surmised that 'rarebit' was the more popular pronunciation in Wales where English is spoken.

The phrase is thought to have originally been intended as a slur or insult, the idea being that the Welsh were too poor to buy rabbit, and instead had to make do with this cheese-and-bread concoction. But it may not even be Welsh at all: Merriam-Webster's dictionary speaks guardedly of an Italian origination.

Wherever it came from, it's certainly a delicious dish. The

cheese – Caerphilly if you're being really Welsh, a good Cheddar if you're not too fussy – is grated, added to beer and melted slowly in a pan or bain-marie. Mustard, paprika or Worcestershire sauce might be added for a bit of a kick. Welsh rabbit is often described as posh cheese on toast, which I feel is rather an insult as it's a far superior dish. It has also got a bit of a reputation as a bachelor's dish, appearing twice in *The Stag Cookbook: Written for Men, by Men* from 1922, perhaps because it uses a splash of beer, leaving the rest of the bottle for drinking. Early recipes describe it as more of a topping taken on toast, even sent to the table in a little pot, whereas ones from the last twenty years or so call for the whole thing to be placed under the grill for browning.

In Wales the dish is known as *Caws Pobi*, literally 'cheese roasted', and mention of it is found in *The Hundred Merry Tales* from 1526. In this book the Welsh are making so much noise that they need to be thrown out of heaven. St Peter stands outside the pearly gates shouting '*Cause bobe*', and as the Welsh all come running he slips in behind them and locks them out. The book, the first example of an English jest book, was apparently read to Queen Elizabeth on her deathbed in 1603, and sounds like the ancestor of *Viz*.

*See also* WORCESTER, WORCESTERSHIRE (p. 317).

## LLANGADOG, CARMARTHENSHIRE
### *Shitake mushrooms from Humungus Fungus*

Consider the mighty 'shroom: always second fiddle to some other ingredient such as chicken, lobbed in as an also-ran, rarely given centre stage on the plate. What is more, out of the hundreds of edible species on the planet, what does your local supermarket or greengrocer sell? Likely as not, bog-standard, bland-as-hell field mushrooms.

Richard and Joy Edwards run Humungus Fungus in the shadow of the Black Mountain, and over the past seven years they have developed and refined a technique for growing shitake mushrooms. They started out selling the mushrooms commercially, but soon found there was more interest in their production technique so they now help set up other growers.

'I think mushrooms can be an answer to a lot of society's problems,' says Richard. 'They're a great food source, they eat sewage and they have

Richard Edwards grows shitake mushrooms on blocks of compressed sawdust

medicinal uses.' The shitake, for example, is revered in Asia for its therapeutic properties. Compare this to the ordinary button mushroom that contains – quite naturally – small amounts of carcinogens, and you can see why the likes of top chef Raymond Blanc might say the following: 'The Chinese and Japanese are laughing at us. While the British consumer is using a huge tonnage of button mushrooms with traces of carcinogenic chemicals, the Chinese and Japanese have through history developed varieties which help to *reduce* the risk of cancer.'

In 2005 Richard helped Blanc set up his grandly titled 'Valley aux champignons' to supply his restaurant, Le Manoir aux Quat' Saisons, with fresh shitake and oyster mushrooms. 'The British haven't had mushrooms in our culture,' Richard says. 'Our children are taught not to play in the woods – they're seen as dark, scary places. In Italy kids are taken into the woods at an early age and encouraged to hunt mushrooms. I've eaten mushrooms that are fantastic – real culinary orgasms. I understand that the Japanese have only two things they refuse to import; one is nuclear waste, the other is shitake mushrooms.'

But just how do you grow mushrooms commercially? Richard explains, 'Mushrooms are the fruit of mycelium; they're only produced when the organism is reproducing.' When I visited, he showed me how he gets it to that stage, leading me through the farm building to an immaculate laboratory complete with microscope and conical flasks. A small amount of mycelium spore is placed on agar jelly in a Petri dish, sealed and allowed to grow. After two to three weeks the agar jelly is cut into eight pieces and dropped into eight bags of wet organic grain. The grain bags have been boiled in a pressure cooker for an hour to kill off any other organisms present. After three weeks the mycelium takes hold. Each bag of grain is then divided between twelve more bags containing sterilised wet sawdust, which are called spawning blocks. It grows in these for a few more weeks and then each is divided into twelve more bags containing sterilised sawdust, bran, woodchip and a bit of gypsum to neutralise the acidity in the wood; these are called fruiting blocks.

There are no visible mushrooms at this point, just lots of white mouldy bags. They can be held like this for some time in a dry room at 22°C. When needed, they are shook up, opened and placed in a cool room with a high humidity. The mycelium thinks all hell has broken loose and in a quest for survival shoots up dozens of mushrooms, which you harvest after a week or so – simple. So, in the case of shitake, one agar plate gets you 1,252 fruiting blocks, each producing about 400 grams, and the whole process takes just twenty weeks.

Richard's other technique is to take the spawning blocks and impregnate logs with them. This results in a much slower growing, almost wild, mushroom that has a more robust flavour; however, this can't be done all year round as the mushrooms are exposed to the elements, and the hungry local wildlife. When Richard threw me a large log, I was astonished to discover that it was as light as balsa wood. 'Over three years the mushrooms have sucked every bit of moisture out of it,' he said. A squeeze of my hand and it buckled and crumbled to bits.

*See also* HEBRON, CARMARTHENSHIRE (p. 67); LYMINGTON, HAMPSHIRE (p. 486); WINTERSLOW, WILTSHIRE (p. 49).

## NEATH, NEATH PORT TALBOT
### The Welsh pig

Wales is often thought of as sheep country, but there is also a strong tradition of pig husbandry, and it even boasts its own breed called 'the Welsh' (lest there be any doubt about its origin). The animal is lop-eared, meaning its ears fall in front of its face. In the eighteenth and nineteenth centuries, pigs from Wales and the borders were often moved into Cheshire for fattening up on milk by-products.

The Welsh, fast-growing and large, became popular after the Second World War, and the numbers of licensed Welsh boars jumped from 41 in 1949 to 1,363 in 1954. But still more pork was needed, so in 1950 the Landrace pig was introduced from Sweden. Pig farmer George Eglington took three Landrace gilts (young female pigs that have produced fewer than two litters) and a Welsh boar and set to work improving the Welsh lines. It is from his handiwork that the modern Welsh breeds come. Mr Eglington described the perfect Welsh as 'pear shaped when viewed from either the side or from above'. Unfortunately, the pear-shaped pig couldn't continue to keep up with the drive for cheaper, leaner carcasses, and the breed became endangered.

In 2002 only eighty-two Welsh pigs were registered, and they remain on the Rare Breeds Survival Trust watch list. However, numbers are beginning to rise again and the animal is being reintroduced thanks to breeders such as Chris Beck and his brother Bleddyn of Panorama Pedigree pigs. After keeping a range of breeds on their grandparents' farm, the boys eventually settled on the Welsh as the one for them: 'It was by far the tastiest and the easiest to keep.' As well as selling the meat, Chris is also a breeder, and his boars command prices in the region of £500 each. He has also reintroduced the Large White, which was the breed his grandparents had kept until the 1950s. Interestingly, his grandparents had left a book on stockmanship, complete with handwritten notes and observations in the margins. It has no doubt provided some ancestral guidance over the past few years.

*See also* LLANDINAM, POWYS (p. 75); LOWICK, NORTHUMBERLAND (p. 216); MARYLEBONE, WESTMINSTER (p. 387); MEOPHAM, KENT (p. 489); PEASENHALL, SUFFOLK (p. 452).

*See also* LLANDINAM, POWYS (p. 75); LOWICK, NORTHUMBERLAND (p. 216); MARYLEBONE, WESTMINSTER (p. 387); MEOPHAM, KENT (p. 489); PEASENHALL, SUFFOLK (p. 452).

## PEMBROKE DOCK, PEMBROKESHIRE
# The Pembrokeshire Tea Company

When you think of tea plantations, you think of the humid mountains of Sri Lanka, Kenya or India, not, it's fair to say, West Wales. Tea has been grown in other parts of the UK before – the Tregothnan estate in Cornwall, for example – but never in Wales.

'Usually, the closer you can grow tea to sea level, the better quality it is. The reason it's often grown up in mountains is that those countries are too hot,' says Tony Malone of the Pembrokeshire Tea Company. So the growing conditions in the mountains of Sri Lanka are cool and rainy – pretty much the conditions at sea level in West Wales. 'The only problem we do have is the wind, but we're working on that. We're looking at developing our own strains that are a bit more hardy.' Pembrokeshire, as well as Cornwall, benefits from the jet-stream currents, which bring warmth in the winter and cool air in the summer, 'So we don't get these extremes of weather, such as the harsh heat of the south-east or the cold of the rest of the country,' adds Tony.

In 2009 Tony, a closet gardener who'd kept a few tea bushes in his student days and had a job in a tea shop, started the business with partner Michael Ward. At present they're blending their fledgling tea plants with imported leaves, but the plan is to have the plantation fully operational and self-sufficient by 2014.

The teas themselves come in a selection of flavours. Pembrokeshire Rose, for example, is a black tea (but you can drink it with milk) made with 60 per cent of their own tea blended with Darjeeling and flavoured with tea roses. It has a floral and refreshing aftertaste. The Sailor's Tea blend, on the

Tea, normally grown high up in cool, wet regions of Asia, is quite at home on the tip of Wales

other hand, nods to the history of tea procurement. The great tea race of 1866 saw tea clippers racing back to London with the first harvest of the season. According to the *Daily Telegraph*'s 12 December edition, the ships were neck and neck practically all the way of the three-month voyage. The winner, the *Taeping*, arrived with just a twenty-minute lead. Sailor's Tea was drunk aboard the clippers, and was black tea enlivened with a slug of the rum ration (fresh milk, obviously, being in extremely short supply). Tony's version is non-alcoholic, but does include the spicy flavour of rum by using similar flavourings to complement the leaves.

Of course, a cup of tea just looks lonely without an accompaniment. Pembrokeshire Tea has teamed up with other small producers, including the Y Felin Watermill, one of the last in Wales, and now offers cakes, pikelets and breakfast oats. Flexibility and pulling together are small businesses' greatest assets, and there's plenty of both going on in Pembrokeshire, it seems. 'There's a fantastic food ethic round here, it's great!' says Tony.

*See also* APPLEDORE, KENT (p. 466); HARROGATE, NORTH YORKSHIRE (p. 250); NEW GALLOWAY, DUMFRIES & GALLOWAY (p. 184); YORK, NORTH YORKSHIRE (p. 270).

# Welsh whisky

The distilling of whisky in Wales has an interesting history, shot through with rumour and legend. The name of Bardsey Island, off the Llŷn Peninsula, crops up in various accounts as home to a distillery, along with the name of a fourth-century monk called Reault Hir. However, the late archaeologist Mary Kitson Clark, whose final work in 1993 was a thorough document of the religious significance of the island, could find no trace of him.

In modern times, distilling was last carried out at the Fron-goch Distillery on the edge of Snowdonia in 1897 by Mr R. Lloyd Price and Robert Willis. An advert for their product describes it thus: 'the most wonderful whisky that ever drove the skeleton from the feast, or painted landscapes in the brain of man'.

Sadly, the venture didn't last long, and during the First World War the building was used as a POW camp. It even housed insurrectionists captured during the Irish Easter Uprising of 1916.

George Bennett's, a wine merchant in Pembrokeshire, managed to track down the last eight remaining bottles of Fron-goch. One was presented to Prince Charles in 1969 while he was aboard *Britannia*, then moored in Fishguard Bay, and he donated it to what is now the Welsh Folk Museum at St Fagans.

Now, in the twenty-first century, after an absence of almost 100 years, Wales has a distillery in production again, this time in Brecon, South Wales. Friends Brian Morgan, Tony James and Alun Evans, owner of the Glancynon Inn, came up with the idea for the Penderyn Distillery over a few drinks in the pub. Morgan is Professor of Entrepreneurship at the University of Wales in Cardiff and practises what he preaches, it seems.

They got funding and brought other backers on board – the distillery is still privately owned, something of a rarity in this day and age – and started distilling in 2000. The spirit is first matured in ex-bourbon barrels before being 'finished' in Madeira barrels for the final six months. The process, of course, takes time, and the first bottles were available for sale in 2004. Production is now up to 100,000 bottles a year. On a visit to open a new visitor centre in 2008, Prince Charles was again presented with a bottle.

Their limited-edition single casks are worthy of note; these see the spirit finished off in various types of barrels that have previously held other drinks.

What is more, they are cask strength, coming in at around 60 per cent. Their limited-edition (207 bottles) port wood single cask, for example, bowled over whisky expert Jim Murray, who said, 'If you have five minutes to try a great whisky, don't bother with this one. This is a full half-an-hour job. At least. One of those malts which never sits still, changing shape and form and refusing to tell quite the same story twice.' High praise indeed, although at £275 a bottle many of us will have to take Jim's word for it.

*See also* DUMGOYNE, STIRLING (p. 162).

## QUEENSFERRY, FLINTSHIRE
### *Really Welsh leeks*

Wales is a big place, covering an area approximately the size of Wales. And yet in 2005 Tesco were unable to find a commercial grower of leeks to supply their Welsh stores anywhere in the country. Leeks, as you're probably aware, are the national symbol of Wales, and sit alongside the shamrock, the thistle and the rose as emblems of the component parts of this sceptred isle. (The daffodil, by the way, is a bit of a Johnny-come-lately, popularised at the turn of the last century.) So come St David's day, when children and adults get all patriotic, they have been affixing to their breasts leeks grown in Lincolnshire, and Dutch- or Cornish-grown daffodils, which rather spectacularly undermines the point.

To right this wrong, Really Welsh was formed in 2005. Colin Bailey, an Englishman with Welsh blood in his veins, farms leeks in Lincolnshire. It was he who responded to the call from Tesco, who said they had no local produce growing in Wales. Having previously been MD at Puffin Produce in West Wales, he thought he should give it a go, and began by growing cauliflowers in the Vale of Glamorgan. This expanded to daffodils, and then leeks, which are grown for the company by Charlie Lightbown on his 160-acre farm in Flintshire, North Wales. 'Charlie's done a really good job farming, and leeks are a durable crop,' says brand manager Rhiannon Williams. Charlie has increased the growing season and now harvests forty tonnes a week – by hand – from late July through to the following May. That means he's out there in the middle of winter, when the ground is rock solid and the air temperature is –6°C. That's dedication.

Patriotism aside, leeks suffer a bit in the kitchen due to the fact that people don't get adventurous enough with them. The late food writer Dorothy Hartley says in her 1953 book *Food in England*, 'Leeks are better braised than boiled' and suggests cooking them in a little stock or water with seasoning and butter. Slicing them into discs is also rather dull. Paul Askew at the London Carriage Works in Liverpool cuts them into two-inch sections, before halving them lengthways and slicing very finely. You're left with julienned leeks that cook in under a minute but keep their bite. Head chef Robert Mace at the Crown in Suffolk uses them like cannelloni, cutting them into two-inch sections, and popping out the core before stuffing and roasting the resulting tube.

But if all this sounds like too much hard work there's always cawl (*see* p. 68): best made, if possible, with Welsh ingredients.

*See also* EAST ANGLIAN PARSNIPS (p. 444); PEA HARVEST (p. 332).

RIVER DEE, FLINTSHIRE
## *Cockles*

Cockles seem to attract trouble. In 2004 in Morecambe Bay, nineteen illegal Chinese workers drowned while out collecting cockles. A year later in South Wales, around 1,000 cockle pickers descended on Llansteffan beach as the cockle beds were open for the first time in four years. Luckily, there were none of the fights witnessed in the nearby Towy estuary in 1993, but a great deal of concern was expressed at the rapine nature of the harvest. Tractors and trucks tore up and down the beach as teams came from all over the UK to stake a claim. And if that wasn't enough, in 2008 a mystery disease killed 6,000 tonnes of the shellfish off the Gower peninsula further to the south.

In North Wales, the cockle beds on the River Dee began to recover after the demise of heavy industry in the 1980s, which over time led to a rise in water quality. This led to a free-for-all in 2005, during which the beds were picked clean and had to be closed. So in 2008, Defra and the Welsh Assembly instigated a licensing scheme to regulate the harvest. The area is carefully monitored, and only fifty fishermen have the right to remove cockles from the beds, a situation that doesn't please everyone. But, thanks to this scheme, the beds have been open for the past three years, with the season running from July to December, and numbers are stable. According to David Edwell from the Environment Agency, 'This is all part of managing fishery properly so the cocklers get a good, regular income from the beds.'

The picking of cockles has gone on in Wales for centuries, the work normally being done by women and children who could take advantage of this easily reachable and free food. Once picked, the cockles are shelled, washed and boiled. Most are destined for export, or a spell in pickling liquor.

The traditional way to eat them is with a splash of vinegar and a dusting of cheap pepper, but they can then be put to a myriad of culinary uses. Bacon is a popular chaperone between cockles and laver bread, and at the Swan Inn in Little Haven, Pembrokeshire, they've been known to serve Penclawdd laver bread and cockle risotto, *cocos ac wyau* (cockles and scrambled eggs) and cockles chowder. With structured, careful management the cockle beds can be a productive resource, not only for the cocklers, but also for those who love seafood.

RUTHIN, DENBIGHSHIRE
## Patchwork Pâté

As initial business capital investments go, £9 is hardly generous. However, Margaret Carter managed with just that in 1982, when she found herself divorced with three kids to look after. Her son, Rufus, tells the tale: 'My mother needed cash. As well as making pâté, she also had six other jobs, including making peg dolls, babysitting, a milk round and waitressing. An opportunity came up to make pâté for the restaurant where she was working and things grew from there.' He means Patchwork Pâté, a successful business based in Ruthin. 'My mother will tell you she's retired and that I'm in charge now, but little happens around here without her knowing,' he adds with a smile.

Margaret started her business from home, in the kitchen, and the first pâté she made was a classic: chicken liver, brandy and herb. They still make it today, and it remains their most popular product. The range itself now extends to something like thirty-five varieties, together with over twenty seasonal variations. 'I think even we've lost count of how many we produce!' says Rufus.

Patchwork's meat comes from the UK, where chicken livers and pork are plentiful, and it also gets through fifty-three tonnes of onion a year. The provenance of its ingredients is extremely important to Rufus: 'If it says Guinness on the label, it's a can of Guinness that gets opened, likewise Cointreau.' Some years ago, while seeking the top level of production accreditation from the British Retail Consortium, Patchwork was advised to switch to liquid pasteurised egg. 'If we're going to use liquid eggs we might as well use powdered Guinness. You can't say to your production team, "Take tremendous care in this area, but then just pour the egg out of the container," it wasn't congruent with what we were trying to do.' Today the company is cracking eggs out of their shells, the way you would at home.

The history of pâté is interesting: in Old French it means pastry, i.e. the casing around a meaty filling which is then baked, but over time the word evolved to become associated with the filling. These days, in contemporary French, *pâté en croûte* denotes a pâté made in a crust, and *pâté en terrine* a version made in a ceramic dish. There are many regional variations in France, as well as similar products around the rest of Europe, probably because pâté, alongside its even less refined cousin, rillettes, are a good way to use up leftovers and offal.

Of course, this simple rustic pleasure got the gourmet treatment in the 1800s, with people adding such things as cognac, truffles, foie gras, and other rich flavours and tastes. In *Chambers Journal* (1853–60) the author offers the advice:

> The recipe of a French reprobate for killing off a rich uncle, was to give him (a gourmand, it may be presumed) a dish of pâté de foie gras of extraordinary richness, and to announce during the process of laborious digestion the failure of his banker.

In spite of food writer Carol Cutler's 1983 book *Pâté: The New Main Course for the '80s*, pâté has remained a starter dish. Today we're most likely to serve it with a slice or two of rustic country bread, as befits its origins, rather than Melba toast, which would seem a little old-fashioned.

Cheaply produced pâté tends to taste of little more than fat and offers nothing but a one-dimensional mouth-grouting. Patchwork's offerings actually taste of carefully assembled ingredients, skilfully highlighted by the added flavourings. As Rufus says, 'People should put it in their mouths and it should change their world.'

SWANSEA, SWANSEA
## Welsh cakes

Welsh cakes are made from butter (or lard in the cheaper versions), self-raising flour, eggs, sugar and currants. They're about the size of a scone, though flatter and much denser in mass and texture. Once the ingredients are mixed and the cakes shaped and cut out – a crenulated edge from a pastry cutter is traditional – they're cooked quickly on a hot plate known as a

Welsh cakes being made at Swansea Market

bakestone. This seals and toasts the surface far better than baking or grilling would do. If you want that authentic experience you can now order a traditionally made cast-iron griddle pan from the Welsh Griddle Company; another option is to use a dry frying pan.

I tried some of these hot filling cakes at a stall in Swansea market, where they were to be had for 30p each or five for £1.25. I don't think you can even buy a chocolate bar for 30p these days. I supersized it and went for five. 'Sugar?' the lady asked, dropping them into a bag. 'Or . . . ?' I said, thinking perhaps they're like popcorn and come in a sweet or salty version. 'Well, nothing really. Go on, have some sugar,' she said in a long-drawn-out Welsh accent and shook a load on. They turned out to be incredibly moreish in a way only warm pastry products can be; soft on the inside with a firmer biscuity bite on the edge. The currants go a little chewy and sticky from the heat of the plate, and the sugar gets plastered all over your fingers and face. I stupidly ate all five in quick succession. Exactly three minutes later, I staggered to the nearest bench for a sit-down, groaning like Dylan Thomas's Captain Cat in his dream.

If you can't get to Swansea market or anywhere else in Wales, Maddocks', run by Anthony and Pat Maddocks, do them mail order. Or for the full Dylan

Thomas experience, have some in the small tea room attached to the boathouse where he lived in Laugharne.

*See also* LARDY CAKES (p. 26); ALBERT EMBANKMENT, LAMBETH (p. 368); ALDERLEY EDGE, CHESHIRE (p. 96); BISHOP AUCKLAND, COUNTY DURHAM (p. 201); ECCLES, GREATER MANCHESTER (p. 103); HOOK NORTON, OXFORDSHIRE (p. 328); LLANDEILO, CARMARTHENSHIRE (p. 74); MANCHESTER, GREATER MANCHESTER (p. 119); MELTON MOWBRAY, LEICESTERSHIRE (p. 341); NAVENBY, LINCOLNSHIRE (p. 344); OTLEY, WEST YORKSHIRE (p. 252); STANBRIDGE, BEDFORDSHIRE (p. 360); WHITBY, NORTH YORKSHIRE (p. 269).

## TALLEY, CARMARTHENSHIRE
# *Cothi Valley Goats*

Goats occupy a funny position in Britain. They're familiar, having been here for centuries, yet are seldom thought of as part of the British farming tradition. To look a goat in the eye is to come face to face with Pan himself; no animal's stare is quite as spooky as that of a goat. They do get a bad press for their destructive nature, but contrary to popular belief they don't eat everything. They just enjoy more fibrous food than lush grass; weeds, stalks and hedgerows, for example.

The rise in cow's milk intolerance has seen goat's milk become increasingly available, but this hasn't spread to goat meat, which is seldom seen in butchers' shops despite probably being one of the most consumed meats in the world. You're extremely unlikely to find it in a fine-dining establishment, even under its French name of *chèvre*, but Caribbean restaurants will sometimes serve it up as goat curry – the most popular goat-based dish in the UK.

Of all goat-related products, however, goat's cheese remains the most readily available. In Llandeilo, South Wales – a region traditionally associated with sheep – you can find a herd of 400 goats kept by Lynn and Richard Beard of Cothi Valley Goats. They've been breeding them for over thirty years, originally starting out in Kent. As well as a large range of cheeses, from spanking fresh two-day-old Twayblade to hard ones like Ranscombe and Drunken Dragon, which is washed in Welsh cider, they also make the only Welsh halloumi, using a recipe taught to Richard by a Sicilian friend. They also produce a blue-veined goat's cheese called Talley Las, and there aren't too many producers of those in the UK.

*See also* BRITISH CHEESE (p. 290).

## Cawl competition

Since 2000 the town of Saundersfoot has held a cawl competition every year in late February. The winner takes the title of 'Cawl Cooking Champion of the World ... and Elsewhere' – just in case cawl is made anywhere else in the universe. For the full story of cawl, *see* p. 68.

WHITLAND, CARMARTHENSHIRE
## Milk in a bag from Calon Wen

Do you remember when, if the blue tits hadn't already got to it, milk on the doorstep would have a layer of cream floating under the foil lid at the top of the glass bottle? I'll confess, as a child I didn't like it much: it left funny white flecks all over my cornflakes. Now, of course, I regret not making the most of it. Milk these days is shiny white and all the same right down to the last drop.

The milk from Calon Wen dairies in Wales, however, still has the tell-tale layer of cream on the top. This is because, unlike nearly all the rest of the industry, it doesn't use homogenisation. Milk, being an emulsion of fat and water, naturally settles with the cream on the top. Homogenisation sees the milk forced through nozzles, not unlike a shower head, which breaks down the fat molecules so they distribute evenly throughout. The result is more even-looking milk, but without the delicious cream floating at the top.

Calon Wen is owned by twenty farming families – large and small – from across Wales, who banded together to sell their own organic milk to local people. They just wanted to have more of a say in how the milk was produced, and it's clear that ethics and environmental concerns run throughout the company. Plastic milk bottles use a lot of energy, so Calon Wen has pioneered the 'eco-pak', which holds four pints of milk and requires nothing more than a reuseable jug to support it and a pair of scissors to snip it open. In terms of space and energy it's a real saver: 'We managed to fit seventy-five empty bags in a one-litre plastic milk bottle,' says marketing manager Elen Morris. The technique is not new, and was tried in the 1970s, 'But milkmen would throw them at people's doorsteps, making them burst,' says Elen. The milkman is a dying breed these days, as we buy nearly all of our milk from supermarkets. Calon Wen milk is available in most large supermarkets in

Wales as well as in London, which is good news for fans of creamy-topped organic milk, but bad news for the blue tits.

*See also* TREEN, CORNWALL (p. 43)

*See also* TREEN, CORNWALL (p. 43)

## WREXHAM, WREXHAM
### *British saffron*

Yes, you read that right. Saffron, that musky perfumed aromatic derived from the dried stigmas of the *Crocus sativus* flower, is still produced today in North Wales. For me, steeped saffron has a sweet, earthy smell, with just a hint of the back of the rabbit hutch. I love it. It's the most valuable spice in the world, so much so that there was even a fourteen-week war over it in the thirteenth century when a 360-kilo shipment of it was hijacked. So precious was the stuff that the adultery and dilution of it was severely punished during the reign of Henry VIII. Nowadays you're more likely to get a fine and community service, like the Bradford man caught cutting La Mancha saffron from Spain with other ingredients in 2000.

Growing your own saffron is not as outlandish as it sounds

It has been grown off and on in this country from Roman times up to the sixteenth and seventeenth centuries. Indeed, the Romans really let rip with it: Nero ordered the streets sprinkled with saffron for his entry into Rome. And if you were of high standing and trying to impress on a first date in medieval times, you got the saffron out to show your wealth and prowess.

Historically, the village of Stratton in Cornwall produced some, along with other herbs. But the most famous example was the town of Chipping Walden in Essex, which became so well known for the spice in the late sixteenth century that the town fathers ditched the Chipping and prefixed the town with 'Saffron', no doubt a great bit of ye olde publick relations.

These days, for commercial British saffron you have to look to the unlikely region of North Wales, where production happens thanks to the green fingers of Caroline and John Riden. The Ridens set up British Saffron in 1985, selling not only the finished product, but also the plants themselves so that customers could grow it at home. Their starter kit retails at £30, and includes a booklet about growing and drying saffron along with recipe suggestions and twenty mature corms. These you plant in the summer months at a depth and spacing of five inches, and by October the flowers with their long stems bloom for about three weeks. Once you've picked your stigmas – preferably at dawn – you need to wrap them in absorbent kitchen paper and dry them in an airing cupboard for a couple of days. Bear in mind, however, that it takes the stigmas of 150 flowers to produce one gram of saffron. 'Although it is difficult to grow regularly on a large scale in the British climate, our vision is for individual cultivation so that gardeners can produce enough for domestic needs,' says Caroline. It's a long way from the heat of Iran to the wet Welsh borders, and no matter where it's grown, saffron remains labour-intensive to produce, but its unique flavour makes it worthwhile. As for uses, Caroline suggests saffron drop scones with home-made elderberry jelly. Or for a main course, you could try saffron mashed potato on top of a good fish pie, or put the fish in saffron sauce. Well worth fighting over, at least on the dinner table.

*See also* ST JUST, CORNWALL (p. 37).

# 3 | The North-West and the Isle of Man

★

Isle of Man

○

*Douglas*

*I r i s h*

*S e a*

*Isle of*
*Anglesey*

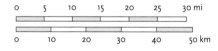

# Katja's Kupcakes

The moment New York City cupcakes went global can be traced back to a late 1990s episode of *Sex and the City*, where Carrie and Miranda scoff one each in the Magnolia Bakery while discussing their latest sexual peccadilloes. They then became a must-have foodie fashion accessory for anyone clicking about town in Manolo Blahniks. Inevitably, a backlash followed; but ten years later things have settled down and now they're just one of the many cake options in your well-stocked urban bakery. I wonder if the initial noughties rise in popularity was due to the fact that the cupcake represents the ultimate in cake individualism – it's a me, me, me cake that allows you to have your cake and eat it, rather than share a socialist slice of a larger communal one.

In a small baking unit on Horseshoe Farm in Alderley Edge, you can find

Katja Seaton is a dab hand at icing everything from cupcakes to wedding cakes

Katja Seaton, who as well as doing some excellent cake decoration also has a nice line in cupcakes. Trained at New York's Cupcake Café, Katja has decorated cakes for the likes of Madonna, Bill Clinton and Oprah Winfrey. In 2001 she swapped the honks of New York taxis for the gentle bleating of sheep on the rolling Cheshire plains, and now decorates both cupcakes and larger cakes for private commissions as well as supplying nearby Davenport Farm Tea Rooms.

The cakes themselves come in a variety of flavours: chocolate, vanilla, lemon and ginger, and Katja decorates them using rich buttercream coloured with concentrated natural food dyes specially imported from the USA. The buttercream is actually more of a custard: it starts with heated sugar, to which is added eggs and butter, plus a dash of vanilla essence.

You have to work quickly. When I visited I watched transfixed as a few deftly squeezed blobs of pink and white butter icing suddenly burst forth into a rose, and then a few dabs became the centre of a daisy. It was very impressive. You know that point when you get closer to a painting in a gallery and what was recognisable is suddenly visible as mere brushstrokes? The same thing happens here, with butter icing replacing the artists' paints. Of course, all this creativity is for naught if the cake underneath is as dry and soulless as old bath sponge. Katja's cakes are made on site by Duncan Poyser, ex-chef turned baker; they're small and light, with a moist, rich interior. A perfect plinth, then, for Katja's creations.

*See also* ALBERT EMBANKMENT, LAMBETH (p. 368); BISHOP AUCKLAND, COUNTY DURHAM (p. 201); ECCLES, GREATER MANCHESTER (p. 103); HOOK NORTON, OXFORDSHIRE (p. 328); LLANDEILO, CARMARTHENSHIRE (p. 74); MANCHESTER, GREATER MANCHESTER (p. 119); MELTON MOWBRAY, LEICESTERSHIRE (p. 341); NAVENBY, LINCOLNSHIRE (p. 344); OTLEY, WEST YORKSHIRE (p. 252); STANBRIDGE, BEDFORDSHIRE (p. 360); WHITBY, NORTH YORKSHIRE (p. 269).

## ALDERLEY EDGE, CHESHIRE
### *Pullet eggs from Horseshoe Farm*

Andy Morrison started out selling eggs door to door over twenty-five years ago when his job as a dairyman wasn't working out; he subsequently became known as Andy the Egg Man. This led to people asking if he had any chicken meat to sell, so he took on more hens. Soon after, he bought the land he was renting and added geese, then cows, then pigs, then a few sheep. By that

Andy Morrison's free-range eggs

point he needed somewhere to sell all this produce, so he built a farm shop, a butcher's and bought more land.

Eggs, however, remain at the heart of the business, and his flock produces 5,000 free-range eggs a day. The chickens he uses are a commercial breed called ISA Brown, hybridised from the crossing of Rhode Island Reds and Rhode Island Whites. They are prolific layers, each averaging over 300 eggs a year. As well as the medium and large sizes, Andy sells the pullet egg, and is keen to explain to people its joys. These are produced during the first thirteen or so weeks of the juvenile bird's egg-laying life. 'They have a different flavour from the bigger ones as more of the chicken's food goes into producing the egg rather than sustaining its body,' says Andy. You never see these in the shops, and we're almost conditioned to think that bigger is better, but in the case of eggs, good things sometimes come in smaller packages.

In 2008 he entered *Britain's Best Dish* on ITV1 with a deep-fried poached egg, but was (strangely) beaten by a taco. And if all this isn't enough, he has also built his own four-bedroom farmhouse – from scratch. In summing up these exhaustive achievements, Andy tells me, 'I believe anybody can do anything if they listen to others and use a bit of common sense.'

*See also* BELFORD, NORTHUMBERLAND (p. 200).

# Lancashire hotpot

The DNA of a Lancashire hotpot starts in the hills of the Pennines, runs down to Liverpool, with its scouse (*see* p. 116), and carries on across the Irish Sea until it reaches the Emerald Isle and its Irish stew. Though all these dishes differ in presentation and method, they might be considered part of the same family. And it's a family with very little spare cash as hotpot, like its cousins, is a dish born of necessity, made from cheap ingredients – just lamb, potatoes and onion – prepared quickly and cooked long and slow.

I can't help but wonder about all this slow cooking malarkey, however. How did it work in days of yore? Not only could you not have tended the dish while the household was at work in both pit and mill, but even if someone was home, think of the fuel bill. One possible method could have been a rapid cooking first thing in the morning when the range was hot for breakfast and hot water was needed for washing. The hotpot would then, perhaps, have spent the rest of the day in a hay box, well insulated so that the residual heat would be kept in until teatime, when a quick heat up on the evening's fire was all that was needed.

Lancashire-born Nigel Haworth now makes a classic hotpot at his Northcote restaurant, and a version of it won the main course in 2009's *Great British Menu* cook-off for returning troops. Nigel's recipe eschews contemporary additions like garlic, wine, and even the Worcestershire sauce that you see in most recipes, and allows the true flavours of seasoned lamb, onion and potato to shine out. Similarly, if you're attempting the dish at home you would be wise to invest in some decent tasty lamb that has got the flavour to give. Alas, fewer and fewer people are cooking hotpot at home. A Tesco survey of 2008 identified the hotpot as one of the UK's ten most endangered dishes. Luckily, there's no sign of that at Nigel's restaurant, where pre-ordered hotpots are a firm favourite with guests.

*See also* CAWL (p. 68).

# Black pudding

In 2002 Dr Neil Haslam of the Fairfield General Hospital investigated whether black pudding consumption produced false positives in colorectal cancer screenings. As well as proving that it does, his results showed that 63

Chadwick's black pudding at Bury Market

per cent of the inhabitants of Bury consume the savoury treat on a regular basis, such is the love for black pudding in this town.

Bury's fantastic market is a great place to buy one; indeed, you can find two excellent producers there: Chadwick's Original Black Puddings and the Bury Black Pudding Company. Each claims to be original, each has its own fans, and each has its own secret family recipe that has been passed down through the ages. No one would reveal it to me, of course, or even tell me what it contains, but you can bet there's blood (probably dried, as these days fresh is hard to come by), as well as little cubes of pork fat, and no doubt the obligatory secret blend of seasonings and spices – pennyroyal is a traditional inclusion. Each pudding is stuffed in a case about the size of a large sausage. They are eaten whole, rather than sliced into the ice hockey pucks you get in your average greasy spoon, and they are not fried or grilled but boiled and split lengthways so that the contents can be scooped out – sometimes with a blob of piccalilli or smear of mustard.

So much for the similarities. What of the differences? Chadwick's pudding is moist and jet black like a dog's nose. It packs a fine peppery punch and has large soft nuggets of fat dispersed throughout. There's the option of a lean one, but that's surely for wimps? The Bury Black Pudding Company's offering is firmer, more solid, and doesn't quite yield to the fork like Chadwick's. Also, the fat nuggets are bigger but less frequently found, and there's a greater range of condiments on offer, including Lancashire sauce, a mildly spicy vinegar-based offering from the Entwistle family in nearby Ramsbottom.

And which is best? Well, it's different strokes for different folks, so I would recommend you go to Bury Market and make up your own mind. For me, though, I preferred Chadwick's by a nose.

See also DINGWALL, HIGHLAND (p. 160); HAROME, NORTH YORKSHIRE (p. 249); HEREFORD, HEREFORDSHIRE (p. 296); SMITHFIELD, ISLINGTON (p. 401); STONEHALL COMMON, WORCESTERSHIRE (p. 312).

CLITHEROE, LANCASHIRE
## Cowman's Famous Sausage Shop

Fifth-generation butcher Cliff Cowburn owns Cowman's butcher's in the picturesque town of Clitheroe. His compact shop on the high street is every inch the traditional butcher's, the wares in the window shaded by a red and white awning. As well as offering joints, chickens and all the usual butcher's fare, Cliff has devoted much of the last thirty years to the British banger. He now offers over fifty varieties and flavours to suit every occasion and taste.

Cowman's had been a butcher's shop in Clitheroe for over 170 years, until his father Ted Cowburn bought it in 1957. 'I left school at fifteen in 1970 and came into the family business. Back then the supermarkets were just getting going and the butcher's business wasn't about the quality you could buy, but how cheap you could buy it.'

It's no coincidence that around this time the use of rind emulsions in sausages became popular. This is pork skin chopped and blended into a white slurry emulsion. Ditto the introduction of MRM (mechanically recovered meat), for which carcasses of many species of animal are blasted with water and the resulting liquid sieved to produce slurry. Yet both these ingredients are still classed as 'meat' when analysed. 'Originally, this procedure was used to make dog food,' says Cliff.

The proclamation on Cliff's shop window reads, 'Our sausages contain no slurry, slurp or goo, just quality meat'. In the late 1970s, Cliff's father, Ted, found a book belonging to his great-grandfather that contained old recipes not only for pork sausages, but also for those made with beef and lamb. They made up a batch and they sold well. Then Cliff had a go, concentrating on county sausages: the Somerset featured pork, apples and cider; the Mercian featured herbs, as did the Lincolnshire. 'That's when I got the bug,' says Cliff.

Since then, Cliff has added such varieties as pork and walnut, smoked pork, as well as the more adventurous curried beef, merguez lamb, and even chicken spiced with lemon grass. For those with a large appetite there's the giant plain pork, which is over eight inches long. Cliff even takes on bespoke commissions: 'We have a Greek doctor based in Stockport who orders five kilos at a time, made to his own recipe. What makes us different is that a lot of our seasonings aren't bought in, we develop them ourselves.' Many butchers, even good ones, buy a dried pre-made seasoning mix and just add it to the pork when mincing.

Though much has changed in the world of butchering and retailing in the past thirty years, Cliff's customers have remained loyal. 'I had a lady come in and tell me that for some reason she wasn't able to get to me last week and so bought some sausages from a supermarket. When the family sat down to dinner they all said, "These aren't Cliff's!"' he chuckles. 'My father's philosophy was, "Don't sell anything you wouldn't eat yourself" and it's a good philosophy is that.'

See also SAUSAGES (p. 122).

## DERWENTWATER, CUMBRIA
# Vendace fish

Picture the scene. It's a time of great environmental upheaval, the world is rapidly changing around you, the ice is melting, the landscape changing. Such a fate befell the vendace fish at the end of the last Ice Age, when as the glaciers retreated and the land dried out, the fish were left in a few lakes in Cumbria and a handful of lochs in Scotland.

They then became fair game for every hungry human who could throw a net or reel in a line, and this continued from the Stone Age right up to the beginning of the last century. The 1903 edition of Webster's dictionary lists the vendace as 'a European lake whitefish, native of certain lakes in Scotland and England. It is regarded as a delicate food fish.' And even Bernard Darwin's *Receipts and Relishes* (1950) lists it as a freshwater herring, and therefore good for the pan or the pot; this from the grandson of the famous naturalist.

Nowadays, however, it's teetering on the brink of extinction. There is no sign of any in Lake Bassenthwaite any more, leaving Derwentwater as the last English location where the fish may be found. A project to introduce it into Scottish lochs has, however, been successful.

'It's at the very edge of its range,' says Dr Roger Sweeting of the Freshwater Biological Association. The vendace, like the char and other members of the *Salmonidae* family, likes clear, clean, well-oxygenated water. As climate change warms the water, its ability to hold dissolved oxygen diminishes. Add to this the problem of predators, not to mention silt clouding the water, and you can see why the fish is in real trouble. It wasn't always the case, though. There was commercial char fishing on Lake Windermere until 1924.

It's still commercially available in Scandinavia, where the waters are deeper, colder and less polluted. In Finland it's known as *muikku*, and is given the usual herring treatment: either salted, poached or smoked. Sometimes they bake it inside a pie crust or rye-bread dough. At other times it's simply fried in a little butter and eaten with mashed potatoes and pickles, and vendace roe is regarded as a great delicacy.

It was a climatic change that left the vendace marooned in a handful of English and Scottish lakes 10,000 years ago, and it's climate change again that may cause it to die out here altogether. Indeed, all of Britain's sixty or so species of freshwater fish face a triumvirate of problems: climate change, habitat loss and competition from non-native invaders. The chance to eat vendace in the UK has long since past, and if we're not careful the chance to even see them may pass too.

*See also* DOVER, KENT (p. 473); GLOUCESTER, GLOUCESTERSHIRE (p. 288); HASTINGS, EAST SUSSEX (p. 483); MARKET HARBOROUGH, LEICESTERSHIRE (p. 340); NEWLYN, CORNWALL (pp. 32 and 34); RIVER SEVERN, GLOUCESTERSHIRE (p. 305); SCOURIE, HIGHLAND (p. 187); SOUTHEND-ON-SEA, ESSEX (p. 455); WANSFORD, EAST YORKSHIRE (p. 261); WHITBURN, TYNE & WEAR (p. 228).

ECCLES, GREATER MANCHESTER
# Eccles cake

One James Birch is credited with popularising Eccles cakes in around 1793 from his shop in the town, and they have remained a firm favourite in this neck of the woods ever since. With a self-mocking affection that only a northerner could muster, locally they're known as 'dead fly pies', after the little chewy raisins contained within. These raisins are mixed with a bit of candied

Eccles cake (or dead fly pie) served with Lancashire cheese

peel, sugar and sometimes a touch of cinnamon or nutmeg. The keen-eyed among you will have noticed a similarity to the modern mince-pie filling, and they are indeed very similar, although suet doesn't feature. A large dollop of this filling is placed in a flaky pastry case, the top is slit three times to provide vents that will let the steam out, and, if you're lucky, offer a peep at the raisins' last resting place within. The cake is then glazed with egg and a light crust of granulated sugar applied. This melts and turns crunchy like glass in a fire after the pies come out of the oven. When the cakes are cooled and I bite into one, I like to find a little bit of air between the filling and the top of the pastry, a sweet taste in my mouth and flakes of golden pastry all down my jumper. There are those, however, who incorporate the filling into the pastry, roll and cut it into rounds and bake solid-style Eccles cake – but to them I give short shrift.

The Edmonds family bakery, based in Ardwick, Manchester, make 'Real Lancashire Eccles cakes' using lots of lovely butter, the finest Vostizza currants from Greece, demerara sugar and a pinch of salt. Each cake is then fashioned by hand.

Twenty-odd miles to the north-west of Eccles is the town of Chorley, home to the Eccles cake's cousin, the Chorley cake. This uses the same filling and encases it in unsweetened shortcrust rather than flaky pastry. The result is a more solid cake – enjoyable, but in a different way from an Eccles. It lacks the dusting of sugar on top too, so to make up for this some say a smear of butter should be added. What complements either cake from these Lancashire towns is a nice big slice of the county's cheese (*see* p. 128).

See also MINCEMEAT (p. 202); ALBERT EMBANKMENT, LAMBETH (p. 368); ALDERLEY EDGE, CHESHIRE (p. 96); BISHOP AUCKLAND, COUNTY DURHAM (p. 201); HOOK NORTON, OXFORDSHIRE (p. 328); LLANDEILO, CARMARTHENSHIRE (p. 74); MANCHESTER, GREATER MANCHESTER (p. 119); MELTON MOWBRAY, LEICESTERSHIRE (p. 341); NAVENBY, LINCOLNSHIRE (p. 344); OTLEY, WEST YORKSHIRE (p. 252); STANBRIDGE, BEDFORDSHIRE (p. 360); WHITBY, NORTH YORKSHIRE (p. 269).

## FLEETWOOD, LANCASHIRE
# *Fisherman's Friend*

Fisherman's Friend lozenges are as much a British institution as the shipping forecast. Even the packet conjures up the image of a sou'wester-clad fisherman hauling in a net during a 'storm ten' somewhere between Dogger and German Bite, the fiery lozenge clamped between his gritted teeth. Their history began in 1865 in the fishing town of Fleetwood, Lancashire, where a pharmacist named James Lofthouse developed a mix of menthol and eucalyptus oil aimed at relieving colds, sore throats and other respiratory problems suffered by the men of the fishing fleet while at sea. A teaspoon of the medicine was probably rather hard to administer, even with a good pair of sea legs, and so Lofthouse soon hit upon the idea of turning it into a lozenge, which was much more transportable and easier to use. Fishermen began to refer to these as their 'friends', and wouldn't sail without them – the name stuck.

Today, each small light-brown oval pastille is a combination of sugar, liquorice powder, menthol and eucalyptus oil, with six tiny pinpricks on one side. The initial smell is of liquorice – still used as an expectorant to this day – then once in the mouth it's full steam ahead as all the other flavours are released and your taste buds batten down the hatches. You can only admire the advice on the packet that states, 'This product is not suitable for children under five.'

Fisherman's Friend is still made by Lofthouse's of Fleetwood, and according to the company, 4 billion lozenges are consumed each year, which, given the size of the UK fishing fleet (approximately 10,000 men), means many a fan of Fisherman's Friend are landlubbers, seeking, as the little paper packet puts it, a 'soothing effect in extreme conditions'.

*See also* PONTEFRACT, WEST YORKSHIRE (p. 254).


## GOOSNARGH, LANCASHIRE
# *Goosnargh duck*

Today the Goosnargh (pronounced *gooze-ner*) duck is something of a celebrity in the avian world, gracing the tables of Hibiscus, Corrigan's and Roast in London, the World Service at Nottingham, the Yew Tree Inn at Newbury and many more. It is the duck professional chefs call for when they wish to display their anatine artistry. (In Douglas Adams's humorous dictionary *The Meaning of Liff*, Goosnargh was defined thus: GOOSNARGH (n.) Something left over from preparing or eating a meal, which you store in the fridge despite the fact that you know full well you will never ever use it.)

Farmers Reg Johnson and Bud Swarbrick initially began raising chickens, rather than ducks, in the mid 1980s on their farm near the Ribble Valley. Local chef, since turned restaurateur, Paul Heathcote played midwife to the fledgling business, as he was keen to improve on the quality of the chickens he served. That gave Reg and Bud the break and support they needed, and they took on ducks a year or two later.

The breed they eventually settled on, after some trial and error, was an Aylesbury and Peking cross. The Aylesbury was developed in said town during the eighteenth century, while the Peking (aka. Pekin) was introduced from China in 1873. Both breeds are white-plumed, and they are often cross-bred.

The farm now processes 2,500 ducks a week. Day-old chicks are bought from specialist hatcheries and brought on until they're ready for slaughter at either nine or twelve weeks. 'Any time in between those dates and you'll end up with something that resembles a hedgehog,' says Reg. They're stunned and killed, and the wing and tail feathers are taken off by a machine that is basically like a giant Epilady. Then it's into a hot wax bath, followed by a cold water bath to set it, before the wax is removed by another machine, taking the last of the feathers with it.

If you want to go and see the ducks you're more than welcome to arrange a visit. 'We do encourage our customers to come and have a look,' says Reg.

If, however, you can't make it to the beautiful Lancashire village of Goosnargh, keep an eye out for the bird in your local restaurant. If the chef has done their job right, you will be served wonderful, juicy meat with a rich flavour. Just remember to pronounce it correctly to the waiter.

*See also* HARLOW, ESSEX (p. 436); HINDOLVESTON, NORFOLK (p. 437); KING'S NYMPTON, DEVON (p. 20); MAIDENHEAD, BERKSHIRE (p. 487); THUXTON, NORFOLK (p. 458).

GRANGE-OVER-SANDS, CUMBRIA
# Cumberland Rum Nicky and rum butter

It's a long way from the tropical heat of the Caribbean to the cold coast of Cumbria, but the exotic products that made the journey in the seventeenth and eighteenth centuries went on to become part of the food landscape of the region. Rum, spices, sugar: all feature heavily in every course of the cooking of the region. So after potted shrimp to start, and Cumberland sausage for the main, what better for dessert than Cumberland Rum Nicky? This pudding, created at the high-water mark of the region's trade in the 1800s, marries rum and sugar from the West with dates and ginger from the East. This fruity, boozy mix is placed in a shortcrust pastry case and, more often than not, topped with a latticework of pastry similar to a treacle tart's (*see* p. 442). However, whereas treacle tart was scraped together from rather meagre ingredients, a Rum Nicky said one thing: 'I'm rich enough to afford these luxury goods.'

Dorothy Stubley, owner of the Hazelmere tea rooms in Grange-over-Sands, Cumbria, has served Cumberland Rum Nicky since opening day in 1984. 'Cumberland Rum Nicky is one of those puddings that each family makes differently,' says Dorothy. Her version takes rum butter, stem ginger, dates and cherries, and incorporates them in a cake mixture. This gooey mix is then placed in a sweet shortcrust pastry case. A latticework of pastry is popped over the top, and the pie is baked and given a final apricot glaze. Other recipes, particularly from further north in the county, contain more dried fruit. 'We sell it all year round, but it's particularly popular during the cooler months and around Christmas,' says Dorothy. Dorothy serves it with crème fraiche, which provides a creamy yet tart counterpoint to the sweet stickiness of the cake.

As for the name, Dorothy has no idea where it comes from, although she suggests that perhaps a 'nicky' could mean 'a little bit of something sweet'. Personally, I'm rather taken with the idea that this devilishly moreish cake is actually named for the Devil himself, Old Nick being a colloquial term for him.

Rum features not only in Rum Nicky, but in another dish of the region, Cumberland rum butter (which Dorothy adds to her Rum Nicky). This is a mixture of butter and rum to which a little spice and plenty of brown sugar has been added. It can be used in a similar way to brandy butter, and was often made to celebrate the birth of a baby, when it was served with oatcakes and, no doubt, more rum. Once the guests had cooed over the new arrival, they would deposit coins in the empty butter bowl as a good-luck gift.

*See also* ALNWICK, NORTHUMBERLAND (p. 196).

## GREAT CLIFTON, CUMBRIA
# Cumberland sausage

Cumberland sausage is a relatively recent addition to the food of the north-west, gaining popularity in the eighteenth century and featuring the spices so beloved of that wild county, namely mace, nutmeg, and white and black pepper. It was traditionally made with meat from the Cumberland pig, but the last of these became extinct in the 1960s, a fate mirrored by the county itself when it was merged with neighbouring Westmorland to form Cumbria in 1974. Yet its first mention in print comes as recently as 1911 in E. J. Jackson's tome *Reliable Guide to the Curing of Cumberland Hams and Bacon and the Preparation of the Offal in the Cumberland Style*.

Today it's difficult to find producers with skills and knowledge that stretch back to the turn of the last century, but in Stuart Flett there is just such a man. Stuart learned the art of making the famous sausage from his father, Rodney, who in turn learned from a gentleman butcher called Billy Clague, who had been making them since the 1920s.

Rodney retired in 2000, but found that his peace was often disturbed by people asking for sausages. In the end he decided to buy the village store in Great Clifton and begin production. Stuart, meanwhile, still makes sausages for his family and friends. 'Mine are better than me dad's,' he says. They both follow the same recipe, but Stuart believes he's got a better eye for making them. 'It's about judging the fat to lean correctly.' Stuart uses only the belly, and believes the meat texture should be coarse and the fat level high so that it can cook the sausage from within as it melts.

There are other tricks to learn: he strips off the leaf lard found near the animal's kidneys as he believes it gives the sausage a greasy, waxy taste; and

The Cumberland sausage, coiled like a cobra and ready to strike your taste buds

he sources his pepper from one specific Indonesian island (the identity of which remains a secret – like the island in *Lost*). 'Their pepper has a sweeter-tasting husk,' says Stuart. Also of note is his use of breadcrumbs – all British-style sausages need a little crumb to bind the stuffing and absorb some of the fat during cooking. Rodney adds a given amount per pound of meat, but Stuart has an improved method. He won't tell me what it is, though.

I couldn't resist asking the most important question: 'How big is your sausage?' After we both regained our composure, Stuart told me that his Cumberlands are about an inch thick, and when coiled up are about six inches in diameter. 'Originally they were sold by length, and so a good Cumberland should be a foot long when uncoiled.'

Stuart eats his with Cumberland sauce (a traditional accompaniment to meats, made with redcurrants, port, mustard and orange and served rather runny and cold), but on occasion he's eaten it with a blob of jam or marmalade – a contemporary version of the medieval diet, when meat and sweet often shared the same plate.

Stuart makes his sausages as much as a hobby as a business. There are other well-known larger producers in the area, Richard Woodhall of Waberthwaite being worthy of note (in fact he has the Royal Warrant for his sausages), as is Peter Gott of Sillifield Farm (*see* p. 114). Recently, they and others formed the Traditional Cumberland Sausage Association to try to secure the Cumberland EU PGI (Protected Geographical Indication) status. And until that comes through, anyone is at liberty to make Cumberlands the length and breadth of the land. However, they're never better, I think, than in the area that lends them their name.

*See also* SAUSAGES (p. 122).

## THE ISLE OF MAN
### *Loaghtan sheep*

The Manx Loaghtan (pronounced *lock-tan*) is a prehistoric short-tailed breed thought to have inhabited the island since the time of the Celts. It has remained unchanged since those days, enduring the tough conditions on the

Meat from the rugged Loaghtan is dark and flavourful

island for over 1,000 years, perfectly at home in the rugged terrain and salty sea air. The name *Loaghtan* is a portmanteau of two Manx words: *lugh* (mouse) and *dhoan* (brown), which is the colour of its fleece as an adult. Interestingly, the lambs are born with jet-black coats that lighten as they are weaned.

As for the flesh, you'd think that Manx farmers, sitting as they do between Irish stew to the west and scouse and hotpot to the east would be well placed to sell their wares. But the characteristics we now value – slow-growing, rich, flavourful – were the very ones that caused the breed almost to die out as farmers switched to faster-growing commercial breeds. By the 1950s numbers had fallen to a mere handful.

Thankfully, common sense prevailed and the Loaghtan didn't go the way of the Cumberland pig or the Limestone sheep. It recently received PDO (Protected Designation of Origin) status, which governs not only the breed, but also the production method. Manx farmers let wildflowers and herbs grow on in the summer, no sheds are used, or 'cake' – a concentrated block of animal feed – and the animals are out all year.

They are amazing beasts, with huge horns – sometimes two, sometimes four – and golden-brown fleeces. The meat itself differs from commercial lamb too; it's more like venison, with a rich ruby colour and a gamey flavour. Strong, but never brutish, to me it tastes of red wine. There are Loaghtan breeders on the mainland, but only the Manx meat that is born, raised and slaughtered on the island has PDO status.

*See also* ELAN VALLEY, POWYS (p. 64); ELWY VALLEY, DENBIGHSHIRE (p. 65); HIMBLETON, WORCESTERSHIRE (p. 297).

KENDAL, CUMBRIA
## *Kendal mint cake*

Going on a yomp around the hills and waters of the Lake District without a bar of Kendal mint cake is like going to see a trashy summer blockbuster without a bucket of popcorn. And although we all entertain notions of its energy-giving survivalist powers and its ability to keep us alive and fuel our triumphant trek over harsh terrain, in reality it's just a nice treat to have on the way round before popping into a tea room for a cuppa and a bun.

Kendal mint cake has fuelled many a legitimate expedition, the most famous being Hillary and Tenzing's conquest of Everest in 1953, as well as

# Clipping-Time Pudding

Clipping-time pudding is one of those regional dishes for which plenty of recipes exist, yet a portion of it for sale is as rare as hen's teeth. It is – quite literally – a beefed-up version of rice pudding that contains pudding rice, currants, raisins, egg, cinnamon and bone marrow. It used to be eaten in the Cumbria region when it was time for sheep shearing – or clipping. Back then, and indeed up until the early twentieth century, the shearing of sheep was done by hand using a tool that resembled a giant pair of scissors. As the work was seasonal and done by hand, highly skilled men would come from far and wide to assist farmers in removing the fleeces. In some cases bed and board might be provided, and the completion of the task was almost always used as an excuse for a celebration.

Elizabeth Gaskell gives an account of the process and the following festivities in an 1853 article entitled 'Cumberland Sheep Shearers':

> The busy women were dishing up great smoking rounds of beef; and in addition to all the provision I had seen in the boilers, large-mouthed ovens were disgorging berry pies without end, and rice-puddings stuck full of almonds and raisins.

The last of these could be our dish, despite the fact that there's no mention of the key ingredient of bone marrow. Though Gaskell was writing in the 1850s, adding bone marrow to puddings was commonplace across the country in medieval times, as was combining the flavours of almonds, mace and cinnamon. Interestingly, food historian Ivan Day makes the point that the Lake District was one of the first tourism destinations, and consequently when the likes of Coleridge and Wordsworth turned up, and later Gaskell and the Victorians, the locals were no doubt keen to show off their 'traditional' dishes, even though they might not be that historic. A modern comparison would be apple crumble, a pud many consider 'traditional' but which is thought to have originated around the time of the Second World War.

Today many clipping-time festivities have died out, and sheep are sheared by electric razor. Fleeces, which once contributed to farmers' incomes, are now worth only a few pence each, whereas it can cost up to £1 to shear a sheep. That said, you can still enjoy a celebration of all things ovine every June at Woolfest, which is held near Cockermouth. Here they host everything from sheep shearing to knitting demonstrations, but, sadly, there has so far been no sign of our extinct pud. Perhaps bone-marrow rice pudding is a bit too challenging for festival goers? Of course, nowadays it would easily grace the menu of St John in Smithfield, mirroring their signature roast bone-marrow salad starter nicely. Or maybe, like its medieval predecessors, its fate is just to slip away quietly.

See also HEREFORD, HEREFORDSHIRE (p. 296).

(more recently) Ewan McGregor and Charley Boorman's motorcycle trip around the world in 2004. After taking out an advert in a climbing magazine, founder of Romney's Kendal mint cakes Sam Clark was approached by the team organising the ascent of Everest. Hillary and Tenzing are said to have had a bite of the cake on the summit of the world, with Tenzing leaving a small piece to appease the gods.

Like many recipes, Kendal mint cake is said to have been discovered in error. When Victorian confectioner Joseph Wiper was trying to make clear 'glacier' mints he took his eye off the pot and the mixture became opaque and grainy. The mint cake was born. Wipers started trading in 1869, but was eventually bought out by Romney in 1987. The other producers in the region are Wilson's, established in 1913, and Quiggin's, established in 1880. As with Stilton producers, each company's mint cakes taste slightly different – owing to the strength of flavour and proportion of glucose to sugar, for example – and some are more 'grainy' than others. All, though, have a history and connection to the area.

John Barron is the current MD of Romney's. 'Eighty per cent of our business is done in the Lake District,' he tells me. The production method remains the same: sugar is combined with glucose and water and boiled, then peppermint oil is added – about 14ml per 18kg of mix. Nowadays mint cake comes in a variety of flavours: original, extra strong, butter mint candy, and rum and butter. John has also produced some special versions for certain clients, including a chilli one. Perfect, perhaps, for tackling a climb in the Andes.

See also HOW RECIPES BEGIN (p. 496).


KENDAL, CUMBRIA
## Peter Gott's wild boar

Peter Gott is what you might call a celebrity producer. He's been fêted by the likes of Jamie Oliver and he's appeared many times on TV and radio; however, this hasn't insulated him from the practical issues that all farmers face. In fact, it may have even contributed to the vandalising of his farm by animal rights extremists, which led to the death of four animals. Still, he remains upbeat.

Peter has had a stall at Borough Market for years, and every Wednesday loads a van with meat, pies and Cumberland sausage for the long drive down

Peter Gott's wild boar in their eighteen-acre enclosure

to London. His farm specialises in rare-breed, slow-grown pigs; the herd is made up of most of our old native breeds: Saddleback, Tamworth, Duroc, Gloucester Old Spot and Middle White. It is meat from these animals that goes into his stunning dry-cured bacon, as well as his Cumberland sausages, ham and pies.

The farm is also home to over 150 wild boar, which Peter started farming in 1993 when his brother gave him four wild boar gilts (young females) as a joke. The boar roam free in an eighteen-acre wooded area, living for up to two years before being butchered and, in some cases, dried and cured. His wild-boar prosciutto, for example, is matured for two years, and after handling the meat your fingers glisten with a fragrant sheen of fat. Indeed, one of the factors that differentiates wild boar from other pigs is the second layer of fat under the skin, and we all know that fat means flavour. As for the smell and taste, well there's that unmistakable 'tang' that boar meat has, a sharp, pleasant gamey flavour that gores its way up your nose and wallows in the back of the throat. His salt-cured boar bacon, for example, comes from a two-year-old animal and when raw is the colour of beef or even venison – that dark matt purple. Once cooked it becomes pinker, but not nearly as much as bacon made from traditional pig breeds. The texture, too, is much closer and fine grained, much like the recalcitrant animal it came from.

*See also* ACOMB, NORTHUMBERLAND (p. 195); AUCHTERMUCHTY, FIFE (p. 144); BLAXHALL, SUFFOLK (p. 419); BROMPTON-ON-SWALE, NORTH YORKSHIRE (p. 236); CHIPPENHAM, WILTSHIRE (p. 9); FRILSHAM, BERKSHIRE (p. 479).

## LIVERPOOL, MERSEYSIDE
# Scouse

Scouse, the iconic stew of Liverpool, gave Scousers their name. The word is thought to derive from *lobscouse*, a sailors' stew from Northern Europe, and the dish itself contains lamb, potatoes, vegetables and other ingredients that have been readily available to Liverpudlians for hundreds of years. When William Black visited the city recently to research his book *The Land that Thyme Forgot*, he professed he couldn't find any scouse. This may be because it's an everyday family dish, the sort of thing that graces a kitchen table midweek, not a restaurant specials menu. That, however, may be about to change.

Like many regional dishes, these days there are a plethora of recipes. Generally scouse is made with lamb, though there are recipes featuring beef. There's a strong geographical argument for lamb being more authentic: to the west of Liverpool you'll find Irish stew, made with lamb. To the east there's the Lancashire hotpot, also made with lamb. But, if born-in-the-shadow-of-the-Liver-Building scousers prefer to use beef, who am I to argue? Some recipes call for swede, others still for tomatoes, both of which hold no dice with me. Some recommend allowing the potatoes to break down so that they can thicken the dish; others prefer them whole. And there are even some that state scouse must be made with leftover lamb from the Sunday joint rather than fresh meat.

Although scouse is home cooking at its best, you can try it at Maggie May's Café in the city. There, they make it with beef, and even sell it in cans for you to take away. Alternatively, if you're after a more luxurious setting, you can take a table at the Malmaison Hotel where head chef Adam Townsley serves it. Adam is an Australian by birth but his wife is from the Wirral, which is what brought him to Merseyside. His version is refined but simple: 'We make it with local ingredients, beautifully tender neck of lamb, carrots, potatoes and onions. To that we add a bit of lamb stock and seasoning and that's it. We don't muck about with it.' The dish is served in a bowl on a board with some bread and pickled beetroot. Classic scouse in a contemporary fine-dining setting – and why not?

*See also* CAWL (p. 68).

*See also* CAWL (p. 68).

LYTH AND WINSTER VALLEYS, CUMBRIA
# *Damsons*

It's a long way from the roadsides of Damascus to the Lyth and Winster valleys in the Lake District, and yet the damson seems to have made the transition just fine. This area, formerly Westmorland but now absorbed into Cumbria, has been known for its damsons since at least medieval times. At one time, most farms had one or two acres of damson trees, which meant that during the spring, both of the ten-mile-long valleys would be festooned with blossom. The fruit was then harvested in the first two weeks of September, which fitted in well with the region's agricultural cycle as by then hay making would have been over.

There are, of course, small areas of damson production in other parts of

Damsons straight from the orchard being turned into vibrant jam

the UK: Shropshire, the Vale of Evesham and parts of Kent. 'We don't think they're as good as our damsons, to be honest,' says Bill Bradford of the Westmorland Damson Association. 'They may be bigger, but they've not got the tangy flavour of the Westmorland damson.' According to Bill, damsons were initially grown in the area not for the tastiness of the fruit, but for their value as a dyeing agent. In the Middle Ages Kendal was a textile town and produced worsted cloth and stockings, many of which were dyed using a mix of woad (a plant that when fermented produces blue dye), dyer's greenweed (another plant, which produces a yellow dye) and damson juice. This colour became known as Kendal green, said to have been worn by archers at Agincourt and mentioned in Shakespeare's *Henry IV, Pt I*.

After the Industrial Revolution the textile industry moved south to Lancashire and away from natural dyes. The damson orchards were kept going haphazardly by the farmers themselves, some of the fruits sold at the roadside and some to jam factories. But in the last fifty years, with the price going down along with demand, many farmers just gave up maintaining the orchards commercially. 'An awful lot of fruit ended up on the floor,' says Bill.

Then in April 1996 Peter Cartmell formed the Westmorland Damson Association, with the help of other local producers who wished to preserve the orchards. They encourage people to plant the trees with grants. 'The tree is rather unusual in that it throws suckers up, and if they're not eaten by livestock, they can be detached from the parent tree and planted, so you know you've got a perfect clone of that tree,' says Bill.

The association is also connecting pickers and commercial companies with farmers who can't harvest all their fruit, marketing the fruit to chefs and jam companies, and buying damsons at a fixed price. Helen Bromley at Low Farm keeps five tonnes of frozen stock of damsons to ensure their availability all year round.

As for the eating, damsons need heat to release their unique flavour. Bill tells of a local chap who makes damson ice cream, and the association's chairman Oliver Barratt and his wife make a damson gin which is stocked in Fortnum & Mason. But for me you can't beat a dollop of the classic damson jam, sweet at first followed by a slight sharpness, and deep, deep purple.

*See also* CORBRIDGE, NORTHUMBERLAND (p. 207); EGTON BRIDGE, NORTH YORKSHIRE (p. 243); HAMPRESTON, DORSET (p. 14); HONITON, DEVON (p. 17); INVERGOWRIE, PERTH & KINROSS (p. 180); NORTHIAM, EAST SUSSEX (p. 492); WALMERSLEY, GREATER MANCHESTER (p. 137); WIMBLEDON, MERTON (p. 415).

# Malt loaf

Hello, my name is Andrew and I have a malt loaf problem. I used to be able to buy a malt loaf and cut off a few slices, rather enjoying the way it sort of squashed as you put the knife to it. Occasionally I'd even take time to butter it, like normal people, but that didn't last. Now I can't wait to tear off the packaging and chew on the whole damn thing like a toddler gnawing a Lego brick. Consequently, I can no longer have it in the house.

Top baker Dan Lepard calls malt loaf the original energy bar because it's high in calories and low in fat. *The Ultimate Hiking Skills Manual* quantifies this, saying that a malt loaf weighs 225 grams and contains 697 calories, of which 146 grams are carbohydrates and only 5 grams fat. I've never tried to make malt loaf, because, I pretend to myself, malt extract is too tricky an ingredient to track down; in truth, I'm really just scared that I'll like it even more than a mass-produced one. Malt loaf is my guilty secret – don't worry, I'll get help.

The most familiar brand in the shops is Soreen, reputedly created by the Sorensen family in Manchester. Warburtons owned the business from 1959, before selling it to Inter Link Foods in 2003. That firm was taken over by an Irish company called McCambridge in 2007, who still make it today in Manchester.

The malt in malt loaf comes from germinating grain – commonly barley – in water so that the starches begin to turn to sugar. Before the grain can start to use them to grow, the process is halted by drying or heating them rapidly. This malted grain is used to make beer, whisky and Horlicks, which incidentally are another three of my favourite things.

In the late nineteenth and early twentieth centuries, malt extract was one of those things, like cod liver oil, considered good for you. It was fortifying and full of vitamins, especially when added to milk, and a spoonful of it was often given to children. Malt producers, keen to see their product in as many places as possible, penned recipes telling us how to use it. The Decatur Brewing Company in the USA, which during Prohibition switched to producing malt extract under the blue ribbon label, even produced the book *Tested Recipes with Blue Ribbon Malt Extract*. This handy kitchen tome guided the housewives of America to add malt to just about everything. There's even a recipe for cabbage au gratin featuring the stuff, if you're feeling particularly adventurous. Mind you, in 1894 the same company had an advert that read, 'Have you a good appetite? If not, drink a glass of Decatur Brewing Company's "Pilsner" Lager Beer before each meal. It is cheaper than medicine, much more agreeable to the taste and a splendid appetizer. Try it.' Which though true, probably wouldn't clear the Advertising Standards Authority's code of practice today.

*See also* ALBERT EMBANKMENT, LAMBETH (p. 368); ALDERLEY EDGE, CHESHIRE (p. 96); BISHOP AUCKLAND, COUNTY DURHAM (p. 201); ECCLES, GREATER MANCHESTER (p. 103); HOOK NORTON, OXFORDSHIRE (p. 328); LLANDEILO, CARMARTHENSHIRE (p. 74); MELTON MOWBRAY, LEICESTERSHIRE (p. 341); NAVENBY, LINCOLNSHIRE (p. 344); OTLEY, WEST YORKSHIRE (p. 252); STANBRIDGE, BEDFORDSHIRE (p. 360); WHITBY, NORTH YORKSHIRE (p. 269).

## MANCHESTER, GREATER MANCHESTER
# The Manchester sausage

Most have heard of the Cumberland sausage, the long curled-up sausage flavoured with pepper and spices (*see* p. 108). And many know about the Lincolnshire sausage, flavoured with plenty of sage. Others still may be au fait with the intellectual powerhouses of the Oxford and Cambridge sausages. But did you know about the Manchester sausage? That's right – Manchester has its own sausage, and the key ingredients are sage, cloves, nutmeg and ginger, according to food writer Alan Davidson. These are added to finely ground pork, salt and white pepper, and that's about it.

In 2007 I was lucky enough to find some for sale in Homestead Farm Shop, Pott Shrigley, Macclesfield. Joyce Dalton, who served me, said her recipe came from an eighteenth-century cookbook that belonged to a family friend and that he never let anybody else read. Eventually, he moved to Australia and said to his friends, 'You can have ten minutes with the book,' and so they frantically wrote down whatever recipes they could, including the one for the Manchester sausage, before the book was packed in a tea chest and shipped away to a new life down under. Since then Joyce has retired, selling the farm and shop, although she still has the recipe somewhere.

Riley's Sausages in Openshaw, Manchester, have been making a product called the Manchester sausage for the last few years. There is a nice yarn on their website about how the recipe came to the family, via a great-uncle who was a pawnbroker by trade and who once took in a pig for cash from a customer. Around the neck of the animal was tied a recipe for their Manchester sausage; the ingredients contained both belly meat and shoulder, rusk, a spice mix, herbs and mustard. It's available in supermarkets throughout the north-west, but is a different beast to Joyce's. Hers was a real home-made, beautiful banger, with a strong spicy nutmeg flavour writ large in the mouth. Alas, it is no more.

See also SAUSAGES (p. 122).

See also SAUSAGES (p. 122).

MORECAMBE BAY, LANCASHIRE
## Morecambe Bay potted shrimp

Morecambe Bay and its mudflats are rich in seafood. This attracts not only wildlife, but also hungry humans. When the tide is out, it's easy to lose your sense of direction, and when it comes in, it's easy to lose your life, earning it the nickname of the wet Sahara.

Shrimp boats have worked the bay for generations, searching for the tiny shrimps that are the size of a baby's finger and just as plump. They pack a rich flavour that belies their size. The word 'shrimp' originally came from Old German and meant anything that is smaller than average; it is related to 'scrimp', 'skimpy' and 'shrink'. Interestingly, the French word for shrimp is *crevette*, meaning 'little goat', as they sort of resemble a leaping goat when they move.

Shrimps have long been preserved in dishes under a layer of flavoured butter. Mace, pepper, cayenne and nutmeg are all used, reflecting the region's love of spices and all things windward. There are many producers of potted shrimps around the bay, stretching as far down as Southport and Blackpool, but Baxters of Morecambe is worthy of note, as it's had the Royal Warrant for over thirty years. Started by James Baxter in 1799, it's still going strong today, with business mainly done by mail order.

Baxters has six fishermen who supply it. The shrimps are caught in small boats operating locally, and once hauled up on to the boat they're boiled immediately in the seawater then picked from the shell. There's no denying this is fiddly work, demanding the concentration of a watchmaker and the speed of a checkout girl. Nowadays some are done by machine, but two-thirds of Baxters' shrimps are still peeled by hand. If you attempt the dish at home, an hour's picking and peeling will give you just about enough shrimp to fill a ramekin.

## Sausages

According to the British Sausage Week website, sausages are the number-one 'in-home meal'; ahead of a cheese and ham sandwich, apparently. I can well believe it: the sausage is, after all, a much-loved, cost-effective family favourite. There are a number of excellent regional variations across the UK, from the Lincolnshire – heavily flavoured with sage – to the coiled-up Cumberland – highly spiced. Then there's the foppish Oxford – skinless and flavoured with veal – the porky geezer that is the Epping sausage, and the neck-and-neck race that defines the Newmarket sausage. If you look hard enough, nearly every region, county and town has a historical sausage, which often evolved hand in hand with another industry such as beer production or cheese-making, as the waste products from these were frequently mopped up by pigs (who will eat anything).

The product itself was designed to use up all the random little bits of leftovers from the butchery process: the awkwardly shaped cuts and the fiddly bits of trim. Today it is the shoulder and belly that are most commonly used. When it's made from well-kept pork using these cuts and a bit of seasoning, a good sausage can't be beaten – indeed, few things in life are finer. But when it comes in a bag of twenty for £1 and is made of mechanically separated meat, there's not much worse – for the pig or for you. And it's the sausage's forgiving form that leads unscrupulous folk to consider debasing it. It's hard to cheat with a joint of meat (but not impossible: some have been known to inject it with water to bulk up the weight) but a sausage's minced-up filling can hide a great many sins. A sausage remains a good weathervane of how competent butchers are at the basic stuff; if they can't get this right, I wouldn't put much store by the rest of their offerings.

Stephen Plume is a man who knows a thing or two about the British banger. His website Sausagefans.com was started in 2001 to promote independent butchers and great sausages. 'We have over 500 types of sausage in the UK. They're good for breakfast, lunch and dinner, and work in everything from a fry-up to a winter casserole to a summer barbeque,' he says. 'Unfortunately, lax labelling laws mean that it is possible for consumers to be hoodwinked into buying inferior imported pork from countries where welfare standards are much lower.' This happened in late 2009 when Wall's were – quite legally – importing pork produced on the Continent to a factory in Manchester and calling the resulting sausages Lincolnshire.

Assuming you've done a bit of research and snagged yourself a well-made banger, what is the best way to cook it? Well, there's the grill, or perhaps the slow, shallow fry. Personally, I'm rather partial to roasting them in the oven on a bed of onions for an evening meal (putting the oven on at breakfast seems strange). I find this lets the sausages get nice and sticky, and the fat that comes out as they cook flavours the onions, helping the gravy along. As A. P. Herbert once wrote, 'When love is dead,/ Ambition fled,/ And pleasure, lad, and pash,/ You'll still enjoy/ A sausage, boy,/ A sausage, boy,/ and mash.'

*See also* ABERTHIN, VALE OF GLAMORGAN (p. 55); CLITHEROE, LANCASHIRE (p. 101); CONWY, CONWY (p. 60); EPPING, ESSEX (p. 427); GREAT CLIFTON, CUMBRIA (p. 108); LOUTH, LINCOLNSHIRE (p. 336); LOWICK, NORTHUMBERLAND (p. 216); MANCHESTER, GREATER MANCHESTER (p. 120); MELTON CONSTABLE, NORFOLK (p. 447); NEWMARKET, SUFFOLK (p. 450); OXFORD, OXFORDSHIRE (p. 352); ULLAPOOL, HIGHLAND (p. 191).

Baxters makes up the shrimps in 30 lb amounts at a time. The shrimps are added to butter and then the spices follow. It's a very light and delicate spicing that allows the flavour of the shrimp to take the lead. I did ask for the recipe, but received the politest of knock-backs: 'Susan Baxter is the only one who knows what's in it. And that's the way it's going to stay.'

*See also* BUCKIE, MORAY (p. 149); CHINATOWN, WESTMINSTER (p. 374); CROMER, NORFOLK (p. 426); LITTLE HAVEN, PEMBROKESHIRE (p. 70); SALTHOUSE, NORFOLK (p. 454).

## NANTWICH, CHESHIRE
# A. T. Welch — the longest deli in the world?

Nantwich, like anywhere in the UK ending in 'wich', was famed for its salt production in Saxon times, but there are plenty of other foodie things going on nowadays. One place that is definitely worth a visit is A. T. Welch's, the foodie equivalent of the TARDIS. A simple bay window and nondescript front door lead to a corridor of edible delights that just keeps on going. It's like a food drag race: at 145 feet long and yet just 12 feet at the widest point and only 8 feet at its narrowest, this oblong outlet must surely be the longest deli in the world.

Once in the door you pass the meat counter, where there is a fine selection of hams and a good range of pâtés. Onwards through the grocery and condiment section packed with jars and tins of many things, before eventually hitting the cheese counter at the end, where you will find Applebee's Cheshire cheese, Shropshire Blue, Hawes Wensleydale and Lancashire in both mild and mature versions.

The shop was established in 1922 and bought from the Welch family by brothers Bill and Bronwen Austin in 1966. Just before you hit the cheese counter there is a left turn that leads to Austin's Yesteryear Grocers Shoppe, which, despite the medieval name, contains a fascinating collection of grocery hardware, signs and memorabilia from the past. For food fans as well as social history buffs it's a great place to wile away a few moments, thinking about what food retailing used to be like: bacon sliced to order, oats sold by weight out of a huge barrel and no plastic packaging.

Austin's Yesteryear Grocer's Shoppe and the café at A. T. Welch

## Great Tasting Meat Company's lamb portmanteau

A portmanteau is a large leather suitcase or travel bag, popular in the nineteenth century. Larger ones tended to have a flat bottom and a rounded top, similar to an old doctor's bag, while smaller ones were almost entirely round and fitted behind a rider's saddle. The word comes from the French *porter*, meaning 'to carry', and *manteau*, meaning a 'coat' or 'cover'. As well as referring to luggage, the word was also annexed by Lewis Carroll in *Through the Looking Glass* to describe terms such as 'galumphing' and 'outgrabe' in *Jabberwocky*. As Humpty Dumpty explained, 'You see, it's like a portmanteau – there are two meanings packed up into one word.'

Amazingly, both these meanings come together in the lamb portmanteau – a lamb chop stuffed with mushrooms and chicken livers. Why only lamb should be described thus is a mystery. There are, after all, many other stuffed meats: chicken cordon bleu, stuffed with ham and cheese; or chicken Kiev, which includes garlic butter. Or even the carpetbag steak, which continues the luggage theme, but involves a perfectly good steak being ruined by the insertion of an oyster.

Many recipes for portmanteau call for a thick lamb chop from the loin to be sliced to the bone from the fat side (through the eye of the meat) and the resulting pocket stuffed with a mix of chicken livers, mushrooms and seasoning. It's then held closed with a stick, breadcrumbed, and fried or baked until golden. However, Andrew Jackson's Great Tasting Meat Company do it a little differently (and better, in my opinion). Instead of individual chops, they take a double loin of lamb about eight inches long and bone it out. They then take a pâté-style mix of lamb's liver, mushrooms, onions, tomato paste and the company's own cooked, cooled, oak-smoked bacon and stuff the joint with it, before coating in Parmesan breadcrumbs. Delicious!

*See also* BROMYARD, HEREFORDSHIRE (p. 283); CAMBRIDGE, CAMBRIDGESHIRE (p. 422); CONWY, CONWY (p. 60); FORRES, MORAY (p. 173); LOUTH, LINCOLNSHIRE (p. 336); MARYLEBONE, WESTMINSTER (p. 387); MELTON CONSTABLE, NORFOLK (p. 447); WOODHALL SPA, LINCOLNSHIRE (p. 364); YORK, NORTH YORKSHIRE (p. 271).

The tools of a master butcher's trade on display at the Great Tasting Meat Company

# Sticky toffee pudding from the Sharrow Bay Hotel

The sticky toffee pudding appears on menus all over the UK, and I like to think that how a pub or restaurant handles the dish is a good indicator of the skill of the kitchen. Mind you, if you're ordering pudding you should already have a fair idea of their talents. When done badly, sticky toffee puddings come microwave-hot, strangely dry inside (despite being covered in sauce) and, more often than not, completely missing the dates, a vital ingredient. When done well, however, a moist, rich, sugary mouth-warmer arrives that really does ensure you leave the table full. Ideally, then, it should be a dark sponge containing chopped dates, with toffee sauce and a large helping of cream.

As ever in these things, as soon as one person or place lays claim to having invented a dish, another person heads for the library to find what the Intellectual Property Office calls 'prior art'. I'll nail my colours to the mast and side with the majority who think the pud (originally called 'icky sticky toffee pudding') was first created in the Lake District, by the late Francis Coulson, original owner of the Sharrow Bay Hotel. When Francis opened the doors in 1948, it was the first of what became known as country-house hotels.

Interestingly, archive footage on a DVD produced for the sixtieth anniversary shows Francis in the 1960s or early 1970s making the sponge mix in loaf tins. These would be baked as a whole cake and sliced into portions with the sauces applied. Sharrow Bay also make a retail version to take home, which is the familiar dome pudding shape.

Of course, another long-time maker of fantastic sticky toffee puds in the region is Cartmel, founded by Jean and Howard Johns. They first came across the pud at the Uplands Hotel in the early 1980s, which was run at that time by Tom and Di Peter. Tom had previously worked at Miller Howe on Windermere, which was another country hotel in the style of Sharrow Bay. 'We used to go to Uplands on a Sunday evening. Tom always used to serve sticky toffee pudding for Sunday lunch, and I'd ask him to keep a piece back for me,' says Jean. Though he would drop hints here and there, Tom would never reveal his recipe to Jean and Howard. Then in 1989 they took over Cartmel village shop, and because they had experience of running a restaurant, they began to bake puddings as well as tray bakes, tea breads and ready meals for the shop. They perfected their own recipe, and today you can find their puddings in Waitrose, Budgens, and Fortnum & Mason, as well as many a good deli. Now in their late sixties, Jean and Howard have taken a back seat and entrusted the company to others, including their daughter. 'We wouldn't have a village shop if we didn't have the pudding. It's been good to us,' says Jean, adding, 'You can't help but like it, can you?'

The sticky toffee pudding, then, perfectly illustrates how recipes develop. Good chefs, bakers, restaurateurs and shopkeepers often sample each other's wares, and emulate each other's ideas, taking them forward and adapting them, which ultimately brings the dishes to a wider audience.

*See also* BAKEWELL, DERBYSHIRE (p. 277); MICKLETON, GLOUCESTERSHIRE (p. 304); PETERBOROUGH, CAMBRIDGESHIRE (p. 352); POLEGATE, EAST SUSSEX (p. 494).

## PRESTON, LANCASHIRE
## Lancashire cheese

Lancashire cheese has some powerful enemies. *Guardian* restaurant critic Jay Rayner said online in 2008, 'I seriously bloody hate Lancashire cheese. I would rather stay in and chew my own toenails than have to eat the stuff.' Perhaps worse than outright hatred by a few is apathy by the many, and just as Lancashire is eclipsed by other, better-known cheeses in the supermarket, it is also often denied counter space in the growing number of specialist cheesemongers and delis in the UK.

All of which is a shame, particularly as there are still some fantastic people making it. One is Ruth Kirkham, who has been making Lancashire cheese for over thirty years using unpasteurised milk from her herd of Holstein Friesian cows. The Kirkhams originally made just four twenty-kilo cheeses a day, which were sold through a wholesaler. When they went bust in the 1980s, they began selling direct, and one of their early customers was Randolph Hodgson of Neal's Yard Dairy, which had started a few years previously. Another fan of the cheese, and all things Lancastrian, is chef Nigel Haworth, owner of the Three Fishes in Mitton. Such is the diversity of cheese made in the area that he is able to offer a cheeseboard featuring six entirely different cheeses all from within the county.

Lancashire cheese comes in many forms, young to old, acidic to creamy, nearly all of them produced in a small region north of Preston. It can generally be defined as 'crumbly', 'creamy' or 'tasty', and can range in age from six weeks to twelve months. The younger the cheese, the more crumbly it is; creaminess comes at around three to four months of age. 'Creamy' and 'tasty' are the original variants, and the cheese was traditionally made from curd produced over a number of days. Smallholders in the region probably only had a few cows, and wouldn't be able to collect enough spare milk in one go to make a large cheese. They would therefore process it into curd so it would keep a little longer, and add to it the curd from the next few days. 'Crumbly' is the modern interloper, and was introduced in the 1950s when the industry was trying to get back on its feet after the war. It's this version that is most readily available in supermarkets.

Alongside the Kirkhams there are many other producers, all making different styles of Lancashire cheese. Butler's Tasty, for example, is aged for twelve months and is exactly as the name suggests. Leagram Organic Dairy produces not only a creamy, crumbly and mature version, but also a soft Lancashire. Meanwhile, Dewlay Dairy has taken its Lancashire-making know-how and evolved it to produce Garstang Blue Lancashire, which has all the creaminess of a Lancashire with the addition of a touch of blue.

Traditional Lancashire is a great cheese for toasting, crumbled straight on to the 'raw' side of toast once the reverse has been shown the grill. Dewlay also produces 'the Lancs Toaster', which is its ordinary Lancashire cheese pre-sliced into thick wedges ready for the grill. What's more, you could mount a flavour raid over the hills to Yorkshire and add a splash of Henderson's Relish (*see* p. 258), which would make matters much more interesting. It's a great cheese to use in a Welsh rabbit (*see* p. 76), or paired with an Eccles cake (*see* p. 103), which once tried is never forgotten.

See also BRITISH CHEESE (p. 290).


RAWTENSTALL, LANCASHIRE
## *Fitzpatrick's Temperance Bar*

'When I read about the evils of drinking, I gave up reading,' said comedian and king of the one-liners Henry Youngman. And I don't mind telling you I'm also a chap who likes a tipple, sometimes a gulp, definitely a slurp and

Beverages aimed at keeping the demon drink at bay

occasionally even a large snifter. I think well-made booze is wonderful stuff – *in vino, civitas*. However, I was prepared to take the pledge (albeit temporarily) when I visited Fitzpatrick's Temperance Bar in Rawtenstall, the last genuine temperance bar in the UK.

The temperance movement began in Preston in March 1832, when Joseph Livesey required followers to sign a pledge of total abstinence from what he believed was the root of all evil, drink. It can be easy to forget that the spectre of the demon drink loomed over our great-great-grandparents just as binge-drinking does over us today.

By 1890 the movement had gathered momentum, and Fitzpatrick's was just one of twenty-four bars the family owned in Lancashire. Like many others up and down the country, it also acted as a sweet shop, herbalist and chemist. It was all about health and well-being and getting the population off the booze. Realising, perhaps, that man's natural condition is to lean on a bar and talk, they recreated the pub set-up, just leaving out the booze and replacing it with tonic drinks. The Industrial Revolution – often blamed for the development of mass alcoholism as the working classes sought to forget the misery of machine-like employment – was also responsible for the development of safe, affordable non-alcoholic drinks and the creation of the soft drink. It was a time that saw the mass development of the soda fountain, of healthy mineral waters and drinks like Coca-Cola (invented in the 1880s). In the UK, root-based drinks like sarsaparilla and dandelion and burdock aimed, through their dark colour and rooty tastes, to offer a simulacrum of beer.

Nowadays, however, current owner Chris Wall has moved with the times and offers smoothies, juices, teas and coffees, in addition to the traditional cordials. There's also a small food shelf featuring chutneys, cheeses and condiments. Elsewhere in the shop are other things I'd forgotten still existed, such as liquorice laces, bon bons and midget gems. And all this is set against adverts and paraphernalia from yesteryear, my favourite being an advert for menthol snuff, which 'clears the head, invigorates the brain, and strengthens the nose'. Despite the modern additions, stepping into Fitzpatrick's is like stepping back in time, and well worth a visit if you're in the area. I left with a bottle of their award-winning sarsaparilla to enjoy later – perhaps as a mixer?

ROSSENDALE, LANCASHIRE
## Lancashire Pineapple Chutney

Just before Christmas 2007, Derek Rice-Jones was made redundant from his job in asset rental. Having always had an interest in food, he made chutneys and relishes that year as presents for his friends and family. The response was good, and so Derek and wife Judy decided to turn a hobby into an occupation and founded the Heritage Kitchen in their cottage in the Rossendale Valley, Lancashire. They're now producing over 150 jars a week.

The range runs to fourteen flavours of chutney, with four extra ones made at Christmas, and includes the ironically named Lancashire Pineapple Chutney. It doesn't actually contain pineapple, but yellow beetroot grown by vegetable farmer Peter Ashcroft of Worthington's Farm, Tarleton. Derek tells the story: 'I met Peter at an event for food producers, and after chatting he said, "Have a bash at making some chutney with these, then," thrusting a box of yellow beetroot into my hands.' Peter jokingly refers to yellow beetroots as 'Lancashire pineapples' due to their bright-yellow interior. Yellow beetroot, once popular in Victorian times, is slowly catching the eyes of chefs as it offers something a bit different from the usual varieties, and of course it doesn't bleed and stain like its red cousin. As for Derek's chutney, it's a classic tangy and sweet combination, with a lovely crunch and beetroot flavour, and a fine accompaniment to cheese or ham.

See also BISHOP'S STORTFORD, HERTFORDSHIRE (p. 321); EASTON GREY, WILTSHIRE (p. 11); EDINBURGH, EDINBURGH (p. 167); FAVERSHAM, KENT (p. 477); MOFFAT, DUMFRIES & GALLOWAY (p. 183); NORWICH, NORFOLK (p. 451); OXFORD, OXFORDSHIRE (p. 351); ST HELENS, MERSEYSIDE (p. 132); SHEFFIELD, SOUTH YORKSHIRE (p. 258); SPENNYMOOR, COUNTY DURHAM (p. 227); WORCESTER, WORCESTERSHIRE (p. 317).

## ST HELENS, MERSEYSIDE
## Piccalilli

Though pickling is an age-old kitchen skill, the first specific mention of a 'piccalillo' was in Elizabeth Raffald's 1769 book, *The Experienced English Housekeeper*. Raffald was born in Doncaster but spent most of her working life in the north-west, where her occupations were housekeeper to the gentry, pub landlady, shopkeeper, author, wife and mother. In culinary matters Mrs Raffald was clearly a woman who knew her onions – quite literally when it came to pickles and relishes, as her book gives many recipes for them. Her piccalillo recipe calls for cabbage, cucumbers and the traditional 'colly-flower' in addition to kidney beans and beetroot, which would, one suspect, give a rather redder hue to the final product. She recommends salting the vegetables first for three days, then adding the traditional double act of punchy mustard (in the form of seeds) and yellow-hued turmeric.

Barton's Pickles of St Helens maintains the north-west's link with this relish. Edmund Barton and his wife Lydia began making pickles in the back garden of their house in Lascelles Street, St Helens, in 1905. Edmund Barton Fairhurst is the third generation to be involved in the family business, which has not only left the recipe untouched but hasn't even moved location in over 100 years. They take onions, diced into 20mm pieces, and mix them 50/50 with cauliflower. The sauce, made from turmeric and mustard powder, is then added. The firm count the Prince of Wales as a fan, and he paid a visit to Barton's in 2005 as part of their centenary celebrations. Though rooted in tradition, there's still room for development, and in 2006 Barton's launched Chillililli, a chilli-based version of the classic condiment, and current favourite of Edmund.

Further north at Bury Market, piccalilli is still served on top of a split black pudding (*see* p. 99). And if you cross the hills to Yorkshire you can enjoy it with cold ham or pork pies. Meanwhile, all the way down south in Wiltshire, Tracklements make an award-winning version that's well worth a place on your plate.

*See also* BISHOP'S STORTFORD, HERTFORDSHIRE (p. 321); EASTON GREY, WILTSHIRE (p. 11); EDINBURGH, EDINBURGH (p. 167); FAVERSHAM, KENT (p. 477); MOFFAT, DUMFRIES & GALLOWAY (p. 183); NORWICH, NORFOLK (p. 451); OXFORD, OXFORDSHIRE (p. 351); ROSSENDALE, LANCASHIRE (p. 131); SHEFFIELD, SOUTH YORKSHIRE (p. 258); SPENNYMOOR, COUNTY DURHAM (p. 227); WORCESTER, WORCESTERSHIRE (p. 317).

SIZERGH, CUMBRIA
# *Growing Well*

There's a simple joy to be had in planting a seed and seeing it grow, and Growing Well, a community-focused farm staffed by volunteers, is keen to pass this feeling on to all who work for them. They produce salad and veg-etables on six acres of land at Low Sizergh Farm, with outdoor crops that include potatoes, cabbages, leeks, fennel, broad beans and squashes, and polytunnels that house salad leaves, tomatoes, cucumbers, chillies and rocket in the summer, and salads such as radicchio and winter purslane in the cooler months.

What's special about the farm is that it uses its business to help people recovering from mental-health problems to reintegrate themselves into employment. 'It's a stepping stone back into work,' says Pauline Sprott, education co-ordinator for Growing Well. 'A lot of people can become very lonely and isolated when suffering from such things as depression.' Growing Well provides a structure, but as Pauline makes clear, they're not a soft touch: in the summer months they have big orders to get out. However, that's part of the challenge: to ensure that the volunteers feel part of a team, and that people are relying on them. Coupled with all this is the safety net of support. 'You give people pride, support and responsibility, but on top of this is the rewarding therapeutic quality.'

The company was started by Beren Aldridge, a fully trained psychother-apist, who teamed up with dairy farmer Alison Park in 2005. The farm has a shop housed in an eighteenth-century stone barn to showcase its own products and the best from the region. There's also a crop-share scheme, where £7.50 a week gets you a pot-luck bag of vegetables that you collect from the farm. Even if the volunteers aren't so green-fingered, they can still join in. 'We had one volunteer who had an IT background, and completely rebuilt our customer database,' says Pauline.

TEBAY, CUMBRIA

## The UK's only independent family-owned service station

As motorways go, the M6 has many things to recommend it. It happens to be the longest motorway in the UK, as well as one of the most scenic. It's also the busiest, and contains the Preston Bypass, the first section of

Not your average grab-and-go service station. Why can't they all be like this?

motorway ever built in the UK. However, it has one other unique feature: Tebay Services, the only independent family-owned service station in the UK. Every other motorway service station is owned by half a dozen large corporations, the majority of which seem to offer a 'choice' of chicken-based fast food or burger-based fast food.

So how did this independent, family-owned, food-friendly oasis come to be? Well, in the 1970s, when the M6 was being extended near John and Barbara Dunning's farmland, John sold the land to the government but asked to bid for the right to run the service station along with the other big players of the day like Trusthouse Forte and Granada. The Dunnings did their homework and won with their plans for a shop and café supplied mainly from their own farm and other food producers in the surrounding area.

Today, Tebay has grown considerably. There's still a farm shop, selling local and regional produce such as fresh vegetables, over forty British farmhouse cheeses, and pies from John Lomas of the Upper Crust Pie Company in Manchester, not to mention Neil and Penny Chambers's handmade Scotch eggs (*see* p. 281). The best thing, however, is the fully stocked butcher's counter on the southbound side, beautifully laid out with steaks, beef olives, chops, joints for roasting and braising, and offal. The meat still comes from the Dunning's family farm: the beef is provided by Galloway and Blue Grey breeds; and the lamb is mainly Herdwick, but also includes other hardy types that cope well with the surrounding harsh hilly landscape of the Lake District.

The landscape is part of the experience, and you can enjoy the beautiful views as you eat either outside in one of the barbecue shacks or in the café, whose dining tables look out on to a small rippling lake surrounded by mountains. Add to this a hotel, caravan park, dog-walking trail, gift shop, picnic spots and children's play area, and the whole place begins to feel like a destination in itself rather than a waypoint on your journey. It's not hard to see why so many people from the south and the Midlands choose Tebay to break their journey to Scotland. There should be a sign a couple of miles before the exit ramp that reads, 'Food monotony can kill, take a break.'

The elusive bilberry, spotted here at a Ludlow greengrocer's

# Bilberries from the Park Farm Shop and Tearooms

Like Jason Bourne, the elusive and seldom-seen bilberry has a number of aliases – whortleberry, blaeberry, whinberry – depending on who's doing the asking. In Lancashire these small blue-black fruit go by the name of wimberries, and the *Cottager's Monthly Visitor* periodical for January 1835 described them thus:

> The berries are agreeable and wholesome, which last is a fortunate circumstance, as they are much eaten by children when in season; and their being ripe is generally announced in neighbourhoods where they abound by the black mouths and faces of all the little people one meets.

As well as being delicious fresh, they also make an excellent pie filling or jam. The season is short, from late June to July, pushing into August and early September if you're lucky. They are not cultivated in the UK, to my knowledge, but in the wild the plant is found on high heath and moorland with very acidic soils, which accounts for its restricted distribution to parts of Cumbria, and the Yorkshire Dales, or further south in places like Dartmoor or the Welsh Marshes. Indeed, I've only ever seen the berries for sale in Ludlow in Shropshire.

They remain a firm favourite for folk 'in the know' in the north, however; folk such as Judith Lees, who runs the Park Farm Tearooms at Walmersley, just north of Bury. 'When we were kids – there were six of us – and we lived on a farm, my mum would send us up Holcombe Hill picking wimberries that she would then bake into a pie, but we'd always have eaten more than we brought back.'

As no one is growing them in the UK, and child labour is frowned upon these days, Park Farm import wimberries from Poland, freezing them so that they last a little longer. 'For the past four years they've been difficult to harvest: it's either been too wet or too dry for the pickers to pick them.' When there are some available, they're washed and picked over to ensure there are no leaves or bits in the crop, then they're stewed down with sugar and baked in a sweet shortcrust pastry. You can either buy a whole pie to take home from the farm shop, or have a slice in the tea rooms with cream, ice cream or custard. 'It's only Lancashire people, and only those who live within a small vicinity, who've heard of a wimberry pie.' Indeed, when Sir

Ken Morrison retired as chairman of his supermarket chain, he said that whatever happened, Morrison's would remain true to its northern roots, adding that they would definitely keep selling bilberries. 'You ask lots of people and they'll have never heard of a wimberry pie,' adds Judith. You have now.

*See also* CORBRIDGE, NORTHUMBERLAND (p. 207); EGTON BRIDGE, NORTH YORKSHIRE (p. 243); HAMPRESTON, DORSET (p. 14); HONITON, DEVON (p. 17); INVERGOWRIE, PERTH & KINROSS (p. 180); LYTH AND WINSTER VALLEYS, CUMBRIA (p. 117); NORTHIAM, EAST SUSSEX (p. 492); WIMBLEDON, MERTON (p. 415).

# 4 | Scotland

## KEY

| | |
|---|---|
| CL. | CLACKMANNANSHIRE |
| EA. | EAST AYRSHIRE |
| ED. | EAST DUNBARTONSHIRE |
| EL. | EAST LOTHIAN |
| ER. | EAST RENFREWSHIRE |
| FK. | FALKIRK |
| IN. | INVERCLYDE |
| ML. | MIDLOTHIAN |
| NA. | NORTH AYRSHIRE |
| NL. | NORTH LANARKSHIRE |
| RN. | RENFREWSHIRE |
| SA. | SOUTH AYRSHIRE |
| SL. | SOUTH LANARKSHIRE |
| WD. | WEST DUNBARTONSHIRE |
| WL. | WEST LOTHIAN |

EILEAN
SIAR

*Atlantic Ocean*

Coleraine

Londonderry

NORTHER
IRELAND

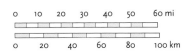

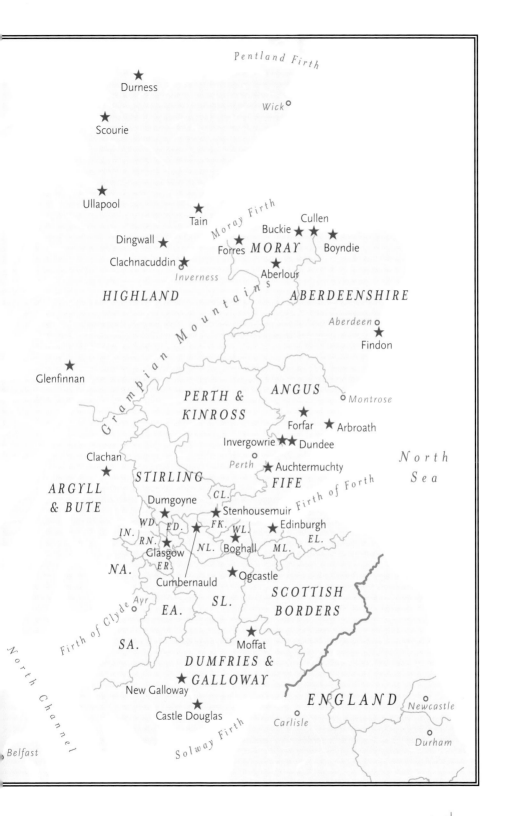

Pentland Firth

Durness

Wick ○

Scourie

Ullapool

Tain

Moray Firth

Cullen

Dingwall

Buckie ★ ★

Boyndie

Forres

MORAY

Clachnacuddin

Inverness

Aberlour

HIGHLAND

Aberdeen ○

ABERDEENSHIRE

Findon

Glenfinnan

Grampian Mountains

Montrose ○

PERTH &
KINROSS

ANGUS

Forfar

Arbroath

Invergowrie ★ ★ Dundee

Clachan

Perth ○

Auchtermuchty

STIRLING

FIFE

North
Sea

Dumgoyne

CL.

ARGYLL
& BUTE

WD.

Stenhousemuir

Firth of Forth

IN.

ED.

FK.

WL.

Edinburgh

RN.

NL.

Boghall

EL.

Glasgow

ER.

Cumbernauld

NA.

Ogcastle

SCOTTISH
BORDERS

Firth of Clyde

Ayr ○

EA.

SL.

SA.

Moffat

DUMFRIES &
GALLOWAY

New Galloway

ENGLAND

Newcastle ○

Castle Douglas

Carlisle ○

North Channel

Durham ○

Belfast ○

Solway Firth

## ABERLOUR, MORAY
# Walkers shortbread

My maternal grandmother came down to the Midlands from Glasgow during the war to work in the factories, and the tartan tin of shortbread was a regular fixture in my grandparents' house at Christmas time. To me, shortbread always seemed more special than ordinary biscuits. Despite the word 'bread' appearing in its name, shortbread is actually a simple biscuit traditionally made from flour, butter and sugar. The 'short' part comes from its crumbly texture (a similar naming exists in *short*crust pastry).

One of the oldest family firms still making shortbread is Walkers, based in Aberlour on Spey, up in the Highlands. Walkers uses 33 per cent real butter in its recipe, the other ingredients being just flour, sugar and a pinch of salt. The resulting mix can be fashioned or cut into many shapes. Walkers offers the traditional shortbread fingers, as well as petticoat tails and round versions. Whatever the shape, each biscuit is baked on a low heat so that it does not brown. With the appliance of saliva and heat, their shortbread comes alive in the mouth; a light dusting of sugar hits the lips first, then the biscuit crumbles at the slightest pressure from your teeth, before melting into a lovely buttery finish.

The firm began when Joseph Walker opened his bakery shop in the town in 1898, and his reputation for quality shortbread soon spread. Today Jim Walker, along with brother Joe, are the third generation of Walkers and still use their grandfather's recipe. The business has long outgrown the original shop, however, and is now based in a custom-built factory just outside the town. With a workforce of over 1,200, for whom they offer free bus transport, they're the biggest employer in the area. One of the things they're most proud of is that more than half of the senior management have risen through the ranks. Some have only ever worked for the company after leaving school, and some local families have worked for the firm for generations. 'Integrity plays a strong part in how we run the company; we try to look after our people very well,' says Jim.

The product range has expanded to include Duchy Originals shortbread, its own-brand biscuits, cakes, and Ecclefechan Tarts – a Scottish rival to the mince pie. When it comes to shortbread, however, the company remains steadfast in its approach and follows Joseph Walker's recipe to the letter. When butter prices shot up, and many producers switched to cheaper fats like margarine, Walkers stuck to its guns and continued to use butter.

Walkers shortbread still comes in tartan-covered tins and boxes with romantic artwork featuring wild glens, thistles, claymores, and tartan-clad heros and heroines. There are those who say that the tartan shortbread tin isn't the modern contemporary face Scotland should be presenting to the world. Jim Walker disagrees. 'It makes me furious. It's unique in the world, there's no other country that has its own iconic fabric.' As for what's in the tin, he adds, 'We don't need a clever marketing person to tell the story; we simply tell the truth.'

*See also* BERMONDSEY, SOUTHWARK (p. 369).

*See also* BERMONDSEY, SOUTHWARK (p. 369).

ARBROATH, ANGUS
## *Spink's Arbroath smokies*

Iain Spink comes from a long line of fishmongers, but after being in the business for twenty-four years, and seeing the small family firm he worked in swallowed up by a larger corporation, he decided to pack it in and study for a degree in Environmental Sciences. Fishing runs deep in the blood, however, and the new experience of being a student short of cash led him to look around for an earner. 'I'd done demonstrations with the smokie barrel at local events like the Arbroath sea festival, so I thought I'd give it a bash for a summer spell.' He started attending Highland games and food festivals, and things went from there. He's now something of a travelling ambassador for the product, going to farmers' markets with his custom-made portable smoking barrels and selling direct.

Even though the preparatory processing, cleaning, tying and salting is done in Arbroath, because the fish are smoked outside the town this means that technically Iain can't call them Arbroath smokies; 'However, there are not many people who have a problem with what I'm doing,' he laughs. This is because it was Iain's father who practically single-handedly campaigned for the Arbroath smokie's PGI (Protected Geographical Indication) status. 'He was the one who saw the true potential of the smokie,' says Iain. Part of the reason for seeking the PGI was to put an end to what Iain describes as 'the appalling so-called Arbroath smokies' being made elsewhere in the UK. 'The problem we had was what was being sold was a million miles from the real thing. The quality was, in a word, crap.'

To make them, Iain uses the best whole haddock from Aberdeen,

Peterhead or occasionally Orkney. 'I don't like to go further afield. You can get haddock from Norway but it smokes like a totally different fish.' The fish are gutted at sea as quickly as possible so that the guts don't taint the flesh, then Iain buys them at the market, takes them back to his unit, removes the head and cleans them up. Then they're dry-salted for a variable amount of time, depending on the size and freshness of the fish. When this process is complete, the salt is washed off, and the fish are matched up into pairs and tied by the tail with jute string. They are then placed on a triangular stick over a barrel with a hardwood fire in the bottom. The top is covered with damp hessian, which quells the fire and seals the top. This is where Iain's skill and experience come in. He'll often have to move them around, as the fire never burns completely evenly. After around fifty minutes they're ready.

'Since I've started doing it, I've seen a huge increase in people's interest in where food comes from and how it's made.' And it's certainly the case that the traditional skill of smokie-making is a spectacle much appreciated at Highland games, game fairs and farmers' markets. It delivers something that tastes great, too: 'The smokie is a very simple thing: a haddock, a bit of salt and a bit of smoke that's cooked over a fire. Folk love that. It goes down very well as an alternative to hot dogs and burgers,' says Iain.

See also CLEY NEXT THE SEA, NORFOLK (p. 424); FINDON, ABERDEENSHIRE (p. 169); GREAT YARMOUTH, NORFOLK (p. 433); HAMBRIDGE, SOMERSET (p. 13); NIDDERDALE, NORTH YORKSHIRE (p. 251); SEAHOUSES, NORTHUMBERLAND (p. 224); WHITBY, NORTH YORKSHIRE (p. 268).

## AUCHTERMUCHTY, FIFE
### Fletcher's venison

Fletcher's eighty-acre deer farm is owned by John Fletcher, who trained as a vet and is an expert in deer and their behaviour, and his wife Nichola, a food writer and cook. They farm red deer, and moved to their current location in the 1970s when they began converting the two-room farmhouse and started up a mail-order business. 'We used to send the venison by Red Star delivery on the train, wrapped in muslin and hay in a box, with a piece of ginger to deter the flies,' remembers John. Nowadays it's all vacuum-packed and picked up from the farm by courier.

There are, of course, differences between wild and farmed venison, as Nichola explained to me. 'Wild deer is a by-product of sport or population

John Fletcher's humanely farmed deer

control, and I'm convinced that the wild flavour is in part due to the skin, which is left on as it comes down the mountain, affecting the taste of the flesh.' What's more, the quality of the meat can vary depending on the season. Sport shooters in particular often want to bag a big stag, but these can be older and a bit tougher, and you certainly wouldn't want to eat a rutting stag.

Farmed venison, meanwhile, offers the consistency of supply, portion size and production control that suits the supermarket's needs. With farmed you're sure that each piece will taste the same and be the same age, things that aren't really controllable with wild venison.

John has fought hard for the right to slaughter the animals in the field, believing quite rightly that this is the quickest and most humane form of dispatch possible, a luxury not often afforded to other animals we eat. At Fletcher's, it is slaughterman and stockman David Stewart who does the deed. He has the responsibility of killing three animals a week, and he's clearly a man who cares deeply for his charges. He first puts down a bit of barley to occupy them, then selects his quarry, aiming for a clean head shot and instant kill. The other deer don't bolt or flee when one of them drops, as they have no frame of reference for what has just happened. Dave then moves over to the animal and slits its throat to begin draining the blood. That may all sound gruesome, but if you eat meat (and 98 per cent of us do) you owe it to yourself to understand how that animal has got to your plate.

The carcass is then handed over to master butcher Graeme Braids, who skins and cleans out the animal before hanging it for a minimum of fourteen days. It's then broken down into the relevant joints and cuts ready for market or mail order. There's very little waste, too; even the tails and testicles are not squandered, being sent to China for use in medicine. The consumption of venison is tiny compared to that of other domestic animals, but as John points out, humans have eaten deer for far longer than they've eaten cattle or sheep, with evidence found from neolithic times.

See also ACOMB, NORTHUMBERLAND (p. 195); BLAXHALL, SUFFOLK (p. 419); BROMPTON-ON-SWALE, NORTH YORKSHIRE (p. 236); CHIPPENHAM, WILTSHIRE (p. 9); FRILSHAM, BERKSHIRE (p. 479); KENDAL, CUMBRIA (p. 114).

## BOGHALL, WEST LOTHIAN
### Paul Boyle's Scotch pies

Boghall butcher Paul Boyle's website bears the line 'Go on, say aye tae a pie, ye know ye want tae!' and, with over 2,500 sales a week, it seems that many people do. One of the most popular is his Scotch pie, which has picked up a brace of trophies in the annual Scotch Pie Competition. In the past these were workmen's pies, cheap and cheerful and made with finely minced mutton to use up the tougher cuts and scraggy bits that were fit for little else.

Nowadays, nearly all Scotch pies are made with beef and traditional hot-water pastry, where the fat – often lard or beef dripping – is dissolved in hot water and the flour then added. This method gives a malleable paste to work with that can then be shaped by hand or machine. Once this case is made, the filling is added and a little lid placed on top. 'Our filling is made with minced flank of beef, and we blend our own seasoning – white and black pepper, salt, ginger and a few other secret ingredients,' says Paul.

His filling, along with a firm crust, is key to the success of his pie. That and the fact that he makes them throughout the day, with fresh ones arriving every thirty minutes – perfect when they're best enjoyed hot. When Paul's father started the butcher's shop in the 1970s, Bathgate was in the centre of a housing estate. It's a close community to this day: 'The shop is a meeting place for people in the area, who really get involved in what we're doing.' After winning the Scotch Pie Award in 2005, Paul added a bakery, and in 2009 his fish pie took gold at

Paul Boyle and his award-winning Scotch pies

the UK Pie Awards in Melton Mowbray. 'When other competitions come along, you get more ideas and push yourself forward. That's what these competitions do, after all – keep an interest in the trade and in this community.'

*See also* CORNISH PASTIES (p. 18).

BOYNDIE, ABERDEENSHIRE
## *Hamlyns porridge*

'Oats: a grain, which in England is generally given to horses, but in Scotland supports the people.' Dr Johnson's 1755 dictionary definition of oats may be well known, along with the reply, often attributed to Boswell but actually said by Sir Walter Scott: 'Yes, and where else will you see such horses and such men?' (In fact, Johnson confessed to Boswell that he enjoyed eating dry oatmeal as a boy.)

Similar statements attesting to the prowess of an oat diet were made in the March 1845 edition of *Blackwood's Edinburgh*, with the author going on to offer a bet that ten Scottish ploughmen fed on oats could best their wheat-fed English counterparts. Like a foodie version of *Braveheart* the diatribe ends with: 'We swear by the oatcake and the porridge, the substantial bannock and the brose – long may Scotland produce them, and Scotchmen live and fight upon them!'

Strong stuff, then, but so is porridge, which has always had an aura of rugged strength about it. Alan Meikle, managing director of Hamlyns of Scotland – one of Scotland's largest oat millers – has been involved in the industry for over fifteen years. The company was founded in 1965, and declares it's the only brand of porridge oats and oatmeal guaranteed to be 100 per cent Scottish from seed to mill to finished product.

Of the annual Scottish crop, which weighs in at about 250,000 tons, roughly 70 per cent goes into porridge production. Oats come with a protective husk, and at Hamlyns this is removed by passing the grain through a revolving drum which bounces it against a rubber surface. The vibration separates the oat from the husk, and the latter goes off for animal feed. The oats are washed clean and then stabilised, a process that sees them heated to 100 °C for twenty minutes to stop enzyme activity and give them a longer shelf-life. What's then left is called a groat, which is put through a kiln and baked for three hours before being stone-ground into oatmeal, or squashed into oat flakes. These are left whole for jumbo flakes, or cut into three and squashed for the standard size. At Hamlyns it's a fully enclosed, modern production process. 'You won't actually see very much happening,' says Alan, but though there's a lot of shiny stainless steel, the principal processing method remains the same. 'When we make it, we add nothing to it, and take nothing away, it's what was in the field, just cleaned and heated, that's it. I've just explained about £15 million worth of kit to you!' laughs Alan.

Porridge has gone from mocked peasant fodder to the pole position of healthy eating, as it can help to tackle obesity and heart disease. It's the original super-food, admired even before we had all become amateur dieticians obsessing about detoxing and antioxidants. Many other breakfast cereals, according to the *Which?* reports of 2004 and 2006, are significantly higher in salt, sugar and fat. Small wonder when Hamlyns' packaging lists just one ingredient: 100 per cent Scottish oats.

Horses' diets aside, there are many marked differences between how we take our porridge in Britain. There's the whole debate over adding milk or water, and another over salt or sugar, and some people believe it's best eaten standing up. There are even differences in the raw ingredient: 'If I were to go to the south of England, I bet 98 per cent would choose oat flakes; if you go to the north of Scotland it's the complete reversal, with most people preferring oatmeal,' says Alan. When asked what he thinks is the best way to eat porridge, Alan plays it safe: 'It's like whisky: there's no such thing as bad porridge. We're happy to provide for all of them.'

## Lobsters and langoustines

The Romans called lobsters '*locusta*', which is the same word they used for locusts, despite some pretty major differences between the two species. This was because they followed Aristotle's categorisation of animals into red-blooded ones, like mammals, and blue-blooded ones, like lobsters, locusts and spiders. Like oysters, lobsters used to be gathered and consumed by the poor, but somehow both the crustacean and the bivalve have seen their fates reversed to become luxury items.

There are many species in the lobster family, but the three most commonly eaten are the American or Canadian lobster, the European lobster and the Norwegian lobster. The American is more common and faster-growing than its European cousins, but the European commands a better price and, according to some, has a better flavour. To the untrained eye, they're tricky to tell apart, and the key is to look for the horn: American lobsters have a pronounced horn between their eyes, while the European ones do not. The former also has slightly larger claws, but this only helps if you've got examples of the species at the same age side by side to compare.

The Norwegian lobster goes by the name of *langoustine* in both France and the UK (and is also known as the 'Dublin Bay prawn'), and *scampo* in Italy, and is the key ingredient in proper scampi. European and Norwegian lobsters can be found all around the UK, but the cool, clear waters off the coast of Scotland are noted for their particularly fine specimens. The Scottish shellfish industry landed 32,765 tonnes of Norwegian lobsters in 2008, which amounts to a market value of nearly £95.5 million. Meanwhile 1,026 tonnes of European lobster was landed, valued at £10.95 million. If you're a mental arithmetic whizz, you'll have seen that the pound-per-kilo value of live lobster is £10.67, which, when compared to mackerel at 75p, shows that there's definitely cash in crustaceans.

Moray Seafoods, based in Buckie, Moray, have been working the North Sea since 1958, with scampi as their core business. In the 1970s they established a sister company in Spain, and the export market remains strong today, with their langoustines travelling as far afield as the Burj Al Arab in Dubai. What has changed over the years is the public's demand for, and appreciation of, high-quality seafood. We expect a lot more than scampi in breadcrumbs today. 'We get told time and time again by chefs throughout the country that you can't get excellent seafood, yet we're an island,' says Euan, the company spokesman. To put this right, Moray take advantage of the UK's improved logistics network and advances in technology and processing to move lobster from the sea to your plate in twenty-four hours, and as well as supplying the truculent chefs, they offer a mail-order service to the public.

Local fishermen bring in the lobsters, which are killed, blast-frozen, vac-packed and dispatched in an ice-filled foam box. Euan contends that this is far preferable to the tanks of lobster you see in some coastal fishmongers. 'People have a perception that if the lobsters are killed fresh, then they're the best. But once an animal is out of its natural environment it suffers degradation.' A lobster that's been kicking its claws in a tank for two or three days is going to be very stressed, so it's far better to hoik them out of the sea and process them quickly.

Moray's lobsters come in a variety of sizes and prices, ranging from 400 grams to 600 grams to an absolute denizen-of-the-deep whopper at 1 to 1.2 kilos that will happily feed four. 'Scottish lobster offers a much better dining experience. By selling direct to people who love seafood you reduce waste and deliver them mature species that look brilliant on the table,' Euan says. No doubt your guests will fall upon your labours like a swarm of locusts, while you regale them with the idiosyncrasies of the Aristotelian classification system.

See also CHINATOWN, WESTMINSTER (p. 374); CROMER, NORFOLK (p. 426); LITTLE HAVEN, PEMBROKESHIRE (p. 70); MORECAMBE BAY, LANCASHIRE (p. 121); SALTHOUSE, NORFOLK (p. 454).

## *Cream o' Galloway ice cream*

Ice-cream maker Cream o' Galloway is a great example of how, with deter-
mination, small businesses can not only survive, but even thrive. The dairy
farm and creamery is run by David and Wilma Finlay; David is the third generation to farm this site. They met sixteen years ago, around the same time
David's father retired. The farm was traditionally a cheese and milk producer,
but when David took over from his father, he began to think about how to
survive. 'It was our third date when he presented me with a business plan!'
she laughs.

They did some research into ice-cream production in Devon, and went
for it in 1994, with Wilma concentrating on recipes and packaging and David
managing the herd of Ayrshire dairy cattle. David swore he would never have
the public on the farm, but soon Wilma persuaded him and they started with
a small shop and some swings for the kids, hoping to catch the passing trade.
Its has now grown to offer a café, nature trail, activity centre and cycle routes.
'Our attitude nowadays is never say never,' says Wilma. It's not just me that

The Finlays' efficient production line churns out 200,000 litres of ice cream a year

thinks what they're making – and just as importantly how they make it – is worthy of note; others do, too. In 2006 Wilma received an MBE in recognition of her services to tourism, as well as the prestigious BBC Radio 4 *Food and Farming* 'Farmer of the Year' award.

One other thing that attracted me to Cream o' Galloway is their attitude to fair trade and sustainability. Ice cream can use a lot of foreign produce: vanilla, sugar, cocoa, chocolate and so on. As Wilma explains, 'It's no good me complaining that we can't get a good price for our milk, if I'm doing over some other producer elsewhere in the world.' Consequently their Made Fair range offers a fair deal for Third World growers, UK dairy farmers and the environment.

Their vanilla ice-cream – a good test of a brand as there's nowhere to hide with vanilla – is particularly good, being rich and creamy and bespeckled with vanilla seeds. Also of note is the cone it comes in. It's a proper baked biscuity one, not one that looks like it's made from reformed styrofoam. 'We like these ones – they cost a bit more though,' says Wilma. A cone is so much more than a mere edible cup to hold the ice cream; it is part of the dish itself. Good ice cream on a poor cone is like a good pie filling inside substandard pastry.

Prior to the cone's invention, ice cream was served in small glass cups known as 'licks' that you handed back to the vendor after you'd finished eating so that they could be washed up. By the end of a long hot day they weren't always that clean. Various other items were also tried, including metal and paper cones, as well as wafers and waffles in many of Europe's capital cities. Tracing the ice-cream cone's evolution is difficult, as pastry cones, cornets and horns were also fashioned to hold fruits, creams and other sweet embellishments. By no means the first description is that given in Agnes B. Marshall's *Cookery Book* from 1888, which reads, 'the cornets were made with almonds and baked in the oven, not pressed between irons.' Mrs Marshall was the Prue Leith of her day, writing books and running a cookery school in Mortimer Street, London. Her other books included *The Book of Ices* (1885) and *Fancy Ices* (1894), so it's fair to say she knew a thing or two about working with ice. Cones at this time would have all been made and baked by hand, but by the turn of the twentieth century, patents for machines to manufacture cones on a mass scale were granted. By 1904 and the St Louis World Fair, we were easily getting to grips with the edible cone.

But back to Cream o' Galloway, who are now producing 200,000 litres of ice cream a year, in over twenty flavours. Their ice cream is now offered –

*sans* cone but in a lovely tub – by Virgin Airlines. 'Only in first and business class, mind, so I wouldn't know,' says Wilma with a smile.

*See also* WHITSTABLE, KENT (p. 500); WOOLER, NORTHUMBERLAND (p. 230).

## CLACHAN, DUMFRIES & GALLOWAY
### *Loch Fyne oysters*

In 2008 the Loch Fyne Oyster Company celebrated its pearl anniversary: thirty years. The enterprise was started by Johnny Noble, the uncle of Loch Fyne's current marketing manager Virginia Sumsion. The loch – which is the UK's largest sea loch – was good for shellfish, as the combination of saltwater and freshwater gives the oysters and mussels their sweetness. So he teamed up with his marine-biologist friend Andrew Lane, and they started out with a small hut by the side of the road and a 'let's do it' attitude. 'Andrew said to Johnny, "I think you could grow oysters here," and so they seeded some, and in the first year they all died,' says Virginia. Next year they tried again, and this time the oysters took. They take a long time to grow, and with cash flow not looking great, Johnny and Andrew turned their hand to smoking fish as well. 'This soon became the mainstay of the business, but

A dozen oysters served on the shore of Loch Fyne

the oysters remain our soul,' says Virginia. She also added a tip regarding oysters. 'If you shake an oyster and there's lots of water coming out, that means it's not so fresh.' Fresh ones are sealed tight.

In the 1990s the company opened restaurants in Nottingham and Peterborough, 'Because Andy had family there and he thought, "Well, at least they'll turn up to eat,"' says Virginia.

Johnny died suddenly in 2002, and instead of seeking a new buyer, the 100 or so staff borrowed £2m from the Baxi Partnership – a trust to help fund more employee-owned businesses – and around £1m from the Royal Bank of Scotland to buy the company for themselves. In 2007 the restaurant arm of the business – which had grown to over thirty sites – was sold to the pub retailer and brewer Greene King, although part of that deal was the commitment that the restaurants still take their stock from the loch.

The remaining Loch Fyne Oyster Company is still employee-owned, however, which ensures everyone gets a say in the running of the business as well as a share in any profits. It also gives employees a sense of security and makes the business more transparent and accountable. Since the buyout, staff turnover has fallen dramatically. I'm a real fan of Loch Fyne's food, as well as their 'employee-owned' ethos. It's an example of a small firm that has grown up through a genuine love of what they do.

*See also* EDINBURGH, EDINBURGH (p. 168); LINDISFARNE, NORTHUMBERLAND (p. 214); WEST MERSEA, ESSEX (p. 459); WHITSTABLE, KENT (p. 500).

## CLACHNACUDDIN, HIGHLAND
# *Football pies*

Standing on the terraces on a cold winter's evening, your team losing 3–0 and down to ten men by half-time, a man needs a little pick-me-up. It has to be something hot, cheap, meaty and filling, and traditionally one dish fitted all those requirements: pie. The pie-and-football partnership hails from a different era. Forget the multi-million-pound Premier League, think rattles, rosettes and half-time oranges. Top-flight clubs, particularly those in the south, are more Pad Thai than pie now – Arsenal even offers crêpes outside the ground – and even those more down-to-earth clubs are more likely to serve burgers, as they're much cheaper and easier to produce than pies.

Head north, though, or down into the lower leagues, and you'll find pies.

Not all of them palatable, if some of the entries in the inaugural British Pie Awards held in Melton Mowbray in 2009 were anything to go by, but pies nonetheless. At this celebration of all things pastry, pies from grounds all over the UK contested the prize of the best football pie, and in a fine example of giant-slaying worthy of the FA cup fifth round, a pie from Clachnacuddin FC in Inverness lifted the trophy, beating entrants from 105 English league clubs and twenty-five Scottish ones, including the likes of Ipswich, Reading and Aston Villa. The pie is made by James Dyce at MacDoughall and Hastie Butchers in Clachnacuddin. 'The club asked us to supply the park with pies, so I took out a large steak-and-gravy pie mix, put it in a Scotch pie shell, then topped it all with puff pastry.' The result is pie that can be eaten without the need for a plate, knife and fork. 'The hardest part was getting the gravy right. All we did was make a regular batch and select the three best-looking ones to send to the competition,' says James.

David MacDoughall and Stephen Hastie set up their shop in 1992, and in 1994 moved to the current premises, where James, who had been working part-time, came on board as a partner. The new premises had a kitchen upstairs, and so James began to experiment with making pies. As well as pies and hot food to take away they also do weekly specials: beef olives filled with haggis; black, white and fruit pudding; and game such as rabbit, which James catches himself using ferrets. As for Clachnacuddin FC, they'll no doubt be hoping for glory in the Highland Football League, the fans fuelled by MacDoughall and Hastie pies: 'Come on you Lilywhites!'

*See also* CORNISH PASTIES (p. 18).

CULLEN, MORAY
## Cullen skink

Cullen is a small seaside town in Moray, on the north-east coast of Scotland. Established in the Middle Ages, its boom came with the fishing trade of the 1800s, and it gives its name to the soup Cullen skink – proudly, it seems, as even the town's sign declares it to be 'Home of Cullen Skink'. The word 'skink' means 'knuckle' or 'shin' and is normally applied to beef bones, but the town's fishing background meant haddock was the more readily available ingredient. The key to getting the most flavour out of the soup is using really good, naturally smoked haddock, to which you add potatoes, onion and cream. It's a phenomenally easy dish to make, but is very comforting

# Clootie Dumpling

To see a clootie dumpling being made is the culinary equivalent of being present at the birth of a child. Cloths, muslin, hot water – and lots of it – are all called for; and after hours of effort you're presented with a 5 lb wobbly, squidgy bundle of joy. Clootie is an old Scottish word for cloth, in which the pudding mix is boiled. This stems from a time when few households had ovens, and most food was boiled in a pot over a fire. The cloth held all the ingredients together.

The ingredients in a clootie can vary, but flour, breadcrumbs, currants, suet, eggs, sugar and spices such as cinnamon, nutmeg and ginger are present in various amounts, while in Fife and along the East Coast treacle is sometimes used, resulting in a much darker dumpling. Whatever you choose to put in, the dry ingredients are first mixed together, perhaps moistened with a drop of milk, then placed on the cloth, which is tied up tight in a ball. The key to a successful clootie is to boil the muslin cloth first, not only to make sure it's clean, but also to stop the pudding mix sticking. A liberal sprinkling of flour helps too; indeed, this actually forms a sort of skin on the finished pudding. Once out of the water and cool enough to handle, your newborn pud is traditionally dried before the fire, or, if you have one, in an oven. The resulting sponge is good rib-coating stuff, and surprisingly not as soggy or stodgy as you might think. Flavour comes from the spices and dried fruits, supported by the sponge.

Another tradition associated with the dish is that of adding a coin to the mix, as we often do with a Christmas pudding. Indeed, the clootie is a close relative of this seasonal belly-filler and has much in common with it.

Clootie dumpling is widely available, especially during the cooler months. Of course, this being Scotland, there are those who wet the baby's head with a nip of booze. The Cranachan Café (itself named after another Scottish dessert) in Princes Square, Glasgow, offers a range of Scottish dishes, including clootie dumpling with Drambuie custard. Meanwhile, Ghillie Dhu, a traditional Scottish pub and live music venue in Edinburgh, offers clootie dumpling with Glayva (a blend of whisky and aromatics) ice cream. For a clootie dumpling served in a more rural location, the Ceilidh Place, a restaurant, art gallery, bookshop and hotel in Ullapool, way over in the far west of the country, regularly have it on the menu.

Of course, it takes skill to make a clootie properly and not end up with a cake-mix-covered cloth floating in hot water (Nick Nairn's *New Scottish Cookery* suggests using an old pillowcase). Consequently there are those who omit the 'clootie' entirely, preferring instead to steam the pudding in a bowl, but that's just cheating.

See also PETERBOROUGH, CAMBRIDGESHIRE (p. 352).

and filling. Of course, other ingredients have had cameo roles to play, too. The white part of leeks, for example, though these are not traditional, and my dad, who wasn't Scottish but was a chef, used to make it thicker than normal and top it with breadcrumbs, turning it into a very loose fish stew with a golden toasted crust. The Cullen Bay Hotel serves the soup in its restaurant 365 days of the year. 'It's a rustic soup, very thick, just diced potatoes, haddock, milk and a splash of cream,' says owner Douglas Tucker.

When Boswell and Dr Johnson stopped off in Cullen on their tour of Scotland, they were offered broiled dried haddock at an inn. Boswell tucked in; Johnson, however, was 'disgusted by the sight of them, so they were removed'. The duo pressed on to Elgin, where they again entered the best tavern in the town and, in Johnson's words 'a dinner was set before us, which we could not eat'. He added, 'This was the first time, and except one, the last, that I found any reason to complain of a Scottish table.' You have to rather feel sorry for the puppy-like Boswell: all eager to please yet having to drag this grumpy Sassenach pensioner around.

See also GLASGOW, GLASGOW (p. 177); STRAND, WESTMINSTER (p. 409).

## CUMBERNAULD, NORTH LANARKSHIRE
# Irn-Bru

Irn-Bru is worthy of a place in the pantheon of great British beverages for being that last man standing after the blitzkrieg invasion of carbonated soft drinks from the USA. Ginger beer, lemonade, tonics and cordials may all still be available, and thoroughly enjoyable, but their sales numbers are no threat to the big boys, and they seem to have lost their cultural resonance. They may be occasionally reached for, but they're not *longed* for, and there is none of the pride the Scots take in drinking their Irn-Bru. There are very few countries where a native soft drink still competes with the likes of Coca-Cola and PepsiCo, but Scotland is one (and Malta another, where Kinnie, a bitter orange drink, is much loved locally). When McDonald's opened in Scotland in 1987 and didn't serve Irn-Bru, uproar ensued and the beverage was added sharpish.

A. G. Barr, makers of Irn-Bru, started out as cork cutters in Falkirk in 1830. The family firm began developing a range of carbonated beverages, and in 1901 Andrew Barr developed the recipe for Iron Brew, as the drink was originally called. There were many of these brews on the market at that time, and most, including Barr's, contained small traces of iron. (This is still true today: Irn-Bru contains 0.002% ammonium ferric citrate.) They were touted as health-giving tonics, and as an alternative to alcohol. Sadly Andrew Barr died just two years later, so didn't see the fruits of his labours.

Production stopped during the Second World War, started up again post-war, and then in 1947 the government began developing new food-labelling legislation, aimed at tightening up the claims that food companies made. In a bid to pre-empt the bill, the company's then chairman – Robert Barr – changed the name to Irn-Bru, thus getting around the fact that the drinks weren't actually 'brewed'. In the end the legislation was amended and the change wasn't necessary, but by that point the new name had begun to catch on, giving the product a degree of brand distinction, one that seems remarkably prescient when you consider today's texting generation and our lackadaisical attitude to grammar in brand names.

In 1995 the company secured the franchise to produce Orangina here in the UK. This led to the construction of a new 122,000-square-foot factory in Cumbernauld, where it and Irn-Bru are made today.

The recipe is known by former chairman Robin Barr and one other A. G. Barr board director whose identity remains confidential. Robin stepped down as chairman in 2009, although he continues to mix the essence that goes into the drink. Although a secret, it's known that thirty-two ingredients feature in it. The final taste is, well, yes, sweet, as there's over a third of your recommended daily sugar allowance in each 300 ml can. But also present is some citrus bite, and finally an ever-so-slightly metallic taste. A *Guardian* Guide article in 2010 once unfavourably described it as a mix of orange juice and rusty Brillo pads, which is a little unfair.

Irn-Bru even has a culinary use, as in 2008 John Sinclair of H. M. Sheridan butchers in Ballater, Aberdeenshire, developed Irn-Bru-cured bacon. This sees the bacon dry-cured in salt and sugar first, before adding Irn-Bru and being vacuum-packed and left to marinate for five days. 'You get the taste of the drink coming through, particularly the sweetness,' says John adding, 'The same people keep coming back for it.'

And so though strong and much loved in its homeland north of the border, the drink still meets with rather nonplussed lips south of Gretna Green. It is, however, quite popular in Russia, where it's produced under licence and also considered a luxury, often being mixed with vodka.

*See also* NEWCASTLE, TYNE & WEAR (p. 221).

## DINGWALL, HIGHLAND

# *Haggis*

In August 2009, food and cookery writer Catherine Brown provoked ire when she had the temerity to suggest that haggis might be an English invention. Meanwhile, in her book *The Haggis: A Little History* Clarissa Dickson Wright offers evidence of a Scandinavian origin. Still others point to the Romans bringing it here. Food historian Ivan Day states that they were once eaten all over Britain, and that recipes appear in Robert May's *The Accomplisht Cook* from 1660.

Does it really matter who first put the animal's bits in its own stomach? I don't think so. Unlike the carcass itself, the heart, liver and lungs of a slaughtered beast go bad quickly, and consequently they need to be used as quickly as possible. The haggis is merely the most famous incarnation of a variety of dishes from all over Europe that feature offal cooked in the stomach of the animal; black pudding is another example that's still popular south of the border. The haggis belongs to Scotland if only by virtue of the fact that it's still eaten regularly there, and not just for high days, holidays and Burns' Night.

This fact is backed up by the phenomenal success of George Cockburn & Son in Dingwall, Inverness, who sell over 1,500 a week. The shop was set up in 1955 by George Cockburn, changed hands a few times in the 1970s, then in the early 1980s the then owner Mr McCallum wanted to retire and so sold the place to Fraser McGregor, who had been working there since he was fifteen years old. To this day, Fraser still uses the recipe taught to him by Mr McCallum. 'First we cook the meats slowly overnight, then we pick over it while it's still hot ['warm reekin', as Burns might say], then it's into a grinder with onions and suet.' This is then hand-mixed with oatmeal and a secret blend of seasoning to give the final stuffing. Casings come in two types: an artificial, plastic one, which a lot of producers use nowadays, or a natural one made from a cow's stomach, each end tied by hand with string rather than Burns's 'pin to mend a mill in time o' need'.

I find haggis has a wonderful earthy offal taste, often backed up with a good hit of pepper, and that the oatmeal gives a soft comforting feel in the mouth. Alongside mashed potatoes it's as comforting as you can get on a cold night at the fag end of January.

Haggis, then, is one of those things – like pancakes – that I eat once a

Haggis at George Cockburn & Son in Dingwall

year and say to myself, 'Blimey, that was utterly delicious, I must eat that more often,' but somehow never quite get round to doing so. I intend to change my ways and gaze a little more into its 'honest, sonsie face'.

See also BATH, SOMERSET (p. 4); BURY MARKET, GREATER MANCHESTER (p. 99); HAROME, NORTH YORKSHIRE (p. 249); HEREFORD, HEREFORDSHIRE (p. 296); SMITHFIELD, ISLINGTON (p. 401); STONEHALL COMMON, WORCESTERSHIRE (p. 312).

## DUMGOYNE, STIRLING
# Glengoyne whisky

One could spend a lifetime exploring the wonderful world of Scotch, but sadly (for me at least) such an in-depth journey lies outside the scope of this book. However, it would be remiss not to at least pause for a wee dram. Of course, Scotland isn't the only place in Britain that makes whisky. The Penderyn Distillery in Wales (*see* p. 83) have been very successful, and the fledgling English Whisky Company based in Norfolk produced their first batch in 2009, but Scotland remains by far the home of the liquid gold.

Highland, Lowland, Island, Speyside, Islay and Campbelltown are the distinct regional variants, and labelling legislation that arrived in late 2009 defines all Scotch whisky as either single malt Scotch, single grain Scotch, blended malt Scotch, blended grain Scotch or blended Scotch. Malts are made only with malted barley, while grain whiskies can contain unmalted barley and other grains such as corn or maize.

There is a huge range of tastes and flavours to choose from, and as ever the best advice for a novice is to visit a specialist shop and ask for a recommendation. Jura is a good Island malt to begin with, while Talisker will take you in at the deep end. Compass Box make some wonderful new-style blended whiskies, where maybe three single malts are blended together, like a wine-maker would use types of grape. Monkey Shoulder are doing something similar.

However, if you want something really interesting and unique, you could do worse than try a drop or two of Glengoyne. The distillery – built in 1833 and in continuous use ever since – straddles the Highland Line, resulting in its stills being in the Highlands, while its casks are in the Lowlands. Furthermore, it's one of only two distilleries in Scotland to use Golden

Promise barley, which was traditionally the barley of choice. It stands up to the strong wind, ripens early and gives a rich malt flavour, but the trade-off is that it gives a lower yield – not ideal as whisky production grew. As well as using an older variety of barley, Glengoyne also air-dry their crop rather than using peat smoke, which adds a further layer of complexity and smooth subtlety. And if you thought wine descriptions were flowery, try this one for Glengoyne, courtesy of an online whisky aficionado: 'The taste of a lullaby.'

Opinion is divided about how best to enjoy this lullaby, however. There are those who would swear that neat is the only way, while others believe a dash of water releases the flavour. Me, I like to run my fingers under a cold tap and then hold them over the glass, allowing just a few drops to mix with the whisky, then sit back and enjoy.

*See also* PENDERYN, RHONDDA CYNON TAF (p. 83).

DUNDEE, ANGUS
### *Dundee marmalade*

The mythology and folklore surrounding Dundee marmalade is almost as thick as the product itself. Sometime in the 1700s, James Keiller is said to have bought a job lot of oranges from a Spanish ship that had docked in the town's port. Unfortunately, they were the bitter, Seville kind that aren't especially nice to eat, and so his enterprising wife got busy with a knife and some sugar, and Dundee marmalade was born. Mrs Keiller was obviously pre-empting Marlene Dietrich's dictum 'Once a woman has forgiven her man, she must not reheat his sins for breakfast.'

This is not an unfamiliar tale, and versions of it are repeated all over the country to explain the provenance of various local spreads and jams. Indeed, the same tale is told for both Frank Cooper's marmalade (*see* p. 350) and Paisley grocer George Robertson, who in 1864 is said to have bought a job lot of oranges which, you've guessed it, his wife made into marmalade.

There are, however, flecks of truth to be discerned in the Dundee story. The Keillers did exist, and owned a sweet shop, so probably already knew about preserving fruit, making jams and working with sugar, but however the marmalade originated, by 1779 they had set up full production, and the product rode the wave of Empire to become famous throughout the world.

There have, of course, been many marmalade producers over the years, but the only one still left making Dundee marmalade is Mackays. Originally founded in 1938 by the Mackay Brothers, the company was acquired in the 1970s by United Biscuits in order to make their biscuits' jam filling. It was then bought as a going concern by the current owner, Martin Grant's father, Paul, who had worked for United Biscuits for twenty-six years. What attracted him was the fact that they still used the open-pan method of jam and marmalade making. When the contract with United ended, Paul set about building the brand and developing recipes with Les Nicholson, who went by the nickname 'Mr Marmalade' and had worked for the Keillers, the original producers of Dundee marmalade, for many years.

As well as making it in batches by hand, it's the ingredients that make Mackays' marmalade different. Seville oranges, of course, are traditional, but they also use raw cane sugar: 'It costs a bit more, but the taste is worth it. Other than that, we add a bit of lemon juice and some pectin derived from apples, and that's it,' says current owner Martin. Thankfully, tales involving job lots of 'bargain' oranges from Spanish sailors or blokes down the pub do not feature in the establishment of Mackays, but making things the old-fashioned way does.

*See also* GREAT DUNHAM, NORFOLK (p. 431); OXFORD, OXFORDSHIRE (p. 350); WATLINGTON, OXFORDSHIRE (p. 361).

## DURNESS, HIGHLAND
# *Hot chocolate at Cocoa Mountain*

Cocoa Mountain can probably lay claim to being the most northerly chocolate producer in Britain, situated, as it is, in the top west corner of Scotland, half a mile on from the village of Durness. It was started by James Findley and Paul Maden in 2006 on a 1955 RAF Cold War early-warning base that was never used. In the 1960s the local council decided to turn it into a craft village and spread some peace and love. It's now home to a bookshop, a bistro, a print maker, a painter, a woodworker and our two chocolatiers.

You might think them both mad for situating their business right at the top of the country, but James and Paul have a great relationship with their local postmaster, who during busy periods like Christmas and Easter comes three or four times a day. They reckon they can get a box of their chocs anywhere in the UK in twenty-four hours.

This stunning hot chocolate is almost a meal in itself

Their handiwork comes in a great many wonderful flavours, with their white chocolate with chilli and lemon grass being my favourite combination, just pipping the strawberry and black pepper.

However, it was their mug of hot chocolate that really impressed me. Was there ever a drink so badly made as hot chocolate? Often it's an afterthought for coffee shops and cafés, made with two teaspoons of powder and topped up with hot water and a dash of milk. The result is a watery drink that somehow manages still to taste of powder.

Cocoa Mountain's hot chocolate, on the other hand, is almost a meal in itself, and comes topped with liquid chocolate deliberately running over the edge and down the sides. Served in a handless cup handmade by the potter next door, which means it needs cupping with both hands like soup, it's the sort of drink you have to get stuck into. No wonder it proves popular with walkers and day-trippers looking for an energy hit and something to warm their bones after a bracing walk along the coast.

The boys are tight-lipped on their recipes and techniques, and rightly so, but as for the future, 'We're going to start looking at caramel,' says Paul. 'We're interested in the whole burnt sugar thing.' I'm sure whatever they do, it'll be interesting. Consider this your early warning.

## *Freshly ground coffee from Artisan Roast*

Artisan Roast was established by New Zealander Mike Wilson and his Chilean business partner Gustavo Pardo in 2007 to bring top-notch artisanal specialist coffee to the people of Edinburgh. 'We were on a mission to improve the coffee in Edinburgh,' says Mike, who did four years in the army before leaving to try something new. 'I've a low boredom threshold, and window-shopped through life. Prior to the army I was a rock star in Syria with long curly hair!' These days he devotes his time to coffee, to improving the café and to developing new methods of production, including chill-filtration, which borrows from whisky production methods and gives quite a different taste to the coffee.

Artisan Roast must be one of the few places in the country that roasts the green coffee beans right there in the shop. 'Fatima', the £10,000 roasting machine, and 'Mustapha', his coffee grinder, have recently been joined by 'Cimba', six times larger than Fatima and able to take the increase in demand.

Mike Wilson checks that his coffee beans are roasted to perfection

'We do all our roasting by scent,' says Mike, which is made possible by the fact that they roast in small batches.

His approach to producing a cup of coffee borders on the clinically obsessive. The first step is cleanliness. Artisan Roast deep-clean their machinery at the end of every day. Many places don't, and the result can be a build-up of oils and dirt that can taint the taste and reduce the crema layer in the cup. Grinding is another area where many people go wrong. 'Coffee starts to go stale after five days,' says Mike, 'so it's important to grind only when you need it.' Next there's a whole host of options to consider in the placing of the grounds in the basket, all to ensure you get a good 'puck'. Water takes the path of least resistance, and in a coffee machine is hitting the puck at nine to ten bars of pressure. If your grounds aren't compacted or 'tamped' into a solid puck, the water will just punch a hole through and the resulting coffee will be bitter and weak. Once you've done this correctly, the resulting pour should only last around twenty to thirty-five seconds, because after that time what's coming out is destroying the taste of the coffee too. Most coffee on the Continent is drunk as black espresso, with cappuccino and latte only being drunk at breakfast time. Of course here in the UK most people are still only just learning this, and we still like lots of milk with our coffee. Then there's not only the choice of milk but the optimum temperature to heat it to; skimmed milk produces a more stable foam, but full-fat milk tastes nicer, and will contain more micro bubbles, making it feel more creamy than airy.

The final result of all this minute care and attention is a truly magnificent cup of coffee: smooth, flavourful and complex, you really can taste the oils, the smoke, the richness and the effort. It's quite delicious.

EDINBURGH, EDINBURGH
## Chippie sauce

Edinburgh is the epicentre of chippie sauce. It can't be found just forty minutes' drive away in Glasgow, although recently it has managed to cross the Firth of Forth and it's even been spotted in Dunfermline. True aficionados believe the sauce should be found on every self-respecting chip shop's counter, housed in an old glass Irn-Bru bottle with holes punched in the screw cap. Various myths abound as to what's actually in it, but the general consensus is that it's the cheapest brown sauce available at the cash and carry (the Gold Star brand being the favourite), diluted with tap water or perhaps vinegar. Quite how it came about is anyone's guess, although the watering down suggests it was originally an idea to make the bottle go further – after all, it's not like you can charge for condiments, unless you're selling it in a bottle to take home, as the Golden Sea on Ferry Road do at £2.20 a litre.

So beloved is chippie sauce that it more often than not takes the place of vinegar in Edinburgh's chip shops, with customers being asked if they want 'salt 'n' soss' on their portions. Naturally various Internet groups can be found singing its praises. Chippie sauce, then, hasn't the history or heritage of Worcestershire sauce (*see* p. 317) or Henderson's Relish (*see* p. 258), but it's loved by the hungry denizens of Auld Reekie all the same.

*See also* BISHOP'S STORTFORD, HERTFORDSHIRE (p. 321); EASTON GREY, WILTSHIRE (p. 11); FAVERSHAM, KENT (p. 477); MOFFAT, DUMFRIES & GALLOWAY (p. 183); NORWICH, NORFOLK (p. 451); OXFORD, OXFORDSHIRE (p. 351); ROSSENDALE, LANCASHIRE (p. 131); ST HELENS, MERSEYSIDE (p. 132); SHEFFIELD, SOUTH YORKSHIRE (p. 258); SPENNYMOOR, COUNTY DURHAM (p. 227); WORCESTER, WORCESTERSHIRE (p. 317).

## EDINBURGH, EDINBURGH
# Oysters and champagne

The Café Royal in Edinburgh is tucked round the back of busy Princes Street and was built in 1861 as a showroom for the latest gas and home fittings. The interior is a stunning example of Edinburgh's Victorian past, when it was known as the Athens of the North. The décor has changed little since then, perhaps because it's been respected and valued by its many owners, with the notable exception of Grand Metropolitan (now merged with Guinness and called Diageo), who bought the café in 1965 and tried to sell it to Woolworths. Woolworths wanted to knock it down so they could expand their Princes Street store, but the city planning officer disagreed, which led to the whole building and its interior being listed on 27 February 1970.

What the café is really noted for, though, is its oysters. In the quieter months they sell around 500 a week, but this can rise to over 900 a week during the summer and the Edinburgh Festival. The standard way to serve them is opened and on ice with lemon, and this accounts for over 75 per cent of the oysters sold. There are, however, some alternative options; Oysters Rockefeller, for example, a recipe that originated in Antoine's Restaurant in New Orleans, founded in 1840 by Antoine Alciatore and the USA's oldest family-run restaurant. His son, Jules Alciatore, developed the recipe and named it after John D. Rockefeller, the richest man in America at the time. For this dish, the oysters are opened, topped with a green-flecked sauce and breadcrumbs, then popped under the grill. The exact recipe has remained a secret for all these years, much to the annoyance of food historians. Some say the sauce features spinach, while others say the green comes from spring onions or parsley. Pernod is mentioned as an ingredient, and butter's in there for sure. For the Café Royal version they're grilled in the half shell on spinach, then topped with mornay sauce and sprinkled with Parmesan.

Another dish worth trying is Oysters Kilpatrick, in which the oysters are wrapped in bacon, grilled and drizzled with balsamic vinegar (older recipes feature Worcestershire sauce). This dish seems to be an Australian invention, and bears a striking similarity to Oysters Kirkpatrick, which also features bacon and cheese. The Kirkpatrick version was created in honour of Colonel John C. Kirkpatrick, who managed the Palace Hotel, San Francisco, where they were created.

To wash all this heritage and history down, the Café Royal also has a small but seafood-friendly wine list featuring champagnes such as Lanson Rose NV and Veuve Clicquot Brut NV, as well as a Sancerre, a Chablis and an Albarino. All of which makes ordering a drink and some shellfish in the Café Royal a mini historical tour as well as a relaxing break from shopping or the festival.

*See also* CLACHAN, DUMFRIES & GALLOWAY (p. 153); LINDISFARNE, NORTHUMBER-LAND (p. 214); WEST MERSEA, ESSEX (p. 459); WHITSTABLE, KENT (p. 500).

FINDON, ABERDEENSHIRE
## Finnan haddie

A finnan haddie is a haddock that's been split open, brined and then smoked. But how did such a thing come to be named? Well, there's always a story, and finnan haddie's goes like this. One day a fire started in one of the smoking houses in the small village of Findon near Aberdeen, the men put the fire out, and when the owner examined his damaged stock he saw a haddock, smelt it – it smelt good – and ate it. Others came to taste it, and before long, Findon, which is pronounced 'Finnan' locally, became famous for its smoked haddock. You'll notice the origin of kippers – indeed, most smoked foods –

# Kedgeree

The roots of kedgeree lie in the Indian dish of *khichri* (also spelt *khichdi*), made with rice and lentils. The word means 'a mix-up', similar to 'hodge-podge' in English. Writing in Bombay in 1809, the young Maria, Lady Callcott in her *Journal of a Residence in India* declared:

> The fish is excellent but the larger kinds are not very plentiful. The bumbelo is like a large sand eel. It is dried in the sun and is usually eaten at breakfast with kedgeree, a dish of rice boiled with dol (split country peas) and coloured with turmeric.

In 1845 Eliza Acton (who never went to India) gives us a recipe that not only features cayenne instead of turmeric, but also has eggs cracked into it and cooked, to make something more akin to a sauce. And it is to Acton that we must attribute the promotion of smoked haddock, as she declares it the best fish to use. David Burton, author of *The Raj at the Table* (1994), explains that smoked Scottish haddock were becoming more available nationally at this time, and so were subsequently added to the dish here in Britain, haddock not being native to the seas surrounding the subcontinent.

In 1861 Mrs Beeton claimed that cold fish would do, and opted for mustard as the heat-giving ingredient, despite curry powder featuring regularly elsewhere in her cookery tome. In contrast, Arthur

Kenny-Herbert, writing in 1885 in his *Culinary Jottings for Madras* under the pseudonym 'Wyvern', said, 'Kegeree [*sic*] of the English type is composed of boiled rice, chopped hard-boiled egg, cold minced fish and a lump of fresh butter.' This he suggested heating in a frying pan before adding salt and pepper and a few bits of green such as cress or parsley. Note his lack of curry powder, turmeric or, indeed, anything else Indian bar the rice. Equally, the fish isn't described as smoked in this 'English type'.

The beauty of kedgeree was that it took the previous day's leftover rice and fish, added boiled egg and in doing so gave those enterprising Victorians a whole new breakfast dish. Nowadays it's normally made fresh, and often for lunch or the evening meal as few of us fancy, or indeed have time for, curried egg and fish for breakfast.

Over the years, other additions and embellishments have been added, most having the effect of making it feel more Indian or substantial. So alongside curry powder we see peas, sultanas, mango chutney and lemon wedges.

Kedgeree, then, is an Indian-inspired dish now made with British ingredients that was once eaten for breakfast but now isn't. It is perhaps, though, the first Anglo-Indian dish, and blazed a trail for the likes of tikka masala and balti.

bears a striking similarity (*see* p. 224). Traditionally it would have been smoked over either peat or seaweed, but nowadays it's very rare to find either of these two methods being used commercially.

Finnan haddie are great for breakfast alongside a poached egg, or you could cook them in a shallow tin with a little milk, water and butter to moisten. Once cooked through, you can remove the fish and thicken the cooking liquor to make a sauce. You can even poach an egg in the tin, making a 'haddyanegg'. Fishers restaurant in Leith on the outskirts of Edinburgh serves them in a slightly different way: grilled, then topped with goat's cheese and cherry tomatoes. Not traditional by any means, but still rather nice.

See also ARBROATH, ANGUS (p. 143); CLEY NEXT THE SEA, NORFOLK (p. 424); GREAT YARMOUTH, NORFOLK (p. 433); HAMBRIDGE, SOMERSET (p. 13); NIDDERDALE, NORTH YORKSHIRE (p. 251); SEAHOUSES, NORTHUMBERLAND (p. 224); WHITBY, NORTH YORKSHIRE (p. 268).

## FORFAR, ANGUS
### *The bridie*

The bridie, along with the Scotch pie, is another example of the Scottish love of meat in pastry. The town of Forfar in Angus lays claim to being its home. A traditional Forfar bridie consists of minced beef and onion, encased in a horseshoe-shaped pastry crust. Shortcrust is traditional in the town itself, but puff pastry is also used.

As for its origins, most think it likely that it takes its name from one Maggie Bridie from nearby Glamis, who travelled the region selling food. Regional food expert Matthew O'Callaghan has been researching its history and has discovered more details about the headstone bearing the name Margaret Bridie in St Fergus's kirkyard in the town. 'When you trace back the history of that Margaret Bridie, though related to people in the town, she actually spent all her life in Muthill in Perthshire. It's a good story, and I have to say the vicar of the church was disappointed, but it's not the right Margaret Bridie. There's only one Margaret Bridie who fits the picture and she goes back to 1680, which makes the Forfar bridie 100 years older than first thought.'

Interesting stuff. More recently J. M. Barrie, born in nearby Kirriemuir, mentions them in *Sentimental Tommy*, published in 1896, and by 1930 they're mentioned not as miners' or labourers' food, but as lunch for both 'beater and gun' in Patrick Chalmers's *Field Sports of Scotland*. He ends with the adage 'a bridie is apt to be awfu' clotty aboot the lugs,' meaning they're so big and hearty that as you bite into the middle, the two ends of the horseshoe are apt to leave your ears daubed in gravy.

With Matthew's help Angus Council have begun a process, similar to their colleagues in Cornwall, to seek PGI (Protected Geographical Indication) status for the Forfar bridie, which means agreeing upon a set recipe, production process and defined area for the dish. To this end they're working with the two bakers in the town who make them: McLaren & Son, who have been making bridies since 1893; and Saddlers, established in 1897.

Meanwhile, non-Forfar bridies are still being made all over Scotland. Alan Devlin runs Sugar & Spice bakery in Auchterarder, about fifty miles south of Forfar. He's a trained chef, rather than a butcher or a baker, and his bridies are a bit different: there's the steak bridie, which is simply steak encased in a puff-pastry shell, or the onion bridie, which is minced steak with plenty of chopped onion. And then there are his extremely non-traditional goat's cheese and ratatouille or venison and pickled walnut versions, and a breakfast bridie, containing air-dried bacon, sausage, beans and a free-range egg.

*See also* CORNISH PASTIES (p. 18).

FORRES, MORAY
## Macbeth's Butchers

Macbeth's Butchers in Forres, Moray, was bought by the Gibson family in 1986 as an outlet for the beef produced on their farm. 'We thought about changing the name, but Gibsons' is not as good as Macbeth's, is it?' laughs shop manager Jock Gibson. The farm is a twenty-minute drive away in the tiny village of Dallas, 800 feet above the Moray Firth in the Highlands of Scotland. It was started by Jock's parents, Michael and Susan, in the 1970s, and began with a pedigree herd of Highland cattle. It was focused largely on the export market, which meant that when the BSE disease restrictions came into play in the late 1980s they had to rethink their business model radically, and turned to beef and butchery rather than breeding. The Gibsons' beef is Highland crossed with Beef Shorthorn, and a bit of Aberdeen Angus thrown in. A Scottish slaughterman once told me that if you want some scrubland cleaning up and making good, the best thing to do is put a 'Highland coo' on it, as they are renowned for eating things that other cows wouldn't give space to in one of their four stomachs. Their ability to make the most of poor pasture, to calve outdoors, and to brave the elements means they thrive in the wilds of Scotland, and with their eyes hidden under a floppy fringe of reddish blond hair, they're stunning-looking creatures.

The Beef Shorthorn, meanwhile, became a distinct breed in 1958. Before that, the Shorthorn was an all-rounder, used for beef and milking, and was bred from the cattle of the north-east of England in the eighteenth century. Incidentally, the Beef Shorthorn's sibling, the Dairy Shorthorn, is listed in the 'critical' category on the Rare Breed Survival Trust's watchlist, with only thirty-five females remaining. By the 1970s, breeders had become concerned that the Shorthorn was under threat from bigger Continental breeds such as the Charolais or Limousin, so the Shorthorn Society sanctioned the introduction of bloodlines from the Maine-Anjou breed to literally beef them up. This was subsequently halted in 2001.

Macbeth's sell a range of meat – beef, pork, lamb and game. You can even order their food from their website. While you're online, you might want to browse their 'meat mentor' section. This nifty idea came from the sheer number of questions they received about how best to cook and prepare the meat. So there's information on such basics as 'how much meat will I need to feed eight people?', as well as a visual guide to cooking steaks correctly, and tips and advice on how to carve it at the table so you don't end up swinging your knife around like a claymore and hacking all your hard work to pieces.

*See also* BROMYARD, HEREFORDSHIRE (p. 283); CAMBRIDGE, CAMBRIDGESHIRE (p. 422); CONWY, CONWY (p. 60); LOUTH, LINCOLNSHIRE (p. 336); MARYLEBONE, WESTMINSTER (p. 387); MELTON CONSTABLE, NORFOLK (p. 447); NANTWICH, CHESHIRE (p. 125); WOODHALL SPA, LINCOLNSHIRE (p. 364); YORK, NORTH YORKSHIRE (p. 271).

## GLASGOW, GLASGOW
# Café Gandolfi

Café Gandolfi has been something of a Glasgow institution for the best part of thirty years. It was started by photographer Ian Mackenzie, whose love of the bespoke camera manufacturers the Gandolfi brothers gave the café its name. When the café opened, the surrounding area – the Merchant City

Café Gandolfi, a much-loved Glaswegian institution

– wasn't the haunt of lawyers, architects and designers it is today, but an area on the wane, the merchants having long since sold up and left. But the café survived, and eventually thrived, and gradually other restaurants and cafés, many of which are Italian in theme, followed in its wake. But Café Gandolfi remains at the heart of it all, and has a loyal following. According to manager Lynne Parker, 'People have often had their first experiences here – their first cappuccino, their first date, first kiss, marriage proposals, all sorts.'

The café is spread over a couple of floors and enjoys the high ceilings and large windows so beloved by the Victorians. The chunky wooden furniture, designed by the late artist and designer Tim Stead, has been here since the café opened. It's a testament both to him and his handiwork that his creations have survived not only the fickle nature of fashion, but also nearly thirty years of Glaswegian bums, hands and feet.

The current owner is Seumas MacInnes, who's expanded upstairs with an Attic bar and opened up the Gandolfi Fish restaurant a few doors down. 'What we have here is something that caters to your mood, from coffee and home-made scones in the morning, lunches, light bites and lazing in the afternoon, to a full sit-down restaurant dinner or simpler gastropub-style food, and on to evening snacking and drinking,' says Lynne.

In the kitchen are chefs Kenny, Bruce and head chef Jamie, who's been here ten years. The café menu has a good range of dishes, including some traditional Scottish flavours: Cullen skink; Stornoway black pudding; and haggis, neeps and tatties. However, I opted for Rannoch Moor smoked venison with gratin dauphinoise, a dish perhaps echoing the 'Auld Alliance' between Scotland and France and something of a Gandolfi standard. The cold, thinly sliced smoked venison is to die for, rich and earthy without being overpowered by the smoke. The dauphs, on the other hand, are warm and creamy. All this is contrasted by the accompaniment of some sliced avocado, which is neither Scottish nor French but somehow stands its ground on the plate taste-wise. I really liked Café Gandolfi; it's the sort of place that's able to shapeshift to match your mood and the company you're with.

## GLASGOW, GLASGOW
### Chicken tikka masala

The Glaswegian curry scene in the mid 1970s was as vibrant as the sauces that accompanied it. It still is today, and the city has won 'Curry Capital of Britain' three times in the last decade. It is in this febrile and fecund environment that the chicken tikka is said to have been created. The story – which I'm sure you're familiar with – goes like this. Ali Asif Aslam, owner and chef of the Shish Mahal restaurant, added a sauce made from, among other things, Campbell's condensed tomato soup to a chicken dish after a customer complained it was too dry. Ali is now in his sixties, but the restaurant, which he initially established at another location in 1964, is still in family hands. The presence of the tinned soup is attributed to the fact that Ali was suffering from a stomach ulcer at the time and so was eating bland food.

In the summer of 2009, Mohammed Sarwar, Labour MP for Glasgow Central, put forth an Early Day Motion calling not only for the city to be duly recognised as the birthplace of the dish, but for the dish to have PDO (Protected Designation of Origin) protection. Many media outlets reported the story, and knowing that curry always tastes great the next day, rehashed it with counter opinions, such as that of Zaeemuddin Ahmad, chef at Delhi's Karim Hotel who said, 'Chicken tikka masala is an authentic

Mughlai recipe prepared by our forefathers who were royal chefs in the Mughal period.' As we've seen with banoffi pie (p. 494), fish and chips (p. 396), and other examples, recipes are seldom plucked from the air. They come about through evolution and happenstance. And so although chicken tikka masala may have some roots on the subcontinent, it's British-Asian now. What's more, it's often the case that others have similar ideas around the same time. A 1965 edition of Mrs Baibir Singh's *Indian Cookery* lists a recipe for 'makhani murgh' – tandoori chicken cooked in butter and tomato sauce – which from the list of ingredients and method is near identical to chicken tikka masala.

These days the dish is a curry-house staple, perhaps because it's warm, comforting and safe, like the baby pool at the swimming baths. A 1998 survey by *The Real Curry Restaurant Guide* found forty-eight different recipes for the dish, with the only common ingredient being chicken. The flavour has subsequently been added to a range of our other favourite foodstuffs, and you can now find chicken tikka crisps, pizzas, Kievs, pies and baked beans on supermarket shelves.

Still, I can't help but wonder who that first refusenik was who sent back his chicken at Shish Mahal. It is to them, that man on the Kelvingrove omnibus who so summed up our tastes with 'I'd like some gravy with that,' that we must give thanks. Which just goes to show that the customer is always right.

See also HOW RECIPES BEGIN (p. 496); BIRMINGHAM, WEST MIDLANDS (p. 279); MARYLEBONE, WESTMINSTER (p. 389); WHITECHAPEL, TOWER HAMLETS (p. 414).

GLASGOW, GLASGOW
## Cock-a-leekie

When a friend once asked me, 'What's in cock-a-leekie soup?' I replied, somewhat facetiously, 'Prunes.' Unsurprisingly, this resulted in a nonplussed look, so I then listed the two primary ingredients that give the dish its name. It's a great combination: an old chicken, like some ageing Lothario, is pepped up by the addition of some young fresh leeks. However, various other ingredients have featured in the dish from time to time, the main one being the aforementioned prunes. What's more, various rumours abounded about the poor cock, including the slightly fanciful one that it was often the loser in a cockfight.

Cock-a-leekie first appears in Fynes Moryson's 1598 description of his journey around Scotland, where he dines with a knight's household on 'Pullet with some prunes in the broth'. The chicken would have been eaten separately, after some of the liquid had been drunk. The addition of stewed fruits is typically medieval, possibly a French influence due to the Auld Alliance, although in later years they came to be omitted. *The Master Books of Soups* (1902) by Henry Smith mentions this, adding, 'The French like to add a few cooked prunes; why, goodness only knows!'

Earlier, Christian Isobel Johnstone (who went by the pseudonym of Meg Dods, a name she took from a Walter Scott novel) declares in *The Cook and Housewife's Manual* (1826) that beef should be used to make the stock before adding a capon or old fowl. She ends the description with 'prunes won't be put to this'. Johnstone also talks about how some cooks thicken the soup with oatmeal, others with pearl barley. Anne Mulhern from the Willow Tea Rooms in Glasgow puts rice in hers, and a few chopped prunes, while Scottish chef Sue Lawrence makes a version with coriander and avocado. Surely the gloves are off!

So who's right? Who knows? Who cares? What's really interesting is that cock-a-leekie perfectly illustrates the changing ebb and flow of recipes over time as tastes and fashions change. For me, though, I'll throw my lot in with Johnstone. Of Scottish soup, she declares, 'We hold as maxims, that the French take the lead of all European people in soups and broths, that the Scotch rank second, the Welsh next, and that the English, as a nation, are at the very bottom of the scale.'

*See also* CULLEN, MORAY (p. 155); STRAND, WESTMINSTER (p. 409).


GLASGOW, GLASGOW

## Rook pie

The world, it seems, has turned on its head. Some of the best places to eat esoteric country fare, such as game, are restaurants in the larger cities, while pubs and inns in the countryside are fitting imported wood-fired pizza ovens or churning out poorly made Pad Thai and Goan curries. Nothing perhaps illustrates this situation better than rook pie.

The recipe itself is nothing new and is mentioned in most cookery books from the Victorian era. The general consensus is that in May (the 12th is said to be the optimum day, but this may just be because of the similar date for grouse) young rooks or 'branchers' are shot. They're then skinned, and the breast is removed and soaked in milk. Mrs Beeton's recipe calls for rump steak too, which makes me wonder why anyone who could afford steak would be eating rook. The Second World War cookbook *They Can't Ration These* (1940) by Viscount de Mauduit features a recipe for stewed rooks as well as rook pie; no sign of steak, obviously.

Rook pie was eaten in patches all over the UK, but particularly in the southern counties; indeed, the Fox and Hounds in Acton Turville used to make a pie once a year until quite recently.

In Glasgow, too, the rook appears fleetingly each May on the specials board at Stravaigin restaurant. Here it's not made into a pie, but treated in a similar way to pigeon. The breast is roasted rare, the leg confited, and both are served with a beetroot rosti, liquorice carrot purée and a cherry jus. 'We're very lucky in that our clientele are willing to try new and different things,' says general manager Calum Robertson. 'Someone working in our head office down in Ayrshire who we get pheasant and venison from was approached by a farmer who was culling a few birds. We went through about forty-eight birds.'

According to the British Trust for Ornithology, there are over 1.2 million breeding pairs of rooks in the UK. They're plentiful, easy to shoot and need culling anyway – pass the pastry, I say. However, in the interests of balance I'll leave you with the 100th maxim of Morgan O'Doherty (a pseudonym of Captain Thomas Hamilton, and later Dr William Maginn; under this nom de plume the two issued forth curmudgeonly and bombastic opinions, like a Victorian Jeremy Clarkson), published in the September issue of *Blackwood's* magazine in 1824. It reads thus:

The best of all pies is a grouse pie, the second a black-cock pie, the third a woodcock pie with plenty of spices, the fourth a chicken pie (ditto). As for a pigeon pie it is not worthy of a place upon any table so long as there are chickens in the world. A rook pie is a bad imitation of that bad article and a beef steak pie is really abominable. A good pie is excellent when hot but the test of a good pie is how does it eat cold? Apply this to the examples above cited and you will find I am correct.

*See also* CARDIFF, CARDIFF (p. 59); CHINLEY, DERBYSHIRE (p. 285); DENBY DALE, WEST YORKSHIRE (p. 240); GREENWICH, GREENWICH (p. 380); MOUSEHOLE, CORNWALL (p. 31).

# 'Steamed' vegetables from the Prince's House Hotel

Kieron Kelly, owner and chef of the Prince's Head Hotel in the Highlands of Scotland, must be one of the only chefs in the country to get his raw ingredients delivered to him by steam train. During the summer months, salad leaves grown by the Lochaber Horticultural Association make the twenty-five-mile journey along the West Highland line – as used by the *Hogwarts Express* in the *Harry Potter* series of films – to Glenfinnan, where he picks them up. 'It wouldn't really be possible without the train,' says Kieron.

One ingredient that Kieron is able to get his hands on more readily is chanterelle mushrooms, and he uses them in a warm salad of pigeon breasts. They grow in the lanes and back garden all around the house, and his two sons pick them for him. 'My supplier will sometimes say, "I've got chanterelles for £20 a kilo," and I'll say, "I've got them for free 400 yards up the road."' With food prices rising, chefs are becoming ever more resourceful at stocking their fridges and larders. 'Because we're small and the menu changes daily, we can be flexible. One of the locals might come in with a tiny punnet of wild alpine strawberries and I'll think, "Great, let's use these!" Sometimes I'm still writing the menu at a quarter to seven.'

# Scottish raspberries

Raspberries feature in a number of Scottish dishes, with cranachan (*see* p. 190) being the most well known. However, production only really got started at the turn of the twentieth century, when growers decided to move from strawberries to raspberries and take advantage of the growing season, which was later than the south's. Few outside the world of soft-fruit production have heard of Derek Jennings, yet if you've eaten any soft fruit produced in the UK, the legacy of his handiwork has more than likely danced on your tongue. In the 1950s, Derek was the head of fruit breeding and genetics at the Scottish Crop Research Institute on the banks of the River Tay. The institute, spun out of the University of Dundee, was at the forefront of research into soft-fruit cultivars, disease resistance and improving yields, and Derek's particular area of expertise was the raspberry.

Wild raspberries picked on the banks of Loch Lomond

'Raspberries were actually a bit of a comedown for me. I was in East Africa doing research into the cassava, which is the fifth most used crop in the world; raspberries aren't even on the list!' he jokes. The act of developing new breeds of raspberry is a long process. Derek and the team would make a cross in the spring, harvest that seed and germinate the seed in the winter. He'd plant it the following year, but it wouldn't fruit until the year after that, so taking three years just to get a single crossed plant. He'd then propagate from that, which adds another three years. 'It's like kids in a school: all of them are different and most of them are duffers. I'm looking for the high flyers,' says Derek. 'You'd raise progenies of 2,000 or 3,000 plants from which you'd pick the best thirty or so, then cross those ones, and so on. After six or seven years you end up with something new and hopefully better. People ask me what's the main requirement of a raspberry breeder and I say, "Longevity!"'

Derek's team developed the Glen range: breeds of raspberries with improved health, firmness, flavour and a longer growing season. They're all named after his favourite beauty spots: Glen Clova, Glen Moy, Glen Isla, Glen Ample. Having hopped through the glens, he switched nomenclature to ladies in the family: his wife, daughter-in-law and so on. 'I'm running out of women,' he says. SCRI-bred cultivars currently occupy 96 per cent of the raspberry market in Scotland, and Glen Ample, released in 1996, is the most widely grown raspberry cultivar in the UK at present. Although the Glen range was developed in the 1970s, you and I weren't able to buy them in the shops until the late 1990s.

After working on the raspberry he turned his attentions to the blackberry, taking attributes from varieties found on the West Coast of America and crossing them with a raspberry to produce the tayberry, named after the River Tay. One day he got a call from Ben Radvan in Buckinghamshire, saying that he had tayberries on his allotment, one of which, by some genetic fluke, had no spines (thorns). Derek hopped in the car with a spade and took a sample; thus the Buckingham Tayberry was born. Tayberries don't have a long shelf life, so you rarely see them in supermarkets, but you can try horticulturists or grow your own.

As for the present, raspberry responsibility has been passed to another Jennings. When Nikki Jennings – no relation – started at the institute fourteen years ago, the industry was still geared up towards the processing market (jams, pulp, juices and so on). It was also in a rapid state of decline due to competition from Eastern Europe. In the 1990s the demand from supermarkets for fresh fruit led to growers filling this need, and moving back to hand harvesting. There's still plenty of competition, but the rapid decline has been nipped in the bud.

New varieties are being developed, the newest being genotype 9062E-1, or to give it its family name, Glen Fyne. This has a good sweet flavour throughout the growing season, the classic, slightly conical shape people expect and a shelf life as good as Glen Ample. The newest area of research is genetics. 'We're now concentrating on molecular markers to identify root rot,' says Nikki. 'Growers are desperate for something that's resistant to this but has good eating quality.'

There are many people like Derek and Nikki across all areas of agriculture who toil away improving disease resistance as well as taste and yield. By selecting and reselecting desirable attributes in plants, they give us something desirable on our plates.

See also CORBRIDGE, NORTHUMBERLAND (p. 207); EGTON BRIDGE, NORTH YORKSHIRE (p. 243); HAMPRESTON, DORSET (p. 14); HONITON, DEVON (p. 17); LYTH AND WINSTER VALLEYS, CUMBRIA (p. 117); NORTHIAM, EAST SUSSEX (p. 492); WALMERSLEY, GREATER MANCHESTER (p. 137); WIMBLEDON, MERTON (p. 415).

# Uncle Roy's sauces and condiments

'I don't like English mustard,' says Roy Anderton-Tyers, the Roy behind Uncle Roy's Comestible Concoctions. It's an odd position for someone in the condiment business. 'Having said that, I've always believed it's a useful spice. Mustard doesn't always have to be hot and horrid.' What Roy doesn't like is the blow-your-head-off kind of mustard, and he likes to tell the story of when his sister-in-law came over from Sweden to work as a waitress, and was asked to fill up mustard pots. After completing the job she made the mistake of licking the spoon – not an experience to be repeated.

Roy started producing mild mustard in 2000 when he ran a deli. He was getting fed up with people coming in asking for French mustard, so he set about making a good, mild mustard, before expanding to a few more styles and sauces. Add to this a low boredom threshold, and you can see why his product range now runs to over 250 items. 'I don't like piccalilli much, and I thought, "Can't I come up with something better?"' He wasn't sure what to call the result. 'Was it a chutney or a pickle?' So he called it a chuckle.

Another condiment he produces is Uncle Roy's Gravy Salt. 'We used to get people coming in the deli and asking for Burdall's salts.' Burdall's is a West Midlands firm that stopped production in the 1990s, and tins of their salt are now available for sale on eBay. Gravy browning is another condiment that's rather falling out of favour as gravy purists make theirs entirely from scratch, while can't-be-bothereds boil the kettle for the instant-coffee-style granules. And yet if you ask around, there are still plenty of fans of gravy salt. Many swear by it to give their sauce a much-loved savoury hit.

All traditional foods have a complementary condiment: ham and mustard, beef and horseradish, lamb and mint. We tend to put a great deal of effort into sourcing good ingredients for the main dish itself, yet put precious little into finding new and interesting sauces. Uncle Roy and many others like him are doing some exciting things with condiments, all of which are well worth a blob on the side of your plate.

*See also* BISHOP'S STORTFORD, HERTFORDSHIRE (p. 321); EASTON GREY, WILTSHIRE (p. 11); EDINBURGH, EDINBURGH (p. 167); FAVERSHAM, KENT (p. 477); NORWICH, NORFOLK (p. 451); OXFORD, OXFORDSHIRE (p. 351); ROSSENDALE, LANCASHIRE (p. 131); ST HELENS, MERSEYSIDE (p. 132); SHEFFIELD, SOUTH YORKSHIRE (p. 258); SPENNYMOOR, COUNTY DURHAM (p. 227); WORCESTER, WORCESTERSHIRE (p. 317).

## NEW GALLOWAY, DUMFRIES & GALLOWAY
# Kitty's Tea Room

Kitty's in New Galloway is a traditional tea room and the total antithesis to the grab-and-go urban coffee culture. You'll find no skinny double Frappuccinos to go here. The cups, plates and saucers are all original antiques, some bought, but many more donated by customers, with one set rumoured to have belonged to the late Queen Mother. Indeed, when you walk into Kitty's you feel, well . . . polite. Squint, and you could be on the set of an Agatha Christie episode where Miss Marple confides in a friend that she's about to unmask the murderer.

'We get all sorts of customers; we get a lot of bikers,' says Kitty's owner Sylvia Brown, and the thought of a group of chunky, leather-clad road warriors gripping the tiny porcelain teacups in their huge hairy hands is an enduring image. The nearby A82 winds alongside lochs and up over

A pot of Scottish blend and a slice of 'Sophie's Sin'

mountains, so it's no wonder bikers as well as everyone else take a short detour into New Galloway for a bit of a pit stop.

The tea room itself has a long history. It was a private house in 1840, and the beautiful fluted wooden ceiling came from the captain's mess in a merchant ship that was broken up in Glasgow. It was brought here and took local carpenters over a year to fix in place. Later on, the building became a temperance hotel, followed by a short spell as a greengrocer's, before finally becoming Kitty's just under twenty years ago.

Sylvia does all the cooking in the back, leaving her daughter Julie and sister Isobel to handle the front of house. Teas come in the familiar blends – English breakfast, Earl and Lady Grey – but also a robust Scottish blend. I tried the latter, as I like my tea so strong you can varnish a fence with it. It had that lip-puckering yet refreshing thwack-in-the-mouth dry tannin feel. To somewhat counter this, there's a range of brilliant cakes all made by Sylvia, including one named Sophie's Sin. It's a rich chocolate sponge soaked in Amaretto liqueur with chocolate ganache in the centre. On top is a layer of white whipped cream dusted with cocoa powder. I don't know who Sophie was, and Sylvia had dashed off so I couldn't ask her, but I'm glad she sinned and her transgressions were immortalised in the medium of cake.

See also APPLEDORE, KENT (p. 466); HARROGATE, NORTH YORKSHIRE (p. 250); NEW GALLOWAY, DUMFRIES & GALLOWAY (p. 184); PEMBROKE DOCK, PEMBROKESHIRE (p. 81); YORK, NORTH YORKSHIRE (p. 270).

OGCASTLE, SOUTH LANARKSHIRE

# *Blaand*

As you no doubt know, cheese is made from curds, the solid substance formed when rennet is added to milk to curdle it. These are then shaped, moulded, dried and aged before going on to the fame and glory of the cheese-board. What's left is a pale, watery, runny liquid known as whey. Of course, it has some uses. Most large cheese producers send it off for processing, where it's dried and turned into whey powder so that it can be added to other foods. Historically in England it went to the pigs, who lapped it up. Scotland, however, didn't have a great tradition of pig farming, and though whey is a by-product, it's still too valuable a foodstuff to simply throw away – but what to do with it?

This very question plagued Humphrey Errington as he lugged cans of whey left over from producing his Lanark Blue cheese (*see* below) out to his farm animals. 'The cattle and the sheep like drinking it, but I'm not sure it does them any good, unlike my pigs.' Fortunately, he found a better use for it in F. Marian McNeill's 1929 book *The Scots Kitchen*: he could turn it into blaand.

Never one to waste a drop of anything fermentable and potentially alcoholic, the fond-of-a-drink Vikings introduced blaand to Scotland over 1,000 years ago. Its production was never commercialised, being more akin to poitín as a source of illicit booze for crofters and farmers and made on the quiet. There's some evidence it was popular in Shetland, where one imagines other brewing materials are hard to come by, while sheep's milk was plentiful.

The production process is, Humphrey admits, a bit crazy. 'It's a completely uneconomical product!' he says. First, the whey is filtered. Historically this would have been done through a cheesecloth; however, this would still have let through particles of fat and protein, which alters and discolours the final result. Today Humphrey filters the whey through a very fine plastic mesh. 'You're looking to ferment the lactose in the whey,' he says, a process that takes a year. It's then transferred to an oak cask and left to age for a further two years. Only then is the resulting clear liquid bottled, and labelled as Fallachan (meaning 'hidden treasure' in Gaelic), ready to be sold.

As for the taste, well, it's an odd one, the closest thing being perhaps sherry. Naturally, Humphrey recommends this fermented whey be served with its former solid counterpart, a slice of his Lanark Blue cheese.


OGCASTLE, SOUTH LANARKSHIRE

## Lanark Blue

Scotland isn't really well known for its cheeses, which is strange as it has a long tradition of making sheep's milk cheese. At the beginning of the seventeenth century, women made hard sheep's milk cheeses and used them both to pay rents and tributes, as well as to see them through the long winter. The Industrial Revolution in eighteenth-century mill towns saw women leave the land to work in the mills, and as cheese-making was seen as women's work, the skill began to die out. In fact, women were in such demand that between 1740 and 1800, wages for farm girls went up 400 per cent. This, coupled with the Scottish Enlightenment's promotion of modern, Cheddar-style production, saw the amount of farmhouse cheese made from sheep's milk greatly reduced.

Today, Cheddar-style hard cheeses make up the majority of Scottish cheese production, and there are some very good ones too, including the Reades' on the Isle of Mull. As for sheep's milk cheese, look no further than Humphrey Errington's Lanark Blue, said to be the first blue sheep's cheese made in Britain for over a century.

It's made from the milk of Humphrey's own flock of 400 sheep, which are kept high on the hills. The *Penicillium roqueforti* (Humphrey won't tell me which particular strain) mould is added at the beginning of the production process, along with rennet, and once the curds have separated and been shaped they are dipped in brine twice. After four weeks they're wrapped in foil to stall further mould growth, and left to mature, being turned three times a week.

People have described the cheese as a Scottish Roquefort, something Humphrey doesn't necessarily agree with. 'The climate, the sheep and the soil are totally different there.' In the mouth it has an almost rusty, coppery tang, the mould possessing a much greener hue than most blue cheeses. This is balanced with a pillow-soft creaminess. Humphrey's cheeses are all a little bit different, depending on the mood of the sheep, the weather, the time of year and many other factors. On the business of making cheese he says, 'Sometimes your job is more that of an attentive observer; there's not too much you can do.'

See also BRITISH CHEESE (p. 290).

SCOURIE, HIGHLAND
# *Loch Duart salmon*

Salmon is often regarded as the king of fish, and as Scottish as the stag on land and the eagle in the air. It's perhaps for this reason that while the domestication and farming of cattle and sheep started in the UK around 4000 BC, the farming of salmon only began in the 1960s. The technique was developed in Norway, and Norwegian firms still dominate the industry, which produces around 1.5 million tons of farmed salmon a year. There is a great deal of concern about the process: farmed salmon can have a detrimental effect on the wild population by spreading disease; and food for the carnivorous salmon is difficult to source sustainably.

Loch Duart salmon are farmed as sustainably as possible

Swimming against this tide, then, is Loch Duart, who have put responsible environmental and welfare policies at the heart of their business. The company was formed in 1999 by Nick Joy and Andy Bing, who met at and later bought out Joseph Johnson's, a salmon netting company that began farming in 1975. Immediately, Nick set about implementing unique production methods. 'Nick's aim was to find a system that was the best for the fish and best for the environment. The economic and commercial requirements were put to one side while this was worked out,' says Andy. The most important step they took was allowing sites to lie fallow for a whole year, much longer than the statutory six to eight weeks required between batches. 'This means we come back to pristine waters, and as a result get better growth rates and a massively reduced risk of spreading any disease or contamination.' Another key step was to reduce stocking densities, giving the fish more room to move, grow and exercise. Finally, they addressed the thorny issue of the fishes' food by sourcing it from sustainable populations of other fish as defined by the United Nations Food and Agriculture Organization. The result of all this effort was the RSPCA Freedom Foods endorsement for their fish in 2002.

All of this obviously has an impact on costs, and Loch Duart salmon costs about 30 per cent more than the market price. 'We have the environmental, ethical and welfare policies that please our customers, but if it doesn't taste nice or any better than something 30 per cent cheaper, it's no good,' says Andy. Luckily, their methods also make for a superior product, and it's no surprise that chefs who are serious about flavour and taste call for Loch Duart. It's the salmon of choice in the Loch Fyne Smokehouse, and the Brown and Forrest smokery in Somerset. Loch Duart then, take the long view. 'We take as a yardstick the idea that we want to be doing this in 200 years' time,' says Andy. The only way to ensure that will happen is by the continued use of their sustainable practices.

See also DERWENTWATER, CUMBRIA (p. 102); DOVER, KENT (p. 473); GLOUCESTER, GLOUCESTERSHIRE (p. 288); HASTINGS, EAST SUSSEX (p. 483); MARKET HARBOROUGH, LEICESTERSHIRE (p. 340); NEWLYN, CORNWALL (pp. 32 and 34); RIVER SEVERN, GLOUCESTERSHIRE (p. 305); SOUTHEND-ON-SEA, ESSEX (p. 455); WANSFORD, EAST YORKSHIRE (p. 261); WHITBURN, TYNE & WEAR (p. 228).

STENHOUSEMUIR, FALKIRK

# Highland Toffee and Wham bars

When I was a child, an ice-cream van that went by the name of Levaggi's used to visit the neighbourhood. All the kids in the area would immediately stop playing or fighting and run after it as if it were the Pied Piper. Twenty-five pence bought you an ice-cream cone, and left enough change for a Highland Toffee bar. After the softness of the ice cream, the bar was something to get your teeth into, or more likely out of, as its chewy sticking power was apt to relieve you of your milk teeth if you weren't careful. This fine attribute was noted in verse by the poet Bruce C. Dick:

> *Nae Curlywurlys or sherbet dabs, or cissy sweeties please,*
> *Gie me something that dislocates ma jaw,*
> *An draws fillings, like shelling peas.*

Highland Toffee bars are made by the New McCowan's Scotland, which started in 1844 when John Millar, a baker, began selling sweets as a sideline. The business has since been owned by Nestlé, and the Dutch confectioner Phideas. It's now owned by businessmen Graham Wallace and Andy Allan.

Highland Toffee was originally called a 'penny dainty', and over the years has evolved from the slab you had to break on the kerb to more of a chewing toffee that provides a workout for your jaw and tongue.

However, the stables of McCowan's harbour another confectionery thoroughbred and childhood favourite that is as modern and futuristic as Highland Toffee is traditional: the Wham bar. Invented in 1982 around the same time Messrs Michael and Ridgeley were debuting on *Top of the Pops*, it is instantly recognisable to anyone who grew up in the 1980s. Chewy, Day-Glo pink and studded throughout with fizzing sugar nuggets, it was the taste of the future.

It cost 10p back then, and although it's only 20p today, its size has been reduced by a third. The original flavour was raspberry, mainly thanks to the presence of E122, E124, E104 and E133. Today the company make over half a million Wham bars a week in a range of flavours, which means there must be a whole new generation discovering its sugary, chewy, space-dust-flavoured high.

*See also* EVENWOOD, COUNTY DURHAM (p. 210); GREAT YARMOUTH, NORFOLK (p. 432).

TAIN, HIGHLAND
## Cranachan, or cream crowdie

With ingredients including oatmeal, double cream, raspberries, honey and whisky, cranachan is all the best bits of Scotland in one pudding. It makes for a truly delicious and decadent dessert, one you'll often see at a Scottish wedding banquet, or at a Burns' Night dinner in darkest January (at which it isn't particularly seasonal). People do play fast and loose with the recipe, though. Blueberries or strawberries – indeed any soft fruit – often usurp the raspberry, and straight whisky regularly contends with its sweetened cousin Drambuie as an addition. Traditionally, cranachan was eaten in late summer at harvest time, and would have been a much more modest concoction. Wild berries were there for the picking and there would have been plenty of oatmeal available, but a crofter's supply of whisky would have been too important to use in a mere pudding, and instead of double cream, crowdie cheese would have been used. Indeed, the pudding still goes by the name 'cream crowdie' in some parts.

Crowdie is a soft cheese, creamy yet crumbly, not unlike a thick cottage cheese but with a lemony level of acidity. A simple cheese known from Viking times, it would have been made every day by the crofters of the Highlands, as it would have been a great way to preserve surplus milk. First the cream was removed and churned into butter for use in the kitchen, then the remaining skimmed milk was warmed gently by the fire, where it would sour and set. The curds were then separated off, lightly salted and sometimes added to buttermilk or fresh cream, which would result in crowdie.

As with much of our native artisan cheese-making, crowdie production all but died out after the Second World War. Credited with its survival and resurgence in the 1960s, however, is one Susannah Stone, from the village of Tain, Highland. She was, by her son Rory's admission, 'a lousy dairy farmer', and one day when the Milk Marketing Board refused to take her milk she decided to have a go at turning it into crowdie. 'She brought a ten-gallon pail into the house and set it in warm water in the bath for three days,' says Rory. The addition of some rennet helped it to set, and the curds were hung to drain in a pillowcase over the same bath. 'At the time my father often complained that you couldn't get crowdie any more, but even he didn't want that much, so they wrapped some in wax paper and sold it to the local greengrocer.' From this haphazard start the small business grew into Highland Fine Cheeses, and Rory still makes Highland Crowdie, as well as some other excellent cheeses including Strathdon Blue. 'Crowdie's not really a gourmet cheese, though – it's rather simple.' Other cheese producers have also tried their hand at making crowdie, and although its future looks more rosy, Rory cautions, 'We still need more Scottish cheese-makers, there aren't enough of us!'

See also BRITISH CHEESE (p. 290).

ULLAPOOL, HIGHLAND
## The Lorne sausage

The Lorne sausage is one of those Scottish foods that you would have thought would cross easily into England – like porridge and whisky. However, it's rarely seen south of the border. Why should this be so? It is simply beef (or sometimes pork) minced, seasoned, patted into a loaf tin and set in the fridge before being taken out, sliced, then grilled or fried. It's certainly a Scottish delicacy, albeit one that's not particularly delicate. 'Years ago, Lorne's what you'd make after you'd made everything else,' jokes Jonathan Crombie of

Crombie's in Edinburgh, who sell Lorne alongside around forty other types of sausage. They are a bit of an anomaly, though, as Lorne is primarily a west-coast dish.

Dave Gordon of Ullapool is a fan. His Lorne took the award for best sliced Scottish sausage in a Scottish Federation of Meat Traders competition in 2008. Dave cuts his Lorne to roughly two and a half centimetres, which is a lot thicker than the normal slice of just over one centimetre. 'When it's thin, you really notice if it shrinks in the pan, and you can tell it's not made from the best ingredients,' he tells me.

It's a dish that's ripe for tweaks and reinvention, and Patrick's of Camelon in Falkirk offer a couple of interesting riffs on the theme: 'Black heart sausage', which is steak sliced sausage with black pudding running through the middle, and 'Brave heart sausage', which features haggis.

The commonly held view – though probably apocryphal – is that it's named after Tommy Lorne (1890–1935), a comedian born in Kirkintilloch and raised in Cowcaddens, Glasgow. Tommy wore a kilt and Glengarry cap on stage and delivered killer catchphrases like 'Sausages are the boys!' and 'In the name of the wee man!' in a shrill, high-pitched voice. When he died after a lifelong battle with the booze, over 3,000 people came to his funeral. In all likelihood, however, it was around before Tommy; indeed, it goes by the name of square sausage, sliced sausage or even Larne sausage elsewhere in the country, particularly on the west coast. The town of Larne sits just across the Irish Sea in Northern Ireland, to the north of Belfast.

Nevertheless, no matter how it got its name, the point remains that a Lorne sausage, like its cylindrical brothers, can be made either well or badly. We're beginning to get a taste for well-made versions of Britain's regional sausages, and maybe soon the well-made Lorne will head south.

*See also* SAUSAGES (p. 122).

# 5 | The North-East

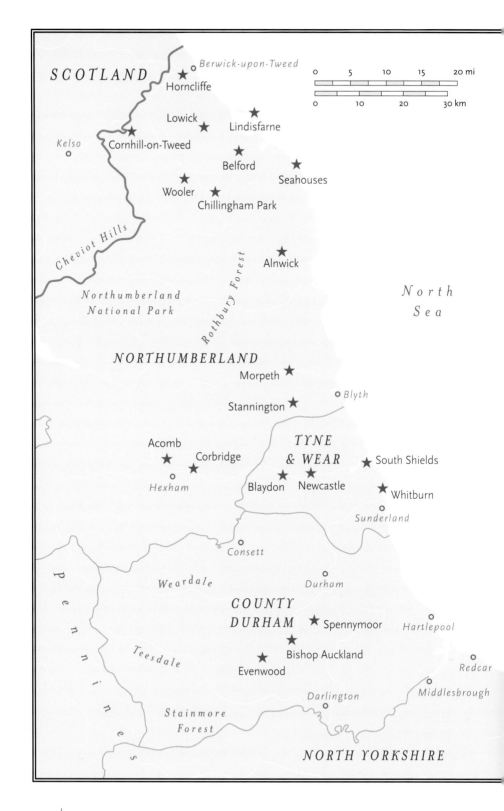

SCOTLAND

Berwick-upon-Tweed
★○
Horncliffe

Kelso
○

Lowick
★
Lindisfarne
★

Cornhill-on-Tweed
★

Belford
★

Seahouses
★

Wooler
★

Chillingham Park
★

Cheviot Hills

Northumberland
National Park

Rothbury Forest

Alnwick
★

North
Sea

NORTHUMBERLAND

Morpeth
★

Stannington
★

Blyth
○

Acomb
★

Corbridge
★

Hexham
○

TYNE
& WEAR

Blaydon
★

Newcastle
★

South Shields
★

Whitburn
★

Sunderland
○

Consett
○

Weardale

Durham
○

Pennines

COUNTY
DURHAM

Spennymoor
★

Hartlepool
○

Teesdale

Evenwood
★

Bishop Auckland
★

Darlington
○

Redcar
○

Middlesbrough
○

Stainmore
Forest

NORTH YORKSHIRE

# Squirrel from Ridley's Fish and Game

Everyone knows that the American grey squirrel has, like some furry William the Conqueror, been driving the native red squirrel out of England, and that the north-east is home to one of the last remaining populations in England. As with the mitten crab in the Thames (*see* p. 374), one idea for checking the progress of the interloper is to eat it. Previously the only people who would countenance this were those survivalist types who were probably more into the killing and preparation of the meat than the eating. Searches for recipes often tend to throw up things like Cajun squirrel stew and other good ol' boy cookin'. However, around the time of the Second World War, the Vicomte de Mauduit, a French nobleman, published *They Can't Ration These*, in which he describes the squirrel as 'more tasty and tender than chicken', and recommends treating it in a similar manner. The egg-laying chicken, after all, would have been far too precious to kill.

David and Carolyn Ridley of Ridley's Fish and Game sell whole skinned grey squirrel for £3.95 alongside a great deal more game and fish. 'They're tricky to skin,' says Carolyn. The best technique they've found is to singe the fur with a blowtorch (this also does away with any fleas the animal may have), which loosens the skin, allowing it to come off in one piece. The squirrels come from all over the north-east and are caught in booby-trapped cages, then dispatched with a swift shot with an air gun to the head. Most of the interest in them comes from the south, particularly London chefs looking for something different to put on the menu – so much so it's hard to keep up with demand.

The Ridleys can be found in the shop unit near Hexham most days, and at farmers' markets and fairs throughout the year. They can also be found in London's Borough Market on occasion. They took on the firm in 1991, and since then have moved off the high street to their new unit, where everything is under one roof.

One of the easiest ways to try their game is to buy one of Carolyn's ready-made dishes: game pie; pheasant and apricot terrine; pheasant with Madeira casserole. If you fancy playing with game yourself, there are pheasant, woodcock, snipe, hares, venison, teal, widgeon, grouse, as well as squirrel for sale. It's fair to say that Ridley's really isn't your average kettle of fish.

*See also* AUCHTERMUCHTY, FIFE (p. 144); BLAXHALL, SUFFOLK (p. 419); BROMPTON-ON-SWALE, NORTH YORKSHIRE (p. 236); CHIPPENHAM, WILTSHIRE (p. 9); FRILSHAM, BERKSHIRE (p. 479); KENDAL, CUMBRIA (p. 114).

## ALNWICK, NORTHUMBERLAND
# *Alnwick Rum*

'Passionate' is a much-debased and overused word in the food business. However, in the spectrum of dedication to a cause, Ian Linsley of the Alnwick Rum Company has gone right through passionate into the ultraviolet of obsession and devotion. He not only demonstrates this fervent attitude towards his product – something that plenty of people also do towards theirs – but towards the resurrection of a company and its history, and to finish the work begun by his late father. With Ian it's personal: family pride and honour is very much at stake.

But first the story: when the Alnwick Brewery was formed in 1890, it produced many beers, including an Indian pale ale, as well as soft drinks such as ginger beer and mineral water. With the coming of the First World War, many of the brewery's raw ingredients became scarce, and so the company, like many others, turned to producing spirits imported from the West Indies. Thus Alnwick Rum was born. The company changed hands, another war came, and in 1978 Drybroughs Brewery took over, and the business lapsed and ceased trading in 1986.

Ian's father was the last chairman of the brewery, and died in 2001. The original recipe for the rum was found among his papers. By then the brewery had been demolished, and all traces of brewing beer and ageing rum in the town expunged.

Ian has devoted himself to bringing it back. He worked with Julian Falk, one of the top blenders in the country, on recreating the recipe. Alnwick is a dark rum, blended from twelve different rums from Guyana and Jamaica. At present it is blended by a company in Holland. 'There's nothing quite like it anywhere else in the world,' says Ian. He has recreated the brewery's beers too, working with Eric Lucas and the team at the Daleside Brewery in Harrogate, Yorkshire. 'I've got nothing but praise for him and his organisation,' says Ian. So the drinks are being made again; however Ian's not stopping there. 'What I really want to do is bring production back to Alnwick, all under one roof,' he says.

Interestingly, there were nine other dark rum recipes, as well as one for a white rum, among Ian's father's papers. The story of Alnwick's historic drinks isn't quite over yet.

*See also* GRANGE-OVER-SANDS, CUMBRIA (p. 107).

*See also* GRANGE-OVER-SANDS, CUMBRIA (p. 107).

ALNWICK, NORTHUMBERLAND
## *Alnwick Treehouse restaurant*

Like many a stately home, Alnwick Castle once had within its grounds a garden that would have provided fruit and vegetables for the house's occupants and staff. The small rise in temperature and shelter that a walled garden provided meant that even peaches could, with care, be grown. The technology employed ranged from simple – enclosing the space to make it warmer – to the complex, such as fires within the walls and removable bricks to regulate the air.

With most families selling up post-war, and no mouths to feed, the walled gardens often fell into a state of disrepair, and many were knocked

The Alnwick Treehouse restaurant is perched sixty feet in the air

down, turfed over or reclaimed by nature. Alnwick was no different, and was completely overrun with weeds when the current duchess of Northumberland first saw it in 1997. Since then she has set about restoring and transforming it into one of the top visitor attractions in the north-east. It now boasts the largest collection of European plants in an ornamental garden (16,500) and, uniquely, a poison garden containing belladonna, tobacco, mandrake and, by Home Office licence (and kept behind bars), the cannabis and coca plants.

It must be both a blessing and a curse for any chef whose food has to compete with such a stunning setting, but head chef Kelvin Gallagher, whose menu is enjoyed sixty feet up in the air in the Alnwick Treehouse restaurant, has literally risen to the challenge. Not only are the diners in the canopy, but his kitchens are too. This, one imagines, makes a refreshing change from the hot dark basements that form most chef's lairs.

The menu is modern and easy-going: roast lamb rump with bubble-and-squeak mash; sausages from nearby butchers Turnbull's, with white beans; and individual smoked salmon quiche, for example. 'The food's not fussy, but simple and robust,' says Kelvin. The Treehouse, while of course happy to refresh visitors to the gardens, is keen to stand tall as a destination in itself. As well as the sausages, all their meat is supplied by Turnbull's in the town, their eggs by Sunny Hill Eggs (*see* p. 200), and their smoked fish by Swallows in Seahouses (*see* p. 224). They do grow some herbs and vegetables in the adjoining gardens, but Kelvin adds, 'We could never grow enough unless we took over half the gardens, and there's no way that'll happen as the roses are much more important.'

Being a family-friendly place, children are looked after, with not only toddler-friendly pasta but also the option to have any main course half-sized at half the price for older kids. Why more places don't offer this I don't know; children, after all, are customers too. Normally, eateries attached to tourist 'destinations' are dreadful clip joints that will stiff you for your cash in return for some mediocre grub, knowing that you will probably not come back any time soon. The Treehouse is nothing like that. It's a destination in its own right that works with the best local suppliers and producers in the area. I never had a Treehouse as a child, but if I could have, I'd have wanted one like this.

# *Pease pudding*

*Pease porridge hot,*
*Pease porridge cold,*
*Pease porridge in the pot,*
*Nine days old.*

So went the old nursery rhyme, displaying blatant disregard for basic food hygiene. Pease pudding is made from split yellow peas, cooked long and slow, often with a smoked ham hock for some extra meaty body. If you like mushy peas (and you should), you'll love pease pudding; same goes if you like pulses, legumes and lentils in general. There's a comforting sloppy nuttiness to the dish, backed up by the onion, and a smokiness from the hock that seals the deal. It's great served with even more ham.

Eliza Leslie in *Miss Leslie's Complete Cookery* (1837) recommends boiling the peas in a cloth until tender, pushing them through a sieve, and then placing the mush in a clean, floured cloth and boiling for another hour; the resulting ball is then sent to the table. Pease pudding is often described as a 'traditional' dish, i.e. it was eaten by the poor, who no doubt hankered for something else, probably meat. Its main area of popularity remains the north-east, although in a thinner form it becomes a London Particular (*see* p. 409). For the full Northumberland on-the-hoof eating experience you should have it slathered over a stottie (*see* p. 222), the traditional large white bap of the region, and top it with a slice or two of ham.

Owing to the addition of ham hocks as a flavouring, pease pudding was often sold in butchers' shops, and indeed it still can be found in some. Mark Turnbull is the fifth Turnbull behind the counter at Turnbull's butchers in Alnwick. Here they sell maybe two dozen pease-pudding-and-ham sandwiches a day, as well as pies, meats and the full range of quality meat you would expect from a Q Guild-registered butcher (an organisation noted for extolling the skill and quality of traditional independent butchers, it is the premiere league of butchery in the UK). Mark also sells pease pudding in tubs ready to reheat, and has been experimenting with selling a pease pudding kit. 'The way we do pease pudding is just yellow split peas boiled in ham stock.' The peas are put in a cooking sack, which is a commercial product, and so Mark is working on finding one suitable for home use. 'What I'm trying to do is take what we do commercially and make it compatible with the home cook.' At the end of the day, pease pudding is cooked pulses, flavoured with additions and reduced to a smooth consistency; just think of it as hot Geordie hummus, pet.

*See also* STOTTIES (p. 222); AMBERGATE, DERBYSHIRE (p. 275); STRAND, WESTMINSTER (p. 409).

BELFORD, NORTHUMBERLAND
## Chickens from Sunny Hill Eggs

When I was a child we kept chickens in the garden and I used to love collecting the eggs – this wasn't in some rural idyll, however: just inner-city Coventry. Someone who has to collect slightly more eggs than I did is Christine Jackson of Sunny Hill Eggs in Northumberland. Her free-range flock of 57,000 hens produces around 340,000 eggs a week. 'After foot and mouth, DEFRA offered farmers a health check on their farms and suggested ways to improve the business. The chap suggested free-range hens, and Dad just laughed at him, but then the idea developed,' she says. Christine spent some time learning how to look after hens and had planned to help her family set up the business, and then get a proper job. 'But it didn't really happen like that,' she laughs.

The cunning fox is the nemesis of free-range chickens everywhere, and so the Jacksons mix the hens in with sheep. 'If there's other livestock in the paddock it gives them security to range further.' And just in case any foxes get past them, there are two pet llamas backing them up. 'Llamas are very protective of their area,' she adds.

'You really want to keep your grass lush in the summer, as this attracts more wildlife, most of which the hens like to eat,' Christine told me. Insects, worms, grass, seeds and even pecking around sheep droppings all make for tasty eggs. Christine explained how to get the best out of them: 'Eggs are 90 per cent water, and over time this evaporates through the shell.' If your egg is spanking fresh, poaching is a doddle. The white will be firm and hold together. Consequently if your egg's getting on a bit, it's best to boil. Shelling a freshly laid egg that's been boiled is a nightmare as it'll all stick to the shell.'

As for the chickens, when they go off the lay it's not the back of the outhouse door for them, but the food services industry, to be made into pies or soup. Some, however, Christine gives to customers as pets. 'If we can keep the hen happy, it'll keep us happy. If the hen has no stress it'll produce really good-quality eggs, and that's what we're all about.'

*See also* ALDERLEY EDGE, CHESHIRE (p. 97).

BISHOP AUCKLAND, COUNTY DURHAM
## Northumberland rice cake

'When I was a child I can remember at Christmas you always offered visitors a slice of rice cake, a slice of fruit cake and a piece of cheese,' says Ann Hustwitt, former home economics teacher and, more recently, artisan cake baker.

Ann started the business in the 1990s with fellow farmer's wife Hilary Jenkins, who has since retired. Initially, she did all the baking at home in her farmhouse kitchen, but as the orders grew she moved to a commercial kitchen at Bishop Auckland in the Dales.

She makes traditional North Country cakes based on old family recipes, of which her rice cake is just one. In the past it would have just been called rice cake, but Ann added the 'Northumberland' prefix so people would know where it's from.

'I've noticed in the shops that there are things called rice cakes,' she says of the styrofoam-style discs munched by dieters. 'Well, they're not our rice cakes . . . they're not very interesting at all.' Ann's is a plain cake – no icing or other adornment – with an almost al dente texture. It's light as a feather but with some of that molar-filling chewiness you sometimes get when eating risotto. Ann uses ground rice rather than the rice flour called for in some recipes, as well as ordinary self-raising flour to give it some lift. The only other ingredients are butter, sugar, fresh farm eggs and ground almonds.

The history of the dish is an interesting one, and various recipes abound. Edinburgh cookery teacher Mrs I. Williamson's *The Practice of Cookery and Pastry* (1854) contains three different ones. *The Housekeepers' Guide* (1838) by Esther Copley also contains a recipe, and points out that 'the cake is often used for holding a trifle'. Some other recipes over the years have called for lemon juice to be added. The cake always appears to have been associated with the festive period, perhaps because it was a nice, light cake that went down well after Christmas dinner.

# Mincemeat

The first bite of the first mince pie of Christmas kicks off a month of eating, drinking and making merry. The crumbly pastry gives way to a boozy aroma, after which comes the sticky, sweet and tangy taste of the mincemeat. The elegance of the filling is that it represents a culmination of the year's produce. Its main ingredients come from the balmy days of summer: firm-fleshed grapes that go on to become wizened raisins and sultanas; bright, acidic lemon and orange that mellow to become candied peel. To these, autumn's apples and plums are added, along with nutmeg, ginger and cinnamon, and all this comes together to be enjoyed in the depths of winter.

The ancestor of today's dainty individual mince pies is the medieval Christmas pie, made with a filling of finely chopped beef, shredded suet and apples. To these were added more costly ingredients such as raisins, spices and sugar. However, in the late 1800s, tastes shifted and the meatless version we're all familiar with today became more popular. Yet the name of mincemeat remains, a situation that must wind up today's trading standards officers no end. The last trace of anything animal in a mince pie today is the suet in the filling. This is made from the fat surrounding the animal's kidneys, although more often than not these days this is replaced with a vegetarian substitute.

Despite being associated solely with Christmas, mincemeat (or at least something very similar to it) features all year round in the Eccles cake (*see* p. 103) and its near neighbour the Chorley cake. The Banbury cake also features a spiced currant mixture (*see* p. 321), as do Coventry God Cakes (*see* p. 287) and baked apples. The food writer Nigel Slater believes mincemeat is well worth using throughout all of the winter months, and has a recipe for a mincemeat crumble cake.

Mince-pie fan Stephen Greenslade begins his annual appraisal of commercial mince pies sometime around mid September, when the first pies start appearing in the supermarkets. Stephen runs www.mincepieclub.co.uk, where every year since 2006 he and his fellow members have sampled, tasted, evaluated and scored as many mince pies as possible. 'The worst ones are the diet versions or budget lines. The pastry's poor and the mincemeat is little more than brown goo,' says Stephen. At the other end of the scale sit the more gourmet offerings of luxury brands. 'A good mince pie should have a dusting of granulated sugar, pastry that won't crumble too much and a filling that's not too sweet. You should be able to taste the fruit and the spice.'

Ann and the ladies who work for her have a combined age of . . . well, let's call it a wealth of experience gleaned from life. They come from a generation for whom baking was an everyday task, and the cakes they produce – Ann's Dales fruit cake is another sterling example – are imbued with know-how. They are, to borrow a phrase, exceedingly good.

*See also* ALBERT EMBANKMENT, LAMBETH (p. 368); ALDERLEY EDGE, CHESHIRE (p. 96); ECCLES, GREATER MANCHESTER (p. 103); HOOK NORTON, OXFORDSHIRE (p. 328); LLANDEILO, CARMARTHENSHIRE (p. 74); MANCHESTER, GREATER MANCHESTER (p. 119); MELTON MOWBRAY, LEICESTERSHIRE (p. 341); NAVENBY, LINCOLNSHIRE (p. 344); OTLEY, WEST YORKSHIRE (p. 252); STANBRIDGE, BEDFORDSHIRE (p. 360); WHITBY, NORTH YORKSHIRE (p. 269).

## BLAYDON, TYNE & WEAR
### Sorbet from Beckleberry's

Sorbets were the original ice-based desserts, made from fruit and other flavourings such as honey, and mixed with snow. *Larousse Gastronomique*, the French tome on everything culinary, tells us that they came to Persia via the Chinese, and indeed the word is derived from the Arabic for 'drink'.

Today we take readily available ice for granted, but in pre-refrigeration times owning an ice house, and serving sorbet as part of your lavish dinner in the height of summer, was a bold statement. Refreshing and simple, modern sorbets are tempered with sugar and a spirit of some description, the booze lowering the melting point of the ice and providing a bit of 'warmth' in the mouth. They were often served between courses in large banquets and formal dinners to cleanse the palate.

With our modern triumvirate of starter, main course and pudding there would appear to be little room for the traditional role played by the sorbet. Peter Craig of Beckleberry's in Blaydon begs to differ. He started the business in 1996 with his father, Ian. Neither had any experience in food production: Ian had just retired from the National Coal Board and Peter had just sat his A levels. Initially they produced ice creams, followed by patisserie and desserts in 1999 and sorbets soon after. His father applied his engineering mind to their production. The process takes water, sugar and dextrose up to boiling point before being homogenised and cooled to form a base mix. It's to this that the final flavours are added, mixed and left to freeze.

Sorbet, once a status symbol, is now refreshingly simple

If you're after something special, Peter even accepts commissions to produce bespoke flavours. Not all are a good idea, however: 'We turned down a request to produce a tobacco sorbet,' he laughs. The request came at the time of the introduction of the smoking ban in England.

Peter tells me his sorbets work as desserts, amuse-bouches, or accompaniments to other ingredients in a complete dish. Their blackcurrant and kirsch sorbet beat off 4,755 products to be named Supreme Champion at the Great Taste Awards in 2008. Their other sorbets include mango, chilli and ginger, which can accompany something like grilled spicy tiger prawns, and a gin and tonic one, which would work equally well before dinner began, or even with oysters. Think of them as grown-up ice pops.

## CHILLINGHAM PARK, NORTHUMBERLAND
## *Wild cattle*

In the UK today, there are some fabulous examples of ancient rare-breed and wild meats for those looking for a taste of the past. You can now get wild boar, Manx Loaghtan sheep (*see* p. 110), and of course feathered and furred game easily. For beef, traditional breeds such as the Highland and the Longhorn are still farmed, but for a really rare breed you need look no further than the Chillingham herd in Northumberland. These animals are now too rare to eat, but in the past they would have graced many a Northumberland table. The herd is looked after by a charitable trust, and Richard Marsh, who spent fifteen years as a prison officer, is their current warden. 'They've not been bred with other cattle and have evolved a genetic system which is quite separate. They've survived inbreeding depression, and now they are effectively all identical twins.'

The borderland between England and Scotland was a lawless place from medieval times right up until the Tudor dynasty. Chillingham Castle, under the Grey family and later the Earls of Tankerville, was a staging post for many English attacks on Scotland, and consequently was often besieged by Scottish armies bent on revenge. With the terrain unsuitable for farming crops, keeping cattle – and the capture and theft of them by reivers on both sides – became the norm. And so the ancestors of the Chillingham herd existed in a tough and wild environment. Some say they're descended from pre-Roman, even Ice Age, breeds; others think they're more recent; but they've been at Chillingham for at least the past 700 years, and the wild Northumbrian landscape has played its part in shaping them. In the harsh winter of 1947 the herd was reduced to just thirteen animals, but they pulled back and survived. Today, they remain the most feral cattle in the country. 'We can't get near them – get in under twenty yards and they'll charge,' says Richard, adding, 'To stand twenty yards away from two bulls who are fighting is incredible. Farmers today pay £5,000, £6,000 for a stud bull. They're not going to want another bull to come up and bash it about. Whereas in our field we've got fifty bulls. And of course the strongest ones get to breed and pass on their genes, which has helped them survive.' Indeed, Charles Darwin even mentioned these animals in his studies on evolution. 'They're lean-looking animals, with no fat on them,' says Richard.

The Northumbrian herd now numbers eighty-eight (there is another herd: after an outbreak of foot-and-mouth in the 1960s, a bull and two heifers were moved to Scotland; they've now bred and this herd numbers twenty animals), and so the population doesn't get too dense in the Chillingham corral, there may have to be a cull. Wild, untamed, feral, and smaller than today's domesticated cattle, these animals would have provided meat that the very rich would have eaten at feasts and banquets. Indeed, Richard tells me there are references to them being killed to feed the local population in the 1750s, and occasionally for Christmas in the nineteenth century. I wonder what the meat tastes like?

*See also* STONELEIGH PARK, WARWICKSHIRE (p. 313).

CORBRIDGE, NORTHUMBERLAND
## *Pick your own strawberries at Brocksbushes*

Farmers have been unfairly stigmatised as grumpy curmudgeons prone to shout 'Geroff moi laaand!' at would-be wanderers. The fact, though, is that many farmers have been saying 'Please come on to my land and pick some fruit' for years now. Pick-your-own became popular with the rise of the environmental movement of the 1970s, with around 10,000 farms offering some form of self-service option (it's perhaps no coincidence that there was a fuel crisis and recession around at that time, too).

A change in affluence and the move by supermarkets to year-round stocking saw a number of farmers quit the practice, and now there are only about 1,000 pick-your-own venues in the UK. Brocksbushes in the Tyne Valley is one. The farm is situated near one of the A69's roundabouts, so is very easy to reach. Caroline Dickinson and her late husband started with a few strawberry bushes. A farm shop soon followed, selling other local foods. Then, perhaps unsurprisingly, people kept asking for a cup of tea, so they put a vending machine in the shop. Caroline, who trained as a chef, then battled the council for planning permission to build a tea room. Staff numbers have increased, new products and recipes have been developed and now she's running one of the north-east's top destinations for a day out.

Between July and October you can pick strawberries, raspberries, gooseberries, tayberries, plums and blackcurrants, as well as seasonal vegetables. Caroline doesn't even mind if you help yourself to a few while going round, considering it her 'try before you buy' policy. It's not often you can do that in a shop, is it? But it makes sense in the field: fruit is never going to be as fresh or as sweet as when it's just been plucked from a bush.

After you've toiled in the field and harvested nature's bounty, you can fortify yourself with a nice cup of tea and a sit-down in their café, before picking up a few things in the farm shop next door. A slice of home-made cake or a scone served with jam made with fruit from the farm wouldn't hurt either. Today, the benefits of PYO have never been more apparent. It's like slow shopping: you can take your time, get some fresh air and sunshine, and appreciate how harvesting the ingredient can be part of the enjoyment. In short, it is good for the soul.

*See also* EGTON BRIDGE, NORTH YORKSHIRE (p. 243); HAMPRESTON, DORSET (p. 14); HONITON, DEVON (p. 17); INVERGOWRIE, PERTH & KINROSS (p. 180); LYTH AND WINSTER VALLEYS, CUMBRIA (p. 117); NORTHIAM, EAST SUSSEX (p. 492); WALMERSLEY, GREATER MANCHESTER (p. 137); WIMBLEDON, MERTON (p. 415).

## CORNHILL-ON-TWEED, NORTHUMBERLAND
### *Heritage potatoes from Tiptoe Farm*

The potato is a great staple food, able to provide a large amount of our daily dietary needs. It's easy to grow and produces more calories per acre than any other crop in any climate – no wonder it's popular. In 2007, potato farmers harvested more than 325 million tonnes on an estimated 193,000 square kilometres of farmland – the equivalent of all the world's potatoes being grown on land about the size of England and Scotland put together. There are many different varieties of potato, some bearing higher yields, and some

Carroll's potatoes come in all shapes, sizes and colours

cropping less often but tasting better; commercial farming, perhaps unsurprisingly, tends to favour the former.

Anthony Carroll's family have farmed the same sixty-acre site at Tiptoe Farm in the River Till Valley since the 1930s, growing modern commercial potatoes and selling them via a potato co-operative. In 1986, when he and his wife Lucy took over, they began to realise that sixty acres was, well, small potatoes, and that if they wanted to make any kind of decent return on the commercial varieties they would have to start dealing in much larger numbers. They had been growing a few heritage varieties in the garden for their own use, and in 2002 they decided to try an acre or two of these varieties and take them to the nearby farmers' market at Berwick-upon-Tweed. They proved a big hit with people looking for something new and different.

The French call the potato 'the apple of the earth', and like the apple, the potato has some fantastically named specimens: Pink Fir, Red Duke of York, Salad Blue and Dumbarton Rover sound like the starting line at the 3.30 at Doncaster. But if you want to try something local to the north-east (insofar as a tuber of Peruvian origin can be), try Mr Littles's Yetholm Gypsy. This variety was said to have been bought by William Little, a shepherd in the village of Yetholm, from a Gypsy at the first Yetholm Fair in the 1940s, although the variety probably existed long before then. It is unusual because it is the only potato with a red, white and blue skin. Lucy recommends boiling or steaming it with the skin on to show off the colours, which remain bright even after cooking.

*See also* MARAZION, CORNWALL (p. 28); NEWCASTLE, TYNE & WEAR (p. 218); SHEFFIELD, SOUTH YORKSHIRE (p. 260).

## EVENWOOD, COUNTY DURHAM
### *Loopy Lisa's Fudge*

There was once a Lord Snooty comic strip in the *Beano* where Aunt Matilda beat the eponymous aristo at an arm wrestle. She attributed her strength to constantly mixing cake for Snooty and his pals to scoff. I'm not certain, but Lisa Hodgson of Loopy Lisa's Fudge would probably do rather well in an arm wrestle too, as she mixes and beats all her fudge by hand. Quite a feat when you consider that each batch needs stirring, on and off, for hours, and that at any one time there will be six batches on the go. 'Everything is done by hand. When it's in the pan and coming to heat you need to stir it fast so it doesn't catch.' However, speed on its own isn't enough. 'When the mix is cooling and setting and you're adding more flavours, such as nuts, you need strength too.' The pan of liquid fudge can weigh nearly two kilos, which has to be lifted with one hand while it is scraped out with the other. All this handiwork is worth it, though, because this interaction with the mix lets Lisa judge when things are ready.

Lisa began making fudge while at university and continued making small batches as a hobby until 2004, when she decided to go into business. Initially she sold it to a few local shops. But things took off a year later when she had her first pitch at the Dales Festival of Food and Drink. 'I ended my office job on a Wednesday, made lots of fudge over the Thursday and Friday and on the Saturday started selling,' says Lisa.

The most popular flavour is vanilla, which contains Madagascan vanilla extract and accounts for 40 per cent of Lisa's trade. Then there are interesting chocolate or nut versions, such as the cardamom and pistachio, and, for the very adventurous, chilli fudge. 'We've gone for flavour over heat, which is why we use dried smokey chipotle chillies,' says Lisa. However, the most intriguing for me has to be her beer fudge, in which beer replaces the water added to the sugar, butter and condensed milk. 'The first time we tried it we just put the beer in, but as the mix came to the boil a frothy head formed and it began to boil over.' It was out with the elbow grease to clean the sticky beery mess from the cooker. Undaunted, they tried another technique, namely simmering the beer to remove a lot of the gas before adding it to the fudge mix.

Some of the finest food historians have lost huge chunks of their lives in the search for the definitive history of fudge. They emerge blinking in the daylight years later, and still none the wiser. There is anecdotal and circumstantial evidence of it being made in women's Ivy League colleges on the American East Coast. Others link it to Scottish tablet (a medium-hard confection traditionally made from sugar and cream). Lisa's fudge is crumbly in the mouth with a dry texture, rather than the smooth chewy version you often see in Devon tourist shops. Initially, you get a wham of sweetness from the sugar, but after that the added flavour lingers: the raspberry ripple leaves a tartness; the rum and raisin a little chewy morsel in your molars. You can perform your own, less strenuous arm-workout exercise by moving pieces of it repeatedly to your mouth.

*See also* GREAT YARMOUTH, NORFOLK (p. 432); STENHOUSEMUIR, FALKIRK (p. 189).

## Chain Bridge Honey Farm

Willie Robson, aged sixty-three, comes from a long line of beekeepers, and has been dealing in all things bee-related for most of his working life. Over the years, Willie and his family have built their honey farm, Chain Bridge, into a food destination. They have added a fascinating visitor centre, a café, a shop and two Routemaster buses (including a Number 12, which I used to catch to Camberwell in my twenties). The hives – over 2,000 of them – are scattered around Northumbria and parts of southern Scotland in a forty-mile radius, and the bees are moved three times a year. In spring they're placed near oilseed rape and wildflowers, which produces a light sweet honey, and in July they're moved to heather moors, which produces a darker, richer honey; then during the autumn they're put in a sheltered spot so that they will survive the cold winter months.

The visitor-centre walls are decorated with panels illustrated by calligrapher Dorien Irving and intricate murals painted by artist Tony Johnson, which lends the whole place a religious feel, almost as if it were a chapel

Chain Bridge's honey varieties are drawn from over 2,000 hives

dedicated to the bee. There are exhibits on mead, on the bee in coats of arms (including that of Manchester, where it is a symbol of Manchester's industry), and on bee-keeping in medieval times, as well as a blow-by-blow account of modern honey production. At Chain Bridge, though, they don't stop at honey: candles, furniture polish and cosmetics such as lip balms and ointments are also produced; nothing is wasted.

As some of you are no doubt aware, all is not well in the world of bee-keeping at the moment. 'Disease is the biggest problem,' says Willie. The most worrying of these is caused by varroa, a mite that lives on the bee and weakens it by feeding on its blood. On top of that there is the effect of insecticides and organophosphates used by other agricultural sectors, not to mention a dwindling supply of experience and knowledge in the industry. And like any other type of farming, bee-keeping is very much beholden to the British weather. A cold winter, followed by a damp spring or summer, and the bees can't get out to collect the pollen they need, which can result in the hive starving. The bees in Willie's hives (*Apis mellifera*) are native to Northern Europe and are, for now at least, doing OK. 'We've got to study all we've learned in a lifetime and stick to these principles,' says Willie.

*See also* LINDISFARNE, NORTHUMBERLAND (p. 213); TOWER BRIDGE (p. 411).

# Lindisfarne Mead

Mead, an alcoholic drink made from honey fermented with yeast and water, was your average Viking's lubricant of choice. It conjures up images of the epic *Beowulf*, and the telling of sagas of great and noble deeds in mead halls. It is probably the first booze mankind ever brewed, probably because it is incredibly easy to make, and for those who fancy getting sticky, a quick trawl of the Internet reveals plenty of tutorials. It has a long history here in the UK, and a lovely chapter in Joseph Warder's *The true Amazons: or, the monarchy of bees* (1713) entitled 'To make English Canary no way inferior to the best of Spanish Wines' tells the reader how it can be used in possets. In France it was known as *hydromel*, but in the UK this tended to denote low-alcohol versions.

Mead is interesting because it's a product that can work in a number of ways: in the summer you can chill it down and enjoy it almost like a refreshing dessert wine or limoncello; come winter, warm it slightly and it is perfect for keeping the cold from your nose round a bonfire or Christmas tree.

Mead production today tends to be a hobby craft for apiarists and specialist brewers, although a few commercial producers do remain. The largest and most well known is Lindisfarne Mead, on the Holy Island off the Northumberland coast. The company was established in the 1960s and is now headed up by Lindsay Hackett. To produce the mead, Lindsay brings in a high-quality fermented alcoholic base from Europe, which is then used to host the flavours of the honey and secret blend of herbs. Water from an artesian well is also added.

Producing a honey-based product, the Hacketts are, of course, drastically affected by the problems facing bees. Indeed, the world shortage of honey means that its price has doubled in the last six years. At present they import South American and Eastern European honey, and are also looking at products from Africa and India. Lindsay is now producing around 15,000 to 20,000 litres a year.

As well as selling the product, the brewery itself is a tourist attraction. Lindsay opened the doors to the public in 1968 (impressively ahead of the curve – nowadays nearly all breweries and distilleries offer a tour) and today around 200,000 people a year pay it a visit to see the vats. Lindsay has also developed the shop, which offers damson and sloe gin, and over

140 whiskies on the off chance that mead isn't your thing. Afterwards you can pay a visit to the nearby monastic ruins of Lindisfarne Abbey, which in 793 was razed by Viking raiders (who were no doubt under the influence).

*See also* HORNCLIFFE, NORTHUMBERLAND (p. 211); TOWER BRIDGE (p. 411);

## LINDISFARNE, NORTHUMBERLAND
### *Lindisfarne Oysters*

Christopher Sutherland's farm is surrounded on three sides by water; it's his own private peninsula. It started life as a cattle and sheep farm, but in 1989 Chris's father, John, decided to extend right down to the waves and start oyster farming on the mudflats. He was by no means the first. The monks of nearby Holy Island were the first to grow oysters here in the fourteenth century, and the practice continued for 500 years until the financial woes of the then owner Lord Tankerville put an end to it.

Christopher and his wife Helen took over in 2003 and have expanded

The Lindisfarne oyster beds with Holy Island in the background

the business. They buy oyster fry from a producer in Guernsey and seed them in nylon bags on raised trestles so that they get a good flow of water around them. As they grow, the bags are thinned out. 'It's important to give the oysters plenty of room,' says Chris.

In 2007 they shelled out for a specialist French oyster boat. This flat-bottomed barge has retractable wheels, allowing Chris and Helen to drive it out on the flats right up to the trestles and bring everything in in one go. 'It's transformed how we do things; the whole process is much more efficient,' says Chris. Before that they were doing it in small batches using a Land Rover, and it took many trips to get everything up to the shore.

Christopher farms the Pacific oyster, which, as its name suggests, is native to Japan and the Pacific coast of Asia. It long ago left its ancestral home and is now found all over the globe. Considered in some parts of the world to be detrimental to native species, it nevertheless makes up the vast majority of oysters farmed in the UK and is quite happy in our waters: the Shellfish Association of Great Britain estimates that nearly 1,300 tonnes were produced last year in 2009. It grows quicker than the native, but still takes up to two years to reach marketable size and quality. A good oyster like Chris's should be plump in the shell, and served sitting in its own personal rockpool of slightly salty water. The taste should be a little saline, and the texture of the flesh, creamy and yielding. I tend not to bolt them down, nor chew them repeatedly, but just push them against the roof of my mouth with my tongue and give them a little squeeze before swallowing.

And that's it: over two years to grow, and a mere two seconds in the mouth. 'What you get out after two years is only as good as the amount of work you put in,' says Chris.

*See also* CLACHAN, DUMFRIES & GALLOWAY (p. 153); EDINBURGH, EDINBURGH (p. 168); WEST MERSEA, ESSEX (p. 459); WHITSTABLE, KENT (p. 500).

LINDISFARNE, NORTHUMBERLAND
## *Northumberland mussels*

'It's like one big marine compost heap of their own making, but the mussels love it.' In 2004, Stephen Oldale happened across some disused mussel beds off Holy Island and obtained permission to harvest them. It is a perfect location: sheltered, yet a five-knot tide passes through, bringing plenty of algae and plankton, which is the mussels' main source of food. Owing to this diet, bottom-grown wild mussels tend to have a more mineral flavour and a deeper apricot colour. They need less salt when cooking, too.

In the eighteenth and nineteenth centuries, mussels were harvested not for food but for baiting long lines, and it wasn't until the Second World War when the decline in the fishing fleet due to U-boats and a lack of manpower made people turn once more to picking shellfish from the shore. By the 1950s, Sheffield alone was importing ten tons of mussels from Conwy in Wales each week, with many people – including Stephen's mum – cooking them as a Saturday treat for tea.

The season for mussels runs from September until about March or April, when they spawn and lose a considerable amount of their body mass. The harvest can dip in winter, though, if a lack of sunlight leads to a reduction in the amount of plankton. The old rule of thumb about only eating mussels during months with an 'R' is partly due to the season, and partly because the potential for toxins to build up is at its lowest during those months. However, the Shellfish Association of Great Britain doesn't recommend picking shellfish, especially bivalves, directly from the beach and taking them home, as all shellfish need to be purified before they're ready for sale.

Stephen harvests his by hand, picking maybe fifty kilos a time, which then spend forty-two hours in special purification tanks. Once that is done, they're checked and ready to be sold at farmers' markets, or supplied to restaurants in the area and pubs such as the Feathers Inn in Stocksfield. Mindful that these are a wild resource, he's careful about the amount he harvests, never taking too much. 'I manage rather than farm the mussels,' he says.

## LOWICK, NORTHUMBERLAND
### English chorizo from Piperfield Pork

In the late 1990s, Graham Head and his wife started Piperfield Pork with just two Middle White pigs. The Middle White has a face only a mother could love, but what it lacks in good looks, it more than makes up for in flavour. Heston Blumenthal chose Piperfield's Middle White when he made the 'perfect sausage' in his TV series *In Search of Perfection*. The small farm, which sits on an outcrop with views to the Cheviot Hills to the west and Holy Island to the east, is now home to a breeding herd of twenty-five pigs, who live in large grassy paddocks during spring and summer, and in airy pens with straw beds during the colder, wetter months.

The Middle White, according to the archives, first received official recognition in 1852 when one Joseph Tuley exhibited his pigs in the Keighley Agricultural Show in West Yorkshire. Some were deemed to be not big enough for the Large White category, but too small for the Small White, thus the 'Middle' breed was established. Sadly, the Small White became extinct in 1912, perhaps in part because the Middle White was gaining popularity due to its excellent taste. It was popular all over the UK, particularly in the capital, where it earned the nickname of 'the London Porker' as it supplied much of the city's pork. After the war, newer breeds gazumped the Middle White, and now the Rare Breeds Survival Trust has listed it as 'endangered'.

Graham's pigs are ready after thirty-two weeks (fourteen more than the standard eighteen most intensively reared ones get). The meat, which is fine grained with a good amount of fat, goes into sausages, hams, Scotch eggs, gammon and bacon, as well as being sold as pork. But it is Graham's air-dried chorizo and charcuterie, which is hung to dry in an old dovecote, that I think is most interesting. A handful of producers are beginning to address this gap in the UK market, and that can only be a good thing.

*See also* SAUSAGES (p. 122).

## *British beef jerky*

Beef jerky is one of those things that either you get or leaves you completely nonplussed. I'll be honest and say I used to fall in the latter camp until I tried Brian Bradley's British beef jerky and, like Saul on the dusty trail to Damascus, became a convert.

The 'jerking' of meat is the ancient practice of salting or drying it so it will last, and it has been practised by nearly all societies around the world. The word 'jerky' comes from the Inca word *charqui*, via the Spanish. It first appeared in English courtesy of Captain John Smith, Elizabethan explorer of the New World, whose life was once saved by Pocahontas. He referred to it as 'jerkin beef'. The jerking process became a favourite of cowboys and pioneers, and today we still associate jerky with the American Wild West. However, if there's one bit of England that feels even a tiny bit American, it's under the big skies of the north-east.

In the town of Morpeth, Northumberland, Brian Bradley makes his beef jerky. Brian was born in Lancashire, but spent time in Kansas. 'Jerky's very popular over there, my kids loved it, but when we came back to the UK in 2004 we couldn't find a good beef jerky, just this mass-produced stuff from South America,' says Brian. All his beef comes from the catering butchers Warren Butterworth in Throckley, Newcastle upon Tyne, and Brian and his small team use fifty kilos of beef a day. 'We use the knuckle,' says Brian, a cut that also goes by the name of 'thick flank' and is from the upper back leg of the animal. 'Butterworth's prepare and slice the meat for us, then it's marinated.' Their original jerky is flavoured with nothing more than salt water, but other versions include pepper, barbecue sauce, and the Cajun hot, which believe me lives up to its name. All Brian's marinades are made by hand, and contain no additives. Then it's into the drying machine, the process taking about eighteen hours, during which time the slices of beef will lose about two-thirds of their weight.

Beef jerky is never going to win any competitions for its looks: it's simply shards of thin, dry brown meat. However, even before you put it in your mouth, there is a slight umami smell to Brian's jerky, like the sort emanating from the stickiness in the bottom of the pan when you've roasted a joint. When the jerky first hits the mouth it's still quite hard; however, as you begin to chew it comes to life, releasing a burst of meaty, beefy, almost Marmitey flavour as it rehydrates, which gets your saliva glands working even more. It is literally mouth-watering.

Like jerky of old, Brian's product is a small ambient (i.e. storable at room temperature) product that is easily transportable, and so over half of his sales are via mail order. He has mailed jerky to over twenty-four different countries: 'We send a lot to troops serving in Afghanistan and Iraq.' The one country he can't send it to, however, is America, as sadly the US Department of Agriculture still have a ban on British beef.

## NEWCASTLE, TYNE & WEAR
### Pan haggerty

You've probably had Spanish potato tortilla in the UK, and many a fine-dining restaurant offers well-made potato dauphinoise. But have you ever tried pan haggerty? In the UK today there is more chance of finding Continental sliced potato-based dishes than our native one. The Potato Council's own website features recipes for layered tuna potato salad, potato pizza, farmhouse potato omelette and potato dauphinoise, but, alas, no pan haggerty.

The dish is a classic recipe born of necessity, and at its foundations is the need to use simple ingredients that will not only feed as many people as possible but also be easy to cook. First, a pan is coated with dripping, then thinly sliced potatoes, sliced onions, grated hard cheese such as Cheddar and a good twist of seasoning are built up in layers.

It's primarily associated with Northumberland (despite the county not being renowned for its hard-cheese production) but it does also have cousins to the south. Nell Heaton's 1951 book, *Traditional Recipes of the British Isles*, gives two similar 'pan' dishes attributed to the residents of County Durham, although probably enjoyed all over the north-east and Yorkshire. 'Panackelty' (sometimes spelled without the k) contains cut and diced cold meat (beef or bacon) fried with some onions and any leftover cooked vegetables. In Nell's recipe, cooked gravy or water is added, and the top covered in sliced potatoes. The lid is then fastened and the whole is cooked slowly on the range until the potatoes are tender. Another variation is 'panjotheram', which contains – yes, you've guessed it – slices of potatoes layered in a deep pie dish and moistened with boiling water. A mutton chop per person is then perched on the top and the dish is covered and baked slowly in an oven for two hours.

A symbol, perhaps, of new-found pride in our historic regional dishes, pan haggerty gives its name to a restaurant in Newcastle opened by Craig Potts and Mike Morley in October 2008. They brought in head chef Simon Wood and began to work out the menu – simple, British and tasty. 'The name came last of all,' says Craig, after Simon added it to the menu as a side dish. The staff still have to explain to many of the younger Novocastrians exactly what's in the dish, although older ones remember it from their childhoods. Simon makes his pan haggerty in large deep trays in the oven. First they're buttered, then the potato slices are layered with onions, seasoning and cheese, before a final brush of melted butter on top. 'We layer them about three inches high, then cut and portion for service,' says Craig. Of course, because it's a restaurant they have to add a little bit of showmanship, so when ordered as a starter the pan haggerty comes topped with a poached duck egg.

Ten years ago pan haggerty would have been on the critically endangered list. It's still as rare as a red squirrel, but just like those little critters it's definitely fighting back.

*See also* CORNHILL-ON-TWEED, NORTHUMBERLAND (p. 208); MARAZION, CORNWALL (p. 28); SHEFFIELD, SOUTH YORKSHIRE (p. 260).

# Newcastle Brown Ale

In 2009 the brewing of Newcastle Brown Ale (now owned by Heineken UK) moved from its ancestral home in the north-east down the A1 to Tadcaster in Yorkshire. This ended eighty-three years of brewing on Tyneside and marked either a new chapter or a final fall from grace for the iconic brown beverage.

Colonel J. Porter (originally from Burton upon Trent) began work on its development in 1925 at the Newcastle Brewery, but it took three years to get it right and the launch came in 1927, just in time for Geordies to celebrate Newcastle United winning the League that year. It was an instant hit, scooping a clutch of medals at the International Brewers' Exhibition in London the following year, and kicking off a close personal relationship between the city and the drink for most of the twentieth century. The iconic blue star featured on the bottle adorned the chests of Alan Shearer and the players at Newcastle United *circa* 1995 to 2000; indeed, the brewery was located across the road from St James' Park.

The new millennium was when things started to wobble. The word 'ale' was dropped from the label as some marketing johnny thought it sounded too olde worlde and was driving away younger consumers. However, a mere four years later it was quietly reinstated as the rebrand had had no effect on sales whatsoever. In 2000, Newcastle Brown was awarded PGI (Protected Geographical Indication) status, ensuring a quality product made to a specific recipe in a defined local area. This, however, had to be surrendered when the brewery moved out of Newcastle and across the Tyne to facilities in Gateshead in 2004.

And so with the move to Tadcaster it is now gone completely from the city. When the move to Yorkshire was announced, Jim Merrington, former commercial director at the old Newcastle brewery, said to the BBC, 'It's a very sad day for Tyneside. Not only is it the end of Newcastle Brown Ale being brewed here, it's also the end of the brewing heritage on Tyneside. There will be no major brewing plant left and it will all be small breweries again.'

And perhaps that's no bad thing, for when a large tree is felled it lets in sunlight. The Hadrian & Border Brewery do a seasonal, full-bodied nutty Tyneside Brown Ale at 4.7 per cent, and the occasional Byker Brown at 4.3 per cent, while the Northumberland Brewery do their Northumbrian Brown in a bottle.

Meanwhile, with Newcastle Brown Ale being exported to over forty countries, and a large portion of production going to the USA, current owners Heineken see potential for the brand to become a global player. But then would we just be drinking in the advertising?

*See also* ASTLEY, WARWICKSHIRE (p. 276); GREENWICH, GREENWICH (p. 378); KNIGHTWICK, WORCESTERSHIRE (p. 299); NEWCASTLE, TYNE & WEAR (BELOW); WOOLER, NORTHUMBERLAND (p. 230).

NEWCASTLE, TYNE & WEAR
## *Fentimans Botanically Brewed Beverages*

When Thomas Fentiman started making soft drinks in 1905 he chose a portrait of his Alsatian dog, Fearless, to be his company logo. By the 1950s he had five factories and offered a full range of soft drinks, including lemonade, orangeade, fruit juices, tonic waters – as well as vinegar. At the far end of one factory they brewed botanical beverages such as old-fashioned ginger beer and hop ale. These were sold in half-gallon stone jars called 'grey hens'. When the arrival of the PET (polyethylene terephthalate) plastic bottle heralded the end of smaller regional drinks makers, who couldn't afford to retool their plants, and the door-to-door pop-man method of distribution took a turn for the worse, Fentimans, like many others, hit hard times. Their last factory closed in 1970.

Then, in 1994, after working in the pub and beverage trade, Eldon Robson, current master brewer and a descendant of the founder, vowed to bring the company back to life. He decided to concentrate on the brewed botanical drinks, as the market for adult-orientated soft drinks such as Aqua Libra and Purdey's was growing in the mid 1990s. 'They were new-age products with fancy ingredients but they were still adult-orientated soft drinks,' says Eldon. 'I decided it was time to bring back the original adult soft drink. After all, brewed botanicals are live products – the real ale of soft drinks.' To do this, he needed the help and advice of a brewery, and after much searching found one in Stockport, Greater Manchester, where the drink is still produced to this day, although the company offices and research department remain in the north-east.

He began by producing 4,000 litres of brewed ginger beer, and today he brews 600,000 litres a month. Taking just under a week to brew, the drinks are ever so slightly alcoholic, at around 0.5 per cent. Unlike most soft drinks, though, their taste isn't one of cloying saccharine sweetness, just fiery ginger that is both complex and flavourful and leaves your lips tingling. Other flavourings besides ginger include capsicum, lemon and the herbs speedwell,

## Stotties

The stottie cake (known colloquially as a Tyneside croissant) is seldom seen outside its traditional habitat of the north-east. The name comes from the Geordie word 'stott', meaning 'to bounce', the theory being that these buns were so tough that they would bounce when dropped. Andrew Whitley in *Bread Matters* (2006) says his Scottish mother taught him the word, and that any potential for bouncing comes from when the stottie is flipped over halfway through the cooking process, giving it a crust on both sides.

Stotties are made from normal bread dough left over from making loaves that has only risen once. Consequently, they have a tight crumb and rise only a little. Of course, all that structural rigidity means that when used in a sandwich they are able to take fillings and toppings that would cause lesser breads to disintegrate, with pease pudding and bacon being traditional. The stottie's firmness and wide diameter makes it perfect for a chip butty: it'll take nearly a full portion of chips and probably the gravy too. It's an unforgettable eating experience. (Careful, mind, lest you get the bready bullet stuck in your gullet.) The stottie is, in effect, a great big firm bun, larger, stronger and thicker set than most of the other breads of Britain.

Around the turn of the last century, they seem to have gone by the name of 'fadges' or 'stottie fadges', although this word is today more associated with potato bread. Of course, there are those who say the stottie is merely a larger oven-bottom muffin of the kind found regularly in Lancashire, and indeed there are similarities. But words and recipes constantly evolve over time, and names for bread products are often the trickiest to pin down.

Claiming credit for the 'revival' of the stottie is Greggs the bakers, which began when one John Gregg opened a small shop in Gosforth, Tyneside, in 1951. Greggs now sell stotties in all their north-east stores, but have yet to offer them nationwide. What is certain, though, is that today a fully loaded stottie is the sustenance most beloved and pined for by expat Novocastrians from all walks of life. In 2010, when Cheryl Cole was recovering from a bout of malaria, her mam apparently rushed down to her bedside in leafy Surrey armed with Northumberland produce such as Craster kippers, pease pudding and a couple of stottie cakes.

*See also* ALNWICK, NORTHUMBERLAND (p. 199).

juniper and yarrow. Due to the brewed nature of the Fentimans range, there's often a tiny amount of sediment found at the bottom of the bottle, which is easily dispersed with a quick shake. Stable mates of the ginger beer include Rose Lemonade, Mandarin and Seville Orange Jigger, Dandelion and Burdock, and Curiosity Cola.

Their products are available in supermarkets as well as cafés, restaurants and gastropubs, and one of their biggest clients is the National Trust. The business is putting a few tentative roots into Europe, with Germany and Spain being popular markets, as well as setting up a small franchise in America. Fentimans is a brand with a great personality – indeed, when Eldon reincarnated the business, he kept the logo featuring the founder's famous panting pooch as testament to the fact that you can't teach an old dog new tricks when it comes to brewing traditional refreshing beverages.

*See also* CUMBERNAULD, NORTH LANARKSHIRE (p. 158).

## SEAHOUSES, NORTHUMBERLAND
# *Northumberland kippers*

Time was, Swallow Fish Smokehouse in Seahouses was just one of many smokehouses in the town. Now, like Fortune's in Whitby (*see* p. 268), it's the last one left. 'We've been smoking here since 1842,' says Patrick Wilkin. Patrick took over the business in 1999 from the previous owner, the late John Swallow, having worked there as a young lad before becoming a fisherman. John and his wife Pauline had put a great deal of restoration work into the place during the 1980s, and the history of the town and its industry is spread across the shop walls in framed photos and postcards they collected over the years.

Seahouses sat on the herring route that ran from Aberdeen right down the east coast to Great Yarmouth in East Anglia. The 1800s were a boom time for towns like Seahouses, Craster and Whitby. The fishwives would follow the fleets, who were following the fish down the coast. Now, of course, the fishwives have long gone, as have most of the fishermen and, indeed, most of the fish.

'We've a machine now for splitting the fish in two, where at one time there were a lot of fisherlassies doing that,' says Patrick. The split fish are brined for fifteen minutes, then hung on tenterhooks to drip-dry a little bit. They're then hung in the smoker for twelve to fifteen hours for cold smoking. What come out are kippers. The word 'kipper' comes from *cypera*, which is Old English for a spawning salmon, which itself comes from *cyperen*, which means copper, the colour of the fish during mating. The process of kippering, along with brining, has been practised since medieval times, and it's thought salmon were the first fish given this treatment.

The invention of kippering is said – apocryphally, no doubt – to have happened in Seahouses. One John Woodger left some fish in a room with a burning stove with predictably serendipitous results. As food writer Mark Kurlansky says in *Salt: A World History*, 'Smoked foods almost always carry with them legends about their having been created by accident.'

See also ARBROATH, ANGUS (p. 143); CLEY NEXT THE SEA, NORFOLK (p. 424); FINDON, ABERDEENSHIRE (p. 169); GREAT YARMOUTH, NORFOLK (p. 433); HAMBRIDGE, SOMERSET (p. 13); NIDDERDALE, NORTH YORKSHIRE (p. 251); WHITBY, NORTH YORKSHIRE (p. 268).

## SOUTH SHIELDS, TYNE & WEAR
### *Fish and chips from Colman's*

Richard Ord's great-grandfather started Colman's in a small hut on the beach at South Shields in 1905. In 1926 he moved to a shop on Ocean Road, and the family business has remained happily ensconced there ever since. During that time the make-up of the road has changed to reflect modern Britain. Gone are the tea rooms and dance halls, and in has come the vibrancy of cuisines from every corner of the globe: kebab shops, curry houses, chop-suey joints, pizza parlours and burger bars. And in the middle of it all the original and the best: Colman's.

Richard visits the quay in nearby Sunderland every morning to select fish for his restaurant from the day boats. His haddock and cod are line-caught in Icelandic waters, all fished from sustainable areas. Other species on the menu include halibut, lemon sole, plaice and monkfish, all fresh and caught less than twelve hours ago. Gurnard and haddock are his particular favourites. It's not often you see that much choice in your average chippie. But then, Richard believes in trying to encourage the public to try other just-as-tasty types of fish and breaking our addiction to cod. 'We've got to start looking after the fish,' he says of his sustainable sourcing policy. For a number of years now he's been working with an organisation called Sea Fish that promotes sustainable fishing, and in 2009 he signed up to Greenpeace's Seafish Sea Life campaign. Indeed, the environmental group went so far as to name Colman's the closest thing to an eco-chippie you could find.

Colman's chips resting after a second go in the fryer

It's not just the environmental impact of the fish that Richard has an eye on, either; his winning of UKTV's Food Hero award in 2008 netted him the top prize of £40,000, which he used to buy another ecological frying range. Made in Holland, these high-tech ranges keep the oil at a constant temperature, ensuring a better fry as well as using approximately 20 per cent less oil. When spent, the waste oil from the ranges is sent away to be made into biodiesel. Add to this biodegradable packaging, menus and napkins, and takeaway cutlery made from potato starch, and you have a sustainable ethical product cooked and served in an environmentally sustainable way.

And so to the dish itself. 'Cooking fish is easy – you need a hot frying medium and your batter as cold as you can get it.' You can coat nearly all white fish in batter (north of the border you can coat anything in batter). It acts as a protective casing around the fish, shielding it from the 190°C oil. After cooking, the batter should be crunchy and firm, almost brittle. This allows the fish to steam on the inside in its own juices, which means that the delicate flavour is preserved, along with the vitamins and nutrients. 'I always say fish and chips isn't fast food,' says Richard. 'It's fresh food cooked fast. What's more, it's a wild food. Where else can you get fresh wild food cooked – steamed actually – in nothing more than a flour-and-water batter with freshly cooked potatoes, for around a fiver?'

*See also* SAFFRON HILL, CAMDEN (p. 396).

# Sedgewick's Original Durham Mustard

In 1720 one Mrs Clements hit upon the idea of milling mustard seeds like flour to produce a fine powder, and modern English mustard was born. Prior to Clements's production method, mustard seeds, which have been grown all over Eurasia throughout history, were simply pounded in a pestle and mortar and mixed with verjuice (an acidic juice made from unripe grapes popular in the Middle Ages) or vinegar, water probably being too bland – or too dangerous – to consume. By first drying the oily mustard seeds and then grinding them to a fine powder you expose more of their surface area. This in turn exposes your tongue to more of the enzyme myrosin, which gives mustard its heat.

Mrs Clements did rather well out of the process, and kept her technique sufficiently secret to amass a pretty penny. Durham mustard, as it became known, began to grace the table of the gentry.

Over the years, various other firms tried to emulate the process both in Durham and elsewhere, the most noted of which was Keens in London, established in 1742. (Incidentally, the phrase 'keen as mustard' is found as far back as 1672, according to the *OED*.) Keens was eventually bought out by Colman's of Norwich in 1905, and so by the turn of the twentieth century Norwich had become the home of English mustard.

*See also* NORWICH, NORFOLK (p. 451).

# Moorhouse Farm Shop

The mark of any good farm shop is that it contains lots of things produced by the farmer who owns it. Moorhouse scores well on this count as there's a well-stocked meat counter featuring pork, beef and lamb, all reared on the farm. The owners are Victoria and Ian Byatt, who bought the current site and set up the farm shop five years ago. 'Our core product is the butchery,' says Victoria, but the shop also acts as a hub for other producers in the area, such as local vegetable grower Nick Craig.

They also run a series of events in a specially built marquee to the side of the shop, including talks on such topics as how to glaze a ham, or demonstrations of artisan bread-baking from the nearby Castle Bakery in Ogle. The shop's butcher also gives talks on steak – where they come from and how best to cook them – and demonstrations of how to make burgers and sausages.

'These demos are something that smaller shops and supermarkets just can't provide. They offer something new and remind our customers and people in the area that we're here, and that we're farmers,' says Ian. 'They're also a great day out,' adds Victoria. Ian sums up his business: 'We're not organic and we haven't gone down the rare-breed route. We're just keen to prove that you can be a commercial farmer serving the local community and make a success of it.' And by the looks of it, he's doing just that.

See also CANTERBURY, KENT (p. 469); COLSTON BASSETT, NOTTINGHAMSHIRE (p. 325); HOOK, HAMPSHIRE (p. 484); IPSWICH, SUFFOLK (p. 441); RUSHWICK, WORCESTERSHIRE (p. 309); WELBECK, NOTTINGHAMSHIRE (p. 362).

## WHITBURN, TYNE & WEAR
### Latimer's Fish Deli

Rob Latimer is very much a man who leads from the front – of his shop, in this case. Not for him the world of the back office and spreadsheets, Rob is a man who is never happier than when preparing, serving and selling the fruits of the ocean. Latimer's Fish Deli and Café is converted from an old petrol station right on the seafront, which was built by Rob's grandfather in 1957. Rob himself was born in the house at the back of the shop, and eventually the family saw the writing on the wall for small independent filling stations, and decided to convert to a fishmonger's instead. What might seem an odd career move from fuel to fish is explained by the fact that in his youth Rob had worked as a fisherman on the west coast of Scotland, but had returned home as the quotas got tougher and the work dried up.

Inside the shop is a long display counter groaning with fish and seafood, including hake, whiting, turbot, cod, haddock, langoustines, lobsters, scallops and oysters. Rob sells whatever the day boats bring in, and this is dependent on the tides, the weather and the time of year. 'I love getting up at 4 a.m. and going to meet the boats,' says Rob genuinely. This is supplemented with produce such as prepared anchovies and some fish from further afield; the oysters, for example, come from Carlingford Lough, an inlet of the Irish Sea. The day I saw him he even had some megrim, which is normally found in the south-west. Pebble-sized monkfish cheeks are also sometimes available. You don't see these much as monkfish are often filleted at sea; the tails – the main edible part –

A small selection of Latimer's ready-to-eat seafood

make up only a third of the animal, the massive mouth and heavy head often being chucked overboard to save space and weight.

Crab is a particular favourite of both Rob and his customers, and his come from the region. It is traditionally presented dressed and back in its shell: the brown meat, which comes from the body of the animal, is placed on either side and in the centre sits the flakier white meat, which is taken from the crab's claws. Crabs are quite easy to take apart and dress yourself, but one key thing to avoid are the gills, or 'dead man's fingers', which if eaten will give you a bit of a gippy tum. For some the brown meat is an acquired taste, but stick with it. As with chicken and turkey, the brown meat is where the flavour is. If, however, you can't be bothered with all that faff, Rob sells tubs of finest dressed crabmeat for a mere £1.50, or you can enjoy it in the wonderful café next door with a view over the North Sea.

*See also* DERWENTWATER, CUMBRIA (p. 102); DOVER, KENT (p. 473); GLOUCESTER, GLOUCESTERSHIRE (p. 288); HASTINGS, EAST SUSSEX (p. 483); MARKET HARBOROUGH, LEICESTERSHIRE (p. 340); NEWLYN, CORNWALL (pp. 32 and 34); RIVER SEVERN, GLOUCESTERSHIRE (p. 305); SCOURIE, HIGHLAND (p. 187); SOUTHEND-ON-SEA, ESSEX (p. 455); WANSFORD, EAST YORKSHIRE (p. 261).

# Doddington Dairy — a cheese and ice-cream farm

Doddington Dairy is really two companies in one. Neill and Jackie Maxwell use milk from the herd to make ice cream, Neill's sister Maggie uses it to make a range of cheeses, and brothers John and Bobbie look after the cows.

The herd had been established for over fifty years when Neill brought home a chunk of unpasteurised Cheddar for everyone to taste. 'We totally fell in love with it,' says Maggie, 'and we started experimenting, basically in the kitchen sink as all farmhouse producers do.' Friends and relatives proved willing guinea pigs, and they set about scaling the steep learning curve for a couple of years. 'We made sure that we didn't sell anything before we were sure that people would love it.'

The unpasteurised milk that goes into the cheese is from the morning milking only, rather than being mixed with the evening milk. Morning milk has a higher fat content, and there's more of it. 'It's warm, fresh and sweet; there's a lot of lactose and sugars in there,' says Maggie.

A Cheddar-style cheese was produced first, with others added to the range over the years. In 2007 they produced Admiral Collingwood, a semi-soft cheese named after the famous naval officer (and Nelson's number two) who was born in Newcastle. The cheese, fairly firm, is rind-washed regularly in Newcastle Brown Ale (see p. 220), which lends it its pungent flavour. However, for my money their Baltic cheese, softer, lighter and washed in Baltic Summer Ale from Liverpool, just pips it.

Newcastle Brown Ale features in another Doddington dairy product, the Admiral Collingwood ice cream. After its success, which garnered interest from all over the world when launched, Neill and Jackie developed an ice cream flavoured with Alnwick rum (*see* p. 196), as well as one using honey from Chain Bridge Honey Farm (*see* p. 211).

Small businesses looking to diversify would do well to take a slice out of the Doddington business model. By working with other small (and even large) businesses like their own, producers can become stronger. 'With ice cream you can start experimenting with products from other producers and have something in a day or two; with cheese it can take months. You learn patience as a cheese-maker,' says Maggie.

*See also* BRITISH CHEESE (p. 290).

# 6 | Yorkshire

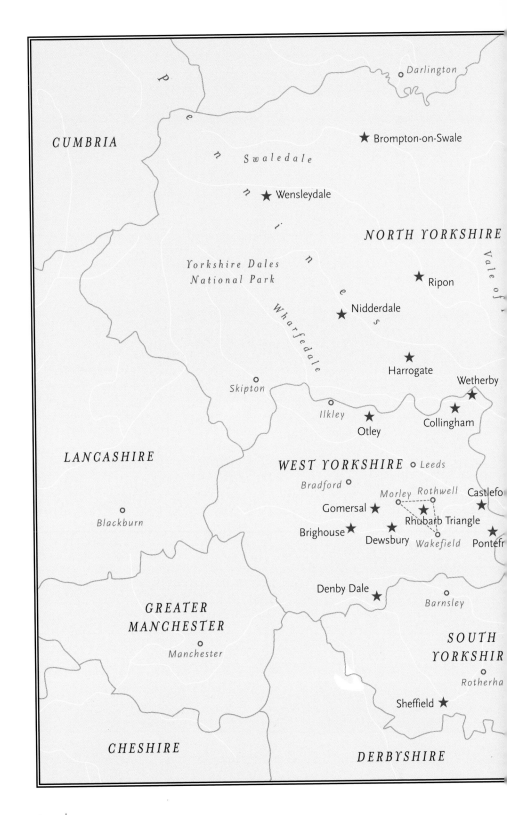

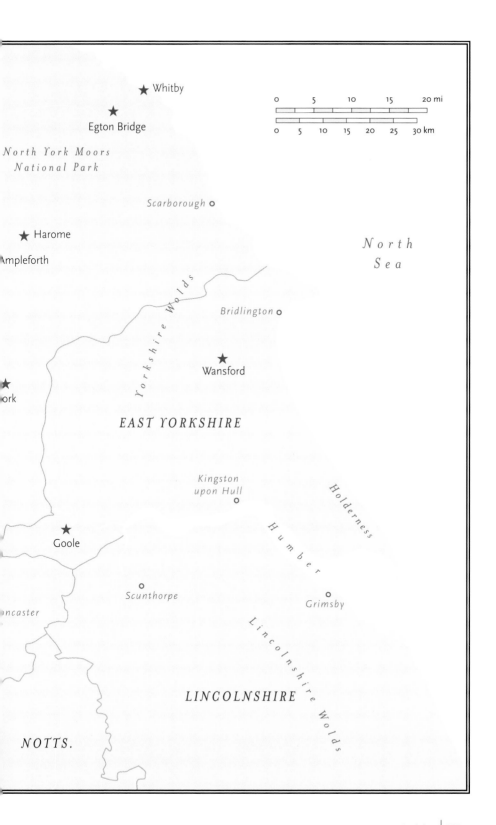

★ Whitby

★
Egton Bridge

*North York Moors*
*National Park*

Scarborough ○

★ Harome

Ampleforth

*N o r t h*
*S e a*

*Yorkshire Wolds*

Bridlington ○

★
Wansford

**EAST YORKSHIRE**

★
ork

Kingston
upon Hull
○

*Holderness*

★
Goole

*H u m b e r*

○
Scunthorpe

○
Grimsby

ncaster

*Lincolnshire Wolds*

**LINCOLNSHIRE**

*NOTTS.*

| 0 | 5 | 10 | 15 | 20 mi |

| 0 | 5 | 10 | 15 | 20 | 25 | 30 km |

# Apples, cider and cider brandy from Ampleforth Abbey

Apples get a bit of a bad press in the Good Book: taking the blame for mankind's fall when in fact the peckish Eve ate 'fruit' from the Tree of Knowledge and what form that fruit took is known only to the Almighty. However, this hasn't stopped church institutions over the years indulging in a bit of ecclesiastical apple-growing, and Father Rainer Verborg at Ampleforth Abbey is carrying on that august tradition.

Benedictine monks founded the abbey – and planted its original orchards – over 200 years ago, and in 1902 Abbot Smith reorganised and replanted the apple trees. Two of the trees from that planting survive; 'The apples from them aren't particularly nice, however,' says Father Rainer with a chuckle. Most of the trees in his orchard are between thirty and seventy years old, and there are now nearly fifty varieties. In the nineteenth and even the twentieth centuries the orchard supplied the abbey, the school next door and nearby villages.

Since becoming custodian of the orchard, Father Rainer has struck up partnerships with businesses and the wider community. Apples are either sold at the abbey gate, or to a fruit merchant who supplies hotels and shops in the area. Apples that don't meet the grade to sell as fresh are made into juice and cider, and some of the latter heads down to Julian Temperley at the Cider Brandy Company in Somerset to be distilled.

As for why they do it, Father Rainer points out that monasteries still have to earn their living. 'We're also giving something back to the community by running a juicing co-operative.' This allows people in the area to bring in their apples and get them pressed and pasteurised into juice; 'It started as an idea to help people prevent waste.' Moreover, the monks are fulfilling the rules of St Benedict, who said, 'When they live by the labour of their hands, then they are really monks.' As Father Rainer says, 'It's a lot of work, it's hard work, but by its nature it is contemplative, so you get into a rhythm and you can fill that rhythm with prayer.'

There's a long tradition of monastic horticulture on mainland Europe, particularly in brewing; one need only think of the Trappist beers of Belgium. And in the UK the monks of Buckfast Abbey in Devon achieved a certain notoriety with their tonic wine, known in Scotland as 'Wreck the hoose juice'. I asked Father Rainer if his cider brandy will follow the same path. 'No, because we do everything by hand. It's rather expensive, I'm afraid; it's not really in the same league. Also, we don't produce 30 million litres a year; we only make 1500 bottles at present.'

*See also* FAVERSHAM, KENT (p. 475); HOLT HEATH, WORCESTERSHIRE (p. 298); MARTOCK, SOMERSET (p. 29); SOUTHWELL, NOTTINGHAMSHIRE (p. 359).

BRIGHOUSE, WEST YORKSHIRE
## *Figit pie from Andrew Jones*

Andrew Jones is nothing if not resilient. When I first met him in 2008 he was manning his stall at the Huddersfield Food and Drink Festival, business was good and he was looking to move to new premises, having outgrown the factory in the city centre. Then, in April 2009, tragedy struck as a gas explosion from the ovens tore the factory apart, killing one employee and seriously injuring another. The blast affected everyone in the close-knit company very deeply: a lot of his team had been there for years. At this point Andrew could have packed it all in, and who could blame him, but there were

Pies being made by hand in Andrew Jones's old factory

thirty-odd people's livelihoods to think about, and it's a testament to the strength of the team that Andrew was back in production within weeks. The kitchens at the back of his two butcher's shops were put into service to ensure that orders were met as best they could, and Andrew got a friend with counselling experience to come in for both his staff and himself.

He founded the firm in 1988, when a butcher's shop on the outskirts of Huddersfield came up for sale. It was small, but it produced twenty dozen pies a week. His big break came three years later when his Cornish pasty won a contest run by the National Federation of Meat and Food Traders. The regional media went mad for the story. 'We were swamped with orders. We went from doing a couple of hundred to three thousand a week.'

His other championship thoroughbred is the figit (sometimes spelled fidgit) pie. These herald from the East Midlands, specifically the historical county of Huntingdonshire (now part of Cambridgeshire), although it's extremely hard to find one there these days. Andrew's version contains pork meat topped with a layer of stuffing and apple sauce, finished with a lattice pastry top. It won 'Supreme Product' in the 2008–9 Deliciouslyorkshire food awards, and Andrew is also listed as a Master Pie Maker by the Pork Pie Appreciation Society, a group of die-hard pie fans on a quest to find the ultimate pie.

Of course, good pastry is just as important as a good filling when it comes to pies. Andrew's pork pies are made with a hot-water pastry; the lard is added to the boiling water before combining with the flour. He uses Italian lard as it gives a better pastry and is better for boiling. The exact measurements and methods Andrew won't reveal, but what he ends up with is a sort of crispy rather than crumbly pastry. It's then put in pie tins, pressed into shape and filled by hand.

After coping with a disaster that saw his business all but destroyed, Andrew and his team of pre-eminent pie makers are back up and baking again. Good luck to them.

*See also* CORNISH PASTIES (p. 18).

BROMPTON-ON-SWALE, NORTH YORKSHIRE
## Yorkshire Game Ltd

If you've eaten game in any of London's top restaurants, chances are it came from Richard Townsend at Yorkshire Game Ltd. He sums things up thus: 'If it's legal to shoot it, we can get it.' The most popular quarry by far is venison, specifically red deer, which are all stalked on Scottish estates that manage their deer populations. Farmed deer is also available, and in this country they are descended from wild deer caught in the 1980s – not that far removed from the wild population. Restaurants take nearly all Richard's wild venison, while supermarkets prefer the farmed as it's more consistent and regular in supply and the production is traceable.

At the start of the decade it seemed as though everyone wanted venison strip loin and fillet – the expensive bits. Then, with the credit crunch, chefs drifted towards the cheaper cuts: the shanks, steaks and the haunch. 'Fillet practically priced itself out of the market,' says Richard.

The most popular birds are pheasants – again because they are so numerous – followed by wood pigeon and mallard, for similar reasons. Next comes rabbit, again all wild: 'There are plagues of the things in this part of the world,' says Richard, and adds as an example that one of the estates he buys from sent four gamekeepers over with 25,000 rabbits in just six months. Since the introduction of the fatal disease myxomatosis in the 1960s to curb their numbers, rabbits have built up an immunity and the population is now expanding.

Yorkshire Game also sells more esoteric items, such as woodcock. 'For every 200 pheasants we get in, we'll get around one woodcock. Their numbers are dependent on the weather in Scandinavia and the Baltic states: if it's cold there, they'll move west.' As a result, they're also the most expensive of the game birds, with a trade price of around £8.50 – a hell of a lot for a small bird. Yorkshire Game also supply restaurants with teal, coots and waterhens, which are legal quarry in season. You can visit any urban park with a pond and see these species. Their flesh is green, and so traditionally they're soaked in milk overnight before cooking.

But it's not just fancy restaurants who are interested in Richard's wares. He's also beginning to supply supermarkets, pub chains and ready-meal manufacturers, all of whom demand much larger volumes. 'People like game because it has flavour, it has provenance, it has had a totally wild life . . . what's more, it's had a sporting chance to get away.' It looks like game is about to go mainstream.

*See also* ACOMB, NORTHUMBERLAND (p. 195); AUCHTERMUCHTY, FIFE (p. 144); BLAXHALL, SUFFOLK (p. 419); CHIPPENHAM, WILTSHIRE (p. 9); FRILSHAM, BERKSHIRE (p. 479); KENDAL, CUMBRIA (p. 114).

## *After Eight dinner mints*

In *Adrian Mole: The Cappuccino Years,* Sue Townsend's eponymous hero gets a job as head chef in a restaurant in Soho called Hoi Polloy. The menu – 'Traditional English, No Choice' – features Heinz tomato soup (with white bread floaters); grey lamb chops with boiled cabbage, potatoes and gravy; spotted dick with Bird's custard (skin £6 extra); and Cheddar cheese, cream crackers, Nescafé and a single After Eight mint. Of course the joke is that the London intelligentsia lap up this postmodern irony and the place is booked out six weeks in advance.

The lampooning of the After Eight marks a fall from grace for this once rather gourmet product. A 1965 advert features two girls in a fast car – the epitome of Swinging London – and a caption that reads, 'I always take a box of After Eight in the Ferrari.'

Created in 1962 and made in Castleford, West Yorkshire, their construction used some of the most advanced engineering and manufacturing ever seen. First, Rowntree & Co had to figure out how to keep the gooey mint fondant from mingling with the chocolate. The answer came in the form of invertase, an ingredient derived from yeast that keeps the fondant stiff while it's being coated in chocolate, but then over time – around a few weeks – changes the fondant back to a liquid form. While stiff, the squares are coated in chocolate, with the excess being blown off by a jet of air; this gives the surface the distinctive ripple. After Eight are, of course, stored vertically – like no other chocolate that had gone before – in little paper envelopes. Douglas Adams in *The Meaning of Liff* (1983) defined 'cannock chase' as 'the process by which, no matter which part of the box you insert your fingers into, or how often, you will always extract most of the empty sachets before pinning down an actual mint, or cannock'.

The After Eight and its ilk are British postprandial petit fours, created to be simulacra of the tiny chocolates, cakes and French patisserie served with coffee at the end of a meal. Mint is there to perhaps freshen the breath and ease digestion. The idea of a little something to nibble on while your dinner goes down isn't a new one. The word 'dessert' is derived from the Old French *desservir*, meaning 'to clear the table', and once formed part of the closing ceremony of any large multi-course meal. Even up until the turn of the last century it still featured on menus. It consisted of fruit, maybe nuts, and other little things taken either at the table or, if there was space, in another room.

Today few of us make our own petit fours or lay on proper dessert. Effort and labour are put into the starter, main and pudding, and that's your lot. But when we do there is something rather Pavlovian about bringing out a few little treats, even though your guests are stuffed to the gunnels with your culinary efforts. In the words of Monty Python's French waiter addressing Mr Creosote, 'And finally, monsieur, a wafer-thin mint?'

COLLINGHAM, WEST YORKSHIRE
## Wharfe Valley rapeseed oil

One of the key images in the TV-led foodie revolution of the 1990s was the sight of extra-virgin olive oil being glugged into hot, waiting frying pans. Since then, we've been so hooked on this one time earwax remover as the de facto 'healthy' oil that frying or dressing a salad in anything else – say, rapeseed oil – now seems strange. It shouldn't, however, and it's worth

Stephen Kilby explains the production process for his rapeseed oil

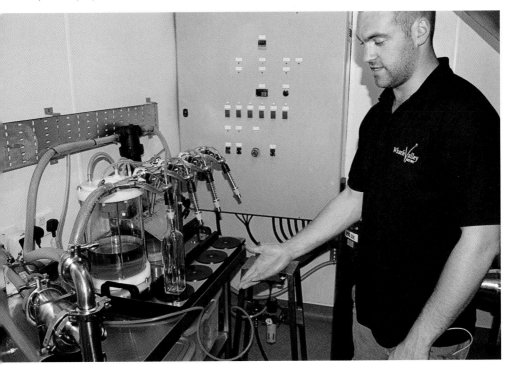

remembering that unlike olives, the raw ingredient for rapeseed oil can be grown right here in the UK.

The Kilbys have been growing the unmistakable bright yellow crop on their Wharfe Valley Farm since the late 1980s, alongside other rotation crops. Like many farming families, in 2005 they looked into diversification, and so they began to press, produce and bottle their own cold-pressed virgin rapeseed oil rather than simply selling the seeds to market and letting someone else add the value.

One ton of rapeseed provides 200 litres of oil. The seed goes through a sorter to remove any impurities, and then into a crusher which separates the oil from the 'meal' – the compressed outer casing, which is sold as animal feed. It is possible to extract the oil using a heated chemical process, but this leaves the meal completely without nutrients, looking like and tasting of sand. After separation, the oil goes through various filtering processes, culminating in a final press that can filter out anything over five microns in weight, which ensures the product stays clear.

Rapeseed is a member of the brassica family (the name coming from the Latin for turnip, *rapum*) along with cabbage and mustard, and you can taste this heritage in the oil's peppery notes. Wharfe Valley Farm produce three different varieties, including an oak-smoked version, which infuses the oil with a subtle background flavour that provides a point of reference for the main ingredient.

Rapeseed oil is richer in colour and more viscous than olive oil, and has half the saturated fat and ten times the omega-3. For those who like to cook hot and hard, for example in a stir-fry, it's also got a higher smoking point than olive oil – 230°C as opposed to 180°C – meaning it can take a beating in the pan and still perform. This versatility, as well as its flavour and taste, have made it popular with big name chefs, such as Lawrence Keogh at Roast in Borough Market, and fellow Yorkshireman James Martin, who makes a mayonnaise with it.

## DENBY DALE, WEST YORKSHIRE
### *Denby Dale pies*

Denby Dale in West Yorkshire is famous for its celebratory pies, which are baked on very special occasions, each one bigger than the previous. The first was to celebrate George III regaining a modicum of sanity in 1788. 'Huzzah!'

cried the town, and celebrated, a little prematurely. On that occasion the pie featured game, an ingredient that would later bring ignominy to the town.

The next pie celebrated victory at Waterloo, and pride of place was afforded to local soldier George Wilby, who fought in the battle and had recently returned home. Rumour has it he carved the pie with his own sword. The year 1846 saw the repeal of the Corn Laws: this event wasn't such a huge success as the stage holding the pie collapsed after the crowd stampeded; residents of nearby Clayton West were blamed with sabotage. However, worse was to come.

The year 1887 saw the Golden Jubilee of Queen Victoria, and the biggest pie yet was planned. Eight feet in diameter and two feet deep, it contained 1,581 lb of beef, 163 lb of veal, 180 lb of lamb, 180 lb of mutton, 250 lb of lean pork, 67 rabbits and hares and 153 game birds and poultry, as well as potatoes. The meat was displayed in local butchers' shops before being cooked in batches, with raw game birds being tucked in around the edges. Once cooked, there was again a stampede, only this time in the other direction as when the pastry was opened the diners recoiled at the stench of rotting meat: the game had gone off. The pie was taken to the woods and buried.

A new pie was made, and game never again featured in a Denby Dale pie. In the last century, pies were made to celebrate victory in the First World War, royal births, bicentenaries and the millennium, all increasing in size. The last one, in the year 2000, was twelve metres long, two and a half wide and over one metre deep, and featured 5,000 kilos of British beef, 2,000 kilos of potatoes and 1,000 kilos of onions. Who knows when the next Denby Dale pie will be? The Coronation of King Charles – or King William? The first Briton on Mars? The events happen roughly every twenty-five years, so keep your eye out around 2025.

If you fancy a more manageably sized pie in the meantime, you can always try the Denby Dale Pie Company. Janet Purcell, her husband and family friends the Worsleys aren't anything to do with the giant pies, they just happen to make nice small ones. Janet started making a few pies for friends, and things grew from there. What is interesting about her meat and potato pies is that layers of potato sit atop the meat mix, just under the pastry: 'That's the way me mother did it, though I do get letters from people in Sheffield saying the potato should be mixed in as chunks,' says Janet, who's sticking to family tradition.

*See also* CARDIFF, CARDIFF (p. 59); CHINLEY, DERBYSHIRE (p. 285); GLASGOW, GLASGOW (p. 178); GREENWICH, GREENWICH (p. 380); MOUSEHOLE, CORNWALL (p. 31).

# Tripe from R. Hey & Sons

I meet a great deal of people who would happily describe themselves as foodies. They seek out the obscure ingredients, respect historical and traditional methods and subscribe to increasing the breadth of our national menu by eating the lesser-known cuts. And nearly every one of them has stopped short of tripe.

Despite the nation's praetorian guard of chefs' best efforts, it remains perhaps a bite too far. If these trailblazers aren't mad keen for it, what hope for the rest of the chicken-eating masses? And yet salvation may come from an unlikely source. It's a well-known dictum that we often use other cultures' cuisines to switch us on to ingredients that have been here all along, and so perhaps the Spanish dish of *callos*, which sees tripe paired with chickpeas, chorizo and paprika, might bring us round. Or perhaps as we begin to explore true regional Chinese cuisine, their fiery *fuqi feipian* (literally 'married couple's slices of lung'), which features tripe as well as other sorts of meats, will become the new vindaloo-style dare for the gourmet elite?

All of this is a long way from tripe's homeland in the north of England, where bleached, blanched cows' stomachs were once an everyday thing. R. Hey & Sons was established by Ronald Hey in 1953, and today son Christopher along with grandson Daniel are at the helm. They supply shops, markets and wholesalers throughout the north of England with cooked tripe, and are one of only three tripe dressers left in the country.

Hey's get their tripe from abattoirs in Yorkshire; they clean it in a warm chemical mixture to remove the black lining, then leave it to cool. There are seams of fat running through the stomachs, so these need to be opened up with a knife before the stomachs are cleaned again. At that point they are ready for export, particularly to Eastern Europe, which is a large market. For the UK market, the stomachs are boiled for just over an hour, then put in a mixture of water, bleach and a dash of caustic soda in a cold room to tenderise. Hey's produce three tons a week.

Cows have one stomach with four compartments (the rumen, reticulum, omasum and abomasum). Hey's mainly process the rumen, which gives us blank or smooth tripe, and the reticulum, which gives us honeycomb tripe. The latter is the best seller in the UK. Much like squid, tripe is best used to host other flavours. Tripe with onions and milk sauce might be traditional, but in this day and age it's a bit bland. Surely we can do better? How about tripe braised slowly in wine or beer, or cooked with garlic, onions and fresh tomatoes, as in Italy? And if that doesn't work, we can always fall back on the old British mantra of 'if in doubt, batter it'.

## *The Old Gooseberry Society*

There exists in Egton Bridge, North Yorkshire, an ancient and venerable society with but one aim: to find the heaviest gooseberry the world has ever seen. Masterminding this task is Eric Preston, aged eighty-one, who has been chairman of the Egton Bridge Old Gooseberry Society for twenty-five years. He's been a member for a lot longer, and has been showing gooseberries for over thirty years, yet he's never won the top prize. 'The really big one's evaded me, but my turn'll come.'

Gooseberry shows were popular in many industrial areas during the nineteenth century, particularly in Lancashire (with textile workers) and Yorkshire. In 1831 there were 722 varieties of gooseberries grown, and in 1845 there were over 171 gooseberry shows all around the country. Thanks to a post-First World War decline, there are now only two left, Egton Bridge's, and one in Holmes Chapel in Cheshire.

Unfortunately, it's not only the gooseberry shows, but also the berries themselves that are seldom seen these days. Eric explains: 'It's such a time-consuming crop to pick, and they seem to have disappeared from the shops all together. I get people ringing me up asking where they can get hold of some gooseberries.' This is a shame, because they have so many uses in cooking. Their sharp acidity is often used by chefs as a contrast against oily fish such as mackerel or meats like duck.

As for the show gooseberries, Eric tells me they seemed to have reached a peak. 'They aren't all that heavier than they were 200 years ago. You'd have thought with all these modern fertilisers they'd be growing giant ones!' The weighing is done on an old pair of apothecary scales, bought in 1937, which are so sensitive they can weigh a feather. Egton switched some time ago to the avoirdupois system of weights, and use ounces, drams and grains, with 27.34 grains to one dram and 16 drams to an ounce. Holmes Chapel still weigh in pennyweights and troy pounds. This caused controversy in 2009, when what was thought to have been a heavier berry was shown there. An expert had to be called in to do the complex conversion between the two

## Yorkshire Pudding

Ask people to name a food heralding from Yorkshire and chances are they'll suggest the county's famous pudding, sitting puffed and proud next to the beef and potatoes in the Great British Sunday roast, quietly soaking up all the gravy. I remember I once made Yorkshire puddings for an American family I visited. They ate them with cottage cheese and peaches and said they liked them. At the time I was filled with abhorrence, but I've since learned that Yorkshire folk have been known to eat them as a pudding with jam or honey. There was also once a custom of sending out the pudding as a first course with the gravy, and once that had been eaten, sending out the beef with parsley sauce, leading to the saying 'Those who ate most pudding get most beef.'

Yorkshire puddings started to appear in the late seventeenth century – around the time of a boom in the availability of flour. The first written recipe we can find appeared in *The Whole Duty of a Woman* in 1737 and was entitled 'Dripping pudding'. Eight years later, Hannah Glass's recipe calls it 'Yorkshire pudding'; as does John Farley, principal cook at the London Tavern, in his book of 1787. By 1830, *The Cooks Oracle* says, 'The true Yorkshire pudding is about half an inch thick when done; but it is the fashion in London to make them full twice that thickness.'

Interestingly, all these early recipes call for the pudding to be flipped halfway through cooking so that both sides may be browned, and that the pudding be made in a single pan or tray placed under the meat and before the fire. Extra fat was probably used, though, as there's no way a joint could give out enough fat to stop the batter sticking to the pan. Nowadays we've moved on from roasting our meat on jacks in front of fires with pans of batter below. We no longer flip over our Yorkshires nor make a single giant pudding for sharing, but bake them, individually, to the size of bath sponges, and woe betide the cook who omits them.

But it is the giant version of the Yorkshire pudding that lends itself to perhaps the most ingenious usage of the product: toad-in-the-hole. Charles Elme Francatelli mentions this dish in his *Plain Cookery Book for the Working Classes* (1852), in which he advises using any meat available rather than sausages specifically. The dish also makes a rather premature appearance in James Orchard Halliwell-Phillips' *A Dictionary of archaic and provincial words, obsolete phrases, proverbs and customs from the fourteenth century* (1847) as 'beefsteaks baked in batter'. Toad-in-the-hole remains a homely, comforting dish to this day, although bangers have taken the place of beefsteaks. Indeed, perhaps we can surmise from all this that we Brits love the combination of fat and batter as much as, if not more than, the meat that comes with it.

Competitors prepare their entries for the annual gooseberry weigh-in

systems, and eventually the berry from Egton Bridge was declared the heaviest, by one grain. I did ask Eric – somewhat anticipating the answer – whether it might not all be simpler if everyone went metric. 'Oh, no no no no! This is the whole atmosphere of the show, the weighing with the old weights and ways.'

On the day of the show – which is always the first Tuesday in August – the berries are weighed between 8.30 a.m. and 1 p.m., then the doors are flung open to the public from 2 p.m. The local brass turn up and do a few numbers, then it's off to either the Postgate Inn or the Horseshoe Hotel for refreshments. What could be more British than folk getting together to find the heaviest fruit using a set of apothecary scales and eighteenth-century imperial measurements, before listening to a brass band and then having a few drinks in the pub? The whole thing has a wonderful charm to it, so much so that I felt compelled to join the Egton Bridge Old Gooseberry Society there and then – membership fee £3. There are only three meetings a year: the

AGM on Easter Tuesday, then one a fortnight before the show and another a fortnight after. 'It's pretty laid-back; time moves very slowly up here,' says Eric. Still waters run deep under Egton Bridge, I'll wager.

*See also* CORBRIDGE, NORTHUMBERLAND (p. 207); HAMPRESTON, DORSET (p. 14); HONITON, DEVON (p. 17); INVERGOWRIE, PERTH & KINROSS (p. 180); LYTH AND WINSTER VALLEYS, CUMBRIA (p. 117); NORTHIAM, EAST SUSSEX (p. 492); WALMERSLEY, GREATER MANCHESTER (p. 137); WIMBLEDON, MERTON (p. 415).

GOMERSAL, WEST YORKSHIRE
## *W. S. Bentley's cress*

Hands up who grew cress at school. On a piece of cotton wool in an eggshell with a face on it, all balanced on a toilet-roll tube. For most of us, this was possibly our first experience of horticulture. Now ask yourself when you last ate cress. Chances are, the little leaves were smothered by claggy egg and mayonnaise in a sandwich, providing the odd green fleck in an otherwise wholly off-white culinary experience. This is a shame because cress is the original micro leaf. Given a bit of room, cress's peppery, mustard notes can sing out from those delicate little leaves.

Jan Bentley, of W. S. Bentley, used to get so many requests for advice from schoolchildren on how to grow cress that he added a page to his company's website about cress cultivation and production. Jan's father started the farm in the 1950s, growing vegetables and salads, but gradually began to specialise in cress, mainly wholesale, with perhaps 3 per cent going to the likes of Morrison's. Times have changed since then, and W. S. Bentley now supply nearly 90 per cent of their cress to the supermarkets. The production process is a little more advanced than the primary-school windowsill, however.

The seed is first pre-germinated, then added to a growing line, where peat is added before it's put into a high-humidity germination room for two days. This ensures all the seeds will come up at the same time. It then goes to a greenhouse for two days, after which it's transferred to a punnet and sent off to the shops and restaurants. Growing time is five days; four in summer, which means that Jan's able to grow three crops a week – speed farming.

Mindful of the future and keen to explore new markets, W. S. Bentley have taken all their cress-growing know-how and diversified into other sprouting seeds such as alfalfa, peas and mixed beans. They sell direct under their own brand name, and also supply Boots, Spar and Waitrose. These have yet to enter the canon of British sandwich fillings, but if you come across an egg-and-alfalfa-shoots butty, remember that you heard it here first. Class dismissed.

*See also* CHICHESTER, WEST SUSSEX (p. 471); CRYMYCH, PEMBROKESHIRE (p. 63); WINCANTON, SOMERSET (p. 48).

*See also* CHICHESTER, WEST SUSSEX (p. 471); CRYMYCH, PEMBROKESHIRE (p. 63); WINCANTON, SOMERSET (p. 48).

## GOOLE, EAST YORKSHIRE
# Carrots from Poskitt Farm

Humble carrots – those big, ever-present orange sticks you see in the shops – weren't always thus. History is sketchy about just how this staple crop came to be, and for much of it they are confused with parsnips. They came from the East and were known to the Egyptians, Greeks and then the Romans, though their use was nearly always medicinal or aphrodisiacal.

Thanks to the efforts of the empires of the classical era, cultivated species of carrots were left across Europe. In the tenth century, carrots, along with parsnips and brassicas, were being served for dinner by the Vikings, according to archaeological evidence unearthed at York. The carrot then, along with maybe a handful of other vegetables, spans nearly all of human history and all major Eurasian cultures. Perhaps this is why we consider it such a staple.

As for our present-day orange carrots, the Dutch are thought to have popularised this type in the 1500s, although there are texts depicting orange carrots from the eleventh century and even as far back as AD 500. Prior to Dutch efforts, carrots ranged in colour from white through to a deep purple. These heritage varieties are available from specialist seeds shops and growers, but you're far more than likely to encounter the orange ones today.

Unlike nearly anything else you care to mention – apples, lamb and berries, to name but three – nearly 95 per cent of the carrots we eat are grown here, with around 9,000 hectares dedicated to their production. Guy Poskitt manages quite a few of those hectares in Yorkshire, Suffolk and Scotland, producing carrots for the food services sector and the supermarkets. He supplies half of all Asda's conventional carrots and all of their organic ones. 'The best time to eat carrots is from September to Christmas: the sugar levels are just right,' he says. Guy, like many growers, uses the popular variety Nairobi, a good all-rounder. He also grows other varieties such as Yokon, which is good for early lifting, and Bangor, which is good for battoning as it grows straight all the way down and doesn't taper. He is able to meet year-round demand through a variety of techniques. Early carrots, ready in August, are started in the new year under plastic, which is removed around May after the last frost. The main crop is sown in April, ready to begin the harvest in September. Summer hits the south first, and so production gradually moves up the country as the crops are ready. In the autumn, hay is put down to protect the tops from frost, and in the depths of winter plastic sheeting is added. Then it's back to the start. In 2009 there was a gap of three days between seasons; ten years ago, it lasted six weeks.

See also EAST ANGLIAN PARSNIPS (p. 444); PEA HARVEST (p. 332).

HAROME, NORTH YORKSHIRE

# Black pudding and foie gras from the Star Inn

Andrew Pern and his wife Jacquie took over derelict pub the Star in 1996, with Andrew's signature dish being black pudding and foie gras. It's also the name of his self-published cookery book (the only book I've ever seen bound in chocolate-brown velvet: very classy). The thinking behind the dish is that it's 'rich man, poor man' (black pudding is a North Country staple, and foie gras is a real luxury), which very much blends in with the clientele and ethos of the restaurant. It's been on the menu for over ten years, so Andrew can pretty much make it in his sleep.

The base is a thin circle of scrumpy reduction, to which are added five tiny blobs of apple chutney, each dotted with a few leaves of chervil. Some watercress from the nearby town of Pickering is added, and a fried ring of black pudding is balanced on top. 'You can grill it,' says Andrew, 'which is slightly healthier . . . but I don't think that's a concern when you're having foie gras.' The goose liver is then fried in a separate pan before being placed on top, then a second ring of fried black pudding on top of that. Crowning the dish is a thin slice of apple covered with caramelised caster sugar.

And what a magnificent construction: the wobbly, unctuous foie gras is smooth and delicate, the black pudding peppery and punchy; it's as if your mouth has met the girl of your dreams flanked by her two big brothers. The caramelised apple adds a sweetness to the meeting, and with one or two chews we're all getting along famously. It's a great little dish.

See also BATH, SOMERSET (p. 4); BURY MARKET, GREATER MANCHESTER (p. 99); DINGWALL, HIGHLAND (p. 160); HEREFORD, HEREFORDSHIRE (p. 296); SMITHFIELD, ISLINGTON (p. 401); STONEHALL COMMON, WORCESTERSHIRE (p. 312).

# Tea from Taylor's of Harrogate

'At four o'clock it was time for tea . . .' went the old advert for Yorkshire Tea, which became something of a mantra in our house, despite growing up t'other side o' t' hills. Yorkshire Tea is only one blend made by Taylor's of Harrogate, based just outside the town. Charles Taylor was originally a sales agent for the Ashby family's London-based tea company. He noticed that water in different areas of the country affected the quality and taste of the tea, and set about developing specific blends for the south-west region, where he was based. They didn't sell and Taylor was sacked.

Convinced he was on to something, and with elder brother Llewellyn acting as a silent partner, he established his own business in the booming spa town of Harrogate in 1886. The tea warehouse included a kiosk, where buyers could taste the blends before purchasing. Over time this became a café, and was frequented by businessmen. He opened the Café Imperial in Ilkley in 1896, and another one in Harrogate in 1905. Neither Charles nor Llewellyn had children to take over the business, and so brought in their

Tea brewed by the experts

nephew James to manage the firm. James had no children either, and so with the business declining, he decided to sell in 1962.

Local rival Bettys (*see* p. 270) bought the business, and converted the cafés to their own brand. Bettys managing director Victor Wild, who oversaw the purchase, wrote in his diary, 'A big step for Bettys! In the right direction, I hope.'

Wild refocused Taylor's on the original business, that of being a top-class tea and coffee importer. Today, still owned by Wild's descendants, the company remains one of the few family-owned tea and coffee merchants in the country. Highlights include Taylor's own afternoon tea blend, which is great after a day on your feet, being strong, tannin-rich and tasty. At the other end of the spectrum is a single estate Darjeeling – the champagne of teas, which is light and delicate. For those who like unusual flavours there is Blue Sapphire, which has a sweet honey taste that is totally unexpected.

Taylor's taste their tea with specially brought in hard water, the water around Harrogate being soft as a baby's cheek. 'It's so we can judge the flavour better,' says tea buyer Suzy Garraghan. In a nod to their founder's mantra of specific blends for different areas, Taylor's Yorkshire Tea comes in hard and soft blends. It really is tea like it used to be.

*See also* APPLEDORE, KENT (p. 466); NEW GALLOWAY, DUMFRIES & GALLOWAY (p. 184); PEMBROKE DOCK, PEMBROKESHIRE (p. 81); YORK, NORTH YORKSHIRE (p. 270).

NIDDERDALE, NORTH YORKSHIRE
# Mackenzie's Yorkshire Smokehouse

Mackenzie's Yorkshire Smokehouse is nestled up the hill from the Fewston reservoir on the Blubberhouses moor, and on a rainy day it looms out of the mist like some sort of Yorkshire Brigadoon. Its current owner is Stella Crowson, who bought the business with her husband Robert after the death of founder Peter Mackenzie, who gave the company its name. Mackenzie started the business in the 1980s when he decided he couldn't get any decent smoked salmon and so started to smoke his own in the basement of his son-in-law's restaurant. He sent a sample to Fortnum & Mason in London, where it won a blind taste test, and he then had to peddle fast and set up a unit as the orders started to pile in. Sadly, a few years later he succumbed to cancer, and Stella bought the ailing business from his stepson in 1997.

They are now one of the largest smokers in the region, smoking everything from salmon and haddock to duck, venison, goose and ostrich, as well as traditional York hams. Cheese also gets the treatment, with smoked Cheddar, Wensleydale and even Parmesan on offer in the shop. They use both hot smoking, which sees the food smoked quickly and ready to eat, and cold smoking, in which a lower-temperature fire imparts a smoked flavour but leaves the product raw. For both processes they use either oak or beech wood or a combination of the two.

'I wanted a restaurant,' claims Stella, 'but my husband said, "Over my dead body," so I bought the smokehouse and developed a restaurant on the side.' Crafty, eh? Over the years, they've totally upgraded and refitted the premises, and the new-look restaurant of fifty-five covers opened for breakfast, lunch and afternoon tea in January 2008. It's a smart but laid-back affair, drawing on the best that the smokehouse next door has to offer, and is something of a destination for well-heeled Yorkshire folk.

*See also* ARBROATH, ANGUS (p. 143); CLEY NEXT THE SEA, NORFOLK (p. 424); FINDON, ABERDEENSHIRE (p. 169); GREAT YARMOUTH, NORFOLK (p. 433); HAMBRIDGE, SOMERSET (p. 13); SEAHOUSES, NORTHUMBERLAND (p. 224); WHITBY, NORTH YORKSHIRE (p. 268).

## OTLEY, WEST YORKSHIRE
# Yorkshire curd tarts from Bondgate Bakery

Yorkshire curd tarts are just one of the many teatime treats to be found in this proudest of counties. Indeed, the good people of Yorkshire are apt to turn their hands to near infinite types of breads, buns, rolls, cakes, slices, flans, tarts, bakes, puddings and pies, leaving you with the impression that teatime in 'God's own county' is a meal given proper credence and respect.

This love of all things pastry obviously requires a good number of bakeries, and they don't come much more representative of the resurgence in quality baking than the Bondgate Bakery in Otley, owned by Stephen Taylor. Stephen trained as a biochemist and after university had a lab position with the NHS in London, but soon left for his native Yorkshire, where, with partner Sally Hinchliffe, he set up the bakery with an enterprise loan. 'Baking is a sort of chemistry, when you think about it,' he claims. That was back in 1984, and he's been there ever since, scooping up local fans as well as being voted 'best local food retailer' by Radio 4's *Food Programme* in 2004.

It takes a certain temperament to work with pastry and breads. Most chefs like to cook with passion, flamboyance and derring-do; all qualities that will lead to flat, hard or tasteless results if applied to baking. Add to this almost scientific approach the unsocial hours – most bakers start work very early in the morning – and you gain a new respect for those who make our daily bread, tarts and cakes. 'When you're starting work at 4 a.m., sometimes 2 a.m., you've got to have a sense of humour,' says Stephen, who likes to shout Klingon battle oaths to fellow baker Hartley. Distinctly lacking in the shop – and the products – are additives and artificial 'improvers', as Stephen's been making additive-free bread from the get-go.

One of Stephen's specialities is the region's curd tart. Curds are made by separating milk into its watery whey and the solid curds using either rennet – a coagulant derived from calves' stomachs – or an acid such as lemon juice. Cottage cheese, for example, is washed curds with a little of the whey left in.

The other ingredients for the filling are margarine or butter, eggs, lemon juice and currants. Stephen uses Greek Vostizza currants in his curd mix. Made from the Black Corinth grape, they are some of the finest produced in Greece. Indeed the very word 'currants' is a corruption of the ancient Greek city-state of Corinth, which makes you wonder whether the first trader to bring them to these shores suffered from a lisp. Anyway, dried using the slow traditional method of short spells in the sun and then the shade, these tiny seedless grapes pack a big sweet punch (when it comes to currants, the smaller the better is a good rule of thumb). Indeed, so good is the Vostizza currant that it has been protected under the EU Protected Designation of Origin scheme since 1993.

For the base of the tart, Stephen uses shortcrust pastry, enriching it with egg yolks and sugar, and pricking it with what he calls 'a docker', which is an eight-inch disc of wood with a dozen clean nails knocked through it and a handle attached. The curd mix – along with the pastry – can be made beforehand and in fact they both benefit from a night in the fridge. In the morning, the currants will have traded some of their sweetness for the lemon and curd's tangy sour sharpness, swelling a little during the process.

After thirty minutes at 200°C the tart is done. At first you're struck by the contrasting smells of warm buttery pastry against the still-present tang of the lemon and sour note of the curds. You can't really smell any sweetness at this stage, but the effect of the sugar and the juicy currants comes through as it hits the tip of your tongue, which is home to your sweet taste buds, after your first bite. The texture is still crumbly, although the free-range eggs in the mix have done their best to bind it. The enriched pastry seems more silken, what with its own added egg, which of course also beefs up the colour. Finally the top crust has turned a rich mahogany brown, flecked with the odd currant, like knots in wood.

So eight inches of enriched pastry, free-range eggs, the finest Greek currants and local curds, all baked together with love and care for just £5. It's really rather good, and a great centrepiece for an afternoon tea.

*See also* ALBERT EMBANKMENT, LAMBETH (p. 368); ALDERLEY EDGE, CHESHIRE (p. 96); BISHOP AUCKLAND, COUNTY DURHAM (p. 201); ECCLES, GREATER MANCHESTER (p. 103); HOOK NORTON, OXFORDSHIRE (p. 328); LLANDEILO, CARMARTHENSHIRE (p. 74); MANCHESTER, GREATER MANCHESTER (p. 119); MELTON MOWBRAY, LEICESTERSHIRE (p. 341); NAVENBY, LINCOLNSHIRE (p. 344); STANBRIDGE, BEDFORDSHIRE (p. 360); WHITBY, NORTH YORKSHIRE (p. 269).

## PONTEFRACT, WEST YORKSHIRE
# *Liquorice*

According to Bassett's, their most famous selection of liquorice sweets was created by accident in 1899. Salesman Charlie Thompson is said to have tripped over while carrying a tray of sweet samples, mixing them all up. The buyer, apparently, liked the look of the mixture, and asked Thompson to name the new creation. He called it 'Liquorice Allsorts', and the rest is history. Personally, my favourite Liquorice Allsort is the round one covered in blue hundreds and thousands, which is odd as it's the only one that doesn't contain any liquorice but instead has a centre of aniseed jelly.

The town of Pontefract is the liquorice capital of the UK. They started growing the plant in the soft soil there – the root is what's actually used – hundreds of years ago. Production finally petered out in the nineteenth century thanks to competition from cheaper imports. The original uses of liquorice were medicinal, and it is still used as an expectorant today. In the early 1600s, liquorice extract was being made into small lozenges, each stamped with a seal. Then, in 1760, an apothecary called George Dunhill had the idea of adding sugar to the lozenges, thus the Pontefract cake as we know it today was born. They were all made – and stamped – by hand until the late 1960s. In 1974 John Betjeman wrote *The Liquorice Fields of Pontefract*, where he and his love did steal a moment together. At the turn of the last century the number of liquorice manufacturers in the town was in double figures, yet over 100 years later the number stands at just two: Haribo and Tangerine. The latter uses Middle Eastern liquorice, although they do maintain some specially kept plants around the flagpole outside the factory's main reception.

Liquorice in sweets is slowly falling out of favour these days, as most newsagent's 'sweets' selections are predominantly chocolate-based and aimed at adults. Of course that doesn't mean liquorice is not being put to use elsewhere, and if anything, confectionery's loss is quality cuisine's gain. At the Fat Duck, Heston Blumenthal serves a salmon fillet wrapped in a liquorice jelly, which is remarkably mild and delicate. Visually, it's mesmerising: garlanded by grapefruit seeds, it rests on the plate and quivers expectantly, like a fish with a rubber fetish. And liquorice works with more than just fish. Chef Glynn Purnell at Purnell's restaurant in Birmingham has used it with duck breast and beef, and TV chef Jean-Christophe Novelli has used it in a sauce for sticky cuts of beef like oxtail. Alternatively, if you fancy something a little more mainstream, you could try one of Farmer Copley's liquorice sausages, which are available at the Pontefract Liquorice Festival, held every July in the town, as well as all year round in the Copley's brilliant farm shop just outside the town.

*See also* HOW RECIPES BEGIN (p. 496); FLEETWOOD, LANCASHIRE (p. 105).

RHUBARB TRIANGLE, WEST YORKSHIRE
## Forced rhubarb

As a child, I loved eating raw rhubarb dipped in a cup of sugar. This, apparently, was a hangover from the post-war contrivance of literally sugar-coating the plant's vitamins and nutrients in order to get kids to eat the sour scarlet stick. For most of its life, it seems, rhubarb has rather suffered from being thought of as 'good for you' rather than delicious, and it was used medicinally by the Chinese. Going by the name of Rhacoma root, it was used to treat gut and liver problems, and in 1657 its asking price was three times that of opium.

In the UK, production is centred on the 'rhubarb triangle' drawn between the towns of Wakefield, Morley and Rothwell in West Yorkshire. Once the area was much larger, supporting over 200 producers, but now there are only under a dozen fighting to keep the tradition alive. Leading that charge is Janet Oldroyd, of E. Oldroyd's in Wakefield, who runs 200 acres. These are divided into an area for outdoor grown rhubarb, an area for forced rhubarb and the rest for propagation – to grow next year's roots. Once rhubarb is in the ground you can't harvest it for the first year, and after three years of harvesting the roots need to be grubbed up and the land rested and reset by growing something else – normally a brassica.

The roots that will go on to be forced spend a lot of time in the ground absorbing and storing energy, which is absolutely critical for a good crop. They're very gently extracted by hand, washed and made ready for planting in the forcing sheds, where they will be grown in total darkness (the candles that appear in photographs are only there so that workers can see to harvest the crop). The plant is fooled into thinking it's spring by heating the shed, something that was done in the past using braziers fuelled with coal from Yorkshire mines. The plant puts out young, tender stems as it would in spring, but as it's growing in darkness it is stopped from photosynthesising sunlight and toughening up. Instead, the growth is fuelled by the stored energy in the roots.

Forcing rhubarb gave people a fresh, vitamin-enriched vegetable in the depths of winter when there was little else around. Producing it is very labour-intensive, and now that we have access to fresh fruit and vegetables from all over the globe all year round, you might be forgiven for wondering why it's still worth the bother. My answer to that would be that this is part of our agricultural heritage; it is a regional speciality that should be championed. Once the last eleven producers are gone, their sheds flattened and their fields dug up, their knowledge will fade and England will be a little dimmer. Moreover, although we live in an age of plenty where you can taste flavours from all over the world, forced rhubarb is easily as good as any of them, its tender stalks packing a refreshing tartness that belies their tender form. Forced Yorkshire rhubarb is unique, and Janet sums up why: 'The soil's to be right, the climate's to be right, and everything comes together here in Yorkshire. We grow it slower than they do in Holland. We do it steady.'

## *Stocks from True Food Ltd*

Despite the oft-repeated mantra that all good cooking starts with good stock, the reality is that few of us can manage to maintain a sixty-litre stockpot constantly bubbling away in our kitchen. *Larousse Gastronomique* suggests simmering beef stock for a minimum of six hours, although most professional kitchens prefer to do it for longer; reduce and pass, reduce and pass, this is the world of the commis chef. Unless the restaurant is a 24-hour operation, leaving the stockpot on probably invalidates insurance, and with kitchens getting smaller and labour and fuel costs only going up, it's no wonder that some restaurants look for a high-quality alternative.

And Mitch Mitchell at True Foods Ltd provides one. Training as a commis chef in his native Scotland, he did stints for various hotels and clients, and rose to be the personal chef to King Hussein of Jordan. Consultancy work followed, but eventually he decided he wanted to do his own thing. One day, while out shopping with his wife, when he claimed he could make a much better stock than the one in the tub on the shelf, his wife replied, 'Well, why don't you do that?' So in went the life savings, and a month later True Foods was born. 'We spent longer deciding the right colour of our lounge curtains,' says Mitch. True Foods have since expanded to soups, pâtés and terrines after asking themselves, 'What can we do while these stocks are cooking for the next twelve hours?'

Good bones are where good stocks start, and Mitch likes to use a selection from all over the animal. 'Neck bones still have a lot of meat left on them for flavour, while ribs and marrow bones give gelatinous quality.' These are roasted in a 250 °C oven to colour, before being put into a large boiler with water, seasoning, bay leaves, and, thyme, and left to simmer. The stock is then strained by hand through a muslin and reduced again (for wholesale into restaurants he reduces it even further), then strained once more, before being blast-chilled.

As for domestic cooks, not many enjoy the prospect of that kind of commitment. It's not so much a complicated task as a time-consuming one, so probably best attempted on a weekend. Or you could always have a lie-in and let Mitch do the work for you.

## Henderson's Relish

The mighty Roman Empire had garum, billions of Chinese have soy sauce and the people of Sheffield have Henderson's Relish. More than a mere condiment, it's an elixir of life found in every café and chippie worth its salt in the region. The relish is shipped to homesick ex-pats all over the world, and counts among its fans Sean Bean, David Blunkett, the Arctic Monkeys and, um, Peter Stringfellow. One Andrew Green even tattooed a picture of a bottle on to his calf as a wedding present from his bride-to-be Tara – now that's devotion.

The current owner of Henderson's, Dr Kenneth 'Doc' Freeman, remains sweetly nonplussed and yet extremely grateful for all this adoration. 'Doc' only came into the business through marriage after retiring as a GP in 1991. 'I left my surgery on the Friday and was here on Monday,' he says.

Originally started as a sideline by general stores owner Henry Henderson in the late nineteenth century, the sauce soon became his core business. It

The humble office and factory where Henderson's Relish is made

was later sold to Shaws of Huddersfield in 1910, before coming under the control of Charles Hinksman in the 1940s, and finally ending up with his nephew, Doc Freeman. Henderson's Relish has been made in a little well-worn building since the 1940s, when it moved there from the original site just half a mile away. Around the small red-brick building the landscape has changed utterly beyond recognition. The University of Sheffield has developed the area and it now houses bright shiny buildings for the improvement of bright shiny minds, throwing the old Henderson's building into even greater contrast.

Inside, the production machinery is Heath Robinsonesque as the bottles roll gently into waiting hands to be packed up and dispatched in boxes of twelve. And yet despite this simple, small-scale set-up, Henderson's still sell over 750,000 bottles of the sauce a year. One could say Doc has a steady hand on the tiller, mindful of growing too quickly or too broadly. The sauce was little-known outside the city initially, but in the past ten years has become a firm Yorkshire favourite. Rather than launching new products (oh, the imagined horrors of a 'lite' version), Henderson's prefer establishing relationships with other producers. So, for example, they have put together a deal with the Yorkshire Crisp Company (*see* p. 260), who do a Henderson's flavour. In its traditional, liquid form it's also becoming more readily available in supermarkets nationwide. This may be down in part to Sheffield's numerous university students becoming hooked, then returning to their hometowns and demanding it.

As you would expect, the recipe is a secret. I wasn't even allowed past the bottling machine into the mixing room in case I saw something I shouldn't. Suffice to say it has a sweet yet tart taste, egged on perhaps by the heat from the spices. So sugar and vinegar play their part, as do the pepper and the sour tang of tamarind. And in the gaps between all this, there is room for the flavour of the thing you're adding the sauce to. Because to truly appreciate Hendo's (as the locals call it), you've got to splash it on summat.

*See also* BISHOP'S STORTFORD, HERTFORDSHIRE (p. 321); EASTON GREY, WILTSHIRE (p. 11); EDINBURGH, EDINBURGH (p. 167); FAVERSHAM, KENT (p. 477); MOFFAT, DUMFRIES & GALLOWAY (p. 183); NORWICH, NORFOLK (p. 451); OXFORD, OXFORDSHIRE (p. 351); ROSSENDALE, LANCASHIRE (p. 131); ST HELENS, MERSEYSIDE (p. 132); SPENNYMOOR, COUNTY DURHAM (p. 227); WORCESTER, WORCESTERSHIRE (p. 317).

## Yorkshire Crisps

The Yorkshire Crisp Company's website bears the phrase 'When God made Yorkshire he was just showing off' and, unlike the crisps, I reckon most Yorkshire folk don't take this with a pinch of salt. The Yorkshire Crisp Company was started by Tony Bishop and Ashley Turner in 2004. As small-scale producers, they decided to target the growing luxury end of the crisps market, and haven't looked back since. From an initial four basic flavours, they have now expanded to nine, including plain 'Nowt On' style and Henderson's Relish flavour (*see* p. 258). They also do parsnip crisps, despite the fact that it's very tricky to get a parsnip to crisp up due to their much higher sugar content, which can burn easily in the fryer. Apparently, the guys ruined two tons of parsnips before getting it right. The environmental impact of making the crisps is also taken into account. All the factory's waste products go to a local pig farmer, and the spent oil is refined into the biodiesel that fuels the delivery vans.

The paddles at the back of the fryer dunk the crisps under the oil

But back to the muddy spuds. The chaps use Hermes, a main-crop potato that's great for making crisps. According to the British Potato Council, Hermes have a high 'dry' content and a good fry colour. Once picked, the potatoes are simply washed and sliced with the peel left on (which is where a lot of the flavour is) before being fried at 172°C in pure sunflower oil. Because a potato is roughly 80 per cent water and 20 per cent dry matter, when frying, the necessary by-product is a good deal of steam. Once the potatoes have crisped up, they are removed, drained and passed through a drum that coats them with the flavour of choice. From there they get a final check over before being bagged, packed and dispatched to everywhere from local farm shops to Fortnum & Mason's food hall. Included in the ingredients listed on the bags is 'tender loving care', and you can definitely taste it.

*See also* CORNHILL-ON-TWEED, NORTHUMBERLAND (p. 208); MARAZION, CORNWALL (p. 28); NEWCASTLE, TYNE & WEAR (p. 218).

WANSFORD, EAST YORKSHIRE
## *Rainbow trout*

On the one hand we're told to eat more fish, on the other wild fish stocks are a cause for concern, so what's to be done? Well, Erik Jensen at Wansford trout farm thinks he may have an answer. 'Rainbow trout is an often over-looked fish which is high in omega-3 and low in fat. What's more, its market price is generally much lower than its cousin the salmon, but it's equally as nutritious and tasty.' Erik's farm supplies the major supermarkets with 600 tonnes of trout for their fish counters each year.

The farm – one of the first fish farms to be built in the UK – was started by a Danish entrepreneur in 1955 and is still owned by the Jøker family. Erik's father worked for them for forty-five years, and when he retired Erik took over as manager. The farm draws water from the Driffield West Beck chalk stream, described by locals as 'gin clear', and itself prized by fishermen for its plentiful stocks of native grayling and brown trout. The farm's fish are housed in large pens about the size of a tennis court, and are stocked at a level well below the recommended average, ensuring they have plenty of room. This low density coupled with filtering means waste water is returned to the stream from the farm as clean as when it left.

# Parkin

Parkin is a warm, filling cake for cold winter evenings. According to food historian Jennifer Stead, parkin may be derived from older, honey-sweetened oatcakes eaten during Celtic and Viking celebrations for the arrival of winter in early November. Oats still feature as parkin's main ingredient, which is understandable as they grow well in the cool conditions across the north of Britain.

All the other ingredients in parkin, though, are products of the Victorian era of mass import, export and production, from an empire greater than the Vikings could have imagined. Raw cane sugar was brought from the West Indies and refined into the granulated form, but also into treacle and golden syrup. These ingredients not only add sweetness to parkin, but also a sticky texture and, in the case of treacle, a dark-brown colour. Lots of powdered ginger and sometimes mace and nutmeg give the cake a fiery taste, and these would have come from the spice markets of the East. The Victorians made parkin to celebrate Guy Fawkes Night – an appropriate cake for the occasion, as a proper parkin should have something of the snap of gunpowder about it in flavour. The first written mention of parkin according to *OED* is in the diary of Dorothy Wordsworth, sister of the poet, who baked some on 6 November 1800.

Parkin comes in both Yorkshire and Lancashire versions, and so could be described as the War of the Roses re-enacted in baking. Indeed, it is not at all well known outside those counties. Traditionally, Yorkshire parkin is made with course oatmeal and dripping (or a mixture of dripping and butter), while Lancashire parkin contains finer oatmeal, a bit more flour and only uses butter. Those under the banner of the white rose would no doubt call it soft. Indeed, it was so admired up north that the first Sunday of November was known as Parkin Sunday in the West Riding of Yorkshire. Ideally, parkin should be left for a few days after baking, quietly resting in a tin. This allows it to get a little sticky and fermented. You can find parkin in practically every bakery in the north of England, especially during the autumnal and winter months, though in the south you'll have much more trouble tracking it down.

*See also* MARKET DRAYTON, SHROPSHIRE (p. 302).

Erik Jensen nets rainbow trout from one of the pens on his farm

On cooking them, Erik says, 'The best way is in a foil bag. Stuff the cavity with lemon and thyme, pour in a drop of wine, fold it up and pop in a hot oven for twelve to fifteen minutes.' Trout has a delicate flavour, which means it's a very good host to other flavours such as fennel, garlic and even bacon. Vegetables that complement it include cucumbers, spring onions, and other light greens and salads. Of course, if you want to get fancy you could always try making a mousseline, which sees the puréed fish added to whipped cream, resulting in a light delicate texture. Or you could take a leaf out of the Portuguese approach to trout, and cook it with a sprig of juniper in the cavity.

See also DERWENTWATER, CUMBRIA (p. 102); DOVER, KENT (p. 473); GLOUCESTER, GLOUCESTERSHIRE (p. 288); HASTINGS, EAST SUSSEX (p. 483); MARKET HARBOROUGH, LEICESTERSHIRE (p. 340); NEWLYN, CORNWALL (pp. 32 and 34); RIVER SEVERN, GLOUCESTERSHIRE (p. 305); SCOURIE, HIGHLAND (p. 187); SOUTHEND-ON-SEA, ESSEX (p. 455); WHITBURN, TYNE & WEAR (p. 228).

## WENSLEYDALE, NORTH YORKSHIRE
### *Wensleydale cheese*

When Cistercian monks came over from Roquefort in 1156 to found Jervaulx Abbey, they brought some of their cheese-making knowledge to the town of Ripon, producing a blue sheep's milk cheese similar to the Roquefort they had known in France. The Cistercian order were not only at the cutting edge of farming technology and food production methods, they were also, in the words of Evan Fraser and Andrew Rimas, authors of *Empires of Food* (2010), 'savvy agricultural managers . . . who . . . despite their professed zeal, became fabulously wealthy landlords' and their know-how quickly spread throughout the community. In the 1500s the Dissolution of the Monasteries saw the back of the monks, but their ex-tenant farmers continued to make cheese in their smallholdings, by then using primarily cow's milk. According to author and cheese expert Patrick Rance, when natural rennet – made from a cow's stomach – wasn't available, a black snail was apparently used. The prefix 'Wensleydale' was added to the cheese in the nineteenth century as people started to sell it nationally.

It must have been a popular ingredient, because in 1897 Edward Chapman bought surplus milk from farms and began making the cheese commercially in the Wensleydale Creamery in Hawes, although his business faltered in the Depression of the 1930s. One of the farmers, Kit Calvert, managed to raise enough money and take the business on, but he in turn ran into trouble as the Second World War broke out. Wartime rationing and food control meant that all cheese production was annexed to the standard Government Cheddar, and the dairy, like so many others after the war, never really recovered. In 1966 the Milk Marketing Board purchased the dairy, and it came under the control of its processing division, Dairy Crest. In 1992 they closed the dairy in Hawes and transferred production to Lancashire. The good people of the Dales had taken the Dissolution, the Depression and war in their stride, but this, this was the ultimate insult, and breaking out the pitchforks (metaphorically at least), four previous managers at the dairy staged a management buyout. Former members of the workforce were rehired and cheese production started again.

The taste is soft and milky, despite fourteen months' ageing, with a slightly sour flavour resting on top of it; while the texture looks solid, but then crumbles and gives easily. The cheese received an unexpected marketing boost thanks to the films of Nick Park, whose hero Wallace and faithful sidekick Gromit adore cheese, especially Wensleydale. Interestingly, though, Wallace is from Lancashire; Wigan, in fact.

*See also* BRITISH CHEESE (p. 290).

WETHERBY, WEST YORKSHIRE
## Cream cakes from Market Place Deli

It's a pub-quiz factoid that Salman Rushdie wrote the 'Naughty, but nice' line for the fresh cream cake advert commissioned by the National Dairy Council in the 1980s. It could equally, however, be applied today to the cakes on offer in the Market Place Deli owned by Ian Giddings. Ian studied catering and bakery management at college before working for a company that imported specialist foods. Made redundant at twenty-six, he was walking past an estate agent's when he noticed a deli that was up for sale, and went for it. That was over fifteen years ago, and he's not looked back since. Staffing the deli is a real family affair, with his wife Sam and his daughter helping in the shop.

The oven in the deli is nearly ninety years old and was made in Leeds

Naughty but nice: strawberry tarts being given a final glaze

by a Mr G. Tweedale. 'It's gas-powered but works a bit like an Aga,' says Ian. 'You get it hot, and can then pretty much switch it off yet keep cooking in it all day.' As for what comes out of it, well, there are savoury things such as salmon en croute, lovely-looking quiches over an inch high (though around these parts they're known as flans) and a range of pies and pastries. Aside from the strawberry and cream tarts, there is lemon cheesecake, baked raspberry and blueberry cheesecake, double chocolate roulard, fruit tarts, tarte au citron, fresh cream pavlova and summer pudding gateaux. 'People tend to favour chocolate things when it's cold, and fresh fruit when it's warm,' says Ian. Ian gets all his fruit for the cakes and desserts fresh from the greengrocer's in the town each morning. A delicious strawberry tart, then, would count towards one of your five a day. Not so naughty, but definitely nice.

# Whitby kippers

In the eighteenth and nineteenth centuries the herring industry stretched from Aberdeen in Scotland, down through Northumberland and Yorkshire to East Anglia. As ships became bigger, the herring became less numerous, and as a consequence North Sea herring fishing was banned in the 1970s to allow stocks to recover. At that time many fishermen quit, or found work on the rigs, and shore-based industries, including kipper manufacturers, had to adjust accordingly.

William Fortune first hung kippers over smouldering woodchips in Whitby in 1872. The smokehouse – a tiny, garage-sized building – sits on a cobbled street leading to the 199 steps that connect to the ruins of Whitby Abbey. An image of William's daughter-in-law Ellen, from the turn of the last century, hangs outside the shop, and a sign behind her advertises the fact that six kippers can be posted anywhere in the UK for 2/-, about 10p in today's money.

Nowadays the business, along with its more realistic mail-order prices, is run by Derek and Barry Fortune, the fifth generation of Fortunes to smoke the fish. 'Our herring has come from Norway for the last thirty years,' says Barry, 'but the process remains unchanged.' In the shop the fish is gutted and cut by hand, washed, then lightly brined for forty minutes or so. Then they are hung in the smoker, the dripping walls as black as a chain-smoker's lung, and cold-smoked over a mixture of oak and beech for twelve to twenty-four hours.

Once the process is complete, they are moved into the shop for sale. To cook them, you can poach them in water (this is known as jugging), which mitigates the strong aroma – but hell's teeth, the smell is part of the joy of kippers – or you can bake them in foil in the oven, barbecue or even microwave them. Derek favours showing them the grill, as do I, ideally for breakfast, with nothing more than a poached egg and brown bread and butter.

Robert Louis Stevenson once said, 'An aim in life is the only fortune worth finding,' and it seems the Fortune brothers have found theirs. 'We're going to keep doing what we're doing, because at the end of the day we like what we do.' No doubt great-great-grandfather William would approve.

*See also* ARBROATH, ANGUS (p. 143); CLEY NEXT THE SEA, NORFOLK (p. 424); FINDON, ABERDEENSHIRE (p. 169); GREAT YARMOUTH, NORFOLK (p. 433); HAMBRIDGE, SOMERSET (p. 13); NIDDERDALE, NORTH YORKSHIRE (p. 251); SEAHOUSES, NORTHUMBERLAND (p. 224).

WHITBY, NORTH YORKSHIRE

# Whitby lemon buns from Bothams

'The correct way to eat a Whitby lemon bun,' claims fourth-generation baker Jo Botham, 'is to tear – never cut – it in half, then tear down the side and fold it over.' This inverting process creates a sort of lemon sandwich. However, most folk just bite into them. Bothams have been baking lemon buns, and a good deal of other delectable delights, since Elizabeth Botham started selling cakes door to door in 1865. She was the second wife of one John Botham, a shepherd and farmer near Driffield. After his first wife died, a plague of anthrax wiped out his flock, leaving him a broken man, so the family moved to Whitby and Elizabeth set about making ends meet. With the coming of the railway, Whitby became a tourist destination for the well-heeled from all over the region, who came to take the air. After a few lungfuls of the North Sea's finest, people were apt to get a bit peckish, and luckily Elizabeth was on hand to sell them some tea and cake, exactly as her descendants do today.

There's a picture of Elizabeth hanging in the entrance to the tea shop, watching over her offspring, that projects an aura of firm politeness. With broad shoulders and strong arms, she looks like the sort of Yorkshire woman who would do everything properly and wouldn't have countenanced anything second rate or any messing about. As well as the bakery and tea rooms, she also found time to run a pub, and gave birth to fourteen children, not all of whom survived – a strong woman in anyone's book.

But back to the buns. They are made fresh every day from a rich fermented bread dough and sultanas, along with icing flavoured with Sicilian lemon oil. Unlike the fruit cake, tea bread and plum loaf Bothams make, which get better with age, lemon buns are best eaten as soon as possible. Malcolm Baker, the author and former editor of the *Yorkshire Evening Post*, once said, 'It's not physically possible to get a lemon bun out of Whitby.' He is right in that they don't travel well; but mainly it's because the temptation to eat them, correctly or not, is just too strong.

*See also* ALBERT EMBANKMENT, LAMBETH (p. 368); ALDERLEY EDGE, CHESHIRE (p. 96); BISHOP AUCKLAND, COUNTY DURHAM (p. 201); ECCLES, GREATER MANCHESTER (p. 103); HOOK NORTON, OXFORDSHIRE (p. 328); LLANDEILO, CARMARTHENSHIRE (p. 74); MANCHESTER, GREATER MANCHESTER (p. 119); MELTON MOWBRAY, LEICESTERSHIRE (p. 341); NAVENBY, LINCOLNSHIRE (p. 344); OTLEY, WEST YORKSHIRE (p. 252); STANBRIDGE, BEDFORDSHIRE (p. 360).

## YORK, NORTH YORKSHIRE
### *Bettys tea rooms*

A cup of tea in the morning is the reason most of us get out of bed. Personally, I can't function until I've wetted my whistle with one. In contrast to my wee-hour, bleary-eyed shuffle around the kitchen, though, there is the fine institution of afternoon tea. And there are few places better to get one than Bettys in York. Yes, there's no apostrophe, but what they lack in correct grammar they more than make up for in what my mum would call 'a good

A 'fat rascal' fixing you with his cherry eyes

spread'. On three-tier display stands you'll find sandwiches (crusts off and cut into fingers), scones with Yorkshire clotted cream and strawberry jam, and a selection of cakes including fruit flan, chocolate profiteroles and some lovely lemon madeleines. These are accompanied by loose-leaf tea in a hot teapot, a small jug of milk and two dainty cups. But if there is one cake that sums up the institution that is Bettys, it's the fat rascal. Similar to a scone, but much more primordial in texture, each rascal contains citrus peel and raisins, is shaped roughly into a mound, and decorated with two glacé cherry eyes and a mischievous rictus mouth fashioned in almonds. It is simply a delight.

Bettys' Swiss founder Fritz Bützer arrived in England in 1907 penniless and speaking not a word of English but determined to seek his fortune. After some muddled exchange he ended up on a train to Bradford, where he found work. By 1919 he had moved to Harrogate, anglicised his name to Frederick Belmont and opened a tea shop.

Subsequent branches opened in York, which became popular with servicemen in the Second World War. A merger in 1962 with Taylor's added more outlets, yet the firm remains resolute in staying rooted in Yorkshire, with no designs or desires to leave the county. This may be in part because of their wish to keep a watchful eye on every small detail, with everything made by their own bakery and delivered to store fresh each morning.

I am a huge fan of tea rooms. A proper cup of well-made tea and a slice of cake is surely up there with the rule of law, freedom of the press and democracy as a hallmark of civilisation. OK, that may be a little grand, but a few moments taken for tea, a nibble and a sit-down is always time well spent in my book.

*See also* APPLEDORE, KENT (p. 466); HARROGATE, NORTH YORKSHIRE (p. 250); NEW GALLOWAY, DUMFRIES & GALLOWAY (p. 184); PEMBROKE DOCK, PEMBROKESHIRE (p. 81).

YORK, NORTH YORKSHIRE
## York ham

Despite the resurgence of interest in all things local and traditional, it's worth remembering that there are those who sometimes fall by the wayside. In 2008, as I stood in front of Scott's butcher's in York, bluebottles crawled across the handwritten notice in the window announcing that they had ceased trading. With their demise, the last place within the old city walls where you could buy York ham was lost after 130 years of trading.

A number of factors were to blame, according to Scott's owner and manager William Anderson, including increasing red tape and problems with access for delivery, not to mention a real slump in the retail side of things. The shop was a stone's throw away from the historic York Minster, a huge tourist attraction, but sadly it seems that the visitors ambling through the lanes had no time for the historic ham, which once stood hock to hock with the *jamón* and *prosciutto* of Europe.

When a butcher called Robert Burrow Atkinson opened a shop in a brand-new building on Blossom Street, York, around 1860, he soon discovered that the cellar was perfect for maturing hams that proved exceedingly popular with locals and visitors alike. Thus, the York ham was born. The Large White pig, first recognised in 1868 and itself descended from an older Yorkshire breed, was no doubt the pig of choice. The back leg and haunch were cut from the carcass and rubbed with a mix of salt, saltpetre and sugar. Then it was hung and left to mature for anything from ten weeks to two years. The joy of it is in its simplicity and subtlety.

There are still some producers based outside of the city who make proper York ham. Dukeshill, in Shropshire, make a fantastic version, cut long off the pig, salted and left for three weeks, during which time it shrinks by a considerable margin. It is then washed, dried and left to air-dry for three months.

The gourmet Jean Anthelme Brillat-Savarin famously said, 'The discovery of a new dish does more for human happiness than the discovery of a new star.' One might equally take the view that the loss of a dish, recipe or traditional method unleashes a supernova of despondency, or worse, apathy.

*See also* BROMYARD, HEREFORDSHIRE (p. 283); CAMBRIDGE, CAMBRIDGESHIRE (p. 422); CONWY, CONWY (p. 60); FORRES, MORAY (p. 173); LOUTH, LINCOLNSHIRE (p. 336); MARYLEBONE, WESTMINSTER (p. 387); MELTON CONSTABLE, NORFOLK (p. 447); NANTWICH, CHESHIRE (p. 125); WOODHALL SPA, LINCOLNSHIRE (p. 364).

# 7 | The West Midlands

# Lockwoods mushy peas

Having grown up in the north, I naturally take mushy peas, along with a slice or two of bread and butter, with my fish and chips. The plate just looks wrong without them; it should be bread, gold and green, to paraphrase Boy George's 'Karma Chameleon'.

And what a green it can be. When it comes to bright-green foodstuffs, the colour of British mushies, particularly the tinned incarnations, beats guacamole and wasabi hands down, which is surprising given the British knack of boiling the hell out of veg. The bright colour is actually due to performance-enhancing additions: Brilliant Blue FCF (E133), a dye made from coal tar; and tartrazine (E102), a synthetic yellow dye. Good chip shops may eschew the additives, meaning their peas will still be green, but edging towards olive every hour, reaching khaki by the time the owner shuts up shop for the night.

Mushy peas should be made from dried marrowfat peas, soaked in a little baking soda and simmered slowly. This is how Lockwoods in Derbyshire still make theirs today. The firm began in the 1960s, selling packs of dried marrowfat peas along with a tablet of bicarbonate of soda at the market in Heanor, Derbyshire. These could then be taken home, soaked overnight and cooked the next day. The downside of this is that you would have had to plan your mushy peas twenty-four hours in advance. Various improvements in production followed, and now the firm produce a tub of peas you can heat in a microwave oven.

In September 2009 Lockwoods stopped using artificial colouring completely. 'I have the view that those two additives will be banned by Europe eventually, so we bit the bullet and removed them,' says general manager Iain Sands. 'We've had a few comments but that's the natural pea colour.' Until 2008 all their peas came from the UK, but a bad harvest forced them to open accounts with growers in America and Canada. In 2009 some 90 per cent of their peas came once more from the UK.

People who don't like mushy peas are just plain weird in my book, and this is my book. So for all you naysayers, all I am saying is, give peas a chance.

*See also* ALNWICK, NORTHUMBERLAND (p. 199); STRAND, WESTMINSTER (p. 409).

# Real ale from the Tunnel microbrewery

Behind most boozers you're most likely to find pub debris, smokers, fights and car-park smoochers. The Lord Nelson in Astley, however, boasts what must be one of the smallest microbreweries in the country, tucked away between its beer garden and car park. The Tunnel Brewery is manned by just Bob Yates and Mike Walsh – Bob takes on the business side of things, and Mike handles all matters zymological – but what it lacks in staff numbers it makes up for in top-drawer brews.

When I met them, though, what was occupying their minds was not their location, but that of a ship from New Zealand carrying a precious cargo of Pacific Gem hops. These Kiwi hops are a key ingredient in Light at the End of the Tunnel, their dark-golden session bitter much beloved by the regulars in the pub next door and the surrounding region. They have to come from New Zealand: 'Hops are like grapes: they have a *terroir*,' says Mike. It's the Pacific hops's high alpha-acid content yet subtle flavour that is their strength. 'It's one of over twenty hops we use, but an important one,' says Mike. Luckily, they had enough to keep them going for some time, but it was certainly

Mike and Bob and a vat of one of their lovingly made brews

uplifting to witness them taking such care in the sourcing and forward-planning of their beer production. Another of Tunnel's charms is the story on the back of each bottle describing how the beer came about, written by Bob, and featuring artwork commissioned from a local artist. It adds to the sense that each bottle or cask is crafted with love, care and attention to detail. Mike, too, is something of an artist; though water is his canvas and the other ingredients are his paints.

Bob believes people seek out their beer because they're looking for depth, flavour and complexity. 'Mass-produced beers might use rice or sweetcorn instead of barley to get the required starches and sugars, but these are flavour neutralisers,' says Mike.

*See also* BRITISH PUBS (p. 434); GREENWICH, GREENWICH (p. 378); KNIGHTWICK, WORCESTERSHIRE (p. 299); NEWCASTLE, TYNE & WEAR (p. 220); SOUTHWOLD, SUFFOLK (p. 457).

BAKEWELL, DERBYSHIRE
## Bakewell puddings

The early history of many recipes often starts with a story, and the Bakewell pudding is no different. Enter then, stage left, Mrs Gervase, landlady in the 1860s of the White Horse coaching inn in fair Bakewell, where we lay our scene. (I'm imagining Mrs Miggins from *Blackadder III*.) As Mrs Gervase entertains her guests, the cooking is left to a kitchen minion who, like a nervous contestant on *Masterchef*, fluffs the recipe, omits the eggs and sugar in the pastry and tries to fix the mistake by adding them on top. Knees tremble as the dish is sent up to the guests. Our comedy of errors ends with all the diners loving this new creation and our landlady taking the applause.

True? Well, that's for you to decide. What is true is that, however it came about, Bakewell pudding is best made and enjoyed in Bakewell. 'I'm happy with the facts that the pudding recipe originates in the UK, and the first people mass-producing it as we do with great ingredients were in Bakewell,' says Jemma Pheasey of the Old Original Pudding Company. Jemma has joined forces with Marion Wright at Bloomers bakery in the town, who also make puddings, to apply for EU PDO (Protected Designation of Origin) status. The first step to PDO status is the hardest, as it requires you to get round a table with your competitors and agree to work together. The next is to come up with a workable definition. Jemma explains, 'For the application,

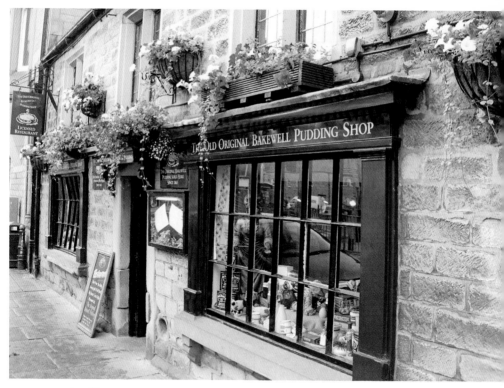

The Old Original Bakewell Pudding Shop

I've even been asked to describe what the texture in the mouth is, and how it breaks down. The recipe we want to submit isn't limited to our versions – for example, we say it can be made with strawberry or raspberry jam – we're just trying to protect the dish.'

The basic recipe calls for a smear of jam on a puff pastry base, topped with a mix of eggs, almonds, butter and sugar, plus the obligatory secret ingredient. It then spends forty minutes in the oven. 'It should be made from the best ingredients, eaten as fresh as possible, hot or cold (though hot is best), with custard or cream,' says Jemma.

A recipe for Bakewell pudding appears in *The Housekeeper's Book*, published in New York in 1837, and Eliza Acton has a recipe in her *Modern Cookery for Private Families* from 1845, where she haughtily observes, 'This is a rich and expensive, but not a very refined pudding. A variation of it, known in the south as Alderman's pudding, is, we think, superior.'

'Ooooo, get her!' as they might say in Bakewell.

*See also* HOW RECIPES BEGIN (p. 496); MICKLETON, GLOUCESTERSHIRE (p. 304); PENRITH, CUMBRIA (p. 127); PETERBOROUGH, CAMBRIDGESHIRE (p. 352); POLEGATE, EAST SUSSEX (p. 494).

## *The balti*

As with chicken tikka masala (*see* p. 176), the invention of the balti remains shrouded in mystery. It is said to have been created in the late 1970s in Birmingham by Pakistani émigrés, and the city is still the UK epicentre of all things balti, quite rightly claiming the dish as its own. The dish has spread all over the country, from the Ganges Balti House in Penzance right up to the Stornoway Balti House in the Outer Hebrides. However, for a proper balti, you need to go to Birmingham's balti triangle.

One man who knows a great deal about the balti is Andy Munro. Andy works for Birmingham Council during the day, and in the evenings moonlights as a balti guru. Other people collect stamps or play golf; Andy enjoys baltis. There are many fine restaurants in the triangle, but not all serve what – in Andy's opinion – is an authentic balti. As for which is best, well, that rather depends on who you're with and what mood you're in. Al Frash on Ladypool Road, for example, is bright and modern, whereas Shabab, a bit further along, is a more traditional affair. As Andy says, 'If balti houses were listed, Shabab would be Grade I.'

The word 'balti' comes from the Urdu for bucket, and refers to the wok-shaped steel pan the dish is both cooked and served in. In Birmingham the balti dishes were initially all made by one man, Mr Tara Singh, now sadly passed away, who was a Sikh engineer with a machine shop near Smethwick. He was approached by one of the restaurant owners (history does not record which) in the late 1970s to make a thin metal dish. This dish was similar to a karahi used in Pakistani and Indian cooking, but smaller, meaning it could be sent to the table. Ironically, despite the balti dish being a UK-grown Pakistani invention, it's now cheaper to have them made in India or China and shipped to the UK. 'You can always spot an original balti dish: it'll be well worn; it might even be missing a handle,' says Andy.

The metal pan is not only a key part of the experience, it also contributes to the taste of the food. Because it cooks the ingredients very quickly – almost stir-frying them – rather than allowing them to simmer in a large amount of sauce, the cooking method really brings out the freshness and flavour. You can even find Birmingham balti houses that serve kidney curry, the quick cooking technique keeping the offal nice and pink. Most baltis, as a result, are served quite dry compared to other curries, with just a small amount of sauce, and importantly they use vegetable oil rather than ghee, which gives a cleaner taste.

Baltis should be eaten without cutlery, using the naan to pick up the meat and mop up any other bits. Naans in balti houses are often, therefore, much bigger than those in your average curry house. And the karak, or family, naan can approach the size of a child's duvet.

Andy believes – and I agree – that there's something special about the Birmingham balti, about its base ingredients and unique cooking method. 'I hate it when I see a balti cook-in sauce. That's just not balti.' He's currently seeking advice on how to get EU recognition, and I hope he's successful. It's all too easy to dismiss balti as just a type of curry, something to soak up the booze, but that would be a mistake. It's a brilliant example of multicultural Britain and one of our great success stories. I think it deserves recognition for that, as well as for being damn tasty.

*See also* GLASGOW, GLASGOW (p. 176); MARYLEBONE, WESTMINSTER (p. 389); WHITECHAPEL, TOWER HAMLETS (p. 414).


## BIRMINGHAM, WEST MIDLANDS
# Bird's Custard

Custard is the oil in the engine of the British pudding machine, so good that it's one of the few culinary things that the French actually attribute to us by name, *crème anglaise*, which is very kind of them. To most of us over thirty, custard means one thing: Bird's Custard powder made in, and often served out of, a Pyrex measuring jug. It was invented in 1837 by Alfred Bird, a chemist from Birmingham, for his wife, who was a bit of a fussy eater and unable to tolerate anything made with wheat or eggs. Bird, one imagines, nipped off to the lab to apply some fine Victorian logic to the problem. The result was a powder that contains no eggs, but uses corn starch and colouring to achieve a thick, yellow-coloured sauce when you add hot milk and sugar. Sadly, history does not relate if Alfred went on to invent the wheat-free sponge pudding, so one rather wonders what Mrs Bird poured her husband's invention over.

One hundred and fifty years later and Bird's invention had become a British staple. It was cheap, didn't need fresh eggs, never split and could be poured on everything. Gradually its popularity waned: ice cream became better in quality and cream more readily available.

These days, custard powder is seen as positively anachronistic and we can't even be bothered to heat up the milk to make it. Bird's (now owned by Premiere Foods) has moved with the times, and introduced a ready-made UHT version in a carton that can be stored at room temperature. If you want 'fresh' custard it's to be found in most supermarket chiller cabinets, the more costly ones flecked with vanilla. This wasn't always the flavouring of choice, though, and old recipes suggest adding cinnamon, lemon peel, brandy and peach water, among other flavours.

*See also* MICKLETON, GLOUCESTERSHIRE (p. 304).

## *The Handmade Scotch Egg Company*

The culinary Fabergé behind the Handmade Scotch Egg Company is Neil Chambers, and the firm is based not in the rugged Highlands of Caledonia but the rolling hills of Herefordshire. It very quickly became clear that if Neil embodies the 'company' in the business name, his wife Penny is the

The Black Watch: a free-range egg enveloped in black pudding and sausage meat

'handmade'. Up until very recently she produced every Scotch egg they made, six days a week. They make over thirty different flavours, but my favourite has to be the Black Watch. Underneath its blond-brown outer crust of breadcrumbs lies a dark mixture of sausage meat mixed with black pudding – utterly delicious.

Penny told me how they're made. 'First you make a sort of pattie, before gently pushing your egg into the middle and building up the sides around it,' she said as she enveloped the egg in the sausage-and-black-pudding mix and rolled it around in her hands. I had a go, and what happened next was like something out of *The Generation Game*. She had knocked out half a dozen while I'd only managed a single slightly larger, slightly wonky one. Penny then started the process of coating the eggs in breadcrumbs, dispensing a pearl of wisdom. 'You should always have a wet hand in the egg wash and a dry hand in the breadcrumbs.' She then dropped them slowly into the fryer. The stopwatch by the side counted down six minutes, then out they came, looking like newly formed planets, yet still squishy and quivering like a newborn baby's head.

The delicate way to eat a Scotch egg is to first slice it into two, then bite the front edge, but I have a jaw like a python and just tend to take a good bite while it's whole. I love that peppery, back-of-the-nose hit you get from the black pudding, and visually the rich dark-red meat contrasts nicely with the white and yellow of the egg. Our national love of the Scotch egg comes from the fact that, despite the name, they are a portable full English breakfast. At the core is your egg, wrapped in sausage, and then bread, albeit in the form of crumbs.

The eggs Neil and Penny use come from a local producer called Brian Taylor, and crucially have to be a week old, otherwise they're a bugger to peel. The pork Neil and Penny buy is from Rochford Company Meats in Tenbury Wells, set up by farmer-turned-butcher Andrew Keysell. Indeed, Neil pays Andrew regular visits so that he can 'meet the meat'. There are a handful of other suppliers, mostly small outfits like Penny and Neil's.

They take a 'jazz' approach to the Scotch egg: constantly riffing on the format, adding little flourishes, classic flavour combinations and seasonal ingredients while somehow never losing sight of the original melody, the tune of egg and pork. One of the great strengths of the business is that either of them can wake up in the middle of the night with a brainwave, and then sell it from the on-site shop by lunchtime. Often, they do seasonal specials and one-offs. One such example is the 'yoat', made with only the yolk, wrapped in pork, and finished with Scottish oats – hence the portmanteau name. 'It's essentially using up a waste product, as once in a while when you peel an egg, you'll catch the white and it'll tear so it can't be used.' So what's next? 'Well . . . we're thinking of launching a range of meatballs.' Scotch eggs without the egg . . . clever!

The history of the Scotch egg is interesting. Like a great many recipes and food inventions, its exact appearance cannot be dated with any accuracy. Not present in Hannah Glasse's *The Art of Cookery* in 1774, Scotch eggs do make an appearance thirty years later in Maria Eliza Ketelby Rundell's *A New System of Domestic Cookery*, and stay with us all the way through to today's TV chefs. Eggs were, of course, put in the middle of many things to improve their appearance; thus their addition to a pork pie gives us the gala pie. It's highly likely they found mass appeal during the Victorian era with the Victorians' love both of 'a savory' and of picnics. Although they don't make Mrs Beeton's list of things to take for a 'picnic for 40' (where practically everything else does), her book does include a recipe for them, served at dinner with gravy as you would faggots or savoury ducks. No matter what their history, a well-made Scotch egg is a thing of wonder, vastly superior to the cheap, mass-produced knock-offs that have all the taste and texture of a sawdust cricket ball.

BROMYARD, HEREFORDSHIRE
## Legge's butchers

Hanging in the corner of Anthony Legge's Bromyard butcher's shop and deli is a laminated poster advertising the distance travelled by some of the key produce sold there. The furthest distance on the list was Tyrrell's crisps, at a princely seventeen miles. Customers at Anthony's shop can also see exactly how their meat is handled, as the butchering area is situated at the rear, and the cold store, where Anthony's beef is hung and displayed like the Crown jewels, is visible through a window. His beef is hung on the bone for four weeks, and in that time it shrinks by 20 per cent, and therein lies the flavour. The sausages are all made on-site, which means that Anthony can adapt to whatever is around. He's experimented with pork, pear and perry sausages, rather than the traditional apple accompaniment; and when a local farmer shot eight wild hares and brought them in, Anthony created hare and pear sausage, just because he could.

Legge's have been known to push the boat out and do something a bit special when asked, too. For a special dinner at the Royal Naval College they put together a crown of beef: two sets of cows' ribs looped round to form a crown. 'It was three-quarters of a metre high and over a metre long,' says Anthony. 'It took two blokes to lift it.' God knows how they cooked it. It's not just the Admiralty that source from Legge's; they regularly get customers from Nottingham, Bristol and Birmingham coming to fill up the car boot. It seems sometimes the clientele have come from further afield than the produce.

*See also* CAMBRIDGE, CAMBRIDGESHIRE (p. 422); CONWY, CONWY (p. 60); FORRES, MORAY (p. 173); LOUTH, LINCOLNSHIRE (p. 336); MARYLEBONE, WESTMINSTER (p. 387); MELTON CONSTABLE, NORFOLK (p. 447); NANTWICH, CHESHIRE (p. 125); WOODHALL SPA, LINCOLNSHIRE (p. 364); YORK, NORTH YORKSHIRE (p. 271).

## BURTON UPON TRENT, STAFFORDSHIRE
# Marmite

Marmite, along with supermarket taramasalata, is one of the few foodstuffs I can't stand, so much so that it actually makes me gag. This is odd, because I tend to like yeasty and umami flavours, and I'm even oddly partial to Twiglets, but when it comes to Marmite itself I am firmly in the 'hate' camp. Many people aren't, though, and the product remains one of Britain's best-loved brands. For those of you who don't know what it is, and it can only be one or two of you, Marmite is a thick, black paste made from concentrated yeast extract. It's normally found spoiling – in my mind at least – that other great British invention, toast, although it has a range of other uses, and I've heard tales of it being stirred into pasta or served with cheese.

It was a German chemist, Justus von Liebig, who developed the process of extracting essences of ingredients, particularly from meat. Liebig built on Louis Pasteur's work on yeast, figuring out that it could self-digest and produce an edible paste. This was at a time when the science of nutrition was in its infancy, and essences, elixirs and extracts were where the action was. Liebig died in 1873, although not before he founded the Liebig's Extract of Meat Company, which gave the world the Oxo cube.

Meanwhile, a British firm named the Marmite Food Extract Company ran with Liebig's yeast extract research and foisted the black spread upon an unsuspecting nation in 1902. As the yeast was a by-product of the brewing industry, the company set up a factory in Burton upon Trent, home then, as now, to British brewing. Vitamins were discovered in 1912, and Marmite contains a large amount of them, which certainly helped its image and popularity. An advert for Marmite in *The Epicure* from the turn of the century declares that it 'contains all the valuable constituents of the best meat extracts' and that it is 'completely soluble, delicate in flavour and low in price'.

Today the company is owned by Unilever, whose advertising centres not on its healthy benefits, but on the love–hate relationship we have with the stuff. In recent years many special editions have been produced, but for the real lovers 2010 saw the launch of Marmite XO, a specially brewed extra-strong version. Its health-giving properties still have its modern proponents, though, including American food writer Michele Kayal: 'It settles a queasy tummy. It gives a boost of energy. And there is nothing – nothing – that takes care of a hangover like a spoonful of Marmite.' All these afflictions I know well, but they're still not enough to turn me on to the black spread.

## *Steak and kidney pudding at the Old Hall Inn*

When I was a child I loved nothing more than those cheap meat puddings you get in chip shops. One prick of the fork and the off-white industrial pastry bubble would burst, releasing a magma of mince, often of dubious origin. I still love a good pie and the Old Hall Inn in Chinley, Derbyshire, has an absolutely stunning one on its menu. The pub is the sort of place tourists come to England in search of but seldom find as they never venture north of Marylebone. For 400 years or so, one half was the old Red Cow coaching inn, while the other half began life as an Elizabethan manor house. In 1926 they were joined in administration, if not structure, when Mr J. Peatfield bought both and created the Old Hall Hotel.

When Dan Capper took over the business from his parents in 2008, he hired head chef Mark Atkinson to man the stoves. Mark has been making the puddings, by hand, since day one. The steak and the kidneys come from renowned butchers J. W. Mettrick in nearby Glossop, and the mix is slowly braised for four hours before being placed in a suet pastry and steamed for ninety minutes. Mark is particularly good at judging the amount of gravy in each pudding: neither too much so that things get sloppy, nor too little so that the filling is too dry and hard to swallow. He makes twenty to twenty-five fresh each day and once they're gone that's it, so it's best to book one.

Steak and kidney pudding with peas: Northern Soul food

What constitutes a pudding has been through many evolutions. Puddings were initially encased in animal gut, either the intestines or stomach. Then in the seventeenth century the pudding cloth came into use, which allowed all sorts of things to be bundled up and boiled without the need to stuff them into a natural casing, of which the Scottish clootie dumpling (*see* p. 156) is perhaps the last vestige. This method endured until the late nineteenth century, when it was replaced by using a basin lined with suet and part submerged in water, with foil or greaseproof paper tied over the top.

As for the filling, Mrs Beeton advises us that 'beef steak pudding may be very much enriched by adding a few oysters or mushrooms,' and Rules restaurant in Covent Garden in London still serve a version like that. The widespread addition of kidney – normally lamb's, as pig kidney can taste a little bitter – was no doubt made so that the steak would go further.

If there's one dish we should be able to do well, one dish we invented that someone else hasn't done better, and one thing that makes us feel good inside, it's a suet-crust steak and kidney pudding.

*See also* CARDIFF, CARDIFF (p. 59); DENBY DALE, WEST YORKSHIRE (p. 240); GLASGOW, GLASGOW (p. 178); GREENWICH, GREENWICH (p. 380); MOUSEHOLE, CORNWALL (p. 31).

## Coventry God Cakes

Coventry God Cakes were traditionally given by godparents to their god-children (or vice versa) at Christmas or Easter time. They consisted of a triangular-shaped puff pastry casing with a mincemeat-style filling, the three corners of the triangle symbolising the Holy Trinity. These days they are, according to food historian Laura Mason, pretty much extinct. They made a brief comeback in 2001 for a re-creation of Dame Godiva Day, which cele-brated the efforts of the city's most famous bareback rider. Alongside traditional God Cakes, a new version was on offer using an apple filling made from Wyken Pippin apples, which once grew locally.

As the cakes were small gifts offered by godparents and children, I suspect they would have primarily been homemade rather than available commer-cially. Nowadays not only are we a more secular society, but even those godparents who are observant probably buy their charges something plastic and noisy. However, that's still no reason not to make a few cakes, and being that puff pastry and dried fruits are available in most corner shops these days, why not go medieval and get the kids familiar with the business end of the pastry brush?

*See also* MINCEMEAT (p. 202).

## Snails

If there's one recent British dish that has attempted to reclaim snails for the UK, it's Heston Blumenthal's signature snail porridge. Infamous for its 'uurgh' factor and conjuring up images of Ready Brek with added slugs, the dish itself is actually more like a sort of risotto, with oats cooked in garlic, parsley and butter that are consequently a vivid green. The dish is finished off with tiny shavings of Jabugo ham, some pickled fennel and plump snails arranged on top. Personally, I thought it was great, but I love snails: to me they're like little musky scallops.

What's more, they're grown in the UK. There are a handful of growers, in Kent, Scotland and Devon. But the ones the Fat Duck use are from the aptly named L'Escargot Anglais in Herefordshire, because snails – along with frogs' legs and garlic – are as French as French can be. We may eat around 150 tonnes of snails a year in the UK, but the French consume 20,000 tonnes. In fact, to meet demand, France now imports nearly all its snails from Eastern Europe. What's worse, over 40 per cent of snails sold in France are actually chopped-up pieces of the Giant African land snail, proof (if it were needed) that our Gallic brothers' food is just as susceptible to adulteration as ours.

L'Escargot Anglais is run by Tony Vaughan, who started the business after forty years in the army. He quickly realised there was a demand from top chefs, but found that snails – he uses *Helix aspersa*, the common garden snail – were mainly served in the winter months when they naturally want to hibernate. To combat that, he rears them in heated conditions indoors or small areas outdoors, so that he can provide them fresh.

He supplies live as well as pre-prepared snails not only to the kitchens of the Fat Duck, but also those of La Gavroche and L'Escargot, among others. You can also find his snails in delis and specialist food shops, although if you're ordering a large amount, you can always ring him direct. If you fancy trying them at home, remember that snails are gastropods, so treat them like their seafaring cousins squid and octopus and you'll soon be enjoying the original slow food.

## GLOUCESTER, GLOUCESTERSHIRE
# Lampreys

The lamprey, a primordial fish, seems a little out of place in this modern age, being the last survivor of the Agnathan – jawless – stage of vertebrate evolution. There it was in the Late Devonian period some 500 million years ago, happy as the day is long, then suddenly some of its fellow sea creatures evolve jaws and lungs, crawl on to dry land and in no time at all are putting lampreys in their pies.

Lampreys were much valued in the medieval period, when people ate a lot more freshwater fish – indeed fish in general, what with the Catholic ban on meat-eating that took up nearly a third of the days in the year. The season for lampreys is from March to May, and the town of Gloucester, which sits on the Severn, was the centre of lamprey fishing as they came up the river to spawn.

Royalty were fond – sometimes overfond – of the lamprey; Henry I, for example, died from food poisoning after eating 'a surfeit of lampreys'. In the battle for the throne that followed, his daughter Matilda was supported by Robert, 1st Earl of Gloucester. Matilda's son, Henry II, granted a charter and various rights to the city of Gloucester, and perhaps in return for this loyalty the city began sending a lamprey pie to the royal household at Christmas. It is often the case that where blue blood goes, others follow, and Samuel Pepys twice mentions lamprey pie in his diary, declaring it 'most rare'. Lady Mary Cressy's recipe in *The Whole Duty of a Woman* from 1695 includes 'salt, pepper, currants, dates, beaten cinnamon, candied lemon-peel and sugar', which, when baked, are combined into a sauce made of lampreys' blood mixed with white wine.

Expense brought an end to the royal Christmas pie in 1836, although the town honoured Queen Victoria with a pie in 1893, and Queen Elizabeth II with a Silver Jubilee pie in 1977. Although lampreys are now threatened more by pollution and river obstacles than by royal appetites, they are making a comeback. Numbers are on the rise in the River Tamar and River Wear, and as they're extremely sensitive to pollution, their presence indicates a high water quality.

If you want to eat them in the UK today, your best bet is to either catch them yourself, or buy them in a fishing bait shop, where they're highly rated as pike bait.

*See also* DERWENTWATER, CUMBRIA (p. 102); DOVER, KENT (p. 473); HASTINGS, EAST SUSSEX (p. 483); MARKET HARBOROUGH, LEICESTERSHIRE (p. 340); NEWLYN, CORNWALL (pp. 32 and 34); RIVER SEVERN, GLOUCESTERSHIRE (p. 305); SCOURIE, HIGHLAND (p. 187); SOUTHEND-ON-SEA, ESSEX (p. 455); WANSFORD, EAST YORKSHIRE (p. 261); WHITBURN, TYNE & WEAR (p. 228).

GLOUCESTER, GLOUCESTERSHIRE
## Single and Double Gloucester from Smart's Farm

Double Gloucester is one of the better known British territorial cheeses – more popular, certainly, than its sibling Single Gloucester. Single Gloucester is made when the cows' evening milk is skimmed of its cream and left overnight before being added to the morning milk and turned into cheese. Double Gloucester, meanwhile, uses whole milk from the evening and morning milkings. Single is aged for something approaching three months,

# British Cheese

Once, while lunching at Raymond Blanc's stunning Le Manoir aux Quat'Saisons, I was presented with a cheese trolley so large I should have heard a 'Beep beep! Attention, this cheese trolley is reversing' safety signal as the two waitresses slowly backed it into view. However, among its myriad delightful contents (and they were many) I could only find one or two British cheeses.

Today, if there is one area of gastronomy where Britain can at least surely contend with France, it is in the area of cheese. The French take a quick win on wine, and bread, we pull one back with beer, but with cheese it could at least go to extra time.

The British interest in cheese took a long time to build up after the Second World War. Strangely, the fight against fascist Germany not only cost lives, it also left our native cheese industry utterly decimated. For the duration of the war all milk went into producing 'Government Cheddar', and even that was in terribly short supply. Paxton and Whitfield, a cheese shop established in 1797 in Jermyn Street, London, became an ordinary grocer's temporarily, such were the shortages. Postwar there was the inevitable loss of manpower, but by then centuries of 'farmhouse' production seemed already to be at an end.

The shoots of recovery started with the founding of the environmental movement in the 1970s, but it took the efforts of people like the late cheese expert Patrick Rance to bring things to the fore. In 1973, Rance was asked by the tourist board to write an article on British cheese, and his findings upset him greatly. He wrote, 'The hard cheeses of England and her firm-crusted blues are the finest in the world. Apart from Stilton, they are also the least known.'

By the late 1990s the end of the Milk Marketing Board brought about a shakedown in the dairy industry; there were those who lost out, of course, but there were also opportunities. Not only were dairy farmers diversifying into cheese production, but new people – with no herds of their own; no farming experience, in some cases – were having a crack at making cheese. Wiping the slate clean may have destroyed a cheese heritage that stretched back hundreds of years, but it also meant the rules were reset, the playing field was level and the customers were either ignorant of or, at the very least, unburdened by tradition.

Todd Trethowan, who makes Gorwydd (pronounced *Gor-with*) Caerphilly in Wales, sums up the situation we're in today: 'In France the cheesemonger is the king; here it's the producer.' Now there are some truly brilliant cheeses being produced, particularly in England. The West Country – ancestral home of Cheddar – also now gives us sloe tavy, the Midlands Little Urn and the classic Cheshire, while the north offers Wensleydale from Yorkshire and Baltic from the north-east. Even Kent is getting in on the act.

So a thousand flowers have bloomed, but the state of affairs is still a delicately balanced ecosystem. Artisan cheeses are also still on the periphery – a glance at the nation's shop shelves will reveal that they're still largely stocked with orange industrial 'Cheddar'. Good cheese, real cheese, needs character and individuality, both in the maker and in the finished product, and these just can't be achieved by mass production.

*See also* PLOUGHMAN'S LUNCH (p. 480).

while Double reaches almost six. It would be wrong to think that Single is merely an inferior version of the Double, though – in fact it's an altogether different cheese: lighter and more creamy. And unlike its well-known sibling, it has PDO (Protected Designation of Origin) status.

Very few people make either of the Gloucester cheeses by hand in the county these days, but Diana Smart does. She began cheese-making in 1987 aged sixty, having wanted to try her hand at it for a long time, but knowing nothing about it. When a local cheese-maker put his business up for sale, she enquired about it, but 'He was making Double Gloucester and I said, "Oh, I don't want to make that rubbish!" as I'd only ever tasted the supermarket version. But he gave me a piece of one he'd made six months previously and I thought, "Boy if I can make Double Gloucester like that, I do want to make it."'

Cheese-making was intended to be, as Diana puts it, 'a quiet little business to keep me out of mischief', but within six months it had taken over completely. Diana's cheese is made with milk from her own herd of over sixty cattle, which includes Holstein, Brown Swiss, Meuse Rhine Issel and some Gloucesters. Unsurprisingly, it was this last breed of cow that was traditionally used for making the cheese.

It is to Diana's Double Gloucester that the organisers of the Cooper's Hill cheese-rolling event have turned since 1988. The cheeses (four or five, depending on how many races there are) weigh a full 7 or 8 lbs, and are 'dressed' with blue and red ribbons. The annual – when safety conditions allow – event held every Whit Monday sees her cheese rolled down the steep hill pursued by men and women all wishing to sprain a muscle or twist an ankle. The first to cross the line at the bottom of the hill claims the cheese as a prize.

Sitting alongside the twin cheeses of Gloucester in Diana's dairy is another cheese, called Harefield. This is Diana's own invention, made in a similar way to her Single Gloucester, but aged for eighteen months so that it has a strong, nutty flavour. This Diana calls her super-special cheese. The name has an interesting story attached to it. 'A chap used to come and buy cheese from us early in the morning, and one day he said, "I saw a couple of hares in your field this morning and that's supposed to be the sign of a good cheese-making farm," and so we called it that!' she says. Despite loving making cheese, at eighty-two Diana admits she is getting on a bit; consequently, son Rod now does much of the work and is, in the words of his mother, 'a fine cheese-maker'.

*See also* BRITISH CHEESE (p. 290).

# *Asparagus from Goodman's Geese*

The Vale of Evesham and its surrounding area is prime asparagus country, and at Great Witley you can find a poultry farm known as Goodman's Geese that has a very good sideline in the delicious green spears. The Goodmans have been on the farm since 1962, originally as dairy farmers, but switched to geese in 1982 and asparagus in 1987. They currently plant twenty-one acres of the stuff.

It is an incredible plant in many respects, taking two years from the initial planting of the 'crown' or root structure to harvesting the spears. At the end of the first year the plant is allowed to 'bolt', and it consequently grows like the clappers, reaching up to a metre high. Twelve months later and, dependent on the weather, the shoots once again push through the clay earth. They can grow as much as a centimetre in twenty-four hours, which means that the crop has to be harvested swiftly. The Goodmans use a special electric buggy that drives along the field steered by the picker's feet, leaving the hands free to cut the spears. The rapidity with which it is picked also applies when you get it home: you must cook and eat it as soon as possible. Days spent rattling around the vegetable drawer in the fridge will leave it tasting woody,

Asparagus takes two years to grow and then we only eat the top six inches

rather than uniquely earthy. It is best steamed rather than boiled, and eaten lukewarm. Although hollandaise is a traditional accompaniment, plenty of other sauces work with it too, as indeed does a boiled egg, with the spears taking the place of the usual bread soldiers.

Asparagus is all very well for the early summer months, but in the cooler months from Michaelmas (29 September) to Christmas the Goodmans switch to producing their geese. They initially took them on as a hobby, but now under the original mother goose, Judy Goodman, they are producing around 4,000 a year, as well as their 4,000 bronze turkeys. Until 2010 Judy was the chairwoman of the British Geese Producers. Judy's geese are bought by people looking for something a bit different for Christmas. The flesh is succulent, and the fat that comes out of the bird can be used for much more than just the roasting of potatoes. 'Jamie Oliver still has a bird off me each year,' says Judy, and chef Mark Hix has it on his Chop House menus in season. Moreover, unlike perhaps turkey, goose is a great thing to eat in late autumn, served with the aptly named gooseberry sauce or, even better, Bramley apple sauce. If you do go for goose this winter, Judy has a tip: 'Make sure you cover the legs with foil when you're cooking it, otherwise it'll burn; the leg meat is delicious.'

*See also* EAST ANGLIAN PARSNIPS (p. 444); PEA HARVEST (p. 332).

GRINDLEFORD, DERBYSHIRE
## The Grindleford Café

There are those who don't get the ethos of the Grindleford station café, those who are offended by the myriad handwritten signs and directives such as 'One napkin per customer' or 'If you want to be a fire guard, join the fire brigade' (the latter pinned above the fireplace). The hand that penned these belonged to one-time chippie, bouncer and debt-collector Philip Eastwood, who ran the café for over thirty years. He died in 2007, and his son Phil left his Business Management degree in Leeds to come home and run the place. Philip senior didn't like mushrooms and neither does Philip junior, so another sign says, 'Mushrooms: we don't sell them, so don't ask for them.'

The café caters for bikers and hikers, and doesn't give a monkey's about soya milk, polyunsaturated fats or nut allergies. It serves large portions of food, much of it fried, to hungry men and women at minimal cost. The menu is a riff played on a five-note culinary scale: eggs, bacon, sausages, chips and beans. It is a solid British caff.

Russell Davies, who, despite being Britain's foremost authority on caffs would be reluctant to call himself that, has devoted many a mealtime (and website and book) to eating eggs, bacon, chips and beans all over the UK. The reason for Russell's love of this quartet stems from his days in a band. After gigging in London and returning up north, they would all stop at Leicester Forest East, where the 'Set 2' from the café menu, featuring egg, bacon, chips and beans, became his usual. 'It's the same phenomenon as when at some point in your twenties you get a haircut you like the look of, and then you just get that for the rest of your life.' Other reasons include not having to talk too much about the food, because, as Russell admits, he's more into the café than the cuisine. 'Cafés are a great place to stop and have a think as well as get a good cheap meal,' says Russell, adding, 'They're very democratic.' In cities, Russell recommends looking out for cafés where traffic wardens or blokes clad in high-vis gather: these people know a good café.

Of the Grindleford he says, 'Great little chips, small, so there's greater proportion of surface area and therefore more friedness. Big, thick bacon and a pale egg.' But my favourite tale about the place has to be this comment left on Russell's blog: 'The owner cuffed me around the head when I asked if he had any Worcestershire sauce. I'm from Canada and I've never been treated like that where I come from. I will never return to Europe because of this man.' Philip Eastwood must be chortling from beyond the grave.

*See also* LLANBERIS, GWYNEDD (p. 71); WEST KNOYLE, WILTSHIRE (p. 47).

HAWKSTONE, SHROPSHIRE
## Cheshire cheese

The lush, flat Cheshire plain with its wet summers and mild winters was, indeed still is, ideal dairy country. Here, as Holsteins chew the cud, cheesemakers ruminate on the art of making great cheese from the resulting milk. William Camden in his *Brittania* of 1586 said, '. . . the grasse and fodder there is of that goodness and vertue that the cheeses bee made here in great number of a most pleasing and delicate taste.' A number of other factors no doubt helped: the nearby town of Nantwich was famous for its production of salt – a key ingredient in cheese-making – and, a few centuries later, the hungry industrial towns to the north provided a market for the product.

Traditionally, it was left to the farmer's wife and daughters to get on with the business of making cheese, as well as the bread, the jam and the butter, all of which needed to be balanced with childcare and doing the laundry. The farmer and his sons, meanwhile, would be out tending land and beast. When daughters married, their cheese-making skills went with them, ensuring that a way with whey was as much of a desirable attribute in a spouse as a GSOH and all your own teeth.

Cheshire cheese of the seventeenth century would have been matured for much longer than it is today, and consequently stronger tasting. It remains one of the most popular cheeses in the UK and comes in patriotic red, white and blue varieties. White is by far the commonest, and red is essentially the same but with added annatto – an orange dye obtained from the pulp of a tropical fruit – for colour. Then there is the rarely seen blue version, whose bright golden interior is penetrated with lovely veins of blue mould. Production of the blue had died out in the late twentieth century, but luckily cheese-maker Joseph Heler based at Nantwich has led a revival and now produces it.

A good white Cheshire should be a creamy light-ivory colour and have a noticeable acid tang. 'It should be velvety, too,' says Adrian Rhodes of Carron Lodge in Preston, who not only makes his own but wholesales many others across the UK. Another popular maker in the area is Appleby's. Started by Lucy Appleby, MBE, at Hawkstone Abbey Farm in 1952, the company still make the cheese in their own way from their own unpasteurised milk. 'The cheeses are calico-bound by hand and stored in on-farm storerooms,' says third-generation Clare Downes (née Appleby), who is part of the family firm. Appleby's recommend eating their Cheshire at around four months' maturation, but if you leave it for longer the taste will become more complex. Randolph Hodgson at Neal's Yard Dairy does just this, buying Appleby's and taking the cheese to six to twelve months old to give a final distinctive flavour.

*See also* BRITISH CHEESE (p. 290).

## HEREFORD, HEREFORDSHIRE
# *Love in Disguise*

A local dish that is quite hard to find these days, unless Fergus Henderson's St John restaurant includes it in his Valentine's Day menu, Love in Disguise hails from Hereford and the Welsh borders from the eighteenth century. It consists of a stuffed calf's heart sitting in a pool of tomato sauce. The stuffing is made from breadcrumbs flavoured with marjoram and parsley; mustard is added for some extra oomph. Some recipes call for a coating of pre-cooked, broken-up vermicelli, bound to the heart with egg wash. This sounds very tricky indeed: imagine trying to get half-centimetre chunks of cooked, coagulated pasta to cling to a heart. Presumably, being British, it would be served with potatoes and vegetables.

I'll be honest: it's not enticing, is it? It's not so much the ingredients – hearts are among some of the best offal – it's the image (in my mind at least) of the poor soul eating it. Perhaps a lonely, lovelorn bachelor stolidly chewing his way through. Hereford is certainly beef-producing country, so perhaps there were a lot of lonely cattle hands? Or, given that in times past it was women who did the cooking, was it invented by a smitten young country lass as a culinary come-on, to be served to the one whom *her* heart desired?

This is one of those regional dishes you would have a very hard time finding. Maybe what this dish needs is some heat and passion in there. A tasty meaty mix stuffed in the heart, some chilli in the sauce, drop the pasta coating and love could once again be in the air.

*See also* CLIPPING-TIME PUDDING (p. 112); BATH, SOMERSET (p. 4); BURY MARKET, GREATER MANCHESTER (p. 99); DINGWALL, HIGHLAND (p. 160); HAROME, NORTH YORKSHIRE (p. 249); SMITHFIELD, ISLINGTON (p. 401); STONEHALL COMMON, WORCESTERSHIRE (p. 312).

HIMBLETON, WORCESTERSHIRE
## English mutton

Rob Havard's family have farmed Phepson Farm, a traditional mixed farm with 500 commercial ewes, 30 suckler cows and arable land, since 1919. When in 2005 Rob took on twenty Wiltshire Horn sheep, he shook things up a bit, moving from supplying standard commercial lamb, which goes to slaughter aged eighteen weeks at the most, to hogget, which is slaughtered at twelve months, and mutton, from sheep between three and five years old.

The Wiltshire Horn is Britain's only native sheep with hair instead of wool. The breed was popular all over the county and in the Wiltshire Downs, but by 1900 was nearly extinct because it didn't produce a fleece. 'Wiltshires are fantastic in terms of management. You don't need to shear them or dag them, and they also don't get fly strike, which is the worst ectoparasite to affect sheep,' says Rob. Dagging is the twice-yearly activity of removing the clumps of dung and dirt that have become caught on the wool near the sheep's bum. You can imagine Rob's joy at not having to do this. And the sheep don't require shearing because the hair just falls off naturally during the spring, leaving wisps about the paddock that the birds use for nest-building. Finally, sheep stocks are kept low, meaning the animals have more space and less chance of getting any foot diseases. These occur frequently in conventional intensive sheep farming, and would normally be treated with chemicals and drugs.

'We rent some land off the Wildlife Trust, and some of these pastures have over 200 types of plants species in them, wild thyme and such,' says Rob. This diet, along with the ageing, adds to the flavour. Yes, there is a fair bit of fat on, say, one of the chops, but if you look at the eye muscle you'll see a lovely marbling of fat through there.

As we're slowly coming to realise, lean meat is boring meat. What's the first thing we do with a bit of lean meat at the cooker? Add a slug of olive oil or a knob of butter in an attempt to get some taste back in there. 'As someone once told me, fat is like sediment in wine. You don't have to drink it, but it adds flavour,' says Rob.

*See also* ELAN VALLEY, POWYS (p. 64); ELWY VALLEY, DENBIGHSHIRE (p. 65); THE ISLE OF MAN (p. 110).

## HOLT HEATH, WORCESTERSHIRE
# Worcester Pearmains from Broomfield's Fruit Farm

In the old agriculture calendar, there was an apple for every month: aromatic, crisp Discoveries at the end of July, temperamental but delicious Cox's Orange Pippins in September and, most importantly for this part of the world, Worcester Pearmains around August. This apple was first raised by Mr Hale of Swan Pool, near Worcester, possibly from a seedling Devonshire Quarrenden. It was then named and marketed by Richard Smith, and around 1875 it received a first-class certificate from the Royal Horticultural Society.

Today Broomfield's are the largest producers of the variety in the region. The farm is currently run by Colin Broomfield, whose great-grandfather started the business in 1910. When times were tough in the 1970s, Colin's father had the idea of opening a farm shop, which they think was the first in the area. Throughout their history they've always entered apples into the Great Malvern Show, and have won in most categories.

Colin Broomfield and his award-winning apples and pears

The apple's flesh is firm, a little juicy and sweet, with a light, pleasant flavour. There's more often than not a hint of strawberry in the taste, although the intensity can vary. The downside of the Pearmain is that its season is rather short: half a dozen weeks if you're lucky. It is, however, a pretty reliable cropper, Colin tells me. Once picked, though, it doesn't keep that well. This, combined with its short season, makes it rather an awkward thing for the main supermarkets to stock. Best, then, pay a visit to Colin.

*See also* AMPLEFORTH, NORTH YORKSHIRE (p. 234); FAVERSHAM, KENT (p. 475); SOUTHWELL, NOTTINGHAMSHIRE (p. 359).

KNIGHTWICK, WORCESTERSHIRE
## 'This', 'That' and game pie at the Talbot

There can't be many inns in the UK that can boast not only rooms, a restaurant, an on-site brewery, but also a monthly farmers' market in the garden. The Talbot public house in Knightwick can, though, and I'd say you'd be hard pushed to find a better example of a pub serving the interests and enterprises of the community.

Perched on the bank of the River Teme, the 'Tolly', as it's known, has been run by the Clift family for over twenty-five years. The pub's restaurant makes the most of what's available locally, from the vegetables grown in the garden to wild foods gathered from the surrounding hedgerows and fields. For the bigger ingredients, such as meat, the Clifts prefer small producers from the region. The only exception to the 'local' rule is fish, which is rather hard to come by in landlocked Worcestershire, notwithstanding the pike and trout in the Teme outside the front door, and so fresh fish are delivered from Cornwall and Wales regularly.

The matriarch of the Clift clan is the current manager Annie's indefatigable mother, Jean, who runs a stall at the monthly market selling terrines, pies, breads and meats. Her game pies, packed with rabbit, pheasant and pigeon, are the stuff of local legend – they're over four inches high and the circumference of an LP record.

To wash down all this local tucker you can't do better than a pint from the attached Teme Valley Brewery. Opened in 1997 to brew small batches for the pub, it is now growing and sells directly to off-licences and pubs all over the West Midlands. The Clift family were hops growers in these parts in the nineteenth century, and consequently the brewery use only UK Maris Otter malt and Worcestershire hops like Challenger, Fuggles and Goldings in their beers. In a practical piece of nomenclature their three main draught bitters are called 'This', 'That' and 'T'Other', the T'Other being an exceptionally light and easy drinking ale perfect for summer at only 3.2 per cent.

The Talbot has been here since the fourteenth century, the market only since 1998. Still, that makes it one of the oldest farmers' markets in the UK. And if the crowds are anything to go by, the pub, the brewery and the market have got plenty of years ahead of them yet.

*See also* ASTLEY, WARWICKSHIRE (p. 276); GREENWICH, GREENWICH (p. 378); NEWCASTLE, TYNE & WEAR (p. 220); SOUTHWOLD, SUFFOLK (p. 457).

## LOWER BROADHEATH, WORCESTERSHIRE
# Mud City Cheddar from Lightwood Cheeses

In my experience, cheese-makers are a special breed. Not for them the visceral butcher's block or the warmth of the baker's oven. Theirs is a cool, sterile world. After all, cheeses, hard in particular, are an exercise in gentle ageing and slow decay, often measured in many months. It takes a patient man to make cheese.

Phil Hulland and his rind-washed Cheddar

Phil Hulland is just such a man. Phil has got a small range of regular cheeses, including the smashing Little Urn, named in honour of England's 2005 Ashes victory and made with ewes' milk. It's medium strength, and similar in style to a Spanish Manchego. His eleven-kilo truckle takes over a year to mature, 'But you do get a better flavour,' says Phil. 'We don't make Little Urn very often; sheep's milk is fiendishly expensive to buy: it costs about as much as petrol.'

But by far my favourite is his Mud City Cheddar. It's Phil's classic Elgar Cheddar, which, like all his cheeses, is made with unpasteurised milk. It's covered in vegetable fat, bound in cloth and then left to age for a few months, then washed once a fortnight up to twelve times in the Sadler's Mud City stout. Sadler's is a family-run microbrewery with a long history. It was first opened in 1900 by Thomas Alexander Sadler and supplied a handful of pubs in the area. Brewing came to an end in 1927; however, it was reopened by the family in 2004, and in 2006 the family opened the Windsor Castle Inn to showcase their beers. The name Mud City comes from a nickname for the shanty town built by refugees and other displaced people in the seventeenth century on the area now known as Lye Waste. Some of the mud houses were still standing well into the 1960s.

The stout not only adds a wonderful mahogany patina to each truckle, but also a delicate, sweet, malty taste to the rind. 'I always tell people to eat the rind. It can be the best bit of the cheese sometimes,' says Phil. The Cheddar itself is superb, leaving a strong tang in the nose followed by a smoothness as it reaches the back of the mouth. It's a well-produced cheese and only available from Phil in his cool, clean cheese parlour or in the warmth and conviviality of the Sadler family's Windsor Castle Inn, where it sits proudly on their cheeseboard.

*See also* BRITISH CHEESE (p. 290).

## MARKET DRAYTON, SHROPSHIRE
# Gingerbread

Ginger is thought to have been introduced to Britain, along with a good many other things, by the Romans. It has since been taken up enthusiastically to flavour all sorts of dishes from savoury sauces and meat cures to sweet cakes, biscuits and bread. Drinks also get the ginger treatment, with ginger ale, beer and 'wine' being old favourites. Part of its enduring popularity is no doubt due to the fact that it works equally well in sweet and savoury dishes, and in times past sweet and savoury sat side by side on the same plate far more frequently than they do today.

Mrs Beeton gives four recipes for gingerbread in her *Book of Household Management* (1861), and all seem to be for cake-sized items. But since the publication of 'The Gingerbread Man' in an American children's magazine in 1875, the idea of gingerbread as more of a cookie or biscuit has slowly gained ground.

Salopians, as Shropshire people are wont to be called, have had a long love affair with the warmer spices from overseas, and king among these is ginger – despite living in one of the most landlocked counties, with no access to a trading port. What makes the traditional Market Drayton gingerbread so special is that it includes a good splash of rum. What's more, the resulting mix is baked into long finger biscuits so that the end can be repeatedly dipped into a glass of port; a similar technique is used with Italian biscotti and Vin Santo dessert wine.

Records point to one Roland Lateward being the first 'maltster and gingerbread baker' in the town, in 1793, and by the turn of the nineteenth century he had plenty of competition. The recipe seems to have passed through many bakers in the town, a sort of bready equivalent of the masons, and Billington's, established in 1817, is the oldest surviving brand. John and May Hayward Hughes of Cheswardine produced gingerbread to the Billington's recipe for over sixty years before retiring in 1995, when the recipe was bought by Terry McCarthy. Eventually the McCarthys moved to Yorkshire, where they still make the Billington's recipe.

The last of the pre-war bakers all died out in the 1980s, but Tim and Sarah Hopcroft took up the torch in 1986 when they bought Reid's bakery, which they ran successfully for a decade. In the 1990s, seeing the writing on the wall and a shift in people's shopping habits, they sold up the retail bakery, and now concentrate on supplying the local tourist information centre, the National Trust, Waitrose and London department stores with their little gingerbread chaps. They also produce bespoke gingerbread for weddings, birthdays and special events, carrying on in some small way the medieval tradition of shaping it into crowns, flowers and notable persons. As Adolphe Thiers, the nineteenth-century French prime minister said, 'No man can truly call himself great until seen in gingerbread.'

*See also* PARKIN (p. 262).

# The Pudding Club at the Three Ways House Hotel

In 1985 the choice of 'pudding' in many restaurants was still between little more than a Black Forest gateaux, a cheesecake and oranges in caramel, all served from the diabolical device known as the sweet trolley. The couple that ran the Three Ways House Hotel at the time, Keith and Jean Turner, decided to do something about it, and held an evening dinner featuring seven classic British puddings. There were twenty or so attendees. At the do, some bright spark suggested they all vote for their favourite, and thus the Pudding Club was born.

Simon and Jill Coombe and their business partner Peter Henderson took over the hotel in 1995, and built on the Turners' success. Such was the demand that they increased Pudding Club evenings from monthly to weekly, added pudding-themed bedrooms, and upped attendance to over seventy. The tradition of seven puddings only was also maintained, and the Pudding Club rules – such as they are – were formalised: first, only one pudding in your bowl at a time; and second, you can only have another helping of pudding when you've finished the previous portion. There is now an ever-changing seasonal repertoire of over 100 hot puddings.

They also made it a year-round institution, rather than just a September

Some of the puddings served up at the Pudding Club

to May event. 'For the first one in the summertime we did seven cold puddings, and it was a disaster. People kept asking, "Where's the treacle sponge pudding? Where's the jam roly poly?"' They quickly corrected matters for the next event, and now there are three cold puddings – fools, perhaps, or maybe a syllabub or trifle – and four hot. On the night of a Pudding Club event, a modest main course is served – nothing too heavy or large, so as to leave ample space – then the puddings are introduced one at a time. As the final entrant is brought in, diners stand and salute it with their spoons.

As you can imagine, the hotel gets through a fair amount of custard. 'We use nine gallons of custard at each event,' says Simon. When the Turners first started the Pudding Club they made proper egg custard, but within a few weeks people were asking for custard with the skin on. 'And so now we use Bird's. We're probably one of their biggest customers, I should think.'

Most of the puddings are made by a local woman named Sheila Vincent, who has been at the hotel since the early 1990s. 'We call her the queen of puddings. She'll do the things that can be made earlier in the day, then our chefs make the more last-minute things.' Sheila's predecessor was a lady of seventy, who had only come out to work when her husband had retired, because she was fed up of being in the house with him.

Only the British really understand pudding. Granted, there's some fine French patisserie and such on the Continent, but the sweet pud is a British invention born out of our industrial and imperial past. More than that, though, puddings are in our soul. I always think that anyone who doesn't like puddings is bound to be a bit mean-spirited.

*See also* BAKEWELL, DERBYSHIRE (p. 277); BIRMINGHAM, WEST MIDLANDS (p. 280); PENRITH, CUMBRIA (p. 127); PETERBOROUGH, CAMBRIDGESHIRE (p. 352); POLEGATE, EAST SUSSEX (p. 494).

RIVER SEVERN, GLOUCESTERSHIRE

*Elvers*

The journey of the elver, a juvenile eel, is one worthy of the attentions of David Attenborough. Thought to spawn in the Sargasso Sea – a huge clump of seaweed in the middle of the Atlantic – they can take three years to make the 2,000 miles to the rivers of Europe. The rivers of western England are most famously associated with elvers, although the little beasts have also

# Trifle

There's an old routine by one of those comedy acts from yesteryear where an amorous man pants to his beloved, 'Darling, I want to cover you in cream and custard and smother you in jelly!' To which she sobs in return, 'I won't be trifled with!'

For me, there has always been something slightly bawdy about a good trifle; it's a show-off party pud and it knows it. If Madonna were a pudding she would be a trifle; it's a pud that has constantly reinvented itself over the years. It appeals to children and adults alike, it can be homely and messy or mass-produced, boozy and grown-up or sugary and innocent. And so what constitutes a trifle has shifted with the ages. A recipe for one appears in Thomas Dawson's *The Huswife's Jewell* from 1596, but this describes something more akin to a fool. Slowly, over the next 100 years, trifles went from being delicate fruit-and-cream concoctions to much bolder, solid, boozier affairs.

By 1751 Hannah Glasse had taken up the cause, adding custard and cakes soaked in sack (sherry). Then in came solid pieces of fruit, comfits and jelly, even though there are those who believe a trifle should be made without the latter. Scotland has a similar dish to the trifle that goes by the name of Tipsy Laird, in which the sponge fingers are soaked not in sherry or Madeira but whisky or Drambuie.

Today, few of us would make every component of a trifle entirely from scratch, baking the biscuits, making a proper custard, combining gelatin and fruit for the jelly. More likely, we would approach trifle-making as a celebration of industrial food production prowess, combining weapons-grade custard, rock-steady jelly and ultra-absorbent sponge soaked in some mystery liquor with tinned fruit, angelica, glacé cherries, and hundreds and thousands. Everything, then, but the kitchen sink.

It was one of the first puddings produced by Leeds-based Northern Foods when they single-handedly invented chilled products and meals for Marks & Spencer in the mid 1980s. The firm had a strong dairy background, and when chairman (now Lord) Christopher Haskins found himself sat next to the M&S chairman on a flight to Belfast, he managed to get a foot in the door to begin supplying them with milk. This, in turn, led to orders for more dairy-based products. In a 2001 interview in the *Sunday Times*, Lord Haskins described the complexities of keeping the ingredients from mixing, curdling and spoiling, admitting that 'the company lost a fortune on that trifle'.

Then there is Bird's trifle mix, a kit-form trifle that comes in a small box containing five sachets, one filled with custard powder, one with jelly crystals, another housing something called 'dream topping', one containing sponge fingers and finally a packet of brown trifle decorations. Like an alchemist with a sweet tooth, you add to these milk, water and sugar, before assembling in layers and leaving to set.

Trifle should always be made in a glass bowl, so that you can see the layers of ingredients – whichever you choose – through the side of the dish. Alan Davidson and Helen Saberi, in their book on the subject, liken the construction of a trifle to architecture, and it goes without saying that once the structural integrity of the pud is compromised by the first round of portioning out, it will start to collapse. A returned-to trifle never quite maintains the magic of its uncut previous state.

These days, trifle can sometimes look a little lost – like an old lush nudged out by more decadent sunken chocolate or warm, homely pastry desserts. This is a shame, as a proper trifle is, in my book, if not the king of puds then one of the crown princes.

been known to appear in the rivers of Sussex and Kent. Tales are told of elvers turning the margins of the rivers black with their sheer numbers. The poor weren't going to let this huge heaving mass of free protein swim by, and so elver fishing began.

On 16 March 2009 at Cheltenham Magistrates' Court, three men from Gloucester pleaded guilty to a charge relating to illegal fishing for elvers. Owing to dwindling stocks, elver fishermen must now have a valid elver fishing licence, and there are also restrictions on the equipment they can use. Thanks to the work of the Environment Agency (EA), illegal fishing is now being stamped out. Al Watson, the Environmental Crime team leader, explains, 'We've got much better enforcement and targeting of offenders. The other big factor is there have been so few elvers in the river it's not been worth their while getting involved.' There are, of course, many licensed fishermen who abide by the rules and work with the EA, including Richard Cook, whose family have been fishing salmon and elvers from the Severn for years using traditional methods.

Today, the EA estimates that eel populations have crashed by over 95 per cent across Europe. There's no one single cause; it could be a combination of environmental conditions, a change in the position of the Gulf Stream and overfishing. What's for sure is that the days of frying them in bacon fat are pretty much over. In recent years most were sent to Asia, where they were reared on fish farms, but now even that trade has tailed off and most go to European stocking projects, Lough Neagh in Northern Ireland being one. 'Once an elver goes to Asia, there's no way it's going to complete its life cycle, whereas in here, a proportion will escape from Lough Neagh and make it back to the Sargasso,' says Al Watson.

In the future, it's likely that there will be a season declared on elvers. There is a natural season anyway, from January to May, but plans are afoot to limit catching to a window within this. 'There's still so much we don't know about eels. Up until recently people thought it a scientific fact that they came from the hair from horses' tails and there was therefore no point doing any research,' adds Al.

See also DERWENTWATER, CUMBRIA (p. 102); DOVER, KENT (p. 473); GLOUCESTER, GLOUCESTERSHIRE (p. 288); HASTINGS, EAST SUSSEX (p. 483); MARKET HARBOROUGH, LEICESTERSHIRE (p. 340); NEWLYN, CORNWALL (pp. 32 and 34); SCOURIE, HIGHLAND (p. 187); SOUTHEND-ON-SEA, ESSEX (p. 455); WANSFORD, EAST YORKSHIRE (p. 261); WHITBURN, TYNE & WEAR (p. 228).

## *Roots Farm Shop*

Which came first, the chicken or the egg? In the case of Will and Meg Edmonds, it was definitely the egg. They started their farm shop in 2000, selling seasonal veg, lamb and beef. They had always had eggs for the farm, and whenever they had the odd box spare they put them on the counter to sell. People kept asking them for more eggs, and so along came 200 Black Rock hens, which live in a field right next to the shop.

The Black Rock is a fantastic chicken for this sort of set-up. A cross of the Rhode Island Red and Plymouth Rock, and produced by only one man, Peter Siddons of Muirfield Hatchery, Scotland, the breed is a prolific layer, averaging 280 eggs a year, with beautiful jet-black feathers with a chestnut-brown bib. It's a robust, well-insulated bird that is perfect for a life outdoors.

The eggs are collected fresh each morning and offered for sale in the shop. The Edmondses even sell the smaller pullets' eggs, which make a great addition to dishes featuring boiled eggs that would benefit from something a little more delicate; think a classy salad Niçoise perhaps.

Although the egg came first, the chicken for eating wasn't far behind.

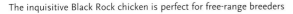

The inquisitive Black Rock chicken is perfect for free-range breeders

What makes Roots almost unique, however, is that they kill and process the birds on-site, something which very few people do these days. Even organic chicken is likely to have been taken to a central processing plant that handles all sorts of birds on one long conveyor belt. What's more, it will have been wet-plucked by machines, and eviscerated by a high-powered jet of water that forces out the innards into a chute (this is why you rarely get the animal's gravy-enhancing giblets).

At Roots, the birds are dry-plucked and the giblets carefully removed, bagged up and kept with the actual chicken they came from. The birds are eighty days old, meaning more flavour and great bones for stock. The skin is thicker and has a layer of fat to keep the small but well-worked breast meat moist, and the two muscly legs are firm in texture – no doubt from all that free-range running about under cherry trees.

*See also* CANTERBURY, KENT (p. 469); COLSTON BASSETT, NOTTINGHAMSHIRE (p. 325); HOOK, HAMPSHIRE (p. 484); IPSWICH, SUFFOLK (p. 441); RUSHWICK, WORCESTERSHIRE (p. 309); STANNINGTON, NORTHUMBERLAND (p. 227); WELBECK, NOTTINGHAMSHIRE (p. 362).


## STOKE-ON-TRENT, STAFFORDSHIRE
# *Staffordshire oatcakes*

Stoke-on-Trent is the epicentre of the Staffordshire oatcake, also known as the 'Potteries popadom'. It comprises a soft pancake about nine inches across made with oat flour, water, yeast and a pinch of salt and sugar. The resulting runny mix is dropped on to a hotplate called a baxton, where it's cooked quickly for a minute and a half on each side before being cooled. You can eat it like this, or reheat it with a filling such as egg, bacon or cheese, so it goes a bit crispier.

There are various accounts of its history, from marching Roman armies heading north, to Jacobite rebels heading south. Things start to get a little more factual in the eighteenth century, when the main industry of the region was pots, pits and steel. Oatcakes are the original fast food, and helped to feed this workforce. They were (indeed still are) cheap to make, quick to cook and edible for long afterwards. With the loss of those industries you might have expected the oatcake to quietly slip away, but not a bit of it.

Local Bill Pearson guided me on a tour of the remaining oatcake shops in the town. First we visited Burslem Oatcakes on Waterloo Road, where I

The Staffordshire oatcake, also known as the 'Potteries popadom'

had a double oatcake with cheese and bacon. The secondary cooking gave this a slightly crunchy and biscuity texture, with a fair amount of salt and fat coming from the melting industrial Cheddar cheese, which was all right by me. Darren Hughes is the current owner and told me the shop has been here for over thirty years. 'In the past the queue would go out the door,' he says. 'We used to sleep in the shop on a Friday night to be ready for Saturday.' There's still a fair rate of trade, mind, with postal workers and truck drivers stopping in for a hot cheap snack. And cheap it is. A mere 67p buys you a cheese-filled oatcake.

Foley Oatcakes on King Street is owned by Martin Smith and staffed by Laura, Beth and Emma. Here again there's a brisk breakfast trade of young lads and dads getting egg, bacon and cheese oatcakes. In the rear of the shop is an eighteen-year-old machine that moves along the baxton, dropping the mix. Then they're flipped by hand. 'We've made 220 dozen, and today's a quiet day. Thursday's we do double that as we have a stall on the market too,' says Martin. That's nearly 5,000 oatcakes on one day! And this is just one of forty oatcake shops in the area, so you can see how much they love their oatcakes round here. At Foley's a cheese oatcake comes rolled rather than flat and quartered, and the oatcake itself is more moist than Burslem's.

Finally I headed to Oatcakes and Pikelets in Hanley, run by another Smith family. Pikelets are sweeter, thicker versions of oatcakes, often containing dried fruit. 'They're like your pudding,' chips in a customer who was getting half a dozen breakfast versions for his family. It tastes like a Scotch pancake crossed with a drop scone – rather sweet, but not bad at all.

As you would expect, each venue has their own secret family recipe, which no one would tell me. 'It's got oats in it' was as far as I got. It's clear the people of the Potteries love their oatcakes, but unlike that other regional working-class industrial staple the pasty, the oatcake has yet to take the world by storm. If these were sold as crêpes filled with Gruyère cheese out of a rustic Citroën van at posh food markets they would be £5 a go. But they're not yet, and perhaps they're best made by and enjoyed by the people who love them the most.

*See also* OLNEY, BUCKINGHAMSHIRE (p. 347).

## STONEHALL COMMON, WORCESTERSHIRE
# *Faggots*

If I see faggots on a menu, my interest is piqued. A word with the waitress or waiter to check a few details follows: Are they home-made? Are they wrapped in caul? Is the offal count high? If the returning news from the kitchen is no to any of the above, I find it best to leave well alone rather than be disappointed. Faggots, despite being cheap to make, take time, patience and skill to make properly – but what a pleasure when done correctly. Antony Worrall Thompson famously burned the bottom of his faggots in the first ever series of the *Great British Menu*, and was consequently beaten by Galton Blackiston. 'I rather feel I won by default!' Galton once told me.

Although at one time a national dish, faggots, like red squirrels, are under threat, and you can now only find them in a few isolated pockets centred around Wales, Lancashire and the once-industrial heartland of the Midlands. In the latter they are known as ducks, whereas in Lancashire they are called savoury ducks. A stall at Bury Market had them for sale when I last visited, but they were the tallish, square kind, rather than the ball-shaped ones I prefer, which should be as large as your fist.

But what's in them? Well, proper faggots should be made from minced pork, chopped pig's heart, liver, onion, seasoning and, occasionally, bread-crumbs. The resulting patties are then wrapped in caul fat (the lacy membrane that surrounds the pig's organs). This is exactly how head chef Dwight Clayton at the Inn at Stonehall, Worcester, makes them. 'They sell very well. Either people don't have the time to make them properly at home, or those skills have been lost.' The feedback from diners runs along the lines of, 'They taste just like the ones my mother used to make.' Indeed, Dwight once had a couple come in and order not only some for themselves, but also another portion wrapped to take away for their folks.

For some, faggots do evoke the 'eww!' factor, partly because they're made with offal, but also because of the name. However, if you've eaten pâté, or even cheap sausages, you've probably eaten this sort of ingredient before. And the name simply refers to the fact that the dish is a collection of ingredients held together by a caul. 'Faggot' originally meant a bundle of something, commonly sticks or wood, and has been around since the fourteenth century. The word was once used as an insult for old women – particularly those thin enough to resemble a bundle of bones wrapped in a shawl – and has, since the early twentieth century, been in use as a pejorative term for a homosexual. Unfortunate connotations, then. But if you see proper home-made faggots served with peas, potato and gravy on a menu, and you've checked that they're the genuine article, I would heartily recommend ordering them and striking a blow for nose-to-tail eating as well as common sense.

*See also* BATH, SOMERSET (p. 4); BURY MARKET, GREATER MANCHESTER (p. 99); DINGWALL, HIGHLAND (p. 160); HAROME, NORTH YORKSHIRE (p. 249); HEREFORD, HEREFORDSHIRE (p. 296); SMITHFIELD, ISLINGTON (p. 401).

STONELEIGH PARK, WARWICKSHIRE
## *The Rare Breed Survival Trust*

After the Second World War, farming, particularly the cattle industry, went through a huge upheaval as the market demanded lots of beef at low, low prices. To meet this demand, larger cattle were introduced from Europe, mainly breeds that were fed on concentrated commercial feeds rather than grasses and that could put on weight quickly and produce lean meat. In this industrialisation of the cattle-farming process, taste and flavour had to take a bit of a back seat, and at the same time our original native breeds were pushed towards extinction. In the 1970s, with the emergence of the conservation movement, we all learned about the plight of the giant panda, the Siberian tiger and the black rhino, but few of us stopped to consider the plight of our domesticated native animals. And yet between 1900 and 1973, twenty-six native breeds became extinct in the UK, including Goonhilly ponies from Cornwall, Limestone sheep and the Cumberland pig, which was the original pork used in the county's famous sausage (*see* p. 108). To right this wrong, the Rare Breeds Survival Trust (RBST) was founded in 1973, by a group comprising scientists, breeders and enthusiasts.

Since then, they have fought tirelessly to communicate the message that our native breeds are not only part of our heritage, but are also perfectly attuned to their landscape and environment, making them much more sustainable in the long term. Good examples include the Highland cow and the Herdwick and Swaledale sheep of the Lake District, all perfectly adapted for life on tough wild grasses in harsh weather that other species would find intolerable. One recent triumph is a farmer who has moved from Holstein – the traditional black and white dairy cow – to the rare breed Irish Moiled. They live happily on grass, and so he no longer has to import corn or soya (often grown on deforested Amazon land) to feed his cattle. What's more, Irish Moiled are a dual-purpose breed, and work equally well as dairy animals or those raised for beef.

Of course, these are commercial animals, and as such they need to work in everyday farms. Sometimes, as in the case of the endangered Whitebred Shorthorn, this means they're mostly used for cross-breeding. A Whitebred put to a Galloway cow produces a Blue Grey, which is more able to suckle calves on rougher grazing and still produce good quality meat. 'In the past we'd never have talked about crossing – it was always about keeping the lines pure as we needed to build up numbers, but now we're at the stage where we need to look at the commercial application of these animals,' says Sally Renshaw from the RBST.

Thanks to the work of the Trust, shoppers and diners are becoming more familiar with some of our native breeds. Most people have now heard of the Gloucester Old Spot pig, for example, a breed that has become something of a poster child for the movement – so much so that it's nearly moved off the Trust's list and into the regular native breeds. Other animals still at threat, however, are the original native population of Aberdeen Angus, the Leicester Longwool sheep and the Croad Langshan chicken. In each case, the Trust works to emphasise the breed's taste and texture as well as its history – this, after all, is the model that worked for the Gloucester Old Spot. The Trust is certainly not a sentimental organisation, one that is trying to preserve animals like zoo exhibits; they carry out extensive DNA and genetic work, they monitor populations and advise on breeding, but most of all, they get the message out that it's worth opting for slow-grown native meat whenever you can. Ultimately, unlike tigers, pandas and rhinos, these animals were bred for eating, and we've got to eat them to keep them.

*See also* CHILLINGHAM PARK, NORTHUMBERLAND (p. 206); THE ISLE OF MAN (p. 110); MEOPHAM, KENT (p. 489); NEATH, NEATH PORT TALBOT (p. 80).

UPTON UPON SEVERN, WORCESTERSHIRE
## *Pegoty Hedge organic beef*

Pegoty Hedge is a fourth-generation family farm that, like so many producers and shopkeepers, is adapting to the rapidly changing needs of consumers and the world at large. When I visited, Peter Surman and his son Oliver very obligingly took me round the farm when they should have been making silage. Pegoty Hedge went organic in 2001, a time when agriculture was in crisis with the countryside having just suffered the devastating effects of foot-and-mouth.

The price difference between standard and organic produce has lessened of late, with the former now costing nearly as much to produce. That makes starting the transition from scratch more difficult. 'It's not such an advantage

Pegoty Hedge's Aberdeen Angus cattle

as it was.' Peter doesn't regret it, however, as organic produce is still something a lot of customers look for.

Their beef is Aberdeen Angus, and looks amazing: deep red with a marbling of delicate fat running throughout. Oliver and Peter began to think how they could remain competitive in today's market and generate more revenue from each animal. 'The trouble with beef is that you only get a few [high-value] steaks off each animal, but a lot more of the cheaper cuts,' says Oliver. To make the most of what they have, they've developed a series of ready-made organic meaty dishes using those tasty but harder-to-sell cuts. The first move was to bring in Dwight Clayton, head chef at the Glasshouse brasserie in nearby Worcester (which they supply with beef). Together, they developed the recipes for such classics as cottage pie, meatballs, beef casserole, goulash and lasagne. They produce all their own stocks from scratch, with the vegetables coming from a nearby local box scheme in Ledbury, which also sells the finished product.

'When we were just doing meat, we were essentially distributors. The meat would come back from the abattoir cut and packed and we'd sell it wholesale,' says Oliver. 'Now we've moved into food production, there's a raft of legislation and inspection to deal with.' It's been a sharp learning curve, but one they seem to be surmounting. 'We wanted to grow slowly, rather than pitching for a 10,000-meals-a-week deal with someone like Waitrose on day one.'

*See also* CORWEN, DENBIGHSHIRE (p. 62).

## WEM, SHROPSHIRE
## *Alternative Meats*

In the past twenty years there has been an influx of new species brought to the UK to be commercially farmed: bison, water buffalo, alpaca, llama and ostrich, to name but a few. Alongside this, there has been a growing interest in eating a broader range of meat from native animals such as goat, venison, veal and wild boar. Finally, foreign holidays, travelling experiences and a growing 'Walkabout' community – particularly in London and the south-east – have created a demand for such exotic meats as kangaroo, crocodile, springbok and zebra.

It is to these three markets that Jeanette Edgar and Rachel Godwin's company, Alternative Meats, caters. The two met when Rachel was working on her father's ostrich farm in the mid 1990s; Jeanette was recovering from a broken back sustained during a horse-riding accident and was looking for a desk-bound job. She found one selling the meat over the phone. Rachel's father, John, eventually moved on to pastures new, but by this time the two of them had built up a bank of knowledge about unusual meats and the clients interested in them.

They added wild boar, some venison and game, and launched Alternative Meats on 19 February 2001, which just happened to be the day foot-and-mouth was found in an Essex abattoir for the first time in twenty years. Within weeks the countryside was locked down. 'There was no movement – we couldn't get any meat out,' says Jeanette. The silver lining to this particular cloud was that they began importing what they could from Belgium and South Africa.

A redevelopment grant helped to keep things going, and in time the business flourished. They have added products such as whole English suckling pigs, Herdwick mutton from Cumbria, and goat from Tim and Marnie Dobson at Radmore Green Farm in Cheshire, as well as delicacies like frogs' legs and even locusts. 'These meats are never going to replace chicken, beef, lamb and pork,' says Jeanette. But they do provide something different. 'Christmas is so telling; people are searching for something different. People's attitudes have changed amazingly in the past ten years,' she says.

Despite all the exotic meat, however, one of the biggest sellers is rose veal, which comes from Heaves Farm in Cumbria. Jeanette and Rachel have been working hard marketing it since 2004, spurred on, no doubt, by the letter from the Queen they received in November of that year complimenting them on its quality.

*See also* HALKYN, FLINTSHIRE (p. 66).

WORCESTER, WORCESTERSHIRE

# Lea & Perrins Worcestershire Sauce

The tangled story surrounding the most well-known maker of Worcestershire sauce can seemingly top the best Whitehall obfuscation and spin-doctoring. Are you sitting comfortably? Then I'll begin. According to local legend, in 1830 Lord Marcus Sandys, governor of Bengal, returned from India and asked two chemists, John Wheeley Lea and William Perrins, to make him a sauce. Once made, though, the sauce turned out to be vile. Rather than throwing it out, the two chemists conveniently left it in their cellar. A few years later, when clearing the place out, Messrs Lea and Perrins found that the disgusting brew had mellowed into a fine, tangy, slightly sharp sauce.

The tale has more than a note of Victorian press release about it, and is incredibly hard to verify. There appears to be no evidence of any 'Lord Sandys' governing Bengal, and the company's official website has him down as a traveller in the region. Early labels bore the legend '... from the recipe of a nobleman of the county', and some think Arthur Moyses William Sandys (1792–1860) of Ombersley Court may be the man in question.

Whoever supposedly commissioned it, it certainly thrived. On the back of the British Empire, the sauce was exported to all corners of the globe. It kept well, added flavour and provided a taste of home. In 1897 the company moved to a new factory on Midland Road, where they are still based today. You can find it with your eyes closed. As you get nearer, the nasal-hair-twanging smells waft over you. Structurally, the factory has remained the same, but forklift trucks and lorries now move around where once there were men and horses. The sauce is still made to the same recipe, though, and can be found in bars all around the world ready to be added to the red-eyed travelling salesman's Bloody Mary, a drink invented in 1921 at the New York Bar in Paris.

Bloody Marys are a good but not everyday use for the sauce. For this, you could do a lot worse than sprinkling it liberally on cheese on toast. The current Baron Sandys – the seventh – is Richard Michael Oliver Hill. Does he enjoy the sauce his ancestor reputedly commissioned, I wonder.

See also HOW RECIPES BEGIN (p. 496); BISHOP'S STORTFORD, HERTFORDSHIRE (p. 321); EASTON GREY, WILTSHIRE (p. 11); EDINBURGH, EDINBURGH (p. 167); FAVERSHAM, KENT (p. 477); MOFFAT, DUMFRIES & GALLOWAY (p. 183); NORWICH, NORFOLK (p. 451); OXFORD, OXFORDSHIRE (p. 351); ROSSENDALE, LANCASHIRE (p. 131); ST HELENS, MERSEYSIDE (p. 132); SHEFFIELD, SOUTH YORKSHIRE (p. 258); SPENNYMOOR, COUNTY DURHAM (p. 227).

# 8 | The East Midlands

Kirton in Lindsey

Lincolnshire Wolds

Owmby-by-Spital

Louth

Welbeck

Chesterfield

*NOTTS.*

Mansfield

*DERBYS.*

Lincoln

Woodhall Spa

Skegness

Navenby

*LINCOLNSHIRE*

*The*
*Wash*

Southwell

Derby

Nottingham

Boston

Colston Bassett

Melton Mowbray

Spalding

Quorn

*RUTLAND*

*The* *F e n s*

*LEICESTERSHIRE*

Rutland
Water

Leicester

Market
Bosworth

Peterborough

Market
Harborough

Coventry

Kettering

*CAMBRIDGESHIRE*

*NORTHANTS.*

Northampton

Chawston

Cambridge

*WARWICKS.*

Bedford

Olney

Sandy

Banbury

*BEDS.*

Hook Norton

Stanbridge

Luton

Bishop's Stortford

*OXFORDSHIRE*

*BUCKS.*

*HERTFORDSHIRE*

*ESSEX*

St Albans

Oxford

Borehamwood

Watlington

*Chiltern Hills*

High Wycombe

Watford

Henley-
on-Thames

*LONDON*

# Banbury cakes

The Original Cake Shop in Banbury, founded in 1555 and home of the Banbury cake, was sadly pulled down in 1968. The cakes are still being made, fortunately, and you can find the story at HOOK NORTON, OXFORDSHIRE on p. 328.

# The Gentleman's Relish

The Victorian age saw the mass industrialisation of food, thanks in part to developments in glassware, preserving and canning technologies. Added to this was an expanded empire that enabled a huge range of raw materials to be sent back to the motherland, as well as a nascent scientific understanding of flavours, all of which came to a head in the area of sauces, relishes and condiments. George Watkins Mushroom Ketchup (1830), Colman's mustard (1814), Lea & Perrins Worcestershire Sauce (1837), HP Sauce (1896) and others all allowed the handlebar-moustached Victorian gent to enliven his plate with many flavours and preserves. But no product better represents the tastes of the Victorian everyman than 'Patum Peperium', better known by the twentieth-century name 'The Gentleman's Relish', a type of anchovy paste.

For many, it's an acquired taste, perhaps because the initial smell is akin to damp fish food, but others, including me, love the idea of Gentleman's Relish and its role in the savoury course, often just for men, that was tacked on to the end of a seven- or eight-course Victorian dinner. Of anchovy paste in general, Mrs Beeton said, 'This paste is usually eaten spread upon toast, and is said to form an excellent *bonne bouche*, which enables gentlemen at wine-parties to enjoy their port with redoubled gusto' – meaning that it filled the salty-snack-to-accompany-booze role that is nowadays occupied by peanuts and crisps.

Patum Peperium was invented in 1828 by John Osborn, an Englishman living in Paris, and the company stayed in the family until 1971 when the last remaining family member, not having an heir, sold the business to Elsenham Quality Foods (est. 1890). They were bought out by G. Costa in 2001, which in turn was bought by AB World Foods, a subsidiary of Associated British Foods. Howard Morrish is the brand manager for Patum Peperium today, and assures us that the recipe has stayed the same through all these changes of owner. Today, the product is made in small batches in a factory in Poland. They boil 250 kg barrels of Portuguese anchovies for up to five hours and then strain to remove the bones and produce an essence. This is mixed with butter, rusk and the secret blend of herbs and spices (mace and maybe nutmeg is in there, I'm sure). Around 70 per cent of the product – housed in the distinctive plastic tubs – is taken by the supermarkets, and the rest goes to high-end retailers and delis. 'We still make the porcelain containers, and each year we do a special limited edition one, all hand-painted,' says Howard.

The umami taste of Gentleman's Relish is incredibly versatile. It adds depth to dishes, and a tiny amount smeared on a leg of roast lamb is quite delicious. I would stress 'tiny' amount here, as the main mistake people make is using too much. A tub should last you longer than a pair of shoes: the one in my fridge is coming up for its second birthday and I've barely put a dent in it. Even the instructions on the tub say 'use sparingly'. This, then, is not a product for lavish slathering, but for gentlemanly deportment.

*See also* EASTON GREY, WILTSHIRE (p. 11); EDINBURGH, EDINBURGH (p. 167); FAVERSHAM, KENT (p. 477); MOFFAT, DUMFRIES & GALLOWAY (p. 183); NORWICH, NORFOLK (p. 451); OXFORD, OXFORDSHIRE (p. 351); ROSSENDALE, LANCASHIRE (p. 131); ST HELENS, MERSEYSIDE (p. 132); SHEFFIELD, SOUTH YORKSHIRE (p. 258); SPENNYMOOR, COUNTY DURHAM (p. 227).

## BOREHAMWOOD, HERTFORDSHIRE
# Pasta from Ugo Foods

In 1929, Luigi Ugo walked and hitched his way from Italy to London, where he found work at a grocery store. There he was often paid in flour and eggs, which he made into fresh pasta. After a few years he opened his first shop on Gerrard Street, which catered for expat Italians as well as anyone with a taste for Continental foods. Those of you with a knowledge of the environs of the capital will note that Gerrard Street is now the centre of Chinatown. According to Ugo Foods' current managing director, Paul Ugo, Luigi even made noodles for Chinese restaurant Ley Ons on Wardour Street (remodelled into a noodle bar around 1998). This came about after the proprietor was impressed with Luigi's spaghetti making. The company moved from retail into manufacturing and was the first to launch a fresh organic range of pasta as far back as 1967. Today the company makes fresh pasta under its Del Ugo brand name, as well as for Waitrose, in a unit based in Borehamwood, Hertfordshire.

Ugo imports semolina from Altamura in Puglia, on the 'heel' of Italy. This region, set high on a limestone plateau, is one of the few flat areas in the country and produces the best durum (meaning hard) wheat that makes the best pasta. The semolina is mixed with free-range eggs and water and fashioned via extruding or rolling into the familiar shapes of spaghetti, linguine, penne or tagliatelle. Flat sheet pasta is made into lasagne or used to make filled pasta.

It's worth remembering that although there were 11,000 Italians in London in 1921, and Soho was home to Italian restaurants such as Leoni's Quo Vadis in Dean Street, which opened in 1926, at that time pasta was, for a great many people in Britain, something of a foreign novelty. Of course nowadays it's about as exotic as spuds, but that doesn't mean we shouldn't give it the respect it deserves. All too often pasta is considered a mere stage on which other flavours strut their stuff, and many people don't cook it correctly. Paul recommends 'plenty of water at a constant but gentle rolling boil, to keep the pasta moving and ensure it cooks evenly. Too little water and it'll stick together; a good amount of salt is crucial, too.'

BOSTON, LINCOLNSHIRE
## Brussels sprouts

A 2002 survey by MORI into British vegetable consumption found that sprouts were the most hated vegetable in Britain. I can't help but think this result was probably caused by the over-boiled and smelly offerings of many people's childhoods. But hell's teeth, there are loads of drinks and foods we think are yucky in our youth that we then grow to love: beer, coffee and marmalade, to name but a few. And sprouts are one of the true tastes of winter. Not over-boiled, though, as this brings out the tell-tale sulphurous pong caused by the release of glucosinolates (found in all brassicas – cabbage, mustard, broccoli – they're a defence against pests and herbivores). Shredding and stir-frying is a much better cooking method, particularly if you add bacon, butter, chestnuts and maybe a few tablespoons of hot water towards the end. Or you could try an Italian recipe in which you parboil then halve them, before baking them ('al forno') with a topping of bacon and cheese.

Roger Welberry of Kirton Holme near Boston has been farming the Lincolnshire countryside for over fifty years, and, like me, he's worried about the future of the British sprout. Prices are low, customers don't seem to want them and there's the ever-present threat of Dutch imports. They're also a resource-intensive crop, as they need to grow for almost a year, being sown in April and harvested in December. Compare that to broccoli, which is ready in ten weeks, or cauliflower in twelve. The pity of the lack of demand is that the varieties of sprouts that have been developed recently are far more sweet and tender than those from your grandmother's day. Gone are the times when sprouts needed a frost before they could be eaten. 'They're not as winter-hardy as they used to be, these modern varieties,' Roger told me.

There are about 150 growers in the UK, who between them grow 15,000 acres of the crop. The main variety is Evesham Special, which is a good all-rounder but perhaps a little middle-of-the-road flavour-wise. Non-commercial growers such as allotment owners have been known to dabble with varieties such as Mezzo Nano, Red Rubine and the comedically named Long Island Improved. Noisette is the choice of the true aficionado. It's small, nutty and made for eating at Christmas with chestnuts and an open fire.

*See also* EAST ANGLIAN PARSNIPS (p. 444); PEA HARVEST (p. 332).

## CHAWSTON, BEDFORDSHIRE
## *Chillies from Edible Ornamentals*

'Pick your own' (PYO) farms became popular in the 1970s, forming an important part of the burgeoning environmental movement. They are a great day out, and offer both young and old some leisurely yet light activity, harvesting nature's copious bounty. Add to this the fact that you get spanking fresh produce at cheap-as-chips prices, and you can see the appeal. It's fair to say it's a summer activity, with fruits such as berries and vegetables like French beans, onions and tomatoes being the most popular.

Perhaps the newest kid on the PYO block, however, is provided by Joanna Plumb at Edible Ornamentals. In 1994, Joanna, whose husband Shawn is American, spent two years living in San Antonio, the heart of Tex-Mex country, and a place where chillies are taken seriously. Joanna's family are commercial growers of fruit and veg, and when her brother came over for a visit and saw chillies being sold loose like apples, he was inspired to set up a business selling wholesale chillies to the supermarkets back in the UK.

In 2001 a DIY store asked him whether he could grow some chilli plants, but he was simply too busy. 'He asked if I would like to have a go,' says Joanna, 'so I did, sowing several thousands of chilli seeds and growing them on.' Then, disaster struck: the order was cancelled. Joanna's dad suggested just composting the lot as he was fed up with watering them, but Joanna wanted to have a go at selling them, and started first at car boot sales, then food shows and subsequently farmers' markets. And so out of disaster came a fledgling business.

In 2007, Joanna and Shawn moved off the family farm, leaving behind forty years of infrastructure, and bought an old garden nursery, where she started again. By then they were not only selling the plants, but had also developed a range of sauces and condiments. They now grow over forty varieties of chillies, including the Dorset Naga (*see* p. 45) and the Padron, which offers a sort of Russian-roulette eating experience, as one in a dozen or so is super hot.

The PYO notion came about, like the best ideas do, by chance. They had taken a few of their favourite customers into their research and development polytunnel, where they had been trying out new varieties of chilli alongside other crops used in the sauces such as tomatoes and aubergines, and they noticed that people really loved going in there and picking all the fresh produce. They began letting more and more people into this spicy inner sanctum, and in the end opened it to everyone.

It's strange that selecting something from a PYO plant, picking it and putting it in your basket should feel so much more rewarding than choosing produce in a supermarket. Perhaps it's the connection to the soil, or to older forms of collecting food. Perhaps PYO simply lets you indulge a little of your inner hunter-gatherer.

COLSTON BASSETT, NOTTINGHAMSHIRE

## *Colston Bassett Stores*

For a wonderful, if a little dramatic, timeline of our relationship with the institution of the village shop, you need look no further than the rural weathervane that is *The Archers*. Changes such as the introduction of self-service, Sunday opening hours, supermarket competition and the closure of post offices have all been meted out on the people of Ambridge.

Colston Bassett Stores, a picture-postcard village shop

Some of those issues will no doubt strike a chord with Jan and Martin Lindsay of Colston Bassett Stores. Their shop must surely be the prettiest picture-perfect store in all of England. The main part of the oak-beamed building was constructed in the seventeenth century, with later Victorian additions, and a modern conservatory on the side houses the café and restaurant. All this sits in a dreamy English garden, replete with an apple tree whose fruits are often used in crumbles, tarts and charlottes – and how often do you see courgette flowers for sale these days?

Bread for the shop comes from the nearby Hambleton Bakery in Oakham, and includes a fine sourdough and rarely seen manchet breakfast rolls. There's also a wide range of cheeses, including Colston Bassett Stilton made around the corner, and a well stocked off-licence.

Of course, most communities aren't as lucky as the residents of Colston Bassett in having a top-notch deli, grocer's and eatery on their doorstep, and in most parts of the country the traditional village shop is very much under threat. According to the Plunkett Foundation, a charity that helps communities set up or maintain local shops, 400 closed in 2009, and 3,000 British villages now have no shop in them. This is all the more alarming when you consider the lessons of the harsh winter of early 2010, when people were unable to get the car out to the supermarkets, and opted instead to walk to the local shop for essentials.

More than just providing the essentials, though, local stores, like pubs, are a place where the community can come together. The Lindsays have poured their heart and soul into their shop, and the effort and attention to detail oozes out of every nook and cranny. It has, however, worn them out a bit. At the time of writing they're looking to find someone younger to take the business on and move it to the next level, and as residents in the village they're keen to see it prosper. 'We'll probably still be here for years to come!' says Martin.

*See also* CANTERBURY, KENT (p. 469); HOOK, HAMPSHIRE (p. 484); IPSWICH, SUFFOLK (p. 441); RUSHWICK, WORCESTERSHIRE (p. 309); STANNINGTON, NORTHUMBERLAND (p. 227); WELBECK, NOTTINGHAMSHIRE (p. 362).

HENLEY-ON-THAMES, OXFORDSHIRE
## *The Crooked Billet*

The door to the Crooked Billet pub has a sign that reads 'Wanted: local produce. Swop for lunch', which instantly conjures up an image of someone like Michael Elphick's Jake the poacher from *Withnail and I* pulling a rabbit from his pants, laying it on the bar and enquiring about the availability of a table for one at 7 p.m.

It doesn't work quite like that, however. 'We have a list of prices from Henley farmers' market and give people a credit note,' laughs owner Paul Clerehugh. So you can't just turn up with a sack of King Eddies and expect a three-course meal. No, what really gets Paul excited is the more unusual stuff. 'We've had big bags of wild garlic, and some beautiful crayfish which had been purged and were all ready to go. Snails were another one.' Other notable donations include boxes of black figs from Lady Silsoe at nearby Neals Farm, or chilli peppers and apples. Mushrooms are also popular, particularly chanterelles and ceps. 'We check them with the official mushroom handbook, plus I'll eat a couple of them just to make sure, and if I'm all right then we use them.'

Paul bought the pub in 1989. When he approached the bank for a loan he had no experience of running a pub and no security against the loan. Unsurprisingly, the bank said no. Undeterred, he went to a second bank and said the loan was for a sports car, figuring that if he defaulted it would be repossessed. 'Sign here, sir,' was the reply, and he cheekily used the money to buy the Crooked Billet. At the time it was the cheapest pub on the market he could find, a complete wreck and had a tree growing through it.

'Swop for lunch': free meals in return for unusual fresh produce

I love the idea of swapping food for, well, more food. Allotment growers, those with large back gardens and the particularly green-fingered often have a glut of produce left over. Here, it can be traded in and put towards the cost of a nice lunch. Food swapping is one of those slightly 'under the radar' activities that adds a frisson of the unique and interesting to the chef's larder. If you grow excess produce, or if you catch, forage for or shoot something, you'll often find that a good chef will take it off your hands for, at the very least, a couple of glasses of house wine; there's something in it for you, and the chef builds customer loyalty – though, as Paul warns, there is the risk of being visited by the Inland Revenue.

*See also* BRITISH PUBS (p. 434).

## HOOK NORTON, OXFORDSHIRE
## *Banbury cakes*

Banbury cakes are one of those things that you might have imagined had been long ago consigned to the pages of the history books. Fortunately, though, they are still being made and are available both in the town and the surrounding area. Most modern recipes call for an oval puff-pastry casing filled with a mixture of currants, fruit and spices – similar to that of an Eccles cake (*see* p. 103). The top is given a wash of egg and a dusting of sugar, and they are all set for a quick spell in an oven.

The Original Cake Shop on Parson's Street in Banbury was built around 1550 (although one suspects the prefix 'original' was added after some rival started up) and it helped to spread the cake's fame far and wide. Gervase Markham's *The English Huswife* (1615) includes a recipe that features currants, cloves, nutmeg, mace and cinnamon mixed with cream and pastry, then coating this with more pastry. Back in Banbury, E. W. Brown took over the running of the Original Cake Shop in 1868, and descendant Philip Brown still bakes Banbury cakes to this day.

The Original Cake Shop 'was pulled down in the name of progress in 1968 and a brick monstrosity put up in its place,' says Philip – it now houses a Balti restaurant. Philip, meanwhile, has decamped to the back of the village shop in nearby Hook Norton and makes his cakes there. They contain the best Vostizza currants, and a blend of spices that has little changed from Markham's 1615 recipe. 'They must have been expensive items to produce back then as the filling ingredients all had to be imported,' he says. Brown's original Banbury cakes are now available in the café within Banbury museum and various other cafés in the town. 'All I'm doing is keeping the thing going, and I suppose when I turn up my toes, this lot will go as well, but we're doing the best we can at the moment,' says Philip. Banbury cakes: get them while they're hot!

*See also* MINCEMEAT (p. 202); ALBERT EMBANKMENT, LAMBETH (p. 368); ALDERLEY EDGE, CHESHIRE (p. 96); BISHOP AUCKLAND, COUNTY DURHAM (p. 201); ECCLES, GREATER MANCHESTER (p. 103); LLANDEILO, CARMARTHENSHIRE (p. 74); MANCHESTER, GREATER MANCHESTER (p. 119); MELTON MOWBRAY, LEICESTERSHIRE (p. 341); NAVENBY, LINCOLNSHIRE (p. 344); OTLEY, WEST YORKSHIRE (p. 252); STANBRIDGE, BEDFORDSHIRE (p. 360); WHITBY, NORTH YORKSHIRE (p. 269).

## KIRTON IN LINDSEY, LINCOLNSHIRE
# *Mount Pleasant Windmill and the True Loaf Bakery*

Londoner Mervin Austin had a wholesale bakery in London in the 1980s and 1990s, producing bread and rolls for big clients such as the civil service, banks and the Post Office. At one point he employed over 150 people. 'It was all machine-made Chorleywood-process stuff (a high-speed manufacturing process that now accounts for 80 per cent of the bread we eat in the UK) and eventually we had a "divergence of opinion" on which way to go,' says Mervin, who by that time had become bored with the daily grind behind a desk. A management buyout led to him leaving. Then one day a neighbour was leafing through *Farmers Weekly* and came across an advert for a windmill for sale in Lincolnshire. 'How far's that?' he asked. 'Not very far,' came the reply, 'just the other side of Cambridge, I think.' Many hours later, Mervin and wife Marie-Christine arrived in North Humberside and fell in love with the Mount Pleasant Windmill.

The mill was built in 1875 for one Edric Lansdall, and subsequently passed through various hands. The sails were taken down in 1936 and an engine fitted. In 1991 the mill was refurbished by new owners with grants from English Heritage, before coming under the ownership of Mervin and Marie-Christine in 2000. The windmill now has a set of French burr stones (made from strips of quartz cemented together and bound with iron band) and a set of English millstone grit stones (made from one piece) quarried in Derbyshire. They also added an eighteen-ton wood-burning oven, which they brought over from Spain. This took two weeks of near-constant burning to reach the correct baking temperature, but once hot, it stays hot. The wood to fuel it comes from nearby estates or sawmills.

And so Mervin is one of the few bakers who control the whole process. 'I've always liked the idea of being a primary producer, going right from the grain through to the finished product. If I had enough money to buy a farm I'd grow the stuff as well!' he says. With this set-up Mervin bakes a range of over thirty breads, including wholemeal, soda, sourdough, pain paysan, rye, ciabatta, spelt, pain au levain, fougasse and baguettes. The strong French influence may be down in part to Marie-Christine, who is French. She runs the tea shop next to the windmill with typical Gallic aplomb, serving cakes, toast, teas and coffees.

In Mervin's eyes, bread has become a mere commodity, and for many people how it's made is of little interest. But things are beginning to change and people are now starting to ask what exactly is in their bread and looking for something different. 'A few years ago you couldn't sell a sourdough for love nor money up here. "Sour?!" people would say. Now I sell loads because I care about good-quality produce, and just sell on the taste.'

*See also* HOLT, NORFOLK (p. 439).

# Red Leicester cheese

Red Leicester, though still red in colour, was called initially just Leicester cheese, and was described in my 1930s copy of *Law's Grocer's Manual* like this: 'Made in the same way as Derby cheese, the cheeses are smaller than the Cheddars and more flaky in substance, but less so than the Cheshires.'

But why is Red Leicester red at all? Well, it seems it was all a bit of a marketing gimmick. When the cheese first began to be made commercially in the eighteenth century and sold in the London markets, it needed an edge to make it stand out against the big guns of Cheddar to the south, Double Gloucester to the west, and Cheshire and Lancashire to the north. Many cheeses at that time contained a small amount of annatto, giving them an attractive orangey-golden hue that people thought indicative of a good cheese. Annatto is made from the seeds of the achiote tree, native to South America, and it has a nutty peppery taste. In an exercise of one-upmanship, one imagines, the makers of Red Leicester added a good deal more to make their cheese the darkest and richest of them all. Today annatto bears the E number E160b.

A truckle of Sparkenhoe Red Leicester

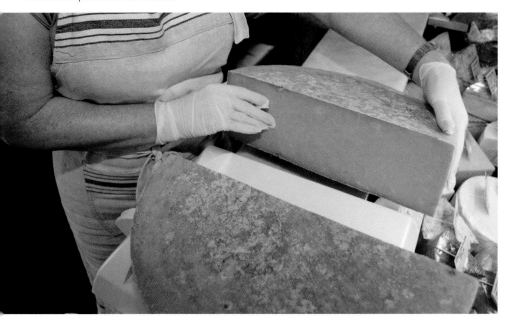

## Pea Harvest

The annual UK pea harvest is a culinary time-trial where a mere 150 minutes separates success from failure. Farmers sow their peas in April or May, looking to hit a specific date in July on which to harvest the crop. As the peas mature, the grower repeatedly takes samples and places them in a machine called a tenderometer, which gently crushes the peas to judge when they're at optimum condition. When that point is reached, the race is on, which makes peas the original British racing greens.

The fields are invaded by specialist harvesting machines, which lift the vines, strip the pods and rattle them through a centrifugal drum to remove the peas. The leftover pods, vines and leaves are all mulched and deposited on the field to be ploughed back into the ground and enrich it, which means that everything leaving the field is edible – no waste. 'You have to put the land in a seven-year rotation, however, otherwise it becomes what's known as pea sick,' says Tim Mudge from the Processed Vegetable Growers Association, which provides commercial support to the majority of pea growers in the UK, nearly all of whom are centred around Yorkshire and North Lincolnshire. 'In the UK we sow about 30,000 hectares of peas each year, which will produce around 130,000 tonnes of peas, nearly all of which are destined for freezing.' It's worth noting that we're also the biggest consumers of the legume in Europe.

In recent years, growers have consolidated into co-operatives, which makes sense as just one pea-harvesting machine can cost up to £300,000, and you might need three or four to work your fields. On the processing side, there are only two large-scale players left: the one you'll no doubt have heard of, Birds Eye, who pack all their own peas at their new plant in Hull, and Pinguin Foods, who pretty much pack everybody else's at their £3m Pinguin plant in King's Lynn, Norfolk.

Despite all this effort, the humble British pea is all too often taken for granted. Fine-dining chefs tend not to use them as they can roll around on the plate making a mess, so while pea shoots are often seen in the best restaurants, peas aren't. Furthermore, our obsession with all things chilled but fresh has led to a fall from grace for this family freezer favourite, which is a shame because they are fresh, as well as tasty and incredibly versatile. 'Over the last few years we've seen some improvement in using peas as an ingredient rather than just an accompaniment,' says Tim. 'You can add them to a stir-fry, or kedgeree (*see* p. 170), or put them in a flan or a tortilla.' And I'll wager you've got a bag in your freezer, nestled at the back. Indeed, when I was a child the freezer was a place where the laws of time had no meaning; the huge white chest in the garage was a stasis chamber into which items would go for months, sometimes years, to be frozen solid like Han Solo in *The Empire Strikes Back*. The biannual defrosting of it always led to a dinner of loose peas, mystery breaded products and a handful of oven chips. 'When you reach in the freezer and pull out a bag of peas in December, you're getting little bits of summer,' says Tim.

See also EAST ANGLIAN PARSNIPS (p. 444); BOSTON, LINCOLNSHIRE (p. 323); GOOLE, EAST YORKSHIRE (p. 248); GREAT WITLEY, WORCESTERSHIRE (p. 293); NEWCHURCH, ISLE OF WIGHT (p. 491); OWMBY-BY-SPITAL, LINCOLNSHIRE (p. 349); QUEENSFERRY, FLINTSHIRE (p. 84).

Production all but stopped during the Second World War when an inferior 'white Leicester' ration cheese was foisted on the public without the distinctive colouring. When the cheese finally reappeared, the prefix 'red' was added to distinguish it from this. However, like many of our post-war county cheeses it was now a shadow of its former self, being little more than an industrial Cheddar clone with all the taste and texture of orange playdough.

There were, however, a faithful few who kept the county cheese-making skills alive, and they were soon joined by new recruits to the cause. David and Jo Clark could be considered just such people. They both have farming backgrounds and together they keep 150 head of pedigree Holstein Friesian cows on their 160-acre farm in Upton, West Leicestershire. In the late 1990s, milk prices fell dramatically, and so, like so many of Britain's farmers, they decided to look into diversification. Having ruled out corporate entertainment and 4x4 off-roading, they turned their hand to cheese-making. Some amateur sleuthing revealed that the last Red Leicester made on a farm was by a Mr Shepherd of Bagworth in the 1950s, and that when he retired no one else was making it within the borders of the county. The Clarks decided to start producing Red Leicester again, poring over old books and recipes to find out how it was done. After a bit of trial and error, the first cheese was ready and Sparkenhoe, named after the farm on which it was made, was born. They are still the only farm-based artisan Red Leicester makers in the county today, although the Long Clawson Dairy, a collective of dairy-farmers-turned-cheese-makers based just north of Melton Mowbray, also make a rather good pasteurised one on a larger scale.

Jo and David's cheese is unpasteurised, which gives it extra depth and flavour. It's made by adding the annatto to the previous day's milk, before the mix is scalded and the whey separated out. The curds are then put into moulds and pressed for forty-eight hours, turning once. The cheeses are bound in cloth and lard and matured for five months at around 10°C. After nearly half a year of waiting, what you're left with is a brilliant, rich cheese the colour of a Turner sunset. Nutty yet creamy, with gentle pressure it flakes gently into generous-sized nuggets. A grocer from the 1930s, bereft of his trusty manual, might be puzzled at the prefix 'red', but he would certainly recognise this as a proper Leicester cheese.

*See also* BRITISH CHEESE (p. 290).

# *Park railings*

Lincolnshire is the only place I've ever seen park railings on a menu. In France the dish is known as Sainte Ménehould, which is the name Hugh Fearnley-Whittingstall gave it in his *Meat* book. It consists of braised meat, primarily lamb, although sometimes beef, cooked, cooled and pressed before being cut into strips and coated in breadcrumbs. Think of it as a fish finger made with meat. The meat needs to be tender, stringy and gelatinous, so the breast of lamb from the front underside of the animal (called brisket on a cow) is the best cut to use.

First cook the joint long and slow in wine or water until it's falling off the bone. Then, while it's still warm, pick the meat off and lay it on a tray between two sheets of cling film, and pop it in the fridge with something heavy on top. The next day you should have a large slab of meat held together by congealed fat – this is a good thing. You then cut it into finger-length strips with a very sharp knife, spread one side with a little mustard, dip in egg and breadcrumbs, and fry. It's probably not easy to attempt at home, but it's a godsend for chefs as it requires extremely cheap cuts, not too much labour and adds value.

I sampled beef park railing as a starter in the Wig and Mitre in Lincoln. This pub dates from the fourteenth century and nestles snugly on the aptly named Steep Hill, which runs between the castle, home to the courts of law (hence the 'Wig'), and the cathedral, home to the clergy (hence the 'Mitre'). They serve a single, warm, large park railing, cut in half lengthways to reveal the dark, meaty interior, and accompanied by crab and tarragon mayonnaise and a few chunks of crunchy radishes and leaves. I'm normally wary of 'surf 'n' turf' combinations, thinking that adding, for example, lobster to a fillet steak just smacks of wealth and gluttony rather than complementary tastes and textures. Here, however, warm bovine and cool crustacean worked extremely well together.

Whether in their lamb or beef incarnation, park railings benefit from something sharp and interesting to provide a contrast to the rich, fatty texture of the meat. In an article for the *Spectator* in 1963, Elizabeth David talked of park railings being a favourite of Eugene Kaufeler, head chef of the Dorchester just after the war. More recently, in his *Great British Menu* entry, chef Mark Broadbent served lamb versions with a piquant sauce featuring anchovies, capers and parsley.

## LOUTH, LINCOLNSHIRE
# *Lincolnshire sausage*

The Lincolnshire sausage is surely one of the UK's top bangers. The area is traditional pig country, with the animals being fed on leftovers from the county's other top crops, cereals and potatoes. What the sausage, alongside haslet, faggots and stuffed chine, shows is that folk around these parts know a thing or two about cylindrical pork products.

Its unique flavouring comes from sage, a member of the mint family, which is the only herb used. Anything else and you've got a herb sausage. 'You see some in the shops made with rosemary or marjoram, but that's not a Lincolnshire,' says Jim Sutcliffe. Jim comes from a farming background and at the age of twenty-four was not only part-owner and manager of a butcher's shop but also the BBC's Young Butcher of the Year 2009. He's also a member of the Lincolnshire Sausage Association and one of over 160 butchers within the historical county's borders who make the sausages.

Naturally, he won't divulge the recipe – suffice to say that it's an old one – but alongside the distinctive sage, you will find pepper, some breadcrumbs and salt. The meat he uses is mainly shoulder. 'Because we produce stuffed chine (*see* p. 337), the butchering to get that off the carcass leaves you with the hand of pork, and it doesn't really make a good joint so all of that goes into the sausage.' This he augments with an occasional bit of belly if it's looking a bit lean. 'We mince in through a wide plate only once,' says Jim. This gives the Lincolnshire its coarse, open texture. It also means that the prior preparation of the meat has to be spot on, with every blood vessel, bit of gristle and vein removed. Casings are natural, as you would expect, and the linking of the finished result is done by hand.

Jim and the other producers have applied for PGI (Protected Geographical Indication) status, which, should it be granted, would mean that Lincolnshire sausages can only be made in Lincolnshire. They are up against some stiff competition, but believe it's worth it so that the public can know what it's buying. Nothing highlights this better than the revelation in the *Daily Telegraph* that Walls were producing a Lincolnshire sausage in Manchester from German, Dutch and Danish frozen pork. All quite legal, but Jim and the rest of the independent butchers in Lincolnshire believe it's wrong, and I, for one, agree with them.

*See also* SAUSAGES (p. 122).

*Stuffed chine*

Sage is first and foremost the herb of Lincolnshire, taking pride of place in the county's sausage. However, there is another pork product made in these parts that stars not sage, but parsley, and lots of it. Stuffed chine sees the backbone and shoulder muscle of the pig removed, and deep slashes made in the meat. It's then cured for ten days or more before being dried off and salted. Then into the slashes a great deal of minced fresh parsley is stuffed, and the joint is wrapped up tightly in cheesecloth and set on a slow boil for four hours. After changing the water mid-way through, and letting the meat cool down in the new water, you are left, after all this effort, with beautiful baby-pink meat and dark green stripes of parsley. Some butchers serve it on the bone, others remove it and slice the chine thinly on the bacon slicer. It is always served cold.

A dash or two of vinegar is the traditional accompaniment, as it's said to counter some of the fat, but as Mrs Poyser says in George Eliot's *Adam Bede* when a guest refuses vinegar, 'Ay, you're i' the right not. It spoils the flavour o' the chine, to my thinking. It's poor eating where the flavour o' the meat lies i' the cruets.'

Chris Smith, a third-generation butcher at Lakings in the Lincolnshire town of Louth, says, 'Traditionally, stuffed chine came from the farming community. It was a celebratory dish eaten around May during the hiring fairs.' These were rural get-togethers where labourers would be hired by farmers to work the summer. 'Traditionally it was prepared on the bone, what we call a neck chine,' says Chris. Today, Lakings produce one on the bone, and one off, depending on circumstance. 'The old hands come in and know what it is, younger people not so much, but they're keen to find out more and try regional specialities.'

*See also* BROMYARD, HEREFORDSHIRE (p. 283); CAMBRIDGE, CAMBRIDGESHIRE (p. 422); CONWY, CONWY (p. 60); FORRES, MORAY (p. 173); MARYLEBONE, WESTMINSTER (p. 387); MELTON CONSTABLE, NORFOLK (p. 447); NANTWICH, CHESHIRE (p. 125); WOODHALL SPA, LINCOLNSHIRE (p. 364); YORK, NORTH YORKSHIRE (p. 271).

## *Stichelton cheese*

Stilton is renowned the world over as the king of British cheeses; famous for not being made in the town itself, synonymous with Christmas, and one of a handful of UK cheeses protected by European PDO (Protected Designation of Origin) status, which means it can only be made to a specific production method in a certain area. PDO protection was awarded after a listeria scare in the late 1970s, which was traced back to unpasteurised cheese production. Everyone panicked, one person died, and large-scale producers switched to using heat-treated milk. The last unpasteurised raw-milk Stilton rolled off the production line at Colston Bassett in 1989. The PDO arrived in 1996.

This is why when Randolph Hodgson from Neal's Yard Dairy teamed up with cheese-maker Joe Schneider to produce a traditional raw-milk Stilton cheese they found they were not, under any circumstances, allowed to call it Stilton. A scour of the history books revealed that Stichelton was an old Saxon name for the town of Stilton, so the chaps plumped for this and a raw-milk

Joe Schneider takes a sample from a truckle of Stichelton

Stilton-style cheese is now back on the menu. It's made slowly and properly from the fresh organic milk of a herd of Friesians on the Welbeck estate in Nottinghamshire, where their production facility is also based (*see* p. 362). It is a joy to taste: incredibly smooth and yet with a little tang on the tongue.

Joe begins by taking curds, milling them into pieces and placing them in the moulds. Stilton isn't pressed, it's just left to sink down – by about half. The next stage is the 'rubbing up', when the outside is sealed by running a butter knife over the outside of the cheese. If this isn't done, the mould will start to appear much too early. The cheeses are then left to mature slowly.

Cheese-making is a meticulous process, and Joe is still refining his. Every little detail must be noted so that eight weeks later he can evaluate the results. Tiny fluctuations in the raw materials and method can develop into noticeable differences in the finished product; the temperature of the milk, the handling of it and the time it was taken from the cow all play a part. 'Colston Bassett has 150 years of cheese-making, so those chaps know that in July the milk alkaline is higher and you need to adjust for that.' Joe and the team are still slowly but surely refining and ironing out these sorts of details, all of which mean that while Stichelton is currently a very good cheese, given a few more years it will be truly great.

*See also* BRITISH CHEESE (p. 290).

MARKET BOSWORTH, LEICESTERSHIRE
## *Bosworth jumbles*

When matters need celebrating, we reach for cakes, pastries and other sweet delicacies. Getting hitched? Time for a wedding cake. Another year older? Have some birthday cake. Killed Richard III in battle, thus crushing the house of York and establishing a Tudor dynasty? Ah, then you and the boys will no doubt want to party with a Bosworth jumble. Apocryphal though it surely is, the story goes that the recipe for Bosworth jumbles was found on the battlefield of Bosworth in Leicestershire; one version of the tale even states that the recipe was prised from the cold, dead hands of Richard III's chef.

The name jumble comes from *gemel*, the Latin for 'twin', and also the name given to a two-fingered ring. Made from butter, sugar, eggs and flour, a common flavouring was caraway seed or occasionally aniseed or almond, either mixed in with the dough or sprinkled on top. The dough was shaped into long rolls, cut into lengths and tied in a loose knot shape or interlaced rings: a medieval pretzel.

Only the wealthy would have worn such jewellery, or been able to afford the sugar to put in jumbles, or indeed have the literacy to read the recipe in *The Good Huswifes Jewell* by Thomas Dawson (1585). Dawson's recipe – he calls them iombils – calls for the dough shapes to be first boiled, before being baked, similar to the way bagels are made:

> Take twenty Egges and put them into a pot both the yolkes & the white, beat them wel, then take a pound of beaten suger and put to them, and stirre them wel together, then put to it a quarter of a peck of flower, and make a hard paste thereof, and then with Anniseede moulde it well, and make it in little rowles beeing long, and tye them in knots, and wet the ends in Rosewater, then put them into a pan of seething water . . . Then take them out with a Skimmer and lay them in a cloth to drie, lay them in a tart panne, the bottome beeing oyled, then put them into a temperat Ouen for one howre, turning them often in the Ouen.

The above recipe makes 100 jumbles, with which to impress your guests after a hard day's battling. Today they are rather hard to come by – they are not even found in the café at the Bosworth Battlefield Heritage Centre.

*See also* HOW RECIPES BEGIN (p. 496).

## MARKET HARBOROUGH, LEICESTERSHIRE
### *Martin Hobbs fishmonger's*

Martin Hobbs is a small fishmonger's in Market Harborough. Sadly, Martin himself passed away a few years ago, and now his daughter Jenny and widow Nora own and run the business. The Hobbs took over in 1971, from Mac Fisheries, a firm established in 1919 by Lord Leverhulme to sell the fish from the Scottish island of Lewis, which he had bought outright for £167,000 in 1918. Mac Fisheries was once a large national chain with over 400 stores, but it was sold off and closed down in the 1970s by its then parent firm Unilever. 'When they closed, they left large parts of the country without any fish,' says Nora.

But the shop's history goes back even further. Nora shows me a picture taken around 1920 in which the owner is one T. B. Hunt and a sign above the shopfront reads, 'est. 1860'. Mr Hunt's piscine produce is laid out for customers to peruse on a huge sloping marble display. The marble was Italian, and despite all these changes of owners, the evolution of fishing itself and today's completely different retail landscape, it's the same marble display that Nora now puts her fish on every day. 'In the 1980s they [health and safety] tried to make us change the block, but Miss Willits, the local conservation officer, helped us save it.' This small fishmonger's piece of three-inch-thick Italian marble has therefore been in constant service for over 150 years. Long may it continue.

*See also* DERWENTWATER, CUMBRIA (p. 102); DOVER, KENT (p. 473); GLOUCESTER, GLOUCESTERSHIRE (p. 288); HASTINGS, EAST SUSSEX (p. 483); MARKET HARBOROUGH, LEICESTERSHIRE (p. 340); NEWLYN, CORNWALL (pp. 32 and 34); RIVER SEVERN, GLOUCESTERSHIRE (p. 305); SCOURIE, HIGHLAND (p. 187); SOUTHEND-ON-SEA, ESSEX (p. 455); WANSFORD, EAST YORKSHIRE (p. 261); WHITBURN, TYNE & WEAR (p. 228).

## MELTON MOWBRAY, LEICESTERSHIRE
# Melton Hunt cake

Before embarking on a day in the saddle pursuing vermin, the landed gentry of Leicestershire required a little something to get them going. The tradition of the stirrup cup, containing port or sherry and often featuring quarry animals in its design, has long been an established part of hunting. However, something a little more filling was required by the members of the Melton Hunt in the nineteenth century. So, in 1854, a baker named Joseph Morris, employed at Melton Mowbray's John Dickinson bakery, invented the Melton Hunt cake.

Morris became a partner in the firm in 1901, and you can still buy Melton Hunt cake from the shop that bears his name to this day. What's more, the recipe hasn't changed one iota. It's still the same mix of sultanas, currants, muscovado sugar, butter, fresh eggs, almonds, glacé cherries and a good slug of Caribbean rum for extra oomph. The texture of the cake is rich, almost sticky, with a nice spicy fermented smell that no doubt comes from the rum.

Indeed, the town has a bit of previous with drunken members of the gentry. In 1837 the Marquis of Waterford, after a successful day at the nearby Croxton Park Races, was refused entry to the town by the Toll Master. Subsequently he and his party found some red paint and began daubing it all over the town, and this may be where the phrase 'painting the town red' originated. There are some sceptics, of course, and it's not unlikely that they decided to get the paintbrushes out as a result of the phrase, but there is strong evidence that the event took place: after a fire damaged the large model swan that adorned the front of the Swan Inn, it was sent for restoration, and in the process the marquis's handiwork was revealed. Equally, some say you can still see flecks of red paint on the older buildings in the town.

Nowadays the cake is perhaps best enjoyed with a cup of tea, rather than as a precursor to blood sports or acts of criminal damage.

*See also* ALBERT EMBANKMENT, LAMBETH (p. 368); ALDERLEY EDGE, CHESHIRE (p. 96); BISHOP AUCKLAND, COUNTY DURHAM (p. 201); ECCLES, GREATER MANCHESTER (p. 103); HOOK NORTON, OXFORDSHIRE (p. 328); LLANDEILO, CARMARTHENSHIRE (p. 74); MANCHESTER, GREATER MANCHESTER (p. 119); NAVENBY, LINCOLNSHIRE (p. 344); OTLEY, WEST YORKSHIRE (p. 252); STANBRIDGE, BEDFORDSHIRE (p. 360); WHITBY, NORTH YORKSHIRE (p. 269).

## MELTON MOWBRAY, LEICESTERSHIRE
# Melton Mowbray Pork Pie

A love of pie stretches throughout this land: the traditional steak pie on New Year's Day in Scotland, meat pies at the footie, cockney pie and mash, West Country pasties – all these prove that bits of an animal cooked in some sort of pastry is guaranteed to appeal wherever you find yourself in Britain.

However, while there may be many regional variations, there is only one protected by European Law: the Melton Mowbray Pork Pie. This is the result of eleven years of hard lobbying, hoop-jumping and paperwork by the Melton Mowbray Pork Pie Association (MMPPA). The association is a collective of the nine producers who all make the pie to strict criteria, which include the pastry being hand-raised rather than made in a mould, and the filling containing cured meat, jelly and a blend of spices.

At the inaugural British Pie Awards in 2009, Sainsbury's 'Taste the Difference' Melton Mowbray Pork Pie made by Walkers Charnwood Bakery took the top prize. In the 2010 competition they did it again, only this time with the one they make for Tesco. The bakery is owned by Samworth Brothers, who also own Ginsters, and Dickinson & Morris, the other big pie producer in town.

Smaller-scale members of the MMPPA, whose pies are just as tasty,

Robert Ross, chairman of the judges at the British Pie Awards, holds aloft a Melton Mowbray Pork Pie

include Mrs Kings, who has a stall at Borough Market in London, Nelson's butchers in Stamford and Northfield Farm at Oakham.

In a town like Melton Mowbray, there is a fair amount of rivalry around pies, but just as there is no one definitive champagne, there is no one definitive pork pie. Each of the producers, both large and small, have their subtle differences. It's all down to taste and preference, and together they take pride in the pies and bring the joy of them to a wider audience.

Britain has too few food successes that make it permanently into the national consciousness, let alone beyond our borders. Sadly, the modern pie – like the sausage – is often mass-produced to a set unit price. It has been debased and reduced to a poor imitation of its former pre-industrial glory. The success story of the Melton Mowbray Pork Pie and its fixture as inimitable outside the region is indeed something to celebrate.

*See also* CORNISH PASTIES (p. 18).

## NAVENBY, LINCOLNSHIRE
# *Lincolnshire plum bread from Welbourne's Bakery*

Pete Welbourne, owner of Welbourne's Bakery in Navenby, once received a letter of complaint from a lady upset that her Lincolnshire plum bread didn't contain one single plum. Pete very kindly wrote back explaining the reason why: 'If we put dried plums in it, by law we'd have to call it prune bread.' Lincolnshire plum bread actually contains no plums; the name comes from the days before refrigeration, when the summer's soft fruit would be dried out to make it last and was known as 'plumed fruits'. Evidence of this can be found in a Mrs Beeton recipe for plum pudding, which also doesn't contain any plums. What a wonderful example of quirky English nomenclature.

Pete's grandfather, Cornelius Welbourne, founded the bakery in 1896, and the place has done its best to weather the onset of time, remaining every inch the small rural bakery. Deliveries to surrounding shops are made on a Wednesday afternoon in a van (the shop still honours half-day closing), but in Pete's father's day they were made using a cart pulled by a one-eyed horse called Nelson.

But back to the bread. So, there are no plums, but what is actually in it? Pete is naturally reluctant to talk in too much detail about the exact quantities in the recipe, but the basic ingredients are currants, sultanas, mixed fruit peel, allspice and cinnamon, eggs, fat, sugar and bread flour. The recipe has

A final sprinkle of flour is added to the plum bread mix

been altered only once since Grandfather Cornelius first broke out his loaf tin and made the first batch, as Welbourne's now use vegetable shortening rather than lard in the mixture so that it's suitable for vegetarians.

There are many plum breads available, and they're all slightly different. Some are little more than ordinary industrial bread with a few bits added and hardly worthy of the name. Welbourne's loaf is a more substantial offering. 'We date it for three months, but it'll keep for longer. In fact, the more you leave it the better the flavour; it matures as it ages.'

It's certainly a weighty loaf: 960 grams and dark, rich and sticky, with a sweet, almost boozy smell reminiscent of Christmas cake, although there is not a drop of the strong stuff in it. Part of the joy of tea breads – and plum loaf is a great example – is that they sit in the culinary spot between sweet and savoury. They act like cakes, but you can treat them like toast. Lincolnshire plum bread tastes great 'neat', with just a simple smear of butter, but Pete also recommends eating it with a slice of Lincolnshire Poacher cheese, or his personal favourite, Cote Hill Blue, which he believes will one day go on to rival Stilton in the nation's affections.

The popularity of the plum loaf has increased in recent years as people have reconnected with regional specialities. Welbourne's now supply John Lewis's food hall, and another local producer, Myers, supply their loaf to

British Airways to be served with the cheese course in first class. With all this new-found adulation there are calls to protect the name under European PDO (Protected Designation of Origin) legislation.

That process does take a while, but a slice of Lincolnshire plum bread with some good cheese, perhaps washed down with a cuppa or something a little stronger, is a very good way to pass the time.

*See also* ALBERT EMBANKMENT, LAMBETH (p. 368); ALDERLEY EDGE, CHESHIRE (p. 96); BISHOP AUCKLAND, COUNTY DURHAM (p. 201); ECCLES, GREATER MANCHESTER (p. 103); HOOK NORTON, OXFORDSHIRE (p. 328); LLANDEILO, CARMARTHENSHIRE (p. 74); MANCHESTER, GREATER MANCHESTER (p. 119); MELTON MOWBRAY, LEICESTERSHIRE (p. 341); OTLEY, WEST YORKSHIRE (p. 252); STANBRIDGE, BEDFORDSHIRE (p. 360); WHITBY, NORTH YORKSHIRE (p. 269).

## NOTTINGHAM, NOTTINGHAMSHIRE
# Iberico World Tapas

Iberico World Tapas is tucked away underneath Nottingham's Halls of Justice in what was once a prison-holding cell for the county court above. Thankfully the decor has been much improved since, with simple clean lines, cream walls and dark woods throughout. The only nod to the Iberian peninsula is the Moorish-inspired mirrors around the edges of the room. How refreshing not to see the castanets, paella pans and stuffed donkeys that are usually found adorning the walls of tapas restaurants. But then, as the name suggests, this restaurant casts its net far and wide in what it defines as tapas.

Owners Daniel Lindsay and Ashley Walter opened Iberico just over three years ago, and being well-travelled chaps, decided to pick key flavours from around the globe that work in small, shareable portions. It's a menu that makes interesting reading. 'The standard of food here means people almost treat it like a tasting menu,' says Ashley. The food is cooked and portioned quickly, and a couple of dishes highlight this speedy approach.

The first is mackerel with pickled fennel, blood-orange sauce and rock chives. The fennel bulbs are finely sliced and pickled in rice-wine vinegar and sugar. The plate is drizzled with the reduced blood-orange sauce and the fennel placed on top. The mackerel, meanwhile, has been grilling under a blisteringly hot salamander, and finally the rock chives are artistically added: simple and tasty.

Or take their approach to belly pork: portioned well in advance, it's

Belly pork with a salad of soya and haricot beans

vacuum-packed and cooked in a water bath gently for sixty hours. When it's needed, it is flash-fried skin side down in a hot pan and finished in the oven. This means that the flesh is very moist and tender, but the skin gets incredibly crispy. It's served with a simple bean salad made from soya beans, haricot beans and tomato concassé (small pieces of skinned, diced tomato), all dressed with parsley and oil. Again, it's all about a few flavours that work well together.

Around the corner from Iberico is its antithesis, a tapas chain restaurant so replete with generic Spanish paraphernalia and a menu straight out of central casting it's like eating in a theme park. So my advice is to dodge past it, nip down the High Pavement and spend an evening with Iberico's multinational team and menu.

OLNEY, BUCKINGHAMSHIRE

## Pancakes

Like haggis, I eat pancakes once a year, and every time I do I think, 'That was delicious, I must eat these more often.' Once, as a child, I ate nine in one sitting, each with a crust of Tate and Lyle's white sugar slowly dissolving in lemon juice, which naturally came from the squeezy plastic lemon. The Jif lemon: what a brilliant example of packaging design. At the time of writing, Sainsbury's sell a 55 ml 'lemon' Jif for 59p and individual lemons for 30p; with a good bit of pummelling an average lemon might yield about 30 ml of fresh juice.

But lemons haven't always been so cheap and readily available. Native to India, and brought west by the Arabs, they weren't widely cultivated by classical civilisations and remained a rarity in Britain until quite recently. The Revd Sidney Smith said of a posting to a parish in deepest Yorkshire in 1809 that he was '12 miles from the nearest lemon'.

But back to pancakes. They are one of the earliest forms of food, needing only some pounded grain, a little water, and a hot stone for cooking on. Versions appear all over the world and through all ages, from Russian blinis and Scottish drop scones to Indian poori and French crêpes. As Ken Albala says in his book *Pancake: A Global History* (2008), 'the pancake would find expression in countless forms.' But in the UK, pancakes will for ever be associated with Shrove Tuesday, when you would use up all the good things in the house like fat and eggs, before embarking on forty days of, if not actual fasting, then at least cutting back a bit for Lent.

The village of Olney in Buckinghamshire has held an annual pancake race on and off since 1445. After various lapses, the latest being during the Second World War, it was revived by the vicar in 1948. The track is 379 metres long, and stretches from the marketplace to the local parish church. The competitors must be women over the age of eighteen who have lived in the town for a minimum of three months. Upon crossing the finish line, the winner has to flip her pancake before receiving the kiss of peace from the vicar and the adulation of the parishioners as they enter the church for the great shriving service. Whether you're racing or not, a key part of the spectacle of pancake-making is the toss. Here you get to demonstrate your sporting prowess, and experience the agony if your pancake hits either the ceiling or the floor, or the ecstasy if you land the perfect flip.

The key strengths of pancakes are that they're quick to prepare, need minimal ingredients and, like toast, can take both sweet and savoury flavours with aplomb. You would have thought that these attributes would have made them the perfect fast food, and indeed on the Continent they are, but in the UK they have to compete in a very crowded field. That's not to say people haven't tried, however. There's a chain called the Pancake Place in Scotland, in London the Dutch Pancake House in Holborn has traded since 1958, and newcomer Crêpeaffair began in Hammersmith in 2004 selling not only the classic lemon and sugar versions, but also savoury ones such as 'The Londoner', featuring scrambled egg, bacon and cheese.

These days, pancakes may seem a bit austere rather than being the gluttonous blow-out of old. Indeed, compared to most of the other food we eat, they're probably quite healthy, as well as being a lot of fun. I really should eat them more often.

*See also* STOKE-ON-TRENT, STAFFORDSHIRE (p. 310).

OWMBY-BY-SPITAL, LINCOLNSHIRE
## *Shallots*

At the height of the credit crunch, a chef I know told me he'd been asked by his boss to cut the kitchen's costs. Looking through the invoices, the boss has asked, 'What about these shallots, can't you just use onions?' much to my culinary friend's dismay. The restaurant survived, but the story highlights the fact that to the man on the Clapham omnibus, shallots are fancy onions that not only cost more, but are a bugger to peel. However, if you want your cooking to taste professional, they're the allium to reach for, a sentiment echoed by chef-at-large Anthony Bourdain in his best-seller *Kitchen Confidential* (2000).

They are best used lightly when you want a sweeter, milder, oniony flavour, as they have twice the sugar levels of their onion cousins. That's not to say they can't take a bit of punishment, however, because they've also got half the water found in your average onion, so hold together structurally during long, slow cooking. All of which explains why they're popular in fine-dining restaurants, if seldom seen in your mum's shepherd's pie.

Aside from western restaurants, many South-East Asian cuisines make use of shallots, particularly Thai food, as this is where shallots originated. The name 'shallot' is ultimately derived from the ancient town of Ashkelon, now in Israel, which was where the ancient Greeks thought shallots came from, when in fact they had journeyed there from much further east.

As with onions and garlic, China leads the world in shallot production; however there are a number of UK producers, such as the aptly named Chris Kitchen of Kitchen Garden Produce, who has been growing shallots in Lincolnshire since 1985. He now has 220 acres of the crop, nearly all of which he supplies to supermarkets, and the business is growing. Kitchen Garden grow a variety called Springfield from offsets, or 'sets', which are clones of a mother plant grown by a specialist breeder in Holland. In the second week of March, Chris's fields are de-stoned and levelled so that the sets can be planted; harvest then happens about fourteen weeks later, from July through to September. The shallots are subsequently stored to ensure a regular supply through the winter. Chris admits they're tricky to grow, susceptible to weed competition and other complicating factors, and so the yield is less than a similar plot of onions, but the flavour more than makes up for it. 'In France they eat ten times the amount we do, but our market is growing. You can't pick up a quality cookery book these days that doesn't call for shallots,' says Chris.

See also EAST ANGLIAN PARSNIPS (p. 444); PEA HARVEST (p. 332).

## OXFORD, OXFORDSHIRE
### Frank Cooper's marmalade

Marmalade has been around since the Romans first noted the Greeks cooking quinces with honey and letting them set firm. Indeed, the quince (*see* p. 361) is still called a *marmelo* in Portugal. In English, marmalade came to mean any preserve or jam made with anything from lemons to onions. In the UK we tend to favour bitter Seville oranges, as they have a high level of pectin, which causes jams and marmalades to set.

It was these oranges that Sara Jane Cooper used in 1874 when, according to legend, she made 76 lb of the stuff, although she was by no means the first. No doubt she got the oranges from her husband Frank's grocery shop downstairs (no wife would make 76 lb of marmalade on a whim unless the marriage was in serious trouble). Maybe Frank had got the oranges cheap, or they were on the turn? In any case, what the family couldn't eat, Frank sold in his shop. You'll notice the similarity between this tale and the one for Dundee marmalade nearly 100 years earlier (*see* p. 163).

Production increased in 1908 with the opening of the Frank Cooper factory near the railway station on Park End Street. The brand became a favourite of embassies and consular offices around the world, as well as with the dons and undergraduates of the colleges in the town. Whenever learned men, diplomats and civil-servant mandarins took breakfast, Frank Cooper's was no doubt on the table, and it still has the royal warrant to this day. A jar of Frank Cooper's marmalade even went to Antarctica with Scott's ill-fated expedition to the South Pole: 'Stiff upper lip, chaps, it's Cooper's on oats this morning!' For the rest of us, marmalade is the taste of sunshine and a great way to start the day.

*See also* DUNDEE, ANGUS (p. 163); GREAT DUNHAM, NORFOLK (p. 431); WATLINGTON, OXFORDSHIRE (p. 361).

OXFORD, OXFORDSHIRE
# Oxford cheese and sauce

Oxford Blue and Oxford Isis cheeses sound as old and venerable as Cheddar and Stilton. In fact you've probably got furniture older than both of them. Oxford Blue came into being in the mid 1990s and Isis followed in 2003.

Oxford Blue is a creamy soft cheese with a delicate mould within it, while Isis is a soft but pungent cheese washed in honey mead. Both, along with a handful of other food-related ventures, are the brainchild of Baron Robert Pouget. They are available in his shop in Oxford's covered market, alongside a large range of other farmhouse cheeses, the majority of which are un-pasteurised and sourced direct from the producer.

Robert is the sort of person one would describe as a character. His first enterprise was called Veggie Heaven in London, a runaway success that sadly went bust and left him broke. Licking his wounds, he came back to Oxford and, at the age of forty, started producing cheeses.

Never one to keep still, Robert also produces Oxford sauce, which is similar to the Cumberland variety. Escoffier's version calls for redcurrant jelly to be dissolved with port and flavoured with shallots, zest of orange and mustard. It's traditionally paired with game and cold meats; the pheasant goujons offered in the Dean Street Townhouse in London would be a ery fine accompaniment, for example. Robert does use his in this way, but he's also not averse to more esoteric uses, such as adding a slug to a Bloody Mary.

*See also* BRITISH CHEESE (p. 290); BISHOP'S STORTFORD, HERTFORDSHIRE (p. 321); EASTON GREY, WILTSHIRE (p. 11); EDINBURGH, EDINBURGH (p. 167); FAVERSHAM, KENT (p. 477); MOFFAT, DUMFRIES & GALLOWAY (p. 183); NORWICH, NORFOLK (p. 451); ROSSENDALE, LANCASHIRE (p. 131) ST HELENS, MERSEYSIDE (p. 132); SHEFFIELD, SOUTH YORKSHIRE (p. 258); SPENNYMOOR, COUNTY DURHAM (p. 227); WORCESTER, WORCESTERSHIRE (p. 317).

## Oxford sausage

A true Oxford sausage is as an effete and foppish a banger as you are ever likely to meet. It's traditionally made with a combination of pork and veal (added for extra luxury, one supposes), and is flavoured with delicate herbs such as thyme, marjoram and savory, as well as lemon rind and a grating of nutmeg. It's also skinless, so needs to be formed into sausage shapes by hand. Hannah Glasse's recipe from 1784 is no doubt the one Mrs Beeton 'borrowed', when she stated, '. . . either put the meat into skins, or, when wanted for table, form it into little cakes, which should be floured and fried'. What you're left with is a chinless wonder of a banger, particularly if you compare it to, say, a wild spicy Cumberland from the north. However, if it tastes great then all is, of course, forgiven.

It's tricky to find a correctly made example under the dreaming spires these days, and heading to the covered market is your best bet as you will find butcher David John there. David's Oxford sausages come with a skin and they don't contain any veal, due, in part, to customer misconceptions about the meat, which is a shame. Still, they've got the correct seasoning and a little citrus note from the lemon. David supplies the Big Bang restaurant in Oxford, Max Mason's temple to top-quality local bangers. Besides the Oxford and other meaty favourites, David also makes vegetarian sausages in a myriad of different flavours. These are skinless, obviously, and probably closer in appearance to a traditional Oxford sausage than the ones he sells. By way of a contrast, he also sells an enormous ring of boerewors sausage that must be twelve inches in diameter. 'Very popular with South African students, that,' says David.

One wonders if a sausage 'boat race' could be staged between the Oxford 'dark blues' sausage and the Cambridge 'light blues' sausage?

*See also* SAUSAGES (p. 122).

## The Old Fashioned Pudding Company

Some years ago (to ask for specifics would reveal a lady's age), Nanna Allen taught her granddaughter Myrtle how to make a Christmas pudding to the

These brown paper packages tied up with string are definitely one of my favourite things

family recipe she had been using all her life. From this grew Myrtle's joy in making not only Christmas puddings, but also all the classic puddings we grew up with: ginger sponge, spotted dick, jam sponge and chocolate sponge. Each of Myrtle's puddings is wrapped in brown paper and tied with string, to which is fastened a large label telling you how to look after it, almost like a little wartime evacuee. You can either simmer it on the hob for thirty minutes, or embrace the white heat of technology and microwave it for three. After that, flip it over on to a plate, watch the jam, syrup or chocolate run down the sides and get ready to enjoy.

The whole enterprise started in 1997. Before then, Nanna Allen made Christmas puddings for all the family, but after the death of her husband she lost heart, and Myrtle asked Nanna to teach her the recipe. After making a few, Myrtle found that she really enjoyed it. Friends and colleagues said they would buy them from her, and things took off from there. But no one wants to buy Christmas pudding all year round, so she diversified into different sorts of sweet sponges and savoury suet meat puddings such as bacon and onion, steak and kidney, and chicken and mushroom. In 2005 she went full-time.

# The United Kingdom of Fry-ups

Were Hogarth alive today, his fat friar at the gates of Calais would no doubt be tucking into a full English while the malnourished French soldiers, rather than carrying a cauldron of *soupe maigre*, would instead be nibbling on a 'Continental' breakfast. Typically, a full English breakfast or fry-up includes some key players, occasionally augmented by a few substitutes. The rock-solid flat back four would be sausage, bacon, eggs (fried) and toast. My own team selection would also include black pudding and mushrooms. Bubble and squeak is welcome, although it can take up too much room. Fried bread is a yearly indulgence, and only if there's good bacon fat to fry it in. I can take or leave tomatoes, I'm not fussed about sugary baked beans, and I regard hash browns as a complete abomination. Finally, the sauce must be brown, although tomato ketchup is permissible for children and the infirm. But that's my version; I'm sure you have your own. Apart from anything else, there are all sorts of regional differences within our devolved Union. A 'full Welsh', for example, contains laver bread and cockles, while the 'full Scottish' includes fried haggis. The 'Ulster fry' of Northern Ireland contains a farl, a potato cake and maybe a Scotch pancake, as well as toast, and sometimes fried bread too.

The fry-up is often the 'main course' of a breakfast, bookended by cereal or porridge first, and fruit or more toast afterwards. The large cooked breakfast is a nineteenth-century invention, and came about when the timings of the other meals shifted around. Dinner, the main meal of the day, was taken at 11 a.m. in the sixteenth century, but had moved to something like 5 p.m. or 6 p.m. by the eighteenth, creating the need not only for a hearty breakfast but also the stopgap of lunch.

In the eighteenth century, then, breakfast began to be taken at

10 a.m., and by 1815 it was still 10 a.m. for those of a leisurely disposition, but 9 a.m. or even 8 a.m. for workers. In 1835, nearly everyone was having breakfast before 9 a.m., and by 1900 it had moved to 8 a.m. for most people.

Of course, the time, size and what constituted your breakfast was dependent on your place in society. The richer you were, the bigger and later you took your breakfast, while many of the poorer went without it entirely. By the late Victorian and Edwardian era, a large cooked breakfast was the hallmark of the upper classes, and although lunch and dinner was served by servants, breakfast was always laid out on a sideboard for the family to help themselves. The latter was, of course, the formal sit-down breakfast taken in the dining room; often the household had already had a provisional breakfast of a hot drink and something bread-based brought to their room by their valets or maids at 8 a.m.

If there was one man who had it in for the large meaty fried breakfast, it was Seventh-Day Adventist and clean-living vegetarian John Harvey Kellogg. His eponymous breakfast cereals fitted the changing times. Of course, nowadays we all know we should be eating slow-release complex carbohydrates like bran and porridge upon waking, preferably after a five-mile run at dawn. You don't need me, the government or anyone else to tell you that eating a fry-up five times a week isn't wise. However, cometh the weekend, cometh the cooked breakfast, even if we're eating it later, and going so far as to call it brunch. To truly appreciate a cooked breakfast requires time, perhaps the weekend papers, and preferably someone else cooking it all for you.

*See also* SAUSAGES (p. 122); TOAST (p. 404); DUNDEE, ANGUS (p. 163); OXFORD, OXFORDSHIRE (p. 350).

Myrtle is the first to admit that there's no secret to her puds: they're made the same way as your grandparents might have made them. Alas, we live in busier times nowadays, and even our grandparents are off bungee jumping or training at the gym, so few of us have the time to make a steamed pudding from scratch. Myrtle's puds are the next best thing.

*See also* CLOOTIE DUMPLING (p. 156); BAKEWELL, DERBYSHIRE (p. 277); MICKLETON, GLOUCESTERSHIRE (p. 304); PENRITH, CUMBRIA (p. 127).

## QUORN, LEICESTERSHIRE
# Quorn — the future food

As a boy I loved the books that described the near future: they made change seem like it was just around the corner. With the help of easy-to-understand sentences and colour pencil drawings of the Syd Mead variety, I could look forward to flying to Australia in an hour, visiting space bases on the moon and making it back in time for a dinner made of strange new foods.

Only the last of these has really come true. The huge oceanic kelp farms from the chapter on futuristic food may never have appeared, but at least the small photograph of a breadcrumbed 'chicken' nugget lived up to expectations. The caption reads, 'This deep-fried breaded chicken is in fact made from mycoprotein, a fibrous substance produced from microfungi.' For the public, it was christened Quorn after a Leicestershire village.

Thus the meat substitute and staple of many a vegetarian's diet was born in the white heat of Macmillan's 1960s, when science was going to feed the world. The population at that time was 3 billion and rising (by 1999 it had doubled). There was a distinct fear of a shortage of protein. Something had to be done, so cometh the hour, cometh the man with a plan. As chairman of the Rank Hovis McDougall group, J. Arthur Rank (also of Rank Films fame) had a lot of leftover starch products, and asked if they could be converted into a protein-rich food that would be safe, nutritional and tasty. Turns out after many years work they couldn't, but the clever chaps that worked on the project had found a fungus that might just do the job. It would give the correct texture (well-cooked porcini, for example, have an almost meaty quality), and so in 1967 some 3,000 soil samples were taken from all over the world. Ironically, the best candidate – *Fusarium venenatum* – was found in a Buckinghamshire field about four miles from the research lab.

By now it was the mid 1970s, and in 1985, having passed a ten-year safety trial, the first Quorn product – a savoury pie – hit the shelves, followed in 1990 by Quorn pieces. Unfortunately, it was unsuitable for vegans, as a small amount of egg white is used in production, and it wasn't until 2005 that free-range egg white was used, at which point the product was finally approved by the Vegetarian Society.

The evidence of the past thirty years has shown that Quorn (now owned by Premiere Foods) didn't manage to solve the issues of starvation and famine, but it has become the favourite veggie meat substitute, with 500,000 Quorn meals eaten in the UK every day (according to Quorn's website).

As for the taste, well, even the most ardent fan would admit it's rather bland. It improves only by having other flavours foisted upon it. It is a simulacrum of meat, lacking the flavour and most importantly the fat. Which is of course its appeal to some people, who use the minced version in dishes that call for ground beef. Furthermore, it seems to be more of an in-home solution, as you hardly ever see it on restaurant menus. Even the Quorn Exchange, a restaurant in the town itself, has roasted butternut squash lasagne as its current veggie option.

## RUTLAND WATER, RUTLAND
### Tap water

The delivery of clean drinking water in the UK is remarkable, but it is so commonplace that we take it completely and utterly for granted. Years ago, when expensive mineral water was all the rage, asking for tap water in restaurants would make you look tight-fisted. Nowadays your digits may still be clenched, but you can justify your cry of 'Tap please!' with your eco-concerns. Ordering a bottle of air-freighted mineral water that tastes as near as damn it to the water we've got here is as big a faux pas as ordering a panda steak well done. There may be those who enjoy the waters of the world as they do wines, focusing on the *terroir*, the softness and the taste in the mouth, but the rest of us mostly just drink it when we're thirsty.

Someone once said (I can't remember who, so in these situations tend to plump for Oscar Wilde) that you should judge a city by the quality of its newspapers and its drinking water. And as anyone who has ever been on holiday in the UK will know, tap water tastes very different depending on where you are. In Manchester, for example, it's very soft and light; in London it's sharp and flat. In a taste test organised in 2008, Severn water was judged the winner, with Anglian water coming second and being described by chef and restaurateur Thomasina Miers as 'delicious, clear and wonderful'.

Anglian water has to supply one of the driest and most demanding areas of the UK. So great was that demand that in 1975 construction was completed on a giant reservoir at the Gwash Valley, which became known as Rutland Water. The villages of Middle and Nether Hambleton were completely submerged, leaving only Upper Hambleton situated on a man-made peninsula as the waters slowly rose. Today the reservoir serves 270 million litres per day to around 500,000 people in five counties across the east of England.

## SANDY, BEDFORDSHIRE
## *Bedfordshire clanger*

The clanger of Bedfordshire has been through some changes over the years. Originally it was a boiled cylindrical suet pudding with a meat filling, and fruit such as raisins studded in the pastry. This evolved over time, and the fruit became a separate filling at one end of the roll. Recipes for the first version appear as recently as 1951, in Nell Heaton's *Traditional Recipes of the British Isles*.

The clanger is often defined in the context of a labourer's lunch, as something filling to take into the fields, being (like the Cornish pasty) a main course and pudding within one meal; this, however, rather romanticises the lifestyle of rural workers in the past. John Burnett in *England Eats Out* (2004) gives a more factual account of their diet and that of the rural poor in the nineteenth century. It consisted of nothing but bread, potatoes, perhaps an onion or piece of cheese, and a few scraps of bacon. Few cottages would have had an oven, and so boiling was the commonest cooking method. One imagines agricultural workers were just grateful for anything filling when out on the land, and weren't too fussed about courses. Furthermore, they not only took 'nuncheon' (a light afternoon snack) in the fields, but also breakfast, elevenses and their afternoon meal. All this food was washed down with beer (up to five pints throughout the day) or tea.

With the demise of mass land labour after the Second World War, the clanger looked set to be confined to history. Then, fifteen years ago, David Gunn of Gunns Bakery in Sandy was invited to set up a stall at the Bedfordshire Festival, and he decided to bring back the clanger for the occasion. Rather than boiling it, David developed a baked version, but still used the suet pastry casing. The filling for the savoury end is made from potatoes, onion and gammon, which he gets from the local butcher, while the pudding end contains stewed apples. So that you can tell which end to start with, two holes are used to indicate the meat end, while three slashes denote the pudding end. And to make sure the flavours don't mix – even though a little of the apple with pork is no bad thing – there's a small pastry wall in the middle of the clanger. Gunns also make a vegetarian version.

To the south, in Hertfordshire, chef Paul Bloxham occasionally has Bedfordshire clanger on the bar-food menu in his two pubs, the Tilbury at Datchworth and the Blue Anchor in St Albans. 'We've lots of great produce around here, but not many well-known dishes, apart from the clanger,' he says. As well as bacon and beef versions, Paul has produced one made with duck, a meat that works really well with fruit, especially plums, although he claims, 'It's the pastry that's the best bit: an old-fashioned water-suet pastry.'

Why the Bedfordshire clanger hasn't gone on to national domination, available in every railway station like the Cornish pasty, I don't know. Maybe its time will come?

*See also* CORNISH PASTIES (p. 18).

SOUTHWELL, NOTTINGHAMSHIRE
## *Bramley apples*

The story of the Bramley apple could have been penned by A. A. Milne or Roald Dahl. It begins in the garden of a small cottage in Southwell, Nottinghamshire, around the year 1809. The cottage was home to Mr and Mrs Brailsford and their two daughters. The eldest, Mary Ann, was playing in the kitchen and decided to plant a few of the pips from some of the apples her mother was preparing. One of these duly grew into a sapling, which then became too big for the plant pot and had to be transferred to the garden. In 1812 Mr Brailsford died, followed by his wife in 1837, and a year later the girls sold the cottage to a local butcher called Matthew Bramley.

In 1856 the hero of the story, seventeen-year-old nurseryman and gardener Henry Merryweather, chanced upon the then vicar's gardener, who had a basket of the fruit. He found out where they were from, and took cuttings from Mary Ann's original tree so that he could commercialise the fruit. As the tree belonged to Mr Bramley, it is his name that Merryweather used. 'He was the first to realise its potential. If you look at old catalogues he's as good at PR as anyone today,' says Celia Stevens of Henry, her great-grandfather. Thanks to Henry's efforts, the Bramley was soon getting noticed, and winning awards. In 1888 it was the star of the show at the Chiswick Fruit Festival.

Bramleys are a uniquely British apple, available all year round and seldom grown anywhere else, although there is a Bramley fan club in Japan; 'I had a lovely Valentine's card from them,' laughs Celia. They are used in many recipes, from classic crumbles, pies and puddings to chutneys and preserves. They're added to cider and juices, and puréed they're the traditional complement to pork.

As for Mary Ann's original tree, it's still there and producing fruit in the small back garden of what is now called Bramley Cottage. The tree is in good shape, considering its age, but a recent attack of honey fungus has taken its toll. In 2002 it was selected by the Tree Council as one of fifty trees to honour the Queen's Golden Jubilee, and to further protect it, Professor Ted Cocking and his team from the University of Nottingham got rid of the honey fungus and took clones. Now twelve direct copies of the original Bramley stand in the Millennium Garden of University Park in Nottingham. As Celia says, 'The Bramley does a good job of flying the flag for Britain, and long may it reign.'

*See also* AMPLEFORTH, NORTH YORKSHIRE (p. 234); FAVERSHAM, KENT (p. 475); HOLT HEATH, WORCESTERSHIRE (p. 298).

## STANBRIDGE, BEDFORDSHIRE
### *Philippa Michie's tea bread*

Philippa Michie makes tea bread on a farm just outside Leighton Buzzard. The Michies were dairy farmers, but the difficulties in that market meant they had to diversify. They converted one barn to holiday cottages, switched to beef cattle production, and almost as a sideline, Philippa started making cakes. Initially Willow's Farm shop in London Colney near St Albans stocked them, but since then Philippa's market has grown and they are now in a handful of delis and shops from Highgate to Hertford.

Philippa's tea bread is as heavy as a house brick and bejewelled with onyx currants and amber raisins, with sticky juices on the inside of the wrapper. Tea bread, as the name suggests, combines a cup of our beloved, highly stewed national brew with the cake mix, so what's not to like? It was just one of the many cakes developed as part of afternoon-tea proceedings. In Wales it is called bara brith (meaning 'speckled bread') and forms part of the food served at a wake as well as for tea. There are two distinct types, one made with yeast and more cake-like, and the other more akin to a loaf. Various recipes abound for either version featuring all sorts of ingredients, but I think Philippa's is one of the best I've had. She simply soaks fruit in hot tea and sugar for a few hours, mixes that with flour and eggs and it all does a spell in the oven. The result is dark and rich like a Christmas cake, yet still moist and chewy; perfect lightly buttered with a cup of tea.

*See also* ALBERT EMBANKMENT, LAMBETH (p. 368); ALDERLEY EDGE, CHESHIRE (p. 96); BISHOP AUCKLAND, COUNTY DURHAM (p. 201); ECCLES, GREATER MANCHESTER (p. 103); HOOK NORTON, OXFORDSHIRE (p. 328); LLANDEILO, CARMARTHENSHIRE (p. 74); MANCHESTER, GREATER MANCHESTER (p. 119); MELTON MOWBRAY, LEICESTERSHIRE (p. 341); NAVENBY, LINCOLNSHIRE (p. 344); OTLEY, WEST YORKSHIRE (p. 252); WHITBY, NORTH YORKSHIRE (p. 269).

WATLINGTON, OXFORDSHIRE
## *Quince Products Ltd*

The story of the quince is peppered with occasions when it is eclipsed by more precocious and brasher family members. You can't eat quince raw (unless you're Jaws from the James Bond films): picked straight from the tree they have the firmness and no doubt the taste of a cricket ball. Unlike their more amenable apple and pear cousins, they are not readily bent to man's dietary needs, and just to annoy us even more they are poisonous to horses.

They remain a noble fruit, however. Show them a bit of heat, introduce some sugar, and the quince's hard, bitter nature mellows considerably. What was once cold, astringent, pink flesh becomes a warm, deep, wine-like red.

It's a process Elspeth Wainwright of Quince Products Ltd knows well. She's been making quince jellies and chutneys since 2003. Her background in food research no doubt helped, but initially the enterprise began as a hobby in an annex of her house in Oxfordshire. 'I shut myself away for six months perfecting recipes,' she says. She now supplies a number of shops nationwide as well as selling the products at the local farmers' market, where retired husband Colin goes by the name of Quince Charming.

Despite successes with her quince jelly in the Accompaniments category at the British Cheese Awards, a growing order book and contracts with top chefs, the process is still very much small scale and the final result a mere handful of jars from each batch. There are a few commercial quince growers in the UK, with many on Elspeth's doorstep, but in 2008 a late frost saw off a lot of the crop and made sourcing the raw ingredient tricky. 'We often get calls from people who've got trees in their garden asking do we want any.' In tough years she has to take all the quinces she can get.

The production process is simplicity itself: the quince are washed, chopped and cooked slowly for up to two hours before being strained through a muslin. The resulting liquid is mixed with sugar and lemon juice – no gelatin, just the natural pectin – and cooked down again before being left to set into the vermillion-coloured jelly.

The pulp, called mash, is reduced with more sugar and goes to make quince 'cheeses' and chutneys. These are best paired with richer meats, especially game. The jellies, too, work with meats and cheeses but also things like ice cream and rice pudding. It's even used in an aioli salad dressing.

Looking to the future, Elspeth has plans to branch out into medlars, a fruit even less well known than the quince. Again, medlars are as hard as bullets when picked, although these need to be 'bletted' – left to go rotten – before they can be eaten. 'The flavour is very distinctive; there's almost a smokiness to it,' she says.

The Spanish and Portuguese version of quince jelly, called *membrillo* (and from which we derive the word 'marmalade'), is traditionally paired with Manchego cheese and has a lighter flavour than the British version. But now that even your average gastropub can put together a decent British cheese-board, is it time we said *'gracias por todo'* to it and used our own?

*See also* DUNDEE, ANGUS (p. 163); GREAT DUNHAM, NORFOLK (p. 431); OXFORD, OXFORDSHIRE (p. 350).

## WELBECK, NOTTINGHAMSHIRE
### Welbeck Estate Farm Shop

Where to start with Welbeck? Not only is there a farm shop, you will also find an art gallery, a café, a garden centre, a cookery school, a bookshop, a cheese dairy and extensive grounds. It remains the family seat of the Duke of Portland. What is now the visitors' car park was once the walled garden. You can still make out the bricked-up holes in the walls every ten metres or so

Welbeck's freshly baked loaves for sale at the shop

that once housed braziers that hastened the ripening of fruit. There was even a peach wall, measuring over 300 metres in length. Stichelton cheese (*see* p. 338) is now produced in one of the estate's dairy buildings.

The farm shop comes under the watchful eye of director Michael Boyle. He's a softly spoken local chap with a background in farming and animal-feed production. He, along with the Parente family who own the estate, set up the farm shop in 2006. 'One hundred per cent of our lamb, eighty per cent of the beef and fifty per cent of our pork comes from farmers on the estate,' says Michael. In season, venison and game all come from the estate too.

Getting that meat butchered to customers' requirements is the job of Mark Brown. 'I can do anything a customer asks for: yesterday I boned out a chicken for someone, and at Christmas, for example, I do a lot of multi-bird roasts.' (The latter are becoming increasingly more popular, *see* p. 20.)

The final string to Welbeck's bow is the School of Artisan Food. This grew out of a bakery housed in the estate's disused fire station. As of 2010 it began offering diplomas and qualifications in artisan food production. The courses cover everything from bread-making to butchery, cheese-making to chocolate. All of the above makes Welbeck unique, in my opinion, and well worth a visit.

*See also* CANTERBURY, KENT (p. 469); COLSTON BASSETT, NOTTINGHAMSHIRE (p. 325); HOOK, HAMPSHIRE (p. 484); IPSWICH, SUFFOLK (p. 441); RUSHWICK, WORCESTERSHIRE (p. 309); STANNINGTON, NORTHUMBERLAND (p. 227).

# Haslet from R. J. Hurst

Haslet is one of those dishes that seems to be made – and even pronounced – differently every forty miles or so along the Great North Road. Although traditional in Lincolnshire and the East Midlands, similar dishes appear all over the UK, perhaps because it's made from pigs' organs, stale bread and seasoning: pretty much universal ingredients whenever a pig is killed.

You can make it with proper cuts of pork – indeed, some recipes call for a bit of pork fat to be added – but using the liver, heart and kidneys gives it that traditional, offally, visceral appearance as well as a distinct taste and texture. A well-made haslet is somewhere between a dry, coarse pâté and a sausage, and it works both as a hot main dish and cold in sandwiches. Once the heart, liver and lungs, known as the pluck, have been chopped and seasoned, the mix is wrapped in caul fat (the lacy membrane that surrounds the animals' organs) and seasoned with salt, pepper and Lincolnshire's favourite herb, sage.

Although I've heard it pronounced *hass-let* (to rhyme with *lass*) and *hace-let* (to rhyme with *race*), butcher Russell Hurst in Woodhall Spa opted for *haze-let*. Russell has been a butcher for over thirty years, and on his shop's back wall were all the wonderful trappings of a life in the trade: postcards from customers and friends, a meat calendar, newspaper clippings, framed awards – all the patina of a life's employment. Russell welcomes a steady stream of customers into his butcher's shop, and sells about eighty haslets a week, proving that at least in this part of the world they still love traditional food from a traditional high-street butcher.

*See also* BROMYARD, HEREFORDSHIRE (p. 283); CAMBRIDGE, CAMBRIDGESHIRE (p. 422); CONWY, CONWY (p. 60); LOUTH, LINCOLNSHIRE (p. 336); FORRES, MORAY (p. 173); MARYLEBONE, WESTMINSTER (p. 387); MELTON CONSTABLE, NORFOLK (p. 447); NANTWICH, CHESHIRE (p. 125); YORK, NORTH YORKSHIRE (p. 271).

# 9 | London

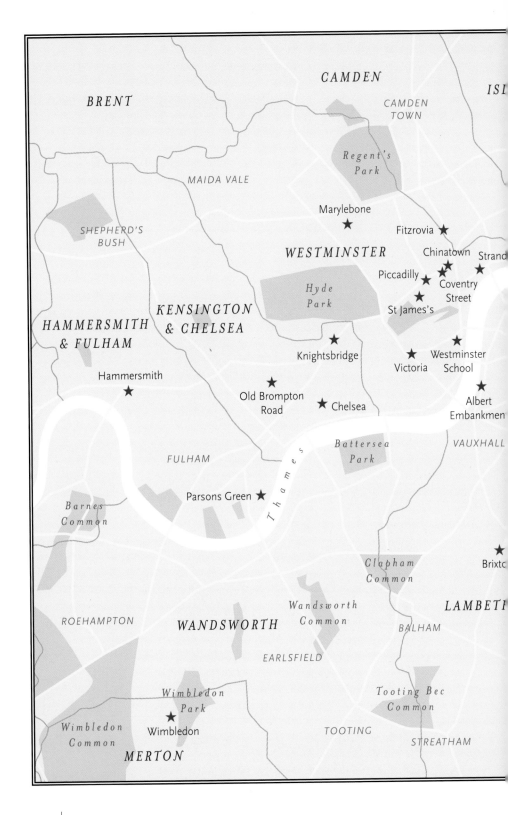

# Portuguese custard tarts from the Madeira Bakery

Stockwell, Vauxhall and the surrounding districts are the main Portuguese neighbourhoods in London, and it's within these areas that you will find one of Portugal's culinary gifts to the world, the *pastéis de nata*. One of the best places to get one is the Madeira, which has a cluster of outlets in the capital, the largest of which sits on the Albert Embankment at Vauxhall.

These small tarts, the case made from a pastry similar to puff or filo and the filling made with egg custard, were originally known as *pastéis de Belém*, after the suburb of Belém in Lisbon. This area was home to the Jerónimos Monastery, which first made the tarts. Following the revolution of 1820, all convents and monasteries were shut down and the clergy within them expelled. Down the Rue de Belém from the monastery was a small sugar refinery and shop and – so the story goes – one of the now homeless brethren offered the shop owner the recipe for the pastries. They're still made there today, as well as all over the world.

Madeira's tarts – nearly 15,000 a week – are all made by hand. 'It's an incredibly time-consuming process, but it's the proper way to do it,' says

The Madeira Bakery's handmade *pastéis de nata*

manager Antonio Luis. The firm supplies not only its own cafés, but many others in the UK, including the Nandos restaurant chain, Harrods and Selfridges. The pastry is made from scratch by sandwiching margarine between layers of dough and rolling, folding and rolling it once more. It's then curled up lengthways into a cylinder and cut into one-inch coils. These coils of pastry – resembling the rings of a tree – are then pressed into a small tart mould and shaped by hand. It is this rather convoluted process that gives *pastéis de nata* their distinctive crinkly edges. Meanwhile, the egg custard is made with liquid egg yolk, sugar, milk and flour, and slowly heated to a stiff consistency. It's then poured on to the pastry case and the tarts are baked in a hot oven (300°C) for twelve minutes.

Each *pastéis de nata* is unique: because the pastry is shaped by hand, no two will ever be the same; and the custard caramelises in dark brown spots in different ways. 'In Portugal they eat them much more caramelised, almost black,' says Antonio. But not all UK outlets want them done to this degree, so Madeira now offers a part-baked blast-frozen version, which allows the deli or restaurant to finish baking them just how they want them.

When you bite into a *pastéis de nata*, you get a delightful sensation of crunchy flakiness that gives way almost instantly to the soft sweet custard. In the café, a dusting of cinnamon is wafted over the top of each one prior to eating, followed by a dusting of icing sugar. The reason why I think these little cakes chime so well with the British palate is for the simple reason that they're made from custard and pastry, which are two things we love in spades.

*See also* ALDERLEY EDGE, CHESHIRE (p. 96); BISHOP AUCKLAND, COUNTY DURHAM (p. 201); ECCLES, GREATER MANCHESTER (p. 103); HOOK NORTON, OXFORDSHIRE (p. 328); LLANDEILO, CARMARTHENSHIRE (p. 74); MANCHESTER, GREATER MANCHESTER (p. 119); MELTON MOWBRAY, LEICESTERSHIRE (p. 341); NAVENBY, LINCOLNSHIRE (p. 344); OTLEY, WEST YORKSHIRE (p. 252); STANBRIDGE, BEDFORDSHIRE (p. 360); WHITBY, NORTH YORKSHIRE (p. 269).

BERMONDSEY, SOUTHWARK
## *Bourbon biscuits*

As a toddler I was often found eating the dog's biscuits; one for pooch, one for me. I forget the brand, but remember they were brown and rectangular. This may explain my love of the Bourbon biscuit. Looking like a baked domino, this solid rectangle of a biscuit has a simplicity that belies its true chocolatey charms.

The Bourbon, for those who don't know (and there can't be many, surely) is two slabs of baked biscuit sandwiched together with a chocolate filling.

It was created in 1910 by James Peek and George Hender Frean, who initially called it the Creola, later renaming it the Bourbon after the House of Bourbon, French royalty presumably adding a touch of class. Their company, Peek Frean, was formed in 1857 and soon moved to Bermondsey, South London, earning the area the nickname 'biscuit town'. In 1861 the dynamic duo, along with one John Carr, had given the world the garibaldi biscuit, named after the Italian general.

In 1921 they formed an alliance with Huntley & Palmers (still the makers of Bath water biscuits, *see* p. 5), to become Associated Biscuit Manufacturers Ltd. Never known to rest on its laurels, the company also gave the world Twiglets, which were created by a French employee, Monsieur Rondalin. He added a Marmite-style yeast extract to dough left over from the manufacture of the company's crispbread, Vitawheat. The resulting knobbly snacks were launched in time for Christmas 1929. At its peak the company employed over 3,000 people, had been granted the royal warrant by George VI and even created Queen Elizabeth II's wedding cake.

In 1960 W. R. Jacob, maker of Jacob's crackers, joined Associated Biscuit Manufacturers Ltd, and in 1982 the US company Nabisco bought the lot, closing the Bermondsey plant in May 1989, before selling everything to Danone in 1994. This attracted little of the hue and cry the sale of Cadbury's was to achieve some thirty years later.

The Bourbon is just one in a stable of true thoroughbred creations baked by James Peek and George Hender Frean. These two titans of the biscuit world are now largely forgotten, although their legacy still sits on every supermarket shelf in the land.

*See also* ABERLOUR, MORAY (p. 142).

## BRIXTON, LAMBETH
## *Pizza from Franco Manca*

When pizza joint Franco Manca opened in Brixton Market in 2008, it was quickly frequented by the habitués of SW2 searching for a quick bite to eat. *Time Out* gave it the award for 'Best Cheap Eats' of that year, and some even said it was the best pizza this side of Naples.

Cheap and popular is how pizza started out. Alexandre Dumas included

The classic Margherita: tomato sauce and mozzarella cheese

a lovely description of pizza and the Neapolitan beggars, or *lazzaroni*, who ate it in his *Sketches on Naples* from 1845: 'At first sight, the pizza appears to be a simple dish, upon examination it proves to be compound. The pizza is prepared with bacon, with lard, with cheese, with tomatoes, with fish. It is the gastronomic thermometer of the market.' Sounds great. However, until recently, the journalist Count Charles Arrivabene's description in his *Italy under Victor Emmanuel* (1862) would have been the commoner view: 'Pizza is a sort of dry cake made of flour, garlic and oil, a horrid composition of which nevertheless the Italians of the South are particularly fond.' Pizza, then, like burgers, fish and chips and noodle soup, started life as poor people's food.

How this simple dish of bread and a cheap topping managed to conquer the world is nothing short of remarkable. Graham Kerr, the 'galloping gourmet' TV chef popular in the 1960s, demonstrated how to make pizza once, from scratch, cooking it in a domestic oven. The show went out live, and after a short piece of film showing how they do it in Italy, with Kerr's ad lib narration, he went to get his own pizza out. After two minutes of hacking at the flan dish with a fish slice, he finally gave up, realising that it had completely stuck. He simply smiled and pulled a funny face. Pizza then was silly, cheap and funny foreign food: Italian cheese on toast.

Although not the first, one of the most interesting Italian pizza restaurants in London was launched by the film director Mario Zampi in the 1950s and was run by his brother and sister-in-law. Called Pizza Express, the restaurant was situated on Wardour Street and the pizzas were made properly in a wood-fired oven. Unfortunately, it didn't last. Zampi was perhaps ahead of his time: the public weren't ready for Neapolitan street food; to them, Italian cooking meant pasta and veal dishes. The restaurant was refitted and renamed 'The Romanella', but after Zampi's death it fell on hard times.

In 1965, Peter Boizot bought the business from Zampi's widow. He had picked up the taste for pizza while travelling and working in Italy in his youth. He brought over a new oven, which didn't fit through the door on arrival, and set about ripping out the plush trattoria interior Zampi had put in a few years before. The nascent *Time Out* magazine subsequently raved about the place. By the 1980s and early 1990s, Pizza Express was the fast-food restaurant of choice for the middle classes. If you were slightly further down the social ladder you might have opted for Pizza Hut (opened in Islington in 1973) or Pizza Land. At the latter in 1975, 49p got you two giant slices of pizza and a jacket potato. As John Dickie says in his history of Italian food *Delizia!*, 'It's a mystery to Italians that the British seem to want everything on one plate. Pizza and salad and garlic bread, and chips.'

I can remember as a malnourished student taking advantage of the Charing Cross Road branch of Pizza Hut's £3.50 all-you-can-eat lunch, the pizza base having all the taste and texture of a mattress. During this time all these firms were cooking their pizzas in tins. And Pizza Express's were the smallest, in my experience. In the twenty-first century new chains opened that eschewed tins and electric pizza ovens and instead used gas or wood-fired ones. Most importantly, the pizza dough came into direct contact with the blisteringly hot stone floor of the oven.

Franco Manca has continued the tradition of shipping in a proper pizza oven. Again it comes from Naples, and can reach 500°C. Owners Giuseppe Mascoli (originally from Naples) and Bridget Hugo (a Brixton-based artist) also brought in specialists to advise their Somerset cheese supplier on improving their mozzarella, and the sourdough used in the bases is said to be made from a batch that has been constantly fermenting for over 200 years. The pizzas have a thin base with a high crust, and the texture is soft and chewy, but not heavy in the mouth.

Buoyed on by their success, the team have opened a more formal offering in leafy Chiswick, but it's the Brixton branch that is the most authentic. The seating is split over the footpath through the market, and next door is Jeffries fishmonger's, which, along with the smell of joss sticks from shops further down, adds some interesting olfactory colour. The food, made quickly and cheaply yet with quality ingredients, and the setting, in a marketplace surrounded by hustle and bustle, are things that someone from Dumas's time would instantly recognise.

CHELSEA, KENSINGTON & CHELSEA
## Chelsea buns

Chelsea has always been known as the posh, well-to-do part of London, playing host to royalty, Russian oligarchs and Sloanes. Accordingly, the Chelsea Bun House was a place where, no doubt festooned in ermine rather than Prada, the nobility of yesteryear such as George II and III would have had their cake and eaten it.

The Bun House was founded sometime in the late seventeenth century by the Hand family, and we know that Gideon Richard Hand and his wife ran it initially, and that it was frequented by George II and George III. Gideon Richard's brother, named Richard Gideon, was an officer in the Staffordshire militia and was called Captain Bun by the troops. Interestingly, Gideon's skeleton, along with that of his brother, was recently exhumed from a Chelsea graveyard. Gideon's was put on display at the Wellcome Trust in London.

The Bun House's exact location isn't clear. Evidence points to the now-demolished Grosvenor Row, although some say it was on Jew's Road, now called Pimlico Road. What's more, it seems to have changed name, and in the 1790s became known as the Royal Bun House, as is revealed in an 1810 illustration of it, at the height of its fame. We also know that a building known as the Old Bun House was pulled down in 1839, yet the Scottish man of letters Thomas Carlyle, who lived at 5 Cheyne Walk, wrote to his mother on 29 March 1850 that: 'I went out for a walk this morning; all was grey, dim, and snell [harsh] as winter: but at the "Original Chelsea Bunhouse" there was a gathering; I stept near, it was poor souls crowding forward for their buns, and Baker and Wife serving them eagerly out of door and window'. Chelsea has altered greatly over the years, although you can still find Bunhouse Place parallel to Pimlico Road – a reminder of the area's culinary past.

The bun itself is made from dough enriched with egg. It's rolled out into a flat sheet, and butter, sugar and dried fruit are placed on top. It's then rolled up, cut, sliced and the resulting swirls are snugly fitted together in a baking tray. Upon leaving the oven they are glazed with golden syrup.

In 1817 the author and publisher Sir Richard Philips waxed lyrical about their 'delicate flavour, lightness, and richness', and more recently Jane Grigson declared them 'the best of all buns, on account of their melting, buttery sweetness' in her *English Food* (1974).

It's certainly their warm, sticky sweetness that wins me over. That and the fact you can eat them almost by uncoiling them, breaking off a piece at a time until you reach the soft chewy centre.

*See also* LARDY CAKE (p. 26); ALBERT EMBANKMENT, LAMBETH (p. 368); ALDERLEY EDGE, CHESHIRE (p. 96); BISHOP AUCKLAND, COUNTY DURHAM (p. 201); ECCLES, GREATER MANCHESTER (p. 103); HOOK NORTON, OXFORDSHIRE (p. 328); LLANDEILO, CARMARTHENSHIRE (p. 74); MANCHESTER, GREATER MANCHESTER (p. 119); MELTON MOWBRAY, LEICESTERSHIRE (p. 341); NAVENBY, LINCOLNSHIRE (p. 344); OTLEY, WEST YORKSHIRE (p. 252); STANBRIDGE, BEDFORDSHIRE (p. 360); WHITBY, NORTH YORKSHIRE (p. 269).

## CHINATOWN, WESTMINSTER
# Mitten crabs

Ever since the Roman invasion, and then the Columbian Exchange, new species of flora and fauna have been introduced to the UK. Garlic and saffron, buffalo and bison, carrots and capons, the list goes on. Some, such as the potato and tomato – in the form of chips and ketchup – have practically become national dishes.

Then there's the Chinese mitten crab, which came here not as an introduction, but by accident. It arrived in the ballast tanks of ships that pump water into their hulls for stabilisation at the beginning of their voyage, then release it at their destination, such as the docks of London. The presence of the mitten crab is by no means a new result of modern shipping practices, however: the first one was spotted in Chelsea in 1935. As far as non-native species go, this means it's been here longer than the blueberry (*see* p. 14).

What people haven't decided in the interceding seventy-odd years, is what to do about it. Mitten crabs have no natural predators here, so just letting nature take its course is simply not working. There are two obvious options:

cull them or eat them. Both come with complications: eradication is tricky and expensive; while eating them requires them to be certified as fit for human consumption by DEFRA. Preliminary tests and field studies carried out by the Natural History Museum seem to indicate that they are edible, but the next step is official approval, which could take years. If you would like to try one now, however, they're sometimes found in Chinatown, where they're imported under the name 'moon crabs'. Alternatively, you could try getting pally with a fisherman on the Medway, Blackwater or Thames and see if he can't find you one.

*See also* BUCKIE, MORAY (p. 149); CHINATOWN, WESTMINSTER (p. 374); CROMER, NORFOLK (p. 426); LITTLE HAVEN, PEMBROKESHIRE (p. 70); MORECAMBE BAY, LANCASHIRE (p. 121); SALTHOUSE, NORFOLK (p. 454).

COVENTRY STREET, WESTMINSTER
## *Wimpy, the first British Burger*

White Castle, the first hamburger joint, opened in 1921 in Wichita, Kansas. By 1940, Dick and Mac McDonald had opened the first branch of McDonald's, and within fifty years American fast food had flooded the world.

Many people don't realize that it was in 1954, around about the time Ray Kroc was expanding and franchising McDonald's in the USA, that Wimpy, the UK's own small contribution to the hamburger's worldwide domination, was founded. Meat had come off the ration, there were plenty of GIs about, rock 'n' roll was in full swing, and so, with an extremely hard sell, American Eddie Gold managed to persuade the venerable British institution that was Lyons to install a Wimpy in their Coventry Street Corner House in London. However, no doubt as a concession to either management or British sensibilities, Wimpy burgers were brought to your table on a plate. When Lyons offered Wimpy burgers at the 1954 Ideal Home Exhibition, it was selling an average of 10,000 a week. Alas, it lost ground to the bigger US chains, and although it does continue to trade it is a shadow of its former self.

Wimpy, McDonald's (first opened in Woolwich in 1974) and Burger King (opened in 1977, on the site of the first Wimpy) were a fresh, casual, youth-friendly alternative to stuffy old restaurants. But over time we got bored of eating in strip-lit neon-plastic fun parks. Consequently, in the twenty-first century, a new batch of restaurants started to look at the basic burger format of meat 'twixt bread and take the experience upmarket.

Gourmet Burger Kitchen, Hamburger Union, Ground and Ultimate Burger are the main runners in the upmarket burger boom, with Byron and Haché perhaps nosing out in front in the style stakes. Byron's meat is grass-fed Aberdeen Angus, Haché's is, as its name suggests, chopped steak.

In all these new-wave burger joints, wine and beer is available, your chair isn't screwed to the floor and, in a nod perhaps to Wimpy and Eddie Gold, your food arrives on a plate rather than in a paper wrapping, and your drink in a glass rather than a paper cup. Knife and forks, though, remain optional. Of course all of this is a far cry from what the burger originally was, namely a quick, cheap and hot bite to eat on the hoof (and possibly featuring bits of hoof too!). The post-war love of Americana may now be history, but burgers are still a popular choice.

FITZROVIA, CAMDEN
## Dim sum at Hakkasan

The habit of having a sit-down and a cup of tea is enjoyed in China just as much as it is in Britain, and is known as *yum cha* in Cantonese. Gradually, little dishes began to be served alongside the tea. These were parcels you could eat to your heart's content, hence the name *dim sum*, which translates as 'touch the heart'. And from those beginnings, what was once a respite from work or a long journey turned into a full-blown eating experience, often spent with friends and family talking about the week's events. Dim sum, then, is afternoon tea crossed with Sunday lunch.

The Chinese community have clearly been doing dim sum for themselves for decades, but until quite recently for most Londoners it remained a mystery. If you knew what to ask for, or had a Chinese friend in the know, you could find it in Chinatown. Chinese food expert and one time food blogger Helen Yuet Ling Pang singles out Golden Dragon on Gerrard Street as a place regularly frequented by Chinese families.

However, when Alan Yau opened Hakkasan in 2001, dim sum went weapons-grade in style, quality and price. The modern era of dim sum had arrived, and Yau's eatery quickly earned a Michelin star for its high-class blending of traditional Chinese elements with a Western dining experience. It soon became a place in which to be seen. Others, such as Ping Pong and Shanghai Blues, followed this freshly blazed trail, catering for a variety of price points, while Yau himself moved on to open Yauatcha, which he sold in 2008.

Scallop shumai at Hakkasan

Helen has noticed changes in the scene over the course of her lifetime. 'When I was a teen I didn't really go with my friends for dim sum, I went with family. Now everybody goes.' Helen highlights, however, the distinction between modern dim sum and the more traditional style: 'I like both approaches, though in a way prefer the modern one a bit more. I like the innovative approach and creativity.' Modern dim sum sees the use of some untraditional ingredients, so at Yauatcha there is Dover sole in black bean, or venison puff, while elsewhere on the menu veal makes an appearance.

Classics available at every venue include prawn dumplings (*har gau*), steamed, semi-translucent dumplings containing shrimp and often flavoured with ginger and bamboo shoots; *char siu bao*, a steamed bun containing meltingly soft barbecued pork meat; and *cheong fun*, rice noodle rolls containing a variety of fillings of both meat and vegetables. Other popular dishes include spare ribs, savoury egg custard and, if you really fancy a challenge, chicken's feet. I've eaten them, and can confirm that there is not much meat on chicken's feet.

At its heart, dim sum combines tasty little well-made dishes, tea and gossip. You can see why it was quickly added to the repertoire of eating experiences in London.

## The Meantime Brewery

It's perhaps fitting that a brewery based in the home of time itself should aim to recreate fantastic examples of some of the seminal beers from the past. Ever since 2000, Alastair Hook's Meantime Brewery has been doing just that, and of particular note is his London Porter and London Indian Pale Ale.

Porter and IPA are two seminal British beers; both were created in London, and both went on to change brewing styles all over the world. Porter was the first modern beer to make the transition between monastic-style, small-scale beer production to modern, often urban, industrial brewing. It was the beer of the eighteenth century.

When Meantime set out to make their Porter in 2005, they did their research, tapping the knowledge of the British Library as well as beer historians and enthusiasts. The Durden Park Beer Circle was consulted, a team of home-brew enthusiasts who have researched and made many old

Meantime Chocolate Ale complements robust flavours such as chicken teriyaki

British beers, particularly those from around 1840 to 1914, the period when, as their website states, a vast range of quality beers were brewed. The resulting products would hopefully be familiar to any market porter from Billingsgate, Smithfield or Covent Garden around 1750, as it is after these men and their fondness for a strong, robust, refreshing drink that Porter is named. Meantime's London Porter is made with seven different malts that imbue it with its rich, bittersweet, chocolatey flavour. As Alastair says, 'Beers are fundamentally solutions to problems. People were looking for something from that product at that time.'

If Porter fuelled the Industrial Revolution and development of commerce in the eighteenth century, IPA was arguably the great beer of the nineteenth century, and did the same for the Empire. It was the first pale beer, using pale malts, a long maturation and a large amount of hops to generate a high alcohol content. This was needed to survive the sea-bound journeys to the subcontinent that lends the beer its name. Today, we may associate IPA with Burton upon Trent, which for centuries was the centre of British brewing thanks to the quality of its waters and brewed much IPA; however, the drink's birthplace was in the capital.

In their day, London brewers were great at using technology to further their business, and so brewers in the capital were the first to adopt such innovations as the thermometer, the hydrometer and the steam engine, as well as advances in the malting and brewing process.

'We think that what we do is consistent with the tradition of brewing in London,' says Alastair. Meantime's ethos may be simple, but they believe they are serving a British consumer who is currently let down by the brewing industry. They don't see themselves as competing against the 600 or so microbreweries up and down the UK; they see their competitors as the likes of Peroni. 'We're in central London making bottled and kegged products for a very tough market,' says Alastair.

Meantime's beers, more than most, seem to work very well when accompanied with food. I remember trying their chocolate beer (which is a Porter with a few of its natural flavours, namely chocolate, enhanced by adding the real thing) paired with chicken teriyaki. In that combination you have something that in two mouthfuls loots tastes from the Far East and South America and comes together in Greenwich. As Alastair says, 'We believe that quality is a function of maturation. Time is an ingredient of good beer.'

*See also* ASTLEY, WARWICKSHIRE (p. 276); KNIGHTWICK, WORCESTERSHIRE (p. 299); NEWCASTLE, TYNE & WEAR (p. 220); SOUTHWOLD, SUFFOLK (p. 457).

## GREENWICH, GREENWICH
### Pie and mash with parsley liquor

Historically, the meal of choice for working-class Londoners was pie and mash with parsley liquor, all washed down with a cup of tea. The first pie and mash shops began to appear in the mid-nineteenth century in East and South-east London. 'No one knows where the first pie and mash shop was, but it was probably an entrepreneurial pie man, traditionally found selling pies in the street, who got enough money to open a shop,' says Mal Vango, who runs the website pie-and-mash.co.uk.

Today, the communities that pie and mash shops once served have become more disparate. Like genuine born-within-the-sound-of-Bow-bells cockneys themselves, pie and mash shops are getting few and far between, and there are now only around seventy-five to eighty shops in London and the south-east – small numbers when compared to the 7,000 or so curry restaurants that can be found within the M25. So are they an endangered species? 'If you'd have asked me a few years ago, I'd have said maybe, but not now,' says Mal. The credit crunch has, in part, helped, as pie and mash often costs under £4.

This iconic London meal is becoming increasingly hard to find

It's a view echoed by Sean Horton from Goddard's pie and mash shop in Greenwich, who has got plans to start supplying his pies wholesale into caffs, pubs and restaurants all over the south-east. Goddard's began in Deptford in 1890, and since the 1950s has had a shop in Greenwich. The pastry-cutting machinery at Goddard's is over sixty years old, and still going strong despite near daily use. The year 2010 saw the firm's 120th anniversary, and the move – for the making of the pies at least – to bigger premises in Sevenoaks, Kent.

Back in the shop, there are numerous flavours of pie on offer, including a vegetarian option. But no matter where you get your pie, the standard beef version should feature only minced beef – no carrots, onions or other additions. In much the same way that vanilla ice cream lets you judge the quality of the ice cream without distractions, so it is with the beef pie.

The mash is made with only the best quality potatoes and perhaps a touch of salt. No cream, butter or milk is added; this isn't *pommes purée*, after all. The final touch, and that which makes it truly a London dish, is parsley liquor. Traditionally, this is made with some of the water that the eels going into eel pies have been stewed in, to which seasoning and plenty of parsley are added. The resulting green-flecked sauce is to pie-and-mash-loving southerners what mushy peas are to northerners. In a nod to changing times, though, many places now offer gravy too.

There are various ways to eat pie and mash. Some prefer a knife and fork; others a fork and spoon. Some turn the pie upside down and start that way, but most just tuck in. 'You eat them the way you were brought up eating them,' says Mal, who favours a knife and eats his the right way up. 'There should be a lot of liquor. I'm a dabber, dipping each bit in the sauce.' In some places you won't see a knife at all, and various rumours abound to explain this, from wartime metal shortages to stopping fights breaking out (the latter, and probably the former, come to think of it, is almost certainly made up). Goddard's offers both knife and spoon. 'You know a die-hard pie-and-mash person when they pick up a spoon,' says Sean.

With the dissolution of the East End out to Essex and Kent, it would be all too easy for pie and mash shops to remain frozen by nostalgia, catering for a smaller and smaller clientele, serving the memory of a community rather than the one outside the shop door. The docks, the factories and the people who worked in them have moved on, and so, it seems, have pie and mash shops. Goddard's and others are aiming to reach new customers and develop new business opportunities, and I wish them the best of luck. In my view, their product, well made and natural, truly deserves its place in the pantheon of British food.

*See also* CARDIFF, CARDIFF (p. 59); CHINLEY, DERBYSHIRE (p. 285); DENBY DALE, WEST YORKSHIRE (p. 240); GLASGOW, GLASGOW (p. 178); MOUSEHOLE, CORNWALL (p. 31).

## HAMMERSMITH, HAMMERSMITH & FULHAM
### Sipsmith London dry gin

Gin appreciation really took off in England when Protestant William of Orange seized the throne from his uncle, James I, in 1688. Soon all things papist, including French brandy, were heavily frowned upon and heavily taxed, while importing and drinking gin from Holland was positively encouraged, and the country went mad for it. By 1751 it had become the vice of the poor, the most famous commentary on which is Hogarth's print *Gin Lane*, a damning indictment of its effects. Plymouth had a long association with gin but if there was ever one city of poor souls who took gin to heart, it was London. When the powers that be eventually decided enough was enough and tried to instigate a form of prohibition in 1736, riots and uproar resulted. When things had calmed down, London dry gin emerged as a specific style. However, today very little is actually produced in the city itself, and no new stills – the apparatus used to distil the drink – had been built since the 1820s.

That is until 2004, when, after years working in the drinks industry, Sam Galsworthy and Fairfax Hall started their own distillery, Sipsmith, in London using a handmade still called 'Prudence'. Into her goes the base spirit, which is gently heated to 78°C so that the alcohol boils and the resulting vapour is captured and condensed back into a liquid, now with a strength of 85 per cent proof. When cooled, this is poured back into Prudence along with the botanicals that give gin its flavour: juniper berries, coriander seed, angelica root, liquorice root, orris root, ground almond, cassia bark, cinnamon and citrus peel. The process is then repeated, and the new liquid cooled and blended with spring water from the source of the Thames in Gloucestershire.

Before Sam and Fairfax could begin, they had to go through the process of getting a licence to distil. This took a tortuous eighteen months, as no one at HM Revenue & Customs knew exactly how to issue a new one. Finally their licence, handwritten on a small piece of paper, arrived, and now hangs framed on the wall. 'We were expecting a scroll with a wax seal,' laughs Sam.

The Sipsmith boys with Prudence

# London's Markets

In 2007 the Mayor's office published a review into all of London's wholesale markets. Their conclusions have yet to be acted on, but the general theme seems to be 'sell up and move out', with the report stating, 'London's five wholesale markets have experienced changes to their historic roles, with increasing competition from supermarkets and more efficient distribution systems. This has, however, partly been offset by the increase of eating out, creating demand for goods from the markets.' The five wholesale markets are London Central Market aka Smithfield, in the City of London, which sells meat and poultry; Billingsgate at Canary Wharf, which deals in fish and seafood; and Spitalfields in Leyton, New Covent Garden in Vauxhall and Western International in Hounslow, all of which deal in fruit, vegetables and flowers.

A visit to Smithfield reveals 800 years of meaty history in desperate need of some love. Horace Jones's original, graceful building has had a string of abusive architect husbands, leaving it battered and scarred. Yet to see the market in full swing at dawn is still a spectacle. Here, white Transit vans cluster around each hole in the market's side, doors open like mouths. Each of these vans is attended by a porter in white overalls and boots – the scene looks like maggots feeding on a giant red-brick slab of meat.

Billingsgate has a similar tale to tell. It was moved from its ancestral riverside home to the then unfashionable Canary Wharf in the 1980s. Now it's a property developer's wet dream, and sits squat under the huge HSBC Tower. The same thing happened to Covent Garden market, once based in the centre of the West End, but shifted in the 1970s to a soulless complex built on an old goods yard in Nine Elms, Vauxhall.

Speak to any trader at one of these London institutions (you will have to be there early, mind) and they will happily talk your ear off about how health and safety, taxes, parking and the congestion charge are killing the markets. One vendor told me that at Christmas they used to put cooked samples out and have some mulled wine on the go, but now they are not allowed: everything has to be sealed. Another said that most traders now want to be gone by 8 a.m. (when the congestion charge kicks in), whereas before they would linger around and pick up a bit of retail trade from early risers and those on their way to work.

So what lies ahead? Well, consolidating all London's wholesale markets into an industrial estate out near the M25 might make sense on paper, but as well as freeing up land to sell and develop in the centre, it would also be the final evisceration of London's food history – a strange decision at a time when levels of interest in British food and where to get it has never been higher. New Covent Garden could be redeveloped as the Tate of food; a market, yes, but also a showcase of our horticultural and agricultural heritage. Once restored to its former glory, the Smithfield site could be a dream location for food fans, diners, catering students and businesses. Just across the street from the market is St John, Hix Oyster & Chop House, Smiths of Smithfield, Comptoir Gascon and many others, all of which trade on the historic location and yet are thoroughly contemporary in outlook and service. What if the big names behind those eateries got together with the traders and the powers that be, and came up with a plan to promote history and heritage hand in hand with produce and provenance? Could Smithfield once again be, as Daniel Defoe described it in 1726, 'Without question, the greatest market in the world'?

*See also* SMITHFIELD, ISLINGTON (p. 401).

Sam and Fairfax were soon joined by Jared Brown, who came on board as master distiller, Prudence was put to work, and not long after, from their tiny lock-up unit in Hammersmith, small quantities of London dry gin emerged. 'We believe things taste better when made properly in small batches,' says Sam.

The taste lingers in the mouth and is incredibly smooth and dry, with the initial perfumed juniper giving way to the citrus flavours. 'It's a gin you can actually sip neat,' says Sam. Of course, it's equally at home in the classic G&T, although Fairfax advises, 'Pack the glass with plenty of ice: too little and it'll melt, diluting the taste.' Or you could make a Lady Grey martini, which sees four teaspoons of Lady Grey tea leaves steeped in a bottle of Sipsmith gin for two hours to impart flavour. To 50 ml of this add 25 ml of lemon juice and 25 ml of simple syrup (equal parts castor sugar and water, well shaken) and the white of an egg. Shake well without ice to build up a frothy creaminess, before shaking again with ice to chill, and serve in a martini glass. This drink, invented by Jared and inspired by New York bar-tending doyenne Audrey Saunders, combines the Brits' love of both tea and gin in a very agreeable way; it's more Park Lane than Gin Lane.

*See also* PLYMOUTH, DEVON (p. 35).

## KNIGHTSBRIDGE, KENSINGTON & CHELSEA
# Harrods Food Hall

Charles Henry Harrod moved his grocer's shop to Knightsbridge from Stepney, East London, in 1849, hoping for an increase in trade from visitors to the Great Exhibition held in 1851 in nearby Hyde Park. The business was expanded under Charles Digby Harrod, and despite a fire in December 1883 (in the aftermath of which he still completed all his Christmas orders), grew rapidly. The current food departments were built in 1925 and today occupy an area of 40,000 square feet, equivalent to fourteen tennis courts. However, the meat hall dates back to 1903 and is one of the most stunning examples of retail architecture you're ever likely to buy half a pound of streaky back bacon in.

The Harrods motto remains *Omnia, Omnibus, Ubique*, or 'All Things for All People, Everywhere'. So much so that during Edwardian times its telegraphic address was simply 'Everything, London'. A lovely description of the store in the 1950s by Gina Mallet can be found in *Last Chance to Eat* (2004):

'Here, it was difficult not to impulse shop, and the salesmen encouraged it. When you saw the raw food, it was impossible to believe British cooking could be bad.' The film director Alfred Hitchcock would order kippers from Harrods to be sent to him when he was in America.

Today Harrods carries 12,000 different food lines, including items exclusive to the store. There is La Via Lattea, a stunning range of artisan goat's cheeses from the Lombardy region in Italy, made with raw milk. These cheese-makers are doing some very interesting things with their cheeses, including goat's cheese with chocolate and a blue Gorgonzola-style goat's cheese with rose petal and woodland berries. On the fruit counter there are some tiny wild alpine strawberries, the price of which will bring a tear to your eye. Closer to home there is Mathers Black Gold Scottish beef, from cattle who graze on the lush grass of Aberdeenshire. As well as being available on the meat counter, this beef is used by Harrods' in-house chefs in dishes for the Harrods Traiteur counter, including the classic beef Wellington. Furthermore, the majority of Harrods patisserie is produced in its very own pastry kitchen.

Other food halls in the capital also worth a browse are to be found in Selfridges and Harvey Nichols, with the newest member being John Lewis, who opened a 1,500-square-metre food hall in partnership with Waitrose in its flagship Oxford Street store in 2007. In the past the likes of Harrods (and Fortnum & Mason) catered to a very specific clientele – indeed they still do – but their exclusivity is now derived not so much from price (though that is still evident) but from the provenance and quality of its food.

*See also* PICCADILLY, WESTMINSTER (p. 395).

MARYLEBONE, WESTMINSTER
## Ginger Pig butchery classes

Tim Wilson is a no-nonsense Yorkshire farmer, although you might ask if there is any other kind. From his farm deep in *Heartbeat* country he produces Tamworth pigs that give the Ginger Pig Company its name, as well as Longhorn cattle and Swaledale sheep. From the bleak moorlands, fields and woods of North Yorkshire, the meat makes its way down to London, where the Ginger Pig have opened a chain of butcher's shops, beginning with a stall in Borough Market in the late 1990s.

Unlike most butcher's shops, however, they afford you the opportunity to

Perry from the Ginger Pig demonstrating how to chine a rib of beef

get up close and personal with their meat in butchery classes which run five nights a week. In charge are Perry and Borut who, like two firm-but-fair drill sergeants, take new recruits and turn them into a butcher's dirty dozen. You and your fellow cadets are let loose on huge sides of beef, whole carcasses of pork and entire lambs with a range of very sharp implements – how often do you get a hacksaw out in your kitchen? All this means you not only come away with a greater insight into the different muscles and anatomy of the animal, but also end up with a large piece of meat you removed, trimmed and tied to take home, too.

Classes from butchery to baking are madly popular these days. It's crazy to think that things our grandparents used to do as a chore, like baking bread, we now do as a recreational pastime. Of course, you could attempt all these things at home, or buy a cookbook and follow its instructions. But that misses the point of a class, which is as much about a communal learning experience at the hands of an expert as the opportunity to meet new people. You also get to use professional equipment in a commercial setting. It may even kick off a career change: I've met a few people who have been bitten by the bug for their chosen profession after getting hooked while on a course. The food, and learning how to make it, is the catalyst that brings like-minded and hungry people together, which is what food is all about.

See also BROMYARD, HEREFORDSHIRE (p. 283); CAMBRIDGE, CAMBRIDGESHIRE (p. 422); CONWY, CONWY (p. 60); FORRES, MORAY (p. 173); LOUTH, LINCOLNSHIRE (p. 336); MELTON CONSTABLE, NORFOLK (p. 447); NANTWICH, CHESHIRE (p. 125); WOODHALL SPA, LINCOLNSHIRE (p. 364); YORK, NORTH YORKSHIRE (p. 271).

MARYLEBONE, WESTMINSTER
## *The first British curry house*

Where to begin with the British and curry? Well, a good place is 34 George Street, Marylebone, London. It was here that Sake Dean Mahomet, along with his Irish Protestant wife Jane, opened the Hindustani Coffee House in 1809. Mahomet was born in Patna, Bengal, and started his career as a camp follower and then subaltern officer in the East India Company, eventually coming to London via Cork (where he met Jane).

His coffee house is now officially recognised as the first Indian restaurant in the UK. And, like most curry houses today, he wasn't catering for expats or Lascars, but us Brits; namely, nabobs and wealthy, self-made businessmen from among his former employers. He served the Indian-style food his patrons would have been familiar with, in decor they would recognise (cane furniture and prints of Indian landscapes). He was, it seems, creating a little piece of the Raj in the capital. His advert in the local press boasted 'the most unequalled curries in England, alongside fine wines and, in a separate room, hoakha pipes filled with real chilm tobacco'.

Sadly for Mahomet, there are some inexorable rules of restauranteuring, and the first is that you have to get the location right. Mahomet was hoping his salon would become a hub of like-minded traders, bankers and merchants, with connections and experience in the subcontinent, which is why he chose an affluent neighbourhood. Unfortunately, though, Marylebone was too far from the Square Mile and the docks, and so despite the restaurant's being well received, he was forced to file for bankruptcy in 1812. Once his debts were cleared, he moved to Brighton, where he opened a bath house that extolled the virtues of 'shampooing' as a form of therapy, and gained a royal warrant as 'shampooing surgeon'.

Meanwhile, others stepped in to meet the demand. In 1927, Edward Palmer opened Veeraswamy's Indian Restaurant on Regent Street, which is still open to this day, and you can now find an Indian restaurant in nearly every town in the land, from Shelina Spice in Thurso in the north of Scotland, to the Taj Mahal in Penzance.

*See also* BIRMINGHAM, WEST MIDLANDS (p. 279); GLASGOW, GLASGOW (p. 176); WHITECHAPEL, TOWER HAMLETS (p. 414).

## NEW CROSS, LEWISHAM
### *Jerk from Smokey Jerky*

Considering the long relationship Britain has had with the West Indies and Africa, Afro-Caribbean food has made none of the inroads into the nation's diet that other cuisines have. Some point to a lack of organisation and accessibility; others to the lack of a figurehead like Madhur Jaffrey or Ken Hom, although Levi Roots has made progress in this regard. And the truth is that very few non-Caribbean chefs will even attempt Caribbean cooking, while many will happily have a crack at curries, Pad Thais and other non-European dishes. Perhaps it's down to the simple fact that white men can't jerk? Or maybe, at its heart, jerk remains a family dish, its recipes like family secrets, handed down, kept safe and seldom shared.

'Proper jerk' in inner London: a selection of chicken, pork and lamb

South-east London is home to a large Afro-Caribbean community, and it's here that you will come across a lot of places to try jerk. 'Every jerk recipe is different,' says Louie Macpherson, owner of Smokey Jerky in New Cross, Lewisham. Louie opened the restaurant in 2004, but has more than thirty years' experience cooking jerk. 'What people call jerk is not really jerk. If a man come and put some chicken in an oven with some spice, that's not jerk, that's gonna be a roast!' he laughs. 'Most shops, that's what you get, really. There are only a few shops that sell proper jerk.' So what is proper jerk? 'For us, it's the kind of seasoning that we use and the way that we prepare it. It's not something that you can just do overnight, it's something you have to learn,' he replies.

There are two styles of jerk: a dry rub, when all the dry ingredients are rubbed over the raw meat; and a marinade, when the meat is submerged in a sauce of wet ingredients for many hours. Louie favours the latter; indeed, he believes this is the only proper way to do it. Common flavourings include allspice berries (called pimento in Jamaica) and chilli, usually fiery Scotch bonnet chillies. Food blogger, resident of Peckham and self-confessed jerk junky Helen Graves advises, 'Grind your own allspice berries, add plenty of sugar to make the marinade sticky, and don't ever, ever be tempted to use different chillies in place of Scotch bonnets. They are the cornerstone of jerk flavour; no other pepper has the same fruity tingle.'

'I don't use Scotch bonnet,' declares Louie, preferring instead cayenne chillies and shattering my preconceptions at a stroke. Like the man said, each recipe is different.

Chicken is the most popular meat to jerk, but belly pork works exceptionally well; goat is usually 'curried' in the West Indies, but can also be jerked, as can fish. 'We do lamb, too,' says Louie. This isn't traditional, but something that has evolved for the UK market, and is stunning nevertheless. In fact, after trying Louie's chicken, pork and lamb I find I like the lamb the best, with pork close second; the fat on the pork chars over the coals, adding a deep flavour and a sticky, crunchy texture. Jerk is normally served with accompanying sauces, and Louie offers his own recipe smokey barbecue sauce and a hot one. The latter is a truly wonderful thing, initially tasting of tomatoes, with an almost yoghurty coolness, but then hitting you with the heat, although never hurting, until the entire taste dies down. You will want more.

Today jerk is cooked over charcoal, often on half an oil drum, split lengthways, the other half forming a lid, rather than in open pits. If you can't get your hands on a steel drum, an ordinary barbecue with a lid is the next best thing. And if you really want to see how seriously people take the cooking of jerk, you can visit the Jerk Cookout Festival held in August in Brockwell, South London, for some lip-tingling jerk action.

## OLD BROMPTON ROAD, KENSINGTON & CHELSEA
# Kebabs

Sadly, the British kebab is often seen as little more than a late-night life buoy for those cast adrift on a sea of booze. It's hardly a life-saver, though: a nationwide investigation by local councils in 2009 revealed that an average doner kebab contains over 1,000 calories. On top of this it contains nearly the entire recommended daily allowance for salt and fat. As for the meat content, it can be a menagerie: lamb, mutton, beef, chicken and turkey all featured. Six samples even contained pork, and two of those were described as halal. So, all in all, not the finest hour for Britain's kebab vendors.

Of course, not all kebab shops serve the awful food described above. Bosphorus Kebabs opened on the Old Brompton Road, South Kensington, in 1974, and has been there ever since. Here you will find things unheard of in your average 'bab house, like side dishes of hummus, kisir and tabbule. The raw meat is deboned in-house, and as well as the usual shish and kofte, there are interesting cuts like lamb saddle chops, which the menu describes as 'the King Kong of Kebabs'. Finally, Bosphorous's doner is made with freshly minced meat, rather than some defrosted mystery elephantine leg from the cash and carry.

A word here on the doner. Although people have been roasting meat on spits since shortly after man invented fire, credit for the creation of the modern doner lies with the late Mahmut Aygün. Aygün was born in Turkey but later moved to Germany. It was he who first conspired – on 2 March 1971 – to put the slices of meat in pitta bread, allowing customers to take their food away with them. Thus the modern kebab was born. He is also credited with inventing the accompanying yoghurt sauce.

Kebabs do get a bad press. Like sausages, they are open to adulteration, but that's not their fault. And when your clientele is mainly three sheets to the wind, you can see why cheaper kebab shops cut corners. Which is a shame, because freshly prepared good-quality meats cooked on a grill or, even better, over coals with salad and bread, can be really enjoyable. Chilli sauce, my friend?

## PARSONS GREEN, HAMMERSMITH & FULHAM
### *Cooking in The Kitchen*

One of the biggest boom areas in food and drink in recent years has been the hands-on cookery event. Beer-and-food matching, wine tasting, butchery, or even bread-making – a household chore to our great-grandparents – there are courses available for all sorts of culinary crafts.

A place that keys into this trend is The Kitchen in Parson's Green, which certainly lives up to its name in that it's a place where you go to prepare food. What it is not, as founders Natalie Richmond and Thierry Laborde will affirm, is a cookery school. The premise is simple: you visit the website, browse the menu and decide what you would like to cook. You then pop along to your chosen session and everything is ready and waiting for you. You have a glass of wine, make the meal, and then your culinary creations are sealed, ready to take home to the cooker, fridge or freezer.

The menu is designed to take in all your home-cooked favourites: fish cakes, stuffed chicken breast, stir-fry, moussaka and Thai curry. The recipes are clear and easy-to-follow, but if you need help, head chef Thierry and sous-chef Claudio are on hand to guide you or show you how to do something. If you want, you can even bring in your own crockery and dishes rather than

Gourmet chefs in the making at The Kitchen's hands-on cookery class

use the trays provided. The Kitchen is unique in that you make not one single dish, but a selection of different meals intended to last the whole week.

These sorts of services and events across the capital and beyond are essentially offering food preparation as a recreational activity, which is by no means a bad thing. Attending one gives you the chance to learn new skills and use new ingredients, all under the watchful eye of a butcher, baker or chef. But it's also about rebelling against food convenience and actually taking the time to enjoy making food, as well as simply eating it.

## PECKHAM, SOUTHWARK
### Baked beans

Incredible as it may seem today, the café staple and student favourite that is baked beans were first launched in the UK as a luxury imported item from the USA. In 1886 Henry J. Heinz walked into Fortnum & Mason in London with some samples which they duly took, and offered for sale at around £1.50 per can in today's money. Fortnum & Mason still sell Heinz beans today, at a more modest 59p per can.

A US company, Heinz can attribute its success in the UK to one Charles E. Helen (he also invented salad cream), who came to England around the turn of the century to oversee expansion into the UK. By 1905 the London office had sales of $163,359, and so Heinz and Helen made the decision to set up production in the UK, a controversial move that at the time was opposed by the board. In 1905 Helen acquired Batty & Co, a pickle and condiment maker based in Peckham, South London. The firm and its products were well respected at the time, and indeed Heinz continued to produce its range of goods for more than a decade after. The move taught Heinz about British tastes and preferences. Over the coming decades, Helen set about making the beans a family favourite with British housewives, downplaying the American connection and extolling their wholesome fibrous virtues. Now that production was in the UK, the cost of a tin of beans dropped considerably. The business moved to larger premises in Harlesden, North London, in 1925, and by the time the Depression hit in the 1930s Heinz was advertising with lines such as 'Every pound of Heinz beans is equal in food value to one pound of prime steak.' Beans were even classified an 'essential food' during the Second World War. Then, in 1959, Heinz opened a factory at Kitts Green, Wigan. Today this is the largest food factory not only in the Heinz empire, but in the world, covering a massive fifty-four acres.

Of course, beans are so cheap and ubiquitous nowadays that money is raised for charity by sitting in a bath of them. Britain's involvement with dried beans of every kind has always been one born of poverty. As any student knows, baked beans are what you eat towards the end of term. A doddle to cook, requiring nothing more than heating up, they can even be eaten cold straight from the can.

During the 1990s, own-label beans were in the front line in a price war between all the major supermarkets, with the cost being reduced to mere pence. As Peter Kay says of Kwik Save, it was 'the only place where the carrier bags cost more than the beans'.

Despite the rival brands and supermarket bean wars, despite various chefs trying to give them a 'twist', and restaurants serving ironic £10 versions, baked beans just refuse to yield to the flows and eddies of fashion, and Heinz still remains the nation's favourite brand. Perhaps you're like me, who will happily buy own-label canned tomatoes, who couldn't give a hoot who makes the kidney beans for a chilli con carne, but if baked beans are coming into the house, it's Heinz or nowt.

Today, we in Britain eat more baked beans per capita than anyone else, even the Americans. They are a foodstuff designed to solve the problem of applying effort; they are the British comfort food of choice. The French may have cassoulet, the Spanish may have fabada, but us Brits have beans, preferably on toast.

*See also* TOAST (p. 404); PICCADILLY, WESTMINSTER (p. 395).

*See also* TOAST (p. 404); PICCADILLY, WESTMINSTER (p. 395).

PICCADILLY, WESTMINSTER
## *Fortnum & Mason*

Food halls are a breed apart from other food shops. All the familiar products are laid out for your perusal as you would expect, but the whole experience has been given the department-store touch. Needless to say, the usual trolley-dash rules do not apply.

The quantity, as well as the quality, of the products is amazing. There is a point of pride between all of them to secure new and exciting produce for their shelves. This is as true today as it was in 1886 when one Mr Heinz first showed samples of his tinned baked beans to Fortnum & Mason, who promptly bought the lot (see p. 394). Fortnum & Mason was established in 1707, when the entrepreneurial William Fortnum, footman at the court of Queen Anne, began a nice sideline in reselling the Queen's half-used candles in a business partnership with his landlord, Hugh Mason.

In 1756 the firm moved around the corner to its present site on Piccadilly. In the eighteenth and nineteenth centuries it catered for those attending the London season, which ran from Easter through to the Glorious Twelfth (of August), which was traditionally the first day of the grouse season and saw the gentry returning to their country piles. Fortnum & Mason even had a bespoke Expeditions Department, which supplied the likes of explorer and adventurer Howard Carter, and for the 1922 Everest expedition provided sixty tins of quail in foie gras and four dozen bottles of champagne; well, one must do these things in style, naturally. Today Fortnum's still caters for those who like to be well provisioned when dining *en plein air*, with a huge offering of hampers and picnic sets. In the store itself the new demonstration kitchen on the first floor holds events from wine tasting and food matching to how to plan a knockout picnic. On the lower ground floor is the grocery department, where you will find such specialities as miniature bananas, elephant garlic from the Isle of Wight, and a meat counter stocked with beef, pork and lamb from Prince Charles's Highgrove estate. Another area where the store excels is preserves. The display of breakfast jams, marmalades, chutneys and relishes is enormous, taking up an entire wall some ten feet long, all housed like specimens in the Natural History Museum on dark oak shelves.

These days, food can be just as much a luxury item and status symbol as handbags, suits or electrical goods, and the procurement of it should be enjoyable rather than a chore.

*See also* KNIGHTSBRIDGE, KENSINGTON & CHELSEA (p. 386).


## SAFFRON HILL, CAMDEN
### The history of fish and chips

The exact origins of fish and chips, like many working-class dishes, are lost to the mists of time. Both London and Lancashire claim the glory for being the home of the dish. A fish-frying warehouse is mentioned in Charles Dickens's *Oliver Twist* (1838), situated on Saffron Hill near Holborn alongside beer houses and filthy shops where Fagin fences his ill-gotten gains, and it's thought that Portuguese Jews arriving from the Iberian

Peninsula and settling in the East End first introduced coated fried fish to the UK, although the Jewish method involves coating the fish in egg and matzo meal, pan-frying it and then serving it cold. Joseph Malin, a Jew born in Eastern Europe, is credited with opening the first fish and chip shop in the East End of the capital in 1860.

But what about the chips? Oddly, we turn again to Dickens, as the *OED* states that the earliest recorded usage of 'chips' is in *A Tale of Two Cities*, published in 1859. They're described as 'husky chips of potatoes, fried with some reluctant drops of oil'. Potatoes were by then the fuel that powered the human cogs and gaskets of the Industrial Revolution, and the hub of that revolution was the north-west of England. Indeed, so sure are they that chips were invented in Lancashire, Oldham Council have even put up a plaque in Tommyfield Market stating, 'The first chips were fried in Oldham around 1860 from which the origins of fish and chip shops and the "fast food" industries can be traced': a bold claim from a boomtown of the Industrial Revolution. What is certain is that fried potatoes were a popular dish in the region, which is perhaps why a traditional potato peeler complete with orange string around the handle is still known as a Lancashire peeler.

So it looks as though the south provided the fish and the north provided the potatoes, but whatever the origin of fish and chips, their union is greater than the sum of their parts, and so the dish remained a working-class staple: hot, cheap and filling. The advent of steam-powered trawlers made sourcing fish a lot easier, and, what's more, those fishermen with their seafaring experience could be drafted into the Navy at a moment's notice during wartime, an unexpected bonus when command of the seas was vital to British interests on the world stage. During the two world wars, fishing decreased and fish stocks were able to recover as fishermen were called up, fuel was rationed and fishing far from shore became too dangerous. And yet, unlike bread, eggs and meat, fish and potatoes remained firmly off the ration book. Churchill's government, obviously, not only recognised just how much they were loved by the working classes, but also how fish and chip shops performed a similar role to the 'National Kitchens' that were set up during the war to ensure the population got some basic nutrition – and, no doubt, as a boost to morale as well. The potential of fish and chips as a gourmet experience, however, was obviously overlooked. As John K. Walton says in *Fish and Chips and the British Working Class, 1870–1940*, which takes a close look at both the dish and the trade, 'Fish and chips became ubiquitous, mundane, inescapable and taken for granted in Britain in the first half of the twentieth century.'

It's a sentiment echoed by Richard Ord of Colman's Fish & Chips in South Shields: 'Fish and chips were underrated and ignored until ten or fifteen years ago. Then top restaurants started putting them on the menu, TV chefs started making them, and the likes of Rick Stein and Tom Aikens started opening chip shops.' It seems that fish and chips were so universal, so much a part of the British way of life, that we took them for granted. Then, as part of the rediscovery of the food of our grandparents in the early 1990s (think lamb shanks, pies and jellied eels), coupled with the celebration of everything working class (think Oasis and the 'mockneys' of Britpop), the fish supper took its place in the pantheon of rediscovered British classics. Everyone loves fish and chips; it's a meal that crosses all cultural and class barriers in the UK and is sought out by tourists and natives alike.

Nowadays, fish and chips are no longer found in filthy Dickensian back alleys; rather they are celebrated internationally. In 2009, Richard Ord was invited to the British Embassy in Rome to cater for a garden party in honour of the Queen's birthday. 'There was a buffet there but everyone – generals, admirals and cardinals – all wanted fish and chips.' But despite the new-found fame, I can't see fish and chips getting above themselves, and there are still few things better suited to staving off the cold of a winter's evening than a warm, paper-wrapped package tucked under your arm as you make your way home.

*See also* SOUTH SHIELDS, TYNE & WEAR (p. 225).

## ST JAMES'S, WESTMINSTER
### *Black velvet — in liquid memoriam*

On 14 December 1861, Prince Albert, the Queen's consort, died in the Blue Room at Windsor. According to his obituary in the *Times*, the event came as a great shock to the nation. The following Monday, all the theatres in the West End were closed, and for the rest of the week, or perhaps on the following Monday – the day of the funeral itself – the steward at Brooks's club, London, informed members that champagne wasn't to be served unless 'dressed' in black. Thus he added Guinness, which, because it is denser than champagne, sank to the bottom of the glass like a black ribbon, and the cocktail black velvet was born.

'We've looked into it and can't find any records in our archive,' says assistant club secretary Alastair Curbbun, which comes as a bit of a blow.

Brooks's club, home of black velvet

Perhaps it was one of those things that was so taken for granted that no one ever bothered to write it down. In the 1960s, to celebrate the 200th anniversary of the club, a set of special 'black velvet' glasses were made. These were hand-blown, with a large chamber about the size of a wine glass to hold the drink, supported on a thick neck by a sturdy base. Sweetings restaurant in the city of London, however, has served black velvet in silver tankards in the past, another traditional vessel.

As well as a bar, Brooks's includes a dining room, and, according to Alastair, the drink has featured in the kitchen's culinary creations of the past, including, apparently, a black velvet crème brûlée. Alastair admits that there is probably the potential to make more of the drink: beef in black velvet is just one suggestion, and of course it would go extremely well with oysters.

It's doubtful that Queen Victoria herself ever drank black velvet, as she's known to have preferred Vin Mariani, a cocaine-based beverage that inspired Coca-Cola. Her other tipple was a dram of Lochnagar whisky, from the distillery situated next to Balmoral which she and Albert toured in 1848. Cocktails are usually such showy, celebratory affairs that it is rare to find one with a dark or sad element. However, if anyone could 'do' death, it was the Victorians.

## *Steaks from Hawksmoor*

Despite all the many breeds of beef cattle in the UK, sitting down to a steak in modern Britain wasn't always a fantastic experience. Why so? Well, it's mostly down to the familiar twentieth-century story of animals being bred for size and yield rather than taste and flavour.

Steakhouses have come a long way since Italian-born Frank Berni converted the Rummer pub in Bristol into the first Berni Inn. Here, the unholy trinity of prawn cocktail, steak and chips (imported Argentinean, of course), and Black Forest gateau sat four-square on the menu and in our stomachs – and it's taken a while for this to pass through.

In 2006, childhood friends Will Beckett and Huw Gott opened Hawksmoor on Commercial Street, London, bringing all their experience of working in various kitchens and running bars (most notably the Redchurch bar off Brick Lane) with them. 'I love meat, and I love it prepared simply,' says Huw, whose family were butchers. 'A hundred years ago we were recognised around the world as producing the best beef.'

Hawksmoor's meat comes from Tim Wilson at the Ginger Pig (*see* p. 387). Before opening, Will and Huw did a whole series of tastings with lots of different suppliers and breeds. Crucially, they didn't look at the prices, lest they subconsciously taint their view, and Tim's Longhorn beef won the contest hands down. It's the main breed used, although it's joined once a month by special guest breeds. Tim has even planted a range of grasses of the type that would have been found in Yorkshire 100 years ago, including white and red clover and cock's-foot grass to name but three. He has consequently seen a difference in the way the animals feed, as well as the taste of the meat. Most farmers in the UK now plant Italian ryegrass, as it's quick growing, stable and produces a large yield for hay or sileage; it's a bit boring for the cows, mind, and it also makes one cow's meat taste a lot like another.

Then there is the butchery. Where once you would only see fillet and rump on menus, nowadays we're all amateur animal anatomists and are prepared to experiment. Hawksmoor offers bone-in prime rib, porterhouse, chateaubriand, rib-eye and bone-in sirloin, all cooked over a charcoal barbecue. 'We tried cooking steaks at different sizes, but they're just much better if they're bigger. That's why steak at lots of restaurants isn't very good: you can't get a decent char on the outside and keep the flavour on the inside.'

Consequently, there are plenty of 'serves two' bits of bovine on Hawksmoor's menu. When I was last there, I had an entire rib cut to myself, knowing full well I was going to make only a dent in it. The kitchen bagged up the rest – including the bones – and I ate it the next day, using the bones to make a stock that then went on to become a French onion soup. So, as you can see, what might seem like a costly outlay can in fact keep you fed for three or four days.

At home, assuming they have got a good steak of a decent size, the problems that bedevil most steak virgins are as follows: they try to cook the meat straight from the fridge, they don't let the pans become hot enough, and afterwards they don't leave enough resting time for the steak to relax. Address these points with room-temperature meat, a pan as hot as it can get, and a resting time nearly equal to cooking time, and matters will improve greatly. A well-raised, -hung and -butchered piece of meat can be ruined by poor cooking, and yet a poor piece of meat can't be improved by correct treatment.

Huw sums things up when he says, 'Really good beef costs lots of money,' and that's just to raise, feed, slaughter and hang it before it even reaches customers.

## *Marrow on toast at St John*

Nothing on the menu at his Smithfield restaurant St John sums up the mild-mannered Fergus Henderson's 'nose-to-tail' philosophy more than roast bone marrow with parsley. Henderson admits, 'It's a bit cheeky, just roasting bones as a signature dish.' Inspiration for the dish struck a few days before the restaurant opened in 1994, when Henderson was watching *La Grande Bouffe* in the Everyman cinema in Hampstead, London. The film, by Marco Ferreri, is a dark satire about four male friends who gather one weekend for a fatal orgy of sex and excessive eating. In one scene, the cast all suck on roasted bones, and 'inspiration struck'. Fergus's wife was a little disapproving of the idea, but he went for it, and it's been on the menu ever since. It's an insanely popular dish – Anthony Bourdain even declared that it would be his last supper – and the restaurant gets through a huge number of bones each week. This means the bones can't all be sourced in the UK. 'They're Dutch, I'm afraid to say. We get some veal meat from Yorkshire, but there just aren't enough leg bones in the UK to meet our needs,' says Fergus.

Fergus Henderson's marvellous marrow on toast

'We sold more of the dish during the BSE crisis of 1997 than at any other time. Blokes would come in and say things like, "We'll show those Johnnies in Brussels," obviously not realising the bones were actually Dutch.'

Since the dish became so popular, it has been much copied, homaged and aped, not only in the UK but also in America. While this revival can be traced directly back to St John, it also continues a long British tradition of eating bone marrow. Charles Elmé Francatelli (an Englishman of Italian extraction) was, along with perhaps Alexis Soyer, the pre-eminent Victorian chef of his day. Francatelli worked in a number of gentlemen's clubs and gambling houses, the sort of place that provoked Mrs Beeton to write, 'Men are so well served out of doors – that in order to compete with the attractions of these places a mistress must be fully aquainted with the theory and practice of cookery.' The Garrick club, home from home for men of letters and learning, was noted for its porterhouse steaks and marrow bones. Francatelli became chef to Queen Victoria and Prince Albert, and although he left after a year, the brief association only enhanced his reputation. He gives a recipe for 'Marrow Toast *à la* Victoria' in his book *The Cook's Guide, and Housekeeper's & Butler's Assistant* (1857) as follows:

Procure a marrow-bone, or get the butcher to break the bone for you – as this is rather an awkward affair for ladies; cut the marrow into small pieces the size of a filbert, and just parboil them in boiling water with a little salt for one minute; it must then be instantly drained upon a sieve, seasoned with a little chopped parsley, pepper and salt, lemon-juice, and a mere suspicion of shallot; toss lightly altogether, spread it out upon squares of hot crisp dry toast, and serve immediately.

As a note, he adds, 'Marrow toast used to be eaten every day at dinner by the Queen at the time when I had the honour of waiting on Her Majesty.' Mrs Beeton also has a version of the dish, although she uses beef bones rather than veal, and recommends plugging each end with pastry and simmering for two hours, which sounds more like a recipe for wallpaper paste than dinner. A quivering lump of marrow is the jewel in the crown of the Milanese dish *osso bucco*, and marrow features in *risotto alla milanese*, along with saffron, two ingredients few of us have kicking about the kitchen, I'll grant you. In the UK, marrow and rice are found together in clipping time pudding from Cumberland (*see* p. 112).

Perhaps the most tantalising Victorian marrow recipe is Francatelli's 'Ox-Piths *à la Ravigotte*', which uses the cow's spinal marrow. This is boiled gently and then left in a pickling sauce, before being dried on a napkin, battered and fried. Sadly, though, this dish we must leave to the pages of history, as the legacy of BSE is that all bovine spinal material must be removed and destroyed.

*See also* TOAST (p. 404); BATH, SOMERSET (p. 4); BURY MARKET, GREATER MANCHESTER (p. 99); DINGWALL, HIGHLAND (p. 160); HAROME, NORTH YORKSHIRE (p. 249); HEREFORD, HEREFORDSHIRE (p. 296); STONEHALL COMMON, WORCESTERSHIRE (p. 312).

SOUTH BANK, SOUTHWARK
## Bubble and squeak from Canteen

Some years ago a company launched a range of cooking sauces with the selling point that because they came in serving sizes for one to two people, there wouldn't be any leftovers to throw out. Personally, I felt my hackles rise, for while I'm not keen on food waste, I'm very much in favour of leftovers.

# Toast

Whether you're after a sixty-second breakfast, a snack, lunch, dinner or supper, or even have the late-night munchies, only one British household favourite fits the bill: toast. Toast is culinarily neutral, inert and non-partisan; it is the Switzerland of foods, able to take sweet or savoury toppings at any time of the day. There is practically nothing you can't put on toast; it is the canvas on which we've all painted bright buttery dawns and mellow marmalade sunsets.

You've got to be a total idiot to get toast wrong, and yet from time to time we all still do. Watchfulness is required when cooking toast; take your eye off it for a second and a beeping smoke alarm is sure to follow. And yet another beauty of toast is that it comes with an 'undo' function. Out with the knife, a quick scrape and lo, your beloved slice is restored to something edible.

The Scandinavian naturalist and student of Carolus Linnaeus, Pehr Kalm, pithily summed up the British approach to toast in his diary entry of March 1748:

> Breakfast . . . consisted in drinking tea. They ate at the same time one or more slices of wheat-bread, which they had first toasted at the fire and when it was very hot had spread butter on it . . . the butter is hard from the cold, and does not easily admit of being spread on the bread, [which perhaps gave] them the idea to thus toast the bread, and then spread the butter on it while it is still hot.

Ahh, dear Pehr, over 200 years later and we all still know this pain. Who hasn't tried to spread butter straight from the fridge, desperately planing it with the knife like a manic carpenter, only to succeed in tearing a hole in the toast when spreading a chunk on?

Some attribute our love of toast to our love of the open fires that we used to cook it over. Equally, though, toasting bread freshens it up, makes it more palatable and stiffens it, so that it can take a topping. Our love of stiff bread with toppings arguably goes back to the medieval trencher, a bread plate from which the nobility ate their meat. Afterwards these 'plates', soaked in meaty juices, would have been given to the poor, who would wait outside if they knew a feast was happening – this meant no washing-up, too.

Toast has magical healing properties. Judaism may have chicken soup, but you need a Jewish mother to make it properly. When you're on your own, ill in your bed, surrounded by a doily of snotty tissues and carrying a hot-water bottle like an expectant mother, far too sick to actually 'cook' anything, you can still – just – manage to make a slice of toast to go with that Lemsip. And when your suffering is of a self-inflicted-kind, toast is the only thing safe to cook.

The Victorians also believed in the healing power of toast. Toast water was a popular quack remedy for all sorts of ills. Most books of the period, and a few into the twentieth century, carry recipes for toast water in the 'caring for an invalid' section. Like some early homeopathic remedy, toast water was made by placing a slice of well-done toast in a glass of boiling water and leaving it to go cold. The water turned brown and the 'goodness' of the toast leeched into it. Sounds revolting, but if you have an upset stomach it's probably worth a pop – I'll bet it tastes nicer than Pepto-Bismol.

*See also* HOLT, NORFOLK (p. 439); KIRTON IN LINDSEY, LINCOLNSHIRE (p. 329); PECKHAM, SOUTHWARK (p. 394); SMITHFIELD, ISLINGTON (p. 401).

First, there is the transmogrifying power of increasing time and decreasing temperature that can take all the hot, busy flavours of a chilli, stew or curry, and, like a headmaster entering a classroom, bring about order and propriety. Liquid-based slow-cooked dishes always taste different the next day, more mellow in the mouth. Then there is the joy of eating from the fridge: reaching for the milk to make a late night cuppa and finding your hand tearing a strip off a chicken carcass or emerging holding a cold roast potato.

And finally there is leftovers redux, and king among these is bubble and squeak. No one sets out to make bubble and squeak from scratch; to do so would be a sign of madness. 'Bubble' only comes about when you have been overgenerous in estimating your diners' appetites. I have always found it prudent to portion for the uninvited guest, although all too often he turns out to be me, a few hours later. But should the leftovers survive the night, glory awaits in the pan the next day. The cold cabbage and roast (or, very rarely, mashed) potato are mixed and mushed up with a fork, and a teaspoon of flour to bind might be added. Then into a hot pan goes butter, and maybe a glug of oil, and then the mixture. I use a small six-inch frying pan and make one pan-sized disc, but others prefer shaping it into fishcake-sized rounds – each to their own. Grated cheese has been known to crown my bubble and squeak. Flipping one can be tricky, so a spell under the grill works to crisp up the top and melt the cheese (should it be present).

Bubble and squeak is a classic that is found all across Britain. Canteen in the Royal Festival Hall on the South Bank of London makes a good version. Here the bubble is fried in meat dripping, and potatoes that have previously been roasted in duck fat are used, as this gives a meatiness to the finished dish. Across all four branches of Canteen in the capital (the other three are at Spitalfields, Baker Street and Canary Wharf), diners eat over 10,000 portions of bubble and squeak a year. Some no doubt will be visitors from abroad, and one can only imagine what they think when they see bubble and squeak on the menu.

## SOUTHWARK BRIDGE ROAD, SOUTHWARK
### Bompas and Parr jellymongers

London has many guilds for the respected trades – butchers, fishmongers, bakers and many more – though not as yet one for the makers of jelly. Perhaps Sam Bompas and Harry Parr should form one, though, because they're the capital's only jellymongers. The boys create bespoke jellies on commission for corporations, organisations and individuals. 'We've had all sorts of clients looking for something special,' says Sam. They built a jelly version of Barajas airport for architect Richard Rogers' birthday, a jelly St Paul's for the London Festival of Architecture, and they regularly take on wedding commissions.

One of their most popular products is a glow-in-the-dark jelly: 'It's made with tonic water, which contains UV-reactive quinine, so it glows brilliantly under a UV light.' They have also made a flameproof jelly, which they set alight like a Christmas pudding.

Fresh fruit from Borough Market (which is just round the corner) is heated up to release its juices, then mixed with leaf gelatin. It's a two-stage process to make the moulds. First, the jelly is modelled on a computer and printed out using a 3D printer. Then the model is put in a vacuum former to make up the negative shape in thin plastic. After a good wash with soapy water, it's ready for the jelly, and the whole thing is then put in the fridge.

Jelly – the ultimate silly party food – used to be made with isinglass. This had to be extracted from the swim bladders of fish such as the beluga sturgeon. Consequently, it was the Russians who perfected, and kept secret, its production method. One Humphrey Jackson, a scientist, gives a lovely account of the difficulties he faced in trying to figure out the method, in a letter to a fellow scientist in 1774: 'In my first attempt to discover the constituent parts and manufacture of isinglass, . . . I found myself constantly disappointed. Glue, not isinglass, was the result of every process.' Eventually the technique was perfected by others, and in 1795 William Murdoch found a way of extracting a similar substance from the swim bladders of cod, which was much more plentiful.

Of course, the other known way to make jelly was to boil the bones, hooves and skin of animals, and then cool the resulting liquid down. Obviously, this left a somewhat savoury-tasting dish, and a small yield. Eventually the process was refined and improved by treating the animal parts to a variety of processes, and gelatin took the lead over isinglass in all culinary preparations. Today, you rarely see the savoury jelly, and eggs, meat and lark's tongues are no longer entombed in aspic jelly, like flies in amber. Of course, Bompas and Parr might be just the chaps to change all that. We shall see.

# Brick Lane bagels

Today, Brick Lane is renowned as London's curry street, but in the eighteenth and nineteenth century it was home to a large Jewish population. Little of that culture remains in the East End today, except perhaps the two bagel shops, one at 155 and the other at 159 Brick Lane.

Sammy Minzly, co-owner of Beigel Bake, is a spritely seventy-four years old. He has seen the area change drastically since the shop – once a kosher butcher's – first opened in 1976. Back then, they opened only in the day, but gradually the hours got later and now the place stays open all night. 'It used to be coppers, cabbies and prostitutes in the early days,' says Sammy.

Now it's almost always completely packed, and there is normally a large and impatient queue. Once inside, then, it's best not to linger with questions and indecision, and just to ask directly for a hot, salt-beef bagel – the name says it all, adhering, as it does, insanely strictly to the Trade Descriptions Act. For your troubles, you will be rewarded with a small chewy bagel – shaped, boiled and baked – that acts as a bready pair of parentheses around the three or four hunks of soft, fibrous beef.

The meat – around 80 kilos a day, and always the brisket cut – is cooked slowly for four hours in a massive pan along with garlic, onions, carrots and pepper. 'When you eat it, you get addicted,' says Sammy. Of course such things need a blob of sauce, and you're invited to slather the little fellas in nasal-clearing English mustard. There is also the very popular salmon and cream cheese bagel: 'For some reason Japanese tourists love these; I can tell when they come in,' says Sammy.

There are some foods that make sense at certain times of the day: a boiled egg, for instance, is perfection itself between the hours of 7 a.m. and 11 a.m., whereas rib-eye steak is not. Salt-beef bagels, although fantastic any time of the day, really come into their own in the small hours. In the early morning of a Saturday or Sunday the place is invariably packed with the demi-monde of London's bars and clubs who have all come out in search of something to eat. Hopper's *Nighthawks* it ain't. Sammy is there every Saturday night from 7 p.m. to 7 a.m., holding forth. Go and see him.

# *A London Particular*

Only in Britain, with our ability to laugh in the face of death itself, would we have named a food after a man-made environmental disaster that at its climax killed 4,000 people in a week. The London Particular – a thick pea-and-ham soup not unlike a runny pease pudding – is named after the infamous smog that once shrouded London. The worst example came in December 1952, when a cold snap meant people burned more coal to keep warm. This, coupled with an unseasonal lack of wind, meant a thick fog settled over the city.

Simpson's-in-the-Strand, which has been serving classic British dishes since 1828, has often had London Particular on the menu in the cooler months. In its recipe, a 'green' (meaning uncured) ham hock is simmered with thyme, carrots, onion, parsley, bay leaves, peppercorns and half a bulb of garlic until the meat starts to fall off the bone. The stock is strained to remove the spent vegetables, and the meat is picked from the bone. Fresh vegetables are then sautéed in olive oil, before the pre-soaked split green peas are added and simmered for another hour. The whole thing is then blitzed in a processor, seasoned, and served with the broken-down ham pieces.

Interestingly, the term 'London Particular' was applied to other things before soup. An advertisement for Messrs Thompson and Fearson of High Holborn from 1827 tells us of their latest shipment of wines, recently arrived at London docks. The itinerary includes 'Vidonia, the old London Particular', of which it goes on to say, 'the character of the old "London Particular" Vidonia being that of a medium between Madeira and Sherry, and possessed of some qualities superior to either'. Madeira was often barrelled and transported by ship to places such as India or 'the Brazils'; the time and rocking motion was said to improve it. It seems that the Victorians were very fond of their fortifying – and fortified – London Particular wines, as this extract from the *New York Times* of July 1855 reveals: 'Port wine is still a favourite medicinal beverage . . . among wines that are given or used "as a medicine" none stand so high as the L. P. or London Particular.' A great endorsement, although sadly no defence against killer smog.

*See also* ALNWICK, NORTHUMBERLAND (p. 199); AMBERGATE, DERBYSHIRE (p. 275).

London's wealth of flora makes it a surprisingly good place to keep bees

## *Up on the bee farm*

London is a massive, never-sated maw that constantly sucks in produce from every region of the country and the world. It's fair to say that it's not a great producer of food. There are a few city farms around the capital, but they're really more about educating inner-city kids than producing anything. However, the idea of 'urban homesteading', which is currently being explored in America and was given a much-needed boost when President Obama planted a vegetable garden at the White House, is also being looked at here – although with London having some of the most expensive real-estate prices in the world, space is at too much of a premium to keep most animals. Except, perhaps, those that fly, such as the honey bee.

Ten years ago, Steve Benbow decided to give up his job as a travel photographer and become a bee farmer instead. He started with hives five storeys up an ex-local-authority block of flats near Tower Bridge, London, and he's now managing over 1,000 hives in London and the rest of the country. In the summer of 2009 he placed four hives of Italian Carniolan bees on the roof of Fortnum & Mason, in Piccadilly. 'London has a lot of green space, and it's fantastic for honey production.' He has over eighty hives in the capital for a number of clients. Each hive can produce, on average, about 100 jars of honey. 'It's also tasty and complex, with a butterscotchy, toffee-like taste,' says Steve.

A look at a Google map of London reveals a lot of roof space which at the moment is only home to the pigeons. And 1,000 jars of honey aren't going to keep many fed for long. They do, however, feed the mind. They show what is possible, and when I read about them, let alone try some, I can't help but stop to consider where our food comes from and how it's made. Steve and I concluded our chat with a shared daydream about another animal happy in an urban environment, the pig. Wouldn't it be great to bring back the London porker?

*See also* HORNCLIFFE, NORTHUMBERLAND (p. 211); LINDISFARNE, NORTHUMBERLAND (p. 213).

# The Vincent Rooms: a restaurant with L plates

In 1908 a training programme was set up by a committee that included Isidore Salmon, director of J. Lyons and Co. tea rooms, noted chef Auguste Escoffier and hotelier Cesar Ritz. Their training school, now part of Westminster Kingsway College, took thirteen-year-old boys and trained them to be the next generation of chefs, waiters and sommeliers for the finest hotels and restaurants of London. 'We needed to ensure we were building skills by learning and by doing rather than looking at a blackboard, so in 1912 we opened a restaurant,' says Geoff Booth, centre director for hospitality. The result was the Vincent Rooms. There were even plans for a fifty-bedroom 'training hotel', and construction had barely begun in 1939 when war put a stop to developments and it was never completed. Sixty years later, things may be about to change, and a training 'boutique' hotel is a very real possibility. The restaurant, meanwhile, has gone from strength to strength, and in 1953, the Escoffier room was added, along with a wine cellar.

All this adds up to one of London's most interesting food venues, in which by the simple act of eating you may be helping train a future superstar of the food world. The Vincent Rooms has a European brasserie menu that changes daily. Diners are served by first-year students, and the food is cooked by second-year students under the supervision of third-years. In the Escoffier room, by contrast, where things are a little more formal, service is performed by second-years and the third-years man the stoves. Starters include *consommé de poisson aux coquilles en croûte*, and smoked trout and salmon terrine, with mains such as poached supreme of turbot with lobster, double-breast poussin supreme *hongroise*-style and whole Dover sole. The fine-dining three-course lunch menu, with canapés and petit fours, is an unbelievable £20 per head. Both kitchens are under the watchful eye of the chef lecturer, but he will only roll up his sleeves in an emergency.

As well as courses for students, this year the college has added leisure courses, so that anyone can spend a day learning techniques such as making a terrine, or sugar work, or butchery. 'It's for the joy of doing it,' says Geoff. 'Ironically, 100 years after our founding, we're still educating thirteen-year-olds on Saturday mornings, though it's for a leisure purpose now – they're learning how to cook and learning about food.' Escoffier et al. would no doubt approve.

## *Coronation chicken*

The year is 1953 and a new sovereign is to be crowned, heralding what some at the time were calling a new Elizabethan age. With 'Zadok the Priest' still ringing in the guests' ears, those who couldn't fit into Buckingham Palace sat down in the Great Hall of Westminster School to a lunch of coronation chicken.

The dish was the creation of Rosemary Hume, co-principal of the Cordon Bleu catering school that she had established with Constance Spry. Spry, a florist, was commissioned to produce the floral displays in the Abbey and along the processional route. The recipe subsequently appeared in their book *The Constance Spry Cookery Book* and so is often accredited to Spry. Inspiration is said to have come from a similar dish of jubilee chicken (chicken in a curried mayonnaise) served for George V's Silver Jubilee eighteen years earlier.

The 1953 version calls for the chicken to be first poached, then left to cool before being removed from the carcass and shredded into bite-sized pieces. It's then incorporated into a light, creamy, curry-flavoured sauce. The dish was served cold, with rice flecked with peas, cucumber and herbs, mixed with a French dressing. Very summery you would imagine, although the weather on that June day was overcast and rainy by all accounts. And while much of the day has been chronicled, there seems to be no contemporary accounts of the food and how it tasted.

According to Hume's niece – and indeed anyone who has eaten it over the interceding fifty years – the dish has been much debased; almonds, sultanas, mango chutney, too much mayonnaise, apricot jam, all have taken their toll. Often too much turmeric is added, turning the sauce a bright yellow, whereas the original called for tomato purée and red wine, which would have given a darker, redder sauce. Coronation chicken has become a mere sandwich filler, a gloopy shadow of its former self. Chicken, once a rare luxury, is now an everyday meat, and curry spices flavour everything from Pot Noodle to crisps.

But in 1950s post-rationing Britain, the dish was, like the monarch it lauded, a fulcrum of Empire on a plate. Apricots, curry, chicken, rice, peas: it was a dish that spanned the world.

## WHITECHAPEL, TOWER HAMLETS
# *Tikka lamb chops*

On a walk through the East End of London on a hot summer's night, your nose will be treated to the heady perfumes of subcontinental spices. The area has been called home by everyone from Huguenot refugees to Ashkenazi Jews to Bangladeshis, and now Brick Lane is regarded as London's curry mile. In 1997 there were ten 'Indian' restaurants, and today there are over fifty, although sadly the hustle for trade seems to have affected the quality and many are (according to curry aficionados) somewhat below par.

There is still plenty of good eating around the wider area though, and a clutch of restaurants have seen their stars rise in recent years. The Tayyab family arrived from the Punjab in 1974, and set up their café in Fieldgate Street. Owner Mohammed Tayyab was the uncle of the proprietor of the Lahore Kebab House around the corner on Umberston Street, which had opened a few years earlier. The current manager, Wasim Tayyab, describes the development of the café: 'There were a lot of men in shared accommodation whose wives were back in Pakistan or Bangladesh. They couldn't cook very well, so my father set up his café to cater for them.'

Nowadays, Tayyabs caters for hungry Londoners who want hot, fresh Punjabi dishes at cheap-as-chapatti prices. Both it, and indeed the Lahore Kebab House, are insanely popular, with queues stretching along the street on busy nights, thus catering to the British love of curry and queues in one evening. Once inside it's a full-on festival of heat and noise. One friend described a meal in Tayyabs as like 'eating in a nightclub', such is the din and neon lighting. But then that frantic rowdy experience, with waiters wielding hot-as-hell iron platters inches from your head as they rush by, is all part of the fun.

The food requires a get-stuck-in attitude, and for this you can't beat the excellent tikka lamb chops, whose spicing is delicious. The rib bone is left long so you have something to hold. If you don't fancy the queues, another option is the Needoo Grill, set up by a former manager of Tayyabs, or the Mirch Masala on Commercial Road.

To British minds, curry has been a catch-all term for an entire continent's cuisine for years. Not so now: with Asian food having gone regional, you can say, 'Anyone fancy popping out for a Punjabi?'

*See also* BIRMINGHAM, WEST MIDLANDS (p. 279); GLASGOW, GLASGOW (p. 176); MARYLEBONE, WESTMINSTER (p. 389).

*See also* BIRMINGHAM, WEST MIDLANDS (p. 279); GLASGOW, GLASGOW (p. 176); MARYLEBONE, WESTMINSTER (p. 389).

WIMBLEDON, MERTON
## Strawberries and tennis

Despite their near year-round availability these days, nothing quite says summertime like the taste of strawberries. The tiny wild varieties, native to Northern Europe and hardly bigger than the caps on your car tyres, pack a flavour hit that practically fizzes on your tongue; they're a devil to find for sale, however. Today we're more used to the commercially grown varieties. Cross-breeding and selectively enhancing attributes in strawberries has been going on since the sixteenth century, giving rise to varieties such as Hautboy (also known as Hautbois), Little Scarlet, Keens' Imperial, Royal Sovereign and Cambridge Favourite, the latter making up 70 per cent of the commercial market in the middle of the last century, as well as modern versions such as Elsanta, which is a touch watery for my liking.

Like many other crops, the railways helped to make the produce of areas such as Kent, Cambridgeshire and Hampshire available to the ever-hungry maw that is London. In 1888, Swanwick station in Hampshire was built with extra-long platforms to facilitate rapid loading and dispatch.

There has always been something regal and high class about the strawberry. Cardinal Wolsey is often named as the first to serve wild strawberries with cream, at a banquet in 1509. It is, however, the All England Lawn Tennis and Croquet Club's tournament in SW19 that is most associated with the fruit. The strawberries eaten at Wimbledon are the Elsanta variety, and are picked daily from Hugh Lowe Farms in Mereworth, Kent. As the oft-repeated quote goes, 'Doubtless God could have made a better berry, but doubtless God never did.' One imagines the team who hull the 27,000 kilos eaten at the Championships each year wish the Almighty had made a strawberry that popped off the plant like a raspberry.

If you want to eat freshly picked strawberries, you can either grow your own, which after some effort might give you enough for a bowlful, or you can pay to take advantage of other people's efforts and find a pick-your-own farm. The latter is a great day out, as well as being cheap and healthy, and you're rewarded with as much fruit as you can eat. However you get your strawberries, I think they're best enjoyed slightly macerated and at room temperature. Give them at least the first set to warm up, only breaking out the cream when the umpire calls, 'New balls please'.

*See also* CORBRIDGE, NORTHUMBERLAND (p. 207); EGTON BRIDGE, NORTH YORKSHIRE (p. 243); HAMPRESTON, DORSET (p. 14); HONITON, DEVON (p. 17); INVERGOWRIE, PERTH & KINROSS (p. 180); LYTH AND WINSTER VALLEYS, CUMBRIA (p. 117); NORTHIAM, EAST SUSSEX (p. 492); WALMERSLEY, GREATER MANCHESTER (p. 137).

# 10 | East Anglia

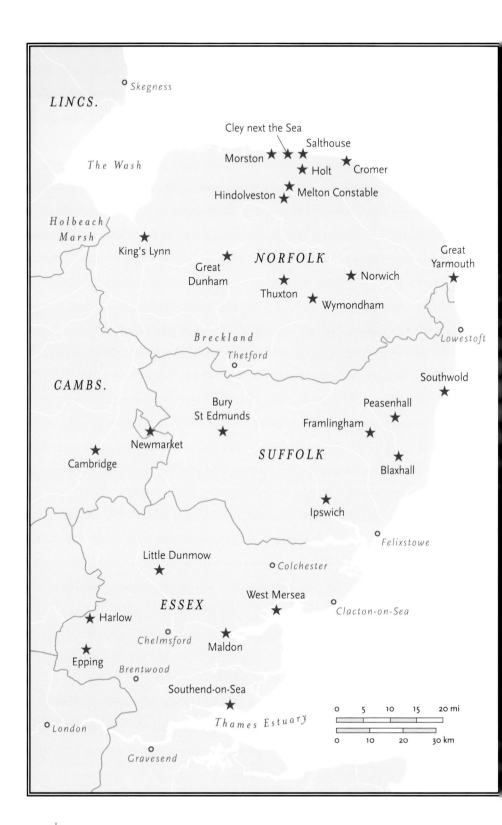

LINCS.

○ *Skegness*

*The Wash*

Cley next the Sea
★ ★ ★ Salthouse
Morston ★ ★
★ Holt ★ Cromer
★ Hindolveston ★ Melton Constable

*Holbeach/*
*Marsh*

★ King's Lynn

NORFOLK

★ Great
Dunham

★ Thuxton
★ Norwich

Great
Yarmouth
★

★ Wymondham

*Breckland*

*Thetford*
○

○ *Lowestoft*

CAMBS.

Southwold
★

Bury
St Edmunds
★

Peasenhall
★

Framlingham ★

SUFFOLK

★ Newmarket

★ Cambridge

★ Blaxhall

★ Ipswich

○ *Felixstowe*

★ Little Dunmow

○ *Colchester*

ESSEX

West Mersea
★

○ *Clacton-on-Sea*

★ Harlow
*Chelmsford*
★ Maldon

★ Epping
*Brentwood*
○

Southend-on-Sea
★

○ *London*

*Thames Estuary*

○ *Gravesend*

| 0 | 5 | 10 | 15 | 20 mi |
| 0 | 10 | 20 | | 30 km |

## Game from the Wild Meat Company

When the Framlingham butcher's shop that Paul Denny was working at closed in 2000 (the last to do so in the town, which once boasted seven), he got together with local farmer Robert Gooch to form the Wild Meat Company. The aim, as they put it, was to take 'the muck and mystery out of buying, preparing and eating game'. Robert handles the marketing and admin, and Paul the production and sourcing. They also teach wild-meat preparation classes as part of the Food Safaris hosted at the Anchor pub in Walberswick.

All the game – pheasant, duck, partridge, rabbit and anything else it's legal to shoot and eat – comes from their own or neighbouring farms and estates, and the area is also on the flight path of many migratory birds, such as wild duck in the autumn and the much-prized woodcock later in winter. The woodcock is, in Robert's eyes, the finest of all game birds. This exclusivity and taste comes at a price – £8.50 for a carcass the size of a poussin – but the taste is incomparable.

'Fifty per cent of what we do is exported; nationally about 70 per cent of all game is exported. We're now beginning to appreciate game, but it's taken some time,' says Robert. If you want to get into game, Robert recommends starting with the white meats first, which means partridge and rabbit. 'Because it's wild it's got very little natural fat, so it's best to use cooking methods that add fat. You don't want to grill game – it's best to pan-fry, casserole or roast it with additional fat.' Suffolk rabbit pie is a particularly good choice as it's cheap, easy to make and, if you feel like cheating, you can buy the meat ready diced. And if making a pie seems like too much effort, Robert and Paul also sell Blaxhall ballotines, named after the nearby town. A ballotine is a boned-out bird that has been stuffed, often with another smaller bird. The chief benefit is you get no bones – as well as no muck or mystery.

*See also* ACOMB, NORTHUMBERLAND (p. 195); BROMPTON-ON-SWALE, NORTH YORKSHIRE (p. 236); CHIPPENHAM, WILTSHIRE (p. 9); FRILSHAM, BERKSHIRE (p. 479); KENDAL, CUMBRIA (p. 114).

## Culinary gadgets and gizmos from Infusions

For sixteen years, John Jackaman was a chef. Then one day he decided he had had enough of working fourteen-hour days, and wanted to do something new. With a network of contacts and an in-depth knowledge of fellow chefs' buying habits, the wholesale supply business beckoned, and Infusions was born. 'Dry goods offered the longest shelf life, and so we borrowed a van and rented a space and got on with it,' explains John.

Infusions started out selling high-value items such as single-estate

A tin of strawberry caviar and some of the scientific-looking kit that created it

balsamic vinegar, bonito (dried Japanese fish) flakes and whole white winter truffles. Soon it dawned on John that only a few chefs in fine-dining restaurants buy these items with any regularity, and so he expanded the range to include the items that feature in nearly every kitchen: rice, pasta, oils, herbs, stocks, pulses and the like. So far, so well-stocked catering supplier. However, John stocks one product line that no one else in the country does: the Texturas range, conceived by internationally renowned (and now semi-retired) super-chef Ferran Adrià. His restaurant, El Bulli, was undeniably the most famous in the world. His cooking and approach to food is revered by practically every top chef in the UK, and he has attained a demigod-like reputation. He is Yoda to Heston Blumenthal's Obi-Wan Kenobi.

Like many a famous chef, Ferran brought out a range of products available to us mere mortals. Launched in 2007, the Texturas range is a set of powders with exotic names such as Algin, Gluco, Xantana, Agar and Lecite. As John explains, all of them are derived from natural sources such as fruit, fungi, seaweed, even bacteria, and have been used in the food industry for years as stabilisers, emulsifiers and flavour enhancers. All Ferran did was bring them into the realm of fine dining and use them in a different, more creative way.

Spherification is one of the more alchemical processes. This uses a combination of the powders to form a skin, turning liquids and purées into spheres, and allowing you to make foods such as strawberry caviar. The technique involves mixing the purée with water, Citras and Algin, then placing it in a syringe and releasing droplets into a bowl containing calcium, which starts the skin-forming reaction. In a couple of seconds you're left with small, soft balls of strawberry purée that look to all intents and purposes like red caviar, ready to be used in a host of different ways.

John and the team regularly take part in exhibitions and events with catering colleges. For him, it's not only enjoyable, but also a way of reaching the customers of tomorrow. 'We try to get the students to think creatively, as this is the environment where they can try stuff out, think out of the box and ask questions,' he explains. But as John says, 'Looked at in the right spirit and treated as a bit of fun, all these things are fantastic. If you take them too seriously, it's not going to revolutionise what you're doing in the kitchen, and it should never get away from great, solid, honest cookery.'

## *Art of Meat*

Butcher Jon West trained as a microbiologist, but now spends his days working with slightly bigger fauna, namely pigs, cows and sheep. Jon established Art of Meat in 2005 after quitting the lab, but when he took over the small shop at the edge of town it wasn't doing that well. His business model was a simple one: the meat should be locally sourced if possible, free-range if possible and the best quality no matter what. That, coupled with high levels of service, meant that within a year he had doubled the turnover.

'We're purely retail. Almost every other butcher has a wholesale side to their business, which can mean having two grades of meat in the shop,' says Jon, and a glance at the display counter reveals the wealth of products he and his team have developed for hungry customers. Worth noting is his porchetta – the stuffed pork belly popular in Italy – as well as feather-blade steak, so called because it has a ridge of fat down the centre that fans out into the meat and melts during cooking. It's from the front of the cow, just behind the shoulder, and is full of flavour, eats as well as the expensive steak cuts, and yet is a third of the cost of sirloin.

A joint of pork from Art of Meat

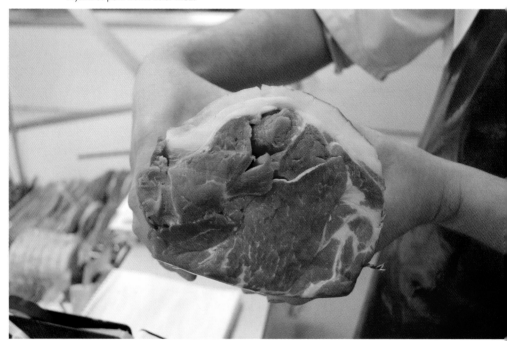

However, nowhere is Jon's attention to detail and quality more evident than in his sausages. The great Prussian statesman Otto von Bismarck may have said, 'People who love sausage and people who believe in justice should never watch either of them being made,' but watching Jon make sausages is fascinating. His pork comes from Dingley Dell Pork in Woodbridge, Suffolk, and is minced in small batches before being mixed with seasonings made from scratch in the shop. Jon even grinds the peppercorns fresh for each batch. One of his – and subsequently now my – favourites is the Italian Stallion, which follows an old recipe given to him by his Auntie Nelda, from Monte Cassino. It has a high meat content within a natural hog-skin casing and is flavoured simply with fennel seeds, salt, sugar, white pepper and a little bit of chilli. The cuts of pork go through the mincer twice, the large bore plate on the front giving the mince a chunky look. The seasoning is added and mixed by hand before being squeezed into the casing.

His Hobson's Choice sausage (named after the famous Cambridge ostler Thomas Hobson) won favour with *Guardian* food writer and broadcaster Matthew Fort when he asked people to write in with examples of great sausages. He described it thus: 'Light texture. Slightly crumbly. Gentle flavour deceptive because it lingers on and on.' High praise indeed.

*See also* BROMYARD, HEREFORDSHIRE (p. 283); CONWY, CONWY (p. 60); FORRES, MORAY (p. 173); LOUTH, LINCOLNSHIRE (p. 336); MARYLEBONE, WESTMINSTER (p. 387); MELTON CONSTABLE, NORFOLK (p. 447); NANTWICH, CHESHIRE (p. 125); WOODHALL SPA, LINCOLNSHIRE (p. 364); YORK, NORTH YORKSHIRE (p. 271).

CAMBRIDGE, CAMBRIDGESHIRE
## Cambridge burnt cream

Many assume this dish is just an English version of crème brûlée, perhaps because the name is a literal translation of the French dish. However, they are mistaken. In England, this sugar-topped custard dish is synonymous with Trinity College Cambridge – founded in 1546 by Henry VIII, a man who knew a thing or two about dining – and the dish still appears regularly on its menus, sometimes with the college crest branded on to the burnt sugar.

Florence White, in her *Good Things in England* (1932), tells us that the recipe came from a country house in Aberdeenshire, and was offered to the

Trinity kitchens around 1849 by an undergraduate and promptly rejected. Thirty years passed and the lowly undergraduate became a fellow, presented the dish again and, surprise surprise, it was speedily taken up, becoming popular in May week, which is held in June. You've got to love the sheer oddness of Oxbridge academia.

But the dish – often called by its French name – was being served in England long before then. As for its origins, well, there is the predictable story that our old friend 'an absent-minded cook' burnt some custard and lo! the dish was created (a similar story explains the creation of Bakewell puddings; *see* p. 277). Simon Hopkinson, in *Roast Chicken and Other Stories* (2007), says that the custard in a perfect Cambridge burnt cream should be made with very little sugar, rather unlike a crème brûlée, because the sweetness as well as the crunchy caramel flavour comes from a thicker topping of burnt sugar. An English topping, then, will require a good wallop with the spoon and should be as brittle as glass, while the French version can be broken with your breath.

Structurally, the dish hasn't changed that much in 400 years, although various flavourings have come and gone. The recipe in T. Williams's 1717 *The Accomplished Housekeeper, and Universal Cook* (1717) suggests adding a little lemon peel and a spoonful of orange-flower water. The recipe ends:

> When it is cold, sift a quarter of a pound of sugar all over it, and brown it with a hot salamander [a piece of metal you get red hot in a fire before holding over what you want to grill], till it looks like a glass plate put over your cream.
>
> *See also* HOW RECIPES BEGIN (p. 496).

## CLEY NEXT THE SEA, NORFOLK
# A *Cley smokie*

East Anglia's best-known contributions to smoked fish are the red herring and the Yarmouth bloater, and both of these are available at the smokehouse in Cley next the Sea (the *e* in Cley is pronounced as an *i*, to rhyme with *fry*) on the North Norfolk coast. Alongside them, however, is a less-well-known dish, the Cley smokie. It's similar to an Arbroath smokie, in that it's a hot smoked haddock, but as it isn't produced in a barrel as they are (*see* p. 143), the chaps at the smokehouse opted to christen it the Cley smokie. Most

The smokehouse in Cley next the Sea

smoked haddock in supermarkets is painted with a smokey, yellow paint, and if it isn't dyed, it's always sold off the bone and cold-smoked, so it needs to be cooked before you can eat it. Here, the fish are sold with only the head and guts removed, and are hot-smoked for about an hour on each side using oak chips.

Herring has been smoked for many years in this country, and it's amazing how many different techniques have built up. There is the bloater, smoked with guts and all; the red herring, which is salted and smoked much harder; the kipper, where the fish is split lengthways, gutted and brined before being cold-smoked over oak to give a succulent and delicate flavour; not to mention buckling, which is a hot-smoked whole herring, guts and head removed.

The benefits of the Cley smokie, and indeed of buckling, is that it's ready to scoff upon leaving the shop. 'We offer this for people who are camping or who are on holiday and don't have anywhere to cook,' says Phil in the shop. So inspired perhaps by the goings on in Arbroath, the smokery in Cley next the Sea has invented a new dish to call its own.

*See also* ARBROATH, ANGUS (p. 143); FINDON, ABERDEENSHIRE (p. 169); GREAT YARMOUTH, NORFOLK (p. 433); HAMBRIDGE, SOMERSET (p. 13); NIDDERDALE, NORTH YORKSHIRE (p. 251); SEAHOUSES, NORTHUMBERLAND (p. 224); WHITBY, NORTH YORKSHIRE (p. 268).

## CROMER, NORFOLK
*Cromer crabs*

Cromer crabs are smaller than other crabs caught around the UK (notwithstanding Cumbria), with a minimum shell size of 115 mm. They are said to have a larger portion of the much-prized white meat, which some say is also sweeter and more tender than that of other crabs. Various reasons have been put forward for this, from the age of the crabs when captured, to a chalk shelf just off the Cromer coast, which may influence their diet.

There are around a dozen boats working out of the town nowadays, and John Lee skippers one of them, hunting for lobster and crab using the traditional pots. Historically, crabbing was a summer occupation, with herring fished in the autumn and cod in the winter. Those trades have somewhat diminished, and with no closed season on crab, fishermen these days tend to concentrate their efforts there.

Once ashore, the crabs are washed, checked over and then boiled for twenty-five minutes. They are then 'dressed': the carapace is removed, the gills – also known as dead man's fingers – taken out, and the meat extracted. Crabs very kindly provide a receptacle for their meat in the form of their own shell, and the moist brown meat is placed either side of the flaky white meat down the centre. John's crabs are available in East Anglia and London via Farm, Park and Wild, an online delivery firm set up by businessman Kent Laws to deliver fresh produce direct from small North Norfolk producers direct to your door.

There are moves afoot to seek protection for Cromer crabs, so that in order to earn the name they must be caught off the coast and processed in Cromer. Some supermarkets stock crabs that have been caught way out in the Atlantic, then frozen and brought back to Cromer for processing, so double-check what you're actually buying. Then you can really enjoy the crab, knowing it's the real thing. I like it with a squeeze of lemon, a blob of mayonnaise and some brown bread, and after I've retrieved every last morsel, and with fingers glistening with oil, I occasionally hold the empty shell to my ear, close my eyes and think of the sea.

*See also* BUCKIE, MORAY (p. 149); CHINATOWN, WESTMINSTER (p. 374); LITTLE HAVEN, PEMBROKESHIRE (p. 70); MORECAMBE BAY, LANCASHIRE (p. 121); SALTHOUSE, NORFOLK (p. 454).

# *The mystery of the Epping sausage*

There is much mystery surrounding the Epping sausage, first and foremost of which is what form it should take: should it be skinless or not? *The Cook and Housewife's Manual* (1827) by Christian Isobel Johnstone opts for skinless, adding beef suet, seasoning, nutmeg and sage to minced pork – bizarrely she also adds some thin bacon rind. However, *The Housekeeper's Guide* (1838) by Esther Copley states that 'Epping sausages are made entirely of lean pork and beef suet, or of fat and lean pork together; the same proportion holds good, two-thirds lean, and one third fat . . . They are always tied in skins.'

In the nineteenth century, Epping was in the countryside, despite being only twenty miles from London. James Greenwood, in *Odd People in Odd Places* (1883), wrote:

> The simple-minded country people dwelling in that rural district knew nothing of the villanous devices of the unscrupulous skin-stuffers of the slums of London. Their pigs were pastured in the leafy glades of the great forest near at hand, and the pork they yielded was of the luscious beech-nut flavour so much admired by the consumer.

However, the charlatans and fakers soon moved in, and impostor sausages flooded the market. Over time the Epping sausage became a byword for cheap and nasty. In the novel *Jacob Faithful* (1838) by sea-story pioneer Frederick Marryat, the hero describes life on a boat thus:

> Indeed, I took all my meals *al fresco*, and unless the nights were intensely cold, slept on deck, in the capacious dog kennel, which had once been tenanted by the large mastiff, but he had been dead some years, was thrown overboard, and, in all probability, had been converted into Epping sausages.

In the late nineteenth century, it seems, the poor sausage had a reputation not wholly unlike today's mystery kebab meat.

Not all producers employed these unscrupulous methods, however. Church's Butchers, in Epping, has been making Epping sausages since 1888, using a recipe from that time. You can still buy them there today. Church's is an old-fashioned retail butcher's shop, which although rebuilt in the 1950s, has occupied the same site since its inception. Paul Parker and David Church (fourth generation) can be found behind the counter. 'We use a mix of belly and shoulder, seasoned with sage, and salt and pepper,' says Paul, 'and the meat we put through the course plate of a mincer twice.' It's similar, then, to a Lincolnshire sausage, particularly as Paul sides with Esther Copley and encases them in natural hog skins. Church's sells 200 to 300 lbs a week, and if you do want to try some, Paul advises patience: 'It's a sausage that gets better as it's kept. If you keep it for three or four days, the sage will flavour the meat much more.'

*See also* SAUSAGES (p. 122).

*See also* SAUSAGES (p. 122).

## FRAMLINGHAM, SUFFOLK
# English wine from Shawsgate Vineyard

If you fancy recreating scenes from the wine-soaked 2004 film *Sideways* but can't afford the trip to California's Santa Ynez Valley, you could do worse than visit some of the 450 or so wineries and vineyards now found in the UK. Nevertheless, British wine remains a niche product and interest – and it wasn't all that long ago that it was little more than a joke to most oenophiles. There is scant evidence of wine-making here prior to the Roman conquest, and 1,000 years later the Domesday Book records around forty vineyards in southern England. Needless to say, wine was drunk by the nobility or by monastic orders, and by the time Henry VIII set about dissolving the latter and increasing the former, there were around 140 large vineyards in England and Wales. British viticulture then declined, probably because it was easier to import cheaper wine from the Continent. The wealthy still drank wine; it was just made elsewhere. The rise of the merchant classes meant London became a great centre for the importing, blending and cellaring of wine. A handful of landowning gentleman enthusiasts and hobbyists grew vines on their estates, but commercial viticulture in Britain was all but dead.

The revival in growing vines in the UK began in the late 1940s and was down to three men: Ray Barrington Brock, George Ordish and Edward Hyams. They came at the subject from an enthusiast's angle, but were armed with science and all three wrote or published books on the subject, Hyams penning *The Grape Vine in England* (1949) and *Vineyards in England*

(1953), Ordish writing *Wine Growing in England* (1953), and Brock the aptly named *Outdoor Grapes in Cold Climates* (1949).

Perhaps inspired by both their words and their research, Major-General Sir Guy Salisbury-Jones, freshly retired from a distinguished career and looking for something to do, planted vines at Hambledon in Hampshire in 1952 and by 1955 the first commercially produced English wine – a dry white – went on sale. Things grew slowly, and by the late 1970s there was a fledgling industry of sorts.

Today English wines are more expensive than wine from Europe or the New World; however, one area in which they can compete and add extra value is tourism. Like breweries and distilleries, many wineries are opening their doors and gates and letting people see what's going on.

One such example is Shawsgate in Suffolk, which grows a mix of red and white grapes. The white grape varieties include Bacchus (which features in many English wines), Reichensteiner, Seyval Blanc, Muller Thurgau and Schonburger, and some of the vines date back to the early 1970s, when the vineyard was set up. As for reds, there are three plots of Acolon and Rondo, the latter, hybridised in 1964, is particularly frost-resistant. This is a key attribute for the changing British weather, as we're not known for our sun-kissed summers.

Grapes for wine-making are normally round and the eating variety oval – not that these ladybirds mind

The grapes are picked by hand in the early autumn, when the sun is on the wane but still strong enough to warm your back. The pickers come from a broad cross-section of society, including locals, mature ladies, travellers and seasonal workers. There is no entrance fee to tour the vineyard, and the whole site is licensed, so you can bring a picnic, buy a bottle and sit between the vines, just like in *Sideways*.

FRAMLINGHAM, SUFFOLK
## Food Safari

When Polly and Tim Robinson decided they had had enough of living in London with their two small children, they returned to Tim's native Suffolk. They had been regular patrons of farmers' markets, and had developed an eye for quality. This got Polly thinking, and in March 2009 the first Food Safari event happened. 'I wanted to facilitate a way of going behind the scenes and meeting the people you might know from a farmers' market,' she says.

The company organises day trips to visit local producers, and participants not only gain new skills, but also reach a better understanding of the knowledge and dedication of those who produce our food. The courses range from a day spent foraging or fishing, to one spent working with game or making cheese. The game course is run with the Wild Meat Company (*see* p. 419), who provide the raw materials, and the butchering and cooking takes place in the kitchens of the Anchor Pub in Walberswick. The cheese course is hosted by Katharine and Jason Salisbury of Suffolk Farmhouse Cheese, and you can also take a tour of Pinney's smokehouse in nearby Orford. One of the most popular days out is visiting pig farmer Alastair Butler from Blythburgh Free Range Pork. Everyone assembles at the pub for a coffee and bacon sandwich, before heading off for a tour of the pigs. Then it's back to the pub with local butcher Ray Kent and a pig carcass, which Ray breaks up, explaining each and every cut. 'One lady said to me when she got home she set about finding her nearest independent butcher because now she had the confidence to go in and ask for things rather than just picking up a packet.' The story is by no means unique.

I would love to see Polly's efforts rolled out around the country. Farmers, although often exceptionally good at what they do, aren't always great at communicating with their customers. Working with someone like Polly allows them to get their message out, to connect with the people who buy their produce and explain why the food looks, costs or tastes the way it does. And the benefits for us as customers are enormous. In supermarkets, it seems, many of us would rather just fling a packet in a trolley than have a chat with the people behind the counters, where the loose items might even be cheaper. It's as though the skill of talking to shopkeepers is dying out, but luckily Food Safari is doing its bit to stop the rot. It is part adventure, then, but also part therapy session.

GREAT DUNHAM, NORFOLK

## *Jam from Essence Foods*

The British go quite doolally about jam; we're obsessed with the science of it. Pectin amounts, fruit content, fructose levels, optimum temperatures and the ominous setting point are all fretted over, often at the expense of the taste. Saucers are repeatedly daubed with a teaspoon of the boiling, seething, blood-red mass – 'Is it set? Is it set?' And the shameful product of failure? Runny jam. The brazen may try to pass it off as Continental and compote-style, but they will meet with short shrift. No, sir: set solid, high-sugar jam is what we British breakfasted on before setting out to forge an empire.

Although the technique of preserving fruits in liquids or reducing them to a solid paste has been with us for centuries, what we now think of as jam is a relatively new process, developed via increased scientific understanding. Lots of good-quality sugar, the key ingredient in jam-making, remained an expensive luxury for many people. But with sugar eventually becoming cheaper in the mid nineteenth century, jam became available even to those at the bottom of the social pile. In the 1880s, according to J. C. Drummond in his book *The Englishman's Food* (1939), in some families two out of three meals were bread and jam. This sounds like a recipe for ill health, but in 2004 a fifteen-year-old called Craig Flatman who had eaten nothing but jam sandwiches for eleven years underwent tests and amazingly was pronounced fit and healthy.

Someone else who loves bread and jam is Sarah Savage of Essence Foods, who makes jams, pickles and chutneys in a small barn conversion in Great Dunham, Norfolk. Available via mail order, her pots of preserves are also found in Waitrose's East Anglian stores. Realising that there is plenty of mass-produced jam out there, Sarah offers something different. Her jams have a high fruit content that she often complements with other flavours. So a classic strawberry jam is paired with Norfolk lavender from the gardens at nearby Heacham. Lavender is a tricky flavouring to pull off in food, but the amount is perfectly judged: a mere high floral kiss as a counterpoint to the richness of the fruit. 'Most jams are so sweet you can't taste the actual fruit,' she says. What's more, her jams are much runnier than most, glistening and slowly sliding off the knife on to your toast. 'People have very set ideas about how set their jam should be. The French tolerate a soft-set jam much better than we do,' says Sarah.

But perhaps nothing could be more English than her strawberry and rose flavour, which contains whole strawberries. A spoon of this in your mouth transports you to a sunlit-dappled cottage garden on a late summer's afternoon.

*See also* DUNDEE, ANGUS (p. 163); OXFORD, OXFORDSHIRE (p. 350); WATLINGTON, OXFORDSHIRE (p. 361).

GREAT YARMOUTH, NORFOLK
## *Rock from Docwra's*

A stick of rock is an integral part of the classic British seaside experience, along with donkeys, seagulls, fried food and a family argument. With its bright colours and high-sugar hit, it's been a firm favourite since the glory days of the great seaside towns Blackpool, Skegness and Great Yarmouth in the 1800s. I loved rock when I was young. I particularly liked the little rectangle of paper in the wrapping that carried a picture of what the resort's view was meant to be like – always sunny, always happy and often in marked contrast to the actual vista.

Stephen Docwra's family have been confectioners and chocolatiers in Great Yarmouth since 1896. Their shop opened in 1922, and when their factory closed in 1985, they moved production into the shop. They now invite the public to watch the rock-making process, particularly the way in which they put the letters in. 'The French put designs in sweets long before we did, flowers and such, but for some reason they never did letters,' says Stephen. Docwra's rock is made in small batches in an open-air pan. The sugar, water and glucose syrup is first heated to 300°C, at which temperature it is clear, and similar to the mix that makes boiled sweets, and then it's tipped out, cooled and machine-aerated, which turns it cloudy white. The various colours can then be added to batches. You get a real sense of history as you watch, as this is the same method that Stephen's grandfather used.

When the main factory closed, the firm also began making handmade chocolates, in part because they are popular all year round, while rock has a seasonal appeal. The company also takes on promotional work: 'We once did a job for the Electoral Commission who wanted fifty thousand three-inch sticks with "vote" running through the middle,' says Stephen, 'only due to a mix-up we got the letters the wrong way round and it said "veto" instead!' He's able to see the funny side now.

The great seaside towns – places like Blackpool, Skegness and Southend – grew up to cater for the working masses. Companies would charter whole trains or a fleet of buses to take their workforce on an annual (and perhaps only) day out. The seaside provided a bracing breath of fresh air and, coupled with dancing, music halls, promenading, donkey rides, fairs and tasty fried or sugary foods, ensured the good times rolled. Blackpool, for example, catered for the textile workers of Lancashire, cockneys flocked to Southend, while Glaswegians went 'doon the watter' to the Firth of Forth. In 1938 the Holiday with Pay Act came into force, giving all workers paid annual leave.

Nowadays our towns and cities are our playgrounds, we have more leisure time than previous generations, and most people, when they do head to the coast, would rather find an unspoilt rural beach than the noise and bustle of these fading Victorian and Edwardian resorts. Me, though, I love the noisy arcades, the dive-bombing seagulls, the salty chips and the sweet stick of rock, an edible souvenir of the British seaside.

*See also* EVENWOOD, COUNTY DURHAM (p. 210); STENHOUSEMUIR, FALKIRK (p. 189).

## GREAT YARMOUTH, NORFOLK
### *Yarmouth bloater*

Great Yarmouth rose to prominence as a centre of herring fishing in the nineteenth century. The fish are in prime condition as they pass the rump of East Anglia, on their way to warmer waters from Scotland. Daniel Defoe visited Yarmouth in 1722, where locals boasted they had cured 40,000 barrels of herring in one season, and by 1880 there were more than sixty curing houses in the town. The processing of the landed fish was done by fishergirls, who came predominantly from Scotland and who followed the fish down the coast. They could gut up to thirty herrings a minute; it takes me that long to get the fish out of the fridge. The industry in the town reached a high point in 1907, when 80 million herrings were landed.

# British Pubs

The uniquely British institution that is the pub grew out of three very different drinking premises: inns, taverns and alehouses. An inn was defined by law as a place for the service of travellers, and the innkeeper had obligations to receive guests and provide for their needs. A tavern, meanwhile (the name coming from the Latin *taberna*, meaning shed or workshop), was a specialist establishment for the sale of wine, often something of an expensive luxury and so taverns were mainly found in London or other large cities. Then there were alehouses, which vastly outnumbered the other two types of establishment and were where the common man supped his ale, which had often been brewed on the premises. Gradually, the boundaries between all three of these blurred, and in the 1700s the term 'public house', from which 'pub' derives, came into common use, partly as a catch-all for all three.

In 1948 journalist Maurice Gorham wrote, 'Progress, reconstruction, town planning, war, all have one thing in common: pubs go down before them like poppies under the scythe,' and today's publicans would no doubt add the smoking ban, alcohol duty and supermarkets selling discounted booze to that list. Figures from the British Pub and Beer Association in 2010 revealed that pubs were closing at a rate of thirty-nine a week, down on the fifty-two that were closing each week in the first half of 2009, but nonetheless quite a statistic. One landlord summed up the situation in a programme called *Last Orders*, broadcast on Radio 4 in 2010: 'Things do change, even pubs have to move wit' times. You've to fit your trade about what people want; it's OK while they keep changing, the sad thing will be when they're not there to change.'

My liver and I have had the privilege of visiting many of the remaining pubs around the UK, confirming my belief that in an age of clone-town Britain, where all the high streets and shopping centres resemble each other, our pubs are the last places that preserve any sense of place and social history. Nothing exemplifies this more than the Crown Inn in Hartest, Norfolk. Inside, it's warm and spacious with thick oak beams running the length of the ceiling. The interior was sympathetically remodelled and modernised in 2003, and the pub is now run by Greene King. Every city, town and village in Britain has a war memorial, but the Crown Inn contains a much more poignant memorial to those who didn't return, a piece of real history. At the outbreak of the First World War those men from the village who had been called up must have had one last night in the pub. Back then, this would have been farming country, a rural backwater, and it's likely that most of those young men hadn't seen a great deal of the world. At some point, one of them must have had an idea. Each man took a coin from his pocket and nailed it on the large black wooden ceiling beam near the fireplace, the intention being that on their return from the war, the men would use the coin to purchase their first pint. A large horseshoe was nailed next to this row of florins and ha'pennies for good luck. Were the men of Hartest excited and full of bravado, relishing the chance to take a pop at the Hun? Or were they absolutely terrified and wanted to mark the occasion somehow? Did they say a prayer, or make solemn oaths and promises? Twenty-five coins are still nailed to that beam, blackened now with age and 100 years of soot from the fire. This is just one example of the history of this nation being written in, and in this case literally nailed to, the walls and ceilings of our pubs. A memento, and a reminder of something that is worth protecting.

*See also* ASTLEY, WARWICKSHIRE (p. 276); HENLEY-ON-THAMES, OXFORDSHIRE (p. 327); KNIGHTWICK, WORCESTERSHIRE (p. 299); LINCOLN, LINCOLNSHIRE (p. 335); WHITSTABLE, KENT (p. 500).

Great Yarmouth lends its name to the Yarmouth bloater. Made from plump herrings, the bloater part of the name comes from the fact that the fish is salted and smoked with the guts in, giving the finished product a certain bloated look. The process is more refined and delicate than the one employed to produce red herring, which are salted and smoked much harder, and were originally sent – unrefrigerated, naturally – to the plantations as food for slaves.

Bloaters were also transported – often inland on a slow-moving, horse-drawn carriage – and yet they have always been salted and smoked for taste rather than shelf life. They are at their best eaten fresh from the smokery, or at least within twenty-four hours. Already cooked by the smoking process, once popped under the grill they reheat quickly, and the fillets are easily removed from the spine, leaving you with a backbone and head straight out of a Tom and Jerry cartoon.

Bloaters can also be made into a fish paste, popular in the high teas of times past, although rather out of favour now. It's all a far cry from the glory days of the bloater, at its height in Victorian times, when the fish no doubt seemed inexhaustible, and the railway transported the product to customers all over the country. So ubiquitous was herring in all its forms that various slang names cropped up to describe it, such as a 'two-eyed steak' or, my personal favourite, a 'Yarmouth capon'.

*See also* ARBROATH, ANGUS (p. 143); CLEY NEXT THE SEA, NORFOLK (p. 424); FINDON, ABERDEENSHIRE (p. 169); HAMBRIDGE, SOMERSET (p. 13); NIDDERDALE, NORTH YORKSHIRE (p. 251); SEAHOUSES, NORTHUMBERLAND (p. 224); WHITBY, NORTH YORKSHIRE (p. 268).

## HARLOW, ESSEX
### Label Anglaise chicken

Consider the chicken dish on a menu in a mediocre restaurant: the safe bet for the unadventurous, normally one step up from the vegetarian option in cost and taste. 'Tastes like chicken' is something people say when they eat something bland, which is a shame because the right bird in the right hands can be a fantastic flavour-filled explosion of taste and texture.

The trick is to pay attention to the breed, age and lifestyle of the poultry on the plate. In the past, British restaurateurs raved about *poulets de Bresse*, the French birds thought to be the best in the world. It was only a matter of time, however, before someone took them on, and Chris Fredericks was the man for the job. He used to be a turkey farmer, and had the opportunity to visit Brittany with a trade organisation. Having seen the different production techniques and ethos, he decided to bring what he had learned back to the UK. Label Anglaise was launched in the late 1990s, aiming itself squarely at quality restaurants and consumers looking for birds that tasted of something.

'We realised that while many of the UK's chicken farms were using mass-production techniques, a higher proportion of French poultry was being raised with higher welfare standards using better breeds.' So in 1998 Chris imported some chicks and tried to grow a better chicken. The birds are Cornish Reds, first developed in the nineteenth century and not rare by any means, although his are bred especially for him at a secret location somewhere in Europe. What Chris adds to this bird is time, space and care. You can even see this in the dressed carcass, which has a more pronounced, higher breastbone reminiscent of Continental types, rather than the broad fat breasts we're used to seeing. 'We started doing 400 a week, and we're now doing a thousand.' Every week the chicks arrive from a specialist breeder and are then put in a brooding area for five weeks before being moved out to range. 'Our birds start the really nice part of their life at the age when a standard chicken would get its throat slit.'

I think you can tell a good chicken by what's in the tray after you've cooked it: if it's swimming in fat and those stringy grey snotty bits, it's been pumped full of rubbish. If, however, there is just a thin coating of fat and one lovely bronzed bird, you're on to a winner. As for the flavour, Chris has found that people need to eat it a few times to gain a full appreciation. 'People don't just open one bottle of decent wine and become a convert. It takes time to pick up the subtlety.'

*See also* GOOSNARGH, LANCASHIRE (p. 106); HINDOLVESTON, NORFOLK (BELOW); KING'S NYMPTON, DEVON (p. 20); MAIDENHEAD, BERKSHIRE (p. 487); THUXTON, NORFOLK (p. 458).

## HINDOLVESTON, NORFOLK
### *Guinea fowl, duck and chicken*

Despite growing up on his family's farm, Jason Peart spent the first ten years of his working life as an electrician. 'When I first left school, my father had the common sense to tell me that farming seventy acres wasn't worth getting into. But once you get farming in your blood it's bloody difficult to get out.' So eventually he returned, and in 2002 took a big cut in wages for a hike in well-being.

These chickens are free-range in the truest sense of the word

Jason produces 200 chickens a week, sold with the gizzards in, as well as ducks and guinea fowl. The incubation and hatching is done by specialist breeders, the ducks and chickens from a firm in Dereham, and the guinea fowl from a breeder in France. Once the day-old chicks come to the farm, here they will stay until they leave in a shopping bag. Jason does all the slaughtering himself and processes the animals on the farm. They are stunned, bled and dipped in a hot water tank before going into a plucking machine. Doing all this himself on-site means he has total control over the process: 'Our birds are cleaner inside and have a cleaner finish because all the while I'm checking them.' This control also extends to the animal feed, for which he uses his own corn, grown on the farm.

Some of his ducks are allowed to grow to over twelve weeks old, whereas most producers stop at seven or eight. 'At seven or eight weeks you get a feather growth on them,' Jason says, 'and when they're in that feather growth you can't pluck them and make them presentable to sell because the skin tears.' However, once past twelve weeks they are pluckable again, and consequently a better-looking bird, which is perhaps why it was Jason's duck that Norfolk chef Galton Blackiston turned to in the first series of *The Great British Menu* in 2006.

The guinea fowl remains something of a specialist product, and Jason only sells about ten a week. I love guinea fowl. It's not as oily and rich as other game birds, but is better than chicken at taking more complex and richer flavours. Keith Floyd paired it with grapes, and it also goes well with rich Madeira sauces and mustards. Jason agrees with me: 'Given the choice I'd rather have a guinea fowl over anything else.'

See also GOOSNARGH, LANCASHIRE (p. 106); HARLOW, ESSEX (p. 436); KING'S NYMPTON, DEVON (p. 20); MAIDENHEAD, BERKSHIRE (p. 487); THUXTON, NORFOLK (p. 458).

## Flour from Letheringsett Water Mill

Standing four storeys high, the red-bricked Letheringsett Mill towers over the flat Norfolk skyline. It was built in 1802 as the principal mill for the surrounding area, as well as the adjoining Letheringsett estate. The current owner, Mike Thurlow, began an extensive restoration program in the 1980s, not only to return the mill to its former glory, but also to make it a viable business and start grinding flour again. 'At one time this mill would have employed two shifts of ten men, as well as the miller, and mill-wright,' says Mike. In the Doomsday Book 580 mills were listed in Norfolk, but by the nineteenth century this had dropped to around eighty, and now Letheringsett is the only water-powered mill in the county that is still producing flour.

Outside, the surface of the mill pond looks completely calm, as you would expect, the only movement on the surface being generated by a flotilla of ducks. But as Mike explains, 'There's enough power from the waterwheel to drive four stones, as well as all the other machinery.' At present, Mike has got one 150-year-old pair of British stones working and is also restoring a set of French burrs that are over 200 years old, as well as taking delivery of a brand-new modern set, made in Holland. This will help him to increase his output and expand; at the moment he's only just able to meet demand. Mike mills a range of flours, including wholewheat and spelt, and dispatches them to outlets all over Norfolk. He even has businesses as far away as Nottingham coming to collect. His flours are also available in local shops and by mail order.

When Mike fires up the machinery, the huge top millstone, which is as big as a café table, begins to turn – slowly at first, but eventually achieving the speed of an LP record. Each stone is cut with grooves running in opposite directions, which act like a pair of scissors: the grain gets trapped between the two and is cut more and more finely. Once dropped into the hole in the middle of the stone, the grain is pushed out over the edge as flour after about two minutes. It then falls down a shoot to be bagged up. Once ground, the flour feels like talc with sand in it – the 'sand' being the good bits. There is a fine balance between the coarse and the fine, and Mike can tell if it's right with what's known as his 'miller's golden thumb'.

Running alongside the commercial aspect of the business is Mike's education programme, and he's reserved an area upstairs where children can be taught about the process of flour production. Adults often need a refresher in the basics, too: 'One American lady came in once and picked up a bag and asked, "What do I do with this?"' he laughs. One suggestion might be to get a bread-maker: 'I've got one myself,' says Mike, 'and I use it every day. When they first came out we had every model in here so that we could test our flour in it.' Bread-making machines give us all the joy of freshly baked bread, and the 'chuck in, switch on, forget' convenience that fits in with our busy lives. I certainly recommend them, particularly as there are few things in the world to rival the smell of freshly baked bread when it's made with Mike's flour.

*See also* KIRTON IN LINDSEY, LINCOLNSHIRE (p. 329).

Grain ready for milling

# Suffolk Food Hall

Oliver Paul and his cousin Robert both have a family background in agri-business. Their predecessors used to own Paul's Malts, which once towered over the Ipswich docks. The boys were working in London at the time, Robert as an accountant and Oliver in sales and marketing. 'He deals with numbers and I do the fluffy stuff,' says Oliver. Home very much remained Suffolk, however, and they would come back for the weekend. 'It was always a little bit frustrating trying to go to farmers' markets around here. You'd know they would have great things on offer, but you could never be sure which Saturday it would be on. Also, while they'd be great for leading ingredients, you'd still have to visit a supermarket to top up on the other things.' With family farmland going untended, the boys decided to create a comprehensive alternative food-retail offering. 'This is where I think farm shops and independents have a real opportunity, to get more sophisticated and offer a full range, so that they are a real alternative to supermarkets.' This accounts for the reason it calls itself a food hall, rather than a farm shop.

Inside the Suffolk Food Hall you will find a range of concessions: fishmonger Crystal Waters – which also travels the region's towns selling fish from its specially adapted forty-foot bus – have a well-stocked counter; and there is also a deli, with cheese selected by London cheesemonger Hamish Johnson; an on-site butchery, led by Gerard King, who won the UK's Best On-Farm Butcher in 2010; as well as a restaurant led by head chef Andy Cole.

Oliver gives an example of the benefits of all these businesses coming and working together under one roof: 'The butcher has a problem getting rid of bones, and has to pay quite a lot to get them taken away by the bone man. Or he can pass them on to the chef, who has a stockpot on the go to produce a *jus*. Not only does this enrich the sauces in the restaurant dishes, but he makes enough to package in Kilner jars and sell back in the shop.' And that's just one of the many little relationships between the different sections.

The restaurant also serves as the venue for Kitchen Club evenings, where a topic or theme is demonstrated, and then dinner and drink served. Autumn saw a 'Nights Drawing In' evening, focusing on slow cooking and stews. 'They're very popular, and are something the supermarkets just can't do,' says Oliver.

The final aim of the Food Hall is to put the fun and joy back into food retail. 'Food shopping is probably the only shopping we don't enjoy; if you're buying clothes, or test-driving a new car, that's good fun. Food shopping should be the same,' says Oliver, reminding me of the old saying 'The French spend their money on food, the Italians on clothes and the British on their gardens.' Oliver and Robert are trying to change that, but if you need a little help making that transition there is also a garden centre next door – everything really is under one roof.

See also CANTERBURY, KENT (p. 469); COLSTON BASSETT, NOTTINGHAMSHIRE (p. 325); HOOK, HAMPSHIRE (p. 484); RUSHWICK, WORCESTERSHIRE (p. 309); STANNINGTON, NORTHUMBERLAND (p. 227); WELBECK, NOTTINGHAMSHIRE (p. 362).

## KING'S LYNN, NORFOLK
## Treacle tart

When J. K. Rowling's Harry Potter gets a whiff of the powerful love potion Amortentia, his nostrils fill with the scent of the thing he loves most in the world: treacle tart. Its warm, sweet faded tones of yellow, brown and cream are the colour of nostalgia; Nigel Slater calls it our national tart.

The word 'treacle' comes from the Greek *theriake*, which means 'an antidote to venom' and arose when medicines were mixed with something sweet to aid ingestion. It is a generic term for all types of syrup that are a by-product of sugar manufacture, and is made when raw sugar cane is crushed and boiled until it has thickened and crystallisation has taken place. These crystals go on to be refined as pure sugar, and the residue used to be discarded until Abram Lyle's firm – and specifically chemist Charles Eastick (who later left to form a rival syrup-making business) – found a way to refine it to give us treacle. Syrup from the first boiling contains about 65 per cent sucrose and was given the name golden syrup; syrup from later boilings is darker, and contains less sucrose. Nowadays in the UK when we say 'treacle' we usually mean the dark black stuff. Black treacle has a very strong taste and flavour, and has been used in a huge variety of food processes, including the Suffolk cure for bacon (*see* p. 452) as well as the classic treacle toffee.

Many modern recipes for treacle tart suggest that you only use golden syrup; however, if you're up for a challenge, a half and half mixture of black treacle and golden syrup always makes things a little more interesting. The everyday version of the dish starts with a standard blind-baked shortcrust case, into which is spooned a mix of stale breadcrumbs, treacle and lemon juice (the tart used to be a good way of using up any leftover crusts of bread). For high days and holidays, though, there is the Norfolk version, or Walpole treacle tart. It's said to have been invented at Houghton Hall, home of the Walpole family, whose most famous member was the first prime minister and 'Norfolk Squire', Robert Walpole. It has a more custardy, wobbly filling, made by adding eggs and cream to the obligatory treacle, and it often omits the latticework found on treacle tarts from other parts of the country.

Although an apple pie would have been familiar to any cook from the 1700s, not so treacle tart. It uses a modern, industrially developed ingredient, a product of Victorian industry, conquest and might. And so, to borrow the phrase from Lyle's tin, 'Out of the Strong Came Forth Sweetness'.

See also HOW RECIPES BEGIN (p. 496).

## LITTLE DUNMOW, ESSEX
### Dunmow Flitch Trials

Marriage is a great institution ('But who wants to live in an institution?' went Groucho Marx's witty rejoinder), the sanctity of which has been observed and rewarded in the Essex village of Little Dunmow since the twelfth century in the form of a trial. Think of it as a medieval version of the game show *Mr and Mrs*. Entrants to the competition must prove that they have not 'wished themselves unwed for a year and a day', and those who can prove their love and companionship under cross-examination win a flitch of bacon. The flitch (an entire side of a pig, including the front and back legs) is generously donated by the two butchers in the town. A court is formed, comprising a judge and a jury of six bachelors and six maidens from the surrounding area. Counsel is appointed, often real-life barristers who live in the region, one of whom represents the happily wedded claimants, and one for the prosecution, who represents the flitch of bacon. It is not a competition between the couples, however, and there is often more than one set of wedded winners. Each couple duly has their relationship cross-examined and taken apart by some of the finest legal minds in Essex. Through example they must impress on the court their devotion to each other, remembering, though, that they are under oath.

## East Anglian Parsnips

Unlike nearly everything else we consider British these days, the parsnip (along with samphire, venison and a handful of other foodstuffs) is actually a true native to these islands. Originally, it was little more than the small root of a plant considered a weed, but cultivation and development over the years led to its being seen as an inferior carrot. The two vegetables even used to share the same name: *pastinaca*, a word derived from a two-pronged garden fork. Parsnips went their separate way around the fourteenth century, becoming known in England as 'parsneps'. Their greatest attribute at the time was in delivering a sweet taste when sugar was exorbitantly expensive; the second greatest was that they could stand up to a frost.

Like carrots, parsnips were considered by some as aphrodisiacal, and Joseph Miller's *Botanicum Officinale* (1722) characterised them in this way: 'Parsneps are more used for Food than Medicine, being a pleasant nourishing Root, though somewhat windy, and thought to be Provokers to Venery' ('venery' meaning the pursuit of sexual gratification. You have to pity the poor, eating root veg because it's the only available, only to have everyone learned thinking they are at it like rabbits).

Carrots got a makeover and a bright new colour over the next 200 years, while parsnips remained little changed, if enlarged, and, as noted above, were thought of as a staple for the poor. Eventually even that role was taken over by the potato, but there remains something honest and salt-of-the-earth about the parsnip.

As with the carrot, the light soil of East Anglia suits the parsnip well, as it grows straight down into the earth. Rocks or heavy clay soil can inhibit growth or cause the root to divide.

It's mainly us Brits and a few other Northern European countries who enjoy parsnips today; according to Alan Davidson in *The Oxford Companion to Food* (1999), their use has all but died out in Southern Europe. In France they are more likely to be found in a trough than at a table, although a 2009 *Le Figaro* article listing the fifty coolest trends of that year included parsnips, stating that they were 'at the top of the hit-parade of forgotten vegetables, with a very subtle taste reminiscent of the artichoke'.

Chefs are apt to get creative with parsnips in the cooler months, and parsnip crisps have become popular as they are seen as healthy as well as tasty. They can take a bit of spice too, as well as making a good thick soup or adding an extra flavour to mashed potato. They can also take salty flavours such as bacon and Parmesan cheese, and can even be used to make wine. A more sophisticated alcoholic application, however, comes courtesy of Esther Medina Cuesta, bar manager at Roast restaurant in London, who makes a gin-based cocktail with apple juice and some parsnip purée, garnished with poppy seeds. For my money, though, the parsnip remains at its best when it's treated simply cored, chopped into wedges and roasted in lots of oil and butter.

See also PEA HARVEST (p. 332); BOSTON, LINCOLNSHIRE (p. 323); GOOLE, EAST YORKSHIRE (p. 248); NEWCHURCH, ISLE OF WIGHT (p. 491); OWMBY-BY-SPITAL, LINCOLNSHIRE (p. 349); QUEENSFERRY, FLINTSHIRE (p. 84).

The trials were originally organised by the Augustinian priory of Little Dunmow, and by the 1400s had become very popular, even being mentioned in Chaucer's *The Wife of Bath's Tale*. The first recorded winner of the flitch of bacon was one Richard Wright from Norwich in 1445, according to documents lodged in the British Museum originally from the priory. After the Dissolution of the Monasteries, the Lord of the Manor took over administration, and continued to stage the contest annually until 1832, when the Steward of Little Dunmow, George Wade, refused to grant the trials, regarding them as 'an idle custom bringing people of indifferent character into the neighbourhood'.

Victorian novelist William Harrison Ainsworth revived them in 1855, and now they take place every four years. In 2008 a couple from the USA were among the winners, and as they were unable to take their winnings home, they donated the flitch to the old people's home. Quite what other happy couples do when they've 'brought home the bacon' history doesn't relate, but one imagines breakfasts, lunches and dinners to be particularly fine under the happy couple's roof.

## MALDON, ESSEX
# Maldon Sea Salt

If there is one ingredient that runs through gastronomy like the background radiation from the Big Bang runs through the universe, it is salt. In Romania, salt mines have been found that date back to Neolithic times, around 6000 BC. Salt is the commonest and most readily available non-metallic mineral in the world, and its use enabled preservation, allowing people to store their food as well as move it around. Without salt there would be no cheese, no kippers, no bacon, and your chips wouldn't taste half as nice.

And so you might be surprised to hear that there are only four salt producers in the UK. One of the store-cupboard ingredients most consistently recommended by British chefs is our very own Maldon Sea Salt. The company is currently run by Steven Osborne, his family having taken over the business in 1922. At Maldon they take water from the middle of the River Blackwater, which due to a combination of wind and tide, is one of the saltiest in England, leave it to settle, so that any mud can sink to the bottom and be removed, then transfer the water to large salt pans. It's then heated at a carefully moderated temperature for sixteen hours, during which time the water slowly evaporates and crystals form. These are then removed, drained and allowed to dry before being packaged and dispatched. That's all there is to it: a completely natural process, and although the technology has changed – no more coke-powered burners, for example – the method would be perfectly familiar to any of Steven's predecessors.

The Food Standards Agency says that excessive salt intake can increase your blood pressure, but then so does commuting on the Northern Line and you don't hear the government telling us to do less of that. However, 65 to 85 per cent of the salt we eat can be found in ready-prepared foods, not in salt added – and, more importantly, controlled and portioned correctly – by you, which accounts for something like 10 to 15 per cent. Many people claim that they can enjoy food perfectly well without salt, but a good-quality salt, sparingly applied, can really bring dishes to life, in my opinion. In recent years chefs have taken up artisan salts as an ingredient in themselves. The crunch of a nugget of tongue-piquing sea salt on salads, or with potatoes, is delicious. Soft, flaky sea salts are as much about texture as taste, and have none of the mouth-puckering harshness of ordinary table salt, but a lot more mineral flavour.

*See also* BRYNSIENCYN, ISLE OF ANGLESEY (p. 58).

*See also* BRYNSIENCYN, ISLE OF ANGLESEY (p. 58).

MELTON CONSTABLE, NORFOLK
## Sausages and pork cheese from M&M Rutland Butchers

Rutland Butchers in Melton Constable is a family affair. Established in a former post office by Mike and Marion Rutland in 1972, the knives are now wielded by son James and three daughters Kit, Carol and Tracy, who sell a beautiful range of products. The provenance of the meat is impeccable: the beef is Aberdeen Angus or Hereford and is raised in East Anglia; the pork is free-range Gloucester Old Spot; and the lamb free-range Suffolk. But it's the attention to detail and the dedication that add an extra something: a loin of lamb stuffed with pâté and mushrooms; handmade chicken Kievs; salt beef; bresaola; pancetta; and faggots.

But being East Anglian, it's the affinity with pork products that allows the Rutlands to demonstrate their skills. Sausages come in a huge variety of flavours: classical varieties such as Lincolnshire and British breakfast are complemented by such creations as rhubarb and sweet chilli, a pizza sausage – flavoured with basil and tomato – and seasonal specials, such as the fruity

Only the finest British meat is sold at M&M Rutland

Christmas sausage, which is given some festive cheer by the addition of sultanas, apple, nutmeg and cinnamon.

'Pork cheese' is also available, which is a dish of cold pork meat – usually from the head – set in jelly from the animal's trotters. In France it's called *fromage de tête*, in Germany it's known as *Presskopf*, and in the USA it goes by the unappetising name of 'head cheese'. No wonder Nigel Slater described it in 2007 as 'currently as unfashionable as any food could possibly be'. However, among a certain type of aficionado it garners respect. The Rutlands' version uses knuckles that have been cooked on the bone for four hours before being minced coarsely, lightly seasoned and left to set in their own jelly. It's cool in the mouth, the jelly wobbly yet full of flavour, and the morsels of meat still juicy and tender. The head cheese fightback starts here. Pass the mustard.

*See also* SAUSAGES (p. 122); BROMYARD, HEREFORDSHIRE (p. 283); CAMBRIDGE, CAMBRIDGESHIRE (p. 422); CONWY, CONWY (p. 60); FORRES, MORAY (p. 173); LOUTH, LINCOLNSHIRE (p. 336); MARYLEBONE, WESTMINSTER (p. 387); NANTWICH, CHESHIRE (p. 125); WOODHALL SPA, LINCOLNSHIRE (p. 364); YORK, NORTH YORKSHIRE (p. 271).

*Norfolk dumplings*

When times are hard and meat expensive, cultures the world over have looked to dumplings to bulk out meals, and the people of Norfolk are no different in this regard. No, where they differ is in the fact that their dumplings contain no suet, just one heaped tablespoon of flour per person, a pinch of salt, and water to bind. Today you would use self-raising flour, but before the manufacture of bicarbonate of soda in the early 1800s, yeast may have played a leavening role. *The History and Antiquities of the City of Norwich* written by Charles Parkin in 1783, said:

> The food of the commonalty consists much of puddings and dumplings, which has produced the proverb of Norfolk dumplings [to describe the populace]. Nor need they to be ashamed of their food, it being certainly the wholesomest and most nourishing to the human body.

Like most gentle mockery and regional nicknames, it eventually became almost a badge of honour.

Norfolk dumplings are known around the region as 'floaters' or 'swimmers', hinting at the fact that their flavour comes in part from the dish they're found floating on top of. In Elizabeth Gaskell's *Cranford* (1853), Mr Holbrook talks of his father's rule 'No broth, no ball, no ball, no beef'; meaning that first you could eat the liquid the joint was boiled in, then the dumplings, then finally – if you weren't full by then – you could move on to the meat.

Nowadays, of course, economy isn't so much of an issue, but taste is. Galton Blackiston, chef and proprietor of Morston Hall in Norfolk, prefers to make his dumplings from leftover bread dough. His version, therefore, contains yeast, which might account for the buoyant nature of the little beauties. Galton also recommends cooking them not in a stew or soup but separately, in rapidly boiling water, as this gives a lighter dumpling. However you cook it, though, a Norfolk dumpling should be as light as a feather, the perfect canvas for the flavours of your stew.

# Newmarket sausage

There are, in fact, not one but two Newmarket sausages, made by two different producers. Both Musk's and Powter's have been making sausages for hungry horse-racing fans for over 120 years. Musk's holds royal warrants and was able to count the Queen Mother among its fans. Powter's, meanwhile, maintains a presence on the high street and has received many awards. There are other differences between the two producers. In 2008, when Chris Sheen of Musk's sought PDO (Protected Designation of Origin) status for the Newmarket sausage, he had to list on the application form a standard set of ingredients and a defined location of production. Grant Powter, however, was understandably unwilling to reveal his recipe and consequently the application faltered, although at the time of writing things may be moving again.

Interestingly, unlike for example the sausage-makers of Lincolnshire and Cumberland who have agreed a list of key ingredients, these two producers use different ingredients and processes, yet historically both use the name Newmarket sausage. Musk's uses the shoulder of pork, a hog-skin casing and a bread binder. Powter's uses meat from the entire carcass, a rusk binder, and mainly a hog-skin or sometimes a beef-collagen case, depending on where the sausages are destined. Each uses a different blend of flavourings; just spices at Musk's, whereas Powter's also adds herbs. So you can see that to protect one recipe and product would exclude the other.

And so we are where we are: neck and neck in a two-horse race. There is no doubting that each sausage is made with care, precision and a great deal of love and pride. Indeed, those very attributes, although perhaps derailing the European protection application, still mean that each sausage is genuine and worthy of the name, as well as a space in your mouth. And as with the gee-gees, it's up to you to pick a winner.

*See also* SAUSAGES (p. 122).

# Colman's Mustard

Colman's is the culinary juggernaut of English mustard. Other brands are available, but Colman's, owned by Unilever since 1995, remains by far the biggest player. Jeremiah Colman, whose previous experience had been in milling flour, bought a mustard-milling business just outside Norwich in 1814, and placed the following advert in the *Norfolk Chronicle*:

> Joseph Colman, having taken the Stock & Trade lately carried on by Mr Edward Ames, respectfully informs his Customers & the Public in general that he will continue the Manufacturing of MUSTARD; & he begs leave to assure those who may be pleased to favour him with their orders that they shall be supplied in such a manner as cannot fail to secure their approbation.

You sense from Mr C. that he's a man who had a strong sense of propriety. The business grew, receiving the royal warrant from Queen Victoria in 1866. Under Jeremiah James Colman, great-nephew of the founder and ever the Victorian industrialist, schools were built for employees' children and healthcare provided for the workforce.

In the nineteenth century, mustard, as well as tea, coffee and a great many other household staples, was sold loose by weight by grocers and so was heavily adulterated. The scientist Arthur Hill Hassall, whose investigations with the newly invented microscope led to a change in the law, tried forty-two times to buy pure mustard from grocers in London, and every batch was 'diluted' with turmeric and flour. To some extent, grocers' adulteration of mustard played a part in the rise of individual, trustworthy brands, many early examples of which traded on quality, purity and provenance. An early advert for Colman's directs the consumer to 'see that the tin bears a yellow label similar to this illustration'. It's also worth noting that tins of Colman's Mustard powder came with a seal.

The acquisition of Keen's in 1903 saw off a major competitor, and an arrangement with Reckitt & Sons in 1913 opened new markets, with the two companies merging fully by 1954. In 1995 the Colman's business was split from Reckitt & Sons and sold to Unilever, and in 2002 it took 53.6 per cent of the UK's mustard market. To commemorate its 150th anniversary in 1973,

Colman's opened a mustard shop in Norwich city centre. When Unilever bought the company, it handed this to the Norwich Heritage Economic and Regeneration Trust, which runs it to this day, partly as a shop but also as a tourist attraction.

Colman's Mustard powder is still available, and one tip is to mix it with milk rather than water, and leave it to rest for ten minutes before eating. Of course, in today's squeezy age it also comes ready-made, in a variety of flavours. The taste of Colman's is very hot, obviously, but it will be tempered by the medium on which it is conveyed, be that bloody beef or a flaky pork pie. Jeremiah Colman is said to have observed that he made his money by the blobs of mustard people left on their plate. But we all come round to mustard, eventually. It is one of those things like marmalade, espresso and dark chocolate that marks the broadening of the palate that we like to think comes with our ascent into adulthood.

*See also* BISHOP'S STORTFORD, HERTFORDSHIRE (p. 321); EASTON GREY, WILTSHIRE (p. 11); EDINBURGH, EDINBURGH (p. 167); FAVERSHAM, KENT (p. 477); MOFFAT, DUMFRIES & GALLOWAY (p. 183); OXFORD, OXFORDSHIRE (p. 351); ROSSENDALE, LANCASHIRE (p. 131); ST HELENS, MERSEYSIDE (p. 132); SHEFFIELD, SOUTH YORKSHIRE (p. 258); SPENNYMOOR, COUNTY DURHAM (p. 227); WORCESTER, WORCESTERSHIRE (p. 317).

## PEASENHALL, SUFFOLK
# Emmett's Suffolk bacon

The village of Peasenhall is laid out along the A1120. On one side, a string of shops; on the other, a ditch, politely called a brook; and beyond that some houses. It's said that houses in the village, and indeed all over Suffolk, were traditionally painted pink using a combination of whitewash and pig's blood. They know a thing or two about pigs and how to use them in this part of the world.

Midway along the main road sits Emmett's Stores, housed comfortably in the same location, indeed in the same building, it has occupied since 1820. You can see the history of the shop in a small section of one of the walls, which has been stripped back to reveal the original structure. The shop had been in the same family for generations, and in 2000 it was bought by Mark Thomas, an ex-Harrods food manager.

Emmett's has always been noted for its black hams, and to this day it does

Where the magic happens: the smokery behind Emmett's Stores

a perfect portion of pork. All the pigs – traditional whites with plenty of fat – come from just four farms, all within twenty-five miles. First, the joints – legs for ham, belly for bacon – are brined in salt water, then they're put into a pickle made from Suffolk beer and other flavourings, where they remain bobbing around for six weeks. Each one is turned by hand every day until they're ready to be taken to the hot smoker, where they spend up to two days, depending on the weather. Then they're left to age, the entire process taking around ten weeks. The smoker itself is a tiny old brick shed, barely five feet high, with a lovely thick tar-like substance coating the interior walls. The small wooden door is stopped by a piece of material, and now and again puffs of white smoke escape through the roof tile as if the pieces of pig have chosen a new pope.

Although good all year round, Christmas is perhaps the best time to appreciate an Emmett's ham, perhaps even their special Christmas cure version, in which brown sugar and treacle are joined by ginger, black pepper, nutmeg and star anise; it's a warming festive way to begin the day.

*See also* LLANDINAM, POWYS (p. 75); LOWICK, NORTHUMBERLAND (p. 216); MARYLEBONE, WESTMINSTER (p. 387); MEOPHAM, KENT (p. 489); NEATH, NEATH PORT TALBOT (p. 80).

# Royal salads from Cookie's Crab Shop

If you ever go to Cookie's Crab Shop, my advice is to go prepared. Prepared to eat some fantastic seafood for sure, but also prepared to take your own drinks, glasses, bread and corkscrew. A thick skin wouldn't go amiss either. Cookie's doesn't have a licence, and it won't charge you corkage if you bring your own booze, but it would also prefer you to bring your own glasses, as this saves on the washing-up. Cookie's certainly isn't a formal restaurant; neither, according to the sign on the door, is it a tea shop, so there's to be no lingering on one of the handful of tables with just a cup of tea. So what is it then? Well, owners Pete and Suzanne McKnespiey were inspired by the street-food outlets they saw on holiday in Australia and the Far East, and they wanted to echo that informality. So Cookie's is a small shack with a handful of tables and a gazebo attached to the side for those who prefer a more alfresco experience. The walls of the building are inset with pebbles from the beach, a particularly East Anglian architectural style. Inside there are paper napkins, plastic chairs, mismatched cutlery, and it's all the better

A royal salad featuring a whole dressed crab, cockles, smoked mackerel and prawns – the face is optional

for it. Cookie's gets very busy during the summer months, when sandwiches and soups are takeaway only, so booking is advisable.

Pete would probably be the first to admit he's got a no-nonsense attitude. 'There's great banter in this place with the regulars. Sometimes I ask, "How was that?" when clearing the table and they reply, "Bloody awful! See you same time next week."' If you're a soft-skinned diner with a delicate nature, this probably isn't the place for you. If, on the other hand, you're a lover of spanking fresh, well-cooked fish and seafood, and not squeamish about tearing crustaceans limb from limb, then you will love it. The crab royal salad, for instance, includes whole dressed crab, prawns, crayfish, mackerel, salmon and cockles served with lettuce, tomato and cucumber, potato salad and coleslaw. All for around £6, which is not much more than a limp prawn sandwich in your favourite sandwich chain. It's a large plate of lovely seafood at a bargain price, and a complete hit of omega-3 goodness.

*See also* BUCKIE, MORAY (p. 149); CHINATOWN, WESTMINSTER (p. 374); CROMER, NORFOLK (p. 426); LITTLE HAVEN, PEMBROKESHIRE (p. 70); MORECAMBE BAY, LANCASHIRE (p. 121).

SOUTHEND-ON-SEA, ESSEX
## *Whitebait*

In the nineteenth century, whitebait were thought to be a distinct species, and were given the name *Clupea alba* by the eminent naturalist William Yarrell. Later on, in 1905, the name was discovered to be a catch-all for any small fish by one Dr James Murie, who studied fish labelled as whitebait and found that some of the boxes contained up to twenty-three species of juvenile fish, including plaice, eel, herring, whiting, sprat and bass. Whitebait are now classed as the young fry of the herring and the sprat, and consequently fishing and eating them isn't really that ecologically sound.

The fishing of them does have a strong heritage, though, and one of the annual responsibilities of Donna Gale, the executive assistant at the Essex Chamber of Commerce, is to organise a lunch to celebrate the humble whitebait. 'It's a quirky English festival, and we're keeping it alive,' she tells me. The history of the lunch goes back – off and on – to 1707, when one was held in honour of a group of landowners in Southend-on-Sea who had helped to restore the river wall following a large breach. The custom continued for many years after this. In 1799 a private dinner featuring whitebait was hosted by Robert Preston, MP for Dover, at his fishing cottage in Essex. The then prime minister, William Pitt the Younger, attended annually, but he and others soon desired to move the dinner closer to London. And so the taverns of Greenwich and Blackwall played host, the Trafalgar Tavern at Greenwich, right on the shore, declaring rather brashly that it only used fish caught from the tavern window. The annual dinner became a regular celebration for the Cabinet shortly before Parliament broke for the summer.

An article in the *Morning Post* of 10 September 1835 reads:

> Yesterday, the Cabinet Ministers went down the river in the Ordnance barges to Lovegrove's 'West India Dock Tavern', Blackwall, to partake of their annual fish dinner. Covers were laid for thirty-five gentlemen.

However, by then commercial fishing in the Thames had all but ceased due to pollution, and the last dinner was held in 1884. The festival was then revived in 1934 by the Southend Chamber of Commerce, Trade and Industry, with the Mayor and notable dignitaries forming the honoured guests. A religious element to the festival developed, and the Mayor's chaplain offered a blessing of the catch.

In the 1990s the lunch was held at McGinty's restaurant on Southend pier. The service took place out on the decking, during which a small portion of the whitebait were returned to the sea (that is if they made it past the assembled seagulls). The pier is nearly 1.3 miles long, and so everyone – including the local brass band and all their equipment – had to muster at the entrance to make the 11.30 train that ran the length of it. After various fires, including one that completely gutted the restaurant in 2005, the event was moved to another location, with Sands Bistro the host in recent years.

Whitebait are now offered as a first-course option rather than the main course in today's whitebait festival at Southend-on-Sea. Meanwhile, Donna is doing her bit for sustainability: 'I don't eat it; I don't like the eyes and the guts and things,' she says.

See also DERWENTWATER, CUMBRIA (p. 102); DOVER, KENT (p. 473); GLOUCESTER, GLOUCESTERSHIRE (p. 288); HASTINGS, EAST SUSSEX (p. 483); MARKET HARBOROUGH, LEICESTERSHIRE (p. 340); NEWLYN, CORNWALL (pp. 32 and 34); RIVER SEVERN, GLOUCESTERSHIRE (p. 305); SCOURIE, HIGHLAND (p. 187); WANSFORD, EAST YORKSHIRE (p. 261); WHITBURN, TYNE & WEAR (p. 228).

# Adnams beer

Southwold is home to the Adnams brewery, and it is said by some that kitchen sinks in the town come with three taps: hot, cold and Adnams. George and Ernest Adnams bought the established Sole Bay brewery in 1872. Ernest continued to build up the business while brother George soon got bored and sought adventure in darkest Africa, where he was apparently eaten by a crocodile.

Today Adnams has a core range of beers, of which Southwold Bitter, Explorer and Broadside are the most popular. These are augmented with some seasonal specials throughout the year, one of the most interesting being Tally Ho. This English barley-wine-style beer has been brewed at the Sole Bay brewery since 1880, and a photograph exists of Ernest and George sitting on a barrel. It's available only in the month of December, and at around 7 per cent ABV it's great for lubricating the wheels of the festive season.

Adnams has also developed the Adnams Cellar & Kitchen Stores, which sells a range of wines, beers and spirits as well as interesting kitchenware and equipment. Since 2002 the company has put its environmental obligations at the heart of its business, and the new stores have won awards for sustainable development, while in 2006 a new distribution centre opened with a living roof and rainwater collection facility. The company has also reduced the weight of the 500 ml bottle from 455 g to 299 g, and in 2008 launched East Green, the UK's first carbon-neutral beer.

In the town itself you can see the barrels rattling around the brewery and get the nose-tingling whiff of a fully operational mash tun on brewing days, but a pub is perhaps the best place to appreciate the brewery's handiwork. Adnams owns and runs a number of pubs and hotels in the town, including the Swan and the Crown. The former has a more formal feel, whereas the latter offers more of a pub experience. Both are on the high street and a mere pebble's throw from the brewery itself.

*See also* ASTLEY, WARWICKSHIRE (p. 276); GREENWICH, GREENWICH (p. 378); KNIGHTWICK, WORCESTERSHIRE (p. 299); NEWCASTLE, TYNE & WEAR (p. 220).

## Norfolk Black turkeys

*The Chronicle of the Kings of England* (1643) states, 'Turkey, carps, hoppes, piccarell and beer,/ Came into England all in one year.' The year in question was 1524 and the birds, originally from the Americas, became associated with Norfolk because it was relatively near to London and already had a thriving goose trade. Allowing the turkeys to fatten up on the fields after the harvest in time for Christmas also made sense, and gradually selective breeding by those early farmers gave rise to the Norfolk Black. In the 1800s faster-growing breeds were developed, like the Cambridge Bronze turkey. Now even that breed has been superseded by the Broad-breasted White, which is the most popular bird today. It has such a large breast and short legs that it is unable to breed naturally, and reproduction happens only through artificial insemination.

The Norfolk Black, meanwhile, slow growing and with a normal body shape, rather fell out of favour in the late twentieth century. It was kept only by a few who knew better, such as Ernest Peele, who started raising black turkeys when he moved to Norfolk from Lincolnshire in 1880.

Today Peele's black turkeys are watched over by his great-grandson James Graham; that's four generations of turkey know-how. In the 1950s, when the future of the Norfolk Black looked bleak, James's grandfather Frank Peele gathered together different specimens from all over the UK and established a strong breeding pool based on four distinct families. Under James's watch this has increased to nine. It's a lovely bird to look at: jet-black plumage and better proportioned than commercial, fast-growing breeds. As well as the Norfolk Black, the farm also breeds the Cambridge Bronze, Lavender, Bourbon Red and Narragansett, as well as Legarth geese. They are all left to reproduce naturally, and the resulting poults are outdoor-reared, feeding on grain, corn and oats that James grows himself.

The turkey, being a game bird, benefits from a bit of hanging after slaughter, and James gives them a week or so to improve the flavour. They're then plucked and sorted (like turkey producers everywhere, the few weeks before Christmas are a blur of feathers), and come 1 p.m. on Christmas Eve it's all done until February, when things start again.

What I like about James's business is that his is a steady hand at the tiller. I get the sense that he's merely the custodian of this flock, and that he's in it for the long term. His customers are, too: 'A customer who came to collect her turkey this year is 100 years old. She's bought a turkey from us regularly for over fifty years.' There are not many producers who can say that.

See also GOOSNARGH, LANCASHIRE (p. 106); HARLOW, ESSEX (p. 436); HINDOLVESTON, NORFOLK (p. 437); KING'S NYMPTON, DEVON (p. 20); MAIDENHEAD, BERKSHIRE (p. 487).

WEST MERSEA, ESSEX

## Colchester oysters from the Company Shed

We all love a simple, rustic, no-frills seafood joint. The call of the sea, the whiff of salt, the flapping of sails. At the Company Shed you get all this and can indulge your inner salty ol' sea dog. You sit where you're told – often sharing tables with complete strangers – and tuck in to the fruits of the sea. It's a noisy, cramped seafood shack and is just perfect because of it.

Nutcrackers are a shellfish-eater's secret weapon

As co-owner (along with her mum, Heather) Caroline Haward explains, 'If you want table service, you can get that elsewhere.' Despite being on the coast, it would be naive to expect everything to be sourced from just outside the back door – after all, there are not many salmon in the Colne estuary. Native Colchester oysters, however – when in season – are provided by Caroline's dad, Richard, and the family can trace its history in the area back over 100 years.

Most people opt for the seafood platter; it's a good all-rounder, giving you a bit of everything: salmon, prawns, cockles from Whitstable, mackerel, crab, and mussels from Norfolk, all for £8. Other menu items include oysters topped with cream and Parmesan, *moules marinière*, rollmop herrings and smoked mackerel. 'We get through fifty stone of crab a week,' says Caroline; what's more, you know it's fresh, because at the back of the shop, the crabs are kept in trays ready for the pot. There is also a fish counter, so you can take things home for your pot if you want more.

Tempted? Well, you're probably not the only one. If after reading this you decide to visit the Company Shed this weekend, my advice is to go early. In fact, skip breakfast, maybe don't even shower, and be banging on the door when it opens. The Company Shed is very popular indeed, particularly at weekends, and unless you're there early you will queue, as I did, for over an hour. The key, however, is to enjoy this and go with the flow, treating lunch as the half-time of an entire day spent walking around the marina, paddling on the beach and generally taking things easy. In their defence, the staff do make every effort by taking names and updating a leader board that shows your position in the queue. During the hour's wait you can go for a nice walk into the village and stock up on bread and wine.

So go, but go early and go pre-armed with bread and booze, and you'll have a whale of a time. After all, there's just something about eating seafood that ensures you drop any airs and graces and get stuck right in.

*See also* CLACHAN, DUMFRIES & GALLOWAY (p. 153); EDINBURGH, EDINBURGH (p. 168); LINDISFARNE, NORTHUMBERLAND (p. 214); WHITSTABLE, KENT (p. 500).

# Norfolk White Lady cheese

When I asked Jane Murray about the name of her cheese, she replied, 'Well, it's made in Norfolk, it's white, and I'm a lady!' She began producing sheep milk for sale in 1986, but in 1999 decided to branch out, into yoghurt at first, then cheese. 'You make what's easy. There was a quick return with something like yoghurt, but of course it didn't have the shelf life.' And so she started making Norfolk White Lady cheese. 'It took me several months to get it right,' she says. After about two years of making White Lady, she found that she

Jane Murray and her sensibly named cheese

couldn't quite keep up with demand and had to turn some customers down. 'There weren't enough hours in the day, what with the sheep taking five hours to milk.' So in 2008 she sold her sheep to a woman up in Lincolnshire, who then sells the milk back to Jane.

Her plans for the future include a blue cheese, but that's under wraps for the moment. To make the White Lady, Jane first pasteurises the milk, then adds the cultures *Penicillium candidum* and *Geotrichum candidum*. These give flavour to the cheese but crucially help form the white mould on the surface. After an hour, she adds vegetarian rennet. 'I don't see the point of using animal rennet – you just end up excluding people. There are a lot of vegetarians and if they're not eating meat, chances are they're eating cheese.' It's then shaped and put into moulds. She makes it on a Monday, and by the following Thursday the white bloom has formed and she can wrap it. Jane puts a seven-week shelf life on it, but the truth is that it simply changes with age. The taste is lovely: light and fresh, Brie-like, but more – how can I put this? – fun, because into this cheese Jane has poured her warmth and humour.

*See also* BRITISH CHEESE (p. 290).

# 11 | The South-East

ESSEX

Clacton-on-Sea ○

○ Harlow

○
Chelmsford

Brentwood
○

Southend-on-Sea
○

_Thames Estuary_

○
Gravesend

★
Meopham

○
Gillingham

★
Whitstable

○
Margate

Wrotham ★
★
St Mary's
Platt

_Maidstone_
○

★
Faversham

★
Canterbury

KENT

Ashford ○

Dover
★

Folkestone ○

_The Weald_

Appledore
★

Horsted Keynes

★
Northiam

_Strait of Dover_

EAST SUSSEX

Polegate
★

★
Hastings

○ Eastbourne

_hannel_

| 0 | 5 | 10 | 15 | 20 mi |

| 0 | 5 | 10 | 15 | 20 | 25 | 30 | 35 km |

## APPLEDORE, KENT
# Miss Mollett's High Class Tea Rooms

Tea, tea, everywhere . . . and yet finding a proper tea shop in this day and age isn't easy. In a bid to fight back against the ubiquity of coffee chains, sisters Alex Cowell and Francis MacDonald set up Miss Mollett's in May 2008 and haven't looked back since. The original Miss Jessie Blanche Mollett ran a tea shop in Appledore between the wars and lived in the village until her death in 1970. After some digging by Sue, their fourth cousin twice removed, they discovered that Miss Mollett was in fact related to them, and so with this pedigree her name was the obvious choice for the fledgling tea shop.

The cakes, pies and quiches are all made by Francis, while Alex makes the soups and the sandwiches, which come in classic flavours: ham, Quickes' farmhouse Cheddar, egg and cress and such. But the food is really only there to accompany the teas, which all come from Kent and Sussex Tea Company, with some, such as the house tea, being blended in-house. The tea is served

A cup of Miss Mollett's house blend tea

in a proper bone-china cup, with a doily between it and the saucer to soak up any spills.

It's amazing to think how we have let the tea room die out in Britain. It slipped away as a community space with no eulogy or minute's silence. The last Lyons tea room, the most famous example of them all, closed in 1981, but the art nouveau design and the waitresses known as 'nippies' went long before that – just after the war in fact. Coffee quickly became the new thing, and how readily we embraced the coffee shop; first the Continental ones, then more recently the American versions. The 'Central Perk' coffee shop from the TV show *Friends*, and the 1990s concept of a 'third space', a place where friends could meet up and relax, made tea rooms seem stuffy and class-ridden in comparison, with all the fun of a doctor's waiting room.

Perhaps things are now swinging back the other way, with people eschewing the noise and bustle of the coffee shop for the quiet contemplation of the tea room. In the former, above the drone of the grinder, the piped music and the thump of enormous mugs on hard benches, you can hardly hear yourself think. Coffee is all about energy and stimulation and lacks the calm, contemplative air of tea taken in a tea room, where heads lean in, eyes check left and right, and sentences begin, 'Well . . .' As Henry Fielding once said, 'Love and scandal are the best sweeteners of tea.'

*See also* HARROGATE, NORTH YORKSHIRE (p. 250); NEW GALLOWAY, DUMFRIES & GALLOWAY (p. 184); PEMBROKE DOCK, PEMBROKESHIRE (p. 81); YORK, NORTH YORKSHIRE (p. 270).

## Vegetarian food from Terre à Terre

The forswearing of eating animal flesh goes back as far as the ancient Greeks. Consequently, up until the nineteenth century, those that did so were known as Pythagoreans, after the famous (and meat-free) mathematician. Then in 1847 the Vegetarian Society was formed, and a year later held its first annual meeting in a hotel in Manchester. In the same town thirty years later Newton Heath LYR, which would eventually become Manchester United, started kicking a ball around. Fast-forward 150 years and out of the 61.4 million people in the UK today, only around 3 per cent (or just shy of 2 million people) call themselves vegetarians. Manchester United fans, on the other hand, number around 5 per cent (or just over 4 million), most of them probably living in Kent.

Brighton, East Sussex | 467

A porcini mushroom pudding served in a fun setting

All this means that vegetarians often get short shrift in most restaurants, the veggie 'option', denoted by that little italicised *v*, frequently a boring-sounding dish at the fag end of the menu. The tick symbol evolved from the *v* in *veritas*, which is Latin for 'truth', and in truth most veggie food in pubs and restaurants is a dreadful afterthought, limited to salad, soup, some bland pasta and cheese thing, or a stuffed pepper if you're lucky; more often than not, it's a Hobson's choice.

Not so at Terre à Terre in Brighton. It first opened its doors fifteen years ago with chefs Amanda Powley and Philip Taylor in the kitchen, and hasn't looked back since. Both Amanda and Philip are classically trained chefs, and when they first opened Terre à Terre no one was really doing restaurant-quality vegetarian food. Moreover, although there have always been veggie cafés and eateries offering good and wholesome food, they've always lacked one vital ingredient: fun. All too often, eating veggie can feel like going to church, or visiting a library: good for the body and soul no doubt, but not exactly party central. And so Philip and Amanda set out to create a bright, fun restaurant where people could enjoy themselves, eat something good, quaff some decent booze and generally have a great time – all without meat. Indeed, Terre à Terre is one of a growing number of restaurants (other examples are Vanilla Black in London, and Banns in Edinburgh) that are offering a fine-dining environment alongside show-stopping meat-free food.

According to manager Vanessa Beard, 'About 50 per cent of our customers are non-veggie [she's a non-veggie herself]. In fact, we've had people come in, sit down and only when they get a menu do they realise we don't serve meat.' One can imagine the scene as they look around in horror thinking, 'But this place looks so normal!' Vanessa continues, 'Some get in a bit of a panic at first, but stay and have a great time.' That great time Vanessa attributes to knowledgeable and friendly front-of-house staff who can reassure people and assuage any fear that they've joined some sort of cult. 'Meat-eaters normally over-order as they think they might not go home full, which isn't the case,' she adds.

Philip and Amanda's menu cherry-picks interesting ingredients and flavours from the Near and Far East as well as the subcontinent, plus a few bits from the West Indies and South America: Fenugreek and argan oil salad; sweet ginger sushi; chilled soba noodles with toasted smoked tofu; chaat spiced poori with chana peas; and finally corn cakes with avocado spice smash and chilli chelly. A lot of Western European food is meat-based – think of all those rich stocks and sauces in French cuisine – and so consequently there's not too much of this on the menu. There is, however, a nod to the British classic of fish and chips, as Terre à Terre is by the seaside. This sees battered halloumi cheese served with pea and mint hash, some pickled quail's eggs and chubby chips.

Another popular dish is the porcini pudding with chestnut purée, soused and braised red cabbage, and mashed potato. Ahh, the mighty porcini, the dreadnought of the fungus world, packed to the gunwales with flavour and possessing a rich, almost meaty texture. The rest of the menu, and indeed cooking, is in a similar vein, playing to the strengths of the main ingredients. Eating there is a joy, and for once I didn't really miss the meat.

CANTERBURY, KENT
## The Goods Shed

The Goods Shed, built around 1846, is situated next to Canterbury West railway station. The building had sat derelict for over twenty years, just another crumbling part of Britain's railway infrastructure, before Suzanna Atkins started her business there in 2002, and now the hiss and clatter of the locomotives has been replaced by the whistle and steam of espresso machines. After leaving the family farm, Suzanna started her working life running a café in Whitstable. After a while she decided she wanted to open a restaurant, and her thoughts ran immediately to the neglected railway shed. It was an excellent space, of course, but far too big for just a restaurant. At about that time the craze for farmers' markets was really taking off, so she decided to build not only her restaurant, but also a space for local producers. 'It's not really a farmers' market any more, it's more of a food hall that majors in local produce,' says Suzanna. 'All the fruit, vegetables and meat are from local farms.' Her efforts saw the enterprise crowned Best Food Market 2009 by the Radio 4 Food and Farming Awards.

Although she would be entitled to rest on her laurels, that's not going to happen. She has just installed a new raw milk vending machine, for instance, bought for €17,000 from Italy. By law only the farmer is allowed to sell milk directly, but obviously, since he's got cows to look after, this is the next best (and legal) thing. You bring your own bottle, insert a coin and fill up with chilled, fresh, buttery-yellow unpasteurised milk. This gives you a lot of possibilities, from knocking together a bowl of stunning porridge, to making your own butter and cheese, something that's just not possible with shop-bought regular milk.

Leftovers and things 'on the turn' are a problem not only for the bottom of your fridge, but also for shops. Mindful of waste and keen to extract both flavour and value from ingredients, Suzanna and some of the chefs have begun using vegetables from the shop that might be a bit past their prime, or if they have a glut, and turning them into preserves, pickles and chutneys; bones and carcasses from the butchers are turned into stocks, all of which are then jarred up and made available for sale.

Food and railways do not always make happy bedfellows, as anyone who ever ate a British Rail sandwich can testify. The Goods Shed, an interchange for producers and those who like to eat good things, bucks that trend. All change please, all change.

*See also* COLSTON BASSETT, NOTTINGHAMSHIRE (p. 325); HOOK, HAMPSHIRE (p. 484); IPSWICH, SUFFOLK (p. 441); RUSHWICK, WORCESTERSHIRE (p. 309); STANNINGTON, NORTHUMBERLAND (p. 227); WELBECK, NOTTINGHAMSHIRE (p. 362).

# *Watercress*

Some say watercress is the new rocket, which just goes to highlight Britain's daft food-faddish nature. The 1951 *Law's Grocer's Manual* has no entry for rocket or arugula, which originally came from the Mediterranean, and yet by the 1990s it was so ubiquitous that some wag christened it the 'Soho weed'. Diners loved its sharp pepperiness, and seemed to have quite forgotten the native leaf that had offered just that for years: watercress. But then it has been long misunderstood, as food writer Dorothy Hartley admonished in *Food in England* (1952): 'This favourite English salad is not understood by the cook who thinks of it as sprigs of garnish.' And I can't help but agree that English watercress is far too good to waste it plugging a cooked bird's derrière.

Watercress production in the UK is centred in the counties of Hampshire and Dorset, although it was first grown commercially in Kent. It doesn't last long when picked, and so was dispatched to London via train on what

Watercress grown in traditional running-water beds

became known as the Watercress Line. Having kept us going during the war, it soon became sidelined thanks to a combination of world trade resuming in the 1950s and the closure of branch lines in the 1960s. In the 1940s, watercress was grown on over 1,000 acres. As the century closed, we were down to 150. These days, production is handled by just a handful of companies. Vitacress, Bakkavor and the Watercress Company are the market leaders, supplying the supermarkets and other retailers.

There are also a few much smaller producers serving local farmers' markets and doing a bit of wholesale trade. Edward Hair of Hairspring is one of them. His ancestor, George Hair, began growing watercress on his Hampshire farm after one of his employees returned from a visit to a similar operation in Kent. Most of the watercress then went back via train to London and Brighton, with horse and cart taking what was left to the local markets. Over the years the watercress beds have improved structurally, and in the 1970s bore holes were sunk to replace the spring-supplied water.

In the autumn of 2009 the National Farmers Union's Watercress Growers' Association, of which all watercress producers both large and small are members, applied for PGI (Protected Geographical Indication) status. They are seeking to protect the production method, which sees watercress grown in beds with gravel bottoms and fed by cool clear water that comes direct from a bore hole or aquifer. They are doing this because some Continental producers grow watercress in soil in polytunnels, and are consequently able to offer a cheaper product. This soil-grown watercress is only three per cent of the market at the moment, but the association is obviously not keen to see it spread much further, not least because it's a lot less tasty.

Proper peppery, water-produced watercress can be used in many different ways, but I think it's best enjoyed raw and as fresh as you can get it, with maybe a bit of crumbly cheese and some good bread. It's also worth remembering that you don't always have to put watercress in the salad drawer of the fridge. It's fine standing or resting in a bowl of water (indeed most herbs and even lettuces benefit from this treatment), and the added bonus is that you can nibble the odd leaf while doing the drying-up.

*See also* CRYMYCH, PEMBROKESHIRE (p. 63); GOMERSAL, WEST YORKSHIRE (p. 247); WINCANTON, SOMERSET (p. 48).

# *Dover sole*

It takes a certain myopia to regard Dover as an 'other Eden' or, indeed, a 'demi-paradise'. These days it's hard to see much past the industrial concrete areas and juggernaut-clogged roads. Whenever I go there it seems to be foggy or raining, or both, which is also how it appeared to Bill Bryson when he first visited England in 1973. And yet, and yet, there's something magical about seeing those cliffs, even wreathed in rain. Another of Shakespeare's lines from *Richard II* springs to mind, 'This fortress built by Nature for herself,' and the white cliffs seem to say, 'You're home, England starts here.'

In culinary matters the town gives its name to Dover sole, as this was where the vast majority of the fish were landed in the nineteenth century, although they were actually caught all along the coast in both directions. No commercial fishing boats operate out of Dover now, so to get your hands on Dover sole you need head along the coast. And if you pick east, you'll soon reach Romney Marsh Fish Market and its owner, Pete Vickerman. Pete has been a fishmonger for years, and his shop has been part of the Haguelands Kent Farm Shop complex since 2006. He prefers to buy local and British, and is supplied from the boats out of nearby Rye and Dungeness.

The Dover sole season runs from June until October. Sole is an interesting fish, because it's one of those rare varieties that you need to let sit for a day or two before using. Straight out of the sea it's too floppy, and when put in the pan it curls up, making for uneven cooking. Letting it stiffen stops this. With sole, less is more: its smooth, firm nature means it doesn't need much done to it: butter, lemon and maybe a caper are the only friends it needs.

*See also* DERWENTWATER, CUMBRIA (p. 102); GLOUCESTER, GLOUCESTERSHIRE (p. 288); HASTINGS, EAST SUSSEX (p. 483); MARKET HARBOROUGH, LEICESTERSHIRE (p. 340); NEWLYN, CORNWALL (pp. 32 and 34); RIVER SEVERN, GLOUCESTERSHIRE (p. 305); SCOURIE, HIGHLAND (p. 187); SOUTHEND-ON-SEA, ESSEX (p. 455); WANSFORD, EAST YORKSHIRE (p. 261); WHITBURN, TYNE & WEAR (p. 228).

## ETON, BERKSHIRE
## *Eton mess*

Even the great Heston Blumenthal, who's got a bit of previous in turning dishes on their heads to create something new and amazing, threw in the towel when it came to Eton mess, saying, 'What is so wonderful about this dessert is that it cannot be improved upon.' Today Eton mess consists of strawberries, bits of meringue and lightly whipped double cream, all mixed together in a bowl. It is summer personified.

As for its provenance, well, Robin Weir, in his book *Recipes from the Dairy* (1995), says Eton mess was served in the 1930s in the school's sock (tuck) shop, and was originally made with either strawberries or bananas mixed with ice cream or cream. Meringue, apparently, was a later addition.

However, a pudding called 'Eton mess aux fraises' appears on the menu of a garden party given at Marlborough House on 5 July 1893. The occasion was the eve of the marriage of Prince George, the Duke of York, to Princess May of Teck. This was an important event, attended by Queen Victoria herself and, being held outside in the middle of English summer, the weather was lousy. Sadly, the menu doesn't go on to describe the dessert in detail, but one can imagine a dainty glass filled with hulled strawberries and whipped cream.

Finally, there is evidence of our old friend serendipity at play with the tale that the dish was created when a Labrador dog sat on a picnic in the back of a car and squashed a rather ornate pudding. Of course, history does not relate the name of the pooch in question, nor what happened subsequently, and the rest of the details are sketchy.

Kirsch is another ingredient often put to the fruit, and chocolate and brandy versions are not unheard of. In my mind it gives summer pudding a run for its money as the top summertime pud. In fact, perhaps its simplicity and ease of assembly gives it the race by a nose.

*See also* HOW RECIPES BEGIN (p. 496).

# The National Fruit Collection at Brogdale

'Kent, sir, everyone knows Kent. Apples, cherries, hops and women,' goes the line in Dickens's *The Pickwick Papers*. The first item on the list is very well served by Brogdale Farm, home to the National Fruit Collection. On this 150-acre site there are over 2,000 different types of apple, nearly 500 types of pears, and apricots, berries, vines and cobnuts. The collection is owned by DEFRA, and the farm is managed by the University of Reading. At one time it was sponsored by Tesco, although that relationship came to an end a few years ago. Its primary purpose is helping scientists and horticulturalists by acting as a gene bank; however, in recent years it's also developed its public-facing side with tours and educational events – over 3,000 people attend its annual autumnal apple week, for instance.

Highlights of the collection include Cox's Orange Pippin, often regarded as the finest dessert apple; although tricky to grow, it rewards with a complex flavour: there's a full-bodied sweetness, almost honeylike, followed by a bubbly fizz on the tongue. Freshly picked, the flesh is as crisp as a newly minted ten-pound note. Lowlights, however, include the Golden Delicious,

My very own apple, with a variety of uses in the kitchen

which just tastes like water. But as head guide Ted Hobday points out, 'They're lunchbox sized, and they travel and keep well.' Interestingly, Golden Delicious are the state fruit of Virginia – you'd have thought they might have picked something more imaginative. Still, the collection is there to preserve everything, not just the varieties that taste nice.

You get a sense of the sheer number of varieties in the visitors' centre, which houses a display of harvested apples and pears whose names are as varied as they are amazing. France's climate lends itself better to pear production than the UK's, so there are also a lot of Gallic names, including a small, mean-looking pear bearing the name 'Napoleon', and also one called 'Green Beurre'. On the apple table you can find Laxton's Royalty, Martini, Chorister Boy, Fireside and the Bedford red. But my favourite has to be the Webb's Kitchen Russett, which apparently has fine, softish flesh with a sweet, sub-acid flavour – just like me.

*See also* AMPLEFORTH, NORTH YORKSHIRE (p. 234); HOLT HEATH, WORCESTERSHIRE (p. 298); SOUTHWELL, NOTTINGHAMSHIRE (p. 359).

FAVERSHAM, KENT
## Ashmore cheese

Historically, Kent isn't a big cheese-producing region, preferring instead to concentrate on perishable produce such as fruit and vegetables, perhaps in part because of its close proximity to London, whose inhabitants were its best customers for decades. Those items had to be packed on produce trains as fresh as could be, whereas cheese, as Clifton Fadiman once said, is 'milk's leap toward immortality'. However, improved logistics means that those items now arrive in the capital from all over the UK, indeed the world, which leaves Kent free to begin producing cheese.

Ashmore cheese, a Cheddar-style cheese full of earthy flavours and with a good natural rind, is made by Jane Bowyer, Teresa Bullock and David Pullen, who go by the collective name of the Cheese Makers of Canterbury. This wasn't always the case, however. The cheese started life in the 1980s when Sussex dairy farmer David Doble decided to have a go at cheese-making using a recipe from a book produced by the North of Scotland College of Agriculture. The Dobles moved to Ashmore, Dorset, where the cheese picked up its name, before moving again to Lord Salisbury's estate at Cranborne Chase. Finally, when David and Pat Doble retired, the business was sold and production moved again – this time to Kent. All of this goes to show the rather random way that cheese comes to be made, and how it can have various incarnations over time.

Ashmore is available at delis and farm shops throughout Kent, including the Cheese Box in Whitstable, which sells nothing but artisan English cheeses. Owner Dawn Hackett says, 'We sell proper English cheese here, and it should be eaten as such, so don't you dare put it near an olive or sundried tomato!'

*See also* BRITISH CHEESE (p. 290).

*See also* BRITISH CHEESE (p. 290).

FAVERSHAM, KENT
## *Cheese and pickle from Macknade Fine Food*

Husband and wife team Renato and Patricia Cuomo run the produce pleasure-palace that is Macknade Fine Food. It has the finesse and detail of an Italian deli, coupled with the honest wholesomeness of a British farm shop. It began life as plain old Fir Tree Farm, and was initially a pick-your-own operation (all the rage in the 1970s). Since then, Renato has drawn on his Mediterranean heritage, adding interesting lines from Italy as well as more British and European stock, including a choice of six different Parma hams, pasta fashioned into the most amazing shapes, and a fine selection of fresh fruit and vegetables. The choice of tomatoes strikes a balance between seasonal English varieties and imported Italian varieties, but when I visited, the most impressive food on offer was the massive Zucca Napolitana, a squash that hogged the shelf space between the cabbages and celeriac like a fat kid in a school photograph. It was without doubt the biggest vegetable I had ever seen: two feet long and ten inches thick, and requiring the strength of a weightlifter to pick it up. Renato often buys things like this on his daily trips to London, partly out of curiosity and partly for the joke, one imagines.

Huge, humorous vegetables aside, there is stuff here that you very rarely get elsewhere, like *soppressata puro suino*, an Italian version of brawn or head cheese. This version consists of large chunks of pork suspended in jelly. Unlike in the UK, where it's made in a pot or a terrine, this version is made in a large sausage shape, and sold in pre-packed slices. Then there is Giacomo Santoleri's Makaira pasta range, produced in small batches in the hills of Abruzzi. Made with durum wheat augmented by barley flour, it's a nuttier, more biscuity pasta than most.

Macknade's tomatoes: beef, plum, salad and cherry

But what really sums the place up is Winterdale Shaw cheese, a traditional, unpasteurised, clothbound Cheddar-style cheese made by Robin Betts less than thirty miles away in Wrotham, accompanied by Pear Mostarda, a single-variety condiment that comes from the Mantovan tradition, made by Paola Calciolari in the north of Italy. The pear is first candied in a syrup that infuses it with sugar and reduces its water content, sweetening and preserving it. Mustard essence is then added to provide a real heat, opening up your senses before dissipating.

The contrast between the shop's products – a local version here, a European one there – makes for a wholly unusual exchange. The combination is an excellent example of the Macknades' skilful blending of Kent and the Continent.

*See also* BRITISH CHEESE (p. 290); BISHOP'S STORTFORD, HERTFORDSHIRE (p. 321); EASTON GREY, WILTSHIRE (p. 11); EDINBURGH, EDINBURGH (p. 167); MOFFAT, DUMFRIES & GALLOWAY (p. 183); NORWICH, NORFOLK (p. 451); OXFORD, OXFORDSHIRE (p. 351); ROSSENDALE, LANCASHIRE (p. 131); ST HELENS, MERSEYSIDE (p. 132); SHEFFIELD, SOUTH YORKSHIRE (p. 258); SPENNYMOOR, COUNTY DURHAM (p. 227); WORCESTER, WORCESTERSHIRE (p. 317).

# *Jugged hare*

Nowadays, jugged hare is tricky to make properly, in part because many old recipes call for the blood of the animal to be added to thicken the sauce. This requires a level of personal intimacy with a butcher, gamekeeper or 'man in the know' on a par with one you would have with your best friend. Few of us have such a person on speed-dial; that said, it is a relationship worth developing. Along with the blood – if you can get it – jugged hare calls for the animal to be cut up into joints and stewed along with juniper berries in red wine and stock.

Hannah Glasse's 1747 recipe for jugged hare is incorrectly remembered for the instruction 'First catch your hare.' The phrase has stuck ever since, even appearing in James Joyce's *Ulysses*, a little mantra when writing about all things hare. Glasse's recipe features no liquid, not even the blood. A few decades later Charlotte Mason, in *The Lady's Assistant for Regulating and Supplying Her Table*, gives us various recipes, including one, 'To dress a hare the Swiss way', that features the liver being pushed through a sieve and the blood being added to the sauce, along with olives and capers. The addition of blood seems to have come from the French *civet de lièvre*, a similar, Continental dish. Later recipes feature port to further enrich the sauce, as well as redcurrant jelly. The jugging is key, too. The receptacle to hold all the ingredients is traditionally a tall jug with paper and a cloth fastened on top, which is set in a saucepan of simmering water. 'Jugging' a dish this way produces tender, falling-off-the-bone meat.

There are two species of hare in the UK: mountain hare, which is native and rare; and brown hare, which, like the pheasant, is a historical introduction from mainland Europe which arrived in classical times. Larger and tasty, it's the brown that you'll see in the shops. There has been some concern about the hare population, which now numbers about a million animals, down from an estimate of 4 million in 1800. The decline is a result of a number of factors, but particularly the change in agricultural practices. Interestingly, the population density is sporadic: barely present in the south-west and Wales, but stable in the south-east.

The area surrounding the Pot Kiln in Berkshire is perfect hare habitat, and Mike Robinson hunts them regularly with a dog and a .22 rifle in the cooler months of the year (the season runs from 1 August to 29 February).

# Ploughman's Lunch

It's such a beautiful piece of deception, you can't help falling for it. The ploughman's lunch was cunningly invented by the English Country Cheese Council (a little-known arm of the government's Milk Marketing Board) in the 1950s. With the war and rationing over, they wanted the public to eat more cheese, and thought the pub was the place to do it; thus they hatched their dastardly plan.

At that time, most rural pubs barely had indoor toilets, let alone a kitchen with a cook, so a ploughman's lunch was designed to include raw ingredients that could be stored easily in the cool of the cellar, and assembled quickly and to order by bar staff. But the real genius of the English Country Cheese Council was to design a dish in which each region could use its own cheese. Cheddar, Cheshire, Red Leicester, Double Gloucester, Stilton, Lancashire, Wensleydale, Derby and Caerphilly were all used initially, with a chunk of bread and blob of pickle for a bit of punch. The name given to the dish conjured up images of honest, red-cheeked tillers of the earth, of England's green and pleasant land gently yielding under the plough.

But these cheeses weren't the farmhouse-made regional versions; they were – like the dish itself – simulacra of bygone traditions, efficiently assembled in bright, modern factories. As Theodore Parker said, 'Kodak sells film, but they don't advertise film. They advertise memories.' A ploughman's works on the same principle: the ECCC didn't say, 'Buy more cheese,' they simply sold it as a memory of a pre-war England, washed down with beer.

And so fifty years later, has knowing this truth set us free? Ploughman's has to compete with pizza and Pad Thai in pubs these days. What's more, it's blossomed from the original bread, cheese and pickle trinity to include a smorgasbord of ingredients. When Keith A. Faulkner researched his book *The Definitive Ploughman's Lunch*, he found that in Devon and Cornwall alone a ploughman's contained on average thirteen separate ingredients, including peppers, gherkins, pickled cabbage, lemon slices, cucumber, olives, beetroot, radishes, sweetcorn and even a Scotch egg. However, despite these variations, Keith points out that the ploughman's can be seen as the true barometer of the standard of everything else on the menu, and I agree with him. Because although the dish was born of dishonesty, it is by no means inherently bad. A wise landlord will know its flexibility, ease of preparation and high profit margin. He will also know that, when unearthed from all the obfuscating ingredients listed above, a plate of good tasty bread, home-made chutney or pickle, and a good wedge of artisan cheese is as simple and tasty a dish as any hungry beer-drinker could wish for, as well as being the most beautiful lie ever told.

*See also* BRITISH CHEESE (p. 290).

'We've fields with fifty to a hundred hares on. And when you think that three adult hares can eat as much as a sheep in a day, you've got to shoot a few,' says Mike. In the restaurant, Mike has developed the recipe to be more like a ragu, still traditionally braised with the blood and other ingredients, but served off the bone.

A Good Food Channel survey of 2006 found that only 1.6 per cent of those aged under twenty-five recognised the dish, with seven out of ten saying they wouldn't eat it. They don't know what they're missing.

*See also* ACOMB, NORTHUMBERLAND (p. 195); AUCHTERMUCHTY, FIFE (p. 144); BLAXHALL, SUFFOLK (p. 419); BROMPTON-ON-SWALE, NORTH YORKSHIRE (p. 236); CHIPPENHAM, WILTSHIRE (p. 9); KENDAL, CUMBRIA (p. 114).

## GUILDFORD, SURREY
# The British Barbecue Society

As soon as the mercury tops 20°C and the sun comes out, someone you know will suggest it: 'Come on over, Dave's doing a barbecue!' Dave will probably be the sort of bloke who never does much cooking and can't see what all the fuss is about. He'll nip off to the supermarket the morning of the big day, load up on lager and cheap sausages, swing by the petrol station for a bag of charcoal, and be handing out health hazards by mid afternoon.

Considering mankind has been cooking over fire since a million years BC, it's amazing how, in the space of a few generations, we have completely lost this skill. Then, of course there is what's actually cooked. Now, I like meat: I love a good steak or spicy lamb chops, and chicken thighs are delicious, as is a good burger or sausage; I love all these things, just not all on the same paper plate. Barbecues in Britain are more often than not, I think it's fair to say, a disaster.

Hoping to right this wrong is the British Barbecue Society, led by Toby Shea. Toby became hooked on the American low- (as in temperature) and slow-cooking style in 2003 while his kitchen was being refitted. 'For a time we had no cooker, so I was looking around and found an offset smoker and I realised that I could put a joint of meat on there, leave it for four, five hours, even all day, to cook,' he says. The result was super-tender and succulent meat. And so what started as a hobby borne of necessity turned into a profession, of sorts, when Toby and friends formed the society in 2008. The style of cooking they favour uses indirect heat and the transmogrifying power of smoke to make simple cuts of meat very, very tasty. They have since gone on to run their own cook-offs in the UK. 'We've four main dishes, which everyone has to complete. Ribs, chicken, pork shoulder, and brisket,' says Toby. Having honed their skills at these events, they have entered a team in both the prestigious American Royal Barbecue competition and the Jack Daniel's World Championship Invitational Barbecue.

It would be wrong to assume that this style of cooking is some brash US import, the culinary equivalent of Monster Truck racing. We do low- and slow-smoking quite well in this country, it's just that it's usually reserved for haddock, kippers and salmon. If you haven't got four or five hours to slow-cook your meat, Toby recommends going for fish, particularly his hot smoked salmon on cedar. Once your fire has died down to white hot coals, move them to the side and place your salmon on a soaked plank of cedar wood big enough to hold it. Put the barbecue lid back on for fifteen to twenty minutes. The wood should slightly catch, hot-smoking your fish as well as cooking it. The key to smoking rather than grilling is to use a good-sized barbecue or a stacked smoker with a lid. It's the smoke and indirect heat that do the work, not the flames. Toby has even cooked paella on his kit, while other members have done cheesecake. 'We want to promote this style of cooking and get more people interested in cooking low and slow. It gives you much better food, and a much better flavour, because smoke is an additional seasoning,' says Toby.

HASTINGS, EAST SUSSEX
## Whiting

Whiting is a member of the cod family that, due to the overfishing of its larger relation, has recently been stepping up to meet our demand for white fish. Some say it's not as exciting as cod and haddock, but it can be just as good if treated delicately. It should be as fresh as possible, and gutted quickly to stop any tainting of the flesh, and for that you could do worse than to live near someone like Sonny Elliot at Rock-a-Nore Fisheries in Hastings.

The shop is situated right on the seafront. As Sonny says, 'I could throw one of our fish and hit the boats that catch them, we're really that close. Fifty paces and you're there.' At least half of his stock comes from the Hastings fleet, and half of that comes from the Adams brothers' boats, a family who have been fishing these waters for generations. In 2007 they got lucky when their new boat was granted the registration number RX1066. They named it *Senlac Jack*, after the hill where Harold stood his army before the Battle of Hastings, and it was the first catamaran to be made in Hastings. Its two hulls make it much lighter and more stable out at sea than a wooden 'clinker'-built boat made from overlapping wooden panels.

In times past, Hastings fishermen might have thrown whiting back, or else sold it for pet food, but these days Sonny sells it for £2.25 per pound, which is a good deal cheaper than cod. Sadly, the fish still doesn't have a great reputation, something Sonny puts down to the fact that it used to be thought of as ideal food for invalids, as borne out by Douglas Chalmers Watson's 1911 book, *Food and Feeding in Health and Disease: A Manual of Practical Dietetics*: 'Raw oysters, whiting, haddock, and sole are the most easily digested members of the fish group.' Now, I love oysters, but not when I'm crook.

*See also* DERWENTWATER, CUMBRIA (p. 102); DOVER, KENT (p. 473); GLOUCESTER, GLOUCESTERSHIRE (p. 288); MARKET HARBOROUGH, LEICESTERSHIRE (p. 340); NEWLYN, CORNWALL (pp. 32 and 34); RIVER SEVERN, GLOUCESTERSHIRE (p. 305); SCOURIE, HIGHLAND (p. 187); SOUTHEND-ON-SEA, ESSEX (p. 455); WANSFORD, EAST YORKSHIRE (p. 261); WHITBURN, TYNE & WEAR (p. 228).


## HOOK, HAMPSHIRE
# Newlyns Farm Shop

Farm shops are an inherently good idea; getting the public on to farms and buying directly from the farmer is beneficial for both parties. They work best, however, when the original farming practices remain at the heart of the business. The Janaway family, who own Newlyns, have been farming 500 acres of the Hampshire countryside for four generations, although they only opened the farm shop in 2004.

'We employ four butchers and all the meat comes from our farm,' says Abby Janaway, who married into the family and now helps to run the shop. There is plenty of work for them too, not only preparing joints, cuts and sausages, but also such favourites as fresh, properly made chicken Kievs. You can buy your meat already marinated too, and the mint-marinated lamb chops come coated in a rich dark green sauce, rather than the bizarre powdery red one that so many butchers seem to use. Call me old-fashioned, but I like my mint-marinated things gloopy and green, please.

What singles Newlyns out for further praise is the beautifully appointed cookery school upstairs. Opened in March 2008, it offers cookery courses and demonstrations for complete beginners, as well as advance training, corporate events and even cooking workshops for kids and teenagers. 'One of our most popular courses was a basics course aimed at men,' says tutor chef Matthew Fleet. Despite all the macho cheffy nonsense on the telly, some fellas still come a cropper in the kitchen. The Men's Introduction course is designed for complete novices, and aims to teach basic skills. In each five-hour session a full menu is put together, featuring bread-making, fish pie, braised sausages with mustard mash, and sticky toffee pudding.

Other culinary sages showing their skills include Indian chef and broadcaster Mirdula Baljekar, and the chefs and staff from Nobu, one of London's best Japanese restaurants, even host a gala evening of food, presentations and music. Newlyns, then, is so much more than a farm shop; it's a foodie arena.

*See also* CANTERBURY, KENT (p. 469); COLSTON BASSETT, NOTTINGHAMSHIRE (p. 325); IPSWICH, SUFFOLK (p. 441); RUSHWICK, WORCESTERSHIRE (p. 309); STANNINGTON, NORTHUMBERLAND (p. 227); WELBECK, NOTTINGHAMSHIRE (p. 362).

HORSTED KEYNES, WEST SUSSEX
# High Weald Dairy

Sarah and Mark Hardy's farm nestles in the High Weald, an area of outstanding natural beauty, in the Sussex countryside. Their farm and dairy was a redundant grain store until they set about transforming it. They make a broad range of cheeses, from both cow's milk – which comes from their own animals – and sheep's milk, which they buy in from specialist producers. Sheep's milk cheese is a popular choice for those who are lactose intolerant. It's also popular with cheese-makers as some of the best and most well-known cheeses from around the world are made with sheep's milk.

The Hardys make two English-style cheeses: Duddleswell, their full-fat hard sheep's milk cheese; and Sussex Slipcote, a soft cheese with a slightly sharp flavour. The latter comes both plain and with herbs such as garlic, basil and mint. 'If you think about it, lamb and mint are great together,' says Mark.

Mark also makes some familiar international cheeses from sheep's milk. Halloumi, the classic salty cheese from the Mediterranean (although made all over Europe), is often made with cow's milk when mass produced. This lowers costs, as sheep are difficult to milk and don't produce nearly as much as a cow, but it also changes the flavour and texture of the cheese. Mark's halloumi uses only sheep milk. Halloumi is famous for being squeaky in the mouth when uncooked, but meltingly moreish after being shown some heat.

Mark Hardy with his Duddleswell cheese

Mark also makes another well-known style of sheep's cheese from the Mediterranean – specifically Greece; it's extremely similar to feta, only he can't call it that. In 1994 feta was one of the first products for which protection was sought under the newly launched European PDO (Protected Designation of Origin) scheme. In 1996 the PDO was granted, but many other European countries, particularly Denmark, which had been making poor-quality cheese using cow's milk and labelling it feta (and even featuring the Greek flag on the packaging), objected. Their argument was that feta is a worldwide generic term, like Cheddar. The debate raged on and on until the gavel slammed down in the ECJ in 2005. Now feta can only be made in specific regions in the Hellenic Republic and nowhere else, which includes West Sussex.

*See also* BRITISH CHEESE (p. 290).

## LYMINGTON, HAMPSHIRE
## *Mrs Tee's wild mushrooms*

Brigitte Tee, known in the trade as Mrs Tee, began supplying some of Britain's greatest chefs and restaurants with wild mushrooms over thirty-five years ago, and in the business she is rightly acknowledged as a master of all things mycelium. In the New Forest, her adopted home, can be found girolles, pied du mouton, chanterelles, hen and chicken of the wood, beefsteak, and the mushroom probably most loved by chefs: ceps. Ceps, known as 'porcini' in Italy, once had the nickname 'penny bun' in England, as their cap, when fully ripe, looks like a small loaf. They have a strong, earthy flavour, and their presence in a dish will rally the taste of lesser mushrooms. They are easy to recognise and can grow quite large – Brigitte once found one that weighed a kilo and a half – and are found in the autumn. If dried, they'll keep all year round.

'2009 was the worst year for mushrooms I have ever known,' says Mrs Tee, describing how the dry September – while great news for late holiday-makers – was extremely bad news for mushrooms. The previous year wasn't much better, as the first sharp frost arrived on 27 September and killed all the ceps. Like farming, foraging is completely dependent on the weather. Unlike farming, however, you can't control where your crops grow. The best spots in the New Forest are stored safely in Brigitte's head – she's never written any locations down, and has only shown her son and daughter a select few. She is the only person in the country with the right to pick commercially in the New Forest, and this only came about after a lengthy set-to with DEFRA and the Forestry Commission, during which Brigitte was arrested. The Forestry Commission complained that her commercial picking was theft and the case went to court, but was eventually thrown out as a waste of time.

As well as narrowly escaping the long arm of the law, Brigitte runs mushroom seminars, where you can learn about fungi, have a nice lunch and get to meet the first lady of 'shrooms, hearing her many tales of a life well-lived, including how her late husband worked with Jimi Hendrix and how she has supplied Michel Roux Jr and Le Gavroche for over twenty years. She has also been known to ask her acolytes this poser: 'Why should you pick mushrooms in the morning?' Answer? 'It's so you get them first!'

See also HEBRON, CARMARTHENSHIRE (p. 67); LLANGADOG, CARMARTHENSHIRE (p. 78); WINTERSLOW, WILTSHIRE (p. 49).

MAIDENHEAD, BERKSHIRE
## Copas turkeys

Turkey, according to the Copas website, is 'the most important part of the most important meal of the year'. I can't help but agree. This dedication to the bird began in 1957, when Tom Copas gave his seventeen-year-old son, also called Tom, some turkeys and told him to get on with it. 'That first year, Dad sold 157 birds,' says Tanya Copas, who along with sisters Sarah and Fenella and brother – the third Tom Copas – runs the family business. Despite the intervening years and growth of the flock, the Copas family's mission remains the same: 'To produce and supply the finest quality, traditional, farm-fresh Christmas turkeys available in the UK, unbeatable in taste, texture and presentation'. They even have a sign above the door proclaiming it.

Apart from a few for Thanksgiving, they only produce for the Christmas market. This means that the turkeys – which enjoy a free-range lifestyle from July – are slow-reared, plump and incredibly tasty. Turkey is essentially a game bird, and the Copases honour this by dry-plucking the carcass and hanging it long legged (fully intact with the head on) for two weeks. This, in combination with the way it was raised, and the various breeds including Norfolk Blacks, Devon Bronze and the Super Mini, gives the meat a rich, mature flavour. Each breed is a different size, which means that customers get the size of bird they want.

The preparation of the Christmas dinner is still a time of huge pressure for whoever is in the kitchen, especially if you've made the effort to buy a bird as good as these ones. To relieve the overworked Christmas cook, the

Copas turkeys spend their days grubbing about in hedgerows

Copases have developed a range of accompaniments: proper gravy, chutneys, sauces and two types of stuffing. They also include a pop-up timing gadget with every bird; you simply stick it in the breast before you put it in the oven, and as the bird cooks the pressure and steam build inside the meat and the top of the gadget slowly rises. When it's fully popped up, the turkey is done.

Across from where the turkeys are gambling around is the processing room, which at Christmas time is a flurry of feathers and activity. 'We have about 300 people working here for two weeks solid,' says Tanya. It's a huge logistical operation to ensure that everyone gets their turkey on time, but each bird goes out the door in its own cardboard box, ready for centre stage – well, centre table – on Christmas Day.

*See also* GOOSNARGH, LANCASHIRE (p. 106); HARLOW, ESSEX (p. 436); HINDOLVESTON, NORFOLK (p. 437); KING'S NYMPTON, DEVON (p. 20); THUXTON, NORFOLK (p. 458).

*See also* GOOSNARGH, LANCASHIRE (p. 106); HARLOW, ESSEX (p. 436); HINDOLVESTON, NORFOLK (p. 437); KING'S NYMPTON, DEVON (p. 20); THUXTON, NORFOLK (p. 458).

MEOPHAM, KENT

# Roundwood Orchard Pig Company

Chris and Bev Brown's pigs are some of the most content, happy and well-fed porkers I've had the pleasure of meeting – and eating – in all of the UK. They are Oxford Sandy & Blacks and Saddleback sows mixed with a splash of Large White from the resident boar. The Oxford and Saddleback are both rare breeds; Oxfords nearly became extinct in the 1980s and were only saved due to a handful of experts, while Saddlebacks are a bit more common. Chris explains the use of the Large White boar: 'We find it gives us that little bit leaner an animal.' It's all a question of fat, it seems; as any food fan knows, fat is where the flavour is, but too much and people can be put off.

The Browns' farm is rented from John Tobutt, who produces soft fruits in the summer, and apples and pears in the autumn. The two enterprises work in a beautiful harmony, with the pigs fertilising the land and eating any windfall or leftover fruit. By moving around different parts of John's land, the pigs also eat slugs, worms and almost anything else they can dig up. 'There's a reason they're known as Nature's plough,' says Chris. The pigs are pretty much left to their own devices, the idea being that their lives should be as natural as a farmed animal's can get. 'We don't even intervene when

Pigs, like dogs, wag their tails when happy, and these are very happy pigs indeed

they're giving birth, unless the sow's in trouble,' says Chris. They just pop their heads around the door to cut the umbilical cord, apply a blob of iodine and let the new mum get on with it. 'When the man from DEFRA came for our first inspection, he stood at the top of the hill, looked at our animals and said, "This is what it's all about!"' adds Bev.

Once a week, Chris selects which ones are ready for the thirty-minute drive to the abattoir. The next day the meat comes back and Brian the butcher comes in to do his work while Chris and Bev make sausages and burgers late into the night. The next day they get up at 5 a.m. to do it all over again. 'You've got to have the passion to do this,' says Chris. 'We never want to get away from feeding and caring for our own animals.'

As ever the proof's in the eating, and these pigs make excellent eating, particularly the crackling. As Chris said before I left, 'To get good crackling, you need a good pig.'

*See also* LLANDINAM, POWYS (p. 75); LOWICK, NORTHUMBERLAND (p. 216); MARYLEBONE, WESTMINSTER (p. 387); NEATH, NEATH PORT TALBOT (p. 80); PEASENHALL, SUFFOLK (p. 452).

# *The Garlic Farm*

Garlic originated from Central Asia's so-called 'garlic crescent', which runs from Eastern Turkey to Kazakhstan. It was thought to have been brought to Britain – along with many other things – by the Romans.

In 1699 the writer and gardener John Evelyn wrote in his *A Discourse of Sallets* (sallets now being called salads), 'We absolutely forbid it entrance into our Salleting, by reason of its intolerable Rankness.' By then the crop was widely regarded as peasant food, unfit for men of status and certainly not to be served to ladies. And this view was still held some 200 years later. There is a wonderful mention of the power of garlic in *The New Family Receipt Book* from 1820: 'The smell of garlic, which is formidable to many ladies, is, perhaps, the most infallible remedy in the world against the *vapours*, and all the nervous disorders to which women are subject.' Mrs Beeton, too, took this line in the 1860s, saying, 'The smell of this plant is generally considered offensive'. So for most of its history on these islands, garlic was persona non grata. Then in 1950 Elizabeth David wrote *A Book of Mediterranean Food* and included in her introduction a quote from chef and restaurateur Marcel Boulestin: 'It is not really an exaggeration to say that peace and happiness begin, geographically, where garlic is used in cooking.'

The rise of the package holiday and the embracing of French and Italian food in the 1960s and 1970s led to garlic slowly gaining acceptance, not because we embraced it in British cooking so much as we simply began to eat more of other people's. Today a summer's evening walk through Soho or down Charlotte Street in London reveals that we've very much fallen in love with the aroma of the 'stinking rose'.

Someone who knows more than most about the world of garlic is Colin Boswell, who owns a garlic farm on the Isle of Wight. What began in 1975 in his mother's kitchen garden has become an obsession as well as a thriving business. He's travelled the world in search of new varieties, and grows twelve varieties commercially each year, while experimenting with a further twenty or thirty. Garlic comes in two distinct types: hard necks, which put up a seed flower; and soft necks, which have been cultivated by man for so long that they have lost this ability. Like chillies, there are garlic varieties that work better with specific cuisines, dishes and ways of cooking. Chinese garlic, for example, is great for quick cooking, but hasn't got the longevity of flavour to work in a cassoulet. Mediterranean-style cooking benefits from the addition of the Iberian Wight.

Garlic bread is most people's first contact with the stuff, which nowadays often amounts to poor-quality garlic mixed with margarine and spread between the sections of industrial, part-baked, half-sliced bread. To make something worthy of the name, Colin recommends you try Purple Moldovan. It's sweet but strong, and has a powerful and beautiful aroma; it's what he uses for the farm's on-site restaurant's garlic bread.

There are few things more satisfying to cook with than good garlic: it has pungency and complexity, and a little goes a long way. I once travelled on a London tube with some home-grown garlic from a friend's allotment in Hackney. Even though it was in my bag, it was so pungent it stank out an entire carriage. Not so pleasant for my fellow commuters, then, but heaven in the frying pan.

*See also* EAST ANGLIAN PARSNIPS (p. 444); PEA HARVEST (p. 332).


NORTHIAM, EAST SUSSEX
## Cherries

Michael Dallaway's father planted cherry trees on the family farm in Kent in 1985. Michael had planned to do a degree in Economics, but he dropped out as he didn't like the course and then his father passed away, so Michael went home and took on the farm instead. 'I decided that cherries were what I wanted to do. We also had apples, but they didn't make much money.'

Michael planted a new bigger orchard in 2003, but it takes three years before a viable crop is produced. Then, around 2006, he had an idea: 'I was pruning the trees one day; you've plenty of hours to think when you're working out there all day.' Michael's idea was to offer the public the opportunity to rent a cherry tree for a year. He knocked up a quick website to test the idea, and found that people were keen. And so for a fixed annual fee of around £50 you get your own cherry tree, which you can visit with a picnic in the spring when the blossom's in bloom and again during summer to collect all the cherries that it produces. 'Some people put tags on them, and give them names. We've a couple of hundred people who've rented since we started and want to pass it on to their children,' he says.

He's now got 2,200 trees in the orchard, of which 1,500 have sponsors.

The 2010 harvest was a superb one, with people going home with over twenty kilos per tree; with supermarkets charging anywhere between £6 to £12 a kilo, that's fantastic value. Often whole families or groups of friends club together to sponsor a tree.

The rest of the 700 or so trees on his land produce cherries which Michael sells at London farmers' markets as well as sending them to New Spitalfields to be wholesaled. 'It's a great package, but it's also a nice bit of security for the farm.'

One of the key factors in Michael's business is the development of the Gisela 5 rootstock. This is a great improvement on the Colt rootstock his father planted, which grew incredibly vigorously, but some years didn't produce any fruit. 'Without the Gisela rootstock I wouldn't be able to guarantee a crop every year.' Michael has also worked with a neighbour on producing cherry brandy, which sells well.

The cherry season, like that of asparagus, is short – a mere six weeks really. It's still a crop that makes you think 'Woo, cherries are in' when you see them, and set about gorging yourself on the glut till deep-purple juice runs down your chin. Cherries have a long history in Britain. In his *History of Domestic Manners and Sentiments in England during the Middle Ages* (1862), Thomas Wright states, 'The cherry appears to have been one of the most popular of fruits in England during the mediæval period. The records of the time contain purchases of cherry-trees for the king's garden in Westminster in 1238 and 1277,' and Wright goes on to describe the great cherry fairs or cherry feasts held at harvest time, which were by all accounts high-spirited occasions. In 1411 the poet Thomas Occleve wrote *De Regimine Principum* (a fictional poem intended to act as a user guide for princely conduct) for the young Henry V, which contains the line 'Thy lyfe, my sone, is but a chery-feire.' Cherry fairs and harvest celebrations were still held in Kent and Worcester in the 1800s.

A few years ago the current plight of the British cherry was highlighted by the Cherry Aid campaign, which declared that we now import around 95 per cent of the cherries we eat in Britain. And although things are beginning to change, there's still much to be done. Fifty years ago in Kent alone there were over seventy-two square kilometres of cherry orchards; there are now less than four in the county.

Schemes like Michael's connect consumers with farming and nature, and at the same time provide a known income at the start of the year. All Michael's trees for 2010 were sponsored, and there's now a waiting list, which goes to prove the demand is there. 'The generation of farmers above me, men of my father's age, can't understand how it works; it's just not on their wavelength,' says Michael.

*See also* CORBRIDGE, NORTHUMBERLAND (p. 207); EGTON BRIDGE, NORTH YORKSHIRE (p. 243); HAMPRESTON, DORSET (p. 14); HONITON, DEVON (p. 17); INVERGOWRIE, PERTH & KINROSS (p. 180); LYTH AND WINSTER VALLEYS, CUMBRIA (p. 117); WALMERSLEY, GREATER MANCHESTER (p. 137); WIMBLEDON, MERTON (p. 415).

## POLEGATE, EAST SUSSEX
### *Banoffi pie at the Hungry Monk*

Very few dishes are invented from absolutely nothing; there is almost always what the Patent Office calls 'prior art'. As Picasso, a man who liked his dinner, once said, 'I begin with an idea and then it becomes something else.' So it was with the banoffi pie. The year is 1972, and Ian Dowding got his first head-chef role at the Hungry Monk in East Sussex. Before this, he had been sous-chef at another restaurant in Berkshire, where the head chef made a dish called 'Blum's Coffee Toffee Pie', named after a restaurant in San Francisco that was famous for its cakes, pies and pastries. The dish was not always successful, though, particularly when the toffee set solid. Left to his own devices at the Hungry Monk, Ian got creative with his menu, adding exciting foreign dishes like taramasalata and ratatouille (remember, this was the 1970s, the era of *Abigail's Party*), and a chance conversation with his sister about boiling unopened cans of condensed milk to create a soft toffee got Ian thinking. He put his head together with the restaurant's owner, Nigel Mackenzie, and they finally struck gold when they added a layer of chopped banana. The name was Nigel's suggestion: a portmanteau of the two major ingredients. It could so easily have been 'toffana pie'. Since then, the dish has been copied and transported around the globe. It's often erroneously thought to be an American invention, a mistake that winds Nigel up so much he offered £10,000 to anyone who could find an earlier reference to the dish.

Banoffi pie, as it's now spelled, is still on the menu at the Hungry Monk, while taramasalata, ratatouille and the like are long gone, replaced with leg of Sussex lamb with flageolet beans, garlic and rosemary, and fillet of pork with black pudding and apple and cider sauce. Also long gone from the stoves of the Hungry Monk is Ian Dowding, who after over thirty-five years in the business now works as a consultant, advising the next generations of chefs and restaurateurs. Who knows what dishes they'll go on to create?

*See also* BAKEWELL, DERBYSHIRE (p. 277); MICKLETON, GLOUCESTERSHIRE (p. 304); PENRITH, CUMBRIA (p. 127); PETERBOROUGH, CAMBRIDGESHIRE (p. 352).

*See also* BAKEWELL, DERBYSHIRE (p. 277); MICKLETON, GLOUCESTERSHIRE (p. 304); PENRITH, CUMBRIA (p. 127); PETERBOROUGH, CAMBRIDGESHIRE (p. 352).

ST MARY'S PLATT, KENT
## Kentish cobnuts

The cobnut has, in a mere 100 years, fallen from the tree of Britain's food knowledge. A great shame for Kent, as large areas of the county used to be given over to its production, according to Alexander W. J. Hunt, chairman of the Kentish Cobnuts Association, who says, 'In the parish of Plaxtol at the turn of the last century, 2,000 acres were grown.' Now, the association's 160 members, who are spread all over the UK, farm only 400 acres in total. But Kent remains the ancestral home of the nut, and the plantations – called platts – are mainly found between Sevenoaks, Tonbridge and Maidstone.

Cobnuts are cultivated varieties of wild hazelnut, and have a distinct shape – more acorn-like than a hazelnut – and a distinct flavour. About sixty-five varieties are known, of which six are grown commercially. Some of the association's members sell into Waitrose and Sainsbury's, but a large majority are sold through farmers' markets and specialist shops or online. 'I sell 25 per cent of my tonnage via my website,' says Alexander, who grows over twenty acres of the crop at St Mary's Platt (the name comes from the village's association with cobnut plantations). 'Every grower sells all of their crop, we never have anything left over. There's great demand from the foodies. It's a very healthy product,' says Alexander.

Cobnuts can be used in any recipe that calls for nuts, so cakes, breads and biscuits are obvious choices, and they can also add body and flavour to stuffing. Being a late summer or early autumn crop, they're a good addition to game dishes, but can also work in soups, or simply toasted. The Victorians favoured them as the post-pudding nibbles sent out after the table had been cleared and the port opened.

The story of the cobnut mirrors so many of our native foods in that it was once much loved but now is hanging by a thread. And Kent itself has seen a

## How Recipes Begin

Serendipity occurs rather too frequently in cooking. Look at the history of any recipe from before the modern age, and more often than not its creation is attributed to chance or error: Lea & Perrins sauce, left 'by chance' to ferment in a basement; Bakewell puddings, the result of a cooking error that just happened to impress the guests; Kendal mint cake, a case of someone trying to make one thing and ending up with another; Liquorice Allsorts, the result of someone falling over. Lady luck, it seems, is a dab hand in the kitchen. The French cheese Rocquefort was said to have been created when a pail of milk was left by a shepherd in the region's caves while he went off to pursue a fair maid. A month later he returned to find his milk had magically turned into cheese (a similar story exists for Cheddar) – lucky him! After a month of heavy-duty wooing, a nice bit of cheese was probably just what he needed. And nearly every smoked item ever invented starts with a conflagration that miraculously leaves the product intact.

Almost as popular as chance and error as generators of recipes and dishes is fable. Here, food is the result of one man's actions, or great victories or tragic loss. So stargazey pie sees a hero battling a stormy sea in order to catch fish to feed the starving village. Sally Lunn buns see a Huguenot refugee try to earn an honest crust on the mean streets of Regency Bath. And Bosworth jumbles see a recipe prised from the cold dead hands of a royal chef. Of course, sometimes the genesis is known and such events turn out to be true. The chicken tikka masala was indeed created when a curry was sent back for being too dry. And the most popular snack food in the world, the humble crisp, was invented when George Crum, the head chef at Moon's Lake House in Saratoga Springs, New York, had a plate of chips sent back for being too thick and soggy. The red mist descended and Drum sliced the potatoes as thinly as possible and added plenty of salt. The diner loved them, and the Saratoga chip, as they were then called, was born.

But these few notable exceptions aside, where are these happy accidents nowadays? Where are the things left unwatched in the oven, or abandoned in basements to transmogrify into something much more? Sometimes modern recipes and products are simulacra of actual dishes. I remember seeing a recipe for Fife miner's stew that began with one tablespoon of olive oil, an ingredient not likely to be present in your average Fife miner's house unless they had blocked ears.

We like the fable, the story and the drama surrounding the creation of food, it gives it substance. As food historian Ivan Day told me, 'For centuries, food was cooked on the fire, which was the heart of the home; the word "focus" means hearth or fireplace. This was not only where cooking was done, but also where stories were told.'

*See also* BAKEWELL, DERBYSHIRE (p. 277); BATH, SOMERSET (p. 5); CAMBRIDGE, CAMBRIDGESHIRE (p. 423); ETON, BERKSHIRE (p. 474); GLASGOW, GLASGOW (p. 176); KENDAL, CUMBRIA (p. 111); KING'S LYNN, NORFOLK (p. 442); MARKET BOSWORTH, LEICESTERSHIRE (p. 339); MOUSEHOLE, CORNWALL (p. 31); PONTEFRACT, WEST YORKSHIRE (p. 254); WORCESTER, WORCESTERSHIRE (p. 317).

great deal of change since 1900: industrial and retail development, transport and housing have all altered the landscape. Yet cobnuts are still there, for now at least, and it seems they are being discovered by a new generation of food fans – unsurprising, really, as they're nutritious, tasty and easy to grow in a domestic garden, although you do have to watch out for grey squirrels eating them before they're fully grown.

## STOCKBRIDGE, HAMPSHIRE
# Orson Welles's cassoulet at the Clos du Marquis

If you're driving from London to the West Country, and fancy some lunch, you would be right to bewail the lack of decent roadside restaurants. However, if you find yourself on the A30, you're in luck, as there sits the Clos du Marquis. The chef patron is Germain Marquis, and his menu is a well-constructed example of classic French roadside cooking, which includes the cassoulet.

Defining a cassoulet is tricky, and there are various schools of thought on what constitutes a correct one. The dish comes from the south of France, but each region makes it with slightly different ingredients. Like so many historical peasant dishes, it has a central theme in which seasonal or local ingredients – or whatever cooks can lay their hands on – play a part.

Essentially, it is a slow-cooked bean stew – the beans being white haricot beans – that features, depending on region, pork sausage, pork meat, mutton, lamb, or, if money is flowing, confit of duck. Finally the dish is topped with breadcrumbs. Germain's cassoulet hails from Les Landes, is topped with mashed beans, rather than the traditional breadcrumbs, and contains lamb as well as pork. Moreover, Germain's cassoulet comes with a story attached. The recipe was taught to Germain in the 1970s by Alain Dutournier in Paris. Dutournier's restaurant was a favourite haunt of Orson Welles whenever he visited the city. 'He used to come especially for that cassoulet,' says Germain. Orson, remember, was a man who let his belly do the thinking. On dining, Welles once said, 'My doctor told me to stop having intimate dinners for four. Unless there are three other people.'

It's a pleasure to find a classical French chef of the *ancien régime* still working hard in the UK and running a good roadside restaurant nestled in the English countryside. In the kitchen, which was gearing up for a busy lunch service, Germain described a sauce he was making for an order. 'Escoffier first made this sauce,' he says. 'Over my dead body will I serve "new-style" food.' Fin.

Steve Graham (overleaf) scoops one of his 'adult' ice cream flavours: Parmesan

## Sundae, Sundae

Steve and Jan Graham's retro ice-cream parlour and sweet shop is 1950s Americana with a dash of public-school tuck shop. Inside you will find proper ice-cream soda, jellies, lollies, hot waffles and some rather interesting ice creams. There are the usual suspects for the kids – vanilla, strawberry and the ever-present chocolate – but for grown-ups, and those after something a little more adventurous, Steve has a different range. His Parmesan ice cream, for example, which doesn't taste too sweet but instead has all the salty notes of the famous cheese. 'It goes great with Parma ham and a tomato salad,' he says, and you can imagine how good that would be on a blisteringly hot day. Then there's a chilli ice cream, which is best left almost to reach melting point before being used as a dip for hot grilled tiger prawns. Other flavours included cracked black pepper and lemon grass. On the sweet side, he offers rhubarb and custard flavour, which amazingly manages to taste of both rhubarb crumble and custard as well as the boiled sweet of the same name. And if you're in need of a little seaside pick-me-up then I'd recommend his *affogato*, an Italian dessert (the name is Italian for 'drowned') in which a large scoop of vanilla is topped with a shot of hot jet black espresso. This is stuff you just do not see at your average Mr Whippy van, and it's brilliant to see someone playing with the idea of what ice cream can be and making new flavours and textures.

*See also* CASTLE DOUGLAS, DUMFRIES & GALLOWAY (p. 151); WOOLER, NORTHUMBERLAND (p. 230).

## Whitstable oysters

As the old saying goes, 'The bravest man the world ever saw was the first to eat an oyster raw.' In Britain, that brave soul may have been a resident of North Kent, perhaps inspired by the Romans, who loved a good oyster, and could even have kick-started the movement that led to Whitstable's becoming famous for oysters. There are many places to eat them in town, including the tiny Wheelers Oyster Bar, which was established in 1856. But for the full Whitstable dining experience, I'd recommend the Sportsman pub. It looks a bit down-at-heel, the paintwork suffering a smidge due to the proximity of the harsh sea elements, but it's much more than a quiet, unassuming boozer stuck in the middle of nowhere. It's home, for my money, to the best cooking you'll ever find in a pub. The menu is chalked up every day on a board to the left of the main bar, as the kitchen takes in produce daily and chef Stephen Harris and his brigade like to make it up as they go along – and I fully intend that as a compliment.

As ever, the joy is to be found in the details: simple, home-made breads with their own churned butter arrive at every table. 'I can't buy better, so I make it myself,' says Stephen. He also makes his own salt, from the sea just twenty metres away. But it's the oysters that kick things off. At the right time of year, they serve native Whitstable ones 'as is', in their broad flat shells, as well as large rock oysters, each sporting a slice of chorizo. All are casually arranged on a tray of shells from the beach. Stephen's oysters are supplied by Phil Guy at the Whitstable Shellfish Company, who also supplies Wheelers and other restaurants in the area. The rock variety comes from Scotland, but the natives he fishes with his own boat. Landed back at Whitstable harbour,

A combination of native (round) and Pacific (teardrop-shaped) oysters

they are cleaned and graded, before spending forty-two hours resting in a purifying tank. Only then are they ready for dispatch.

Stephen's cooking is fantastically accomplished. The entire effect is one of effortless nonchalance, without ever looking cackhanded or thoughtless. It is, quite simply, the best food in a pub I think you'll ever eat, and you can walk it all off along the sea wall afterwards.

*See also* CLACHAN, DUMFRIES & GALLOWAY (p. 153); EDINBURGH, EDINBURGH (p. 168); LINDISFARNE, NORTHUMBERLAND (p. 214); WEST MERSEA, ESSEX (p. 459).

## WINDSOR, BERKSHIRE
### Poor knights of Windsor

Who, in the hung-over, halcyon days of their youth, didn't dredge cheap white bread through some whisked eggs of dubious provenance and fry the resulting sopping slice in vegetable oil? Eggy bread is a favourite for the morning-after, as all the ingredients can be bought from the corner shop along with Lucozade and paracetamol. Little did we realise as we stood at the cooker, heads thumping, that we were standing on the shoulders of giants. Apicius in ancient Rome, Maestro Martino of Como in the fifteenth century, Gervase Markham and Hannah Glasse, among many, many others, all produced recipes for it.

Throughout history, eggy bread has been the canvas on which cooks have painted the tastes of their age. Maestro Martino soaked his in rose water and egg, and topped it with 'a little rose water coloured yellow with saffron'. Markham adds 'cloves, mace, cinnamon, nutmeg and a good store of sugar'. Hannah Glasse first soaks French rolls in sugar and cinnamon-flavoured cream, then turns them in beaten egg. Other additions have been fruit compote, icing sugar, honey, maple syrup and the student's squeeze of ketchup, all of which have graced the surface of eggy bread like a Jackson Pollock canvas.

The dish has had various names through the ages. In France a version is known as *pain perdu* ('lost bread'), as the stale, i.e. lost, bread was revived by the soaking in egg. In Germany it takes the name *arme Ritter* ('poor knights'), and in the UK it's had various names, from gypsy toast, to eggy bread, to 'poor knights of Windsor'. This chivalrous connection is attributed to knights captured at the battle of Crécy, who, after having paid the ransom demanded, were given alms by King Edward III at Windsor Castle. Furthermore, various recipes dictate cutting the stale bread into fingers or 'soldiers' prior to soaking in the egg mix. Other references point to the fact that medieval knights, being members of the gentry – although not always rich – had to serve a pudding, and puddings don't come much cheaper than eggy bread.

## Winterdale Shaw

Winterdale Shaw is an artisan Cheddar-style cheese that is made by Robin Betts's family, who have been dairy-farming on Platt House Farm since 1950. In 2006, Robin made his first batch of cheese with milk from the family herd, and has been an avid evangelist for cheese-making ever since. Every Saturday, between 11 a.m. and 1 p.m., he opens the dairy to show off his wares and his skills. To make his cheese, he takes the milk straight from the cow in the morning, puts it into the cheese vat while still warm, and by mid afternoon the curds have separated, ready to be placed in the moulds before being pressed gently in the wooden cheese press. What happens next is rather special, though: the cheese is left to mature for ten months in chalk caves dug into the North Downs. This keeps the cheese at a constant 10°C to 12°C. Upon emerging and once unwrapped, the final cheese has a full flavour with a subtle sweetness. It's no wonder it took gold at the World Cheese Awards in 2009.

*See also* BRITISH CHEESE (p. 290).

# List of Suppliers

## The South-West

### BATH, SOMERSET

The Garrick's Head, 7–8 St John's Place, Bath, BA1 1ET · 01225 318368 · *www.garricksheadpub.com*

The Albion, Boyces Avenue, Clifton Village, Bristol, BS8 4AA · 01179 733522 · *www.thealbionclifton.co.uk*

Sally Lunn's, Sally Lunn's House, 4 North Parade Passage, Bath, BA1 1NX · 01225 461634 · *www.sallylunns.co.uk*

Huntley & Palmers, PO Box 7830, Sudbury, CO10 8WE · 01440 788873 · *www.huntleyandpalmers.com*

A. E. Eades, 18 Crescent Lane, Bath, Avon, BA1 2PX · 01225 317319

### CHEDDAR, SOMERSET

Keen's Cheddar, Moorhayes Farm, Verrington Lane, Wincanton, BA9 8JR · 01963 32286 · *www.keenscheddar.co.uk*

Montgomery's Cheddar, Manor Farm, North Cadbury, Yeovil, BA22 7DW · 01963 440243 · *www.farmhousecheesemakers.com*

Westcombe Cheddar, Lower Westcombe Farm, Shepton Mallet, BA4 6ER · 01749 830312 · *www.farmhousecheesemakers.com*

Parkham's Farms, Higher Alminstone Farm, Woolsery, Bideford, EX39 5PX · 01237 431246 · *www.parkhamfarms.com*

Denhay Farm, Broadoak, Bridport, DT6 5NP · 01308 458963 · *www.denhay.co.uk*

A. J. & R. G. Barber, Maryland Farm, Ditcheat, Shepton Mallet, BA4 6PR · 01749 860666 · *www.barbers1833.co.uk*

### CHIPPENHAM, WILTSHIRE

The Real Boar Company, Noble Street, Sherston, SN16 0NA · 01249 782861 · *www.therealboar.co.uk*

### EASTON GREY, WILTSHIRE

Tracklements, Whitewalls, Easton Grey, Malmesbury, SN16 0RD · 01666 827044 · *www.tracklements.co.uk*

Continental Delicatessen, The Chequers, Devizes, SN10 1BB · 01380 723355

### HAMBRIDGE, SOMERSET

Brown and Forrest, Bowdens Farm Smokery, Hambridge, TA1 0BP · 01458 250875 · *www.smokedeel.co.uk*

### HAMPRESTON, DORSET

The Dorset Blueberry Company, Trehane Nursery, Ham Lane, Wimborne, BH21 7LT · 01202 873490 · *www.dorset-blueberry.com*

HELSTON, CORNWALL
Gourmet Picnics, Amélies at the
Smokehouse, Harbourside, Porthleven,
TR13 9JS · 08456 210400 ·
*www.gourmetpicnics.co.uk*

HONITON, DEVON
Otter Farm · *www.otterfarm.co.uk*

KING'S NYMPTON, DEVON
Heal Farm, King's Nympton, EX37 9TB ·
01769 574341 · *www.healfarm.co.uk*

LOOE, CORNWALL
Bocaddon Farm Veal, Bocaddon, Lanreath,
Looe, PL13 2PG · 01503 220995 ·
*www.bocaddonfarmveal.com*

LOSTWITHIEL, CORNWALL
Trewithen Dairy, Greymare Farm,
Lostwithiel, PL11 OLW · 01208 872214 ·
*www.cornishfarmdairy.co.uk*

LYME REGIS, DORSET
The Town Mill Bakery, 2 Coombe Street,
Lyme Regis, DT7 3PY · 01297 444035 ·
*www.townmillbakery.com*

MARTOCK, SOMERSET
The Somerset Cider Brandy Company,
Pass Vale Farm, Burrow Hill, Kingsbury
Episcopi, Martock, TA12 6BU · 01460
240782 · *www.ciderbrandy.co.uk*

MOUSEHOLE, CORNWALL
The Ship Inn, South Cliff, Mousehole,
Penzance, TR19 6QX · 01736 731234 ·
*www.shipmousehole.co.uk*

NEWLYN BAY, CORNWALL
Cornish Albacore Tuna · 01736 351050 ·
*www.cornishtuna.com*
M&J Seafood, Enterprise House, Eureka
Business Park, Ashford, TN25 4AG ·
01296 333800 · *www.mjseafood.com*

NEWLYN, CORNWALL
Cornish Sardine Management Association,
The Pilchard Works, Newlyn, Penzance,
TR18 5HW · 07809 609545 ·
*www.cornishsardines.org.uk*

PLYMOUTH, DEVON
Plymouth Gin, Black Friars Distillery,
60 Southside Street, Plymouth,
PL1 2LQ · 01752 665292 ·
*www.plymouthgin.com*

ROCK, CORNWALL
St Enodoc Hotel, Rock, PL27 6LA · 01208
863394 · *www.enodoc-hotel.co.uk*

ST JUST, CORNWALL
W. T. Warren & Son, Boswedden Road, St
Just, Penzance, TR19 7JP · 01736 786195 ·
*www.warrensbakery.co.uk*

STOURHEAD, WILTSHIRE
Stourhead, Stourton, Warminster,
BA12 6QD · 01747 841152 ·
*www.nationaltrust.org.uk/stourhead*

TOTNES, DEVON
Country Cheeses, 1 Ticklemore Street,
Totnes, TQ9 5EJ · 01392 877746 ·
*www.countrycheeses.co.uk*
White Lake Cheeses, Bagborough Farm,
Bagborough Lane, Pylle, Shepton Mallet,
BA4 6SX · 01749 830538

TREEN, CORNWALL
Treen Farm, St Levan, Penzance, TR19
6LF · 01736 810273 ·
*www.treenfarmcampsite.co.uk*

WEST BEXINGTON, DORSET
Peppers by Post, Sea Spring Farm, West
Bexington, Dorchester, DT2 9DD ·
01308 897766 · *www.peppersbypost.biz*

WEST KNOYLE, WILTSHIRE
Willoughby Hedge Café, West Knoyle,
  Warminster, BA12 6AQ · 01747 830803

WINCANTON, SOMERSET
Charles Dowding, Lower Farm, Shepton
  Montague, Wincanton, BA9 8JG · 01749
  812253 · www.charlesdowding.co.uk

WINTERSLOW, WILTSHIRE
The Harrow Inn, Little Bedwyn,
  Marlborough, SN8 3JP · 01672 870871 ·
  www.harrowinn.co.uk

## Wales

ABERCYNON, RHONDDA CYNON TAF
Parsons Pickles, Ashburnham Works,
  Burry Port, SA16 0ET · 01554 833351 ·
  www.parsonspickles.co.uk
Tyddyn Llan, Llandrillo nr. Corwen,
  LL21 0ST · 01490 440264 ·
  www.tyddynllan.co.uk
Sushi Day, 20 Margaret Street, Abercynon,
  CF45 4RE · 01443 741933 ·
  www.sushiday.co.uk

ABERTHIN, VALE OF GLAMORGAN
Greta's Wholefoodies, Cwrt Newydd,
  Aberthin, Cowbridge, CF71 7HE · 01446
  775240 · www.gretaswholefoodies.com

BLAENAFON, TORFAEN
The Blaenafon Cheddar Company,
  80 Broad Street, Blaenafon, NP4 9NF ·
  01495 793123 · www.chunkofcheese.co.uk
First Milk, Cirrus House, Glasgow
  Airport Business Park, Marchburn
  Drive, PA3 2SJ · 01418 876111 ·
  www.firstmilk.co.uk

BRYNSIENCYN, ISLE OF ANGLESEY
Halen Môn, The Anglesey Sea Salt
  Company, Brynsiencyn, LL61 6TQ ·
  01248 430871 · www.seasalt.co.uk

CARDIFF, CARDIFF
Clark's Pies, 23 Bromsgrove Street,
  Grangetown, Cardiff, CF11 7EZ /
  454 Cowbridge Road East, Canton,
  Cardiff, CF5 1BJ · 029 2022 7586 /
  029 2056 2697 · www.clarkspies.co.uk

CONWY, CONWY
Edwards of Conwy, 18 High Street,
  Conwy, LL32 8DE · 01492 592443 ·
  www.edwardsofconwy.co.uk

CORWEN, DENBIGHSHIRE
Rhug Estate Organic Farm, Corwen,
  LL21 0EH · 01490 413000 ·
  www.rhug.co.uk

CRYMYCH, PEMBROKESHIRE
First Leaf Produce, Blaenafon, Brynberian,
  Crymych, SA41 3TN · 077 4861 3444 ·
  www.firstleaf.co.uk

ELAN VALLEY, POWYS
Elan Valley Mutton, Henfron Farm,
  Elan Valley, Rhayader, LD6 5HE ·
  01597 811240 ·
  www.elanvalleymutton.co.uk

ELWY VALLEY, DENBIGHSHIRE
Elwy Valley Welsh Lamb, Rose Hill
  Cottage, Henllan, Denbigh, LL16 5BA ·
  01745 813552 · www.elwyvalleylamb.co.uk

CAWL
Mimosa Kitchen & Bar, Mermaid Quay,
  Cardiff Bay, CF10 5BZ · 02920 491900 ·
  www.mimosakitchen.co.uk
Howells Butchers, 11 Cae Folland,
  Penclawdd, Swansea, SA4 3YJ · 01792
  850371 · www.howellsbutchers.co.uk
Sugarcraft Bakery, 30 Commercial Street,
  Beddau, Pontypridd, CF38 2DB ·
  01443 205114

HALKYN, FLINTSHIRE
North Wales Buffalo, Midlist Farm,
  Halkyn, Holywell, CH8 8DH · 01352
  781695 · www.northwalesbuffalo.co.uk

**HEBRON, CARMARTHENSHIRE**
The Mountain Food Company, Banc Y
Ddol, Hebron, Whitland, SA34 0YR ·
01994 419555 · *www.mountainfood.org*

**LITTLE HAVEN, PEMBROKESHIRE**
DASH Shellfish, Walton West, Little
Haven, Haverfordwest, SA62 3UA · 079
1735 3323 · *www.dashshellfish.co.uk*

**LLANBERIS, GWYNEDD**
Pete's Eats, 40 High Street, Llanberis,
LL55 4EU · 01286 870117 ·
*www.petes-eats.co.uk*

**LLANDDEWI BREFI, CEREDIGION**
Trethowan's Dairy, Gorwydd Farm,
Llanddewi Brefi, Tregaron, SY25 6NY ·
01570 493516 · *www.trethowansdairy.co.uk*
Trethowan's Dairy Shop, 33–34 The Glass
Arcade, St Nicholas Market, Bristol,
BS1 1LJ · 01179 020332

**LLANDEILO, CARMARTHENSHIRE**
Welsh Cottage Cakes, Units 5–6,
Beechwood Industrial Estate, Talley
Road, Llandeilo, SA19 7HR · 01558
824213 · *www.welshcottagecakes.co.uk*
Pemberton's Chocolate Farm, Llanboidy,
SA34 0EX · 01994 448800 ·
*www.welshchocolatefarm.com*

**LLANDINAM, POWYS**
Neuadd Fach Baconry, Llandinam,
SY17 5AS · 01686 688734 ·
*www.baconry.co.uk*

**LLANGADOG, CARMARTHENSHIRE**
Humungus Fungus, Red Pig Farm,
Bethlehem, Llangadog, SA19 9HD ·
01550 740306 ·
*www.humungusfungus.co.uk*

**NEATH, NEATH PORT TALBOT**
Panorama Pedigree Pigs, Tyla Morris,
Gardners Lane, Neath, SA11 2AU ·
01639 644091 · *www.welshpigs.com*

**PEMBROKE DOCK, PEMBROKESHIRE**
The Pembrokeshire Tea Company,
Technium Unit 6, Pembroke Dock,
SA72 6UN · 01437 741671 ·
*www.pembrokeshiretea.co.uk*
Y Felin Mill, Y Felin, St Dogmaels ·
01239 613999 · *www.yfelin.co.uk*

**PENDERYN, RHONDDA CYNON TAF**
The Welsh Whisky Company, Penderyn
Distillery, Pontpren, Penderyn,
CF44 0SX · 01685 810650 ·
*www.welsh-whisky.co.uk /*
*www.penderynstore.com*

**QUEENSFERRY, FLINTSHIRE**
Really Welsh Trading, Wick Road,
Llantwit Major, Cardiff, CF61 1YU ·
01446 796386 ·
*www.reallywelsh.com*

**RIVER DEE, FLINTSHIRE**
The Swan Inn, Point Road, Little Haven,
Haverfordwest, SA62 3UL ·
01437 781880 ·
*www.theswanlittlehaven.co.uk*

**RUTHIN, DENBIGHSHIRE**
Patchwork Paté, Llys Parcwr, Ruthin,
LL15 1NJ · 0845 123 5010 ·
*www.patchwork-pate.co.uk*

**SWANSEA, SWANSEA**
Maddocks' Cakes from Wales, 64
Southgate Road, Southgate, Gower,
Swansea, SA3 2DH · 01792 233447 ·
*www.cakesfromwales.com*

**TALLEY, CARMARTHENSHIRE**
Cothi Valley Goats, Cilwr Farm, Tally,
Llandeilo, SA19 7BQ · 01558 685555

**WHITLAND, CARMARTHENSHIRE**
Calon Wen Organic Milk Co-operative,
Unit 4, Spring Gardens, Whitland,
SA34 0HZ · 01994 241481 ·
*www.calonwen-cymru.com*

WREXHAM, WREXHAM
British Saffron, Caer Estyn Farm, Rhyddyn
Hill, Caergwrle, Wrexham, LL12 9EF ·
01978 761558

## The North-West and the Isle of Man

ALDERLEY EDGE, CHESHIRE
Horseshoe Farm, Horseshoe Lane,
Alderley Edge, SK9 7QP · 01625 590055
Davenports Farm Shop, Florists and Tea
Room, Bridge Farm, Warrington Road,
Bartington, Northwich, CW8 4QU ·
01606 853241 ·
www.davenportsflorists.co.uk

BLACKBURN, LANCASHIRE
Northcote, Northcote Road, Langho,
Blackburn, BB6 8BE · 01254 240555 ·
www.northcote.com

BURY MARKET, GREATER
MANCHESTER
Chadwicks Original Black Puddings, Bury
Market, 1 Murray Rd, Bury, BL9 0BJ ·
01706 226221 ·
www.burymarket.com/stalls/chadwicks
The Bury Black Pudding Company, Unit
12, J2 Business Park, Bridgehall Lane,
Bury, BL9 7NY · 0161 797 0689 ·
www.buryblackpuddings.co.uk

CLITHEROE, LANCASHIRE
Cowman's Famous Sausage Shop,
13 Castle Street, Clitheroe, BB7 2BT ·
01200 423842 ·
www.rcoward.com/cowmans

ECCLES, GREATER MANCHESTER
Lancashire Eccles Cakes, 57 Hyde Road,
Ardwick, Manchester, M12 6BH ·
0161 273 6368 ·
www.lancashireecclescakes.co.uk

GOOSNARGH, LANCASHIRE
Johnson and Swarbrick, Swainson House
Farm, Goosnargh, Preston, PR3 2JU ·
01772 865251 ·
www.jandsgoosnargh.co.uk

GRANGE-OVER-SANDS, CUMBRIA
Hazelmere Café and Bakery,
1–2 Yewbarrow Terrace, Grange-over-
Sands, LA11 6ED · 01539 532972 ·
www.hazelmerecafe.co.uk

GREAT CLIFTON, CUMBRIA
Mr Fletts Cumberland Sausage, The
Chicken Shop, 144 Vulcans Lane,
Workington, CA14 2BP · 01900 604953 ·
www.cumberland-sausage.co.uk
Richard Woodall, Lane End, Waberthwaite
nr. Millom, LA19 5YJ · 01229 717237 ·
www.richardwoodall.co.uk

THE ISLE OF MAN
The Manx Loaghtan Sheep Breeders'
Group, Cannons, Huntley Road,
Tibberton, Gloucester, GL19 3AB ·
01452 790309 ·
www.manxloaghtansheep.org

KENDAL, CUMBRIA
Romney's Kendal Mint Cake, Mintsfeet
Trading Estate, Kendal, LA9 6NA ·
01539 720155 ·
www.kendal.mintcake.co.uk
Sillfield Farm, Endmoor, Kendal,
LA8 0HZ · 01539 567609 ·
www.sillfield.co.uk

LIVERPOOL, MERSEYSIDE
Maggie May's Café, 90 Bold Street,
Liverpool, L1 4HY · 01517 097600

LYTH AND WINSTER VALLEYS,
CUMBRIA
The Westmorland Damson Association,
Lile Yaks, Cartmel Fell, Windermere,
LA23 3PD · 01539 568698 ·
www.lythdamsons.org.uk

Cowmire Damson Gin, Cowmire Hall, Crosthwaite, Kendal, LA8 8JJ · 01539 568200 · www.cowmire.co.uk

### MANCHESTER, GREATER MANCHESTER
Riley's Sausages, C. H. Sausage Company, 9 Cornwall Street, Openshaw, Manchester, M11 2WQ · www.rileysausage.co.uk

### MORECAMBE BAY, LANCASHIRE
Baxters Original Potted Shrimps, Thornton Road, Morecambe, LA4 5PB · 01524 410910 · www.baxterspottedshrimps.co.uk

### NANTWICH, CHESHIRE
Austin's Yesteryear Grocers Shoppe, 45 Hospital Street, Nantwich, CW5 5RL · 01270 625941 · www.atwelch.co.uk
The Great Tasting Meat Company, Gate Farm Shop, Wettenhall Road, Poole, Nantwich, CW5 6AL · 01270 625781 · www.greattastingmeat.co.uk

### PENRITH, CUMBRIA
Sharrow Bay, Lake Ullswater, Penrith, CA10 2LZ · 01768 486301 · www.sharrowbay.co.uk
Cartmel Village Shop, The Square, Cartmel, LA11 6QB · 01539 536280 · www.cartmelvillageshop.co.uk

### PRESTON, LANCASHIRE
Mrs Kirkham's Lancashire Cheese, Beesly Farm, Mill Lane, Goosnargh, Preston, PR3 2FL · 01772 865335 · www.mrskirkhams.com
Leagram Organic Dairy, High Head Farm Buildings, Green Lane, Chipping nr. Preston, PR3 2TQ · 01995 61532 · www.leagramorganicdairy.co.uk

### RAWTENSTALL, LANCASHIRE
Mr Fitzpatrick's Temperance Bar, 5 Bank Street, Rawtenstall, Rossendale, BB4 6QS · 01706 231836 · www.mrfitzpatricks.com

### ROSSENDALE, LANCASHIRE
H&P Ashcroft, Worthington's Farm, Park Lane, Holmes, Tarleton, PR4 6JN · 01772 814465 · www.worthingtonsfarm.co.uk
Heritage Kitchen, Heritage House, 26 Burnley Road, Bacup, OL13 8AB · 01706 873101 · www.heritagekitchen.co.uk

### ST HELENS, MERSEYSIDE
Barton's Pickles, Lascelles Street, St Helens, WA9 1BA · 01744 22593 · www.go-e2.co.uk/bartons

### SIZERGH, CUMBRIA
Growing Well, Low Sizergh Farm, Low Sizergh, Kendal, LA8 8AE · 01539 561777 · www.growingwell.co.uk

### TEBAY, CUMBRIA
Tebay Services, Junction 38 (M6), Penrith, CA10 3SS · 01539 624505 · www.westmorland.com/tebay-services
The Upper Crust Pie Company, 50 Hardmans Road, Whitefield, Manchester, M45 7BD · 0161 766 9744 · www.uppercrustpies.com
The Handmade Scotch Egg Company, Hopscotch, The Old Cookhouse, 5 The Hop Pocket, Bishop's Frome, WR6 5BT · 01885 490520 · www.handmadescotcheggs.co.uk

### WALMERSLEY, GREATER MANCHESTER
Park Farm Shop and Tearooms, Walmersley, Bury, BL9 5NP · 01706 823577 · www.parkfarmshopramsbottom.co.uk

## Scotland

### ARBROATH, ANGUS
Iain R. Spink's Original Arbroath Smokies, Forehills Farmhouse, Carmyllie, by Arbroath, DD11 2RH · 01241 860303 · www.arbroathsmokies.net

**AUCHTERMUCHTY, FIFE**

Fletchers of Auchtermuchty, Reediehill Deer Farm, Auchtermuchty, KY14 7HS · 01337 828369 · www.seriouslygoodvenison.co.uk

**BOGHALL, WEST LOTHIAN**

Boghall Butchers, 65 Margaret Avenue, Boghall, Bathgate, EH48 1SN · 01506 630178 · www.boghallbutchers.co.uk

**BOYNDIE, ABERDEENSHIRE**

Hamlyns of Scotland, Cairnton Road, Boyndie, AB45 2LR · 01261 843330 · www.hamlynsoats.co.uk

**BUCKIE, MORAY**

Moray Seafoods, 3–15 Low Street, Buckie, AB56 1UX · 01542 280086 · www.morayseafoods.co.uk

**CASTLE DOUGLAS, DUMFRIES & GALLOWAY**

Cream o' Galloway, Rainton, Gatehouse of Fleet, Castle Douglas, DG7 2DR · 01557 814040 · www.creamogalloway.co.uk

**CLACHAN, DUMFRIES & GALLOWAY**

Loch Fyne Oysters, Clachan, Cairndow, PA26 8BL · 01499 600264 · www.lochfyne.com

**CLACHNACUDDIN, HIGHLAND**

MacDougall & Hastie Butchers, 4 Queensgate Arcade, Inverness, IV1 1PQ · 01463 715219 · www.macdougallandhastie.co.uk

**CLOOTIE DUMPLING**

Cranachan Café, Unit 51, Princes Square, 48 Buchanan Street, Glasgow, G1 3JN · 01412 486257 · www.cranachancafe.co.uk

Ghillie Dhu, 2 Rutland Place, Edinburgh, EH1 2AD · 0131 222 9930 · www.ghillie-dhu.co.uk

The Ceilidh Place, 14 West Argyle Street, Ullapool, IV26 2TY · 01854 612103 · www.theceilidhplace.com

**CULLEN, MORAY**

Cullen Bay Hotel, Cullen, AB56 4XA · 01542 840432 · www.cullenbayhotel.co.uk

**CUMBERNAULD, NORTH LANARKSHIRE**

H. M. Sheridan, 11 Bridge Street, Ballater, AB35 5QP · 01339 755218 · www.hmsheridan.co.uk

**DINGWALL, HIGHLAND**

George Cockburn & Son, 19 Mill Street, Dingwall, IV15 9PZ · 01349 863512

**DUMGOYNE, STIRLING**

Glengoyne Distillery, Dungoyne nr. Killearn, Glasgow, G63 9LB · 01360 550254 · www.glengoyne.com

**DUNDEE, ANGUS**

Mackays, James Chalmers Road, Arbroath, DD11 3LR · 01241 432500 · www.mackays.com

**DURNESS, HIGHLAND**

Cocoa Mountain, 8 Balnakeil, Durness, Lairg, IV27 4PT · 01971 511233 · www.cocoamountain.co.uk

**EDINBURGH, EDINBURGH**

Artisan Roast, 57 Broughton Street, Edinburgh, EH1 3RJ · 07590 590667 · www.artisanroast.co.uk

The Gold Sea, 139–141 Ferry Road, Edinburgh, EH6 4ET · 0131 554 2195

The Café Royal, 19 West Register Street, Edinburgh, EH2 2AA · 0131 556 1884 · www.caferoyal.org.uk

**FINDON, ABERDEENSHIRE**

Fishers, 1 Shore, Leith, Edinburgh, EH6 7QW · 0131 554 5666 · www.fishersbistros.co.uk

**FORFAR, ANGUS**

James McLaren & Son, 8 The Cross, Forfar, DD8 1BX · 01307 462762 · www.thebridieshop.co.uk

William Saddler & Sons, 96 North Street,
  Forfar, DD8 3BN · 01307 464121
Sugar & Spice, 96 High Street,
  Auchterarder, PH3 1BJ · 01764 661100

FORRES, MORAY
Macbeth's Butchers, 11 Tolbooth Street,
  Forres, IV36 1PH · 01309 672254 ·
  www.macbeths.com

GLASGOW, GLASGOW
Café Gandolfi, 64 Albion Street, Glasgow,
  G1 1NY · 01415 528911 ·
  www.cafegandolfi.com
Shish Mahal, 60–68 Park Road, Glasgow,
  G4 9JF · 01413 347899 ·
  www.shishmahal.co.uk
The Willow Tea Rooms, 217 Sauchiehall
  Street, Glasgow, G2 3EX · 01413 320521 ·
  www.willowtearooms.co.uk
Stravaigin, 28 Gibson Street, Kelvinbridge,
  Glasgow, G12 8NX · 01413 342665 ·
  www.stravaigin.com

GLENFINNAN, HIGHLAND
The Prince's House Hotel, Glenfinnan,
  PH37 4LT · 01397 722246 ·
  www.glenfinnan.co.uk

MOFFAT, DUMFRIES & GALLOWAY
Uncle Roy's Comestible Concoctions,
  6–7 Buccleuch Street, Moffat, DG1 0HA ·
  01683 221076 · www.uncleroys.co.uk

NEW GALLOWAY, DUMFRIES &
GALLOWAY
Kitty's Tea Room, High Street, New
  Galloway, DG7 3RN · 01644 420246

OGCASTLE, SOUTH LANARKSHIRE
H. J. Errington & Co, Walston Braehead
  Farm, Carnwath, ML11 8NF ·
  01899 810257 · www.lanarkblue.com

SCOURIE, HIGHLAND
Loch Duart Salmon, Badcall Salmon
  House, Scourie, Lairg, IV27 4TH ·
  01674 660161 · www.lochduart.com

STENHOUSEMUIR, FALKIRK
Millar McCowan, The New McCowan's,
  44 Tryst Road, Stenhousemuir,
  FK5 4HA · 01324 562158 ·
  www.millar-mccowan.com

TAIN, HIGHLAND
Highland Fine Cheeses, Blairliath Farm,
  Shore Road, Tain, IV19 1EB ·
  01862 892034 · www.hf-cheeses.com

ULLAPOOL, HIGHLAND
Crombies of Edinburgh, 97–101 Broughton
  Street, Edinburgh, EH1 3RZ ·
  0131 557 0111 ·
  www.sausages.co.uk
Patricks of Camelon, 334 Main Street,
  Camelon, FK1 4EG · 01324 612082 ·
  www.patricksofcamelon.com

## The North-East

ACOMB, NORTHUMBERLAND
Ridley's Fish and Game, Unit 15, Acomb
  Industrial Estate, Acomb nr. Hexham,
  NE46 4SA · 01434 609246 ·
  www.ridleysfishandgame.co.uk

ALNWICK, NORTHUMBERLAND
R. Turnball & Sons, 33–35 Market Place,
  Alnwick, NE66 1AT · 01665 602186 ·
  www.turnbullsofalnwick.co.uk
Alnwick Rum, Old Rum, Aydon View,
  Alnwick, NE66 1BF · 01665 604768 ·
  www.alnwickbrewery.com
Daleside Brewery, Camwal Road,
  Harrogate, HG1 4PT · 01423 880022 ·
  www.dalesidebrewery.com
The Treehouse at the Alnwick Garden,
  Denwick Lane, Alnwick,
  NE66 1YU · 01665 511852 ·
  www.alnwickgarden.com/eat/eat-in-the-
  treehouse

BELFORD, NORTHUMBERLAND
Sunny Hill Eggs, Sunny Hill Farm,
   Detchant Farm, Belford, NE70 7PF ·
   01668 219970 · www.sunnyhilleggs.com

BISHOP AUCKLAND, COUNTY
DURHAM
Jenkins & Hustwit Farmhouse Fruit Cakes,
   3b Laurel Way, Bishop Auckland,
   DL14 7NF · 01388 605005 ·
   www.jenkinsandhustwit.com

BLAYDON, TYNE & WEAR
Beckleberry's, Artisan Foods, Cowen Road,
   Blaydon, NE21 5TW · 01914 141180 ·
   www.beckleberrys.com

CHILLINGHAM PARK,
NORTHUMBERLAND
Chillingham Wild Cattle, Chillingham
   Park, A697 between Alnwick and
   Belford, NE66 5NP ·
   www.chillinghamwildcattle.com

CORBRIDGE, NORTHUMBERLAND
Brocksbushes Farm Shop and Tearoom,
   Corbridge, NE43 7UB · 01434 633100 ·
   www.brocksbushes.co.uk

CORNHILL-ON-TWEED,
NORTHUMBERLAND
Carroll's Heritage Potatoes, Tiptoe Farm,
   Cornhill-on-Tweed, TD12 4XD · 01890
   883833 · www.heritage-potatoes.co.uk
Berwick Farmers' Market, The Maltings
   Art Centre, Eastern Lane, Berwick-
   upon-Tweed, TD15 1AJ ·
   www.berwickfarmersmarket.com

EVENWOOD, COUNTY DURHAM
Loopy Lisa's Fudge, 1 Randolph Industrial
   Estate, Evenwood, DL14 9SJ · 01388
   835135 · www.loopylisasfudge.co.uk

HORNCLIFFE, NORTHUMBERLAND
Chain Bridge Honey Farm, Horncliffe,
   Berwick-upon-Tweed, TD15 2XT ·
   01289 386362 ·
   www.chainbridgehoney.co.uk

LINDISFARNE, NORTHUMBERLAND
Lindisfarne Mead, St Aidan's Winery, Holy
   Island, TD15 2RX · 01289 389230 ·
   www.lindisfarne-mead.co.uk
Northumberland Mussels, 15 St Helen's
   Terrace, Spittal, Berwick-upon-Tweed,
   TD15 1RJ · 01289 332216 ·
   www.holyislandmussels.co.uk
The Feathers Inn, Hedley on the Hill,
   Stocksfield, NE43 7SW · 01661 843607 ·
   www.thefeathers.net
Lindisfarne Oysters, West House,
   Ross Farm, Belford, NE70 7EN ·
   01668 213870 ·
   www.lindisfarneoysters.co.uk

LOWICK, NORTHUMBERLAND
Piperfield Pork, The Dovecote, Lowick,
   Berwick-upon-Tweed, TD15 2QE ·
   01289 388543 · www.piperfield.com

MORPETH, NORTHUMBERLAND
British Beef Jerky, 2 Eshott Heugh
   Workshops, Felton, Morpeth,
   NE65 9QH · 01670 787778 ·
   www.britishbeefjerky.co.uk
Warren Butterworth Catering Butchers,
   Unit 5, Westway Industrial Park,
   Ponteland Road, Throckley, NE15 9HW ·
   01912 296060 ·
   www.wbutterworth.plus.com

NEWCASTLE, TYNE & WEAR
Pan Haggerty Restaurant, 21 Queen
   Street, Newcastle, NE1 3UG · 01912
   210904 · www.panhaggerty.com
Hadrian & Border Brewery, Unit 11,
   Hawick Crescent Industrial Estate,
   Newcastle, NE6 1AS · 01912 765302 ·
   www.hadrian-border-brewery.co.uk
Northumberland Brewery, Fuggles Bar,
   Accessory House, Barrington Road,
   Bedlington, NE22 7AP · 01670 822112 ·
   www.northumberlandbrewery.co.uk
Fentimans Botanically Brewed Beverages,
   6 Rear Battle Hill, Hexham, NE46 1BB ·
   01434 609847 · www.fentimans.com

**SEAHOUSES, NORTHUMBERLAND**
Swallow Fish of Seahouses, Fisherman's
Kitchen, 2 South Street, Seahouses,
NE68 7RB · 01665 721052 ·
*www.swallowfish.co.uk*

**SOUTH SHIELDS, TYNE & WEAR**
Colmans Fish and Chips, 182–186 Ocean
Road, South Shields, NE33 2JQ ·
01914 561202 · *www.colmansfishand-
chips.com*

**STANNINGTON, NORTHUMBERLAND**
Moorhouse Farm Shop and Coffee Shop,
21 Station Road, Stannington, Morpeth,
NE61 6DX · 01670 789016 ·
*www.moorhousefarmshop.co.uk*
Castle Bakery, Ogle Castle, Ogle,
NE20 0AT · 01670 775181

**WHITBURN, TYNE & WEAR**
Latimer's Seafood Deli and Café, Shell
Hill, Bents Road, Whitburn, SR6 7NT ·
01915 292200 · *www.latimers.com*

**WOOLER, NORTHUMBERLAND**
Doddington Dairy, North Doddington
Farm, Wooler, NE71 6AN ·
01668 283010 ·
*www.doddingtondairy.co.uk*

## Yorkshire

**AMPLEFORTH, NORTH YORKSHIRE**
Ampleforth Abbey Orchard, Ampleforth
Abbey, Ampleforth, YO62 4EN ·
01439 766899 ·
*www.abbey.ampleforth.org.uk*

**BRIGHOUSE, WEST YORKSHIRE**
Andrew Jones Pies, Units 2–4,
Queens Mill Industrial Estate, Queens
Mill Road, Huddersfield, HD1 3RR ·
01484 548137 ·
*www.andrewjonespies.co.uk*

**BROMPTON-ON-SWALE, NORTH
YORKSHIRE**
Yorkshire Game, Station Road Industrial
Park, Brompton-on-Swale, Richmond,
DL10 7SN · 01748 810212 ·
*www.yorkshiregame.co.uk*

**COLLINGHAM, WEST YORKSHIRE**
Wharfe Valley Farms, Collingham,
LS22 5BA · 01937 572084 ·
*www.wharfevalleyfarms.co.uk*

**DENBY DALE, WEST YORKSHIRE**
The Denby Dale Pie Company, Unit 12,
Denby Dale Business Park, Wakefield
Road, Denby Dale, Huddersfield,
HD8 8QH · 01484 862585 ·
*www.denbydalepiecompany.co.uk*

**DEWSBURY, WEST YORKSHIRE**
R. Hey & Sons Tripe, Meadow Lane,
Dewsbury, WF13 2BE · 01924 463512 ·
*www.heystripe.com*

**EGTON BRIDGE, NORTH YORKSHIRE**
Egton Bridge Old Gooseberry Society ·
*www.egtongooseberryshow.org.uk*

**GOMERSAL, WEST YORKSHIRE**
W. S. Bentley Growers, Cliffe Hill
Nurseries, Cliffe Lane, Gomersal,
BD19 4SX · 01274 851254 ·
*www.wsbentley.co.uk*

**GOOLE, EAST YORKSHIRE**
M. H. Poskitt, The Firs, Kellington nr.
Goole, DN14 0SW · 01977 661236 ·
*www.poskittcarrots.co.uk*

**HAROME, NORTH YORKSHIRE**
The Star Inn, Main Street, Harome nr.
Helmsley, YO62 5JE · 01439 770397 ·
*www.thestaratharome.co.uk*

**HARROGATE, NORTH YORKSHIRE**
Taylors of Harrogate, Pagoda House,
Plumpton Park, Harrogate,
HG2 7LD · 01423 814000 ·
*www.taylorsofharrogate.co.uk*

NIDDERDALE, NORTH YORKSHIRE
Mackenzie's Yorkshire Smokehouse, Units
1–6, Wood Nook Farm, Hardisty Hill,
Blubberhouses, LS21 2PQ ·
01943 880369 ·
www.yorkshiresmokehouse.co.uk

OTLEY, WEST YORKSHIRE
Bondgate Bakery, 30 Bondgate, Otley,
LS21 1AD · 01943 467526 ·
www.bondgatebakery.com

PONTEFRACT, WEST YORKSHIRE
Farmer Copleys, Ravensknowle Farm,
Pontefract Road, Purston, Pontefract,
WF7 5AF · 01977 600200 ·
www.farmercopleys.co.uk

RHUBARB TRIANGLE, WEST
YORKSHIRE
E. Oldroyd and Sons, Hopefield Farm,
The Shutts, Leadwell Lane, Rothwell,
Leeds, LS26 0ST · 01332 822245 ·
www.yorkshirerhubarb.co.uk

RIPON, NORTH YORKSHIRE
True Foods, Unit 9, Hallikeld Close,
Barker Business Park, Melmerby,
HG4 5GZ · 01765 640927 ·
www.true-foodsltd.co.uk

SHEFFIELD, SOUTH YORKSHIRE
Henderson's Relish, Leavygreave Road,
Sheffield, S3 7RA · 01442 725909 ·
www.hendersonsrelish.com
The Yorkshire Crisp Company, 2a
Waleswood Industrial Estate, Wales Bar,
Sheffield, S26 5PY · 01909 774411 ·
www.yorkshire-crisps.co.uk

WANSFORD, EAST YORKSHIRE
Wansford Trout Farm, Whin Hill,
Wansford, Driffield, YO25 8JJ ·
01377 245353

WENSLEYDALE, NORTH YORKSHIRE
The Wensleydale Creamery, Gayle Lane,
Hawes, Wensleydale, DL8 3RN · 01969
667664 · www.wensleydale.co.uk

WETHERBY, WEST YORKSHIRE
The Market Place Delicatessen,
23 Market Place, Wetherby, LS22 6LQ ·
01937 584051

WHITBY, NORTH YORKSHIRE
Fortune's Kippers, 27 Rose Avenue,
Whitby, YO21 3JA · 01947 601659 ·
www.fortuneskippers.co.uk
Bothams of Whitby, 35–39 Skinner Street,
Whitby, YO21 3AH · 01947 602823 ·
www.botham.co.uk

YORK, NORTH YORKSHIRE
Bettys Café Tea Room, 6–8 St Helen's
Square, York, YO1 8QP · 01904 659142 ·
www.bettys.co.uk

## The West Midlands

AMBERGATE, DERBYSHIRE
Lockwoods, Ripley Road, Ambergate,
DE56 2JR · 01773 856686 ·
www.mushypeas.co.uk

ASTLEY, WARWICKSHIRE
The Tunnel Brewery, The Lord Nelson
Inn, Birmingham Road, Astley,
Nuneaton, CV10 9PQ · 02476 394888 ·
www.tunnelbrewery.co.uk

BAKEWELL, DERBYSHIRE
The Old Original Pudding Company, The
Old Original Bakewell Pudding Shop,
The Square, Bakewell, DE45 1BT ·
01629 812193 ·
www.bakewellpuddingshop.co.uk
Bloomers Connoisseurs Bakery, Buxton
Road, Bakewell, DE45 1DA · 01629
812044

**BIRMINGHAM, WEST MIDLANDS**
Al Frash, 186 Ladypool Road, Sparkhill,
Birmingham, B12 8JS · 01217 533120 ·
*www.alfrash.com*
Shabab, 163–165 Ladypool Road,
Sparkbrook, Birmingham, B12 8LQ ·
01214 402893

**BISHOPS FROME, HEREFORDSHIRE**
The Handmade Scotch Egg Company,
The Old Cookhouse, 5 The Hop Pocket,
Bishops Frome, WR6 5BT ·
01885 490520 ·
*www.handmadescotcheggs.co.uk*
Rochford Country Meats, Wood Park
Farm, Rochford, Tenbury Wells,
WR15 8SL · 01584 781586

**BROMYARD, HEREFORDSHIRE**
Legges of Bromyard, Tenbury Road,
Bromyard, HR7 4LW · 01885 482417 ·
*www.leggesofbromyard.com*

**CHINLEY, DERBYSHIRE**
The Old Hall Inn, Whitehough, Chinley,
SK23 6EJ · 01663 750529 ·
*www.old-hall-inn.co.uk*

**CREDENHILL, HEREFORDSHIRE**
L'Escargot Anglais, Credenhill Snail Farm,
Credenhill, HR4 7DN · 01432 760218

**GLOUCESTER, GLOUCESTERSHIRE**
Smart's Traditional Gloucester Cheese, Old
Ley Court, Chapel Lane, Birdwood,
Churcham, GL2 8AR · 01452 750225 ·
*www.smartsgloucestercheese.com*

**GREAT WITLEY, WORCESTERSHIRE**
Goodman's Geese, Walsgrove Farm, Great
Witley, WR6 6JJ · 01299 896272 ·
*www.goodmansgeese.co.uk*

**GRINDLEFORD, DERBYSHIRE**
Grindleford Station Café, Station
Approach, Upper Padley, Bakewell,
S32 2JA · 01433 631011

**HAWKSTONE, SHROPSHIRE**
Joseph Heler Cheese, Laurels Farm,
Hatherton, Nantwich, CW5 7PE ·
01270 841500 · *www.joseph-heler.co.uk*
Carron Lodge Cheese, Park Head Farm,
Carron Lane, Inglewhite, Preston,
PR3 2LN · 01995 640352 ·
*www.carronlodge.com*
Appleby's Cheese, Broadhay Farm, Lower
Heath, Whitchurch, SY13 2BJ · 01948
840387 · *www.applebyscheese.co.uk*

**HIMBLETON, WORCESTERSHIRE**
Phepson Farm, Himbleton nr. Droitwich,
WR9 7JZ · 01905 391205 ·
*www.phepsonfarm.co.uk*

**HOLT HEATH, WORCESTERSHIRE**
Broomfield's Apples, School Plantation,
Holt Heath, WR6 6NF · 01905 620233 ·
*www.broomfieldsfarmshop.co.uk*

**KNIGHTWICK, WORCESTERSHIRE**
The Talbot at Knightwick, Bromyard
Road, Knightwick, WR6 5PH ·
01886 821235 ·
*www.the-talbot.co.uk*

**LOWER BROADHEATH,
WORCESTERSHIRE**
Lightwood Cheese, Heath Grange Farm,
Lower Broadheath, WR2 6RW · 01905
333468 · *www.lightwoodcheese.co.uk*

**MICKLETON, GLOUCESTERSHIRE**
The Pudding Club, Three Ways House
Hotel, Mickleton, Chipping Campden,
GL55 6SB · 01386 438429 ·
*www.puddingclub.com*

**RIVER SEVERN, GLOUCESTERSHIRE**
Severn & Wye Smokery, Chaxhill,
Westbury-on-Severn, GL14 1QW · 01452
760190 · *www.severnandwye.co.uk*

**RUSHWICK, WORCESTERSHIRE**
Roots at Rushwick, Upper Wick Farm,
Bransford Road, Rushwick, R2 5TD ·
01905 421104

STOKE-ON-TRENT, STAFFORDSHIRE
Burslem Oatcakes, 9 Waterloo Road,
Burslem, ST6 2EH · 01782 819718
Foley Oatcakes, 421 King Street, Fenton,
Stoke-on-Trent, ST4 3EE · 01782 599119
Oatcakes & Pikelets, 134 Chell Street,
Stoke-on-Trent, ST1 6BD · 01782 261899

STONEHALL COMMON,
WORCESTERSHIRE
The Inn at Stonehall, Stonehall Common,
WR5 3QG · 01905 820462 ·
*www.theinnatstonehall.com*

UPTON UPON SEVERN,
WORCESTERSHIRE
Pegoty Hedge Organic Beef and Lamb,
Ryalls Court, Upton upon Severn,
WR8 0PF · 0800 0436735 ·
*www.pegotyhedge.co.uk*

WEM, SHROPSHIRE
Alternative Meats, The Dutch Barn,
Highfield Farm, Wem, SY4 5UN ·
0844 545 6070 ·
*www.alternativemeats.co.uk*

## The East Midlands

BOREHAMWOOD, HERTFORDSHIRE
Ugo Foods, 1 Hertsmere Park, Warwick
Road, Borehamwood, WD6 1GT ·
020 8207 0100 ·
*www.ugogroup.co.uk*

BOSTON, LINCOLNSHIRE
Holme Farm, Kirton Holme, Boston,
PE20 3NL · 01205 290470 ·
*www.holmefarmgroup.co.uk*

CHAWSTON, BEDFORDSHIRE
Edible Ornamentals, Cherwood Nursery,
Blue Bells, Chawston, MK44 3BL ·
01480 405663 ·
*www.edibleornamentals.co.uk*

COLSTON BASSETT,
NOTTINGHAMSHIRE
Colston Bassett Store, Church Gate,
Colston Bassett, NG12 3FE ·
01949 81321 ·
*www.colstonbassettstore.com*
Hambleton Bakery, Cottesmore Road,
Exton, Oakham, LE15 8AN ·
01572 812995 ·
*www.hambletonbakery.co.uk*
Colston Bassett Dairy, Harby Lane,
Colston Bassett, NG12 3FN ·
01949 81322 ·
*www.colstonbassettdairy.com*

HENLEY-ON-THAMES,
OXFORDSHIRE
The Crooked Billet, Newlands Lane, Stoke
Row, Henley-on-Thames, RG9 5PU ·
01491 681048 ·
*www.thecrookedbillet.co.uk*

HOOK NORTON, OXFORDSHIRE
The Village Shop, High Street, Hook
Norton, Banbury, OX15 5NQ ·
01608 737245 ·
*www.villageshophooky.com*

KIRTON IN LINDSEY, LINCOLNSHIRE
True Loaf Organic Bakery, Mount Pleasant
Windmill, North Cliff Road, Kirton in
Lindsey, DN21 4NH · 01652 640177 ·
*www.trueloafbakery.co.uk*

LEICESTER, LEICESTERSHIRE
Leicestershire Handmade Cheese
Company, Sparkenhoe Farm, Main
Road, Upton, Nuneaton, CV13 6JX ·
01455 213863 ·
*www.leicestershirecheese.co.uk*
Long Clawson Dairy, Long Clawson,
Melton Mowbray, LE14 4PJ ·
01664 822332 · *www.clawson.co.uk*

LINCOLN, LINCOLNSHIRE
Wig & Mitre, 30–32 Steep Hill, Lincoln,
LN2 1LU · 01522 535190 ·
*www.wigandmitre.com*

## LOUTH, LINCOLNSHIRE

Meridian Meats, 108 Eastgate, Louth,
LN11 9AA · 01507 603357 ·
*www.meridianmeatsshop.co.uk*

Lakings of Louth, 33 Eastgate, Louth,
LN11 9NB · 01507 603186 ·
*www.lakingsoflouth.co.uk*

## MANSFIELD, NOTTINGHAMSHIRE

Stichelton Dairy, Collingthwaite Farm,
Cuckney, Mansfield, NG20 9NP ·
01623 844883 · *www.stichelton.co.uk*

## MARKET HARBOROUGH, LEICESTERSHIRE

Martin Hobbs' Fishmongers, 5 Church
Square, Market Harborough, LE16 7NB ·
01858 464025

## MELTON MOWBRAY, LEICESTERSHIRE

Walkers Charnwood Bakery, 200 Madeline
Road, Beaumont Leys, Leicester,
LE4 1EX · 01162 340033 ·
*www.samworthbrothers.co.uk*

Dickinson & Morris, Ye Olde Pork Pie
Shoppe, 10 Nottingham Street, Melton
Mowbray, LE13 1NW · 01664 482068 ·
*www.porkpie.co.uk*

Mrs King's Pork Pies, Unit 30, Manvers
Business Park, High Hazels Road,
Cotgrave, NG12 3GZ · 0115 9894101 ·
*www.mrskingsporkpies.co.uk*

Nelson's Butchers, The Pork Pie Factory,
Alma Place, North Street, Stamford,
PE9 1EG · 01780 763345 ·
*www.nelsonsbutchers.co.uk*

Northfield Farm, Whissendine Lane, Cold
Overton, Oakham, LE15 7QF ·
01664 474271 ·
*www.northfieldfarm.com*

Joseph Morris Butchers, Walcote Road,
South Kilworth, Lutterworth,
LE17 6EG · 01858 575210 ·
*www.joseph-morris.co.uk*

## NAVENBY, LINCOLNSHIRE

Welbourne's Bakery, 38 High Street,
Navenby, LN5 0DZ · 01522 810239 ·
*www.welbournesbakery.com*

## NOTTINGHAM, NOTTINGHAMSHIRE

Iberico World Tapas, The Shire Hall, High
Pavement, Lace Market, Nottingham,
NG1 1HN · 01159 410410 ·
*www.ibericotapas.com*

## OWMBY-BY-SPITAL, LINCOLNSHIRE

Kitchen Garden Produce, Fen Road,
Owmby-by-Spital, Market Rasen,
LN8 2DR · 01673 878471

## OXFORD, OXFORDSHIRE

The Oxford Cheese Company,
17 The Covered Market, Oxford,
OX1 3DU · 01865 721420 ·
*www.oxford-covered-market.co.uk*

David John, 93–97 The Covered Market,
Oxford, OX1 3DY · 01865 249092

The Big Bang, 124 Walton Street, Oxford,
OX2 6AH · 01865 511441 ·
*www.thebigbangrestaurants.co.uk*

## PETERBOROUGH, CAMBRIDGESHIRE

The Old Fashioned Pudding Company,
127 County Road, Hampton Vale,
Peterborough, PE7 8ET · 01733 248606 ·
*www.oldfashionedpuddings.co.uk*

## SANDY, BEDFORDSHIRE

Gunns Bakery, 8 Market Square, Sandy,
SG19 1HU · 01767 680434 ·
*www.gunns-bakery.co.uk*

The Tilbury, Watton Road, Datchworth,
SG3 6TB · 01438 815550 ·
*www.thetilbury.co.uk*

The Blue Anchor, 145 Fishpool Street, St
Albans, AL3 4RY · 01727 855038 ·
*www.theblueanchorstalbans.co.uk*

## STANBRIDGE, BEDFORDSHIRE

Willows Farm Shop, Coursers Road,
London Colney, St Albans,
AL4 0PF · 0870 129 9718 ·
*www.willowsfarmshop.com*

## WATLINGTON, OXFORDSHIRE

Quince Products Ltd, Watcombe Manor,
Ingham Lane, Watlington, OX49 5EB ·
01491 614664 · *www.quinceproducts.co.uk*

## WELBECK, NOTTINGHAMSHIRE

The Welbeck Farm Shop, Welbeck Estate,
Worksop, S80 3LW · 01909 478725 ·
*www.thewelbeckfarmshop.co.uk*

## WOODHALL SPA, LINCOLNSHIRE

R. J. Hirst Family Butchers, Station Road,
Woodhall Spa, LN10 6QL · 01526 352321 ·
*www.hirstlincolnshiresausages.co.uk*

## *London*

## ALBERT EMBANKMENT, LAMBETH

Madeira Café, 46a Albert Embankment,
London, SE1 7TL · 020 7820 1117 ·
*www.madeiralondon.co.uk*

## BRIXTON, LAMBETH

Franco Manca, Unit 4, Market Row,
Electric Lane, London, SW9 8LD ·
020 7738 3021 · *www.francomanca.co.uk*

## FITZROVIA, CAMDEN

Hakkasan, 8 Hanway Place, London,
W1T 1HD · 020 7927 7000 ·
*www.hakkasan.com*
Yauatcha, 15 Broadwick Street, London,
W1F 0DL · 020 7494 8888 ·
*www.yauatcha.com*

## GREENWICH, GREENWICH

Goddard's Pies, Fountain Court, next to
2 Greenwich Church Street, London,
SE10 9BQ · 0800 862 0400 ·
*www.pieshop.co.uk*
The Meantime Brewing Company,
The Old Brewery, Pepys Building, Old
Royal Naval College, London, SE10 9LW ·
020 3327 1280 ·
*www.oldbrewerygreenwich.com /*
*www.meantimebrewing.com*

## HAMMERSMITH, HAMMERSMITH & FULHAM

Sipsmith Independent Spirits, The
Distillery, 27 Nasmyth Street, London,
W6 0HA · 020 8741 2034 ·
*www.sipsmith.com*

## KNIGHTSBRIDGE, KENSINGTON & CHELSEA

Harrods Food Hall, 87–135 Brompton
Road, London, SW1X 7XL ·
020 7730 1234 · *www.harrods.com*

## MARYLEBONE, WESTMINSTER

The Ginger Pig at Marylebone, 8–10
Moxon Street, London, W1U 4EW ·
020 7935 7788 · *www.thegingerpig.co.uk*
Ginger Pig butchery classes · 01751
460802 · *www.learnbutchery.co.uk*
Veeraswamy, Mezzanine Floor, Victory
House, 99 Regent Street, London,
W1B 4RS · 020 7734 1401 ·
*www.veeraswamy.com*

## NEW CROSS, LEWISHAM

Smokey Jerkey, 158 New Cross Road,
London, SE14 5BA · 020 7639 6204

## OLD BROMPTON ROAD, KENSINGTON & CHELSEA

Bosphorus Kebabs, 59 Old Brompton
Road, London, SW7 3JS ·
020 7584 4048 ·
*www.goodmood.moonfruit.com*

## PARSONS GREEN, HAMMERSMITH & FULHAM

The Kitchen, 275 New King's Road,
London, SW6 4RD · 020 7736 8067 ·
*www.visitthekitchen.com*

## PICCADILLY, WESTMINSTER

Fortnum & Mason, 181 Piccadilly, London,
W1A 1ER · 020 7734 8040 ·
*www.fortnumandmason.com*

SHOREDITCH, HACKNEY
Hawksmoor, 157 Commercial Street,
  London, E1 6BJ · 020 7247 7392 ·
  *www.thehawksmoor.co.uk*

SMITHFIELD, ISLINGTON
St John Bar and Restaurant, 26 St John
  Street, London, EC1M 4AY ·
  020 3301 8069 ·
  *www.stjohnrestaurant.com*

SOUTH BANK, SOUTHWARK
Canteen, Royal Festival Hall, Belvedere
  Road, London, SE1 8XX · 0845 686 1122 ·
  *www.canteen.co.uk*

SOUTHWARK BRIDGE ROAD,
SOUTHWARK
Bompas & Parr, Unit B, Flatiron Yard,
  14 Ayres Street, London, SE1 1ES ·
  020 7403 9403 · *www.jellymongers.co.uk*

SPITALFIELDS, TOWER HAMLETS
Brick Lane Beigel Bake, 159 Brick Lane,
  London, E1 6SB · 020 7729 0616

STRAND, WESTMINSTER
Simpson's-in-the-Strand, 100 Strand,
  London, WC2R 0EW · 020 7836 9112 ·
  *www.simpsonsinthestrand.co.uk*

TOWER BRIDGE
The London Honey Company ·
  07973 744 331 ·
  *www.thelondonhoneycompany.co.uk*

VICTORIA, WESTMINSTER
The Vincent Rooms, Westminster
  Kingsway College, 76 Vincent Square,
  London, SW1P 2PD · 020 7802 8391 ·
  *www.westking.ac.uk*

WHITECHAPEL, TOWER HAMLETS
Lahore Kebab House, 2–10 Umberston
  Street, London, E1 1PY · 020 7481 9737 ·
  *www.lahore-kebabhouse.com*
Tayyabs, 83–89 Fieldgate Street, London,
  E1 1JU · 020 7247 6400 ·
  *www.tayyabs.co.uk*

## East Anglia

BLAXHALL, SUFFOLK
The Wild Meat Company, Lime Tree Farm,
  Blaxhall, Woodbridge, IP12 2DY ·
  01728 663211 · *www.wildmeat.co.uk*

BURY ST EDMUNDS, SUFFOLK
Infusions, 4 Lundy Court, Rougham
  Industrial Estate, Rougham, Bury St
  Edmunds, IP30 9ND · 01359 272577 ·
  *www.infusions4chefs.co.uk*

CAMBRIDGE, CAMBRIDGESHIRE
Art of Meat, 45 Arbury Court, Cambridge,
  CB4 2JQ · 01223 350950

CROMER, NORFOLK
Farm Park & Wild, 1 Douglas Bader
  Close, North Walsham, NR28 0TZ ·
  0844 846 2329 ·
  *www.farmparkwild.co.uk*

EPPING, ESSEX
Church's Butchers, 222–224 High Street,
  Town Centre, Epping, CM16 4AQ ·
  01992 573231

FRAMLINGHAM, SUFFOLK
Shawsgate Vineyard, Badingham Road,
  Framlingham, Woodbridge, IP13 9HZ ·
  01728 724060 · *www.shawsgate.co.uk*
Food Safari, 26 Double Street,
  Framlingham, Woodbridge, IP13 9BN ·
  01728 621380 · *www.foodsafari.co.uk*
The Anchor, Walberswick, Southwold,
  IP18 6UA · 01502 722112 ·
  *www.anchoratwalberswick.com*
Pinney's of Orford, The Old Warehouse,
  Quay Street, Orford, IP12 2NU ·
  01394 459183 ·
  *www.butleyorfordoysterage.co.uk*
Blythburgh Pork, St Margaret's Farm,
  Mells, Halesworth, IP19 9DD ·
  01986 873298 ·
  *www.freerangepork.co.uk*

GREAT DUNHAM, NORFOLK
Essence Foods, PO Box 152, Dereham,
 NR19 9AR · 01362 668844 ·
 *www.essencefoods.co.uk*

GREAT YARMOUTH, NORFOLK
Docwras Rock Factory, 13 Regent Road,
 Great Yarmouth, NR20 2AF ·
 01493 844676

HARLOW, ESSEX
S. J. Frederick & Sons, The Farm Office,
 Temple Farm, Roydon, Harlow,
 CM19 5LW · 01279 792460 ·
 *www.sjfrederick.co.uk*

HINDOLVESTON, NORFOLK
Martins Farm, Hindolveston, NR20 5DB ·
 01263 861241

HOLT, NORFOLK
Letheringsett Watermill, Riverside Road,
 Letheringsett, Holt, NR25 7YD ·
 01263 713153 ·
 *www.letheringsettwatermill.co.uk*

IPSWICH, SUFFOLK
Suffolk Food Hall, Wherstead, Ipswich,
 IP9 2AB · 01473 786610 ·
 *www.suffolkfoodhall.co.uk*

MALDON, ESSEX
The Maldon Crystal Salt Company, Wycke
 Hill Business Park, Maldon, CM9 6UZ ·
 01621 853315 · *www.maldonsalt.co.uk*

MELTON CONSTABLE, NORFOLK
M & M Rutland Butchers, 13 Briston
 Road, Melton Constable, NR24 2DG ·
 01263 860562 ·
*www.rutland-butchers.co.uk*

MORSTON, NORFOLK
Morston Hall Hotel, Morston, Holt,
 NR25 7AA · 01263 741041 ·
 *www.morstonhall.com*

NEWMARKET, SUFFOLK
Musk's Sausages, 4 Goodwin Business
 Park, Newmarket, CB8 7SQ ·
 01638 662626 · *www.musks.com*
Powters, Wellington Street, Newmarket,
 CB8 0HT · 01638 662418 ·
 *www.powters.co.uk*

NORWICH, NORFOLK
The Colman's Mustard Shop, Royal
 Arcade, NR2 1NQ · 01603 627889 ·
 *www.colmansmustardshop.com*

PEASENHALL, SUFFOLK
Emmett's of Peasenhall, Peasenhall,
 Saxmundham, IP17 2HJ · 01728 660250 ·
 *www.emmettsham.co.uk*

SALTHOUSE, NORFOLK
Cookie's Crab Shop, The Green, Salthouse,
 Holt, NR25 7AJ · 01263 740352 ·
 *www.salthouse.org.uk*

SOUTHEND-ON-SEA, ESSEX
Sands Bistro, Western Esplanade,
 Southend-on-Sea, SS1 1EE ·
 01702 468123 · *www.sandsbistro.co.uk*

SOUTHWOLD, SUFFOLK
Adnams Brewery, Sole Bay Brewery,
 Southwold, IP18 6JW · 01502 727200 ·
 *www.adnams.co.uk*
The Swan Hotel, Market Place,
 Southwold, IP18 6EG · 01502 722186 ·
 *www.adnams.co.uk*
The Crown Hotel, High Street, Southwold,
 IP18 6DP · 01502 722275 ·
 *www.adnams.co.uk*

THUXTON, NORFOLK
Peele's Norfolk Black Turkeys, Rookery
 Farm, Thuxton, Norwich, NR9 4QJ ·
 01362 850237 ·
 *www.peelesblackturkeys.co.uk*

WEST MERSEA, ESSEX
The Company Shed, 129 Coast Road,
 West Mersea, Colchester, CO5 8PA ·
 01206 382700

WYMONDHAM, NORFOLK
Norfolk White Lady Cheese, Willow Farm
  House, The Green, Deopham,
  Wymondham, NR18 9DH ·
  01953 853145


## The South-East

APPLEDORE, KENT
Miss Mollett's High Class Tea Room,
  26 The Street, Appledore, TN26 2BX ·
  01233 758555 ·
  *www.missmollettstearoom.co.uk*

BRIGHTON, EAST SUSSEX
Terre à Terre, 71 East Street, Brighton,
  BN1 1HQ · 01273 729051 ·
  *www.terreaterre.co.uk*

CANTERBURY, KENT
The Goods Shed, Station Road West,
  Canterbury, CT2 8AN · 01227 459153 ·
  *www.thegoodsshed.net*

CHICHESTER, WEST SUSSEX
Hairspring Watercress, Mill Farm,
  Hambrook Hill (South), Hambrook,
  Chichester, PO18 8UJ · 01243 572666 ·
  *www.hairspring.org.uk*

DOVER, KENT
Romney Marsh Fish Market, Haguelands
  Farm, Burmarsh, Romney Marsh,
  TN29 0JR · 07854 541675

FAVERSHAM, KENT
Brogdale Farm, Brogdale Road,
  Faversham, ME13 8XZ · 01795 536250 ·
  *www.brogdalecollections.co.uk*
Cheesemakers of Canterbury,
  Lamberhurst Farm, Dargate, Faversham,
  ME13 9ES · 01227 751741 ·
  *www.cheesemakersofcanterbury.co.uk*
Macknade Fine Foods, 4–5 West Street,
  Faversham, ME13 7JE · 01795 537373 ·
  *www.macknade.com*

FRILSHAM, BERKSHIRE
The Pot Kiln Pub and Restaurant,
  Frilsham nr. Yattendon, RG18 0XX ·
  01635 201366 · *www.potkiln.org*

GUILDFORD, SURREY
The British Barbecue Society, Minley
  Nursery, Spoil Lane, Tongham,
  GU10 1PB · *www.bbbqs.com*

HASTINGS, EAST SUSSEX
Rock-a-Nore, Seatoller, St Helens Avenue,
  Hastings, TN34 2JT · 01424 461912 ·
  *www.rockanore.co.uk*

HOOK, HAMPSHIRE
Newlyns Farm Shop, Lodge Farm, North
  Warnborough, Hook, RG29 1HA ·
  01256 704128 ·
  *www.newlyns-farmshop.co.uk*

HORSTED KEYNES, WEST SUSSEX
High Weald Dairy, Tremains Farm,
  Horsted Keynes, RH17 7EA ·
  01825 791636 · *www.highwealddairy.co.uk*

LYMINGTON, HAMPSHIRE
Mrs Tee's Wild Mushrooms, Gorsemeadow,
  Sway Road, Lymington, SO41 8LR ·
  01590 673354 · *www.wildmushrooms.co.uk*

MAIDENHEAD, BERKSHIRE
Copas Traditional Turkeys, Kings Coppice
  Farm, Grubwood Lane, Cookham,
  Maidenhead, SL6 9UB · 01628 499980 ·
  *www.copasturkeys.co.uk*

MEOPHAM, KENT
Roundwood Orchard Pig Company,
  Roundwood House, Ifield Road,
  Meopham, DA13 0QH · 01474 816845 ·
  *www.candbmeats.co.uk*

NEWCHURCH, ISLE OF WIGHT
The Garlic Farm, Mersley Lane,
  Newchurch, PO36 0NR · 01983 865378 ·
  *www.thegarlicfarm.co.uk*

NORTHIAM, EAST SUSSEX

Cooks Yard Farm, New Road, Northiam,
Rye, TN31 6HS · 07905 671114 ·
*www.rentacherrytree.co.uk*

POLEGATE, EAST SUSSEX

The Hungry Monk, Jevington, Polegate,
BN26 5QF · 01323 482178 ·
*www.hungrymonk.co.uk*

ST MARY'S PLATT, KENT

Kentish Cobnuts Association,
Comp Lane, St Mary's Platt, Sevenoaks,
TN15 8NR · 01732 882734 ·
*www.kentishcobnutsassociation.org.uk*

STOCKBRIDGE, HAMPSHIRE

Clos du Marquis, A30 London Road
between Stockbridge and Sutton
Scotney, SO20 6DE · 01264 810738 ·
*www.closdumarquis.co.uk*

WHITSTABLE, KENT

Wheelers Oyster Bar, 8 High Street,
Whitstable, CT5 1BQ · 01227 273311
Sundae Sundae, 62 Harbour Street,
Whitstable, CT5 1AG ·
*www.sundaesundae.co.uk*

WROTHAM, KENT

Winterdale Cheesemakers, Platt House
Farm, Fairseat Lane, Wrotham,
TN15 7QB · 01732 820021 ·
*www.winterdale.co.uk*

# Bibliography and Further Reading

Acton, Eliza, *Modern Cookery for Private Families* (Longman, 1845; revised edition 1868)

Adams, Douglas, *The Meaning of Liff* (Pan Books, 1983)

Albala, Ken, *Pancake: A Global History* (Reaktion Books, 2008)

Arrivabene, Charles, *Italy under Victor Emmanuel* (Hurst and Blackett, 1862)

Bagshaw, Chris, *The Ultimate Hillwalking Skills Manual* (David & Charles, 2006)

Beeching, C. L. T., *Law's Grocer's Manual*, third edition (London, 1930)

Beeton, Isabella, *Mrs Beeton's Book of Household Management* (S. O. Beeton, 1861; repr. OUP, 2008)

Betjeman, Sir John, 'The Licorice Fields at Pontefract' from *A Few Late Chrysanthemums* (John Murray, 1954)

Bevan, Judi, *Trolley Wars: The Battle of the Supermarkets* (Profile Books, 2005)

Black, William, *The Land the Thyme Forgot* (Bantam Press, 2005)

Borrow, George, *Wild Wales* (John Murray, 1862)

Bourdain, Anthony, *Kitchen Confidential* (Bloomsbury, 2000)

Brock, R. Barrington, *Outdoor Grapes in Cold Climates* (Tonbridge, 1949)

Burnett, David, and Saberi, Helen, *The Road to Vindaloo: Curry Cooks & Curry Books* (Prospect Books, 2008)

Burnett, John, *England Eats Out* (Longman, 2004)

Camden, William, *Britannia* (London, 1586)

Carter, Elizabeth, *The Good Food Guide 2010* (Which? Books, 2009)

Cassidy, Nigel, and Lamb, Philippa, *Battenberg Britain* (Michael O'Mara Books, 2009)

Chalmers, Patrick, *Field Sports of Scotland* (Philip Allan & Co., 1936)

Colquhoun, Kate, *Taste: The Story of Britain Through Its Cooking* (Bloomsbury, 2007)

Copley, Esther, *The Housekeeper's Guide* (Longman, 1838)

Cressy, Lady Mary, *The Whole Duty of a Woman* (London, 1695; revised edition 1737)

Croft-Cooke, Rupert, *English Cooking* (W. H. Allen, 1960)

Crowden, James, *Ciderland* (Berlinn, 2008)

Darwin, Bernard, *Receipts and Relishes* (Naldrett Press, 1950)

David, Elizabeth, *A Book of Mediterranean Food* (John Lehmann, 1950; repr. Grub Street, 1999)

David, Elizabeth, *An Omelette and a Glass of Wine* (Robert Hale, 1984; repr. Penguin Books, 1990)

Davidson, Alan, *The Penguin Companion to Food* (Penguin, 2002)

Davies, Jennifer, *The Victorian Kitchen* (BBC Books, 1989)

Davis, Pat R., *Oysters and Champagne* (Robert Hale, 1986)

Dawson, Thomas, *The good huswifes jewell* (London, 1596; repr. as *The Good Housewife's Jewel*, Southover Press, 1996)

de Mauduit, Vicomte, *They Can't Ration These* (Michael Joseph, 1940; repr. Persephone Books, 2004)

Dickie, John, *Delizia! The Epic History of the Italians and Their Food* (Sceptre, 2007)

Dickson Wright, Clarissa, *The Haggis: A Little History* (Appletree Press, 1998)

Digbie, Sir Kenelme, *The Closet of the Eminently Learned Sir Kenelme Digbie Kt. Opened* (London, 1669; repr. Tutis Digital Publishing, 2008)

Douglas, Norman, *Venus in the Kitchen* (Heinemann, 1952)

Drummond, J. C., *The Englishman's Food* (Jonathan Cape, 1939; repr. Pimlico 1994)

Dumas, Alexandre, *Sketches of Naples* (E. Ferrett & Co., 1845)

Easton, Ellen, 'Etiquette Faux Pas and Other Misconceptions About Afternoon Tea' (http://whatscookingamerica.net, 2004)

Elmé Francatelli, Charles, *The Cook's Guide, and Housekeeper's & Butler's Assistant* (Richard Bentley, 1857)

Evelyn, John, *Acetaria: A Discourse of Sallets* (London, 1699; repr. Hard Press, 2006)

Fearnley-Whittingstall, Hugh, and Carr, Fizz, *The River Cottage Family Cookbook* (Hodder & Stoughton, 2005)

Fearnley-Whittingstall, Hugh, *The River Cottage Meat Book* (Hodder & Stoughton, 2004)

Fernandez-Armesto, Felipe, *Food: A History* (Macmillan, 2001)

Fraser, Evan D. G., and Rimas, Andrew, *Empires of Food: Feast, Famine and the Rise and Fall of Civilizations* (Random House Books, 2010)

Freeman, Bobby, *First Catch Your Peacock: The Classic Guide to Welsh Food* (Y Lolfa, 1996; revised edition 2006)

Gaskell, Elizabeth, *Cranford* (London, 1853; repr. Cricket House Books, 2010)

Giles, J. A., *William of Malmesbury's Chronicle of the Kings of England* (London, 1847)

Glasse, Hannah, *The Art of Cookery Made Plain and Easy* (London, 1747)

Green, Frances H., *The Housekeeper's Book* (William Marshall & Co., 1837; repr. Applewood Books, 2008)

Greenwood, James, *Odd People in Odd Places* (F. Warne, 1883; repr. at www.victorianlondon.org)

Grigson, Jane, *English Food* (Macmillan, 1974; repr. Penguin, 1998)

*Gye's Bath Directory* (H. Gye, 1819)

Hartley, Dorothy, *Food in England* (Macdonald, 1954; repr. Little, Brown, 1999)

Hawkins, Sir Christopher, *Observations on the Tin Trade of the Ancients in Cornwall* (J. J. Stockdale, 1811)

Heaton, Nell, *Traditional Recipes of the British Isles* (Faber & Faber, 1951)

Henderson, Fergus, *Nose to Tail Eating: A Kind of British Cooking* (Bloomsbury, 2004)

Hickman, Trevor, *The History of the Melton Mowbray Pork Pie* (Sutton Publishing, 1997; repr. The History Press, 2005)

Hippisley Coxe, Antony D., and Hippisley Coxe, Araminta, *Book of Sausages* (Gollancz, 1994)

Hix, Mark, *British Seasonal Food* (Quadrille Publishing, 2008)

Hopkinson, Simon, *Roast Chicken and Other Stories* (Ebury Press, 1994; revised edition 1999)

Hyams, Edward, *The Grape Vine in England* (Bodley Head, 1949)

Hyams, Edward, *Vineyards in England* (Faber & Faber, 1953)

Jackson, E. J., *Reliable guide to the curing of Cumberland hams and bacon and the preparation of the offal in the Cumberland style* (1911)

Jennings, Paul, *The Local: A History of the English Pub* (The History Press, 2007)

Johnstone, Christian Isobel, *The Cook and Housewife's Manual* (Edinburgh, 1826)

Kettilby, Mary, *A Collection of Above Three Hundred Receipts in Cookery, Physick, and Surgery* (London, 1734)

Kurlansky, Mark, *Salt: A World History* (Jonathan Cape, 2002)

Lampen, Martin, *Sausage in a Basket* (Bloomsbury, 2007)

Leslie, Eliza, *Miss Leslie's Complete Cookery* (Pennsylvania, 1837; repr. Applewood Books, 2008)

Malcolmson, Robert W., and Mastoris, S. N., *The English Pig: A History* (Hambledon Continuum, 1998)

Mallet, Gina, *Last Chance to Eat: The Fate of Taste in a Fast Food World* (W. W. Norton, 2004)

Markham, Gervase, *The English Huswife* (London, 1615; repr. McGill-Queen's University Press, 1986)

Marshall, Agnes B., *Cookery Book* (London, 1888)

Marshall, Agnes B., *Fancy Ices* (London, 1894)

Marshall, Agnes B., *The Book of Ices* (London, 1885)

Mason, Charlotte, *The lady's assistant for regulating and supplying her table* (London, 1773)

Mason, Laura, and Brown, Catherine, *Traditional Foods of Britain* (Prospect Books, 1999; repr. as *The Taste of Britain*, Harper Press, 2007)

May, Robert, *The Accomplisht Cook* (London, 1660)

McNeill, Marian F., *The Scots Kitchen* (Glasgow, 1929; repr. Birlinn, 2010)

Montagné, Prosper, *Larousse Gastronomic* (Editions Larousse, 1938; revised English edition, Hamlyn, 2001)

Morton, Mark, *Cupboard Love* (Blizzard Publishing, 1996; revised edition, Insomniac Press, 2004)

Murphy, Lynda, and Rugg, Julie, *A Food Lover's Treasury* (Frances Lincoln, 2008)

Murray, Sarah, *Moveable Feasts* (Aurum Press, 2007)

*The New Family Receipt Book* (John Murray, 1810)

Nicey and Wifey, *A Nice Cup of Tea and a Sit Down* (Little, Brown, 2004)

Occleve, Thomas, *De regimine principum* (London, 1411)

Ordish, George, *Wine Growing in England* (Rupert Hart-Davies, 1953)

Parkin, Charles, *The history and antiquities of the city of Norwich* (London, 1783)

Pepys, Samuel, *The Diary of Samuel Pepys* (London, 1825)

Premier Malt Products, *Tested Recipes with Blue Ribbon Malt Extract* (Premier Malt Products, 1951)

Prout, Samuel, *Fireside Facts from the Great Exhibition* (Houlston & Stoneman, 1851)

Raffald, Elizabeth, *The Experienced English Housekeeper* (Manchester, 1769; repr. Southover Press, 1996)

Rundell, Maria Eliza Ketelby, *A New System of Domestic Cookery* (John Murray, 1824)

Sambrook, Pamela, *The Staffordshire Oatcake: A History* (Palatine Books, 2009)

Schott, Ben, *Schott's Food and Drink Miscellany* (Bloomsbury, 2003)

Segnit, Niki, *The Flavour Thesaurus* (Bloomsbury, 2010)

Singh, Balbir, *Indian Cookery* (Mills & Boon, 1965; seventh edition 1975)

Slater, Nigel, *Eating for England: The Delights and Eccentricities of the British at Table* (Fourth Estate, 2007)

Smith, Henry, *The Master Books of Soups* (London, 1900; repr. Applewood Books, 2008)

Spencer, Colin, and Clifton, Claire, *The Faber Book of Food* (Faber & Faber, 1994)

Spencer, Colin, *British Food: An Extraordinary Thousand Years of History* (Grub Street, 2002)

Spry, Constance, and Hume, Rosemary, *The Constance Spry Cookery Book* (London, 1956; repr. Grub Street, 2004)

Stein, Rick, *Rick Stein's Guide to the Food Heroes of Britain* (BBC Books, 2003; second edition 2005)

Strong, Roy, *Feast: A History of Grand Eating* (Jonathan Cape, 2002)

Thomas Ellis, Alice, *Fish, Flesh and Good Red Herring: A Gallimaufry* (Virago, 2004)

Toussaint-Samat, Maguelonne, *A History of Food* (Blackwell, 2002; revised edition, Wiley-Blackwell, 2008)

Visser, Margaret, *The Rituals of Dinner: The Origins, Evolution, Eccentricities and the Meaning of Table Manners* (Grove Press, 1991)

Warder, Joseph, *The true Amazons: or, The monarchy of bees* (London, 1713)

Watson, Douglas Chalmers, *Food and feeding in health and disease: a manual of practical dietetics* (Wood, 1911)

White, Florence, *Good things in England* (Jonathan Cape, 1932; repr. Persephone Books, 1999)

Williams, T., *The accomplished housekeeper, and universal cook* (London, 1717)

Williamson, Mrs I., *The practice of cookery and pastry* (John Greig & Son, 1854)

Wright, Thomas, *A History of domestic manners and sentiments in England during the Middle Ages* (London, 1862)

Yeatman, Marwood, *The Last Food of England* (Ebury Press, 2007)

Zuckerman, Larry, *The Potato: The Story of How a Vegetable Changed History* (Macmillan, 1999)

# Acknowledgements

This book would not have been possible without the huge amount of time and knowledge given to me by the people featured in it. Repeatedly I found myself in awe of their expertise, skill and dedication, and to each of them I extend my heartfelt thanks.

I'd like to thank my editors at Random House Books: Sophie Lazar, who brought this book into the world and encouraged me every step of the way before the patter of tiny feet meant Silvia Crompton took up the task with equal aplomb. Thanks, too, to Gemma Wain, who ably assisted them both. Thanks to Jeff Cottenden for the wonderful cover photography, Tim Duckett for the author photo, Richard Marston for the layout, Darren Bennett for the maps and the Random House design and production teams for all their efforts in making it look so superb. A big thank you also goes to Channel 4 for commissioning *The Big British Food Map* back in 2007, which ultimately led to this book.

Many thanks to all my patient family and friends, who regularly enquired about the book only to hear me repeat the mantra 'I've nearly finished it, honest,' and to those who proofread some of the entries. A special thank you to Shannon Moore, who gave me her flat to work in while she was away on business, thus saving me from my own domestic procrastinations such as descaling the kettle or cleaning out the toaster's crumb tray.

Finally, the biggest thank you of all goes to my wife Kate for her unwavering support and encouragement, and to my daughter Matilda, who brightens my days.

# Picture Acknowledgements

Photographs are reproduced by kind permission of: Tracy Denning Smitherman (p. 9); Pembrokeshire Tea Company (p. 82); John Riden (p. 91); Cathie Cassie (p. 110); Boghall Butchers (p. 147); George Cockburn & Son (p. 161); Beckleberry's (p. 205); Lucy Carroll (p. 209); Christopher Sutherland (p. 214); Egton Bridge Old Gooseberry Society (p. 246); The Old Original Pudding Company (p. 278); Three Ways House Hotel (p. 304); Hakkasan/Bacchus PR (p. 377); Goddard's Pies (p. 381); Brooks's club (p. 399); Patricia Niven (p. 402); London Honey Company (p. 410); Mustard Communications (p.471).

All other photographs supplied by the author.

# Index